c.1

The Gates of the Dream

THE GATES
OF THE
DREAM

GÉZA RÓHEIM

INTERNATIONAL UNIVERSITIES PRESS, INC.

New York   New York

This book is dedicated to the memory of

SÁNDOR FERENCZI

Motto

Di, quibus imperium est animarum, umbraeque silentes
Et Chaos et Phlegethon, loca nocte tacentia late
Sit mihi fas audita loqui; sit numine vestro
Pandere res, alta terra, et caligine mersas.

(Aeneid, VI, 263–267.)

INTRODUCTION

Some time ago I was invited to the house of one of my oldest friends. He was talking to a younger colleague and asking quite seriously: Is there such a thing as psychoanalytic anthropology? The younger colleague smiled and looked at me, and I thought: Has my life really been in vain? Not that I really believed it. In fact, in a sense I could say that in this book we have for the first time psychoanalytic anthropology in a different and deeper sense.

Till now I have been telling anthropologists that psychoanalysis is a tool in their field that can explain many things. Now I am telling psychoanalysts that they could use anthropology. The theory of this book could never have been evolved if I had not been a practicing psychoanalyst, but I also could not have understood all the implications of what my patients were saying if I had not been on familiar terms with the *altjiranga mitjina,* "the eternal ones of the dream."

Now this brings me to the first question: Is there such a thing as a psychoanalytic anthropology? From a practical point of view psychoanalysis and anthropology are two different professions. A psychoanalyst sits in his office and receives patients who want to be cured. An anthropologist goes to some tribe in the desert or jungle and tries to understand those people—who certainly do not want to be cured, indeed, they could teach us a lesson in happiness.

However, there has been a tremendous change since 1915 when I first wrote "psychoanalytic anthropology." Many anthropologists have been analyzed. The results have been in a sense more than could have been expected. Anthropology has been transformed at least in America, and "Personality and Culture" is certainly a new science. Curiously enough in Europe, nothing of the kind has taken place, and if psychology there has any influence on anthropology, it is Jungian psychology.

From my own point of view of course, what has been gained in breadth has been lost in depth. With few exceptions—I need not name my most intimate associates here, we have something new that is in many respects revealing but is definitely not psychoanalysis. In 1927, in the discussion about "Lay-analysis," I wrote[1] that in order really to understand anthropology (and the same is valid for allied disciplines) it is not enough to be analyzed. One must also be a practicing psychoanalyst. Freud said: It is easy to descend into the Hades of the unconscious but not so easy to

[1] Róheim, G., *Internationale Zeitschrift für Psychoanalyse,* XIII, pp. 232–233.

stay there. Nobody can stay there without continuous, or at least intermit-
tent, contact with the unconscious. The reader may ask: Well then, according to you what is the solution? Are human problems necessarily solved?
The ideal solution would be lifelong research positions in which the psychoanalytic anthropologist alternates between field work and clinical work.
What now seems impossible may be possible in a distant future.

Ferenczi's thinking in *Thalassa* is one of the influences reflected in
this book. The second is Tylor with his derivation of the gods from animism and animism from the dream. And the third is Laistner's attempt to
explain mythology on the basis of the nightmare.

Géza Róheim

CONTENTS

ACKNOWLEDGMENTS

I wish to thank the following publishers for their generous permission to quote extensively from their publications:

J. J. Augustin; Farrar & Rinehart, Inc.; Grune & Stratton, Inc.; Harper & Bros.; Hermitage Press; Liveright Publishing Corp.; The Macmillan Co.; Museum of Modern Art; W. W. Norton & Co.; Pantheon Books, Inc.; W. B. Saunders Co.; University of Chicago Press; University of Minnesota Press; University of Wisconsin Press.

x

I

THE BASIC DREAM

I. SLEEP

My hypothesis assumes that the dream is primarily a reaction to the fact that we are asleep, or to put it differently, that there is such a thing as a basic dream which represents this reaction. Other layers are then added to the dream and these are derived from our waking life.

If we assume that a type of dreaming is simply due to our being asleep, the question, of course, arises as to what is sleep?

Freud writes:

"Sleep is a reactivation of the intrauterine situation. We have rest, warmth, and absence of stimuli, many people even sleep in the fetal position."[1]

Mazurkiewitz likens the almost continuous sleep of the newborn to a continuation of intrauterine life.[2] According to Kleitman "the newborn baby probably wakes only when it is hungry, cold or otherwise disturbed, falling asleep again after it has been taken care of or the disturbance otherwise removed."[3] According to Gesell during sleep the early body posture is reminiscent of the fetal habitus.[4]

A patient (male) who had periods of dreamy wandering in his youth when asked to make up a story in the analysis replies as follows: "I am walking down a slope. It is like a dream. I am walking into something. It is a cunt."

Another patient, mother of two children, age about thirty, says: "I am falling asleep, I am a little child again."

The following dream of a young woman makes it quite clear that to be asleep is to be in the womb.[4a]

[1] Freud, S., "Metapsychologische Ergänzung zur Traumlehre," *Gesammelte Schriften*, V, pp. 520, 521.

[2] Mazurkiewitz, "L'état de sommeil et de veille au cours de l'homme," *Revue neurologique*, I, 1936, 913 *et. seq.*, quoted by Kleitman, N., *Sleep and Wakefulness*, Chicago, 1939.

[3] Kleitman, *op. cit.*, p. 508.

[4] Gesell, A., Ilg, F. L., Bullis, G. E., *Vision*, New York, 1949, p. 81.

[4a] The patient came after a hysterectomy. Other dreams of the same patient are discussed in this chapter.

1

I dreamed of a little girl not bigger than my hand. She went to sleep in a cellophane globe, inside the globe was urine and in the urine the little girl. People asked whether the urine was not harmful and I said, "No," since she liked it. All she asked for was that her doll should be placed near her so that she could have it on awakening, i.e., on coming out of the cellophane and urine.

She awakened to urinate. The day before the dream was characterized by various frustrations, her mother's sickness, etc. In the dream the hysterectomy is again annulled by uterine regression. She is a little girl who has a fantasy child, a doll. The connection of the vesical and of the birth dream is also very clear. The hand as the measure for the little girl's size means that she sleeps with her hand covering her vagina.

A depressive patient dreams as follows:

I am in two brown cocoons. I feel very cozy, completely relaxed.

The background of the dream was that she was tense for a few days. She felt guilty for not calling her mother and another married woman of her mother's age, to whom she feels obligated. At the same time she resists both obligations and consciously she wants to be independent. After having gotten in touch with both she feels relaxed. The brown color reminds her of mushy feces. In her tense periods she is constipated; in her relaxed periods she has diarrhea. She is in the cocoons like an embryo. Fantasies on the couch about being a baby, walking on all fours, etc. At the end of the hour strong vertigo. She remarks, "It feels as if I had been *asleep* for a whole hour."

A patient analyzed by an analyst I control reports:

I am playing with a woman's breasts. She does not look like my mother. A man beats me up. Then I see my mother's vagina and it feels as if I were falling into it.

Associations and Interpretation: She does not look like my mother—self-explanatory. He used to box with his father. Falling into mother's vagina is the basic dream.

A patient has quarreled with his wife. She told him their marriage was no good and that the best thing would be for him to leave home.

Dream: I am on the ocean in a box, a houseboat, with my daughter Mary. We are drifting away from Los Angeles and I fall asleep. Then we land. I am on shore and awake. A woman is there (I omit the rest of the dream).

The associations to the woman lead him to a famous beauty who had wanted to seduce him when he was a young lad but he could not get an erection, and then to his mother.

Mary is the name of his young daughter and also of his girl friend, but in the dream it seems to be his child.

Falling asleep in the box on the water simply symbolizes the process of falling asleep, i.e., being in a box on the water with a woman (womb). Landing is being born, awakening, and to dream is a partial awakening.

When I talk about uterine symbolism I am not thinking of a direct survival of birth memories that particular night. What I mean is that falling asleep itself is a repetition of the womb situation but is sometimes symbolized by its opposite, i.e., being born. In this case we have both symbols: uterine regression and birth.

Jekels and Bergler explain sleeping and dreaming as the conflict of the death and life principle. They quote Economo and Pötzl on the tendency immanent in the protoplasm to rest and identical with the death impulse,[5] in language and poetry sleep and death are frequently equated. Jekels and Bergler assume that the destructive goal of the Thanatos component is not only neutralized but is actually transformed into the recuperative effect of sleep. Eros transforms the instinct to rest into an instinct to sleep primarily by offering the return to the womb as a pleasure premium. "As a further measure, a heightened degree of defense as it were, Eros invests the ego with all the libido at its disposal. For this it mobilizes even the repressed libido itself—the infantile sexual wishes."

"If then appearances are not deceptive we must add to the well-known function of the dream as the guardian of sleep a second function —the guarding of life." "Sleep is death stirred by dreams, death is dreamless sleep."

When I started writing this book I accepted the Thanatos theory and the Jekels-Bergler theory as my starting point. The difference in my working hypothesis was mainly that instead of life impulse versus death impulse I introduced a new phase: (a) death impulse, (b) dying (sleeping) as uterine regression, (c) body as phallos, emphasis on erotic tension (wishes) to counteract anxiety involved in relinquishing object world.

However, modern biology questions the existence of the death impulse. According to Szász (and the authorities he quotes) the second law of thermodynamics applies only to "closed" systems whereas living organisms are "open" systems. Thus the device by which an organism maintains itself stationary "really consists in continually sucking orderliness from its environment."[6]

"Freud's views regarding the death instinct seemed to have been in-

5 Jekels, L., and Bergler, E., "Instinct Dualism in Dreams," *Psychoanalytic Quarterly*, IX, 1940, pp. 394–398.

6 Szász, Thomas S., "On the Psychoanalytic Theory of Instincts," *Psychoanalytic Quarterly*, XXI, 1952, p. 31.

fluenced by the biological theories current at that time. These theories were largely based in the physics of closed systems." "Since, however, life can appear only in open systems, the principle of entropy is not applicable under these circumstances." "Aging and death thus appear to develop only in response to environmental interferences with the life instinct."[7]

I do not feel I can decide which interpretation of the facts in biology is valid. The anthropological or mythological parallelism, sleep-death may not mean, as Jekels and Bergler think, just what it says, but may be reversed in our fantasy, death is unending sleep. In other words, we have experienced sleep but not death. In my book on "Spiegelzauber" (Vienna 1919) I could show that in the oracular use of the mirror a girl (or boy) might either see the future spouse or their own headless image (pp. 117 ff.). The conflict is here, as in Freud's original theories narcissism versus object love or the regressive versus the progressive trend of the libido.[8]

We shall now discuss the fantasy content of the moment of falling asleep.

II. HYPNAGOGIC AND HYPNOPOMPIC FANTASIES

A young girl, who has had many affairs but seldom achieves orgasm, describes the sensation of falling asleep on the analytic couch:

"I am whirling, my whole body is like a top. I am a dancing dervish. I am falling into a tomb."

The same patient is dozing off on the analytic couch. She says: "I would like to be pregnant. Now I am at the bottom of a well. Space seems infinite, sinking. I can hear my own words but it is as if they come from a distance."

A man of about thirty-five says, "I am floating, my whole body is whirling around. It is a pleasant sensation. I am drowsy."

A married man remembers only a fragment of his dream, "A deep chasm—it was sleep."

We now quote from a famous British psychoanalyst, viz., *Alice in Wonderland*.

"Alice was getting very tired of sitting by her sister on the bank, and of having nothing to do. . . . The hot day made her feel very sleepy and stupid." Suddenly she sees the Rabbit who takes a watch out of its waistcoat pocket, then hurries down the rabbit hole. "In another moment down went Alice after it, never considering how in the world she was to get out

7 *Ibid.*, p. 44.
8 Cf. also Bunker, Henry, A., "Narcissus," in *Psychoanalysis and the Social Sciences*, I, New York, 1948, p. 159.

again. The rabbit-hole went straight on like a tunnel for some way, and then dipped suddenly down, so suddenly that Alice had not a moment to think about stopping herself before she found herself falling down what seemed to be a very deep well."

"Either the well was very deep, or she fell very slowly, for she had plenty of time as she went down to look about her, and to wonder what was going to happen next. First, she tried to look down and make out what she was coming to, but it was too dark to see anything; then she looked at the sides of the well, and noticed that they were filled with cupboards and bookshelves: here and there she saw maps and pictures hung upon pegs. She took down a jar from one of the shelves as she passed, it was labelled 'ORANGE MARMALADE,' but to her great disappointment it was empty; she did not like to drop the jar for fear of killing somebody underneath, so she managed to put it into one of the cupboards as she fell past it." After various other episodes she finds locked doors, then a golden key that opens one of them. "The door led into a small passage, not much larger than a rat-hole, she knelt down and looked along the passage into the loveliest garden you ever saw. How she longed to get out of that dark hall, and wander about among those beds of bright flowers and those cool fountains, but she could not even get her head through the doorway, 'and even if my head would go through,' thought poor Alice, 'it would be of little use without my shoulders. Oh, how I wish I could shut up like a telescope! I think I could, if only I knew how to begin.'" She drinks something, eats something, and suddenly becomes nine feet tall. The end is that Alice awakes from her dream.[9]

In a modern novel, we find a similar hypnagogic fantasy becoming a dream. This is about a nine-year-old son of a Hungarian family about to emigrate to Paris.

"For Jani, worn out and half asleep, is worrying about the boring of tunnels and the blowing of caves. . . . However, robbers escape and hide Jani's tunnels and caves, and the secret flying field he has just built, in his thought, on a hidden plateau between high peaks serves the wicked aims of a master *kidnapper*. . . . His sleep-numbed brain is now busy cutting a bridle path in the forest." Finally he falls asleep.[10]

The following passage is quoted from T. W. White's "The Sword and the Stone."

"The Wart slept well in the woodland nest where he had laid himself down, in that kind of thin but refreshing sleep which people have when they first lie out of doors. At first he only dipped below the surface of sleep, and skimmed along like a salmon in shallow water, so close to the surface

9 Carroll, L., *Alice in Wonderland*, New York, n.d., pp. 1–15.
10 Foldes, J., *The Street of the Fishing Cat*, New York, 1937, pp. 8, 9.

that he fancied himself in air. He thought himself awake when he was already asleep. He saw the stars above his face, whirling round on their silent and sleepless axis, and the leaves of the trees rustling against them, and heard small changes in the grass. These little noises of footsteps and soft-fringed wing-beats and stealthy bellies drawn over grass blades or rattling against the bracken at first frightened or interested him, so that he moved to see what they were (but never saw), then soothed him so that he no longer cared to see what they were but trusted them to be themselves, and finally left him altogether as he swam down deeper and deeper, *nuzzling his nose into the scented turf, into the warm ground, into the unending waters under the earth*"[11] (My italics).

A patient whose depression started at a very early age with the birth of his brother has the following hypnagogic fantasy:

John and I are both in a grave. Even there I am trying to kill him.

Another patient reports the following dream at the moment his alarm clock went off.

I am trying to get back into a cave, but the entrance is blocked (i.e., he is trying to prolong sleep).

The same patient somewhat later has the following fantasy on awakening:

I am struggling to get out of a cauldron, or is it a womb?

Another patient, age thirty-five, married, says:

The dream slipped away. I saw a snake crawling into a rockhole. In this case the dream is clearly genital. Fantasies on the couch may be quite similar. This is a schizoid patient, "I see a girl in a fur coat. She looks like my sister. We go into a shaft or corridor. It keeps getting narrower and progress is always more difficult."

The patient has difficulties in coitus. Conscious masturbation fantasies about his sister. The narrow room is both his mother's womb or vagina and his sister's vagina. *The whole person is in the vagina.*

A depressive patient, a young married woman, has the following hypnagogic fantasy:

There are many holes in the ground. Ropes are hanging down from these holes. I am at the bottom of one of them in the earth.

After this hypnagogic fantasy, she relates another of a more complicated structure.

Blue rings, like smoke or fog or excrement, envelop me. They start to

11 White, T. H., *The Sword and the Stone*, New York, 1939.

encircle me from the feet and move upward very fast. Then I see red rings (sex) and I feel as if I were being turned inside out. It really feels as if I were sinking into my self.

Perhaps this is the real explanation of sleeping, of the hypnagogic fantasy, of the basic element in the dream. "One feels as if one were sinking into oneself."

Falling or sinking are typical hypnagogic sensations. In English we have the expression "to fall asleep," in Hungarian, *álomba merült:* "to dip under into sleep, as into water." But in German we have *einschlafen,* in French *endormir,* "to sleep in," "to turn into oneself." If we can condense these two ways of expressing sleep, we can say that the sleeper turns into himself and falls back into the womb, his own body being the material substratum of the dream-womb. The Yukaghir shaman's drum is a lake into which he dives in order to descend into the spirit world.[12] Gutheil's patient reports a dream flash: "I am falling down a precipice into an endless depth."[13]

Several patients with anxiety relate that they have noticed the moment when the hypnagogic fantasy became a dream. Sometimes they awake with anxiety but with the content of the fantasy lost. One, after a bitter fight with his hysterical wife, retains the following words: "My mother does not love me; other mothers love me," and awakes with anxiety.

A middle-aged woman, analyzed because of certain difficulties in her married life, reports the following recurrent hypnagogic fantasy or dream.

I am rising in the air. Hands of many people are reaching out for me, but I elude them and rise up. I float above a tree or some other object without touching it.

She describes her narcissistic nature and the pleasure she gets from writing poetry, which lifts her above the common herd. She also remarks that this dream or fantasy feels like an orgasm.

Whereas the typical hypnagogic fantasy contains elements of sinking, i.e., falling asleep, and can be interpreted either as coitus or (and) as uterine regression, in this case it is *rising,* a flying dream of a definitely orgastic nature. It seems that the patient is also masturbating in this dream fantasy; we infer this from the "hands" and the "not touching."

A dream analyzed by Gutheil shows some similarities to this one. The dreamer is a married woman of forty, dissatisfied in her marriage.

A dog jumps at me. I cannot defend myself otherwise than by rising into the air. Then I am flying in the air, but I am still within reach of

12 Czaplicka, M. A., *Aboriginal Siberia,* Oxford, 1914, p. 209.
13 Gutheil, E. A., *The Handbook of Dream Analysis,* New York, 1951, p. 280.

the dog which constantly snaps at me. I continue flying till I am suspended over a precipice. Then I fall down and lose consciousness. The
falling down was a pleasant sensation which became intensified after I
hit upon a rock in the ground.[14]

The rising is here coitus, the falling down with loss of consciousness
both sleep and orgasm.

In some not too frequent cases falling asleep is represented as being
fetched by mother.

A young woman whose father has recently got a job has difficulty in
falling asleep. She remembers the following as a hypnagogic fantasy:

A woman dressed in black comes through the door. She carries two
big shopping bags.

Then she dreams:

I see a crate of eggs with the lid off.

Associations: Two shopping bags; that is what mother usually has
when she goes to buy food. There was a big dinner at her father's house.
She recently met two friends, one of whom was pregnant, and the other
asked her when she would be having a child. There are two sisters in the
family. Black = death.

The hypnagogic fantasy shows falling asleep as falling back into
mother's womb, as dying, but also death wishes against mother who comes
to fetch her as a ghost (black).

Associations: Father used to sell eggs. Chicks come out of eggs. The
hypnagogic fantasy is regressive, the dream itself oedipal and genital.

A middle-aged patient, male, married, has the following hypnagogic
fantasy or dream.

A witch is putting some ointment on my eyes to close them. He does
not wake up but remembers this next morning.

The following dream might just as well be (or perhaps is) a hypnagogic fantasy. The dreamer is a young woman (hysteria).

I see a chest of drawers like in a hotel.
She had a good time with X, a girl friend whom she regards with
admiration, at that hotel. It is also like the trunk of another lady friend
who left recently for Europe. The chest of drawers is also like the elevator
that brings her to the analyst.

Analysis is somehow like sleeping or dreaming. The chest or trunk
of her two ideals is an improved maternal womb into which she falls
asleep.

[14] *Ibid.,* p. 211.

Lowy quotes a hypnagogic hallucination of his own which we shall now interpret in accordance with other similar hypnagogic phenomena. Lowy writes:

"During a difficult period of my life, owing to the political circumstances in Czechoslovakia, I went to bed at night, saying to myself, 'I can't bear it any longer.' In the hypnagogic hallucination I see first of all an old Slovak man who is toiling laboriously cutting wood, his undulating locks hide a face covered with sweat. Then I see a heroic figure from a film I once saw. He is the hero of the Slovak people; he fought gloriously against the suppressors of his brethren as he was shown in the film dying in a last heroic fight. *I see him rise proudly from his fetters and shake his locks. Lastly, I see some prone figure (dead?).* Perhaps it is my father (with a beard?). This latter picture is not in accordance with past reality. The meaning content seems to be quite simple: 'This life with its struggle leads to final exhaustion, to an early death.' I may add that in my youth I used to say with regard to some difficult task that 'it was as difficult as cutting wood.' "[15]

We wish to emphasize two main features of the dream or fantasy. The dying of the hero is the process of falling asleep, *the rising in the phallic countermove.* Superimposed on this is, of course, the oedipus conflict, killing father, overcoming difficulties is hard work, cutting wood. The author also quotes a hypnagogic fantasy of Silberer, interpreted by Silberer in a manner which touches only what is conscious. Silberer has just seen *Faust* in the theater. He writes:

"I try to concentrate on the difficult problem of the *Mutter* (mothers) which has given so much heartbreak to interpreters of Goethe's work." He wakes from sleep with the following hallucination:

"I am standing on a solitary promontory projecting far into the *dark sea.* The waves of the sea seem to blend with the dark sky which is mysteriously heavy."[16]

The standing sleeper and the solitary promontory are the *phallos,* the ocean and the sky are the mother. This is the correct solution of the "Mothers' " scene in Faust.

In the Second Part of *Faust,* Act I, we find Faust and Mephisto as magicians at the Emperor's court. The Emperor demands that the shades of Helen and Paris be evoked. Faust tells Mephisto it has to be done, and Mephisto is now telling Faust how it can be accomplished.

[15] Lowy, S., *Psychological and Biological Foundations of Dream Interpretation,* London, 1946, p. 37.

[16] Silberer, H., "Symbolik des Erwachens und Schwellensymbolik," *Jahrbuch für psychoanalytische und psychopathologische Forschungen,* III, 1912, p. 625.

Mephistopheles[17]

Unwilling, I reveal a loftier mystery
In solitude are enthroned the Goddesses,
No Space around them, Place and Time still less;
Only to speak of them embarrasses
They are The Mothers!

• • • • • • •

Faust

Where is the way?

Mephistopheles

No way!—To the Unreachable,
Ne'er to be trodden! A way to the Unbeseechable,
Never to be besought! Art thou prepared?
There are no locks, no latches to be lifted,
Through endless solitudes shalt thou be drifted
Hast thou through solitudes and deserts fared?

• • • • • • •

Here, take this key!

Faust

It glows, it shines,—increases in my hand!

Mephistopheles

How much 'tis worth, thou soon shalt understand
The Key will scent the true place from all others
Follow it down!—'twill lead thee to the Mothers.

• • • • • • •

Descend, then! I could also say, Ascend!
'T were all the same. Escape from the Created
To shapeless forms in liberated spaces!
Enjoy what long ere this was dissipated!
There whirls the press, like clouds on clouds unfolding;
Then with stretched arm swing high the key thou'rt holding

Faust

Good! grasping firm, fresher strength I win
My breast expands, let the great work begin!

Mephistopheles

At last a blazing tripod tells thee this,
That there the utterly deepest bottom is
Its light to thee will then the Mothers show,

• • • • • • •

17 Goethe, J. W., *Faust*. Pt. II, Bayard Taylor, tr. New York, Modern Library ed.,
p. 52.

Composedly mounting, by the luck upborne,
Before they notice it, thou shalt return
When thou the tripod hither hast conveyed,
Then call a hero, a heroine, from the shade,—

. . . .

Faust (sublimely)

Ye Mothers, in your name, who set your Throne
In boundless Space, eternally alone,
And yet companioned! All forms of Being
In movement, lifeless, ye are round you seeing.
Whate'er once was, there burns and brightens free
In splendor—for't would fain eternal be;
And ye allot it, with all potent might
To Day's pavillions and the vaults of Night.

Then we see Paris and Helena whom Faust has brought to life from the Mothers. He descends to the Mothers with the key and ascends bringing up Helen of Troy.

Silberer has recorded some dreams in which awakening appears as coming out of the womb. The dreamer, a woman, falls through a crumbling ceiling and is covered with fragments. The ceiling, or fragments, slips off from her and she is awake.[18]

It is morning, and Silberer is partly trying to stay asleep and partly to awake.

Dream: I am crossing a brook, standing on one foot. I pull my foot back again.[19]
A very characteristic awakening dream.

I have put something in a box, but as I can't reach it there are strings attached to it by means of which I can pull it out at any moment.

The box is evidently the uterus. Coming out of it is awakening. The same interpretation is valid for the following. Silberer writes:

"A little after the alarm clock has gone off, I want to go on sleeping, but noise from the street disturbs me. I want to lock myself in my room, but one door keeps opening."[20]

In another dream the awakening is symbolized by diving into a pool —i.e., by going to sleep.

---

[18] Silberer, H., "Zur Symbolbildung," *Jahrbuch für psychoanalytische und psychopathologische Forschungen,* IV, 1912, p. 677.

[19] *Idem,* "Symbolik des Erwachens und Schwellensymbolik," *Jahrbuch für psychoanalytische und psychopathologische Forschungen,* III, 1912, p. 625.

[20] *Ibid.,* p. 628. In another dream, we also find awakening symbolized by a door opening (p. 647). Cf. also Paul Federn, "The Awakening of the Ego in Dreams," *International Journal of Psycho-Analysis,* XV, 1934, p. 296.

We quote another awakening dream as symbolizing the "upward movement."

I am doing gymnastic exercises with a lady. She is in a kneeling position. I tell her, "Now comes the real difficulty—*to arise*[21] (*Aufstehen*—to awake, but also an erection).

A patient whose conflicts have to do with latent homosexual tendencies reports the following hypnopompic fantasy:

I am talking to a group of young women. Then a little withered old man invites me to come into his house. But he also blocks the way and comes too close to me face to face. I am excited sexually.

The women remind him of several women he has had affairs with. The little old man is like his superior in the office (Father imago). He mentions the fact that before falling asleep he had intercourse with his wife and she stimulated him anally with her foot. He frequently sticks his finger into her rectum.

The father imago prevents his having affairs; instead he invites him into a male vagina, i.e., the rectum. Going into the house (rectum, vagina) means continuing sleep. This, however, is not possible, because of the manifestly homosexual dream content.

The following awakening dream of a patient with schizoid personality shows a clear-cut birth symbolism. The dreamer's wife is pregnant.

I am on a boat that is drifting on the ocean with my friend N. The boat collides with a bridge and I lose my pocket knife. There is a tunnel or arcade on the bridge. A taxi driver has the idea to pull the boat through a narrow opening up on the bridge and then pull it through the arcade on the bridge. A procession forms itself, first the taxi driver, then a baby elephant, then the boat. The taxi driver pulls elephant and boat. I awake.

Associations and Interpretation: The night before they saw a movie. It was about a bull fighter who looses his grip (lost knife, castration). When he was a little boy they called him a baby elephant because he was so fat. The elephant must also be phallic, the trunk. He hopes for a son. The drifting boat is his wife, she is pregnant and the rest follows automatically. In the dream the driver represents the analyst; the analysis will pull him through, i.e., he himself, the boy (with whom he is identical) and his wife (who is now in danger) will all be reborn. The birth symbolism of the awakening and the phallic body is quite clear. I now quote a dream published by Grotjahn.

"In dreams about flying it is of special interest to note the relation of

21 Silberer, *op. cit.,* p. 647.

the volitional Ego function and its importance for the awakening. A male, aged thirty-six, reports the following example of a flying dream.

"In the dream someone is throwing snowballs at me. I get up in the air and try to fly to my balcony which I cannot find. I think 'why don't you awaken, then you could enter the house by the front door.' I am afraid to fall down. I have the feeling that this is no dream, that I can really fly, that I always could have flown if I had wished to strong enough. This is only a question of will power, the last words were thought during awakening."

Grotjahn comments:

"Flying is, even in a dream, connected with a very strong body feeling and this body feeling is already an Ego function and usually the beginning of an awakening state. In the observation the flying is actually felt, the dreamer needs to make a tremendous energetic effort, flying is a problem of will power. This effort too belongs to the volitional part of the Ego."[22]

In my opinion Grotjahn completely misunderstands the structure of the dream. It is true that the ego prompted by the superego is trying to awaken the dreamer, but all the rest is beside the point. The reference to will power is probably used in an inverted sense, it is the reverberation of attempts to *give up masturbation* (question of will power). The flying is an erection or masturbation dream with the body as phallus. The front door is not the door of awakening, it is that of sleep or the womb. "I can really fly"—is typical of erection or masturbation dreams.

A patient of Lowy has the following vision:

"A balloon or Zeppelin is rising, a fighter zooms down."[23]

The fall is falling asleep, the patient is fighting against this (fighter). The rising Zeppelin is again the phallos.

These are Doris Webster's observations on the process of falling asleep. "In trying to trace the change at the turning point of sleep from coherent thought to apparently incoherent nonsense I found that I could catch and bring back impressions from the different layers of attention in which we sink when we fall asleep." She heard the words "mountains not yet flattened out." "The relation to my posture was apparent for I had fallen asleep with my knees raised." Another time in the same position she heard the word "Julia." This was another reference to pushing up a hill.

22 Grotjahn, M., "The Process of Awakening," *Psychoanalytic Review*, 1942, XXIX, pp. 9–10.

23 Lowy, *op. cit.*, pp. 37, 38. Further very clear instances of the hypnagogic fantasy as a uterus are given (but not so interpreted) by E. Bergler. An enquiry into the "material phenomenon," *International Journal of Psycho-Analysis*, XVI, 1935, p. 209 (abyss = vagina), p. 211; lemon, p. 212; medieval fortress, p. 214; sentry box.

"Litchfield" spoken in a tone of exultation referred not only to the hill leading to Litchfield, Connecticut, but also to the famous "show" section of that town. "My hands spread out on the mattress represented those sections."[24]

The hypnagogic fantasy also creates a new environment formed out of the dreamer's body.

III. The Basic Dream

The following is the dream of a patient who is trying to break himself of the habit of taking sedatives. The patient relates:

It is summer. I am at a summer resort and I have decided that this is the best time to eliminate sedatives.

Dream: A young man is lifting a kind of bowl high up. I won't do it. If I take any of the stuff that is in the bowl, I shall become a zombie.[25] (This is because the night before I did not sleep very well and I was tempted to take a sedative again.) If I don't, I'll never be a zombie.

Associations: The young man—*Euthanatos* with the torch. Taking from the contents of the bowl—those who eat the food offered by Persephoneia stay dead;[26] they cannot return to the living world. All the dead are wedded to Persephoneia.

The young man—the picture on the Manhattan telephone directory —the joke about the man who had such an erection he could not get a job, and now he is on the telephone book. The whole figure in the joke is interpreted as a penis, but instead of the bundle of lightning he has a bowl in his hand in the dream. The bowl on top is mother's vagina (displaced upward), and eating is coitus.

The dream reveals anxiety at the moment of falling asleep. It must be the moment in which the hypnagogic fantasy is passing into a dream because of the question: shall I take a sedative? It reveals quite clearly what falling asleep means; it is going into mother, coitus with mother. It is also death (Persephoneia, Zombie) but it is a death *in coitu. Euthanatos*—the Greek mythological image of *good death,* a young man with a torch. The anxiety elements are counterbalanced by phallic magic, the supernatural penis (body) wedded to Persephoneia, one of the immortals. This is why he does not awake but sleeps till morning.

---

24 Webster, D., "The Origin of the Signs of the Zodiac," *American Imago,* I, 1940, pp. 31–47.

25 It is not quite clear whether this is a dream or a hypnagogic fantasy.

26 This is not quite correct, cf. infra.

Freud interprets the following dream:

I see a little house somewhat further back between two castles. The door is closed. My wife takes me to the little house and opens the door. I slip in quite easily into the house where I find a passage that is narrow and goes upward obliquely.

Somewhat further back means a coitus a tergo. The two big buildings or castles are his wife's buttocks. The passageway is the vagina, the small house a young girl in whom he is interested.[27] It is generally accepted that this is the way coitus is symbolized in dreams but the question has never been asked, does it mean anything that the phallus is represented by the whole body of the dreamer?

Our primary concern will be to show that there is a close connection between the hypnagogic fantasy and the dream. The hypnagogic fantasy becomes a dream if not interrupted by anxiety or not repressed. *This reveals the existence of a basic dream valid for mankind in general and also gives us new insight into the nature of dreaming.*

A middle-aged, depressive patient dreams:

While dozing in the afternoon on my couch I was listening to the ball game. This continues in the dream. I am still on a couch listening to the baseball game on the radio. The whole room gradually looks like a funeral parlor. Stein and my wife are in the kitchen doing dishes.
    The ceiling is decorated with green boughs. The boughs are cut off their trunks and suspended mysteriously. They are pointing toward the bulbs and candles.
    Stein goes into the other room. He lights a candle or strikes a match, and again the light increases slowly.

Associations: Stein is an imaginary rival and a father figure. Something dirty is going on between his wife and Stein in the kitchen = the primal scene. In the first phase of the dream the patient is in a funeral parlor—sleep is both death and regression into the womb. Interrupting and sexually stimulating experiences come from the outside and gradually break up the dream. First the primal scene: something dirty is happening outside; father and mother. The boughs and the light are again Christmas, i.e., birth. At the same time they also represent the life impulse gradually returning. Stein who strikes a light in another room is now a duplicate of the dreamer.

He awakes and immediately has intercourse with his wife.

The following dream of a little boy is a typical basic dream in our sense of the word.

27 Freud, *Gesammelte Schriften,* III, p. 117. Cf. VII, p. 198.

I walk downstairs. My mother follows me and pushes me so that I feel dizzy.[28]

A five-year-old boy dreamed:

I was a whale and was coming down the Montblanc bridge. I went underneath it and everyone stared at me.

The child's analyst merely told him: "Well, this time you were bigger than your father."[29] This was, of course, all she could tell him, but the dream is more: the dream of going in and under is falling asleep and also coitus.

The next dream was dreamed by a girl of sixteen:

I am going over a narrow bridge. Suddenly it breaks under me and I plunge into the water. An officer dives in after me and brings me with his strong arms to the bank. Suddenly it seems to me that I am a dead body. The officer looks very pale, like a corpse.[30]

We can distinguish three stages in this basic dream:
(a) Sleep is death.
(b) Sleep is uterine regression.
(c) Sleep is coitus.

Whether sleep is a periodic death depends on whether we accept or reject the death impulse, but that it is a regression into the womb cannot be doubted.

A patient dreams:

I am going into the subway. (It is a tomb or a womb, she says.) I see a big cat and a kitten. The kitten is tied to the big cat by a chain.

Since her problem is her resistance to the analysis and her mother fixation, nothing could be clearer. She hates cats. The cat is her mother, she is the kitten. She is going back into the womb.

A middle-aged woman patient, in a mixture of depression, compulsion neurosis, and strong tendencies toward introversion, dreams:

I am on the edge of a crater. I am afraid of falling because I shall be burned. But as I fall, the feeling is nice and warm, and I land on a cushion. While falling, somebody shows me a stage with four Hallowe'en witches.

Interpretation: "Falling on the cushion" makes it clear that we have to do with a dream that develops directly from a hypnagogic fantasy. The dream shows her anxiety in falling asleep, and also her attempt to

[28] Eisler, M. J., "Geburtstraum eines fünfjahrigen Knaben," *Internationale Zeitschrift für Psychoanalyse*, VIII (1922), p. 343.
[29] Rambert, M. L., *Children in Conflict*, New York, 1949, p. 162.
[30] Campbell, J., *The Hero With a Thousand Faces*, New York, 1948, pp. 103, 104, quoting Stekel, *Die Sprache des Traumes*, p. 200.

prevent herself from falling asleep. She has had a nightmare recently which she forgets in the morning, knowing only she has had a nightmare. The four witches are herself and her three sisters. The sisters have all had rather promiscuous lives—hence, witches' orgies. She has had one isolated sexual experience after a long period of sexual abstinence. This is enough to make her feel guilty. Hence the hell fire at the bottom of the pit and herself as one of the witches. At the same time and on another level, the regression aspect of the dream (i.e., regression into the womb) is countered by libidinization or progression. She is one of the witches, it is nice and warm down in the crater. After the dream she makes a significant remark—it felt like receding into the lining of one's stomach (turning inwards).

The following dream of a woman in narcosis also shows the process of falling asleep:

I dream that I am swinging sustained by a rope across a big space. The rope is attached to the center of the space and I am swinging round the axis. It is most alarming and suddenly the rope breaks and I lose my hold of it and fall with fearful anxiety into vacancy. Unexpectedly I come against a hateful spongy something and bite into it with all my strength in order to hold fast. Previously while falling I may have shrieked.

Stekel writes, "She recognizes that this must be a dream about her mother's womb and that the rope must be the umbilical cord. (She had been trained by the previous analyses.) But to the spongy mass the association was again the rotten apple into which she bit and the fall into sin."

After these associations a memory cropped up. She was seven and the family had just moved into a new flat. Her father was sitting on a chair in one of the rooms and he never noticed that the cord by which the electric chandelier hung was giving way. The lamp fell on his head and cut it open so that the blood streamed from the forehead. The patient was terribly frightened. When we analyze the various associations we see that they supplement one another. The bloody forehead is connected with the antlers. The injury to the father symbolically represented the tragedy of his marriage. (His wife had given him the horns to wear.)[31]

The dream is characteristic for the process of falling asleep, especially the circular swinging or rotating. The rope is not the umbilical cord (as interpreted by the analysis) but the penis (= head, antlers) the fall, the dropping off to sleep, orgasm, and birth in reverse. We shall discuss later the significance of the biting as retarding the fall.

A married man of thirty-five, diffuse anxiety, difficulty in falling asleep, dreams:

31 Stekel, W., *The Interpretation of Dreams,* New York, 1943, II, p. 515.

I am in the foyer of a house. The analyst is *sleeping* in bed with my mother. He need not do that, I tell him. I rush out of the house.

The foyer of the house is the vagina. He frequently identified himself with the analyst. He is entering sleep (mother), and he is also inside, asleep. But he rushes out, i.e., he tries to awaken himself. This would be what we mean by the basic dream. However, that is by no means the whole story. He goes on to talk about his father and finally shows clearly oedipal fantasies. Superimposed on the basic dream we have therefore a dream of the *primal scene*.

Another patient, recently married, does not want to have a child. But his wife insists.

Dream: I jump from a rock to rescue a child in the ocean. By the time I get there it is only a doll. Then I see it on the beach, safe and alive.

The ocean he jumps into is his wife's vagina. The jumping figure is the phallic body and he doubts whether the penis will be alive or dead. The penis and the child are both symbolized by the doll. The dream means coitus, uterine regression and birth on the beach.

A patient whose sister is pregnant dreams:

There are many cookies on a tray. They are offered to my sister. I eat them all. As a punishment I am to be pushed into an oven on a shovel.

Association: The oven reminds her of the chimney where the stork is supposed to bring the children.

Interpretation: Allegedly she envies her sister, but really she wants to be the embryo in the womb. The punishment in the dream is what she desires. Eating the cakes—sibling rivalry. Her sister's unborn child really means her sister unborn.

What follows here is an attempt to deepen our understanding of some universal aspects of the dream, especially in its relatedness to sleep and the moment of transition between waking and sleeping.

In the dream of all human beings we have a clear indication that a phallic double is formed and that the dreamer's environment is built up out of his or her own body.

The dream itself is in its first stage already a compromise, the result of a conflict. For reasons to be explained either on the basis of the death-impulse theory or because sleep as regression into the womb causes anxiety (relinquishing the object world) the regressive trend is transformed into a coitus. Now in coitus itself, as Ferenczi has shown, the male enters the female totally with the sperm, partially with the penis and in fantasy with the body. Incidentally the curious fact may be worth observing that while coitus in the primates has lost its biological function it returns or regains this function is the coitus fantasy, the male becomes a child, i.e., his own child. This is also our basic dream, regression is also progression, i.e., genitality. The conception theories of the Australians with the child found and placed in a dream illustrate this point very neatly.[32] We should expect that when a female patient reports a dream in which she enters a room the meaning of the dream is uterine regression. However, a patient who has recovered her ability to have orgasms reports the following dream:

A little woman with short red hair opens the door and says with a gracious gesture "Enter, please!"

She is about to menstruate and feels a strong sex urge. The short red hair is her own pubic hair.

In coitus she is in her own vagina, i.e., the vagina is cathected.

In other dreams the regressive aspect of space may be more emphasized.

A depressive patient, young woman who has no orgasm:

I see a woman who has a long box-like structure. There is room for a child in it, also a piano and a toilet. I reproach her for keeping a child in such a confined space and I feel anxious. She says, there is a door through which the child can step out.

The woman is her mother. The box means the uterus but also the confining aspects of her neurosis which are due to her mother's personality. Why the piano and the toilet? These are what the child has to play with, i.e., masturbation (the piano) and urethral and anal pleasures. We certainly cannot assume that the embryo masturbates in the womb. But if the box is also her own vulva, uterus and her whole body the dream is understandable. The next dream is mentioned here to show how the dream transforms anxiety (day stimulus) into an erotic situation in which genitality and regression are combined.

The patient is a young woman who is feeling very tired. Her doctor has told her that she suffers from a calcium deficiency. Her last waking thought before falling asleep, I am so tired, it would not matter if I were to die.

Dream: I am in my home town (in Europe). The whole place is very poor but there is one palace in it, the Royal Palace. I peer through the red draperies and I see a grey-haired woman sitting in a room.

She talks about the love affair she had with a young man who was somehow connected with the court. She calls this young man grey-haired. She thinks of her dead father, of the analyst, of her mother. These are

[32] To be discussed infra.

grey-haired. Peering through the drapery; she compares the drapery to her own labia.

The first layer of the dream means mother is in her womb. "I am in my womb or vulva" means genital cathexis. "Mother is in it" means (a) oedipal cathexis, (b) "I am in mother." The emphasis on the red draperies means the room or Royal Palace is also her own genital organ. "If I were to die I would be buried with my father," i.e., the grey-haired figure in her womb is her father as a lover (cf. associations above).

Another essential feature of the dream is fission. Primitive animism says that in the dream the soul leaves the body and travels about. Actually in sleeping all cathexes are withdrawn from the environment that is seemingly external and objective but really libidinal and subjective.

The following dream shows what we mean by saying that the body image in the dream is genital, usually phallic even in the case of a woman.

A young married woman, who enjoys coitus but stops just before orgasm, dreams:

I am walking up a steep flight of stairs in a house that belongs to my mother's best friend, a famous beauty in her youth. I go up to the floor before the last. It is dangerous, it might cave in and I might fall.

The beautiful woman, her mother's best friend, is herself. She is walking up (rising; move of sexual tension in coitus) in her own house, i.e., her own vagina. But she halts before reaching the top, it might cave in (orgasm).

The body image going up the stairs is obviously phallic. On the deepest level the identification of the female's body with a penis is simply a representation of her regressive trends plus the male component of her ambisexuality. In a case analyzed by Fenichel, the author writes:

"Further analysis revealed unequivocally that here too the *Vaterleibsphantasie* covered a *Mutterleibsphantasie* on a deeper level, that the penis corresponded to the idea of the inside of the mother's body, of the embryo in whose place she had fantasied herself."[33]

The next dream of a forty-year-old woman with a schizoid character shows what we mean by saying that the environment into which the dreamer regresses is both her own body and the maternal womb.

I am standing before a building that is an obelisk, a Sphinx and I go inside. It is now a hospital. There is a candy store before the building. My mother is behind me and either she or I wear a peculiar blouse.

Associations and Interpretation: (1) The blouse. Reminds her of a friend, who may be a schizophrenic.

[33] Fenichel, O., "The Symbolic Equation: Girl = Phallus," *Psychoanalytic Quarterly*, 1949, p. 309. However, Fenichel disregards Ferenczi's views and interprets on oral lines.

(2) The obelisk. A penis. Her recurring fantasies, nearly delusions about having a penis. This is connected with a cover memory about father; her penis appears to be father's introjected penis. (This is, of course, an interpretation.)

(3) The Sphinx. Breasts of a woman. Also; man and woman copulating.[34]

The day residue is her indecision about going on with her career or giving up. The latter is symbolized by regression into the maternal womb, the hospital, schizophrenia. She says, "looking at this building is like looking at myself in a mirror."

A young woman whose husband has intercourse with her about once a month dreams as follows:

I am on a dock that juts into the water. There are houses on the dock; each of them has only one room. I am in the last house or room. I have a little girl about one or two years old. She is the most beautiful little girl one can imagine. I look at her, her legs are like my husband's. Then I change my mind, the legs are like mine.

The marvelously beautiful girl is her vagina. She remarks that her husband has a feminine personality while she is more masculine—therefore what is it, a vagina or a penis?

The dream expresses the patient's doubts regarding her role in sex. She is in her own room (cathected vagina) yet she has beautiful legs (fantasy of a penis).

A married man, who has had a quarrel with his wife about his coming home late, dreams after this:

We are going to visit Elsa and Jack. We are in a long hallway (like the waiting room for the analysis), old-fashioned, flat telephone on the wall. Elsa appears crying on her mother's shoulder (or on my mother's). Then I stand opposite the elevator or rather a huge elevator shaft that is open. A man is urinating into it. Then I do the same. Finally a little man cleans the urine off my shoes by pouring water out of a jug.

It is night time, hot. We are at a summer camp for children. Somebody suggests swimming in the nude. I am looking forward to seeing Elsa in the nude, but my wife is jealous and I am afraid the camp director might catch us.

Associations: (1) Elsa and Jack. Friends, a divorced couple. We had been talking before about another divorced couple, now remarried.

(2) The hallway. Like a vagina. (Interpretation: mother's vagina; mother figure appears with wife figure.)

(3) The old-fashioned telephone. When he was a little boy they

34 Cf. Róheim, *The Riddle of the Sphinx,* 1934. (The patient has not read the book.)

taught him to telephone to his father on that kind of apparatus. He used to say, sticking his finger into the telephone, "Father do you see me?" which was very funny.

(4) The elevator shaft. "Our house in the country, anxiety in elevator." (I interpret it as his mother's vagina.) The first man who urinates must be his father. The little old man looks like a man who had the same first name as his father and was in many ways his father's mentor. Then he remarks that his father wanted to make this older man's wife. He comments on women who become mistresses of both father and son.

Interpretation: The dream is undoubtedly a urethral waking dream. It represents the oedipus complex on a urethral level. The third man who washes means *lustration*—it must be all right if generation after generation does it.

The swimming scene is still urethral but partly on a present-day level. The woman involved is really desirable, his wife really jealous. But the camp director and the children's camp point to the infantile past.

He says that his wife is exactly like his mother. He married her not so much out of love but because he thought she would be good for him, keep him from various irregularities.

The association with father and the telephone and the finger is significant. The primal scene, father's penis—there are stations on the way "back into life."

An interesting feature of this dream is that the road to regression, i.e., the mother's vagina, is also the entrance to the analyst's office.

A patient of the depressive type has the fantasy that on arriving at the analyst's office he knocks at the door violently and shouts, "Let me in, you bastard." Analysis reveals that the "bastard" is his younger brother *in utero* and the analyst's room is the womb. A young girl in a depression says that the analytic room is a tomb, completely dark, and she will fall asleep. It is like the grave—no, it is like the womb, and then these fantasies take the opposite course. To sleep is to sleep with the analyst.

A patient, a young woman who comes to analysis after a hysterectomy, dreams:

I am in a cave. There is a silk curtain covering the entrance of the cave. On the other side of the curtain a man is talking. I don't see him. Then he is making love to me. A lot of school children come rushing out of school. I am afraid that they will see us making love. But the man reassures me. I should go deeper into the cave. I am lying in a characteristic position, like my mother lies in bed. My mother is also in the cave and she is in the same position. At the same time I am also having a bowel movement.

Interpretation: The cave is her own vagina and womb. In her dream her womb is always restored and she can give birth to children. This is represented by the children rushing out of school, herself in her mother's position and her bowel movement. The silk curtain is her restored hymen. The analyst is having an affair with her, this reminds her of the many affairs her father had with young girls. Public scandal, i.e., her father being seen in these situations, was a continuous topic in her childhood (the primal scene).

Second part of the dream: A jury of young men is threatening me because of a parcel I made up badly. One of them smiles and relents.

Interpretation: The parcel reminds her of a marriage gift she sent to a relative. It contained a bronze horse. Badly tied = her missing womb. The bronze horse reminds her of her father who used to ride, then of the Trojan horse, i.e., father in her—the oedipus complex is the danger, the Trojan horse. Her husband is the young man who smiles and forgives her attachment to father.

The dream, of course, has many layers. However from the viewpoint of what we call the basic dream it shows clearly the combination or succession of regression (withdrawal into mother's womb) and libidinal cathexis (being in own womb, affair with analyst).

The same patient dreams several months later:

We are to get a new apartment. It is sunny. But as we are in it (she and her husband), I see that it is like a cave with a disgusting fluid oozing from the side of the cave.

The sunny apartment means a new womb. The sun is both the libido and her son (to be). The disgusting fluid is menstruation and means her magically restored femininity. But the point is that here again she is in her own vagina.

Another dream of the patient, six months later:

You (i.e., the analyst) are eating herring in an old-fashioned mansion. It is like the house of my first husband. The entrance is two columns (Greek style), an arch and a door painted red. I am with my husband. Suddenly I notice that it is six o'clock, time for my hour. I am angry that he did not warn me. Now I lose forty-five dollars, I say. I telephone to you that I will be there soon. You tell me on the phone that I am to bring you more herrings. I go to a shop and buy four for you and two for myself and my husband.

Association: My husband came home the night before the dream and told me that his friend's wife is pregnant. In general, most of the wives in our age group are about to have babies. I was jealous the other day when I heard you talking in the living room to the girl who came before me. She seemed to be at home here. But you were eating the herrings in a kind of detached way. The forty-five dollars—as if I were missing the third hour. "My husband does not warn me" means you did not warn me the last hour but only the week before that I should come at a different time on Tuesday.[35] Four reminds me of *fuck*—that is what adults do. Two herrings—number two—defecating. Intercourse is for adults, defecation for children.

Interpretation: The dream mansion is her own womb in its pre-hysterectomy state. The red door—her bleeding or sexually excited vagina. The analyst eating herrings (female sex organs in her) is the phallic body or the *phallos represented as a body*. The three hours she wants are the three siblings in her first husband's family. She would then be her first husband's mother.

Another patient whose husband is impotent, after having started an affair with a young man, dreams as follows:

I am approaching a house. It is built in a U-shape, French colonial style. It is so beautiful that I cry. A young couple are about to separate. To the left there is a room with a woman *sleeping in it*. There are small rubber dolls on a drawer, all in the embryo position. The woman is to get a civil service job in Washington.

Associations: The U-shaped house reminds her that she always thinks her vagina is too big. French style—France means love. The couple who separate are herself and her husband. The sleeping woman is herself, symbolizing the state of being asleep, of introversion. The embryonic dolls—to be asleep is to be in the womb. The trend toward introversion is counterbalanced: she appears in many shapes herself, the young woman, the sleeping woman, the dolls. The other countermove is genitalization. A civil service job in Washington—prostitution. In this dream as also in the following dream of a young man coitus is represented symbolically as the whole body being in the vagina.

There is a *long corridor* in which I am standing. I ask Jane to come and have a *shower* with me. I am afraid her mother might catch us. (Jane is his girl friend.)

The following is the dream of a married man. He is depressed and severely constipated.

I am in a courtyard surrounded by white marble houses. Mausoleums. A young man is with me. I tell him I too would like to live in the country. The white marble is a contrast, association to black excrement. The space is formed out of his own rectum libidinally cathected.

---

[35] She missed an hour that week because she forgot that we had changed the schedule.

The young man is his own penis. Country—cunt. (He would like to get out of his depressive state to genitality.)

A divorced woman after rejecting another suitor dreams:

I am with Tom and Mary. (These two are brother and sister, also unmarried.) We are being pulled by ropes up through a narrow hole. We arrive at a mansion. There is a swimming pool with many swans.— It seems as if I had been there before. I want to help Mary to buy furniture. She refuses to let me.

The transition to sleep is a regression to the womb. The narrow hole—the birth passage. The mansion where she had been before and the pool—the womb. The swan is associated with a love song and with her father. Plurality of swans—many men. Furniture—marriage (the furniture in the room = penis in vagina). Mary is herself who wants it and does not want it.

A young girl who is about to be separated from her boy friend who has now a job in another town:

I look through an opening. A young couple, they are walking upstairs and singing, it is a wedding.

She sees herself having intercourse with her boy friend. The opening is the vagina and is the staircase. Coitus is symbolized by both herself and her friend being in her own vagina.

A married woman who intends to divorce her husband has the following dream (she is menstruating when she dreams this):

I am walking on the beach. A child of about five runs out of the ocean toward me. Another one, a baby, jumps head foremost into the ocean. I catch it, rescue its life. Then I put it to my breast to suckle. It refuses to take the nipple but stands erect in my arms. I carry it jutting forward through a gate into a garden full of red roses. I am careful that it should not be hurt by the thorns.

Interpretation: The dream denies and affirms menstruation. The blood is symbolized by the red roses. But at the same time, she is not bleeding because she is just being delivered (the baby jumps head foremost into the ocean). She is also being born through the analysis. The child's reluctance to suck is her own will to be independent of her husband's income, which may also be true on a conscious, autosymbolic level. Actually, however, the point is that the child symbol becomes a penis symbol. Carrying it through the gate and through the rose bushes means masturbation, coitus with her own menstruating vagina in the male role.

Another patient, a recently married woman, is dissatisfied with her husband. He has intercourse with her very rarely. She also tells me about a medical examination, about the assumption that there is too much organic maleness (androgens) in her, and about her general dissatisfaction with the shape of her own vulva. Her marriage is on the rocks for other reasons also.

Dream: I see a woman in a male overcoat with lace showing under it. It is a rundown place full of junk. I am in a miserable shack. A little boy is seated on the cellar door. I tell him to come into my shack or go back to where he came from.

Interpretation: The woman who is both male and female is herself. The place full of junk is her marriage. The miserable shanty in which she is: her own vulva and her sexual desires. The little boy seated on the door—her husband, her husband's penis. He is to *come in* or go back where he came from.

The house she is in is her own genital organ. This symbolized both the inevitable dream regression and sexual desires.

In the following dream we have a combination of the oral and the uterine. It is dreamed by a husband who on account of his depression has been refraining from intercourse for some time.

I am crossing a bridge with my wife. I look at things through a grid-iron. Under the bridge I see a river. It is flowing with milk. At the same time I *am also in the river.*

Associations: The gridiron is flat. Like the breast after sucking.

Interpretation: The gridiron is the breast. Crossing the bridge with his wife is coitus. "In the milk"—a combination of intrauterine and oral.

The following dream shows what we mean by talking of a double movement, regressive and progressive, in the dream. A patient with latent homosexuality and hypochondria dreams:

In the morning after the alarm bell goes off, he dozes off once more. Then in his state of half-sleep it is as if one pulled something, like a piece of excrement, out of a dark cave—or lost it. It is evident that because of the anal features of his character he is inclined to identify his own rectum with the "dream vagina." But the dream pulled out of a cave is exactly like the theories of antiquity where the dream comes out of a gate. In both cases it means that the dreamer goes into a cave womb. Now for the dream itself.

(1) The whole family is running toward the subway station. My elder daughter jumps, my wife also just makes it. The door closes and I am left on the outside with my younger daughter.

(2) I am in a big house, a broadcasting station. It is like a child's view of the world looking upward. A performance is going on, they are very bad actors. I feel cheated.

Associations and Interpretation: The dreamer recognizes the death wishes against his elder daughter and wife with whom there has been a lot of conflict recently. The younger daughter is his favorite. The elder daughter has taken to thumb sucking (age eight). This and other facts clearly show her desire to regress and be the younger daughter once more. Grave and womb thus become identical. The younger daughter symbolizes regression. Running toward the subway, jumping into the subway, symbolize the basic dream or falling asleep (also coitus). The bad performance and the feeling of being cheated revert to the primal scene.

A depressive young woman, mother of three children, who has so far never achieved orgasm, dreams:

I am driving through a gate with my husband. There are two gates. My husband tells me to drive through the gate that is nearer the middle of the road. We are through now and my husband tells me to show how I park the car. I don't do it very well.

Association: The gate is the gate of the Bronx Zoo. In the Zoo people go and gape at the sex life of the animals. Parking was the difficult thing when she learned to drive a car. "Am I going into my own vagina" she asks.

Interpretation: The other gate is evidently the rectum. She is going into her own vagina. That is precisely what she is doing. The difficult task—the orgasm—is solved in the dream. Where people go to see the sex life of animals—the primal scene.

The following dream is quoted because of the combination of the symbolism and elements derived from a life situation. The dreamer is a business man of forty. He has not been in business for many years because of severe anxiety derived from the oedipus complex and the superego.

Dream: I am on the top of a mountain. I am trying to get off the top and I could do so by getting into a shaft. But the jump from the top to the shaft is dangerous. Two strong young men help me with a rope.

Associations: The top of the mountain—Thomas Mann, *The Magic Mountain*, isolation. He has just concluded a business deal and is upset about it. The two strong young men are his business associates.

Interpretation: The top of the hill—his mother's bosom. The two helpers—his testicles. The rope—his penis. The shaft—his potential wife's (mother's) vagina. The business deal means being potent, making a lot of money, killing father, getting married.

In the next dreamer we have a divorced woman, middle-aged, who wants to get married and resists the idea.

I am traveling in a trolley car. Yet I seem to be the trolley car myself. It turns round and makes marvelous maneuvers in the country.

(Refers to her many affairs, also to masturbation.) Now I am walking up a hill with my brother. Steps, hewn into the rock. At the top of the hill there is a gate. The inscription is *Israel,* as if this were the frontier of Israel. A woman is at the gate. I have no passport, I cannot enter.

Associations: The land beyond the gate is Heaven. Because there is a woman at the gate it is also a womb. She has no passport, it is too early to die. The brother is the one with whom she had sex play as a child.

Interpretation: The cleft in the rock is her vagina. She and her brother are walking up, going in = coitus. This brother figures in her dreams as a substitute for her present fiancé and boy friend. Coitus starts in the vagina and ends in the womb. This is what she fears in marriage, i.e., death (going into womb and dying). One of the spontaneous associations (referring to the absence of a passport) is, of course, I cannot go in, I have no womb. On the association of uterine regression and death, she tells me that her mother was in labor with her for thirty-six hours and nearly died in giving her birth. Her mother used to tell her this very often.

Since the way "up from the womb" is based on *seeing,*[36] the nuclear element represented in the dream is frequently the primal scene.

The patient is a girl with latent homosexuality and a depression. At the present moment she is in an anxiety state and on the verge of falling back into a depression after a manic phase. She reports the following dream.

I am with Mary. We are both *valets* and our masters have left us. We walk on a road and arrive at a tree. A bundle is hanging from the tree. It is wrapped in a Scotch plaid. Then I make two sketches *to bring the masters back*—one for Mary and one for myself. The one for Mary is a *faun.* The one for me, *myself* and a *man boring a stone* and showing off to John. Then I and my friend June are seeing a play. It may be *As You Like It* or *Stromboli* with Ingrid Bergman.

Then another girl friend invites me to come and live with her on an island. Or, as an alternative, she will come and live with me. Then she will imitate me, the way I talk. Then I have to go to the frame-maker.

Associations and Interpretation: She and the other girl both want to get married, but it seems that the men in question do not want them. The other girl is very much like her but better looking and more successful. In a sense, she is the ego ideal, but the ego ideal is also represented by the two phallic images, the faun and the man boring the stone. The road is her vagina, the bundle hanging from the tree a fancied pregnancy. The word Scotch suggests a story about a man in a kilt and 25,000 women who worked in a factory raping him.

---

[36] I.e., eye and mouth are object directed.

The baby in the bundle suggests the nursery rhyme:

Rockabye baby on the tree top
When the wind blows the cradle will rock
When the bough breaks the cradle will fall
Down will come baby, cradle and all.

The patient is the castrating female and the prospective mother who is aborting her child—that is, if she had one. The regressive trend of coitus explains the penis-embryo equation.

The drawing—"meant to show off"—is the primal scene. The one for her idealized self is purely genital—i.e., the faun. The other is genital and narcissistic; she and a man are boring a stone and showing it to another man.

Stromboli is a volcano and Ingrid Bergman is passion (orgasm). In *As You Like It* Rosalind is dressed as a boy.

The girl friend who invites her to the island and the one who will be her duplicate are significant, since we assume that the *fission or double in the dream represents a defense against uterine regression, i.e., death.*

The picture in the frame is the fantasy of a permanent orgasm.

There are other good reasons for the prevalence of primal scene dreams. Since *to dream is to see* and since the central conflict in life is always oedipal, the importance of the primal scene is evident. *Moreover, in seeing the primal scene, i.e., the father entering into the mother, the dreamer is really repeating the basic dream, i.e., himself entering into mother.*

Another dream, that of a patient who thinks she has lost her boy friend but is not quite sure about it and is also wavering between depression and elation, contains the "down" and "up" movements very clearly.

Dream: (1) I am going down into the cellar—that is where the N. family lives. The rooms are shaped like the letter H. There is a red table-cloth.

(2) Then I am with Mary. We are shopping for underwear. We see green and yellow garters.

Associations: The N. family are all very old-maidish. One would hardly believe that they ever had intercourse. The letter H reminds me of Hell. This is why the tablecloth must be red. The cellar also reminds me of our own cellar *where the cat had kittens.*

"In the second part of the dream I am with Mary. This is a girl who is very happily married. The green garters remind me of natives in grass skirts—sexy. Yellow was the favorite color of my former boy friend."

Interpretation: The first episode means introversion (the N. family), regression into the womb (the cat), but also sex (the red tablecloth) and guilt (Hell). In the second scene the direction is clearly "up." Mary, the green and yellow colors of the garters, all indicate this.

We must be asleep in order to dream. Sleep, whatever it really may be, is interpreted[37] as being *in utero*. But that does not mean that the dream as such, especially the dynamically important conflict in the dream, takes place in prenatal life.

A depressive patient who has been analyzed for a long time has failed to remember dreams. He is now starting to remember them. Here is one of his dreams. He is married and has a daughter about eight years old.

Dream: (1) I am in a small room. An elegant, well-dressed man is with me. His attitude is sneering, sarcastic. He says, "You and I are of the same age."
(2) I am on a boat going to Europe. There is danger there, Nazis. Someone says, "Let the children get off first."
(3) A child is lying on its back in flames. I console the mother.

The third scene refers to the main traumatic event of his childhood. When he was about three years old, his brother was born. He was intensely jealous. When his little brother was circumcised and nearly died in consequence, his guilt was terrific. On the other hand, the third scene also refers to his incestuous fantasies regarding his daughter.

About the Nazis in Europe, he observes that they are all tall men. In other words, life is full of dangerous fathers (this corresponds to his actual behavior).

The boat scene he associates with the anxiety he has on the ocean. Although he is a good swimmer, he feels sometimes as if his body were lead—something is pulling him down (regressive trends, withdrawal). The children should get off the boat first—birth.

It is the first scene that interests us here. The sneering, critical person, well-dressed, is evidently the superego. The small room is the womb, but all this means that he is asleep. To follow this through and to say that he had the superego already in the womb is obviously impossible. Sleep is the intrauterine situation, but in dreaming we are already coming out of the womb, out of sleep.

The following dream distinguishes the progressive and the regressive direction in the dream. The dreamer is a married woman, young, whose sex life with her husband upsets her, partly because he has intercourse with her at rare intervals, but also because she does not have an orgasm.

Dream: I am with N. and a music teacher. There is a house with a square window or opening. The music teacher shows us how to get in through the opening and then leaves us.

[37] By "really" I mean biologically, by "interpreted" I mean from the point of view of the unconscious.

There is another opening covered with a velvet curtain. Velvet is old-fashioned. I wish he would also teach us how to get in there.

Associations: She is dissatisfied with the shape of her vagina, that is why the first opening is square. The parchment would be the hymen: in so far as she has no orgasm she is a virgin.

N. is her future lover, or rather a man with whom she would like to have an affair.

The other opening of the house reminds her of her mother's furniture.

It is clear that the two openings represent (a) her own "opening" (she, her lover, and the analyst go in), and (b) the regressive path to her mother. The sentence, "I wish he would teach me the other way," should also be inverted. The "other way," the regressive path, she knows very well, but the "going forward" toward her own vagina is still unknown. But the next scene of the dream represents the two trends (i.e., regressive and coital) as one.

There is a house on the side of the hill. It is a long corridor, I can go in. I am talking to a clear-eyed man. Another one follows me. When we go through the door, the clear-eyed man disappears. I go further in the corridor. There is a cubicle branching off the corridor, and in it a woman is asleep. A man is standing beside her and a little girl.

Associations and Interpretation: The house on the hillside reminds her of Rip van Winkle. She has lost ten years of her life (marriage). The clear-eyed man reminds her of her husband, the other may be the lover she desires. The long corridor is her own vagina, she thinks it is too big. The woman sleeping in the cubicle reminds her of her mother; the man must be her father and she is the little girl.

Mother sleeping and father standing beside her would also be the primal scene. Further, the woman sleeping in the cubicle is the sleeper herself, and the cubicle is the womb.

The following dream was dreamed by a patient whose problem was ejaculatio praecox and was analyzed by Dr. Ruth P. Berkeley. The dream was discussed in a seminar I gave on dream interpretation.[38]

The patient was dozing off and was disturbed in going to sleep by his wife's voice. She was scolding his daughter in the other room and telling her to go to sleep.

Dream: I am driving a car with my wife. She curls up on the back seat, and I drive the car but I do it merely by wriggling my whole body in a semirecumbent posture. We enter a large building, a little boy is skipping merrily in advance. There is an archway, my wife knows I am

[38] The text is abbreviated.

afraid of it and we by-pass it without going through. I awake and in a drowsy state I go and kiss my little daughter.

Associations: The color of the building reminds him of the color of the walls in the analyst's office and of his wife's dress. Later he remembers that he has seen an archway like one in the building and on it he noticed a carved figure in the embryo position.

It is evident that he identifies with his daughter who is told to go to sleep. This *regressive* tendency is represented by the building, the archway and by his wife's curled-up position. But the dream is also coitus, the phallic body image (wriggling, driving) and on awakening he kisses his daughter.

A patient, age twenty-five, in love with a young man, is very sleepy and closes her eyes in the analytic hour. On the couch, she sees herself falling into a bottomless pit, is anxious, wonders whether she is dying, talks of a shaft, a cave, then she thinks this must be marriage to her young man or perhaps this is orgasm.

A young girl whose inability to come to a decision with regard to her boy friends revolves around the oedipal conflict dreams:

From upstairs I telephone downstairs to Mrs. N. (mother's best friend). Mary (the maid, a matronly person) is on the telephone. I tell her I am Mrs. X. (her mother's name). Her face looks blurred, like a cabbage. (*Association:* like the face of a dead person in a novel she has been reading lately.)

Interpretation: She says telephoning *down* is like a *man hole,* a chute, like *falling asleep.* The cabbage—the vagina. Falling asleep is falling into mother's vagina, or death.

The same patient, with anxiety about orgasm, about falling asleep and in general about relaxing, dreams:

I am falling asleep and feel as if I were whirling, there is a buzzing in my ears. I fall into my mother's arms and am greatly relieved when she holds me. (She desires to confess everything to her mother—hence, the feeling of relief.)
There is a long corridor (like the rabbit hole in *Alice in Wonderland*) and a kindly looking Negro woman shows the way. We are now on a raft that is painted green (her mother's favorite color). We *rise* in the air and then *descend,* but this time I do it with very little anxiety. (She nearly achieved orgasm the last time she had intercourse.) Now we are in a summer camp, a lot of very young girls. Mother does not like it. (Masturbation is for the young; mother disapproves.)

A social worker reports in a control hour about a schizophrenic girl (age eighteen), an orphan who is receiving psychotherapy. The girl tells him the following dream:

I am with Mrs. N. in a car. (Mrs. N. is her favorite school teacher.) We go uphill and arrive at a precipice. I fall out of the car into a deep lake.

She adds, furiously, "Don't tell me it is because I want a mother."

Davidson describes the case of a young man who suffers from *ejaculatio praecox* and *drowsiness*.[39]

These attacks of drowsiness were usually preceded by a numbness of the limbs and great fatigue. His arms and legs seemed to "give way" and he fell asleep. He believed during these attacks that he was a little boy and said, "I would like to go into mother's womb." A typical dream of his was: "A woman's legs surrounded me and I went into the vagina."

Dreams following coitus prove my contention that the *upward movement* in the dream is genital.

Dream of a woman analyzed by Eisenstein after an unsuccessful attempt to have intercourse.

My husband and I *started up in an elevator when it got stuck*. I got scared that we would not be able to get out and awoke in a panic.

Another dream of the same patient:

My husband and I were climbing a high narrow passage (vagina). Strewn across the floor were groceries, mostly eggs. I had a feeling in the dream, "How is it possible to get through this narrow passageway without destroying the eggs?"[40]

To avoid misunderstanding I repeat that my interpretation is not Fodor's, who regards what happens in the dream as based on intrauterine life.

As an example I quote a dream dreamed by Fodor himself.[41]

First he remembers this:

"I saw a tiny beetle, about the size of the head of a pin. It opened its wings and now it was a butterfly about an inch-and-a-half long and of a very nice pattern. I was preoccupied with how I would preserve this beetle with outspread wings. I fantasied, half awake, that somebody invented a method of killing it at the moment the wings opened.

"Then the memory of the earlier part of the dream came back with a rush. I was swimming happily in an underground grotto. I had a vivid recollection of the stone vault and the clearness and depth of the water. The swimming could be better described as a darting like a fish. The

39 Davidson, C., "Disturbances in the Sleep Mechanism," *Psychoanalytic Quarterly,* XIV, 1945, pp. 483, 484.

40 Eisenstein, V. W., "Dreams Following Intercourse," *Psychoanalytic Quarterly,* XVIII, 1949, pp. 154–172. Also in *The Yearbook of Psychoanalysis,* Lorand, S., ed., VI, 1950, pp. 136, 137.

41 Fodor, N., *The Search for the Beloved,* New York, 1949, pp. 309, 310, 311.

speed was extraordinary and exhilarating. I had no hands or did not use them. A young boy fast as lightning was always just ahead of me. We both came from somewhere else, waters outside. Then the raiding party came. I vaguely thought they were Russians. The entrance to the grotto was sealed. On the bare, rocky wall, no opening could be seen from the outside. My daughter was with me now and she talked so loud that the raiders heard her and found the entrance. I was fearful they would put me to death. For this my daughter was to blame and I wondered how she would feel on knowing what she had done."

Fodor explains his own dream as follows:

"The meaning of the second part of the dream is transparent. The grotto is the womb and the darting about as if driven by a tail is a reference to the pre-natal development by allusion to the tadpole stage. The grotto is sealed because the womb is sealed during pregnancy and as I associate Russians with the Russian colossus, the raiding party could only stand for the father's penis that threatens to break into the womb and inflict death. My daughter stands for myself as a child illustrating the mother and child-relationship and the innocence with which the unborn faces the fear of death. The purpose of the dream is to reveal that the unborn child is capable of experiencing traumatic shocks before birth.

"Thoughts about the younger boy ahead of me yielded the immediate association of two childhood friends. One was a hunchback, a small misshapen human being, the other alive with a flaming sexual imagination always full of stories about a gigantic penis or an immense vagina. I could not tell what made me think of these two boys but I could readily see that the hunchback was a good association with the embryo, the other with the invader.

"The meaning of the beetle was now beginning to unfold. I collected beetles when I was a child, sticking pins through my prizes. Sometimes they wiggled on the pin for days but it never struck me that the act was cruel or that it was a kind of crucifixion. The dream beetle was too small for a pin. I think it stands for the embryo and the butterfly for the embryo transformed into a human child. The killing of the beetle for purposes of preservation at the moment when the wings opened suggests a reference to the agony caused by parental intercourse in the human stage of gestation. Birth is crucifixion, an experience equivalent to death; but the fear of death as indicated by the dream does not originate in birth alone, it antedates it and is caused by coitus shocks to which the unborn child is exposed."

Thus far the author. We agree in one detail only, namely that the grotto with the water is the female genital organ. The darting movement is, of course, coitus, and when we think of a tail it is certainly more obvious to think of the *membrum virile* than of a tadpole. The young boy fast as lightning ahead of him: clearly the phallos. The associations make this clear to anyone who is not blocked by a preconceived theory. The hunchback (dwarf) and boy who always talked about sex are also phallic images. That the daughter should be the dreamer as an innocent embryo is out of the question. It is really the daughter and represents the dreamer's incestuous wishes. Far from innocent she also stands for guilt feeling, her loud talk is the voice of conscience. The punishment is, of course, carried out by father but not while the dreamer is in the womb—it is when he is having intercourse. (Primal scene in reverse.) And now the beetle and butterfly, the phallic symbol of the psyche. Preserving the butterfly with outstretched wings is maintaining a perpetual erection—but killing it the moment the wings open is castration anxiety.

The following dream of the Hungarian novelist Jókai, quoted by Stekel, shows the significance of *looking* in the dream:

I am in a desert. A little old woman in grey is following me. I thought she is following me because she too would like to get out of this desert. She did not look at me, but when I looked at her face I perceived that her eyes were closed. *She was blind* and only my footsteps guided her. "Mother," I said, "come along, and I will show you the way out." She made no answer and did not move. "Well," I thought, "she must be deaf and blind." I walk away and hear swift steps following me. The woman, as if taken unawares, promptly closed her eyes. Once more she feigned deafness and blindness. It seemed so uncanny that I did not know what to say. The old woman continues her pursuit, to get rid of her I walked in a zig-zag line. At the end of the desert the road led into something quite black. I looked again, it was my grave. "Toward that you are pushing me? Wait a minute, and I'll outwit you." Turning sharply to the right I went in that direction. The woman followed me closely. After some time I looked up once more to see that on the horizon the black pit still awaited me. "I won't let you push me into it, you accursed crone," I exclaimed, and sat down firmly on the ground. There was no longer a sound of footsteps, but I could feel that the woman was still near me. When I now raised my eyes more quietly, it was to see the pit itself coming toward me, slowly at first from afar but more quickly as it drew nearer. Shuddering I jumped to my feet, turned around and close behind me stood the old woman much taller than I. With large, light-colored eyes, now widely opened, she looked at me maliciously, smiling craftily down at me and raised her clawlike fingers over me. I tried to hurl myself against her and while making the effort I awoke.[42]

While not gainsaying the interpretation given by Stekel which may also be valid, we quote this dream because it confirms the viewpoint that the visual element in the dreams is already a partial awakening and returning to life. The old woman, although clearly representing the

[42] Stekel, *The Interpretation of Dreams*, New York, 1940, I, pp. 208–210.

mother, is yet derived from the closed eyes of the dreamer. Going into the womb (mother) and dying are the same thing. Hurling himself against the mother is coitus. Whether anxiety is primarily that of dying, of birth, or of castration is not the point. What we are emphasizing here is that seeing is a partial awakening.

The Aranda say *alkneraka* for being born (*alkna* = eyes, *eraka* = to become). It seems therefore that the Upanishads are correct when they interpret the dream as a stage between waking and sleeping. It says in the Sarva-upanishat-sara that if one perceives all the object in the external world this is being awake. If one is liberated from the impression of being awake and perceives only with four organs, without sound, that is the dreaming of Atman. If all the fourteen organs are quiet and one is not conscious of separate objects, that is sleep.[43]

The hypothesis advanced here is therefore that dreaming is caused by an attempt to regain a partial contact with the environment. The break with the environment is the regression into the womb. The dream environment is formed out of the libidinally cathected body of the sleeper.

We will now let Plato give his version of our theory.

"And now, I said, let me show in a figure how far our nature is enlightened or unenlightened. Behold! human beings living in an underground den, which has a mouth open towards the light and reaching all along the den, here they have been from their childhood and have their legs and necks chained so they cannot move, and can only see before them, being prevented by the chains from turning round their heads. Above and behind them a fire is blazing at a distance and between the fire and the prisoners there is a raised way and you see, if you look, a low wall built along the way like the screen which marionette players have over them, over which they show the puppets."[44]

A very clear instance of this trend *upward* in the dream is the following, dreamed by a patient, after an unsuccessful coitus with her husband.

Dream: I am making salad. Tomato in the middle, with four lettuce leaves. Hard-boiled eggs surround it—between the tomato and the lettuce. There are also two bell peppers.

While relating the dream she is in a state of sexual excitement. The tomato is her vagina. She is not menstruating, the red color indicates sex. The four leaves, labia majora et minora. Eggs, it is her ovulation period. The two bell peppers, she thinks, must be testicles.

In other words, without the bell peppers, we have what I would call

---

[43] Deussen, P., *Sechzig Upanishads des Veda*, Leipzig, 1905, p. 623.

[44] Plato, *The Republic*, B. Jowett, ed., *The Works of Plato*. Tudor Publishing Co., n.d., VII, p. 265.

the basic dream—in its nonregressive form. The erotic world is being built up—based on the sleeper's vagina. With the bell pepper her problem of masculinity versus femininity enters into the dream.

A young man who has anxiety about making his girl friend pregnant and, although he is quite potent, has strong castration anxiety, dreams:

I see a cripple in a bathing suit *coming out of the subway*. He has an umbrella, it is raining. I give him the address of a swimming pool.

The swimming pool. A very tall man is seated at the edge of the pool. His feet are in the water, he has pulled his trousers up. I reproach him for not having changed into swimming trunks, he will contaminate the pool.

I dive into the pool myself, completely dressed, head foremost.

The cripple represents his castration anxiety. The umbrella and the rain; penis and semen. The tall man whose feet are dangling into the pool —the primal scene. Ideas about soiling the woman and making her pregnant. But he dives completely dressed; coitus with a condom.

A patient analyzed by Mr. E. Weil has great anxiety before having intercourse with his wife. He dreams:

My wife is in a swimming pool. I take a head dive. She embraces me and pulls me down under the water. I awake screaming.

He verbalizes his fear of orgasm as fear of merging into his wife, of disappearing completely.

The transition from re-entering the womb to delivery is also the movement upward.

The dreamer of the following dream has no difficulty in having love affairs but can never make up her mind to marry the man she loves. Unhappy marriage of parents, career woman tendencies and other factors contribute to the fundamental oedipal fixation.

Dream: I dive into a rocky pool and swim out to a sandy beach with a breast stroke. The pool is full of women.

Associations: The breast stroke with legs pulled up reminds her of a woman who is giving birth. A friend of hers delivered the day before the dream.

Interpretation: The baby she delivers is herself reborn. She has plenty of time to get married, she is just born.

Another dream of a young woman analyzed for frigidity again shows that she withdraws into her own vagina and then forms a new world made out of her own body.

Dream: I invite my friend Mary to see my new summer house, especially the new porch. It is sunny and newly furnished. She is surprised. I myself am also surprised when I discover a long corridor. It seems to be also a garage through which my husband can drive out in his car. Finally we go into the kitchen, it is black, dirty and still has the old furniture.

Interpretation: Mary is the friend who insisted that she should be analyzed. She is very near to achieving an orgasm now, this new vagina is the sunny porch she shows Mary. But her unconscious wants analysis to endow her with something else, a big penis. That is the long corridor where her husband drives out, something that protrudes from her own body. She is still constipated and constricted in character, that is the black kitchen—her rectum.

In the dream of a married man, with an anxiety neurosis, we find nearly the whole dream made out of his erect penis.

Dream: I scold a little boy for messing his coat sleeves. But it seems that his coat is really my coat. A man comes up to me and says I have no right to scold the boy. I intend to fight, but first I want to show him how strong I am. I take a football and kick it but it goes sideways instead of going in a straight line. The child throws it back but instead of a football it is now a shoe messed with feces. I don't want to kick it back again. I would hurt myself.

Associations and Interpretation: He awakes with an erection. Messing the coat = ejaculation in the bed. The little boy = his penis. The man who is against scolding the boy = the analyst. He will fight for his right to stay neurotic. The powerful kick, however, represents the opposite, a great erection, to ward off the superego. It goes sideways—not to his wife. The shoe: his father used to tell him, "I will throw you out like an old shoe." The feces: he was very small and had smeared himself completely with feces. He was standing at an open window and the danger was that he would *fall out*.

The erection is followed by castration anxiety, kicking his own *balls*. He is only a little child smeared with feces. Or, semen and feces are the same, he is in danger of smearing. Father threatened to throw him out, he might fall out, the semen might fall out.

Months later the same patient who has undergone an operation on his groin reports the following dream:

I am running round a lake, chasing a little boy. I am running to music which has been composed by N. N. There is a grotto with X's wife in it. I go in. There is a discussion with Y (father figure) on the proper method in recording music.

Associations: The lake reminds him of a lake where he used to go to visit his mother's sister with whom he indulged in heavy necking when he was about ten years old. The composer who wrote the music is famous for having affairs with the wives of his friends. The little boy he is running after is his own penis, the grotto is the vagina of N. N.'s wife. He would like to have an affair with her.

Continuation of Dream: There is a ditch between the concrete and the lawn. I am in a car and the problem is how to get the car off the lawn without damaging the ditch.

The concrete is the bandage on the groin, the lawn his pubic hair, the car his penis. Can he have intercourse with the bandage?

I have always found that the *primal scene* plays a very important role in the dreams of most patients. After all, the dream means *seeing something* and on the oedipal level the most important thing to see is the primal scene. I will now quote a primal scene dream I published many years ago.

The analysand, a young married woman with some anxiety but not exactly neurotic, relates the following dream.[45]

I am passing through a narrow door. I get into a room which suddenly broadens out into a hall. A Communist who has left the country and whose name is Star also manages to slip in through the narrow opening. Detectives follow, everybody has to show their papers.

Associations:[46] The name Star (*Csillag* in Hungarian) reminds her of a comet, *a star with a tail.* This reminds her of the nightmares of her childhood. At about the age of three she would awaken with a terrific shock and scream, "The Lion, the Lion!" Father would then take her out of her bed and put her into mother's bed—there she would immediately fall asleep. She remembers sleeping in the parents' bedroom and observing the shadows of the trees that were swayed by the wind. The crown of the trees, the lion with its mane and the tail of the star are all the same thing. She remembers walking arm in arm with her father and seeing Halley's comet.

It is clear that all these tails, manes, trees mean father's penis and that the man called Star, a former boy friend, represents the father. The detectives who ask for identification = the superego. The dream is intercourse with the father—but passing through a narrow door into a room that suddenly broadens out is uterine regression, i.e., the basic dream. The childhood-dream is obviously the primal scene.

Another typically recurring childhood dream, this time from a British analysand:

45 Róheim, G., "Die Urszene im Traume," *Internationale Zeitschrift für Psychoanalyse,* VI, 1920, pp. 337–339.
46 Some of the data published in the German paper are not repeated here as they have no bearing on our main theme.

I am being pursued by a unicorn.[47] I run into a booth or stables. This is very stupid of me, I think in the dream, because this is the stable of the unicorn (i.e., he is bound to come into this booth).

Associations: The unicorn = the British coat of arms. The horn of the unicorn is the father's penis. The dream contains a passive homosexual component: being pierced by the father's "horn." But the latent dream wish and what we have called "the basic dream" are here really identical—"running into mother's vagina." Then we have a "primal scene" element: the unicorn runs into the mother's vagina. Since the essence of the dream is visualization, duplication, projection, *the primal scene may be a "second edition" of the basic dream.* This does not mean that the actual primal scene has nothing to do with primal scene dreams—I am only implying that "father (or father's penis) disappears into mother" may be a new version of the sentence: "I disappear into mother."

Freud writes: "In many dreams, usually connected with anxiety, we find the narrow passage into a room or water. They are based on phantasies of intrauterine life or birth. The following is the dream of a young man who observes parental coitus *in utero.*

" 'I am in a deep gap with a window like in the tunnel in the Semmering. I see first just space, emptiness, and then I project a picture into this space. A field is being plowed deeply and I think of the work that is being done. Then I see a book on pedagogy—and I am astonished that so much space is given in it to the sexual impulses of the child.' "

Freud then quotes the following dream of a woman:

" 'I dive into a deep black lake where the pale moon is reflected in the water.' "

The interpretation given by Freud is that diving into the water is emerging from the water, i.e., being born or reborn in the cure.[48]

The second dream I would not invert but would interpret it as a hypnagogic fantasy or basic dream, i.e., as the moment of falling asleep.

As for the interpretation of the first dream, I am always puzzled by the use of the word "fantasy" in this connection. If we mean an unconscious fantasy then it would seem to be that the explanation is to be sought in the process of sleeping and dreaming itself. I do not think Freud can mean a conscious fantasy because nobody but a schizophrenic or at least a very schizoid person would have a conscious fantasy about re-entering the womb.

The next dreamer is a married man. He has overcome his impotency

[47] Cf. Zeckel, A., "The Totemic Significance of the Unicorn," in *Psychoanalysis and Culture,* Wilbur, G. B., and Muensterberger, W., eds., New York, 1951, pp. 344–360.
[48] Freud, *Gesammelte Schriften,* Vienna, 1925, III, pp. 119, 120.

and can perform coitus but does not dare to look at the vagina and in general still has plenty of castration anxiety.

Dream: I go down a steep staircase to the cellar. I am with mother and we are visiting Professor Sin. Suddenly my mother disappears and I shout in desperation, "Mother, mother!"

I am now at a banquet with a group of non-Jewish biblical scholars. I relate the first part of my dream to my neighbor. He says, "Hush, hush. Professor Sin is now in disgrace with the president." I explain to him that anyone born on "Tishe bof"[49] will be the Messiah.

Associations: The cellar, grave, his dead father. (Mother disappears, she is "sinning" with father.)

The banquet reminds him of the Olympic gods and specifically of the scene where Hephaistos is hurled from the sky.

What happens in the Iliad is this. After the withdrawal of Achilles from the Greeks, his mother Thetis begs Zeus to avenge her son by defeating the Achaians. Hera who is both the protecting goddess of the Achaians and the relentless enemy of the Trojans combines this with her jealousy of Thetis and remonstrates with her husband. Zeus thunders back and tells her his will is supreme, — the gods of Olympos cannot save her if he lays hands upon her.

Hephaistos, her son, tells her not to spoil the festive meal, for nobody can withstand the might of the Thunderer. He refers to the time when Hera was in fetters and suspended in the sky by Zeus, and how he tried to defy the father of gods and men and rescue his mother and was hurled from the sky by Zeus and at sunset landed more dead than alive on the island of Lemnos. Hera smiles and accepts the drink, and when Hephaistos in his overzeal spills the nectar from the cup "Homeric laughter" shakes the whole Olympos. And then when the sun sank in the west, Zeus himself fell asleep beside his divine consort.[50]

Interpretation: The non-Jewish scholars are the Olympic gods. What is the whole Greek mythology but a gigantic primal scene with the amours of the world-shaking Zeus and the futile jealousy of his divine consort? The Professor Sin of the dream is now the revolting son Hephaistos, the fall from the sky is coitus, and the spilt nectar is overflowing semen. The original myth is probably also a dream for the story ends with the sun sinking in the west and the sleep of the gods.

It is interesting to note, however, that in mythology Hephaistos falls twice from the sky, and his fall is clearly the birth trauma. This other version of Hephaistos' fall from the sky makes his mother Hera hurl him from above because of his lameness and he is rescued by Thetis, the sea

49 Jewish fast day, but not the Day of Atonement.
50 *The Iliad,* I, lines 545–611.

goddess, with whom he stays for nine years constructing for her a palace of unequalled beauty.[51] This fall is obviously birth, falling out of the mother, and into the mother nine years in the palace of unequalled beauty. But this birth trauma myth is again hardly a direct repetition of the birth trauma, it is birth (or uterine regression) as falling asleep back for nine months into the beautiful palace of the ocean mother.

Both the descent into the cellar and the fall of Hephaistos are over-determined, the son "falling into" the mother and the father disappearing in the mother (primal scene).

Finally we recognize the meaning of the passage on the Messiah—he is born on a holiday (identification with the Christian Messiah). But when the Messiah comes all that is forbidden will be permitted (quotation from the Talmud). Therefore he too will be able to look at the vagina.

The following dream again shows the sequence: falling asleep, coitus, primal scene. The dreamer is a woman with agoraphobia and the dream was analyzed by Dr. Dollin and discussed when he brought it to me in control analysis.

Dream: I am waiting for my husband. Then I go up in an elevator. I hold on to a pole and swing round and round.

Then I go upstairs. I have to straddle, a puddle of water. I pull my skirt up so that it should not be wet.

I see my daughter falling down a flight of stairs. I run after her to see whether she is not hurt.

I am now in a room with sunlight coming into it like a museum. A woman is weaving. She tells me I will have her money if I do exactly as she does.

Associations: The museum and the sunlight remind her of Greek statues in the museum and fig leaves. The weaving is like a woman who waddles like a duck with legs apart. Her mother-in-law walks like that.

Interpretation: The elevator, the swinging on the pole, the daughter falling downstairs all mean the same—the moment of falling asleep. The genital significance of this moment becomes clear when we consider the puddle—her lubricated vagina.

But what about the sunlight? This is a typical feature of her dreams. The associations she brings about the museum and especially about the Greek gods and fig leaves show what is meant by the sunlight: the primal scene. The weaving motion reminds her of a waddling duck, of legs far apart, of the way a pregnant woman walks or of a woman *in coitu.*

The next dream is also derived from a case analyzed by Dr. Dollin and controlled by me. The case is a pregnant woman with agoraphobia and depersonalization.

[51] *Ibid.,* XVIII, pp. 395–410.

Aunt Blanche is in a cradle asleep with father. I try to wake father and then aunt. Then I am awake.

She recognizes that the cradle must be the womb. Her aunt is much like herself in character (mother's sister). She is replacing the embryo in her womb and at the same time the womb is her own vagina and coitus with father would follow if she did not wake up. In real life she consciously wants to interrupt the analysis and unconsciously her pregnancy.

The following dream is dreamed by an analysand who is being analyzed for professional reasons.[52] This dream has been recurrent with him since early youth.

He has to go from one building to another through a narrow arched passage. He has to get from A to C through B. But he has to get out of the elevator in A at the right moment. He can manage it if he starts out right, but it is difficult. Building B is a private apartment.

"I have to pass unnoticed. I can either go through an auditorium where people are listening to a concert or through an apartment, but in the apartment I must avoid the *bedroom* of a married couple. I am allowed to go through the *dining room* or the *kitchen*. I manage to do this and then *I go down to the basement* where I see some plumbers welding pipes together. Then I get out with my son. It seems he has been with me all the time. We have been in a taxi all night—we must get out unobserved."

Associations: (1) The bedroom—where he is not allowed to go. He happened to go into his parents' bedroom and they were just having intercourse (he was about twelve years old). Father rolled off mother.

(2) The concert. He used to have nightmares and would *scream.* Then he went to his parents' bed (first house) and they wanted to get rid of him. Therefore they sent him to his little sister's bed (she was about three years younger than he). The little sister slept in the parents' bedroom. He went into her bed and had intercourse with her—taking care to withdraw on time.

The patient now sees the following connections. Building A—the parents' bed. Building B—sister's bed. Get out of elevator—*coitus interruptus.*

Interpretation: His screaming is the concert. He can go to the kitchen (anal) or the dining room (oral) but the bedroom is taboo.

There are also other factors involved in the dream. The present-day situation is this: his wife is pregnant and he would like to have a mistress; can he do it unobserved? The analogy with the past is that the coitus with the younger sister was going on while his mother was pregnant.

52 Social worker, married, age thirty-five.

His son was with him in the taxi = his penis. The arched passage between one house and the other is back into mother's womb. Down into the basement = falling asleep or basic dream. There he sees the plumber welding = the primal scene.

The following is the dream of a man, middle-aged, father of two children, analyzed mainly for professional reasons. He has bought them a television set and finds to his surprise that his bank account is considerably depleted. He said, ouch! when he saw the figure.

Dream: I am going down into a cellar. A little grey animal is going before me through the door but as soon as I let it in it comes back again. A man steps on a thumbtack or on the little grey animal and says "Ouch!"

I think now my wife and children can see what a kind man I am.

Before the dream he and his children saw a movie based on the Pied Piper of Hamelin.

Interpretation: "What a kind man I am" is self-irony. The little grey animal he steps on is his son and he is the Pied Piper of Hamelin. But the grey animal and the rats also represent his penis *which goes in* (regression, coitus) and *comes out,* i.e., the dream world is built up. Behind the dream scene—television, i.e., the primal scene.

The next dream shows in a quite convincing way the patient in the intrauterine situation, witnessing the primal scene and identified with his own penis. The situation is this. The patient has been treated for sterility at the request of his wife but he is really very much opposed to the idea of having a son. He has also got rid of a situation which had made him depressed.

Day stimulus: "I fell asleep with an erection."

Dream: I dream that I am in Dr. N.'s office. (Dr. N. is his wife's analyst.) Dr. N. is making a telephone call and I see his figure silhouetted against the wall. The office is like a hothouse full of vines, creepers (they are not real creepers, only made of paper). Dr. N. takes a smear from my penis. I say it is not gonorrhea but either the marks left on it by a woman's hairnet or a chancre.

I and some others are being hoisted up a tall white building. I see dangling ropes. A man from above says: "All those who are hoisted up will be let down at 5 P.M."

Associations: Dr. N.'s office = hothouse, tomb or the womb. He must be telephoning for the undertaker (to take his wife's corpse).

The creepers: "You must know them—it is like in a tropical jungle where you have to cut your way through with a knife." The *creeper,* a baby, he just sneaks in unwanted.

Dr. N. taking a smear—"That is the other doctor who is treating me for sterility." Gonorrhea means physical causation of sterility. The imprint of the hairnet, my mother's hairnet, castration anxiety. Chancre: dangerous penis, keep away.

The white building is father's grave stone. The ropes remind him of a woman's dangling tresses. The story of Rapunzel.[53] Climbing up on his mother's head. 5 P.M.: the day's work is finished, the task is done. He awakes, still has the erection and has intercourse with his wife.

Interpretation: The hothouse office of the other analyst who is analyzing his wife is the *womb.* Going into the womb, regression and coitus are identical. Here we have the explanation of the type of dream in which the patient sees the primal scene in the intrauterine situation. Not because he actually "remembers" father's penis in mother's vagina, but also not on the basis of conscious fantasies. His own desire to regress into mother's womb (*in toto* or *in coitu*) is identified with the primal scene. The creeper is the embryo in the womb. His comment on the use of the knife in the jungle means killing the embryo with his penis.

The part about gonorrhea means that his sterility is not caused by anything physical but by castration anxiety (mother's net) and that his penis is a weapon (chancre). The last dream scene with the "hoisting up" is still the penis erect. He will get into mother (Rapunzel motive is a displacement upward, head instead of vagina), "kill" his father, i.e., make a baby and thus end the analysis.[54]

The ascent (ladder, stairs, etc.) is both coital and emerging from the vagina (birth). A patient with agoraphobia (analyzed by Dr. Dollin) dreams:

I am walking up a ladder. I go through a hole, then I am between a floor and a ceiling, lying on my stomach (the patient associates to this: fucking). The dream is just before awakening.

A young woman who is being analyzed because she has no orgasm dreams:

A sexy woman shows me a brand-new modern house. The interior is newly decorated. The woman takes me into the bathroom. People looking at a television set.

53 Grimm, *Kinder und Hausmärchen* No. 12.
54 The erection as origin of the climbing or ascending dream is quite clear. Cf. for a confused Jungian view, M. Eliade, "Durohana and the Waking Dream" in *Art and Thought, Essays in Honor of D. Ananda K. Coomaraswamy,* London, 1947, pp. 209–213. "Gradual Development to Higher Levels of Consciousness," in C. G. Jung, *Aion,* Zürich, 1951, p. 414. The ladder dream in N. Fodor, *The Search for the Beloved,* New York, 1949, p. 199, is a very obvious masturbation dream with oedipal content.

The modern house is an affair, and her remodeled vagina. The television and the audience are her exhibitionism—if she has an affair everybody should see it.

The next patient is a divorced woman who is having an affair with a divorced man. She enjoys the affair sexually but otherwise thinks he is not the right kind of man for her.

Dream: I am in a truck. There is a truck driver. And in the truck is a *deep sea monkey.* A deep sea movie will be made about the deep sea monkey. I get frightened, jump out and land on my stomach.

Associations and Interpretation: The truck driver is her lover. The deep sea monkey is the embryo in the womb. But what about the deep sea movie? It was father and mother having intercourse which she saw. But since she jumps out and is born, she is identical with the embryo in her own womb. Putting herself into her own womb or vagina means the excitement she feels at witnessing the primal scene. Yes, she does not like her lover, but she gets excited when he inserts the penis.

The entrance to the body may be the mouth instead of the vagina, but this is still a dream of uterine regression.[55]

A middle-aged woman feels that she has lost her grown-up daughter. The daughter who had previously identified with her and loved her even too much has married a man of shady character.

Dream: I am seated on an El train behind Y and T (her daughter and her son-in-law). Suddenly the El train becomes a scenic railway. It rushes down almost in a perpendicular fashion—it feels like an orgasm. I am afraid that I will fall out. Then I lie crosswise to prevent too rapid a fall. We are on a beach. Y and T say they must leave me and go to the theater. It is 9 P.M. They must go to meet an actor who plays King Lear. Now I am lying on the sand, very happy, quiet.

A vault gradually forms above her head. It is made of concrete, it is somewhat like the sky vault but it does not close at the end where her head lies. Beyond the head is the ocean. She crawls out from under this and starts shouting "Didi" (her daughter's pet name), but an echo keeps replying, "Chicago!" (That is where her daughter has gone with her husband.) Then she shouts her daughter's real name. Then there is a little girl beside her who says, "Your daughter is in Chicago."

Associations: The El train reminds her of a love affair previous to her marriage. In many respects her daughter's young husband and this man are identical. She has an orgasm by identifying with her daughter (primal scene reversed). Daughter and son-in-law, i.e., her own youth, leave her at 9 P.M.—that is the moment when the analytic hour ends. What leaves her is her past. They go to see King Lear—her father complex.

55 Cf. Ferenczi, S., *Versuch einer Genitaltheorie*, Wien, 1924, pp. 30–31.

Happiness on the beach—after the orgasm. *"The vault is really like the palate as if she were the tongue in her own mouth."* We then proceed to get further associations. The caressing name of her daughter is Didi = tits (this is interpretation). The echo "Chicago" is important. She was pregnant with her daughter in Chicago and that is where she got the first advice in sex life.

What is the meaning of the dream? The part about her daughter identification and the primal scene in reverse and her father complex (King Lear) we have seen. The vault is here *oral;* instead of being in her own vagina, as so many female dreamers are, she is in her *own mouth.* There is a reason for this—a mother in search of a daughter (mouth-breast organization). However, the associations are about her pregnancy when her daughter was in her—and therefore we could still question whether the mouth is not just displaced upward for vagina and uterus.

But in the case of the hebephrenic patient who dreamed, "I was being chopped up with an axe (just like chopping up your food), with a knife— you know how it is when you fill your mouth with saliva, then draw it back and it is cut off with a knife, your tongue is the knife," we might say that the oral zone is libidinally cathected, that therefore he withdraws "into his mouth" and rebuilds the world on an oral basis. There are plenty of data to confirm this. But there is also an abundance of intra-uterine or birth fantasy material. Could we say that with children in the oral stage the withdrawal really takes place "into the mouth?"

A boy of five, whose father was a baker, is reported to have had the following dreams:

(a) I was in a loaf of bread and a German cut it into little bits and saw me. I flew away. I had wings on me.

(b) I was in a kettle and drank up all the water. Mother could not find me, I went under the gas pipes.[56]

Apart from the possible intrauterine connotation of the kettle these oral dreams are not as simple as they look.

(a) The infant bites the nipple; and (b) experiences talio anxiety and finally identifies with mother's breast.

At any rate the oral and the intrauterine can overlap. As Stone writes, "A striking example of the apposition of the intrauterine and oral fantasies of sleep occurred in a dream of the second analytic period. The patient is swimming alone. He emerges from the water and runs into it backward. Immediately thereafter he is lying on an oblong structure just short of the waves. The structure is like a coffin."[57]

56 Kimmins, C. W., *Children's Dreams*, London, 1937, p. 58.
57 Compare the vault and ocean in the mother-daughter dream quoted above.

The associations deal with his wife's birthday, stomach pains . . .
the analytic couch and a sarcastic remark of a wealthy uncle, "Take an
overdose of my sleeping medicine any time you want." Further associations: his mother's pregnancy, the birth of his sister, etc.[58]

Another patient, a lawyer, age about forty, depressive, dreams:

Cardinal Spellman is always standing before a Little Red Brick
Church. He hangs out in a candy store. A young man who is also there
wants to leave in search of a more profitable occupation. Cardinal Spellman asks for everybody's girl friend. It seems that this is the Virgin
Mary. But she looks like an umbrella or a papal cap.

The Cardinal is red and his name means "spell," i.e., incantation or
magic. He is the Red Man of Magic, i.e., the penis.

The red church is a vagina. In the dream the Cardinal as a personification of the penis is always standing—and the patient is being analyzed
for ejaculatio praecox. The Virgin Mary means the mother, or in general
a fantasied woman. The umbrella or the papal tiara is the condom. The
candy store signifies masturbation: pleasures easily obtainable. The young
man who seeks more profitable occupation is another phallic personification, this time tending toward coitus (more profitable occupation).

In a paper on "The Origin of the Ideal" I have published other
dreams of this type.

A patient, who is nearly cured of his homosexual tendencies and recently married, dreams:

Mother goes to visit my father-in-law. *There is a man who lives with
him.* Father-in-law and mother have slept together. My wife and I slept
on the street or rather, corner of the street near our house. I see my
mother in black with *a young man who excites me.* I want him to come
with me. I awake and masturbate.[59]

Associations and Interpretation: The man who lives with his father-
in-law is the son who is an appendage of his father. Mother in black means
that father is dead. Mother is dragging the young man into a little round
building—the vagina. The young man is his juvenile alter ego and his
penis. He would like to be like the young man or like his own father, i.e.,
completely heterosexual. The key to his homosexuality is the magical
notion that he must refill with semen after losing the semen and this he
achieves through fellatio. His homosexual partners really played the role
of supernatural penises, sources of his own potency.

The next dream is that of a married man. He is having affairs but is
impotent with his wife.

[58] Stone, L., "Transference Sleep in a Neurosis with Duodenal Ulcer," *International
Journal of Psycho-Analysis,* 1947, XXVIII, p. 13.
[59] Róheim, G., "The Origin of the Ideal," *Samiksa,* II, 1948.

My wife goes to sleep in the other room. A young naked man who is with me goes in after her. I am indignant and I enter in time to prevent them from having intercourse.

The young naked man is his penis. He himself is his own superego—always arriving in time to prevent intercourse.

A depressive patient dreams:

I am doing my work and the analyst sits beside me. I chase him out; he is not to supervise me. He comes back in the form of a dwarf who dances and jumps all around the place.

The analyst is first the superego, then a phallic being. At the same time this shows the mechanism of getting rid of a depression.

The next patient is divorced, age about forty, and has no sex life. She dreams:

I am on a raft with lilac bushes. It looks as if it were moving but it is standing still. A cat curls up in a silver dish.

The cat is like a queen or like an embryo. It represents herself or rather her vagina, curled up, narcissistic. The raft is also her vagina; the lilacs represent penises. The patient is Hungarian and the word for lilac is *orgona,* the same as for a church organ.

At any rate it is safe to say that the process of falling asleep is a withdrawal of cathexis while the process of dreaming is rebuilding a libidinal environment.

Several patients who had anxiety dreams told me that they would suddenly awake after having fallen asleep for a second and tell themselves, "Now I was asleep," at the same time feeling that the hypnagogic hallucination was just about to become a dream. The hypnagogic fantasy and the dream have one thing in common: both represent environment as formed out of the dreamer's body.

A young woman, depressive, without orgasm, dreams:

My uncle, who is a doctor, tries to persuade me to exchange the plot I now own for another one. In the middle of this second plot there is a lake with a dark path winding round it. I will have nothing to do with it, I say it is too wet.

Obviously this new plot would be a new vagina, one with an orgasm. The dark path is the pubic hair, the doctor (uncle) the analyst.

The next dream is that of a young woman, married, also without orgasm, but not depressed. It is the husband who has difficulties in coitus.

I am standing on a little donkey. It keeps getting bigger and bigger. Now it is an elephant. Before me is a lane, a clear road, then bushes.

Evidently she is having intercourse with herself. The animal she is riding is her own imaginary penis in erection. The lane, her body (or vagina), the bushes her pubic hair.

The next is a characteristic masturbation dream, dreamed by a menstruating woman of about forty.

I am holding on to a motor car and running after it with great exertion. It is going toward a red light district on the other side of the Hudson over a bridge.

Two women are in the car. I can't hold on any longer. I land near bushes on the other side.

The red light (besides indicating prostitution) is her menstruating vagina. The rushing motion, the car = sexual excitement. Holding on = masturbation. The two women = her two breasts. The bushes are her pubic hair. The exertion in the dream is her anxiety about masturbating which she finally stops—i.e., she lets go.

A young girl, who is having affairs but has a lot of anxiety to contend with, dreams as follows:

Two dogs are brought into my room. One is an Irish setter. John gives it liver—now it is tame. The other one is dangerous. It is a big terrier with black and white spots. The problem is how to get it on a leash. This happens in a store. A shadowy woman is in the background.

The leash is made of foil (fencing foil) and I have to hang on to the point. At the other end of the foil is a ring, in the ring a string and the string is attached to the dog's collar.

(1) The red dog is herself. John is Irish; he is her lover who keeps her tame and not so frightened by having intercourse with her.

(2) The big terrier is the new man who was introduced to her the other day as a husband candidate.

(3) Marriage is the leash. The foil is the penis pointing toward her. (Her father was angry with her yesterday.) The ring is her vagina.

She mentions that she had a hypnagogic fantasy before this dream. *She is struggling with a dog. Both are holding on to a bone and she cannot get loose.*

Considering the competitive nature of her sex life and her phallic fantasies—the hypnagogic hallucination evidently means coitus. But what is perhaps still more important is that it is obviously the introductory phase of a dream.

A middle-aged patient dreams:

Tom and I are exploring a high mountain. It is covered with snow, but the snow melts as Tom goes higher up. We leave provisions as we go along for the next time.

His son Tom is his penis. The mountain is the mons veneris—the snow his wife's frigidity. The provisions left behind means the semen.

A married man who has a fundamentally depressive personality with inferiority feelings dreams especially about potency.

I am swimming out into the ocean showing off how far I can swim. The consistency of the water changes: it becomes like oysters (oysters always remind him of the vagina). My hands are clasped on a pillar and I am just swimming round.
The family of my first analyst are watching from the shore.

The coitus nature of the dream is evident, also the fact that he is masturbating (holding on to his penis). Exhibitionism is an overcompensation of his anxiety.

A middle-aged man who comes to be analyzed for professional purposes quarrels with his hysterical wife. During coitus his wife says, "Get out, I hate you!"

Dream: Many people are hanging from a rope. They are holding on precariously by their fingers. I and another man are taken off the rope. We are to be executed (guillotine).

The dream is practically self-explanatory. His body is his penis hanging on precariously to his wife's vagina. The guillotine is the castration trauma he suffered.

Why many men, or why he and another? These are questions we may be able to answer later.

A middle-aged woman, character disorder, dreams:

I am traveling on a ship. I have to crawl through a very narrow opening into a triangular room.

The rest of the dream does not interest us here but the dream itself is a typical dream beginning—going back into the womb.

Another typical basic dream element is when the environment is formed out of the body.

A young woman who has been pregnant for three months and has a strong transference on her father's brother dreams as follows:

I am eating a turkey with Uncle N.[60] Then I am in a room with one *baby grand piano*. It is a unique piece. It is in the house of another aunt *who never wanted a child*. Then I come to another room with a tree in it. The tree has branches and it is inlaid with mother of pearl. *It is also a unique piece.*

She ate a turkey with this uncle before the dream. The aunt was indignant but her uncle said he and his niece could do whatever they pleased.

[60] The same uncle figured in a previous dream as the Holy Ghost.

It is clear that she has conceived orally from the uncle who represents her father. Although pregnancy is a distinct victory over mother and mother substitutes (or perhaps just for this reason) the emphasis on the baby's uniqueness makes her anxiety clear. She is an only child.

The same patient dreams:

I dream of a woman who is pregnant. It is not me. She has a kind of basket fixed to her stomach and I can see through it. She shows me how to detach it, that is how the child will come out. I look inside but all I can see is seaweed. (The seaweed reminds her of a witch's hair). Then I see a beautiful girl with long blonde tresses. She is pregnant; there is a baby inside.

The seaweed = "long hair." This association again shows obviously her vagina and her mother's womb.

Another patient (female) dreams about a room that is always becoming nicer and nicer and now it is a bedroom with a regular bed in it.

The room is her vagina, and the dream expresses her hopes that the relationship with her lover will improve.

We may assume that these symbols have a twofold meaning: regressive (uterus of mother) and progressive (libidinal). Both are the stuff the dream world is built of.

The following dream is that of a middle-aged patient, a widow with a series of phobias.

Mother is driving my car. Then I take over from her. I let all the pedestrians cross. I stop at the stop sign. Then I drive into a fenced off square. The ground is inundated with soapy water. The fence bulges out at one place. I put my dog into that bulging place and go to sleep in the soapy water. We both [she and the dog] go to sleep and then I sleep till 11 A.M. I wake with a start (i.e., in my dream) and wake up the dog (a bitch). She has foam on her mouth and seems to laugh or smile.

Now I go with the dog into a panelled room. It is English style, like in a house I used to own in England. Tom is there with N.N. I carry the bitch with its vagina turned toward the men and I am angry that they don't notice it is a cat ["chat," French for vagina].

The first part of the dream refers to her mother (the superego) as the driver of her car in the past. She stops at the stop signal. This means that she changes the past, has never had any affairs nor done anything illicit.

The soapy water reminds her of the baths she used to have as a child, of how her mother would put her in soapy water. "The sleep in the dream" motive when we add to it the motives "mother" and "water" certainly proves the intrauterine quality of sleep. Eleven o'clock is the time when her boss will leave. He is taxing her energies, and she can hardly wait to see him leave. So she will sleep a few days (wish). When she wakes up, i.e., in the dream, she takes the bitch out of the bulge; it smiles, it has foam or water in its mouth. Evidently, she is brought back to life once more by the libidinally cathected vagina.

Now we have the panelled room. It refers to past glories. Her former boy friend is there with her, a man who has become rich by making men's underwear (i.e., the rich man, or the genitalia of the rich man). They do not notice her chat (vagina). After Thanatos (sleep) Eros.

The pregnant young woman mentioned earlier also dreamed:

I am going to a castle which is also a restaurant. It is owned by our friends Jack and Irene. Then I see a bossy girl who dominates her husband.

The castle was full of milk pitchers. I recognize a medium-sized green one as mine. Irene says it is not mine. She shows me the basement where many green pitchers of the same kind are being manufactured. I tell her that I can prove that it is mine, that it has my mark at the bottom. My mark is a cross with four circles, a circle at each end of the cross.

If it's mine she has to eat it. So now she starts eating it. But the pitcher becomes sugar, and she enjoys eating it.

The castle-restaurant with the milk pitchers is, of course, her own body and in it the baby she is nourishing. Irene is an aunt who keeps telling her what to do about the child and who in general behaves as if it were her own child. The pitchers are also her breasts. To the cross she associates a nutcracker, and then a woman's legs spread out in coitus. The nuts remind her of testicles.

What about the circle at the end of the cross? It reminds her of a mole, a blind animal underground—the embryo. Eating the pitcher reminds her of the witch in folk tales—Hänsel and Gretel—then another aunt who wants the baby for herself.

The dream reveals many things (among them, her desire to kill the embryo) about herself and her husband, etc. But all we want to know is the first step in the dream—her pregnant womb, her breasts.

The same woman has the following fantasy when in the elevator coming to the analyst.

I am all gum drops. I feel like I am suspended.

Associations: Suspended—the embryo. Gum drops—eggs—babies.
Another dream of the same pregnant woman:

Somebody shows me a graveyard. There are many holes in it. Some go straight down like a well. "That is how we dispose of our dead," a voice said. "We eat them, starting with the foot."

This reminds her of frogs' legs—a frog is like a baby. Again we see the mother's desire to destroy the baby, but the main thing that concerns us here is the environment formed out of the body and the descent into the womb.

A hypochondriac patient, age thirty, dreams:

There are three people in the room: myself, N.N., and my wife. He is very tall and thin. Looks like a prick, and leans toward my wife.

Certain characteristics of N.N. remind him of his father.

N.N. is, of course, his own penis. In this dream, the body as penis is going into the vagina. This is what I call the basic dream. The body (penis) receding into the womb can also be the basic dream of a girl. For instance, the dream quoted above about the girl who rides on an animal that keeps going toward a place grown over with bushes.

The following dream makes it quite clear what we mean by the "down" and "up" movements. The dreamer is a middle-aged married man. Satisfying his young wife sexually is one of his main neurotic problems. Before the dream, he had his penis in her vagina, but she was so dry that the erection collapsed.

Dream: A huge pier juts out into the ocean (penis, wet vagina). It is night time, he is alone. He is going to die. (The "down" or regressive movement.) But he takes hold of the pillars of the pier and pulls himself back to the shore by an overarm movement. The pillars touch his penis. Now he is ashore in a sailor's uniform, quite happy. He goes up to the porch of a hotel; there are many guests there, also his wife.

Pulling with the arms, the penis touching the pillars are clearly masturbation. In the dream he is masturbating and his penis is erect. This is the "up" movement that saves him from death.

The following dream of a young married woman in love for the second time with her first love shows the distinction between the symbolic and the historical dream factors.

I am walking on a bridge that leads to a hayloft. In the hayloft I am sitting with X.X. (the man she is in love with) and the Y couple (parental figures). I lean my head on Y's shoulder. I realize I am too bold, Y and his wife are reconciled now. Why did I do it? A ladder goes down from the hayloft. A taxi with a very elegant lady. When she gets out I want to get in. But a little girl still remains inside. She is a child or a dwarf dressed like an adult.

Associations: There was a bridge like that from the right side of the track to the wrong side in her home village. Hayloft—a roll in the hay.

The associations reveal that Y's wife is really herself—and "Why did I do it?" is guilt feeling. The Y couple = parents; and further, the analyst and his wife. The elegant, sophisticated lady is the way she would like to be. She cannot get into the taxi because she is really a child dressed up as an adult. The beginning of the dream: *bridge, hayloft, ladder*, is the basic dream—but in associating it is the *historical* or personal that interests the patient.

I must modify the interpretation I gave previously of two other dreams of my own. Both were dreamed while I had pneumonia and, as I was later told by my doctor, I was in a critical state for a few days.

"One night I felt very weak. In a reverie I said to myself: Well, there is nothing to be done about it. I am just going to die and that is all there is to it. I was quite resigned. There followed a hypnagogic hallucination.

"I see myself crossing a river. On the other side, a woman in pink, outlines very dim, waiting for me.

"I have the feeling that the dream means death. I shake it off and tell myself, 'Look, this is nonsense. Nobody can die in his own papers.' The reference was to 'Charon and the Obolos,'[61] and 'The Song of the Sirens.' "[62]

Next day, I noticed that my wife put on a pink housecoat when the doctor came. The fantasy must have meant in a symbolic language, "I can still cross the water to my wife." I wrote, "It is very improbable that I should have desired coitus in that extreme state of weakness," and I concluded that the life impulse by a *denominatio a potiori* was coitus. Dreaming of death, in terms of my own papers, means *non omnis moriar*.[63]

Now, I would give a somewhat different interpretation to the one contained in my paper. This is what I now call the *basic dream*, the moment of falling asleep. Fear of dying wakes me up—death and sleep are too similar to each other. Since I was really near to dying, the upward or genitalized movement was not very strong, except in the waking thought. Yet, it is immanent in the dream itself for Odysseus (with whom in my childhood I frequently identified myself in fantasy) is the hero whom the Sirens cannot conquer. He stands *erect* tied to the ship's mast.

The dream of the following night confirms this view.

There is a door ajar—I have to push it quite open with my shoulder so that a little child can go in. I fall back on my cushion in despair. I am too weak, I cannot open it.

However, I am practically certain that there is also another fantasy element in this dream. The little child who is supposed to go in through

61 *The Psychiatric Quarterly Supplement*, XX, 1946, pp. 160–196.
62 *The Psychiatric Quarterly*, XXII, 1948, pp. 18–44.
63 Róheim, G., "The Original of the Ideal," *Samiksa*, II, 1948, pp. 1–13.

the door is connected with a famous hero of the Hungarian Chronicles.

The Hungarians (in the ninth century) are besieging Byzantium. One of them, Botond by name, steps forward to challenge a Greek giant. "Although I am the smallest of the Hungarians," he says, "you had better take two companions with you, one to take care of your corpse and the other for your soul." He lifts his axe and with one stroke smashes such a gap in the iron gate of the city that a child of five could go through. Botond was certainly the favorite hero of my childhood.[64]

The little child going in is quite clear: it is both coitus and regression into the womb. The mention of the cushion shows that it is the moment between a hypnagogic fantasy and a dream.[65] "I am too weak, I dare not fall asleep."

A pneumonia patient, with 105° fever, shortly before her crisis dreams:

I was dozing. The door opened very slowly. Somebody approached my bed as slowly as in a slow motion picture. I felt strange. He walked around my bed and placed his hand on my heart. I woke up bathed in sweat. I had the impression of having seen Death and was afraid to fall asleep again.[66]

The slow motion and the cold are the opposite of fever. This dream is similar to one frequently found among primitives. A relative has come to fetch the dreamer. But again we have the *door,* i.e., *the gates of the dream.*

The following dream will permit us to penetrate into the mechanism of sleep and dreaming.

A middle-aged divorced woman is reluctantly contemplating having an affair with somebody—and also has other plans involving a new kind of work.

Dream: I am running on a covered bridge through a kind of tunnel in great haste. At the same time I am also on the ground looking at myself.

Then I go down black stairs into a completely black room. This is a famous restaurant, my former boy friend took me to this place.

A. is drinking coffee, lapping it up like a dog, bending down. The room is full of very high chairs to sit on. His wife is there. She says I am not to have cake with the coffee because it makes me fat.

Associations: The bridge is like the Ponte dei Sospiri in Venice. This is where the criminals go from their prison to be executed. The associa-

64 Szentpétery, I., *Scriptores Rerum Hungaricarum,* I, 1938, pp. 310, 311.
65 Róheim, "The Origin of the Ideal," *Samiksa,* II, 1948, pp. 1–13.
66 Gutheil, *op. cit.,* p. 81.

tion to the stairs is also significant. Twenty years ago she was hypnotized for a stair phobia.

If we take the arcade-bridge and the stairs together it seems that going to sleep (hypnosis) means dying and therefore causes anxiety. The arcades and the bridge are evidently her own vagina, the very dark restaurant is like her own womb. The name of the restaurant is like her own first name. The tall chairs remind her of penises. A. is being analyzed. She has doubts about his potency. Lapping up must be cunnilingus. A.'s wife is very much like her mother. Mother forbids her to become fat, i.e., pregnant by father.

It is interesting to note that she is also on the ground watching herself running through the arcade-bridge combination.

I assume that what we have called the basic dream originates in an anxiety, a part of the sleeping person is dreaming—in other words, is not quite asleep. It is observing what the other part is doing, but it is seeing it in a symbolic form. It is not a phallos entering a vagina or a child going into its mother's womb, it is the person himself falling or going into a cellar or pool or hole, etc. Is this because of the birth trauma which has to be canceled or repeated every night? This is what Rank and now Fodor would assume.[67] In some cases where the narrow passage is emphasized it seems evident that the act of being born actually leaves mnemonic impressions on the individual. But the main thing seems to be that physiological factors determine this periodicity of sleep and that the withdrawal of cathexis from the environment causes anxiety. Narcissism comes to the rescue, withdrawal into one's own body is withdrawal into the womb.

But the dream is visual. As soon as the world is destroyed by withdrawal of cathexis, it is rebuilt (like in schizophrenia) and the result is a mixture of historical and symbolical elements. The day residue is active, financial worries make her think of getting a lover. Actually, however, she is very narcissistic and scarcely "giving." She may wish for cunnilingus but not for penetration.

However, we are now told by the patient that A.'s wife who always tells her what to do and what not to do, is just like her mother. What is the "mother imago" telling her in this dream? That she may flirt with father but not have an affair with him, not become pregnant by him. In terms of reality this would mean flirting with success but never having an affair. The latent dream thought would be to be pregnant by father. The basic dream would be withdrawing cathexis from environment and falling back into the womb. Yes, but which womb? Mother's womb and

67 Fodor, *op. cit.*

her womb, her vagina, become identical. It is from her vagina or womb that the attempt is made to build up a new world on a libidinal basis.

The moment of falling asleep is the moment in which the soul is born, that phallic personification of the body which in the process of falling asleep is withdrawn from the object world, but in the dream builds up a new world. The way the primitives put it, that it comes out of the body, not that it goes in, is in a sense correct.

From this point of view, we should say that fission or duplication is the first dream mechanism. The dreamer *sees* himself. There is already a duality. The reason for this fission is anxiety. In other words, the dream-body-phallus while it is going in is at the same time coming out of the womb. The following dream, or rather, hypnopompic fantasy was dreamed by a patient in Budapest, a professor of Hungarian literature.

A whole crowd of people rise in the theater. From the stage they hear the words, "A sirt hol nemzet sülyed el a népek veszik körül" ("the grave into which a nation sinks is surrounded by the people of the whole world"). He awakes with an erection.

The quotation is from the *Szózat* (Oration), a poem by Vörösmarty which ranks next to the *Hymnus* (Kölcsey) as a national anthem. The dream is based on an episode in his past. He was in the theater with his girl friend. They were playing the *Hymnus* on the stage. Since it was part of the play it is not customary to rise on such occasions. But he rose from his seat, having always been a Hungarian chauvinist, and thereby compelled all the others to rise too.

But in this dream the quotation is from the *Szózat* and not the *Hymnus*. "The grave into which a nation sinks" is sleep. But the lines that characterize the *Szózat* for every Hungarian are these:

Hazádnak rendületlenül légy hive ó magyar
Ez bölcsöd és majdan sirod is
Mely ápol és eltakar

(Undauntedly be true to thy country, O Hungarian,
This is thy *cradle* and will be thy *grave* that
nurses and covers thee.)

This is an obvious allusion to the womb as beginning and end. "Undauntedly" could also be translated "unshakably" and means the erect penis. The next lines the dreamer thinks of are from the classic of Berzsenyi, *A Magyarokhoz* (To the Hungarians): Nyolc századoknak vérzivatarjai között rongált Budának tornyai állanak ("Amidst the blood and storms of eight centuries *the towers of shattered Buda still stand*") and then, "El magyar áll Buda még" (The Hungarian still lives, the fortress of Buda stands).

The regression into the womb is also coitus with mother. It has the double purpose of regressing into the womb and warding off regression. The majestic lines hide castration anxiety. The many phalloi that stand in the dream are duplications or multiplications conditioned by anxiety. *The formation of a double in the dream is the moment when animism originates.*[68]

I must add that by double I mean not only the duplication of the dreamer, but the dream image itself.

This is the dream of a young woman analyzed because of feelings of inferiority and blushing when in society.

I see Mrs. N. and a second woman seated at a table. The second woman looks just like Mrs. N. She is even fatter. There is a scar on her face. I say to her that it does not matter, that she has the most beautiful voice in the whole world.

Associations: She is menstruating—that is why the woman has a scarred face. The second woman who is even fatter than the first one reminds her of pregnancy. A typical dream of menstruating women: they are pregnant. "The most beautiful voice in the world" reminds her of Bunker's paper, "The Voice as a Female Phallos." The first woman, whose double the second woman is, looks like her mother.

There is a two- or even threefold formation of alter ego here.

(1) The identification with her mother. To her, sex is a problem; her mother was promiscuous.

(2) The pregnant woman. Denial of menstruation.

(3) The beautiful voice—a phallic personification. (Further denial of menstruation.)

Dream of a man whose short stature worries him. To him, it has become the symbol of an inadequate penis.

I see Tom with two women. Next week he will get sixty-five dollars. I think I will give him two five dollar notes I have in my pocket.

Associations: His brother Tom is six foot three and a great lady killer. The patient is unhappy in his marriage. Sixty-five was his house number where he lived before his marriage. Tom is unmarried. The two five dollar notes: masturbation, his testicles, castration anxiety.

Interpretation: He has got rid of his wife, is unmarried and a lady killer like Tom. The tall brother—his phallic double.

The clearest instance of what I mean by the patient retreating into

---

[68] This duplication or repetition in connection with the intrauterine situation is mentioned by Freud, S., *Neue Vorlesungen zur Einführung in die Psychoanalyse*, Wien, 1933, p. 35.

her own vagina and then building up the new world from it is the following dream:

My husband has chosen a new apartment for me. All the rooms are very ugly. I am very angry. Finally, we come into a room where the wall paper is all covered with red blots. I am furious. I see the bathroom; instead of a tub there is a beautiful shell.

I ask the patient whether she is about to menstruate, she confirms this (the red blots). All women dream either of menstruation in a symbolic form or of being pregnant in the premenstrual days or during menstruation because the dream must cancel or symbolize the disappointing fact of the absence of pregnancy. Her husband is responsible for her unsatisfactory sex life, i.e., for her not being pregnant. It is to be emphasized that she is *in* the room that represents her bleeding vagina. The bathroom with the shell reminds her of Aphrodite Anadyomene, the Goddess of Love, rising from the shell—the erotic beginning of a new world.

A similar menstrual dream is that of a young woman who has quarreled with her boy friend about something very unimportant. She is also expecting menstruation.

I am very angry at my date and my mother and won't let myself be examined by the doctor. My house is dirty—let mother clean it, it is her job. I am now about to go upstairs. My brother-in-law and sister are sitting on the steps, many little tame animals surround them. Now I am in a long, tiled bathroom, like a corridor. I am naked and I cover my genitals with a shower curtain. I see the ocean. Under my window I see the devil dressed like a hunter. He asks me for a date and shows me the bloody deer he has just killed.

Associations: The devil looks like her lover, but also like her father. The bloody deer; her bleeding vagina. Won't let the doctor investigate her—is ashamed to tell the analyst what the quarrel was about. The dirty house—again her body. Sister and her husband have several children (tame animals). Long bathroom = her vagina. *The state of being sexually excited is symbolized by her being in her own vagina.*

Another patient, a young widow, narcissistic, apparently not even desirous of coitus, dreams:

I am in a beautiful apartment, thick rugs on the floor colored brown and red. Love seats around the wall. I am flying or floating above the carpet. It is really a long corridor. A married couple—the girl tall and thin, the man tall and athletic. They are looking for the news section. I tell them this is the building of *The New York Times.* I am now in an air plane which is flying in a kind of gap between the hills. I see only the back of the pilot's head; it is roundish.

Associations: The carpet: brown like excrements, red like blood. ("Are you menstruating?" I ask. "No, but in two days, I think.") This is the explanation of *The New York Times* and the news section. The woman *looks like she would like to be* and the man is like one of her past lovers. But the roundish head of the pilot again reminds her of her own buttocks.

For the male dreamer the body appearing in the dream is phallic, space is feminine (uterine, vaginal).

Female patients also symbolize themselves as boys. The same mechanism is revealed in the following dream (penis envy):

A little boy is standing in a lake and I am vomiting into the lake three times.

Associations: Her husband had intercourse with her at three. She is troubled by nausea lately. "The little boy must be me," she says. Then she goes on with fantasies about a wedding and rebirth from the water.

Interpretation: The vomiting is ejaculation. The water she stands in is both her mother's womb and her own erotically cathected vagina.

Confirmation: Yes, she also masturbated after the coitus.

A married man of thirty-five has an affair with a young actress. His problem is, shall he divorce his wife and marry his girl friend? He dreams:

I telephone to a woman who must be quite near because I see her. It is the *wrong connection.* (*My wife, he says.*) I am in the *elevator* with Mary (*name of girl friend*). She *operates the elevator.* I stand erect.

Associations: The space of the elevator is Mary's vagina. The rest is self-evident.

The following dream is that of a young woman. Her phobias have been eliminated, but she still has no orgasm or only rarely.

A canoe is shooting down rapidly into a tunnel. A man is in the canoe; the boat closes over him like a pea in a pod. Then I see myself swimming out of the tunnel. Fred is swimming in the opposite direction.

Associations: The person is like an embryo (folded), like a papoose. After saying several other words beginning with *p* she finally comes to "penis."

Interpretation: The dreamer, identifying her body with her father's penis goes into her own vagina (boat, tunnel) and comes out. This would be an orgasm. Fred, who represents her boy friend, is inept, i.e., she blames it on him.

The dream is visual. Although the first move is a regression into the vagina, the scenery of the dream is certainly not intrauterine, as Fodor might assume. In the dream the dreamer is halfway out of sleep (the uterus) and building up a new world on a libidinal basis. Libido means life, withdrawal of cathexis (uterine regression) means death. The ambi-sexuality that is latent in every human being comes into its own here. The body appears both as a male and as a female genital, *both as moving in space and as forming space.*

Beside the libido in its unadulterated form something else is used to build up a new world and to protect the ego from complete extinction (sleep, dying). These are the memory images of the past. Hence we find all sorts of stages of ontogenesis represented in the dream which travels a long way from the present to the past and from the past to the present. We thus assume that the dream has a double function: to protect sleep from the intrusion of the day worries and to protect the ego from falling asleep completely, i.e., dying.

We shall now try to summarize what we have to say about the dream.

Freud says that dreaming is naturally regressive since sleeping is.[69] The moment of disintegration of the conscious ego or of the holding onto the objects of the external world is interpreted as falling back into the womb.[70] However, since neither the embryo nor the infant in the process of being born can see anything, we must assume (a) that mnemonic traces must exist on an "infraunconscious" level if by unconscious we mean visual images, (b) that the very act of visualizing these memory traces, i.e., *the basic dream,* is *progression* in *regression,* that is to say, the regression into the womb is counteracted, and (c) that our theory clearly implies that regression, although it may later be used as an ego mechanism is originally *an intrinsic part of the id.* It is congenital and inevitable in a foetalized species.[71]

The dreamers show that the womb into which the sleeper or dreamer withdraws is at the same time his own body. The libidinal cathexis withdrawn into the body appears on the scene as a body phallus, i.e., *theoretically, both male and female play both roles,* that of the actor (male) and of the stage (female). It is necessary to emphasize here another aspect of this progression-regression mechanism. In the case of the woman, the womb into which the sleeper withdraws is also her own erotically cathected vagina. In the case of the man, the phallic body is more emphasized. In both, therefore, the regressive dream also means that a new dream environment is being built up—based on genital libido.

This dream theory explains the two main factors of the dream—historical and symbolical. The dream must be symbolical and libidinal

[69] Freud, S., *Gesammelte Schriften,* II, Wien, 1924, p. 490.
[70] Kleitman, N., *Sleep and Wakefulness,* Chicago, 1939, p. 111.
[71] Cf. Róheim, G., *Psychoanalysis and Anthropology,* New York, 1950, Chapter X: "The Unity of Mankind."

because the primary process is the very essence of the dream, the path back to environment. However, the dreamer is not an infant but a fully formed person with a structuralized psyche. It still remains true, therefore, that the starting point of the dream is the *day residue* or rather the superego (reproach) contained in the day residue (Jekels and Bergler). The superego is holding the ego—trying to prevent its disintegration, i.e., falling asleep. When the id in the form of regression gets the upper hand (sleep) or at least a partial upper hand in being partly awake (dream), the id solves these problems by representing a libidinal solution with the secondary aim of also achieving a solution in reality.[72] This is the magical aspect of the dream. But why is this represented on an infantile level? Because regression is the essence of the dream. The anal and oral aspects of the dream are stations of this journey from one terminal to the other, it being not even clear whether they represent stations of the train that goes from the present to the past or from the past to the present. The historical and the symbolic become interwoven and the personal is superimposed on the generic. Since the world is built up again every night on a libidinal basis, all past situations revolving around personal problems in growing up are relived, reseen. From the viewpoint of the id and of the dream as magic the function of these elements is to say, just as I have outgrown, overcome, my problems at the age of two or five or eight I shall triumph in this present situation. But the superego may get the upper hand, guilt transforms wishing into anxiety and the result is, "I feel just as helpless and afraid as I felt at the age of five, etc."—and the magic has failed, we have an anxiety dream.

We speak (following Freud) of neurosis as an archaism, but we should not forget that normal development is also based on a repetition of the past—but a repetition of a different kind.

IV. DREAMS OF PRIMITIVE TRIBES

The following instances are taken from dreams of various non-European (and non-American) dreamers.

Chinchewara, an old woman of the Matuntara tribe (Central Australia), has the following dream:

There was water on both sides, and I climbed up a gum tree. The branch bent down, and I was hanging on it—then I dropped down, and as I fell my mother caught me in her arms and took me away.

Then I went to a place where I saw my mother's grave, and I went up a high rock. There was a gap there, and I passed through the gap.

72 Cf. Róheim, G., "The Magical Function of the Dream," *International Journal of Psycho-Analysis*, XXX, 1949, Part 3.

Two enemy warriors were on the other side lying in wait for me and trying to choke me.

The rest of the dream is of no importance in this connection. But it is clear that the dream opens with the typical birth symbolism and death anxiety. The historical or personal motivation of the death anxiety is contained in the sequel of the dream.[73]

Urkalarkiraka has the following dream:[74]

I was walking across a stream, and there was a deep hole in the middle of the stream. I nearly drowned. Then I awoke.

The following dream of Uran tukutu (Pindupi tribe) shows the urethral and basic dream pattern (dreamed August 24, 1929).

I see a devil (mamu) coming out of a little hole near a tree. It looked like a cat, long red hair, full of blood. Threw my magic stone at it but I missed. Then it disappeared in the ground and came out again at another place. There were flames in a big crack; the demon ran into it, shook itself and got burned.

He was rolling into the fire when he awoke. He went to urinate.

It is necessary to explain that the natives, sleeping near the fire when the night is cold, frequently roll into it and even get wounds before they wake up.

Associations: The place the devil first comes from is Ululura ngurara = Blood wood tree. He comes from a hole near the tree. The demon in the dream looks like Puna tari, his elder brother. Puna tari was a father substitute, because his father was too old to teach him anything. Puna tari taught him how to use the spear and spear thrower, how to catch a kangaroo, etc. He often fought with Puna tari and speared his leg.

The place is also like Ulturpma where one man who stood to him in the relationship of *marutu* (brother-in-law) was cut in a fight by another man who was his *kamuru* (uncle). He (the dreamer) then speared the *kamuru*.

About the cat, he says that at Katilka he sat in a hole made by the flood. Afterward when he went hunting he saw a fire, it was burning in a hole. His dog ran into the fire and it was past rescuing.

Interpretation: The oedipal content is obvious. The fight with the father substitute and the uncle are associations to the dream.

Beyond this we can see that the fire as usual symbolizes urine. The associations mention a flood and on awakening he urinated.

The fire and hole in which the demon (actually the dreamer who rolled into the fire) disappears is the basic dream.

[73] Cf. Róheim, G., "Dream of Women in Central Australia," *Psychiatric Quarterly Supplement*, XXIV, 1950, p. 23.
[74] Field notes.

In Normanby Island, Doketa, the chief of Loboda and Gagajowana, dreams as follows:

I dreamed about a big wind, a storm. The village was covered with water. People were floating, and then they *went down into* the water. I stayed in my room with a light, and then the missionary said, I have not left you.

He talks about various dangers, and then of why he accepted Christianity. Before he became a Christian, he was accused of being a sorcerer (a *barau*), and therefore he might be attacked or sorcery might be practiced on him.

The words spoken by the missionary in the dream were really spoken by a man who wanted to summon him to the Government because of a pig, and the missionary told him he would protect him.

He tells me a myth about the origin of the drum. In the other world there was a self-moving drum and the people danced all the time, they had nothing to do but enjoy themselves. The people of Kelologeia got tired of the eternal music and stole the drum.

The man who stole the drum dove into the sea—and this is how it happens that we enjoy ourselves with women and we dance. But the drums have to be made first; it is not like in the other world.

He talks some more about people who threatened to *barau* him (kill him by magic), and then he says with a smile, "Oh, all right—let them try! Woe to them if they do so! *Then I will show them.*

Another dream was as follows:

Sky angels woke me and said: You come with us. We went to a large house, as big as from here to Bwaruada. We went in one door and came out another. Then we went in the other door again. We opened a door and I saw Dr. Bromilow's shadow. He was sitting there writing at a table with books piled on it. He saw me, stood up, and we shook hands.

"In the Christian way he finds intra-uterine protection or rather a mild father with whom he shakes hands in the uterus. He is taken up to heaven by the same angels who took Christ up, resurrection follows upon death, coitus is not death, there will be another resurrection when the penis comes out of the vagina."[75]

What I add now, however, is that falling asleep means going through a door and dying—Bromilow, the missionary, died many years ago.

Ramoramo, whose dream I have published,[76] reports the following dream:

[75] Róheim, G., "Psycho-Analysis of Primitive Cultural Types," *International Journal of Psycho-Analysis*, XIII, 1932, pp. 151–177.

[76] *Idem*, "Dream Analysis and Field Work," *Psychoanalysis and the Social Sciences*, I, New York, 1947, p. 102.

Dream 8

I went up a big hill. It kept turning round, quicker and quicker. From the moving hill I jumped across to a house. A white man came, and I asked, where did I come from? He raised his hand. You come from my hand, he said, and then I came down to earth.

Associations: The white man was Usubeni, a missionary. He used to ask the native who worked for him, "Did the boar fuck the sow?" If the native said no. Usubeni would threaten to shoot him.

The place where the dream occurred looked like the whole earth. The hill was like a hill at Bwebweso (other world) called Sabedi. This is a witches' hill. A man from Woodlark told him that the witches' hill keeps turning around. Inside the earth there is a trunk that makes the whole earth turn around. A witch went down to the underworld to see this trunk, it is as small as a needle.

He jumps to the house for protection. It is the kind of house they build against enemies. He talks about various dangers, storms, white police, intercourse.[77]

Interpretation: What is the role of the white man in this dream? He is a sort of intermediary between the white man's god and the dreamer. The missionary is the father; he came from his hand. The day stimulus of the dream was the talk with the Bunama people. The white men will come into the country to take their women and land. A storm means famine. Then he tells stories about famines in which people ate their own children. According to the context, being eaten is the punishment for sexual desire.

The whole dream is about the theme, "Where did I come from?" The answer is, "from parental intercourse." (Has the boar fucked the sow?) The trunk of the world tree or the needle would also be the father's penis revolving in the mother, and also the moment of falling asleep. From the primal scene, he jumps into the protecting house (uterine regression).

I have mentioned the case of a patient who feels like a spinning top on the couch. She is falling asleep, going back into the womb, dying—having an orgasm.

Ramoramos' dream is parallel to this state. The revolving is the falling asleep. The whole world is the dreamer himself.

To Iledi, a young boy of Darwuada, had the following dream:

Wadanoj came at night while I slept. She chased me, we ran. I grew wings and I flew up. Then I fell to the ground suddenly and there I was. Flies and ants covered me, and then I fell to the ground. They washed me with hot water and I woke up.

[77] For details, cf. previous publication.

Associations: Wadanoj was his grandmother who used to make much of him in his childhood. But if his mother did not give her a share of the pig, she would chase him. His little brother climbed a tree once and fell down like that. He was unconscious and covered with flies and ants. They washed him with hot water and he revived. People thought the old witch (grandmother) made him fall from the tree because they did not give her enough food. The old witch then healed his brother.[78]

The secondary dream work in this dream is the rearrangement of sequence. The falling from the tree is falling asleep, falling into the womb, dying. Then comes the "flying with the grandmother" as a substitute for the mother. Naturally, the guilt about the brother increases the anxiety in falling asleep and in the dreaming.

Seguragura's wife Ne Duro dreams:

Neijani, my daughter, is being carried away by the water. Her father came, pulled her out of the water and reproached me.

In the dream her daughter is dead. This happens at Waira Kawana. That is where her brother floated away like that on the water. Lobagodu fished the child out, but the child was dead.

Her daughter was engaged to Lomenaj, a boy of about thirteen. But Lomenaj who was notoriously fickle had been playing around with Dadaujo. She reproached Dadaujo for this whereupon the latter swam into the river to commit suicide. Her father fished her out from a canoe.

Her husband reproached her for quarreling with the child. She said the same words to her mother when her little brother died.

Guilt feelings enter into the picture again. She championed her daughter's cause when the daughter's lover was unfaithful, but in the dream it is her daughter who dies. Swimming in the water and being pulled out of the water are probably the birth symbolism of falling asleep. Her daughter is dead in the dream, i.e., she is dead, asleep.

Zakaria, a middle-aged married man from Loboda, dreamed the following after we had visited a newly-made grave.

When they buried the dead man, the oki fruit *kept falling.* I gathered some of the fruit, therefore my hand became broad (like that of witches), but I did not go into the grave, I came out.

The rest of the dream is an anxiety dream about being chased by the dead man. That part is not relevant, but what is important is the *falling* and the denial of having been in the grave.

Tomekera, a middle-aged married man in the village of Boasitoroba dreams:

[78] Field notes.

I wanted to go to work at Sawalawara. They put me on the shore. I asked for Pweromu. He said, Here I am. We shall sleep here today, he said. Let us go to sleep. We got ready to sleep. The house was closing in on us. They were knocking from the outside. I got frightened and awoke.

Day stimulus: His son-in-law Gejdi was telling him about the time when he was working in the mines for the white people. One shift worked only at night, one only in the daytime. If they wanted to go up they had to shout to the people on top to pull them up.

Associations: Knocking means *barau* (sorcerers). His uncle always used to shout, "They are knocking at my house!" meaning the *barau* people. He was always afraid because he had killed many in the wars.

Pweromu is a friend of his, a peaceful man with whom he used to work.

Interpretation: Obviously this is a nightmare having to do with sorcerers. What interests us here is only that sleep is mentioned in the dream and symbolically represented by a house closing in on the sleepers.

The following dream of Bulema was dreamed while he was getting ready for a *sagari* in honor of his wife (i.e., a *mwadare*[79]).

I was climbing a tree for fire wood when a woman called me. She said, "Bring your lime pot."[80] I descended the tree and got pepper. I chewed with her and she asked me, "Are you finished?" I said I was finished. Then come for my pig, for the *sagari*. The woman's name is Gogonore. She calls her sisters and they bring food for the feast. I killed a pig and we ate. But she quarreled with her sisters. She said, "My brother Hirata built a canoe, we are going down to the *numu* world." She said, "Your sisters [i.e., Bulema's sisters] quarreled with me, therefore I am taking my brother-in-law [i.e., Bulema] down to the *numu*[81] world. But my brother [i.e., Hirata] said, "You go up again [i.e., your time to die has not come yet]. So I went up [awoke].

Bulema said he became sick because of this dream, i.e., he was feverish (malaria). Probably he is feverish at the time of the dream.

Associations: Garurej was a woman who followed me when I climbed a tree for flowers. "She called for me, I came down, we chewed together, she took the lime pot home and I spent the night with her. She was my mistress." But the woman in the dream is Gogonore. He calls Gogonore, his mother's elder sister and also a *werabana* (witch). But this does not mean that she was a real woman, she is one of the *tokwa-tokway* (female spirits) of his clan. There is a song about Gogonore.

---

[79] Cf. Róheim, G., *Psychoanalysis and Anthropology,* New York, 1950, p. 178. *Idem,* "Tauhau and the Mwadare," *International Journal of Psycho-Analysis,* XIII, 1932.

[80] The lime pot is a gourd with lime used with a spatula when they chew betel.

[81] Underground realm of the *numu,* fertility spirits.

> Gogonore, Gogonore,
> My anger went away and the pain also
> There you take me round
> I walked, I forgot (poured out) my angry thoughts.

"Anger" is not quite exact as a translation. The text is *Kau siwapa,*
isiwapa means that a man gets angry and commits suicide by going into
enemy territory with the intention of getting killed. The spirits of people
who did this went to the underground realm of the *numu.* "Take me
round *numu* point" would mean bring me back to the living, I am not
angry any more.

Now he describes Gogonore as she appears in the dream. She is short
and broad, not pretty. Looks like Babaidoa, a Trobriand woman, the
wife of a white man. This white man used to send for Babaidoa with his
axe poised for use. Then he examined her vagina; if it was wet he cut his
working boys with the axe. This was because he regarded that as proof
that she had been having intercourse with one of them.

Gogonore has three sisters and Hirata is her brother. Hirata is the
canoe builder of the *numu* world (the mythical character of Gogonore
and Hirata becomes apparent). Hirata has his nose on one side and one
eye is higher up in the face than normal, the other somewhat lower.[82]
The sisters of Gogonore look like Matanogi and Neneora, the two maids
employed by the writer's wife. The quarrel is this: the sisters want to take
the pig to their husband but Gogonore says, "I married later so the pig is
mine." It is customary for the elder to give in to the younger not the other
way round.

He calls Gogonore his "mother," the word usually used in mentioning a witch. In this culture there is always a potential conflict "sister and
wife," i.e., the man's allegiance is divided between these two and the food
distribution ceremony is supposed to overcome this tension. "Sister"
means also "mother," i.e., all the women of the matrilineal *susu* (breast,
clan). The woman in the dream is a mother, the association is a mistress
—death is the penalty for incest. But underlying this there is another
sequence: ascent (tree climbing) coitus, *descent in a canoe (uterine regression).* It is the dream of a sick man with the ending, "I am not going to
die yet." The dream of a man called Lazaro from Loboda follows:

I sat on a boat with my wife and my son. *He was asleep on the out-*
rigger and we went to Kekura. We pulled ashore and both started to go
inland but the child was still asleep in the boat. "What if it falls off," I
said, and we both went back to the canoe. Then I woke.

Associations: They went like that once to Soisoija with the child remaining on the boat. They followed the boat of Deligogo, his sister's hus-

[82] The *nigonigogo* or supernaturals never have normal faces.

band's boat. Deligogo is a great man in the *une*[83] and a great canoe builder. If young men went courting the girls and the girls rejected them he would make fun of them and say, "He came back without fucking."

They pulled up the canoe on the shore of Kekura near the cave of Matakapotaiataia.[84] He mentions the story of Matakapotaiataia, "this is where he was hidden with his mother."

Interpretation: In the myth Matakapotaiataia's mother is pregnant, hides in a cave when everybody is killed by the man-eating monster Tokeduketai and in the cave she is delivered of the future hero Matakapotaiataia. The womb symbolism of the cave is therefore obvious. *The child asleep on the boat and the cave,* taken together, symbolize sleep. Paddling, the association to the courting expeditions of boys, the fact that he is with his wife—all these mean coitus, i.e., the dream. Coming ashore is awakening, going back to the boat, to the sleeping child—prolonged sleep.

The dreams of the people of Alor, published by Cora Du Bois, contain the same typical motives.

Tilapada, a woman, dreams that her soul goes to the other world. Some were being roasted, some sat in chairs like white people. *Someone took me by the wrist and threw me down.* I fell on top of a tree, then another man took me by the wrist and threw me on another and shorter tree till I came down to the ground.[85] [I omit the rest.]

The only comment to make is that the characteristic sensation of falling is here repeatedly connected with a man.

Another dream of hers is this:

Langmai (a kinsman) and Helangmai (her husband's kinswoman) were walking on a cement strip like a path. *On either side there was a dark hole like a ravine. The two fell off the path into the darkness.*[86]

Furthermore:

I dreamed that my soul was returning from Hatoberka. We were in a ravine below the village. *There Mailang and a man from Aila were sleeping (floating) in a pool. Their heads were out of the water resting on the bank.*[87]

We quote this as a functional symbol of sleep as intrauterine regression—omitting the rest of the dream.

The following experience of Rilpada the seer is reported as a vision but it seems very dreamlike to me.

[83] Or *kune,* cf. Róheim, G., *Psychoanalysis and Anthropology,* p. 183.
[84] Actually the cave is quite near the ocean, just a strip of beach between them.
[85] Du Bois, C., *The People of Alor,* Minneapolis, 1944, p. 400.
[86] *Ibid.,* p. 403.
[87] *Ibid.,* p. 431.

I looked and there was a bird flying down in front of the privy doorway. In a little while it flew up in front of the entrance doorway. It was either a *sisak* or a *tintopa* (both birds favored by seers as familiars). I thought, what is this? Maybe people are surrounding the house and want to kill me or steal me. I fetched father's sword. I went to the privy doorway and stuck my head out through the thatch. I thought I could escape that way. Then I pulled my head back and went down by the house ladder onto the verandah. I saw many flies coming out of a sheep's anus. Then they all swarmed up my anus. Spiders came out of the sheep's mouth and then they entered my mouth.[88]

We have all the basic dream elements here. The flying and the descent, "the coming out" (birth), and the anal-oral version of uterine regression (in and out of mouth, of anus).

The following dream of a middle-aged Navaho woman, mother of several children, was not dreamed at the time she told it but many years before. No associations were available—I might say they were not even necessary.

It was winter. I was looking for something far from home. The snow made me lose my way. I was afraid in the *dark* and I was trying to *get back* to where I had started. I saw a pile of dirt and a hole.
Then heat struck me on one side of the body. It came from the hole, it felt good. I went nearer to the hole and looked in. Then I heard noise like somebody breathing. I was not afraid now. "Who is there?" she asked. "Someone" is the reply. I told the man I was lost and that I wanted to go into the hole. "Whoever you are, I want to stay with you for the night," I said. I was invited in. I went a little further, it got light and the room got bigger. Inside it was covered with soft cedar bark and a fire was blazing. Somebody was lying down there and he sat up. It was a man-bear. He asked me where I came from. He said, "All right, granddaughter, lie on that bedding, nobody will hurt you." *I fell asleep.* The bear snored, I was awake. I fell asleep again. The bear began to howl, "Get up!" I fell asleep again. I awoke, the bear patted me on the shoulder and showed me where to go with his paw. I jumped out of the hole and I was awake.[89]

Guessing from other Navaho dream material the bear is probably the father imago. The repeated mentioning *in the dream* of falling asleep and awakening indicate the underlying anxiety because of the oedipal content. The hole into which she creeps and which then becomes a room and her sleeping in the room—this is what we mean by the basic dream.

An old Navaho woman, Tehepaa, dreams:

It was far away at Black Mountain. I was walking from the store with my son and daughter. A dance was being held nearby. Suddenly the earth was open, we fell in it and it closed up again. How shall we get

88 *Ibid.*, p. 240.
89 Field notes, 1947.

out, I thought. There was a path, circular, and many hogans. A man was sitting there (*he looked like you when you are writing*). The man said, "My granddaughter sits right here beside me." The man had a ball and a stick like a rattle. He hit my foot, neck and shoulder and the top of my head on both sides with the rattle.

Then he told me to dance and I stood up and danced. Then he stood up and danced and the children also. He said, "You can go back now!" I asked, "How, there is just fire all over!" He said, "There is a step ladder and a tunnel and that is where your home is." So we climbed up there. Back on earth there was a man fixing a tractor. (*This one looked like you too*), and we asked him where our home was. He said, "There, near the pine tree—the place where you were is hell."

The way the man in the land of the ghosts (or hell) hit her was like the native medicine man touching people with corn pollen. The man was naked—"Perhaps it was Jesus," she remarks. We see in this dream cultural elements both from missionary teaching (Jesus, hell) and from her own religion (the medicine man). But the point is that the sinking and rising, the circular path, the ladder and the tunnel are the traits of the basic dream. The naked medicine man, the stick and the dance are genital, oedipal, transference traits. She sinks both into the womb and into her own vagina.

I quote one of the dreams published by Kluckhohn and Morgan. A Navaho woman living near Flagstaff dreams:

> After my little girl died, I dreamed *I was sleeping* and a little girl just *like her came into the hogan* . . . [italics mine]. And this little girl was kind to me. She didn't speak to me, and she only laid her head on my head. . . .[90]

I conjecture that the combination of sleeping and the little girl going into the hogan means that (a) her dead child is coming back into her womb, (b) she herself is the child going into her own or her mother's womb.

The following dream dreamed by an acculturated "Wolf" Indian and analyzed in its characterological aspects by Devereux clearly shows the structure of what I call the "basic dream." Among the symptoms of the patient we mention only those which might have a bearing on this dream: troubled vision, anxiety attacks, nightmares, compulsive sleeping ritual, difficulties in falling asleep, disturbances in potency.[91]

Dream: Me, my brother and another guy. They left me alone and went ahead. I noticed in a cave some stuff and rags, and I went in to look over this place. The first thing I noticed were these medicine

[90] Kluckhohn, C. and Morgan, W., "Some Notes on Navaho Dreams," *Psychoanalysis and Culture,* New York, 1951, p. 122.

[91] Devereux, G., *Reality and Dream,* New York, 1951, pp. 60–61.

bundles, they have. You know how they are—cloth, hides, buckskin, all mixed up in there—I don't understand it myself. I noticed it was one of those old Indian graves. It was open. You know how they used to put them in caves and cliffs and later on all the flesh decays and only bones are left. All these medicine bundles were piled in there—all rotting. I took a stick and kept punching around, but the others told me to hurry up. I said, I want to look first, I always was told. . . . Another thing that was there was part of an altar among the rubbish. We were all told to believe that these things were so holy and to respect them. The old people have their medicine bundles in the back rooms where they stay. They do not permit anyone to walk in front of it. They must go around it. I was not afraid. I went to look and to take apart a few. These guys kept hollering at me, "Hurry." I said, "Wait, I want to see what is in there." I called them "courage builders" and "altar." "I want to find out what is inside." I thought, "Gee, you think—I was thinking all wrong before this. Why didn't I know before. It will be one thing off my mind when I have finished looking it over." Then I walked out. That is one worry lifted off my mind. Then we started down the cliff. It was so steep, it was almost straight down. It was a hard descent. They said, "We got to get to the bottom—it is up to you to get us down." They looked up constantly. It looked terrible above. I say, "Up there it is all over. It looks rough but that is over. The thing to think of is what is down." The guy said, "What ledge do we jump to next. You see that ledge over there? I think it is the best to jump on next." I said, "It is not the best. We must figure on the next step after that one. If we jump there, we can't go further down and can't get back up but that other ledge leads down by steps. We got to figure ahead." As we started down the other guy worried about how we ever got this far. I said to him, "Forget it!—to hell with that—that is all over." Then we went to the bottom. There was a little stream there and we rested up. I was facing the stream. The other guys tried to talk about the place we came from, but I paid no attention to them.[92]

If we eliminate the dream factors discussed by Devereux which are obviously derived from the treatment, we find here the traits of ascent, descent, the cave, death, voyeurism (his trouble with his eyesight), and the stick (phallic). The denial of the wish to look back at the past implies that wish. And the past is the cave or death. Like many dreams and myths of this type it ends with a stream. The dream of a Manyika medicine man is very similar.

I was in a big mountain with my first father. I don't know his face. I was too small when he died. He showed me a hole in a big stone. He told me, I should go inside this stone. I was afraid to go inside this hole although I wanted to very much. Then he went in first and I followed. I was not afraid then. It was very dark. There was a horn of medicine. There were plenty of horns. There was also a big black snake. He again told me not to be afraid. The snake looks after the horns. I told my father, I know you are dead. How is it you are with me? He answered, "I

92 *Ibid.*, p. 240.

am dead, but I walk and you don't see me." I felt in the dream a bad smell coming from my father, I thought it was his body. Then we came out, father first, and I after him. We went up the mountain. He told me to go on my own. He will look after the medicine. And I went up and up. Then I woke up.[93]

The father image is double: the protecting human father and the dangerous snake in the hole. The horns with medicine are probably the body contents. Going inside a hole and then ascending till he awakes—these are familiar traits.

The following dream of a Kiwai Papuan named Saibu is a very good example of the basic dream showing with great clarity that a dream about coitus is also a dream of total regression into the womb.

Two canoes were sailing on the water with two men steering. *It was quite calm but the canoes sank down* of their own accord, the two men *climbed up* on the masts and the people on the beach were shouting [sinking, climbing, anxiety].

Suddenly he found himself at Mabudavane with a man named Duane, *he saw a small house which was hanging by a rope from the sky.* The wind made the house whirl *round and round,* and in it they saw a man named Dabu. He asked them to come into the house *and he crawled in through a small opening while the house was spinning round* [birth in reverse].

The wind came whirring and tossed the house round and the men had to crouch on all fours in order not to be thrown off. A man up in the air was holding the rope by which the house hung and they heard his voice saying, "That house I make him for wind." A heavy gust of wind carried the roof off the house. The house disappeared. The two other men sailed off in a canoe.

He found a woman who lived in a house. *Underneath the house there was a hole in which she kept a pig but no one else knew of the animal's existence.* [The embryo in the womb.]

She used to cut the hair of men, women and children and gave it to the pig to eat. He wanted to see the pig and at last she showed it to him. The head was a skull with no skin or flesh. The animal had two drums instead of forelegs and on one side of the body it was like a cassowary. She told him it was a secret, not to tell anybody and she closed the hole. [The nightmarish quality of the pig and the haircutting indicate castration anxiety.]

Then she wanted him to have intercourse with her, that would make him keep the secret. He was just getting ready to do so when his son awoke him because he talked in his sleep.[94] [Italics mine.]

Madubavane must be a kind of spirit land though the real spirit land is Adori. The reason for quoting this dream is that sinking, climbing,

---

[93] Sachs, Wulf, *Black Hamlet,* London, 1937, p. 111; cf. p. 24.
[94] Landtman, G., "The Folk Tales of the Kiwai Papuans," *Acta Societatis Scientiarum Fennicae,* XLVII, Helsingfors, 1917, p. 447.

whirling house, crawling in through narrow opening, a secret hole containing a dream animal, are all preliminary symbols of coitus.[95]

Unabelin, a Mountain Arapesh, dreams as follows:

I saw a hanging house shelf. All the ghosts were dancing. Now the shelf fell down. It fell, it fell. Finally it reached the ground. The ghosts said, "Now we will dance on the shelf and one of us will get into the shelf." One of them got on top of the shelf. They hoisted it up and hoisted it up again. It went higher and farther. It went too far. It went altogether out over the sea when the derwick hoists cargo into a big ship. They said, "Alas, this friend has gone altogether."

It was about Laabe's brother (who died subsequently). This dream means that someone will die.[96] The sinking followed by rising, the *going into* and dying indicate the basic dream.

A Somali prostitute, Ewado of the Tumal (smith) caste, dreams:

I was a bird and I flew up to the sky. I came back and then I was in a boat. The boat was wrecked and I sank into the sea. People came and rescued me. Then I saw I was alive. Then I dreamed I was married and was delivered of a child. A Somali stole the child and ate it. No, my husband's cousin, my first suitor was the child's father and it was he who tried to eat it. My husband fought with his cousin and killed him. Then we moved and all the camels died (the child in the dream was white like an Arab).[97]

Flying, sinking, being in a boat, delivery—the sequence of the basic dream. The father as cannibal ogre is parallel to our discussion of ogres. The whiteness of the child is the transference.

She adds that it was her father who put her in the boat but the boat sank. When she flew she was a black crow. Her father is the father of the dream-child and also the cannibal. The loaded camels must be pregnant women, they die instead of her.

The following dream of a woman on the Solomon Islands shows both sleep or dreaming as coitus and coitus as going into the vagina even if the dreamer is a woman.

I dreamed that a ghost ran after me. I went up in the air, my hands were waving about, I had nothing to hold on to. But I did not fall down. Then I made a noise like this (grunting and panting). I was walking along the road with my husband. *I went inside a hole and went to sleep.* Then my husband told me to tell the women to fill the water cocoanuts with pig's fat. I did not want to and said: "I don't want the women to say bad things about me."

95 Cf. another dream of the same man; *ibid.,* p. 444.

96 Mead, M.: "The Mountain Arapesh," V, "The Record of Unabelin," *Anthr. Papers, Am. Mus. Nat. Hist.,* New York, 1949, Vol. 41, Part 3, pp. 363, 364.

97 Róheim, G., "Dreams of a Somali Prostitute," *Journal of Criminal Psychopathology,* II, 1940, p. 166.

Blackwood comments: Cleaned out cocoanut shells serve the women for water bottles. To defile them in the way represented in the dream would be resented. The dreamer was at the time pregnant by another man, not her husband, and there was much gossip about this in the village.[98]

The aerial flight with the hands not touching anything is evidently masturbation ("I had nothing to hold on to" = denial). The grunting, panting shows the sexual excitement beside the fact that she is now walking with her husband. Then she goes into a hole and goes to sleep (sleep as uterine regression). The hollowed-out cocoanut is her own womb: she denies that it has been "defiled" by another man.

The following dream of a Kwakiutl shaman shows (1) the birth significance of going to sleep or of awakening, (2) the genital aspect of the same (i.e., the regressive and progressive aspect of the dream), and (3) the formation of a double in the dream, i.e., the origin of animism.

I dreamed I had gone to the other side of the world, the sky. I went up and saw a house. A beautiful woman came to me. She said, "Thank you, lord: You are the one to whom I refer as husband: Let us go into my father's house." We entered a beautiful house. The father became very angry. He was a very old man and was going to knock me down. I was afraid and I awoke. [Here we have the oedipal element combined with entering a house, i.e., a woman.] I went to sleep again. She said, *"Go into the water of this river* so you may be successful this summer. *My father is the one who takes care of the world."* After I had finished bathing, I woke up. [This part of the dream may be urethral.] Then I dreamed that I had been called by a man to go with him to the upper half of the world, the sky. We went up, he held my right hand. Then we passed through the door in the middle of the upper side of our world. He showed me everything in the house.

Then he went to a hole in the edge of the world. He said, "Through this hole pass the children when they are born, when they come from the upper side of the world. I am going to help you that it may not be hard for you to pass through."[99]

The following two dreams of a woman of the same tribe show the typical "falling asleep" or "basic dream."

I dreamed I fell into the water while we were paddling at the foot of the mountain in deep water. *I was frightened and I awoke.*

I fell from a tree and all my bones were broken. I was dug up by my tribe. I had not yet reached the house when I awoke.[100]

98 Blackwood, Beatrice, *Both Sides of Buka Passage,* Oxford, 1935, p. 579.

99 Lincoln, J. S., *The Dream in Primitive Cultures,* London, 1935, pp. 318–319, quoting from F. Boas and G. Hunt, "Contributions to the Ethnology of the Kwakiutl," *Columbia University Contributions to Anthropology,* III, 1923, pp. 3–54.

100 *Ibid.,* p. 36.

The next dream is that of a Yuma medicine man. The dreamer is Matkwas Humar (Yellow Earth Young), the oldest medicine man of the Yuma (1931),[101] age about seventy-five. With others he used to listen to speeches made by his uncle (*nequi*) who was a mighty chief and a good man. The uncle's speeches consisted of edifying sermons in which the young men of the tribe were exhorted to lead normal lives. They were to try to see the chief in their dreams and to repeat what he said, and then they too would become orators and chiefs. The young man really did succeed in dreaming of his uncle; he saw him standing with the *kovsho* (nose ring) but he never managed to repeat his uncle's words. That is why he never became an orator. But he dreamed another dream and this second dream made him into a medicine man.

I dreamed I was lying asleep in a house.[102] A bird called *uruc* came. First it stood outside and then it took me away. The bird took me to an unknown country. There he told me my name is *Nemesawa Kutcaër* and said, "Now look what I am going to do. I will come to life, I will do it, you shall see it. I will call it 'Night Backward and Forward.' Look at it, it is my shadow." Then the spirit sang a song about the mountain Awi-kwame (the mountain of creation). "Land mountain high, I will make it come to life, I will do it, you shall see, you shall also do it, and he stood up, with his left hand, damp body, you will hold it. So he did it, lying on its back, it came to life, you see it, you shall do it."
I perspired and woke up—he says.

Associations: Nemesawa Kutcaër—this is the name of a fish (i.e., fish spirit). But the fish looked like a human being. It was naked, good look-ing, with long hair (i.e., like the Yuma were in his youth). *In the dream the fish took his own shadow and made a patient out of it.*

He was on Awikwame, the mountain of creation. There was a shade house[103] bigger than any human house he had ever seen. The spirit re-minded him of another dream.

Dream: I was in my mother's womb and I woke up. The same spirit came and he showed me another land and there it rose up before me. It was barren with withered trees. The spirit said, "You will see it. I will bring them to life [meaning the withered trees]. At night I will take you to another house where you can see it, the front of the skirt. You will go into the farthest corner and from there in the house you will look up where the bones join, you will really see it. This is not the true dream but if you are fortunate you will see it later. You will see it in

---

101 Published originally in Róheim, G., "Psychoanalysis of Primitive Cultural Types," *International Journal of Psycho-Analysis*, XIII, 1932, pp. 186, 187.

102 I use my original field notes here and add some details to the first publica-tion.

103 This probably means the original shade house or *karuk,* the mourning house in which Kokomat was burned.

the land of mist of clouds. Little birds standing in a row—it belongs to you and people will laugh at it.

Every real medicine man is supposed to start his dreaming in the womb.[104] As far as my data go, however, this is a misunderstanding. All that is claimed is that the medicine man, really called "dreamer" or future medicine man, is supposed to have dreamed about being in his mother's womb. In this dream the spirit reminds him of a dreamlike experience which he is supposed to have had in his mother's womb, of a *déja vu.* He further explains that "the little birds standing in a row" are the patients he will cure, and the people laughing at him does not mean what it seems to mean but prestige, popularity.

In connection with the dream he also explains the disease and the cure. The disease is called *tinyam kwackawak* (night back and forward) or *tinyam kwaljewish* (night twisting round). The patient is feverish and feels a chill in the chest and abdomen.[105] He (or she) walks up and down looking for a shady and dark place. "If I think I can't cure them I send the patient to another medicine man. *If the patient looks like the person in the dream I can cure her.* I must spend a day and a night with the patient *without falling asleep.* When I think the fever is abaiting I can sleep a little and then go on with the cure." First he feels out the place where the pain is with the left hand, then he presses and blows on it, sucks it till the pain is dispersed in the body. He talks about a case in which he failed and people reproached him for not being careful. Then he says that he always did what the old people told him to do, not run around too much, to sit down, etc. *The dream person would appear again in his dreams whenever he failed in a cure.* (Italics mine.)

Interpretation: Both in the first dream and in the dream he remembers as an association we have the same fundamental situation: *the dreamer is in the womb and sees the primal scene.* In the first dream he is *in a house,* then the bird takes him somewhere (presumably flying). Although he talks about a fish, the *uruc* is the nighthawk which in the mythical songs heralds the dawn and ends the song (an attempt to awake). The spirit is *showing him something, things coming to life,* the manipulation with *the left hand* I interpret as the *primal scene.*

This interpretation is confirmed by what he says about the voice of the spirit in the dream. It sounded just like a man called Cipae Kwawkiu (insect carrying), a relative of his wife's who *had a great many children.* Now we can see what is meant when this representative of the father

---

[104] Cf. J. P. Harrington, "A Yuma Account of Origins," *Journal of American Folk-Lore,* XXI, 1908, pp. 326, 327.

[105] Mostly women have the variety of the disease called *tinyam Kwaljewish* (night twisting round). They cry, shake, twist around and have froth on the mouth.

imago does something with the left hand, when the left hand is bathed in sweat and presses the patient's body. In the intrauterine dream the womb is repeated symbolically in the other house to which he will be transported. But here the emphasis is on the seeing, obviously on seeing the mother's vagina. At the same time the spirit is making the *withered trees come to life,* i.e., the primal scene.

The fact that the shaman has to keep awake all night (and other North American rites of the same type) shows that *sleep is death,* and while the patient sleeps the shaman is awake as his *alter ego.*

Another medicine man, middle-aged, called Wakierhuuk (Shouting Cowboy) tells the following dream:

I was standing beside the water—a mighty stream—and I saw it. It was called Xavil (Colorado). He who called it that sat down and created things, the horse and the ass, and gave them names. He made many things and then he made a woman and a man so that they should multiply. He struck the ground and water came forth. Then he named the tribes and said, "If anyone names the tribes lift up your left hand, hold it over him like this and he will be well." Then the dreamer went on to describe the creation of man and woman in greater detail. In the dream he saw how a penis and how a vagina were added to the two bodies which were otherwise finished. "Kokomat held his hand over the head of a man who looked rather like you!" he said. "Anyway, nobody can convince me that you are not a medicine man." (This is addressed to the writer.)

Use Kochmal (White Mud), another medicine man, related two dreams on which his power was based. In one dream he saw a bird with outspread wings. He seated himself on the bird's back and with four strokes of the bird's wings they reached Awi-kwame. Then he saw how the spirit healed people and heard him summon the wind and the clouds to enter first the spirit and then the patient and thus to cure him.[106] The spirit was called Ashe-uru (i.e., Buzzard = nighthawk; compare with *uruc* above). He appeared in human form as a man with a white hooked nose with a stone ring in it. He looked like his father. Then he laughs in a most unfilial way at the thought of the old man's weakness and helplessness. Instead of associating to the dream he tells a long story about an old man who lived with his two daughters and received Coyote as a "younger brother." By a magic bird which Coyote creates the old man is lifted high up in the air till he reaches the sky and can no longer find his way home. The spirit bird Ashe (same as in his dream) carries him back with four strokes. He tells him that whatever he saw he must keep his

[106] He relates this as a vision, not as a dream.

eyes shut and lie on his face. But he disregards the taboo and sees Coyote raping and mistreating his daughters. Thereupon he finds himself in the sky again. (Primal scene in reverse.)

As a young man he dreamed of the mountain called Sakupaj. There was a road; on it was an old man in a glass house. The old man said, "Turn around to your left!" The young man did so and saw the mountain called Sakupaj. [He pointed to a lamp in the room to explain the shape of the glass house and the lamp looked really like the uterus.] As he climbed up the mountain he saw the trunk of a felled tree and beside it two mountains. With the drum sticks he beat upon the felled tree and the voice of a woman sounded from the tree. "A mystery wind is coming—hurry back into the glass house," she said. She said this and there sat an old man. Then there was a sand storm and he could see nothing. The old man said, "Now go out!" The storm ceased to rage and he could see the sky and the landscape.

He now tells us that there are really two mountains called Sakupaj, one male and one female. Between the two there is a lake like the glass house in his dream.

The glass house or lake is evidently a symbolic representation of the womb. The tree trunk with the female voice is the mother, but in it he finds the old man. The raging storm which prevents him from *seeing* is again obviously father. But whether he himself is in the glass house or the old man, we now know that a man in a house symbolizes not only regression but equally *the penis in the vagina*. Therefore the intrauterine dream combined with the primal scene dream simply mean that the dreamer and the father want to go to the same place. In very archaic terminology, the primal scene means "father going into the womb"; in genital language, a man in a house is a penis in the vagina.

Knowing this it is not astonishing that the closely related Maricopa should have sought dream experiences or magic power in *caves*. One of these was the home of a spirit named *Kukupara*. *One can barely creep through the entrance to this cave;* far inside is a large room and the cave extends indefinitely beyond. "Whenever a man wished to be rich or to become a shaman or to have crops prosper or be a good runner or have many girls about him, he lay in the cave facing the opening and holding his right hand out. Then he heard something coming from the rear of the cave, there was a great draught and the sound of a whirlwind. But if the seeker fled from the cave in fear he would become *blind* and perhaps insane."[107]

A remark made by Forde is significant: the dreams of the Mohave shaman are supernatural in two dimensions.

[107] Spier, L., *Yuman Tribes of the Gila River*, New York, 1933, p. 244.

"Not only did he visit Awikwame but he *had at the same time retraced all time so that the original keruk was in progress when he reached there.*"[108]

We shall return to this remark later. But I must call attention to other significant remarks also to be evaluated in the section on animism.

The mythological personage is formed out of the dreamer. He awakes with perspiration, the left arm of the spirit perspires. The patient in the dream is the "shadow" of the spirit just as the spirit himself is the "shadow" of the dreamer.

The following is the dream of an old woman who lives alone. Her white name is Mrs. Norton, her Yuma name is Chochach Chapuk (1931).

Dream: Last night I dreamed there was a house, a door. I was standing there. My relations came and wanted to give me clothes but I said no.

Associations: She had arrived in the land of the dead. This is a country that lies to the south. They live like we do only a little better. There is always plenty of food and clothes. All the weeds we see on earth are food there. Everything is the reverse: day is night, night is day, flame is smoke and smoke is flame. The relatives thought she was dead and wanted to keep her there.

The house is like a house she had, it was destroyed because a relative died. (It is taboo to tell me what relative, I would infer that it must be her husband.) The persons she sees in her dream are her dead relatives. She had been thinking about them.

After she woke from this dream; then she went to sleep again and dreamed:

I went down a hole. I said, I won't go down. He said, I should go down. After saying this I jumped back to the edge of the hole. The earth was crumbling under my feet. I awoke, I was safe.

Associations: She describes the hole as long and narrow, deeper than a man's height. The people in the hole are mostly people she has never seen. They are all naked as they used to be when she was young. The person with whom she has the discussion about going into the hole is John Dugan. She refuses to say anything improper about him. He is not a medicine man; if he were a medicine man the dream might mean he was bewitching her to make her sick.[109]

I surmise that the hole she is sinking into is her own vagina (= her

108 Forde, C. D., "Ethnography of the Yuma Indians," *University of California Publications in American Archaeology and Ethnology*, XXVIII, 1931, pp. 203, 204. Cf. Kroeber, A. L., "Handbook of the Indians of California," *Bulletin of the Bureau of American Ethnology*, LXXVIII, 1925, pp. 744, 745. Cf. Mohave dreams in Chapter "Dreamers and Shamans" *infra.*
109 Field note in Yuma, 1931.

mother's vagina) and that the improper things she refuses to say about John Dugan must be sexual. He wants her "to go down." For this very old woman sleeping is naturally even more dying than for others, hence the dream deals with anxiety by regression and libidinization.

V. DREAMS OF A SCHIZOPHRENIC PATIENT

A series of dreams collected from a schizophrenic patient might throw further light on the situation.

The dreams I collected from a hebephrenic male patient at Worcester State Hospital in 1938 and 1939 reveal two things quite clearly, that (a) the dream originates through fission, i.e., the dreamer observes himself as doing something and is therefore both subject and object;[110] (b) this fission proliferates, the one person becomes two or more; and (c) the content of the dreams is unmistakably regressing into the womb or coming out of the womb.

Dream, January 21, 1939: It was not a dream, it was like a puzzle. I was in a room all red bricks like a fireplace and no door. How could I get out? And in my mouth there was a bowl with beef stew, but I could not eat it. The stew was covered with wax and I could not get my teeth into it. In the room there was a tall, hairy thing or two, or perhaps more of them. It was a bug with a face like my father. These bugs ran about the room like little dogs. They would pick you up and then put you down just playfully.

A few days later he remarked about this dream:

"The brick room I was in was like a room I had been in before. It was like the fireplace they make at Christmas. I felt as if I were being pulled out."

The place where he had been before, from which he was being pulled out Christmas, the birth of Christ (he often represents himself as Christ in his fantasies)—make it quite clear that he is in the womb and is being born.[111]

He observes, "When there was trouble about the beef stew and about coming home I always felt that I would have to begin everything again, go to school again, etc., and that frightens me."

Nunberg reports a catatonic case who believed that he had been dead. It will take him nine months to get well again or to be born.[112]

---

110 Naturally, this can also be seen in the dreams of neurotic patients, but perhaps not so clearly. Cf. Bleuler, E., *Dementia Praecox, or the Group of Schizophrenias,* New York, 1950, p. 440.

111 Cf. a typical intrauterine fantasy in a case of schizophrenia, "I remember a time when I lived in a castle near the sea but I had to leave it because of an imminent flood." Schreber, P., *Denkwürdigkeiten eines Nervenkranken.* Leipzig, 1903, p. 75.

112 Nunberg, H., "Ueber den katatonischen Anfall," *Internationale Zeitschrift für Psychoanalyse,* VI, 1920, p. 29.

Nunberg shows the identification of the patient both with the mother and with the child that is being born.[113]

What we are trying to show in our case is how in the dreams of the schizophrenic he plays all the roles. Superimposed on these representations of himself we have also object relationships, but the identity of all the persons who appear in the dream is made quite clear.

Dream, March 4, 1939: I was playing football with two or three colored boys or dwarfs. They expected me to pass the ball, but I hung on to it and would not let go.

Associations: It was like the other dream in which he ate beef stew or a corn soup, but could not eat it and could not make himself understood. It was like being dumb, like an animal. He felt hungry but it was not real hunger, only a feeling like hunger, etc.

Asked about the dwarfs in the dream he said, "The dwarfs played so nicely, it looked as if they were only looking not playing." He ought to have passed the ball on to the Black Dwarf but it seemed that the dwarf was not ready to take it, so he hung on to the ball and ran down the field all alone. Then he had the funny feeling of being all alone in the field. The dwarfs on his side were more like himself, only much shorter and black. On the other side there were more real dwarfs who were six feet tall like himself and they looked as if they were no bigger than a child.

The dwarfs probably represent his genital organ while the ball might be both breast and scrotum. The patient says, "The dwarf who ought to have caught the ball was like some of the others in my dream, like Angel Love or Depth Koda. Those dwarfs are supposed to help with my food trouble and be able to *translate* what I say and *know who I am,* like the people up in the place where I was transported by Angel Love."[114]

The "not being able to translate" and all that belong to the syndrome of schizophrenia rather than to the dream. But the important point is that the dream is clearly formed out of the patient and that regression is indicated in the giant who looks no taller than a child.

A Waking Dream, May 3: A Crown Prince dressed all in black with a high hat came and woke me. The Crown Prince handed me a sword to see whether I would fight. There is another Crown Prince dressed in grey and then several others. I wondered whether the Crown Prince would stay with me.

113 *Ibid.,* p. 49. Cf. Stocker, A., "Oedipustraum eines Schizophrenen," *Internationale Zeitschrift für ärztliche Psychoanalyse,* VIII, 1922, p. 67. (Uterine regression, lake symbolism.)

114 These details will be explained later.

He seemed to stay with me after the dream and to take care of me. [Transition from dream to reality.]

Then he said, "I was once allowed to dress like that and was almost a Crown Prince myself."

There were other Crown Princes in grey who were also ready to fight him.

In another dream the Crown Prince looks like his father. The point is that all the "fathers" or "girls" in his dreams look like himself.

Dream, August 11: A horse came to fetch me and carried me to an empty carriage. Then a Crown Prince came and it turned out that the carriage belonged to him. Then another Crown Prince came and took him by the scruff and rushed him up to the doctor's office. "It might have been Dr. Angel or you or Dr. Kant. The Crown Prince looked like you or my father. In the office there was a nurse and a young girl. She looked funny *like thin air* [weak cathexis of object-imagery]. Then I was rushed back again by the Crown Prince or by one of the girls to pull a carriage out of a ditch. The horses had run away and they wanted to see if I could do it." [Pulling out of the ditch is birth or awakening—the rushing is probably coitus.]

Then the Crown Prince came up to the carriage. He was almost French, he was Napoleon Bonaparte. He made me sit beside him as if I were almost a Crown Prince myself.

"I do not like to talk about these things because he or I might be mistaken for the Crown Prince. I had a horse like that once. It went like lightning. It was quite black. It was a white horse. It was dark brown, a kind of black." Then he talks about an awful experience. There was a carriage, a man and a girl in it. The horse broke away like *lightning* and he had to rush to the rescue on another horse and catch it. He jumped into the carriage, took the reins and brought the horse back to normal again.

The horse here is quite obviously the id which has run away with him in his psychosis. He dreams that he can master the situation once more. The origin of the dream images from one person is quite clear.[115]

Another dream: I was being chopped up with an axe (just like chopping your food with a knife). You know how it is when you fill your

---

[115] A dream dreamed by a patient in analysis (not schizophrenic) shows the same mechanism—all the actors represent the dreamer.

I am swimming in a bay with two boys. Three others are shooting at us from an island with a gun. I hope the gun won't go off before I can reach them and stop them. They shoot but it does not go off, I climb ashore, grab his hand, and put it on the muzzle of the gun. I awake.—

This is a masturbation dream. Both trios are penis and testicles. The swimming is the erection or the pulsation in the penis, the gun would be the ejaculation. He covers his penis with his hand and awakes in time to prevent an ejaculation.

mouth with saliva, then draw it back and it is cut off with a knife, your tongue is the knife.

Then he goes on to say how once when he had eaten cheese *this acted like a dream and lifted him right off the bed.*

We shall discuss the *oral* as a dream factor later. What we wish to show for the present is merely that regression and therefore ultimately uterine regression are characteristic aspects of sleeping and dreaming. All this has been said by Freud[116] and he also sees a certain degree of parallelism in dreaming and schizophrenia.[117] It seems that falling asleep is in itself uterine regression but followed immediately (or simultaneously) by the journey back, by rebuilding the world or rather, a libidinal world of its own.

This is what the schizophrenic patient calls his "great dream":[118]

I am trying to come back home but there is a mountain in the way. It is very high and semicircular like the place where I live. The sun sets on the top of the mountain and I have an uneasy feeling, I don't know where it will disappear. A man stands on the ground in a lion's skin like a coat and he is leading a pet lion like a dog. Above the hill in the air there is an angel, a young girl with a face like mine used to be. Still higher up a skeleton hovers in the air, it looked like my father or brother. *Then I had the feeling that something comes out of me just like another self.* It came out of my nostril and it felt as if I had fainted. It was just like myself and it stood before me like an angel.

He regards this dream as the starting point of his illness. Actually it is a recovery dream because the motive "I was trying to get home" reappears in the many fantasies, dreams, etc., and means "I was trying to regain normalcy."

Later on he tells me that *this dream is like Alaska.* He used to live there once, or his grandfather did. "Like a buried country that belonged to another people like Alaska belonged to the Russians or Indians." Nothing remains, only hands to show the way. It is like when he could not get to the food and could not make people understand what he wanted. (This is the usual explanation of the origin of his schizophrenia.) "It is like reaching hands right across from one continent to the other, from here to Russia, but there were many other countries between them where they ate all different kinds of food. But if somebody is hungry it does not matter."

What is the meaning of the mountain? Since his associations always revolve around this dream it is not difficult to find the meaning.

His relation to reality, to the world of objects, is based on his rela-

116 Freud, S., *Gesammelte Schriften,* II, p. 465.
117 *Ibid.,* V, p. 520.
118 I.e., the dream to which he constantly refers as symbolizing his difficulties.

tions to his mother. Each time she visits him in the hospital and leaves again the original trauma is repeated. On the 7th day of July he says his mother visited him on Sunday and he has given up all hope of going home. Whenever his mother brought him things something was torn or lost. On the 25th he says that he stopped thinking about things after his mother's visit. But some days later he began thinking again. He says, "A place is like a big mountain first, but, if it is only a picnic place like you don't want to go back to, it is like a little hill." This is what happened to his home now.

This clarifies the meaning of the word mountain. It represents his mother. The next sentence makes it more specific. He used to try to find out whether the places he used to stay at were right by wandering through these streets in memory and trying to eat at each of these places. It was like a *Christmas dinner,* he left a little of the food so that he would be able to identify himself and find the way back. Sometimes he describes his anxiety in terms of getting lost, then again in terms of losing the object. "What have you been thinking about?" I ask him. He replies, "About the whole trouble, about people not recognizing me and how I got lost when I lived with my grandmother." *The way food disappeared in him was like the way he disappeared when he got lost.* Once he went so fast that people could not see him and that was the same thing as when the food disappears in his inside.

But—it is hardly possible to draw the line between reunion at the breast and regression into the womb.

In the next sentence he says that his feeling is like "when you go into the woods and you go *deeper and deeper* hundreds of miles and you feel heavier and when you come out again you are dazed." Once when he was at home he disappeared—he could see the people but they could not see him.

In another version of his "big dream" he is in Paradise or the Garden of Eden.

Once a priest took me up into the air. I just flew through and disappeared from home and was away for eight or nine years. Up in the sky I found an angel, a woman called Angel Love. She had yellow hair and a body of gold and wings made of feathers that covered her completely. There was an island floating in the air and I came up there when I crashed through stained glass. Nobody did any work. There everybody was just free and easy and they gave me something to eat or drink like orange juice, or berries, or soup.

Another time when he mentions the same dream or fantasy of the eight or nine years' absence in the sky,[119] he continues: "My father and

[119] Nine months of pregnancy, eight or nine, something indefinite, is the way he always talks.

mother wanted me to go to a place beyond the earth." *But the house where he was born is his and nobody can take it from him. Once he found an entrance to the Garden of Eden. It was a hole or ditch in the earth and he fell through. This is the place where he came out,* the place where he was born in the Garden of Eden. "It is as if you were driving in a car through a dark wood[120] *and suddenly you come to a tunnel and fall forward head foremost with great speed." Once upon a time he came out of a place where there was no door. This was before he had a name. Some people thought he was born like that in the desert or wood like a wild animal, or perhaps he was born in the Garden of Eden and had no mother. He came up right through a tunnel, right through the earth near the Mississippi and there was a great mountain to stop him.* He had no name for some time and his *father fought with him and would not let him stay at home.*

The world beyond the mountain is therefore definitely the womb. In relating his big dream he compares the mountain to the bug in the path. The bug in the path, sometimes called by him ape or gorilla, is obviously his father. He used to have a bug like a lion and one like a monkey and they took them away from him because there was no room for them.

"I am afraid to offend the bug," he declares, "because if I did I might not be reborn, you know." The bug that governs birth is the one that has a head like his own and eats the food when it gets into his inside. *This bug looks like his father.*

We are now beginning to understand the dream. It is uterine regression stopped by father.

What is the meaning of the sinking sun on the horizon? We more than suspect that he himself is the sun.

When the trouble caused by the bug started he went to the sun dial, which is opposite the sun and like the sun, and wanted to set something right. The sun dial directs all automobiles and ships.

On the 13th of April, 1939, he tells the story of the sun dial as follows: He was told that time and tide wait for no man. He was allowed to keep track of time by keeping track of ships coming and going from Europe. He did the same with the sun, but then he would look at the line made by the sun or at the railroads, because clocks were not reliable. *Once he was so happy that he flew into space like the sun.* At the same time he moved the sun dial he wanted to take the sun off its course.

Then he says, "All this trouble about losing the wall and things closing in on me is the same as the sun dial. People found that kind of

120 Note above the fantasy about getting deeper and deeper into the wood.

funny, too. I was trying to make it stand straight at 12 o'clock and to stop the sun while hurrying on the sky. There was a girl, she thought it was about her and that I was trying to catch her." The people thought he meant sun-dying, but he was afraid that the sun would die. That meant that he would die or disappear. "The food dies in him like the sun sets in the evening."

A patient studied by Dr. Bak says:

"When after my birth I became conscious, I found myself in a locality in which I saw light and warmth and gave it to others. The bigger the Universe, the more predominant the sun giving becomes. I started sun-shine. At my birth I produced it along with atoms, light and warmth. At the beginning the Universe was a canoe in which I alone had a place, this was the first building and this was also the first universe."[121]

Apart from the thermic interpretation given by Bak (sun heat), the fantasy certainly also involves seeing. The newborn infant sees, he is the sun. The dream about the sinking sun would be himself returning into the womb, dying. But it also means "marrying" and it is because of this meaning that the father or the mountain is in his path as an obstacle. The mountain, therefore, is an overdetermined ambisexual symbol. It means (a) the breast, (b) the mons veneris or vagina (semicircular), and (c) the father.

The disappearing sun is he himself falling asleep, returning into mother's womb.

The man in the lion skin is he himself in the role of father. The pet lion is a repetition of the same symbolism. The lion was originally his chief enemy, i.e., father, and the man in the lion's skin is identification with father. The dangerous enemy becomes also a pet lion or, as the North American Indians would say, a guardian spirit.[122]

When the schizophrenic dreamer dies in the dream which is generally regarded as characteristic of schizophrenia, according to our assumption this is also the psychology of every dream or of falling asleep. When a duplicate of the dreamer comes out of his nostrils this, as we shall see later, is the origin of the soul.

But what is going on up there in the air? His father as *death* and his sister as the angel—we assume that it is the primal scene.

VI. Orality, Sleep and the Dream

Lewin's theory of the dream is different. He writes, "Despite earlier naïve views that a primary wish to return to the mother is operating here

[121] Bak, Robert, "Regression of Ego-Orientation and Libido in Schizophrenia," *International Journal of Psycho-Analysis*, XX, 1939.
[122] Cf. chapter "Dreamers and Shamans" on the guardian spirit.

(viz., in claustrophobia) it can be shown that the oral triad of wishes suffices to explain the claustrophobic fantasy, and it is not necessary to postulate any memories of blissful intrauterine feelings. The intrauterine fantasy in which the child identifies itself with the nursling, is taken into the abdomen and in that location continues its feeding or comes to rest in a sound sleep, is a nursing fantasy with a shift downward from the breast to the abdomen. It is the fantasy of a baby that stands, which Bateson and Mead call the knee baby[123] as distinguished from the younger lap baby. 'For the knee baby's view of the world is lower than the lap baby's. It has factually been displaced downward and it contemplates instead of the mother's breast and arms her lap and abdomen—but not necessarily with any new thoughts or intentions. In its wishful fantasy it nurses itself into the abdomen as it did into the breast or perhaps it fortifies the nursing by biting or other improvements and then goes to sleep.' Prenatal psychology has been a field for rich psychoanalytic speculation and few facts, whereas the sleep of infants that follows nursing is an assured fact and the speculations about it have not been numerous. Undoubtedly the care of small babies seeks to reproduce the physical conditions within the uterus and there is no objection to this sensible and biologically sound idea, but there is nothing besides our imagination to say that the baby is happy in the mother's body."[124]

This theory shows that the author is doing his best to avoid assuming a memory of different kind than that with which we are familiar. I can sympathize with this effort, because I myself have hesitated and sometimes accepted and then again rejected the intrauterine theory.[125] But Lewin himself cannot very well get along without this assumption of some kind of prenatal memory. It is quite obvious that mothers, nurses, etc., do not give the child a situation in which it can be as it is in the uterus because they have decided to do so. If the adults prepare a womb situation for the neonate, it is done unconsciously, i.e., instinctually. Nor can it be believed that dreams with narrow passages, lakes, islands, etc., can be explained on an oral basis. Finally, as we pointed out, the house, cavity, etc., into which the dreamer withdraws may be and often is her own vagina with regression (maternal womb) and erotic cathexis in the same image. "Happy memories" of existing in the womb need not be postulated. Regression is one of the fundamental trends in our foetalized species. Uterine regression is absence of stimuli. We could not have been "happy" in the womb since this would involve the opposite state ("un-

123 Bateson, G. and Mead, M., *Balinese Character*, New York, 1942.
124 Lewin, B. D., *The Psychoanalysis of Elation*, New York, 1950, pp. 109–110.
125 Cf. Róheim, G., "The Song of the Sirens," *Psychiatric Quarterly*, XXII, 1948, p. 21.

happy") but we retroproject a state of happiness into the womb, because of our biologically conditioned regressive tendency.

The wish to eat, the wish to be eaten, and the wish to sleep constitute what Lewin calls the "oral triad." He writes, "Following Freud's implications in *The Problem of Anxiety*, I am inclined to assume a libidinal rather than an aggressive or anxious primary form and to say that the wish to die or to be devoured precedes the fears. The wish would be an expression and formulation of the desire for the relaxation and sleep that originally followed upon uninterrupted nursing. The wish for sleep and rest would be the bedrock of the idea and the aggressive and anxious versions represent later deposits."[126]

With the latter half of this sentence I agree, but that the idea to be devoured is particularly *relaxing* is, to put it orally, hard to swallow. If Dr. Lewin here makes use of Freud's authority, he seems to forget the essence of the theory called *Beyond the Pleasure Principle*. The death impulse is there regarded as the other protagonist of the dualistic scene, in direct opposition to the libido and as the metapsychological background of aggression.[127]

I shall now discuss two constituent elements of Lewin's triad: (a) the oral nature of sleep, and (b) the "wish to be devoured."

Isakower describes hypnagogic hallucinations. He quotes the words of a patient who says, "When I am feverish I get a curious sensation in my palate. Yesterday I noticed it when I was going to sleep although I was not feverish. At the same time I have the feeling as if I were on a *revolving disc*.[128] As if I were lying on something, but this crumpled feeling is in my mouth at the same time. The whole thing begins in the palate. I feel as if I were lying on a crumpled cloth which is winding itself round. The crumpled object is not lying under me but round me and it's disagreeable.

"Then I am small at a point, as if something heavy and large were lying on top of me. It does not crush me and *I generally draw a triangle with my hand*, a triangle with one side missing. I draw it in the lump as if it were dough, then I feel the whole thing in my mouth and in my head. It's like a balloon, a kind of bodiless feeling.

"I only feel something round, I have no idea of what it looks like," etc. "It is as if the whole feeling of childhood were coming back."[129]

Somebody who had heard of a Cossack raid had the following fan-

126 Lewin, *op. cit.*, p. 128.

127 Freud, S., *Gesammelte Werke*, VI, 1924, p. 245.

128 [Frequent sensation of patients on the couch.]

129 Isakower, O., "A Contribution to the Psychopathology of the Phenomena Associated with Falling Asleep," *International Journal of Psycho-Analysis*, XIX, 1938, p. 333.

tasy. He felt as if he were lying on his back or floating in the air, and had a sensation accompanied by anxiety of some tiny objects which became infinitely large. As he did so, he had a pleasant tickling sensation just behind his upper and lower teeth and at the bottom of his mouth. The general feeling was like that in *coitus*—only he and the universe existed, nothing but himself and something infinitely large—he was "inside."

While the first half of the fantasy is oral, the second half is *coitus as uterine regression.*

We are inclined to forget the beginnings of psychoanalysis and therefore I quote from Ferenczi: "Teeth are tools with which the infant wants to bore itself into the mother's inside."[130] And later, "having equated both sleep and coitus with the intrauterine situation, the parallelism of sleep and coitus follows."[131]

Isakower states that the libidinal cathexis of the oral cavity predominates at the oral stage.[132] However, he also adds, "Other descriptions mention characteristics which suggest the power of birth or of the intra-uterine situation."[133]

Lewin seems to advocate an exclusively oral theory of falling asleep. He writes, "The dream screen, as I define it, is the surface on to which a dream appears to be projected. It is the blank background present in the dream though not necessarily seen, and the visually manifest action in ordinary dream content takes place on it or before it."[134]

One case mentioned by Lewin is similar to the dream screen with the gridiron mentioned above. Lewin's patient dreamed of a large iron lattice which stood between her and the landscape. "In analysis this lattice was found to represent the metal frame pad which her mother had worn after an ablation of the breast. The operation took place when the patient was seven."

The patient whose "gridiron" dream we reported has no such experience in his background; in fact, he was never breast fed. But he was certainly "bottle fed," and he, like all other infants, must have fallen asleep after oral satisfaction. Therefore, the gridiron (lattice) would be a combination of disparate elements. One would be to be fed, the other to see or to awake, to have intercourse, to be in the intrauterine situation. However, according to Lewin, there is no such thing as intrauterine regression.

"Thus, in claustrophobia where the retreat to the uterus is used as

130 Ferenczi, *Versuch einer Genitaltheorie*, Vienna, 1924, p. 30.
131 *Ibid.,* p. 100.
132 Isakower, *op. cit.,* pp. 337, 338.
133 *Ibid.,* pp. 341, 342.
134 Lewin, "Sleep, Mouth and the Dream Screen," *Psychoanalytic Quarterly*, XV, 1934, p. 420.

a defense and the fantasy represents a going back into hiding, the mother's body is always pictured as being entered orally, either actively or passively. Either one bites one's way in or one is swallowed by the mother. The foetus with which the claustrophobic identifies is the retroprojective neonate. The fantasy of returning to the mother's body is a secondary fantasy combining the idea of union with the mother at the breast and later impressions."[135] Lewin goes so far as to say that "strict analytic logic compels us to see in the wish to sleep a wish to be eaten up."[136] Following this trend of thought, he draws a parallel between sleep and mania.[137]

Lewin elaborates what he means by the "wish to be eaten." "That the nursling wishes to be devoured only means that toward the end of the act of suckling and with the gradual approach of sleep, the infant has certain perceptions and experiences of yielding, relaxing and falling that leave a strong mnemonic impression and that later on these memories and experiences serve as a nucleus for a cluster of ideas of being eaten in various forms."[138]

In the predormescent phenomena reported by Isakower, the sleeper feels large masses being stuffed into his mouth as he falls asleep. At the same time he has a sense of being enveloped or wrapped into the *breast* as if he were being swallowed by it. In dreams sinking into soft, yielding masses such as snow or bodies of water or, more figuratively, into dense forests or into a crowd repeats this sense of being swallowed or being put to sleep.[139]

In dream or hypnagogic sensations as quoted by Isakower above, the food stuffed into the sleeper's mouth may not be the beginning of sleep, but the last remnant of the stage of being awake. Similarly, thumb sucking, using pacifiers, taking nightcaps, etc., before falling asleep would be holding on to the breast before falling back into the void or womb. Before falling asleep a person may be holding on to pleasure on any level of organization. We have the frequent custom of erotic fantasies or masturbation intended to put the patient to sleep but sometimes achieving the opposite result. An obsessional patient will sit on the toilet for hours before he makes up his mind to go to bed. On another level, it is the superego that prevents falling asleep. "Do your duty, don't relax," and the pleasure obtained before sleep which then merges into sleep may well be id magic against the superego.

[135] *Ibid.*, p. 428.
[136] *Ibid.*, p. 431.
[137] Lewin, *The Psychoanalysis of Elation*, p. 82.
[138] *Ibid.*, p. 104. Cf. also Ferenczi, S., *Thalassa, Psa. Quart.*, II, 1933, p. 383, on the oral and later genital attempt to re-enter the womb.
[139] Lewin, *The Psychoanalysis of Elation*, p. 106.

A patient, a young and not too neurotic married woman reports the following dream:

A tall, red-faced man has two faces, one nice and one ugly. Looks like my husband. It also is like balloons on Mardi Gras or like a penis.

She gives just one association: a painting of Dali's, a huge balloon but tied down. The picture is called Sleep.

It is now clear that the ugly and nice faces express ambivalent feelings about her husband. Sleep, or falling asleep, is represented here as a huge penis. But why? She now tells me what I did not know, that before falling asleep she always feels very "sexy," i.e., her husband's penis is the last remnant of the state "awake."

A young girl is having an affair. She went to sleep after coitus in which she had no orgasm. She owns two cats, both of which are pregnant. She has guilt feelings in connection with the affair and fears of becoming pregnant.

Dream: I am in bed. The cat must have wetted the floor. Something is leaking. How is this possible? She is housebroken, she should go to her box. Perhaps there is another room and she urinated there. I go to find the other box. But how can I be dreaming if I am not in my bed. I faint —this is the only way I can get back to bed. Then I awake.

Associations: She was lubricated on awakening. The other box she is looking for is in a room where there should be no box, i.e., she should not have had the affair.

Interpretation: Looking for the box and wetting means that she is trying to finish the unfinished coitus. But the box is not only her vagina —it is also her mother's uterus, regression, dying, fainting. Hence anxiety that cannot be dealt with by the dream imagery and awakening.

This is my own dream.

I want to drink a glass of water but fall asleep before I can do it. I dream that I am drinking a glass of water.

It is clear that the oral element of the dream is the last remnant of being awake and not the first of being asleep. That the feeling of sinking into something should be interpreted orally instead of birth in reverse is not particularly convincing. After all, the infant does not sink into the bosom. Yet there is another basis for the *oral* theory in interpreting the basic dream, or, rather, I would call it the oral-anal or gastrointestinal theory. In so far as the "womb" into which the sleeper withdraws is his own body, the dreamer may identify himself with the swallowed food or with the feces in his intestines or the urine in his bladder.[140]

140 We shall have to discuss this later in connection with creation myths and myths of the labyrinth.

The basic dream represents both regression into the womb and coitus. But it is the sleeper's own body out of which this womb is formed. If the sleeper is a woman it is her own vulva and uterus that is at the same time her mother's womb. Sometimes also the mouth, which in an adult I would regard as usually a displacement upward. But if the sleeper is a man, mouth or rectum may play the role of the womb and the sleep peregrination may be in the intestines.

A married man dreams that he is sleeping in a tub of water. There are holes at the bottom of the tub and silver medals keep falling through these holes. The tub is his mother and the medals are feces in which form he keeps being born, i.e., makes an effort to wake up.

In this sense then we can accept part of Lewin's theory. (1) Falling asleep is going back into mother's body. (2) At the same time it is also going back into one's own body and thus the entrance may be the mouth, the exit, the rectum. But that sleep is oral I can only accept in a modified sense. Hunger, i.e., orality, is the very thing that *wakes* the sleeper or infant. The infant goes to sleep after being fed because if hungry it could not sleep. For sleep we need a biological explanation and it is certainly not derived from the need for nourishment.

Kleitman remarks, "If the babies are nursed in succession the one that has been fed and has no hunger pangs will easily succumb to the action of the particular concentration of toxins, while the hungry one will remain wide awake under these conditions."[141]

Therefore, if the visitor in the other world eats of the food of the other world, he or she will stay in the other world because awakening is conditioned by hunger.

In the Kalevala Väinämöinen the arch wizard descends to the underworld for the necessary incantations to complete his boat. The old woman of the underworld offers him her beer to drink but he refuses (Kalevala XVI Runo). In a Coos story (North America) a man who is on his way to the other world sees huckleberries. But he does not eat them. His grandmothers offer him food in a pan. The food consists of lice. "My grandson, this thing is usually eaten whenever someone gets here." He did not eat the food, but remembered his children and early in the morning he went home.[142]

The soul of a sick person among the Kiwai went to the other world. The entrance was blocked by two bars which stood up against each other on the road and kept fighting each other. When the woman approached, the bars raised themselves, allowing her to pass. In the other world she

---

[141] Kleitman, *Sleep and Wakefulness,* p. 483.

[142] Frachtenberg, L. I., "Coos Texts," *Columbia University Publications in Anthropology,* I, 1913, pp. 139–149.

found her deceased husband and others. She saw all kinds of food but if she had eaten any she would have died finally and would not have returned home.[143]

In the Banks Islands, the spirits can go to Panoi and return, provided they do not touch the food of the dead.[144]

Persephoneia by command of the Father of Gods and Men is restored to the arms of her mother. "But while Demeter was still holding her dear child in her arms, she asked her, 'My child, tell me, surely you have not tasted any food while you were there below? Speak out and hide nothing but let us both know. . . . If you have tasted food you must go back again amidst the secret places of the earth.' "[145]

Eating in the dream may mean a desire to prolong sleep just like urinating in urethral awakening dreams.[146] In this case eating would mean warding off hunger. But prolonged pleasure of another kind may be symbolized by eating.

A young girl who has had a very successful coitus with her lover falls asleep:

I see something like a screen, then it is the Super Market pushcarts rushing up and down very quickly.

The dream screen has been explained by Lewin. The Super Market is the inexhaustible food supply, while the pushcarts rushing up and down are coitus. She wishes to continue indefinitely what she has experienced before falling asleep.

I think that although the dream is regressive and genital the dream screen may also be in the background, for if the dream, as opposed to sleep, represents the trend back to the object world and the child alternates between sleep and orality (awake) the first dreams of children would be oral.

Here we may discuss another very important question: the role of bisexuality in explaining human behavior.[147] The dream is one of the bridges between biological and psychological bisexuality because here the dreamer sinking into himself certainly plays both roles with object-derived imagos superadded in all cases except those of far regressed schizophrenics.

---

143 Landtman, G., *The Kiwai Papuans of British New Guinea*, London, 1927, p. 289. If the spirits in a dream offer food, it must not be accepted because this would mean death. Mackenzie, D. R., *The Spirit Ridden Konde*, London, 1925, p. 248.

144 Codrington, R. H., *The Melanesians*, Oxford, 1891, p. 277.

145 Hugh G. Evelyn White, *Hesiod, The Homeric Hymns*, Cambridge, Mass., 1943, pp. 317, 390 seq.

146 Cf. *infra* Vesical Dreams and Myths.

147 Cf. Nunberg, H., "Circumcision and the Problems of Bisexuality," *International Journal of Psycho-Analysis*, XXVIII, 1947, pp. 145–179.

The phallic body image is also explained by Lewin as "oral."[148] Lewin writes, "Abraham has answered the question, how does the equation originate (i.e., body phallus). In his *Entwicklungsgeschichte der Libido,* he has published two case reports in which the patients constantly identified their whole body with a penis. These patients unconsciously believed that they had become a penis because they had eaten one. Abraham found that the complete fantasy consisted in a biting off of a penis—that is, killing it—equating it thus to feces, then swallowing it, and by virtue of the swallowing and incorporation, making it one with the eater."[149]

This is, of course, a possibility, but by no means the only one. Ferenczi has called coitus a partly real, partly fantasied return to the womb and orgasm itself a "genitalization of the whole body."[150]

Lewin's data seem to me to prove the exact opposite of what they are supposed to prove. "When the body is used to symbolize the phallus, the mouth may represent the urethra and the ejection of fluid from the mouth an ejaculation or urination." He then gives the following dream of a patient.

"I am sitting with my little girl on my lap. I grasp her tightly by the shoulder and squeeze her. She vomits and the vomitus squirts straight out. I awaken and find I have had an emission."[151]

The oral symbolism is manifest, the genital content latent. When the Aranda ask each other, "Have you eaten?" they mean, "Have you had intercourse?" But it does not work the other way around. It is not as Abraham and Lewin would interpret "a special case of identifying the body with any part"[152] *but the basic unconscious equation of body and phallos (Ferenczi).* The Australian beliefs about finding a child in a dream (to be discussed *infra*) and the dream equation of phallus and child found in clinical analysis obviously confirm Ferenczi's viewpoint.

This genital interpretation of dreams can be challenged from another point of view. The neonate and the infant are obviously dominated by orality, therefore it might be said that the genital as the basic element of the dream might be questioned. There are several answers to this objection. Number one; the dreams in question and the myths we shall interpret as derived from these dreams are myths and dreams of adults not infants. Freud has certainly shown that dreams have an infantile background but this background may go no further than the oedipal organization. Another question arises if we consider what is meant by *"oral."* The

148 Lewin, "The Body as Phallus," *Psychoanalytic Quarterly,* II, 1933, pp. 24–47.
149 *Ibid.,* p. 31.
150 Ferenczi, S., *Versuch einer Genitaltheorie,* pp. 52, 53.
151 Lewin, *op. cit.,* p. 25.
152 *Ibid.,* p. 25.

psychoanalytic view that follows closely in Freud's footsteps regards oral as autoerotic, narcissistic. From this point of view it would be plausible to classify sleep as "oral." Actual experience, however, shows that hunger and sleep are opposed to each other. I feel like reviving the controversy between the Budapest group and Viennese psychoanalysts. The Hungarian school has always emphasized "archaic object love." "A particularly clear picture of this love," according to Alice Bálint "directed especially toward the mother, emerges, in my opinion, from certain quite general phenomena of the transference, which appear in each case independent of age, sex and form of illness and are also to be found in training analyses, i.e., in practically healthy people."[153] The patient loves the analyst but without regarding the analyst as a real person. "The correct way is to assume that there we have to deal with love, with archaic love, the fundamental condition of which is the complete harmony of interests. In this naïve egoism the antagonism that exists between self-interest and the interest of the object is not perceived at all, e.g., when the little child or the patient in this particular state of transference means that the mother (the analyst) must not be ill then it does not mean concern for the well-being of the other but for one's own well-being which might be endangered by the other's illness."[154]

A patient of mine, who had been in analysis for half a year, thought that the summer vacation was a technical device on the part of the analyst. It never occurred to him that the analyst himself might need the vacation.

Endre Petö, a pediatrician and psychoanalyst, writes:

"On the basis of these observations all of which relate to infants in the first three months of life the following facts were established; even at the age of five days (the time of the observation of the youngest baby) object relationships can be proved to exist. If these object relations are disturbed either by inconsiderate behavior or by lack of conscientious nursing by the mother, feeding disorders appear which lead to partial or even complete refusal of food."[155] But if we must assume—and this seems to be evident on a purely behavioristic basis—that the oral is object-directed or that the infant is anaclitic (Spitz),[156] then we can hardly agree with a theory that regards sleep as oral.

Another important factor to be taken into consideration is the over-

153 Bálint, A., "Love for the Mother and Mother Love," *International Journal of Psycho-Analysis*, XXX, 1949, p. 253.

154 *Ibid.*, p. 254.

155 Petö, E., "Infant and Mother," *International Journal of Psycho-Analysis*, XXX, pp. 263–264.

156 Cf. Bálint, A., "Early Developmental States of the Ego," *International Journal of Psycho-Analysis*, XXX, pp. 263–275. Spitz, R., "Autoerotism," *The Psychoanalytic Study of the Child*, III/IV, 1949, pp. 85–120.

lapping or coexistence of the oral and genital. Halverson has described erections in infants practically from the moment of birth. To say that these erections are "nonsexual" seems to me rather a peculiar point of view to take.[157]

Keiser writes: "An erection in infants from a full urinary bladder is common observation, and that the baby fondles that erection most mothers know. Two male infants under one year of age have been observed by me going through the motions of adult intercourse *during a deep sleep.* [My italics.] They were extremely active and might be said aggressive against the bed. The deep sigh and relaxation that followed could only indicate their having had some experience which simulated an orgasm. It would appear that the original danger innate in sexual demands is the equation of death with the momentary unawareness that accompanies orgasm."[158] (Cf. in the dream interpretations coitus and death.) "In view of the presence of the genital drive from infancy it must be recognized that genital union is desired by the child at a much earlier age than has been supposed. This will influence the relationship to parents in that the child not only had an oral dependence on the mother, but also derived genital pleasure from contact with the mother.

"When it is said that the normal child renounces earlier oral and anal gratification for genital supremacy it is implied *that the normal genital drive has always been present.* [My italics.] No new psychological state has developed which might have created the genital tension. The old genital drive is merely being given its greater importance by virtue of withdrawing libido from earlier levels."[159] Kinsey reports, quoting Halverson, that erection may occur immediately after birth and as many observant mothers (and few scientists) know it is practically a daily matter for small boys from earliest infancy.[160] "Orgasm has been observed in boys of every age from five months to adolescence. Orgasm is in our records for a female baby of four months. The orgasm in an infant or other young male is, except for the lack of an ejaculation a striking duplicate of an orgasm in an older adult. There are observations of 16 males up to 11 months of age with such typical orgasm reached in seven cases. In five cases of young pre-adolescents observations were continued over months or years, until the individuals were old enough to make it certain that true orgasm was

157 Halverson, H. M., "Studies in the Grasping Responses of Early Infancy," *Journal of Genetic Psychology,* LI, 1937, pp. 371–449.

158 Keiser, S., "The Fear of Sexual Passivity in the Masochist," *International Journal of Psycho-Analysis,* XXX, 1951, p. 164.

159 *Ibid.,* pp. 170–171.

160 Kinsey, A. C., Pomeroy, W. B. and Martin, C. E., *Sexual Behavior in the Human Male,* Philadelphia and London, 1948, p. 164. Halverson, "Genital and Sphincter Behavior of the Male Infant," *Journal of Genetic Psychology,* LVI, 1942, pp. 95–136.

involved; and in all of these cases the later reactions were so similar to the earlier behavior that there could be no doubt of the orgastic nature of the first experience."[161]

In analyzing the dreams of adults we have distinguished the "progressive" and genital trend from the regressive, although the two may also be condensed in one image of the dream. Obviously the boundaries are not so clear because the genital is also regressive and the regressive (toward the mother) also genital. The trend "toward the mother" is oral and genital in a sense progressive because object directed. But, as everyone knows, the main functions of the neonate are to eat or to sleep. We should therefore say not, as is usually assumed, that human beings at the onset of life are completely dominated by orality *but that they are under the sway of two main trends, regressive (sleep) and object directed (the nipple).* We cannot prove the congenital existence of the regressive trend except on a theoretical basis. Since mankind is a foetalized species,[162] congenitally juvenile, a psychological resistance to the process of growing up is inevitable. In this sense we can justify the birth-trauma theory but not concentrating exclusively on the shock of birth but on the general state of the neonate.[163] What happens later is that man invests the most object-cathected situation (coitus) with regressive fantasies and the most uterine situation (sleep) with genital images (dream). Thus both congenital id trends can serve as defenses against each other. Perhaps the most eloquent illustration of this theory is the study of human play, dominated as it is by oscillation "away from the object toward the new object back toward the old object."[164]

The Kaingang perform a transition rite on the baby called "baby blackening." After having pierced the baby's lips the god-father walks back and forth with the baby. This is called "the baby's making." Following the baby's making they play a game with soft bags which they toss back and forth between the parents and the child's ceremonial parents. The people shout, "Come here, catch my pet,"[165] which makes it very probable that the bags really symbolize the baby.

At Bougainville children tie all kinds of creatures to a string and then let them go a little and pull them back again. They like to get hold of a *mother with its young,* perhaps a flying fox or an opossum and tease both

161 Kinsey, *op. cit.*, p. 177.

162 Cf. Róheim, G., *Psychoanalysis and Anthropology*, Chapter X.

163 Cf. Stern, M. M., "Anxiety, Trauma and Shock," *Psychoanalytic Quarterly*, XX, 1951, p. 189.

164 Cf. Hermann, I., "Sich Anklammern, auf suche gehen," *Internationale Zeitschrift für Psychoanalyse*, XXII, 1936; and Bujtendijk, F. I., *Wesen und Sinn des Spieles*, 1933.

165 Henry, J., *Jungle People, A Kaingang Tribe of the Highlands of Brazil*, New York, 1942, pp. 196, 197.

by letting the young one grip its mother and then putting it away.[166]

In Sipupu little children sit in a group. They represent *taro*. One child is the thief. He steals them one by one. The last child that is left is called mother of the *taro*.[167]

It would take us far from the main stream of our thinking to trace all manifestations of this "to and fro" in clinical analysis, in everyday life, in ritual. It is easy to see basic elements of progression and regression in the curve of libidinal tension. The increase of the curve, the mounting tension would be equated with the progressive or object-seeking trend while the reachieved tension-free state would be equivalent to regression. The oral factor in the dream may be one in which the infant gets in touch with reality. The dream may be "oral" in three distinct ways: (a) Reality has not been completely given up. (b) It is an attempt at re-establishing contact with reality. (c) Since what we have called regressive might also be called introvert and what we have called progressive extrovert—since, in other words, the material substratum of the dream womb is the dreamer's own body, the dreamer may identify with the food or feces passing through the gastrointestinal tract (similarly with the urine). Another important motor of the dream is seeing which in a sense is parallel to eating.

Gesell writes: "When does this newborn baby begin to use his eyes? He is visually sensitive to light from the moment of birth. Although his eyes are prevailingly closed they are far from inactive. The eyeballs frequently make short lateral excursions, even under closed lids. The lids themselves recurrently quiver, or they contract participating in the grimacing which especially involves the ocular and oral regions. The head extends or rotates slightly from time to time."[168]

"Vision has a pre-eminent place in neonatal development. Visual behavior patterns are among the first and most complex to assume form and function."[169] The four-week-old infant wakes not only to feed but to exercise his visual functions. He stares, albeit rather vaguely, at his surroundings.

"In the ensuing months (12–16 weeks) these elaborations lead to a veritable visual heyday. Vision assumes an engrossing and exciting role in the mental life of the infant."[170] "Almost literally he picks up the

[166] Blackwood, B., *Both Sides of Buka Passage,* 1935, p. 180. Cf. the game described by Freud, "Jenseits des Lustprinzips," *Gesammelte Schriften,* VI, p. 201.

[167] Róheim, G., "Children's Games and Rhymes in Duau," *American Anthropologist,* XLV, 1943, p. 102.

[168] Gesell-Ilg-Bullis, *Vision, Its Development in Infant and Child,* p. 78, cf. the rotating motion in the dream.

[169] *Ibid.,* p. 81.

[170] *Ibid.,* pp. 84–85.

object with his eyes, drops it and picks it up again. This is truly a form of ocular prehension, a forerunner of manual prehension. . . . He appropriates with his eyes more successfully than with his hands."[171]

In sleep we close our eyes—regress from the object world. The dream consists of a series of images—a move toward an imaginary object world. In the dreams we have been reviewing we find a regressive (uterine) and a progressive (genital) trend in sequence or condensation. Perhaps we have found the real source of human conflict in this conflict within the id. I emphasize that I do not regard regression as an ego but as an id function although naturally it may also be used as an ego function. Here again a digression would be necessary and we would have to ask what is the id? I am aware of the fact that most psychoanalysts regard such composite phenomena as "oral masochism" (Bergler) or the "desire to be devoured" (Lewin) as belonging to the id. If we do so I cannot see in what the id differs from the unconscious. Freud's first definition of the id makes it practically a new term for the unconscious.[172] But in his last summary of psychoanalysis Freud writes:

"Das älteste dieser psychischen Provinzen oder Instanzen nennen wir das *Es;* sein Inhalt ist alles, was ererbt, bei Geburt mitgebracht, konstitutionell festgelegt ist, vor allem also die aus der Körperorganisation stammenden Triebe, die hier einen ersten uns in seinen Formen unbekannten psychischen Ausdruck finden."[173] ("The oldest of these psychical areas or forms is the id, it contains everything that is inherited, congenital, constitutional.")

It would seem to me better to distinguish id functions from those that depend on the introject and these we would rather call archaic superego.

VII. The Eternal Ones of the Dream

It is here that we go back again to anthropology. When I wrote my book *The Eternal Ones of the Dream* I don't think I quite fathomed the problem.

The life of the "eternal ones of the dream" ends where the dream begins. The typical ending of the myth is that they *borkeraka* and *tjurungeraka,* i.e., got tired and became *tjurunga* in a cave or a hole in the ground. "Became *tjurunga*" means (a) they died, (b) they went to sleep, and (c) they became phalloi.

[171] *Ibid.,* p. 89.
[172] Freud, S., "Das Ich und das Es," *Gesammelte Schriften,* VI, p. 367.
[173] Freud, S., "Abriss der Psychoanalyse," *Internationale Zeitschrift für Psychoanalyse und Imago,* XXV, 1940, p. 9.

The Pitjentara kangaroo myth that starts at Kankana (Crow) ends at Kunamata (Mound of Excrements) where all the kangaroos *went in* and became *kuntanka*. The place is called kangaroo hole or fig hole. There are many fig trees there. If anyone commits a murder he can hide behind the trees and nobody will find him.

In the story of Unami and Yurgna (Testicles and Semen) the two great ancestral kangaroos and all the others went into a cave and became *kuntanka* (*tjurunga*) there. In another version of the story they first put their *kuntanka* in and then became *kuntanka* themselves in the cave (i.e., first the penis goes in). In one of my unpublished myths the emu ancestor makes a cave and then pulls the young emus in after him. There they became *kuntanka*. In another myth they make a big cave in a flat rock, *go down* and become *kuntanka*. Another myth ending is that the emu ancestors come to a *big water* and go in. "Then the old man went *down* into the earth and the young ones went after him. The old man emu called them like an emu calls its young ones, and they all went down at Namban urkun and he went down after them." Pindupi country, that is where the emu ancestors *went in* and became *kuntanka*. A sand wallaby myth told by Kulaia ends with the phrase: "They made a big rock hole, put up a ceremonial pole and went in." A wallaby myth of the Nambutji ends as follows: "He came from the north and went into the middle-sized hole. Then he became a tjurunga and made a cave there." (Abbreviated from field notes.)

In a Yumu myth, the end is connected with anxiety. The sand wallaby ancestors stand there with the ceremonial pole near a water hole. The water hole was inhabited by a mythical serpent. The serpent came out and swallowed them all. They became *tjurunga* in the serpent. An opossum ancestor ends his wanderings on earth by intercourse with his mother-in-law. Then they all *went in* and became *tjurunga*, at Anapita. The story of the wandering of two honey ant men ends: The old man went into a bigger cave and the young one into a smaller cave.

In some of these myths the symbolic form is discarded.

A woman came from Maurungu[174] and gave birth to a child at *Nata* (Lap). The boy became big and walked on all fours looking for his mother. He had a little stick and he kept trying to walk on his two legs aided by the stick. Then he walked on all fours again and finally found his mother's track. One day he went to Maurungu and his mother saw him coming. She opened her legs and put a *tjurunga* on her head. She called him with open arms and she squatted on the ground with her vagina wide open. He went in with his *papa* (stick, child's *tjurunga*) and he *borkeraka* (became tired) and became a *tjurunga in his mother*. In an

174 Cf. Róheim, G., *The Eternal Ones of the Dream*, p. 239.

Aranda myth, an old woman of the Kultja (corkwood blossom) totem was pregnant. She gave birth to twins. The first twin went away and became an *erintja* (demon). He bit people in two and then returned to his mother. She saw that he was dripping with blood and she killed him. She put him into a cradle and then into a pouch. He became a *tjurunga* there. She went to the water hole at Taila and he became quite a grown-up man. Then he became little again and she put him back into the cradle. She covered it with a *tana* (vessel) and next morning the second baby had also become a *tjurunga*. In the ritual that represents the myth the man who plays the role of the mother does the *alknantama* (ceremonial wriggling) also imitates the process of delivery.[175]

A phallic stone was found near Koporilja (Hermannsburg). Koporilja is the rain totem center. The stone was called *kwatja parra*, i.e., water penis and the following myth was told by Rauarinja to H. A. Heinrich, the teacher at Hermannsburg Mission.

West of Koporilja there is a big hill called Nkalla-lutua. There was a rain man there called Nkanjia. He was also a thunderman. In a cave up the creek was another rain man, Eroamba (Big Cloud). At the spring there was a third rain man named Inamana (Big Rain). A little way down from Koporilja there was a fourth rain man whose name was Larkaka (sheet lightning).

Up from Koporilja there was yet another rain man whose name was Kotulba (i.e., lightning that strikes).

One day the rain man Nkanjia said to the rain man Eroamba, "Grow no more." Thereupon the rain man Eroamba grew no bigger and the skies were no longer overcast. Then he said to the rain man Inamana, "You are not to rain all the time." Then he spoke to the rain man Larkaka, "You are no longer to make lightning all the time." Then to Kotulba, "You are not to throw thunderbolts."

Finally he said, "Behold, I am really a great rain man, all the other rain men obey me!" But now he saw another rain man called Imbotna (Hail) who came sneaking up on the four other rain men. Imbotna came quite close to them and undid their hair so that it hung over their shoulders. Then a big rain came. The rain encircled them so that they could not see anything. Imbotna started to drag the four minor rain men to his place.

When Nkanjia saw this he got very angry and talked very loud, i.e., he thundered. They fought, but they both became tired (*borkeraka*) and became *tjurunga*. The other rain men also got tired and became *tjurunga* at various places.

[175] *Ibid.*, pp. 206–208.

From Alkrabanta Larkaka (sheet lightning) went to his aunt who lived at Tjakala. His aunt was an *alknarintja*. When she saw Larkaka approach she danced *shaking her thighs, causing the lips of her vagina to tremble. Lightning came out of her vagina. Larkaka entered her vagina.* When Nkanjia spoke (thundered) his penis became erect[176] and fire came out of his penis setting trees alight.

He then caught hold of his long penis and hit trees, smashing them. One day his penis broke off, was petrified and became a *tjurunga*. Kotulba himself became a *tjurunga* at Njambunga.[177]

It is especially interesting to compare this myth with the previous myth which starts at Maurungu. There the story ends with the mother doing the *alknantama*, the ceremonial trembling while the son is going in. I have repeatedly interpreted the *alknantama* as coitus, here we find no ceremony, just erotic trembling pure and simple. The rain projection is, of course, semen and lubrication, the lightning orgasm.

Another thunder myth is of interest because of its bearing on the *ending* of the life history of these mythical beings and because of what is obviously a representation of the vagina in stone.

In the Mungarai country there is a place called Crescent Lagoon by the whites and Dadba by the natives. There are flat tables like outcrops of sandstone there with several cup-shaped structures in them that look like pounding stones. They are obviously man-made. They vary in size from very small circular depressions, perhaps an inch or two inches in diameter and an eighth to half an inch in depth, to symmetrically shaped roughly hemispherical, cuplike depressions ten to twelve inches in diameter and six to eight inches in depth. These cuplike structures are said to have been made by Namaran, the thunderman. He lived at the bottom of the pool in a hole in a great rock. He made rain that filled the lagoon and used to go in and out of the stone. He had plenty of spirit children with him and if a woman puts her foot into the pool a spirit child will creep up into her. The cups were made by him when he was first trying to open up the rock and go in. But since the rock was too hard, he went into the pool where he lives with the spirit children.[178]

The mythical *ending* is the same as the dream's *beginning;* the penis, or the body as penis, re-enters the mother.

[176] In the texts I have collected we often find the phrase "the penis talks," i.e., it is erect.

[177] Balfour, H. R., "A Phallic Stone from Central Australia," *Mankind*, IV, 1951, pp. 246–249. I have changed the word "spinster" in the text to the original *alknarintja* which is not quite the same thing; cf. Róheim, G., *Psychoanalysis and Anthropology*, pp. 104–105.

[178] Spencer, B., *Native Tribes of the Northern Territory of Australia*, London, 1914, pp. 335–336.

"The time when the ancestors wandered on earth was called *altjiranga nakala,* i.e., ancestor was, in contrast to *ljata nama,* now is. Other expressions were noted as equivalent; these were *inanka nakala* = eternally was. This led us to the etymology of the word *altjiranga mitjina. Mitjina* is an equivalent to *kutata* = eternal. *Nga* is ablative suffix like from or of = the eternal ones of the dream, or, who come from the dream. This was the explanation given by Old Moses, Renana (Nathaniel) and Yirramba who were then (1929) the most reliable bearers of Aranda tradition in Hermannsburg."[179]

Other tribes have similar beliefs in a mythical age. The beings who wander on earth in this period are in a certain sense the ancestors or prototypes of present-day mankind, but in another sense they really are "the people of the dream."

Elkin writes: "They are historical and local, they are significant for the present and the future. They are moral and social in function. They are denoted by a term such as *altjira* (Aranda), *az dzugur* (Aluridja), *bugari* (Karadjeri), *lalau* (Ungarinjin), which has a number of meanings all of which are summed up in the long past time, when the culture heroes and ancestors introduced the tribal culture and instituted its rites and laws."[180]

"The same term also means dreaming or dream. . . . A man's dreaming is his share in the sacred myths or rites of the historical traditions of the old or eternal dream time. . . . The usual term for this past creative period as we have seen means also 'dreaming.' A person's dreaming is his cult totem: in other words, that is his symbol and share of the long past heroic age and indeed his means of access to it."[181] The Mara call this period *intjitja,* the Tjungilli and Binbinga call it *mungai,* the Anula call it *raraku.*[182]

The Wandjina or cave paintings are similar totemic ancestors. The story ends with the Wandjina "lying down," which is another way of saying that he died or (and) that he went to sleep.[183]

Considering all this we must conclude that *the dream nucleus of these stories is quite evident.* We have an environment developing from the human body like in a dream and we have an ending (going into a cave in

179 Róheim, G., *The Eternal Ones of the Dream,* p. 201.

180 Elkin, A. P., "The Secret Life of the Australian Aborigines," *Oceania,* III, 1932, p. 128.

181 *Idem, The Australian Aborigines,* Sydney, 1945, p. 187.

182 Spencer, B., and Gillen, F. J., *The Northern Tribes of Central Australia,* London, 1904, pp. 750, 754, 759.

183 Capell, A., "Mythology in Northern Kimberley, North West Australia," *Oceania,* IX, 1939, pp. 390–391.

phallic form) that corresponds to what we have called the basic dream, i.e., the moment of falling asleep.

If we take any *tjurunga* the analogy becomes even closer. The object itself is supposed to be the *body* of one of these heroes of ancient times. When the marks of the surface are explained we are told that the dots are paintmarks the prehistoric person made when he decorated his own body, straight lines may be cheloids (scars) on his chest. So far this would be quite simple. But this *body* is also a record of the journey he made from his birth to his death. There are a number of concentric circles indicating the place where the hero with others made a camp or a windbreak (*quendja*) at such and such a place, then another concentric circle indicating such and such a place; in other words, the wandering of the mythical hero from birth to death.

Thus the *tjurunga* corresponds very closely to my theory of the dream. A journey in time and space, a body that is also environment, a narrative that ends by "going down," and the hero as a phallic symbol.

Since the people themselves say that all their culture and customs and institutions are derived from these dream beings—maybe they are right and should be taken literally.

Old Yirramba dreams in ceremonies just as he talks ceremonies all day. I quote here only the ending of his dream (No. 2 in my collection).

"On the top of the mountain there was a Kauaua (ceremonial pole) and many novices whirling the bull-roarer.[184] It was a big place. I and the other old man and the novices heard the whirling and we ran around the ceremonial pole shouting, wa! wa! (a part of the ceremony). Then the *Unjiamba* (Hakea flower, a totem related to the Honey Ant)[185] old man began to decorate himself and all the novices embraced him. Then the young men went out again whirling their *namatuna* while the old Unjiamba man got ready for another ceremony. They made a big hole in the sand and then a big cave. It was a *great place* (i.e., totem center) of the Unjiamba. Then they all went down and *tjurungaraka*."

I quote from my notes only the part of the interpretation that concerns us here. He tells me about the part of the dream in which he is "going down." He was very *tjipa tjipa* when they *were all transformed* into *tjurunga* and compares this feeling with the pleasure or ecstasy of an orgasm. This is also *tjipa tjipa*.

This is all we need for the present. The "going down" in the myth is the phallic going down into mother.

Another important fact is that the natives believe that ceremonies can be derived from dreams. Aldinga of the Ngatatara tribe dreamed a

184 This is a dream of an initiation.
185 The dreamer's totem.

ceremony. His soul visited the totemic caves where it saw his double and the double of his brother (a double double formation) performing a ceremony. What he saw in his dream he repeated in reality—but this, although very much like the other rituals, was nevertheless a nonsacred ceremony.

The *iruntarinia*, or spirit doubles, frequently communicate to the head of a group the right time for the performance of ceremonies. They themselves perform such ceremonies and if a plentiful supply of some animal appears before the ceremony has been performed it is due to the ceremonial activity of the spirits belonging to the totem clan.[186]

Anthropologists have been puzzled ever since the days of Captain Grey by the rock paintings of the aborigines of North Kimberley. Owing to Elkin's work[187] we can now attempt to understand the meaning of these cave images.[188]

The natives say they do not make the *wondjina* figures but only repaint them. The figures themselves are called *wondjina made themselves*. They are self-created. There is nothing in the workmanship of these figures that a present-day native could not do although external influence for some of the figures has been repeatedly assumed or hinted at.[189]

"Perspective is mostly absent. This applies to the position of the hands and feet or of the headdress. The feet are depicted as though the soles were in the same plane as the legs. The number of toes and fingers varies from three or four to seven on each hand and foot. What my informants say is that the beard commences at about the level of the armpit.[190] The complete genital organ is depicted in some of the female *wondjina* on the front of the body. Stripes, dots, and dashes are probably paint applied to the body for ceremonial purposes. *The absence of the mouth cannot be explained. The natives say simply that a mouth cannot be made. Apparently the efficacy of the painting is associated with its absence.* [My italics.]

"The first and perhaps primary significance of *wondjina* is that of the power that makes, or which is in, the rain. If a *wondjina* head be retouched, if *wondjina* be made 'pretty fellow,' rain will fall even in the dry season as I have shown. The proper time, of course, for this retouching is at the beginning of the 'wet' (season). . . . *If the headman of the rain*

186 Spencer and Gillen, *Native Tribes*, p. 519.

187 Elkin, "Rock Paintings of North West Australia," *Oceania*, I, 1930, pp. 257–279.

188 Cf. also Elkin, "The Origin and Interpretation of Petroglyphs in South East Australia," *Oceania*, XX, 1949, pp. 119–157.

189 Grey, G., *Journals of Two Expeditions of Discovery*, 1841, I, p. 202. Basedow, H., *The Australian Aboriginal*, Adelaide, 1925, p. 343. Elkin, *op. cit.*, p. 275.

190 According to Elkin, what they think is that the beard is probably a shell ornament hanging from the neck (the *takula*).

*totem dreams that he has visited and 'touched' the wondjina painting in
the gallery of his horde he tells everybody about it."* [My italics.]

After this they expect the rain to come. *To touch this picture in a
dream has the same effect as touching it in actual fact.*

The *Ungud,* a large snake, is either the mate of the *wondjina* or identical with it. Both terms also mean the rainbow serpent. *Ungud* is also
used like *altjera,* meaning the mythical past or dream world.

The retouching or painting of the female *wondjina* causes an increase
of babies for Ungud. The rainbow serpent makes and brings spirit babies
down in the rain to the water holes. A man in the Ungarinjin tribe always
finds his baby "along" water, possibly in the rain as it falls.[191] "One
Ungarinjin informant told me [i.e., Professor Elkin] *that wondjina offers
a man a baby in a dream or a man in his dream* might ask a different
wondjina for a baby until he gets a good child.

"The other function of the *wondjina* is to increase the species they
represent. If the *wondjina* are retouched the species will increase. The
bones of the dead or at least some of them are also deposited in these
caves.[192]

"Man's part is to retouch, perhaps occasionally to paint anew the
wondjina heads and adornments and to paint pictures of the desired objects and species on the *wondjina banja* or rock galleries. The efficacy of
the special paintings is associated with the fact that they are *Ungud,* that
is, belong to the far-past creative times. Preservation of continuity with
this period is essential for present prosperity."

This actually happens in the dream. Elkin says, "It is perhaps per-
missible to regard *wondjina* as the regenerative or reproductive power in
nature and man—a power which is especially associated with rain. I am
not sure whether *wondjina* is *really* thought of in terms of sex. Some of
the paintings are said to be women, while other references to *wondjina*
seem to make them male."[193]

In the meanwhile, however, the caves visited by Grey have been re-
discovered. Four of the images Grey regarded as female from "the mild
expression of their countenances." This was correct. The cave in question forms one of a south to north series of caves and a basaltic hill com-
memorating the sexual experimentation of a hero, Dalimen, and some
young women in the period when all were ignorant of the methods of
coitus and some of the females were immature. The name of the place
is "laughing or tickling place"—an obvious allusion to forepleasure.

[191] Cf. the well-known European stork, and the familiar stories on the origin of
children.
[192] Elkin, *op. cit.,* pp. 276, 277, 278.
[193] *Ibid.,* p. 279.

The name given by the natives to Grey's cave is "drying place," referring to women's cleansing actions after intercourse. Four female Wondjinas are looking at the male Wondjina, evidently Dalimen, desiring intercourse.[194] "Further north is a high hill with a number of upright stones and other broken ones representing the penes of Wondjinas, and one stuck in a crevice representing a mythological event.[195] The hill is named Lowparin, referring to coitus. Some distance from it is another rock the name of which is "sex play." The paintings are almost all said by the natives to represent the vulva. "One Dalimen myth ends with this organ 'becoming a painting' while another ends with the Wondjina after his sex experience saying that he would 'become a painting,' and across the Prince Regent there is said to be a picture of Wondjina Dalimen embracing his wife."[195a]

Some cave pictures represent the bodies of the heroes who became paintings at the close of their exploits and wanderings, that is, dying. Though their spirits went to the nearby *Ungud* pool or spirit home ready to become active again when their pictures are repainted.[196]

According to Elkin and the Berndts, many of the sacred drawings in Arnhem land are derived from dreams and represent the totemic country or the ancestral beings.[197] The principle theme is based on a crocodile from Blue Bay. In the dreaming era, this crocodile made a hut on a ceremonial ground in which the totemic emblems were stored. During the dancing an extraordinary fire sprang up suddenly, burning the emblems and some of the men. The crocodile was burned about its "arms" and escaped to Caledonia Bay taking fire with him. The design represents a variation of the myth seen in a dream by an artist.[198]

About certain songs we are told that the Owl sometimes comes to the sleeper and sings them to him in a dream and listens to the song. Awakening in the night, he sings over to himself the words that he has heard and when he is quite sure of them he sings them aloud to the people.[199]

The galleries of drawings in the Oenpelli caves contain drawings of women with human or reptile heads, with several arms, accentuated breasts and elongated vulvae streaming with semen, women with babes suckling at their breasts, bodies of women showing fetal growth, women dancing, men and women carrying out the sexual act. A series in the form

194 Elkin, "Grey's Northern Kimberley Cave Paintings Re-Found," *Oceania*, XIX, 1949, p. 8.
195 Evidently coitus.
195a Elkin, "Cave Paintings Re-Found," p. 9.
196 *Ibid.*, p. 12.
197 Elkin, and R. and C. Berndt, *Art in Arnhem Land*, Chicago, 1950, p. 50.
198 *Ibid.*, p. 66.
199 *Ibid.*, p. 83.

of bark paintings was collected at Oenpelli, others from Goulburn Islands.[200] Some represent individuals in sexual intercourse, others pregnant women—being imitative magic designed to bring about these situations. Others are black or destructive magic. Thus, a man who has caught his wife in *flagrante delicto* would sketch his wife, call out her name, and then he would draw a composite figure with an animal, human, bird or reptile head—the eagle and the Rainbow Serpent being the most popular ones. Several arms and sting-ray spines are inserted protruding from the body. This would make her feel sick and after a few days kill her.[201]

The hypothesis we now suggest to account for these cave paintings is this. *They were originally dreams born out of the need of a man to communicate his dreams to a fellow man in imagery or narrative form.*

History repeats itself. Modern movements in art openly claim to be based on dreams. "Dali shared the group surrealist faith in sleep as an aid in distracting the vigil of conscious reason. A number of his paintings are literal transcriptions of dreams."[202]

If these primeval beings or myths were originally dreams, primitive man could justly claim that they were "made of themselves." Then if we remember our theory of the basic dream, we can understand the *descent,* the location of the painting in a *cave,* the association with death, and *the ascent, the genital meaning of the dream, the fertility magic and baby finding in the myth, and in the painting. Urethral-erotic waking dreams would explain the connection with rain, and genital libido would explain the connection of the dream or dream cave with the origin of children.*

Lommel tells us that *wondjir* is the word for sperm, and hence it is clearly connected with Wondjina, the god of rain and fertility. The Wondjinas are represented on the rock paintings as roughly anthropomorphic beings. They are believed to cause and to be the rain. They emanate out of *Ungud*—the eternal dream time, a being represented as a snake which unites in it the conception of time as well as that of the creative principle of the world.

"The Wondjina Kalaru threw the first flash of lightning by splitting his penis and letting out the fire and the flash of lightning. He created the fire by turning outside the red inside of the split penis and letting out the fire and a flash of lightning. He can direct the flash of lightning by taking the penis in his left hand and showing the direction he wants the lightning to go with a club in his right hand."[203]

---

[200] The bark paintings are secondary and are derived from the cave paintings.
[201] Elkin, Berndt and Berndt, *op. cit.,* pp. 80–81.
[202] Thrall Soby, J., *Salvadore Dali,* New York, 1941, p. 14.
[203] Lommel, A., "Notes on Sexual Behavior and Initiation, Wunambal Tribe, North Western Australia," *Oceania,* XX, 1949, pp. 160, 164.

The belief that the father must find the pre-existent child in a dream means simply that he must first dream a coitus dream with his wife. The spirit child seen in his dream is his own penis.

In the beliefs of the natives of Australia the child frequently comes in a dream and its previous dwelling is either a pool or a cave. Thus, for instance, around Ooldea, a water hole somewhere to the north in the Spinifex country, is the place where spirit children dwell. There is probably one such water hole in each tribal territory. In each case the children are standing round a fire.

Married women coming to the water would, if they wanted children, sit there with legs wide apart and the spirit child enters through the vagina. The point, however, is that the informants said, "that not rock hole, that vagina." The spirit children call their prospective mother's vagina "rock hole" and say "I am going into a rock hole" and then they intend to be born.[204]

Hence, if we are told that the father fetches the child in a dream from a water hole it is evident that the dream is the kind of dream we are discussing, i.e., the basic dream in which the dreamer *goes into* the mother (i.e., his mother plus his wife).

Kaberry reports some of these child-finding dreams of the natives of the North Kimberley division.

"Wallanang's father swam across the gulf to an island to get pelican and duck. When returning the Rainbow Snake followed him. That night he dreamed of a child which entered his wife."

The function of the dream is to provide the means by which the spirit child enters the womb of the woman.[205] A little girl relates how she was speared by her father prior to birth[206]—an obvious sexual symbolism of the father's dream.

According to Elkin: "A father always 'finds' his child in a dream and in association with water either in a water hole or in the falling rain.

"Even if in the first instance he 'finds' his child in water in waking life he will see it in a dream later on when he is asleep in his camp. In his dream he sees the spirit child standing on his head and catches it in his hand after which it enters his wife."[207]

We have seen above how the dream of the finding of the spirit child is connected with the pictures in the sacred cave. Three tribes of North West Australia, the Bardi, the Nyul-Nyul, and the Djabera Djaber, be-

204 Berndt and Berndt, "A preliminary report on field work in the Ooldea Region," *Oceania*, 1944, XIV, pp. 236–237.
205 Kaberry, P. M., "Spirit Children and Spirit Centres," *Oceania*, VI, 1936, p. 395.
206 *Idem, Aboriginal Woman*, Philadelphia, 1939, p. 74.
207 Elkin, "Totemism in North Western Australia," *Oceania*, III, 1933, pp. 460–461.

lieved that the father finds a spirit child in a dream. One of the Bardi named Nangur relates his own conception as follows. His father was fishing one early morning and picked up a green turtle at which moment the spirit child caught him by the wrist and followed him out of the water. After his father had dreamed of him several times he threw a spear under his father's leg while his father was asleep and then entered his mother's womb.

The spear thrown under the father's leg clarifies everything; the spirit child is the father's penis.

Another Bardi said that a man will dream of a spirit child about ten inches high on the ground, in a tree, or on a stone! Then he dreams that the child is drinking at his wife's breasts. If the mother does not want the child, the latter, who realizes the fact, drops a little spear about four inches long which the father, still dreaming, picks up and throws into some wood or tree from which the spirit child cannot withdraw it.. *The child then stops with the spear.* But some time after this when the man and his wife are walking about seeking food, the former may throw a spear at a turtle (or some other animal). He sees the spirit child who then passes between his legs and enters his wife.[208]

In all these dreams two features are emphasized: the spear and the passing between the legs.

Among the Forrest River tribes we have the following "spirit child" dreams. A man sees a frog when he stops to drink in his dream. He pushes the frog toward his wife and it becomes his child. Or he gives fat emu meat to his wife and that food becomes his child.[209]

However, the spirit child is somehow connected with the rainbow serpent. *Brimurer,* the rainbow serpent, brings the spirit child from the water hole. After a man has found a spirit child in one of the ancestral galleries, Brimurer takes red ochre from the painting which then becomes a new spirit child. The repainting is supposed to restore the "dream time" balance that has been upset by the emanation of the new child.[210]

A man finds the child in a dream, it comes from a pool, is somehow connected with phallic symbols—that is, the conception myth is really based on a dream.[211] Perhaps the natives are right and we should take what they say literally: *the totem is a dream.*

Elkin says that "the dream to the native is a real objective experience

[208] Elkin, A. P., "Totemism in North Western Australia," *Oceania Monographs,* No. 2, 1934, p. 445.

[209] Kaberry, "Spirit Children and Spirit Centres of North Kimberley District," *Oceania,* VI, 1936, p. 395.

[210] *Ibid.,* p. 398.

[211] Cf. Róheim, "The Nescience of the Aranda," *British Journal of Medical Psychology,* 1938, XI, pp. 343–360.

in which time and space are no longer obstacles and in which information of great importance is gained by the dreamer. The information may
refer to the sky world of the Aranda in which time and space are no longer
obstacles, especially if he be a medicine man, or to the earth beneath, to
his fellow tribesmen or even to his child yet unborn. But the great
'dreaming' or dream time was the age of the mighty heroes and ancestors,
who indeed still exist. And so a person's totem links him to that period
and gives him a share in it. Again a totem is also *bugari* dreaming because
it represents the totemite in the dream life of present-day men and
women. To dream of a person's totem is to know that he will come along
in a day or so. . . . Moreover, the totem might well be called 'dreaming'
seeing that a father becomes acquainted with a child's totem by dreaming
of it."[212]

, According to Elkin and the Berndts, the natives of North Australia
live on two planes, symbolical and practical. To those with eyes to see,
rocks and trees, rivers and hills, are "Dreamings," marking the deed of
the mythical heroes and the places where the spirits of men and animals
dwell.

Everything has its shade or soul as distinct from the material vehicle.
The shades must become "infleshed," each in its own kind. Therefore, if
man wants to live he must enter the world of "shades" while still alive.
Just as the natural object is the symbol of the soul within, this "dream
time" world must be entered by means of symbols in the ritual.[213]

Among the Wunambal tribe, the cause of conception is a dream. In
this dream the soul of the father wanders around in the country and
meets somewhere *usually at the water place where his own soul emanated*
a spirit child. In a second dream he hands over this spirit child to his
wife. Or a man has a vision. He "sees" a snake or small fish which disappears suddenly. Now he knows that he has found a child. In the "child
dream" a man goes back to the place he came from, to the water place or
cave where his soul originally emanated,[214] which, however, also becomes
identical with his wife's vulva and womb.

We have assumed that mythical images are in caves because they
are dream images and the dream, or rather sleep, represents a regression
into the womb. But if they had mouths they would not be effective. This
certainly does not tally with the oral dream theory as presented by Lewin.
The mouth in this connection means biting, castration, anxiety, and
therefore the opposite of fertility.

212 Elkin, "Totemism in North Western Australia," *Oceania,* III, 1933, pp. 265,
266.
213 Elkin, Berndt and Berndt, *op. cit.,* p. 14.
214 Lommel, *op. cit.,* p. 162. The author correctly interprets these dreams as showing an unconscious knowledge of paternity.

We have found that the "going down" (falling asleep, regression) and the "coming up" (phallic or vaginal progressive trend, awakening) are the underlying features of all dreams. They are not always remembered and frequently are condensed in one image. If we take Australian myth and ritual as forming a unity (which is indeed the view of the natives themselves), we shall find these mechanisms. The myth, as we have seen, is the "down" and the ritual takes us "up."

Warner writes about the Murngin, "The little babies when they are fish (unborn) live in the same place as the *marikmo* and the *mari* souls (ghosts of the dead). The *marikmo* and *mari* watch us. If we are good and we don't steal or have other men's wives, he sends us fish to our wives. . . . You can't see that spirit when it comes back but you can see it in a dream. . . . The man who has dreamed goes to the leader and says that so and so has come back to look at his children and to bring Yurlunggur (the initiation ceremony). That leader asks the man which way the man in the dream said to make Yurlunggur for this next time because he knows that the man understands from this dream."[215]

Where the mythical ancestors "went down" (i.e., died, regressed into the womb) they "come up" once more to give fertility to human beings and nature.

"As the *pulwaiya* (ancestor) 'went down' into his appropriate *auwa* he assumed 'or caused to be' the form of the totemic object with which he is associated. . . . Myths often have a currency as legends or stories but the real inner meaning of the myths in relation to ritual is known only to a few and is the special property of a clan. . . . One man said that he dreamed the ritual of which he was in charge but that his father had also dreamed it before him. The ritualistic procedure is apparently handed down from one generation to the other relatively intact but it seems that a man 're-dreams' the ritual and so acquires the necessary mystical qualifications for carrying it on."[216]

The bonefish myth tells how the bonefish man in mythical times wandered with his sister. They both hit each other till they bled and were mortally wounded. They "went down" in a flat place where the mangroves grow. Then the bonefish hero joined his brothers again at another place and, bidding them farewell, "went down" under the water there, promising as he did so that the bonefish would "come out" whenever they went to the place to "chase them out."

"In the ritual the bonefish-god 'comes out' of a bloodwood tree. . . . He is both god and bonefish. At his feet kneels the suppliant who fans life

[215] Warner, W. L., *A Black Civilization*, New York, 1937, p. 280.
[216] McConnel, U. H., "Myths of the Wikmunkan and Wiknatara Tribes," *Oceania*, VI, 1935, p. 66.

into the phallus of the god which appears to rise of itself in response. . . .
This fanning of the phallus is apparently the inner meaning of the hitting of trees, stamping of the ground and sweeping of the *auwa* (totemic
holes) with branches which usually accompanies the 'stirring-up' of the
pulwaiya in 'increase' ceremonies at the auwa. Beside the bonefish-god
stands his wife and partner in creation who 'went down' near by."[217]

For further data of this kind I refer to my previous publications.[218]

*It seems that in the dream we have one of the most important
sources of human culture. We might say that the colossal structure of
fantasy we have built up from century to century actually starts in our
dreams, or, more precisely, when one human being finds it necessary to
tell his dream to another, that is, in a prehistoric psychoanalytic situation.*

I do not intend to convey the impression that all myths and beliefs
must have their origin in dreams actually dreamed by somebody. Certainly this book is going to show that this element has not been sufficiently understood so far and that Laistner who held these views had
something of the insight of a genius, though in his days he naturally had
but a very imperfect understanding of the dream.[219]

Many myths deal with conflict situations, oedipal or preoedipal, etc.
But I suspect that the technique of the dream, metamorphosis,[220] wish
fulfillment, double formation (fission) and condensation, displacements
upward, etc., often supplied the raw materials out of which myths were
formed by our dreams. It can, of course, be said that these elements are
present anyway in the primary process, but it is certain that they manifest themselves most clearly in the dream. In a period when dreams were
taken as real events they must have contributed materially to myth formation and to beliefs. Why did the dreams have to be told? This, of
course, we can merely conjecture. Arguing on a present-day basis, one
would take two factors into consideration: (a) the need to communicate
because of the guilt factors in the dream, and (b) the vaunting of the
magical exploits contained in the dream. Perhaps a third factor is important. The dreamer does not know how to make the transition from
dream to waking life. He is not sure about the reality of the dream, and
this reality-unreality situation upsets him and he wants to achieve stabili-
zation by telling another person what had happened at night.[221]

217 *Ibid.*, p. 67.
218 Cf. especially Róheim, *The Eternal Ones of the Dream.*
219 Laistner, L., *Das Rätsel der Sphinx,* 2 vols., Berlin, 1889.
220 Cf. Róheim, "Metamorphosis," *American Imago,* V, 1948.
221 When I told Pukutiwara that flying machines had been invented by the whites,
he remarked that there was nothing remarkable in that, that he flies nearly every
night.

I do not doubt that myths contain historical elements handed down orally from one generation to the other, but in this again they do not differ from dreams which contain "historical" elements determined by the dreamer's life.

As I have hinted before, animism is based on the double seen in the dream.[222] Jensen quotes the following remarks from an unpublished manuscript of Petri on the Ungarinjin in Kimberley: "The 'dream time' is called *Lalan* or *Ungud* (*Ungur*) but also *Ya-yari*. This word seems to be derived from *Yari*, i.e., dream, vision, dream totem. *Ya-yari* also means strength, vitality. *Ya-yari* is what makes us feel, think and perceive. It also means potency because being sexually excited was called *ya-yari*. It is this that enables man to dream and thus to be in contact with the world of the supernatural. *Ya-yari* is the tie that unites the individual and the mythical heroes of the past. A medicine man said, '*Ya-yari* is the part of *Ungur* that is in me.' "[223]

Jekels and Bergler interpreted dreaming as the work of the "life principle" mobilized against the "death principle" as revealed in sleep. We have something to add to this.

The dream image of the dreamer is the phallic double with men, sometimes also with women. In women it may also be the genitally cathected vagina. In more general terms as valid for both sexes, the body cathected with genital libido.

We shall now attempt to summarize the first chapter.

We have come to the conclusion that

(a) In sleep we return to the intrauterine situation.

(b) The dream as such is an attempt to re-establish contact with environment, to rebuild the world. It is the normal parallel to schizophrenia, not to the manic-depressive states.

(c) Falling asleep is both birth in reverse and coitus. Awakening is birth.

(d) Sleep is a combination of regression and introversion. The dream space is both the mother's womb and the dreamer's body.

(e) In our foetalized species conflict or bipolarity is present in the id. The genital drive and regression are both congenital.

(f) Uterine regression is a desire and an anxiety. This is obvious since the neonate both sleeps and feeds and it has to give up the breast in order to sleep.

(g) The dream image is essentially genital (phallic). The dream image is male, the dream space female.

(h) The basic dream is the body flying or descending, genital libido, the

222 Róheim, *Psychoanalysis and Anthropology*, pp. 39, 40.
223 Jensen, A. E., "Mythos und Kult bei Naturvölkern," *Studien zur Kulturkunde*, X, Wiesbaden, 1951, p. 145.

object-directed trend against uterine regression. The visual quality of the dream is also a state of being half awake, a countermove against uterine regression.

(i) Just as in the defense mechanisms that are familiar to us on a higher level of organization, this defense mechanism actually contains whatever it is supposed to ward off. We find such traits in the dream as passing through narrow gates, diving into lakes, caves, etc. Undoubtedly these primordial traces of intrauterine existence are approached through channels of pregenitality and genitality (oral, urethral, anal, genital), yet we cannot very well explain their presence in the dream except by assuming that there is *something to go back to in engrams*. We have already assumed that the intrauterine state is revived in sleep; it would seem that this first step involves the second.

In this journey into the past, the dreamer naturally attempts to rebuild the environment on an infantile level or rather on the level of infantile wishes. It is here that the dream becomes personal and specific, it is here that the ego and the superego of the dreamer intervene and prevent an undisguised manifestation of the latent content.

ADDENDA

A. Regression and Genitality

In a seminar on dream interpretation Miss May Delmar asked whether my dream theory was identical with that of Gutheil.

Gutheil writes: "The awakening—apart from the fact that it is regulated by the sleep center—is prepared by some physiological process. The distention of a urine-filled bladder, the hunger contractions of an empty stomach, the increase of noises, the rise in the body temperature, the retinal reactions to increased influx of light stimulation—all these factors contribute to the conditioning of the cortex for the task of adaptation to daily life.

"In awakening the ego which has thus been prepared by the dream to accept reality rallies to establish normal relations with the outside world. It enters these relations as a well-adjusted agent. The dream has conditioned the ego for such a function by hallucinating a functioning, adaptable and efficient ego.

"As we see the dream is a function of the ego. [My italics.]

"In deep sleep we are unconscious. There is no ego, no thought, no dream. In awakening we are at first not fully conscious, but the conscious is flickering up gradually. The ego is awakening. And it is then that the thought-dream is awakening; at first passing through a prelogical archaic layer and then becoming more conscious and recallable. The closer to awakening the dream is perceived the less distorted is its content.

"During the moments of falling asleep and of awakening the dream forestalls a sudden disintegration of the ego and facilitates its restitution. This function of the ego is particularly important as all rapid transitions entail a danger of a sudden flush of panic and of shock to the individual."[1]

Undoubtedly these ideas have something in common with my own. The dream as a partial awakening, the emphasis put on body stimuli, the defense against total unconsciousness, the function of restitution, are implied in both theoretical views. The main difference lies in the sentence I have italicized. According to Gutheil, *the dream is a function of the ego.*

Gutheil's view has the merit of avoiding the rather startling assumption of *conflict immanent in the id that is in our congenital inheritance.* Moreover, if we regard the ego as the body ego, there is something to be said in favor of this view.

Freud writes: "The ego is primarily a body-ego, a being of the surface, in fact, a projection of this surface."[2]

"It is easy to see that the ego is the part of the id that has been modified by external stimuli through the mediation of perception, a continuation of the differentiation of the surface of the body. The aim of the ego is to represent the influence of environment as against the id, to replace the pleasure principle which reigns supreme in the id by the reality principle. Perception plays the role in the ego which drives play in the id. The ego represents what might be called the rational element in us as opposed to the passions that are the driving force in the id."[3]

It is obvious that the ego as a construct is really used in two senses: one as the libido cathexis of the body or the pleasure ego, the other as the representative of the reality principle.

Fenichel, following Freud, writes: "The surface is differentiated gradually with respect to its functions of stimulus perception and discharge. The product of this differentiation becomes the 'ego.' The ego proceeds selectively in its reception of perceptions as well as in its allowing impulses to gain motility. It operates as an inhibiting apparatus which controls by this inhibiting function the position of the organism in the outside world."[4]

If we use the word ego in this second sense, as the representative of

1 Gutheil, E. A., *The Handbook of Dream Analysis,* New York, 1951, pp. 37–39.
2 Freud, S., "Das Ich und das Es" (The Ego and the Id), *Gesammelte Schriften,* VI, 1924, p. 369.
3 *Ibid.,* pp. 368–369.
4 Fenichel, O., *The Psychoanalytic Theory of Neurosis,* New York, 1945, pp. 15–16.

the reality principle,[5] it is clear that we cannot regard the ego as the power behind the scene in creating the dream but that we must equate it with the secondary elaboration as opposed to the primary process. Yet again, since we assume that the dream is due to an attempt to restore the world of objects and objects can exist only if an ego exists (and vice versa), we might plead in favor of Gutheil's views.[6]

Once more we pause, for there is obviously only the illusion of an ego and object contrast in the dream since even the seemingly object elements are evolved from the body of the dreamer with more or less of the object world superimposed on the symbolization of the body.[7]

Psychoanalysis has attempted to give a psychological explanation of coitus or object love. Freud himself came to the conclusion that the reason why we displace libido from the ego to the object is that too much libido would accumulate in the ego and displacing it to the object is a device to avoid pain or being sick.[8] Jekels and Bergler believe that "in coitus the male, in identification with the phallic mother, overcomes the trauma of weaning through becoming the active rather than the passive participant."[9]

In Ferenczi's theory we have the trauma of birth instead of the trauma of weaning and coitus is explained as an attempt to regress into the womb.[10]

The Jekels-Bergler formula is easily refuted. The authors are probably not aware of the fact that primitive tribes like the Australians have no weaning trauma whatsoever because they wean themselves gradually whenever they please from mother's milk.[11] This, of course, would not apply to the Ferenczi formula. However, we must seriously question whether we are not overstepping the limits of psychology when we attempt to explain our coital pattern on these lines. It is older in evolution than the Genus mammalia. How can we then assume that it *originates* in uterine regression.

We are told by Gantt that certain worms show a great withdrawal from environmental stimuli during copulation. "In the spring from about March through May the whole field is alive with the nuptials of

5 Cf. especially Bally, G., "Die frühkindliche Motorik im Vergleich mit der Motorik der Tiere," *Imago,* XIX, 1933.

6 All this has nothing to do with the ego feeling in Federn's sense of the word. Cf. Federn, P., "Ego Feeling in Dreams," *Psychoanalytic Quarterly,* I, 1932, pp. 511–542.

7 *More* in dreams of normals, *less* in that of schizophrenics.

8 Freud, S., "Zur Einführung des Narzissmus," *Gesammelte Schriften,* VI, pp. 168–169.

9 Jekels, L., and Bergler, E., "Transference and Love," *Psychoanalytic Quarterly,* XVIII, 1949, pp. 343–344.

10 Ferenczi, S., *Versuch einer Genitaltheorie,* Vienna, 1924.

11 Róheim, G., *Psychoanalysis and Anthropology,* New York, 1950, pp. 55–56.

these creatures soon after dawn. About one-fifth of the worm's length remains embedded in the soil while the other four-fifths is extended towards its neighbour who is similarly situated. During the copulatory act, the anterior third of the ventral surfaces of neighbouring worms are applied to each other. Ordinarily when the worms are not copulating they are very alert; they withdraw into their tunnels at the approach of an intruder detecting his footsteps several yards away, apparently through the tactile sense. But during copulation they are as 'deaf' as our friend the *glooharka* (Russian name of a kind of grouse) for not only can they be approached but one may . . . walk boldly up to them and even prick them with a straw, especially if the pricking is done near the copulating end of the body."[12]

We would assume that the genital response is present from the beginning, it is inherited in the genes.[13]

Then what is the value of these theories which describe genital sexuality in terms of pregenital organizations or of uterine regression? Are they null and void? By no means, they describe psychological processes which really take place in our unconscious but which overlay and do not explain that which would take place anyhow for biological reasons, viz., our pattern of copulation. What takes place here is really that we are reluctant to grow up and in the unconscious our already delayed growth rate becomes even more delayed and may be equated with the mother-child relationship or with uterine regression. This process of a gradually slowed down rate of maturation and prolonged span of life does not start with man, but it certainly reaches its climax in the human species.[14] Therefore we must assume that both the regressive trend and the object-directed trend are congenital in our species. To a certain extent these two trends might be equated with an increase in pleasurable tension (libido) and a desire to restore a previous state of things, or homeostasis, i.e., they would be the mounting and the decreasing segment of the same curve. The regressive trend is relatively recent and more specifically primate or human. The copulatory trend is far earlier in evolution.

12 Gantt, W. Horsley, "Psychosexuality in Animals," in *Psychosexual Development in Health and Disease* (edited by Hoch and Zubin), New York, 1949, p. 34.

13 Cf. "As an organ of erogenous sensitivity the genitals are highly effective from birth on." Fenichel, O., *op. cit.*, p. 72. The same viewpoint is valid for sleep also. It is older in evolution than uterine regression can be. Some assume "embryonic" positions (amphibia, etc.), that is, they roll into a ball or "introvert." If the death impulse is equated with eliminating stimuli that would certainly be valid for the animal world in general. On sleep in the animal world cf. Hesse, R., and Doflein, F., *Tierbau and Tierleben*, Leipzig, 1914, II, pp. 892–896.

14 Cf. on this subject Róheim, *Psychoanalysis and Anthropology*, Chapter X, "The Unity of Mankind."

Returning now to the question: "Is the dream in its *origin* an ego function?" the answer would be no. The force is supplied by the object-directed (genital, in very early stages perhaps oral) id trend which then cathects the body of the sleeper and forms the phallic body image—Hermes, the flying dream, the soul. The double vector of sleep versus wakefulness and regression versus genitality is in the id.

One observation emphasized by Greenacre suggests, however, that this antithetical trend may be fused or welded in human beings not only as a life experience (reaction to delayed maturation) but as something that must be congenital. "There is one other phenomenon sometimes associated with birth to which I would now call attention: the frequent appearance in male babies of an erection immediately after birth. There is a possibility . . . that its occurrence immediately following birth is not merely coincidental but is the result of stimulation by the trauma of birth itself."[15]

This would bring us one step closer to Ferenczi's theory of genitality as regression to the womb. Our dream material has clearly shown that regression and genitality may be represented by one "movement" in the dream or may be antithetical to each other. The universal dream symbolism of "a person entering a room" as coitus and as uterine regression certainly proves the emphasis on the regressive aspect of coitus in our species with its delayed growth and premature incidence of sexuality. Still I would look for a causal explanation of coitus in biology and not in psychology.

B. The Problem of Symbolism

The question is whether symbolism is conditioned by repression or whether it is an intrinsic part of the primary process which would exist even if there were no repression. The former may be called the official psychoanalytic theory. According to Jones, "the two cardinal characteristics of symbolism in this sense are (1) that the process is completely unconscious, the word being used in Freud's sense of incapable of conciousness, not as a synonym for subconscious, (2) that the affect investing the symbolized idea has not, in so far as the symbolism is concerned, proved capable of that modification in quality denoted by the term 'sublimation.' "[16]

If we refer the matter back to Freud we can find statements that con-

[15] Greenacre, Phyllis, "The Predisposition to Anxiety," *Psychoanalytic Quarterly*, 1941, X, p. 75.

[16] Jones, E., "The Theory of Symbolism," in *Papers on Psycho-Analysis*, London, 1948, p. 139.

firm this point of view. "Dreams use symbolism in order to represent latent thoughts in a hidden form."[17]

But Freud also writes: "We have found that the distortion of the dream which prevents us from understanding the dream is a consequence of the censorship and directed against unacceptable unconscious wishes. But we do not assert that the censorship is the only factor that causes the distortion of the dream and really a further study of the dream will convince us that there are also other factors at work. This amounts to saying that even if we did not have the dream-censor, other factors would be at work which would prevent us from understanding the dream, that is the manifest dream content would still not be the same as the latent dream content."[18]

If the censor does not account for the use of symbols in dreams then what is the explanation? "Symbolism seems to be a survival of a former identification."[19]

Jones elaborates this viewpoint still further. "The tendency of the primitive mind as observed in children, in savages, in wit, dream, insanity and other products of unconscious functioning—to identify different objects and to fuse together different ideas, to note the resemblances and not the differences, is a universal and most characteristic feature. In explanation of it there are two hypotheses. The one most usually accepted would refer to the phenomenon under discussion, as well as most others of symbolism, to the structure of the undeveloped mind for which reason it might be termed the static hypothesis: the main feature to which they call attention is the intellectual incapacity for discrimination. The second which I shall point out presently has to do with the pleasure-pain principle and the third to which Rank and Sachs call attention to the reality principle."[20]

"The second factor leading to lack of discrimination is that when the primitive mind is presented with a new experience it seizes on the resemblances, however slight, between it and previous experiences, and this for two reasons both of which have to do with the pleasure-pain principle. The first of these is that the mind—above all the primitive mind which is ruled by this principle—notices most what interests it personally, what therefore is most pleasurable or most painful. It ignores distinctions between the ideas when they are indifferent to it and notices only those that are interesting."[21]

[17] Freud, S., *Gesammelte Schriften,* III, p. 69.

[18] Freud, "Vorlesungen zur Einführung in die Psychoanalyse," *Gesammelte Schriften,* VII, 1924, p. 150.

[19] *Ibid.,* III, p. 68.

[20] Jones, *op. cit.,* p. 105.

[21] *Ibid.,* p. 107.

"The third factor in preventing discrimination is not sharply to be distinguished from the last one, though it refers rather to the 'reality principle.' It is clear that the appreciation of resemblances facilitates the assimilation of new experience."[22]

We must first define what is meant by "the primitive mind." If some psychoanalysts think of our primeval ancestors as people who really did not know the difference between their own penis and a stick they picked up or between a cave and a vagina, then all we have to say is that such a concept is so manifestly absurd that it does not even have to be refuted.

But if we mean primitive in the sense of ontogenesis there is much more to be said for such a derivation of symbolism.

If I now delve back in time to my field work among the really primitive Pitjentara, I see little Aldinga, a Pitjentara boy, aged about three, son of their chief Pukutiwara. He beholds our teapot with amazement. Then he discovers how tea can be poured out of it, points to his penis and says, "kalu" (penis). But I doubt whether even this little child of the desert would actually have believed that the teapot was identical with his penis. The next instance I have described in detail. A group of children of the desert tribes (Yumu, Pitjentara, Pindupi) see the toys made by the white man for the first time in their lives. "The first reaction was one of great and general anxiety. Slowly they approach and now they begin to know what they are afraid of. The treatment of the toys is absolutely animistic. They talk to the snake and monkey and begin to threaten them. The monkey is to drop that stick he is holding or they will break his arm. The snake is not to try to bite them or they will kill it. The next phase is that they go into details. Where does the snake eat and where does it defecate? The squeaking india rubber doll with a hole in its back eats and defecates through the hole. They try to feed the dolls with the dried fruit I gave them. But the chief thing is always, "Where does the excrement come out?" And it is really a sight to see the deep perturbation depicted on their faces whenever they find a completely smooth surface with nothing that could be qualified as mouth, anus, vagina or penis. Gradually, however, they find a way out of the difficulty. The paper trumpet and the snake are the first to be picked out as penis symbols and fitted to their own genitals. One after the other all objects, even the most unlikely ones, are called *kalu* (penis) and used accordingly. Finally we see the whole group, about fifteen children, boys and girls rushing after each other and using it in the natural way a penis should be used."[23]

Environment has become genitalized. In an unpublished manuscript

[22] *Ibid.*, p. 108.

[23] Róheim, G., "Psycho-Analysis of Primitive Cultural Types," *The International Journal of Psycho-Analysis*, XIII, 1932, p. 101.

I come to the conclusion that symbolism and magic are simply the same thing. Primitive magic is always "symbolic" and symbolism always magical, that is, it is performed for a purpose.

I shall now quote the extremely interesting data reported by Ronald M. Berndt on the religion of the aboriginals of Northern Australia.

"This religion then is a dominant quality in Yirkalla life and is reflected in all its institutions and conventional forms of behaviour. It concerns itself with the fructification of all living things and in that category human beings themselves are considered the most important. As, however, the Kunapipi cult is especially concerned with the rhythmic sequence of birth and death it is crystalized in a definite concept of a Fertility Mother. Moreover, the cult is concerned with the coming and going of the seasons, the appearance and disappearance of vegetable and plant matter, and the propagation of other natural species—all phenomena which are necessary for the continuance and well-being of the people themselves."[24] The mythical background of this cult is the Djangawul myth. The ancestral beings collectively called Djangawul came from a mythical island which is now the land of the dead.

The leader was Djangawul himself, the two women were his sisters, the younger Maralaitj, the other Pildjiwuraroiju and the other man was called Bralbral. They brought a large conical mat which is now used by the women and certain sticks (rangga, sometimes forked, sometimes pointed) possessing life-giving qualities. *The mat symbolizes the uterus the rangga sticks were penes and when not used ritually were kept hidden in the ngainmara.*[25]

It is to be noted that this is exactly the interpretation I have given regarding the *tjurunga* and the totemic cave, the penis in the vagina (uterus). "As the Djangawul journeyed along the coast they met other ancestral beings but none of them had the procreating powers of the great Djanggawul. Djanggawul had an elongated penis and his two sisters had long clitori which dragged on the ground as they walked. Djanggawul had sexual relations with his sisters, so that they were continually pregnant. From time to time at the camps they stayed he would lift their clitori to one side and put his hand up into the uteri to remove many children of both sexes. The songs represent the perpetual pregnancy of the two sisters, their uteri being likened to the *ngainmara* mats which they brought with them while the embryo removed from them in childbirth are the *rangga.*"[26]

24 Berndt, R. M., *Kunapipi*, New York, 1951, pp. 6, 7.
25 *Ibid.*, p. 7. The interpretation given above is conscious, given by the natives.
26 Berndt, *op. cit.*, p. 7; Elkin, Berndt and Berndt, *Art in Arnhem Land*, Chicago, 1950, p. 29.

According to the Aranda tradition the Wildcat people, especially their leader Malpunga, were endowed with huge phalloi. The spirit children, however, emanated not from these but from the *tjurunga* which they carried with them in sacks or from the feathers that flew off their bodies when they performed the ceremonial *alknantama* (wriggling).

Most of the ritual consists in dancing on the sacred ground where a *nara* hut has been constructed. This hut represents the womb, in it the *rangga* are stored and from it men emerge to posture and dance ritually while holding them.[27] Beside and interwoven with this cycle is the Wauwalak myth and ritual. The Wauwalak are two mythical sisters, one with child, the other a virgin. Berndt writes "aboriginal women are all potential *wauwalak,* and a great deal of their behaviour, particularly at puberty and when menstruation ceases at pregnancy, is said to be based on that of the two sisters."[28]

In Central Australia theoretically every young woman is a potential *alknarintja,* i.e., eyes turn away, a woman who runs away when she sees the men. In some of the *alknarintja* myths I have collected we find two *alknarintja* sisters, one older, the other younger or still a virgin.

The two sisters are, of course, just an off-shoot of the fundamental mother imago (Kunapipi, Kalwadi or Kadjari). Native artists depict human beings flowing into the uterus of the Mother into the round "ring place" for the performance of sacred rites. When the ritual is completed "the Mother" lets them out, they emerge from the ring places and pass once more into ordinary life.

In Central Australia we have the exact parallel. The concentric circle or various deviations from the fundamental pattern is called *ilpintira* which means *ilpaindora*—womb inside or very much in the womb or in the very center of the womb. The concentric circle as ground drawing is *tjalupalupa* which means navel but this is only a euphemism for the vagina. The final phase of the initiation ritual is called *inkura* (hole) because the hole is the central element in the whole ritual.

Inkura, or *nankuru,* is both the name of the ritual and the territory in which it is held.

We see two mounds nicely decorated with gum tree leaves converging northwards. The ceremonies take place between these two mounds. All the performers are decorated with circles which have a reference to the hole or womb. We find one man gradually arising from a hole with the others surrounding him. The one emerging from the hole is a young wallaby, those surrounding him are old male and female wallabys. The

27 Berndt, *Kunapipi,* p. 8.
28 *Ibid.,* p. 9.

song says that the young wallaby comes out of the pouch and they stretch him to make him grow. The rebirth meaning of the ritual is clear, though not as openly stated as in the case of its northern equivalent.[29] In this northern ritual there is a continuous intermingling of male and female symbolism. Retelling the myth of the two sisters briefly we see Julunggul, the female rock python, holding her head high. She spat out lightning until the Wauwalak crouched in fear calling out at each flash. The younger sister dances to keep the approaching python away, for the snake was going to swallow them both. However, the snake comes nearer and nearer and swallows first the baby, then the mother, and then the younger sister.[30]

Warner has a different version. Here Yurlunggur is male; as such he is attracted by the menstrual blood and that is why he swallows the sister.[31]

This may be due to local differences or to a general tendency in this area verging toward ambisexual symbolism. Berndt reports that his old informants said: "You know *when the Yulunggul snake went into the hut we mean that a penis is entering the woman's vagina and this hut is a uterus too* [my italics], that is why we have it on the sacred ground for it reminds us that everything must come from the mother's uterus. That is how we came in the Dreaming [mythical period]; and people still continue to come in that way, don't they? And why do we have that Yulunggul? Well, don't we have to have a penis to open up and inseminate the woman so that she can give birth to children? And when the Yulunggul swallows the Wauwalak that is like a penis being swallowed by a vagina, only we put it the other way around."[32]

We shall simply omit the problem of this bisexual symbolism for the time being because it would lead us into complicated problems connected specifically with the area in question (Arnhem Land) rather than with the meaning of symbolism. But one thing is clear—the swallower is the female, that which is swallowed is the penis, and the bulk of the ritual consists in dances that imitate coitus or in actual coitus.

The ceremonial ground represents the uterus of the great mother. When the ground is completed, snake totem actors dance or writhe in the hole. The two actors, one representing a man, the other a woman, dance the "mating dance." The man has an erect bark penis and moves in pursuit of the woman who is desirous of coitus. They move toward the trench and dance around it and at its entrance they simulate sexual

[29] Cf. Róheim, G., *The Eternal Ones of the Dream*, pp. 102–129.
[30] Berndt, *op. cit.*, p. 22.
[31] Warner, W. L., *A Black Civilization*, p. 252.
[32] Berndt, *op. cit.*, p. 39.

intercourse. "The Mother is said to be present in the *ba'uma* and her life-giving powers are made operative by the actions of the two dancers. [The natives say:] 'The acting of coitus by the two dancers is like the uterus being fertilized: the Mother is having intercourse so that she may produce.' "[33]

While the purpose of the ceremonial dancing, as noted above, is to prevent being swallowed it is also performed in the womb, that is on the ceremonial ground or in the hut, that is symbolically identified with the womb. However, there is more than dancing, there is actual ceremonial coitus.

While the dancing is in progress the partners retire to a specially constructed shade or hut in which the woman accepts one man after another. This hut is again the hut of the mythical Wauwelak sisters,[34] i.e., the womb.

We see here a completely conscious form of symbolism or allegory (if somebody prefers to call it that). Compared to Central Australia, the area I have worked in, the symbolism is quite open. It confirms all my previously given interpretations, and it shows also a striking difference between this area and Central Australia. In the latter the female element is repressed and expressed only in symbols; in the North the male role is not exactly repressed but tends to be obscured.

The next trait we observe is that all this symbolism has a magical purpose, indeed, without this magical purpose it would be meaningless.

"And when the Julunggul swallows the Wauwelak that is like a penis swallowed by a vagina. . . . Now when we hold our big rituals we do the very same things because we want the seasons to come and things to grow and people to be born; that is the real meaning of what we do."[35] The coitus of the performers on the ceremonial ground makes the snakes do the same.[36]

We see then that symbolism in Australia may be conscious or unconscious. Its content, be it manifest or latent, is always genital (regressive), and the genital and the regressive may either be identical (back into the womb through coitus) or opposed (coital ritual to prevent being swallowed). Symbolic ritual is also magic; as in the dream, a new world is created.

Berndt's informants have given him several dreams which are nearly accurate repetitions of the ritual.[37] I had the same experience when I was

33 *Ibid.*, p. 43.
34 *Ibid.*, p. 53.
35 *Ibid.*, p. 39.
36 See *infra* on the role of the snake.
37 Berndt, *op. cit.*, p. 71.

in Central Australia. Berndt believes that his informants really dreamed these dreams. I think that is impossible. But I am not accusing my friend Yirramba banga or any of the others of *mala fides*. For them the boundaries of dream, myth and ritual are not quite clear. To quote Berndt: "Men 'dream out' the meanings of their sacred rituals coming spiritually into direct contact with the ancestral beings. They perform the rituals in dreams. . . . Many sacred designs are altered or added to because of dreams. . . . Sacred songs are influenced by dreams."[38]

I have made an attempt to show that these myths—and I now add, also the rituals—are based on real dreams though, of course, with many modifications due to the wear and tear of generations.[39]

This is the myth as recorded by Berndt: The Wauwalak sisters, one older and one younger left their home. Before leaving the elder sister had incestuous relations with a clansman and thus she became pregnant. They traveled in the direction of the Muruwul sacred waterhole naming all the animals and plants. They walked along killing iguana, opossum, bandicoot, bush rat and kangaroo for food and collecting yams. As they put the animals in their dilly bags they said, "You will be sacred later on," that is, they would become totems.

The elder sister gave birth to her child and they went on to the sacred water hole of Muruwul.

First they placed an opossum on the fire to roast but as soon as the creature grew warm it got up and ran away. The same happens with a bandicoot, an iguana and all other animals.

In the sacred water of Muruwul lived the great Rock Python, the Rainbow snake, the "headman" of all animals and vegetables. The sex of the Rainbow snake varies; according to Berndt, the female interpretation predominates, other field workers have reported the rainbow snake as male. The animals that the Wauwelak were trying to cook knew that the Rainbow Snake was nearby and that the Wauwelak sisters were desecrating the waterhole by dropping afterbirth blood into it. The animals now jump into the well and by doing so become sacred objects or totem animals. The yams don't jump into the water but they turn to ashes which means the same thing.

The sisters decided to *go to sleep.* The Rainbow Serpent, excited by the blood, emerges from the water. It emerges with lightning, rain and flood. The sisters dance to retard the snake's progress. However, this retarded the snake's progress only temporarily. Seeing the woman and the child she sprayed them with saliva from her throat to make them slip-

38 *Ibid.*, p. 72.
39 Róheim, G., "Mythology of Arnhem Land," *American Imago*, VIII, 1951.

pery. This covered their body so that their skin became soft and easy for swallowing. The Rainbow Serpent swallowed first the baby, then the mother, then the younger sister. The snake made a tremendous noise which is now the sound of the bull-roarer.[40]

In the version given by Warner the Rainbow Serpent is definitely male. "They sang Yurlunggur and menstrual blood. When Yurlunggur heard these words he crawled into the camp of the two women and their two children. They had suddenly fallen into a deep sleep from his magic. He licked the women and children all over preparatory to swallowing them. Finally he swallows them and regurgitates them *at daylight*."[41] [My italics.]

The interrelationship of the sexes is confusing. After having been told that the Rainbow Serpent is female we are told that when the serpent enters the hut of the women, "This is like the penis going into the vagina. The whole process of swallowing is interpreted by the natives as an act of coitus. The saliva mentioned above is called *ngal* which means semen. The Rainbow Serpent sprays out the *ngal* like an ejaculation of semen [the head in the woman's hut, the penis in the vagina] and then swallows them [coitus]."

The erectness of the Yulunggul and the other two Pythons is the result of the swallowing interpreted by Berndt's informants as an erect penis.[42]

Another myth reported by Berndt from Western Arnhem Land should be mentioned here.

Jurewadpad, the Rainbow Snake (or the poison snake python) wanted Gulanundeits. Her parents decided that they wanted the Rainbow Snake as their son-in-law so they told their daughter to sleep with him. However, she refused because she wanted a young boy. The Rainbow Snake got angry and he said to his companions, "You stop here and I'll go hunting." He found a large hollow tree and he chopped it down. When he had finished felling the tree he went back and constructed a little hut. "I am going to make that hollow log like a house so that I can go into it," he said and then he added, "I'll make it so narrow that the girl can come in and be right alongside of me, or it can be so narrow that she can sleep under me while I copulate with her as I lie on top of her and we can both play inside there." (This was the first sacred totemic drum uvar.) He invited the girl to come in but she refused. He went into the drum and turned himself into a Rainbow Snake. (Till then he was

40 Berndt, *Kunapipi*, pp. 20–24.
41 Warner, *op. cit.*, pp. 254–259.
42 Berndt, *op. cit.*, p. 25.

in human shape.) The girl peered into the log and the snake darted forward and killed her, then the snake also killed the mother.[43]

There is an obvious confusion in this area in sexual symbolism, male and female symbols seem to alternate. The point is that all over the "primitive" world the mythical being that swallows the initiates and then releases them, from which they are reborn, is supposed to be male, whereas the role is naturally a female role.[44] To symbolize coitus as "being swallowed" (i.e., the female's role in coitus) is also somewhat forced. In the Wauwelak and similar myths the females and young boys are swallowed, the females being classified with the uninitiated (i.e., young male) part of society. The natives call their stories dreams and in the Wauwelak myth quoted above the Wauwelak sisters fall into a magic sleep before being swallowed. I assume, therefore, that the original of the myth was a dream, in which the dreamer falls asleep, i.e., he is swallowed by a supernatural being and re-emerges in the morning, i.e., he is awake.

Initiation, as a drama enacted by the whole tribe, is usually being swallowed by a male being and being reborn. I have commented on the fact that the fathers are here making an unconscious attempt to sublimate the oedipal revolt by assuming a maternal role.[45] It is interesting to note that while Kunapipi, according to Berndt, means the Mother, in certain areas it also means the subincision hole,[46] i.e., the men by subincising themselves become mothers.

But quite apart from these specific traits of North Australian ritual, the remarkable thing is that symbolism is here quite conscious. Thus the long bull-roarer is called the body of the mother, the round wide bull-roarer the mother's uterus or vagina, the long "man" bull-roarer is called the penis and the smaller one the testicles.[47]

In Central Australia the meaning of the symbolism is not as conscious as here. The *tjurunga* is not definitely called a penis, but the first *tjurunga* was Malpunga's penis which was in a state of perpetual erection.[48] But whether symbolism is conscious or preconscious or unconscious, in primitive life *it is always magical*.

One of the Kunapipi songs published by Berndt is obviously connected with rain and water, and fertility is evidently the result of the myth and the associated ritual.

[43] Berndt, R. M. and C. H., "Sexual Behavior in Western Arnhem Land," *Viking Fund Publications in Anthropology*, No. 16, New York, 1951, pp. 120, 121.

[44] Róheim, G., *The Eternal Ones of the Dream*.

[45] *Idem*, "Psychoanalysis of Primitive Cultural Types," p. 72; *idem*, *The Eternal Ones of the Dream*, Chapter VIII; *idem*, "The Symbolism of Subincision," *American Imago*, VI, 1949.

[46] Berndt, *Kunapipi*, p. 16.

[47] *Idem, Sexual Behavior*, p. 140.

[48] Róheim, *The Eternal Ones of the Dream*, p. 85.

I give an abbreviated version. When Kadjari (Mother Imago) emerges from the water the waves break into foam on the sand bar. Several lines describe her emerging from the water, the waters swirl around her. Later the song describes how she is accompanied by a group of young girls. They walk along the banks of the river. As the young girls walk along they discuss each other's bodies. Then the song is about yams. The Kadjari (Mother Imago) who is with the young girls scatters the grass seeds as she goes along. New grass begins to sprout. They approach the ceremonial grounds. The emblem that represents the Rainbow Serpent (phallic) is placed in position at the edge of the ceremonial trench that represents the vulva or uterus of the mother and is made to "play" there (i.e., imitating coitus). Then the song is again about yams, clouds and rain.[49]

The assumed connection of the mythical concepts and ritual with environment is made quite clear by Warner. "When the inland lakes dry up and the small streams disappear and many of the clan water holes are empty then thunder comes and calls out for the rain. The thunder clouds are called male clouds and they meet the female clouds and copulate. At the same time the snakes on the ground put their tails together and copulate also.

"The rainbow is sometimes a snake, sometimes a snake's house (i.e., male or female). The rain is the saliva of the Rainbow Snake with which he swallowed the two sisters.

"The wet and dry seasons are caused by the snakes. During the wet season the snakes curl up and have sexual intercourse: the Great Father Snake does the same. They then come out of the water and want to lay their eggs. This brings on the dry season so that they have a place to lay the eggs.[50] Coitus dances representing copulating snakes are danced in the *kartdjur* (the ceremonial trench that represents the vagina or clitoris of the Mother Imago), another dance represents a single man looking for a mate."[51] "The majority of the dances are related to coitus. The dancers represent male and female wagtails, male and female rock pythons, having intercourse.[52] A part of the ceremonial trench called *kanala* (the river) is also the vagina of the mythical mother. The *jelmalandji* or phallic emblem is placed there 'just like in coitus.'"[53] (Native informant.)

We emphasized the dreamlike elements in the myth of the Wauwelak sisters. If we consider the peculiar trait of inversion of sexes then the trait in which the "dancing" (i.e., coitus) is supposed to delay the swal-

49 Berndt, *op. cit.*, pp. 188–203.
50 Warner, *op. cit.*, pp. 381–384.
51 *Ibid.*, p. 302.
52 Berndt, *op. cit.*, pp. 43, 44.
53 *Ibid.*, p. 83.

lowing would look like our dream theory, sleep is uterine regression, the dream image moving in space a phallic countermove against uterine regression. Since the dream represents coitus as the whole person in the room or cave (i.e., symbolic vagina) the copulating pairs or the one male in search of a mate in the "vagina" or "uterus" is even more dreamlike. I now notice that years ago I had uncovered the meaning of *ngallunga* as the great mystery of the Australian initiation ritual, but then, of course, I could not see its dreamlike quality. The performers of the *ngallunga* ritual run backward in a creek and flick their subincised penises upward while doing so, showing the subincision wound to the boys. The word *creek* that occurs in the songs refers to the wound and creek means a vagina. But it now occurs to me that it may also mean the actual creek in which the ritual is performed and this creek may also symbolize a vagina.[54]

Considering the homosexual symbolism of the ritual (the men offer their female genitals to the younger generation) and the symbolism of running, the running backward might be offering their front, their vagina, to the boys.

The problem that arises is this. Symbolism can be both conscious and unconscious, but it is always magical. The crying of the child is the first form of magic, and it is effective because it results in the mother fulfilling the child's desires. But what we fail to recognize is that all symptoms, defense mechanisms, in fact, personality itself, are a form of magic. They aim (and partly successfully) at influencing environment by subjective factors. Primitives have magic in a conscious form, whereas with us it can function only (excepting certain forms of neurosis or psychosis) if it is unconscious. The dream, even before the censorship sets in, is both magical and symbolic.

Dream symbolism is certainly not conscious. Then we might ask if it is not conditioned by repression, why do we have dream symbolism? It must be synthetic, the result of two forces operating in opposite directions. Now our dream theory assumes that while sleep is perceived by man's unconscious as uterine regression, the dream is a rebuilding of the lost world on a libidinal-narcissistic basis in which phallic and uterine images (symbols) predominate. In other words, the dream room as a womb would be both an attempt to regress into the womb and to get back into this world. Hence the original contrasting elements of *that which is congenital in us* (I purposely avoid using the word id here as the two meanings may not be quite the same) would be the explanation of symbolism.

54 Róheim, *op. cit.*, pp. 155–177.

C. Arnhem Land Mythology

Before they sink into their totemic caves or pools, the "eternal ones of the dream" wander on earth. Their wanderings are always phallic, either in the form of performing phallic ceremonies, or direct cohabitation. All we have to do is to invert the order of events, the sinking and transformation into a tjurunga first, and the rising or erection afterwards and we have the basic dream.

In Arnhem Land mythology we can also find confirmation for the transition from the hypnagogic fantasy to the dream. The ancestors are half awake, half asleep, that is in a hypnagogic state. "Fish" are being caught in the "sacred mats." Fish is esoteric for penis, and "the sacred mats" for the uterus.[1]

[1] Berndt, R. M., *Djangawul*, London, 1952, pp. 156, 157.

II

ANIMISM

We shall now gain deeper insight into the meaning of animism.

The Dieri believe that a man's soul leaves the body while he is asleep but it can also be taken out of the body by evil magic. The Wurunjeri say "when I sleep and snore the soul goes out sometimes to Tharangalk bek (other world) but it cannot get in and it comes back." One of them who had a sick child in the hospital dreamed that the child said to him, "We will go up there, do not be afraid, we shall not fall down." There were two strings hanging down. The dreamer climbed up after his son and they came to a hole where some people were looking down. He went up through the hole. According to the Kurnai the human soul leaves the body and visits its parents in the sky country while asleep. Songs and charms are also received in dreams. One woman reports that she had gone to the sky in her sleep but could not get through the hole.[1] Death there is just an extended sleep or dream, "the permanent disability to return to the body produced by the evil magic of some enemy."[2]

The Euaklayi say that the soul wanders about while its human habitation, the body, sleeps and the things seen in dreams are what the soul sees in its wanderings. This is the time when sorcerers can capture the soul and when this happens the sleeper wakes up tired and languid. Or maybe the soul has had a fight with another soul in its wanderings. Evil sorcerers collect these souls in their medicine bags. If the soul does not return, that is death.[3]

The Murngin believe that when a man dreams his soul is moving about over the country away from the body and observing what is going on at other places. During the hot afternoon the men frequently sleep in the shade and if it becomes necessary to waken one of them this is done slowly, giving the soul time to return to the body. "The soul during these extra-corporeal experiences is in a world where the totems, the unborn totemic children and other extramundane creatures exist. Dreams are definitely associated with black magic, for at times it is difficult for a man

[1] Cf. my own dreams in the first chapter.
[2] Howitt, A. U., *The Native Tribes of South East Australia*, London, 1904, pp. 434–440.
[3] Langloh, P. K., *The Euaklayi Tribe*, London, 1905, pp. 26–29.

134

to determine which is dream and which is waking reality. Munyirir's brother declared that Kimingmulu had attempted to steal his soul. He said that two or three nights before he made his accusation he was lying asleep with his wife in his camp when just before morning someone came along and stepped on his foot. He did not think this was part of his dream but that someone was trying to steal his soul."[4]

My own field data include the journey of the soul theory as a general explanation of the dream. The dreamer in Central Australia or in Normanby Island always mentioned the dream as something that his soul had experienced.

Aldinga of the Ngatatara group had a dream in which his soul and that of his brother went back together to the totemic caves and saw a ceremony performed by the spirits which they then taught the others to perform. Kanakana of the Mularatara group was being initiated into becoming a medicine man by Minyimata. That night he dreamed that Minyimata's soul came and took his soul and put magic stones into it. Then the two souls ran about and saw the *wankas* like light on a tree (caterpillars in which ancestral souls are supposed to travel).

On Cape York every individual has two spirits or souls at birth. One of these called *yorntal* is the throbbing that pulsates in the fontanelle. It resides in the body only during early childhood and with the closing of the suture it goes to a place in the mother's country called the place of the *yorntal*. The other spirit *mipi* remains in the body until death when it joins the *yorntal* with which it is in intimate association during the dream life of the individual.[5] After tooth avulsion his tooth is placed in a palm tree near a waterhole. This is the place of his *yorntal* and to this place he returns again and again in his dream life. You can either ask a man where is your *yorntal* or where do you dream? It amounts to the same thing. The place of the *yorntal* is also called "Dream place," throughout life when a man dreams his *mipi* goes to this place to join the *yorntal* which has preceded the *mipi* shortly after the birth of the child. For this reason he must not be awakened from sleep except by calling his name from a long distance. Their conception of sleep is very close to that of death, in each the *mipi* leaves the body to join the *yorntal* but in sleep *poiya* still animates the body.[6] If a man has a lagoon or watery place as his *yartji yor-tadji* (place of his personal totem) he may dream that he is swimming there with his *yartjimo* (personal totem). If his personal totem is a bird he may dream that he is flying with it. After death the soul definitely joins the

---

4 Warner, *op. cit.*, pp. 511, 512.

5 Thompson, D. F., "The Hero Cult Initiation and Totemism on Cape York," *Journal of the Royal Anthropological Institute*, LXIII, 1933, p. 493.

6 *Poiya* is therefore not identical with *yorntal*.

personal totem at the totem place. The totem place is also the other world where a man is greeted by his mother. The totem places are usually pools or water of any kind.[7]

These data reveal the regressive nature of dreaming. First one "soul" leaves the body and goes back to the maternal water. In the dream it is joined by a second soul. After death they are reunited in the totemic lagoon.

The Solomon Islanders say, "You sleep, something goes out of your head, when you wake it comes back." "The men who died before send dreams to you when you sleep." "In dreams we go and stay with the people who are dead." "I think when we dream our *abin* [shadow, reflection in a glass of water] go and stand up with all the men who fought in the old days."[8]

In Florida the soul of a living person is called *tarunga*. The *tarunga* goes out of him in dreams and returns; at death it returns no more. In Motlav the *talegi* leaves the body only in certain dreams such as leave a vivid impression. When a man faints the *talegi* also leaves and sickness is due to soul catching as usual. In Saa, if a child starts in sleep a ghost is snatching its soul and the doctor undertakes to bring it back.[9]

The Fijians believe that the soul leaves the body in sleep, if a person faints or is unwell and finally leaves it at death. A man may be crying out lustily for his own soul to return if he feels unwell.[10]

The Dayaks believe that the soul leaves the body and travels far in the dream. The Tagalas are careful not to wake the sleeper too suddenly lest the soul fail to return.[11]

According to the Muria the soul leaves the body in the dream.

One day two men went to a blacksmith's shop to rest. One fell asleep, the other sat by his side watching. Presently the soul came out of the sleeper's mouth in the shape of a lizard and went to feed. A dog chased the lizard. The other man covered the sleeper's face with coal dust for a joke. The lizard did not recognize the body and went seeking elsewhere. But when he cleaned the face the lizard quickly entered and became the soul again.[12]

According to Chinese belief the sleeper's soul leaves his body. "When

[7] Thompson, *op. cit.*, pp. 427–429.
[8] Blackwood, B., *Both Sides of Buka Passage*, Oxford, 1935, pp. 546–547.
[9] Codrington, R. H., *The Melanesians*, Oxford, 1891, pp. 249, 250.
[10] Williams, T., *Fiji and the Fijians*, London, 1858, X, pp. 241, 242.
[11] Wilken, G. A., *De Verspreide Geschriften*, III, 1912, *Het Animisme bij de Volken van den Indischen Archipel*, pp. 17, 18; Kruijt, Alb. C., *Het Animisme in den Indischen Archipel*, S. Gravenhage, 1906, p. 72.
[12] Elwin, V., *The Muria and their Ghotul*, Bombay, 1947, p. 475.

someone has a dream diviners say that it is a peregrination of his *hwun* and so if he dreams that he appears before the Emperor of Heaven it must be his *hwun* that ascends to heaven."[13] In fact novels have been written about the adventures of the dream soul.[14]

The Hausa in Nigeria believe that when a person sleeps his soul wanders about; also when a person is daydreaming. "If you dream you know when you wake that your soul has been to visit the people and places seen for the soul can travel as quickly as a spirit. Before the soul has returned a person cannot be awakened. However, they also say that if one touches the body the soul returns as quick as thought.[15] Sometimes a person is thirsty during the night but too sleepy to wake up and get a drink. "This shows that the soul is suffering from thirst and is trying to get out of his body to assuage it. On the person going off to sleep soundly the soul will leave the body and will take the shape of a bird and fly to where there is water. You often hear a 'tweet-tweet-tweet' at night and you know that that is a thirsty soul for the birds sleep at night and do not fly about. Sometimes, however, the soul may fly down a well and not be able to get up again or it may be caught by witch or wizard and shut up in the hollow of a tree."[16] The former is obviously the basic dream while the witch or wizard is acting out this dream belief.

According to the Bakongo the spirit (*mwanda*) of the dreamer leaves the body and visits the persons and places seen in the dream. Should they see any one in a dream that person's spirit has also left its body and come to see them. These people they regard as witches or wizards who have come to squeeze the life out of them while asleep. The wizard or witch can also transform itself into some weird form and sitting on the beam of its victim's house it sings and gloats over its sleeping prey.[17] The Nandi say that during sleep the soul leaves the body and a person must not be awakened roughly because the soul might not find its way back.[18] The following riddle is of interest because it shows that they dream of going into a house.

When I arrived at a certain house and found the occupants dead I died myself. What was the death? Sleep.[19] The soul leaves the body and returns through the gap caused by the extraction of the middle incisor teeth of the lower jaw.[20] According to the Azande, bad dreams are actual

13 Groot, I. I. M. de, *The Religious System of China,* Vol. IV, Book II, 1901, p. 111.
14 *Ibid.,* p. 119.
15 Tremearne, A. J. N., *The Ban of the Bori,* 1914, pp. 131, 132.
16 *Ibid.,* pp. 134, 135.
17 Weeks, J. H., *Among the Primitive Bakongo,* London, 1914, pp. 282, 283.
18 Hollis, A. C., *The Nandi,* Oxford, 1909, p. 82.
19 *Ibid.,* p. 144.
20 *Ibid.,* p. 82.

experiences of witchcraft. A nightmare is proof positive that he has been attacked by witches. In sleep, the soul leaves the body and roams about and meets other spirits. A sleeping witch (or wizard) can send the soul of her witchcraft out to eat *the soul of her victim.* "The hours of sleep are hence an appropriate setting for the psychical battle that witchcraft means for the Azande, a struggle between his soul and the soul of witchcraft when both are free to roam about at will while he and the witch are asleep.[21] A member of the Ibo tribe gave the anthropologist the following explanation of his animism.

"Apart from what our fathers have told us, the way in which we believe in the existence of the soul or spirit is mostly through dreams, those which are good and those which are bad, i.e., nightmares. So we think that when a man is asleep whether at night or in the day his soul goes away and speaks sometimes with the dead, sometimes with the living.

"In this way we compare dreams, prophetic visions, death and sleep together, and always in connection with the soul because it seems to us that one and all of them have the same meaning, i.e., that one is related to the other. For in sleep just as in death, the soul leaves the body and seeing as we do in dreams the souls of those who are living and those who are dead makes us believe that this is really the case."[22]

The Lambas in Northern Rhodesia believe that during sleep the spirit leaves the body and wanders about. If a person is awakened, he may say, "Why did you wake me so suddenly instead of letting me finish dreaming where I went."[23] In Cameroon the dream soul leaves the body during sleep and sees strange lands and strange scenes. On returning to the body, it partly forgets what it has seen and what remains are only the vagaries of a dream,[24] probably an autosymbolic representation of the secondary process. The Bafiote say that if somebody has fainted, he is still alive but his soul has left him, it is wandering. It is dangerous to wake a sleeper too suddenly because his soul may be far away. It must have time to return. In the dream the soul flies like a bird, it rows a canoe and maybe it goes to the tree where the placenta is buried[25] (regression).

The Jukun believe that a wizard steals a person's soul at nighttime. The wizard takes a long time to wake up as his soul is out capturing the souls of sleepers. However, people may also be slow to wake up because their souls have been wandering. Some believe that only a portion of the

[21] Evans Pritchard, E. E., *Witchcraft Oracles and Magic among the Azande,* 1937, p. 136.
[22] Leonard, A. G., *The Lower Niger and its Tribe,* 1906, pp. 145, 146.
[23] Doke, C. M., *The Lambas of Northern Rhodesia,* London, 1931, pp. 217, 218.
[24] Nassau, R. H., *Fetichism in West Africa,* London, 1904, p. 55.
[25] Pechuel Loesche, E., *Die Loango Expedition,* Stuttgart, 1907, III, 2, p. 301.

soul acts this way or that there are two souls. The wizard who has captured the soul secrets it in a pot.[26] (Symbol of the womb.) During sleep a man's soul revisits every place he had been during that day. When anyone is slow in waking up that is because his soul is still absent. One who wakes up quickly has his soul with him at the moment he is aroused. During the daytime somebody may be in a dreamy state and awake out of a reverie with a start. His soul was wandering. There are two souls: one that is capable of being reborn and one that stays in Kindo (other world). The *dindi mba* (soul of birth), in the form of locust bean leaves, enters a man's house while he is having sexual intercourse with his wife. From the leaves, the soul jumps into her womb.[27]

Junod remarks that he saw a Thonga boy praying before going to sleep. He prayed that his soul should come back next morning. They consider the human being as a double capable of unsheathing itself in the dream. There are other more dangerous instances of this unsheathing; when a person is sick the wizards have taken his soul. If he recovers from a fit of unconsciousness, the soul has been brought back. At death the final unsheathing takes place.[28] South Africans in general believe that the shadow or spirit leaves the body during sleep. If this were not the case, how could it survive death?[29]

In Liberia when a person dreams, his *zu* goes walking and tells him what is going on. As it goes it keeps looking back in readiness to return if it sees anyone coming to awaken the person it has left. As soon as it comes back the sleeper awakens. No one ever tries to awaken a person suddenly lest his *zu* fail to get back in time. The first thing a person does in the morning is toss colanuts to learn if his dream spirit has gone to some forbidden place during the night, even though he has not dreamed at all.[30]

This often repeated trait of "give the soul time to return" throws some light on the dream derivation of soul concepts (difficult awakening) and on the animistic origin of spirits of gods.

Vogul gods when called by the shaman always protest, "Why did you call so powerfully? I had to come very quickly, I could not finish my tea!" or something similar.[31] The Saulteux summon the soul of a living man, the Voguls summon an animistic god. The Saulteux conjurer says, "I am calling for the man from Lac Seul." Shortly afterward there was a thump

[26] Meek, C. K., *A Sudanese Kingdom*, New York, 1950, pp. 295, 296.

[27] *Ibid.*, pp. 202, 203.

[28] Junod, H. A., *The Life of a South African Tribe*, Neuchatel 1913, II, pp. 340, 341.

[29] Kidd, D., *The Essential Kafir*, London, 1904, p. 83.

[30] Schwab, G., *Tribes of the Nigerian Hinterland*, Cambridge, 1947, p. 322.

[31] Munkácsi, *op. cit.*, II, p. 0351.

indicating the new arrival and then a strange voice saying, "I was sleeping but I heard you calling me" This was the soul of a noted Lac Seul conjurer.[32]

The Karens explain dreams to be what the soul sees and experiences in its journeys when it has left the body asleep. We are apt to dream of people and places which we knew before because the soul can only go to visit the regions where the body has been before.[33] The Kiwai believe that the soul in a dangerous illness sometimes passes out of the body and may go away altogether. The friends of the sick person light a fire at night outside his house and watch the road the spirits are supposed to take. The watchmen chase the soul back into the house and when it re-enters the body the patient will wake up and be safe for a time.[34] The Bukaua believe that the soul leaves the sleeping body and returns at the moment of the awakening.[35] According to the Trobriand Islanders the soul leaves the body when they sleep and the things it sees and experiences are our dreams.[36] In Malekula (Mewun) when a man is asleep his soul (or double) wanders about and visits other people or places. The people in these localities are unaware of the dreamer's presence, for their souls are also wandering about elsewhere and they are therefore incapable of seeing the visitor.[37] In some cases they do not believe that the body of a dreamer is without a soul, although they think that when they speak to someone in their dreams, they are talking to a person's soul. According to the Oroka-iva it is the *asisi* or spiritual double of the dreamer that travels in the dream.[38] Among the Northern Andaman Islanders *ot-jumulo* means "reflection," "shadow," and *ot-jumu* is "a dream" or "to dream." In a dream the sleeper's soul (*ot-jumulo*) leaves the body and wanders about, therefore it is dangerous to waken a sleeper suddenly, it might cause him to be ill. According to the Fox Indians the soul is in the heart from which it comes forth when one is asleep and wanders around. But it remains in its place when one is awake.[39] The Bakairi think the soul travels about in one's dreams and it is dangerous to wake a sleeper suddenly because the wandering soul might not have time to return and sleep would then become death. This hurried return of the soul explains the headache we

32 Hallowell, A. I., "The Role of Conjuring in Soulteux Society," *Publications of the Philadelphia Anthropological Society*, II, 1942, p. 259.

33 Tylor, E. B., *Primitive Culture*, I, 1903, p. 441.

34 Landtman, G., *The Kiwai Papuans of British New Guinea*, 1927, p. 271.

35 Neuhauss, R., *Deutsch Neu Guinea*, III; Lehner, *Bukaua*, p. 425.

36 Seligman, C. G., *The Melanesians of British New Guinea*, 1910, pp. 734, 735.

37 Deacon, A. B., *Malekula*, 1934, p. 562.

38 Williams, F. E., *Orokaiwa Society*, 1930, p. 261.

39 Jones, W., "Notes on the Fox Indians," *Journal of American Folklore*, XXIV, p. 218.

feel sometimes when we wake.[40] The Kobeua also believe that the soul
leaves the body and goes for a walk. But it does not go far. The soul hovers
near the sleeper's head and then it goes back to the head again and so on.
Finally it returns into the body through the mouth; this is awakening.[41]
The Dayaks think that in sleep the soul sometimes remains in the body
and sometimes leaves it and travels far away and that both when in and
out of the body it sees, hears, and talks.[42]

King Gunthram lies down in the forest and goes to sleep in the lap
of his henchman. A snake emerges from Gunthram's mouth and goes
toward a brook. It cannot cross the water. A servant lays his sword across
the brook as a bridge and then disappears in a mountain. After a time it
emerges from the hill and the way it went out it comes back again into
the sleeper's mouth.[43]

We have here both the belief of the soul *leaving* the sleeper's body
in the dream, the phallic symbolism of the serpent and sword, and the
uterine symbolism of the water and the mountain. The sinking into the
body is represented as coming out of the body, but in the dream setting
the soul is phallic, the environment uterine.

According to the Angami Nagas, nightmares are caused by the souls
of sleeping friends.

A man who had bad nightmares went to sleep with his sabre under
his pillow. He tried to kill the nightmare with the sabre but it escaped
in the form of a butterfly and flew into his friend's house. The other man
said next day that he had been horribly frightened at night by dreaming that a man had tried to kill him with a sabre.[44]

The beliefs of the Wind River Shoshone reveal the essential identity of dream image and soul. "*Mugua* lives inside of you, *navujieip* is in
your head, *boha* is nearly the same as *mugua*. *Mugua* lives after death.
Navujieip is a gift to you and returns after your death to God. It is a
kind of a guide. *Navujieip* comes alive when your body rests; it acts as
a guide and comes in any form: as an insect, an animal or a person and
so on. That is the case when I am dreaming. I see me then in my own
shape or like an animal, a snake, even a tree. *I am acting in my navujieip*. Sometimes it mystifies you; you do the most impossible things in
the shape of your *navujieip*. It gives you advice. *Navujieip* is almost the
same as *mugua*. *Mugua* is what keeps you alive. *Boha* is what advises
you, it comes in you *navujieip*.

40 von den Steinen, K., *Unter den Naturvölkern Central Brasiliens*, 1894, p. 340.
(Cf. pp. 435, 510.)
41 Koch-Grunberg, T., *Zwei Jahre unter den Indianern*, 1910, pp. 151, 152.
42 Spenser St. J., *Life in the Forests of the Far East*, 1862, I, p. 189.
43 Grimm, J., *Deutsche Mythologie*, II, 4th ed., Gütersloh, 1875, p. 905.
44 Hutton, J. H., *The Angami Nagas*, London, 1921, pp. 246, 247.

"Mugua is active during the day, *navujieip* at night. When *mugua* is asleep *navujieip* is in a strange place. Only the medicine man's *mugua* can liberate itself in his lifetime and wander about and for example pay visits in the realm of the dead.

"When I slept my soul left my body and I could see the body lying on my bed and I went to the land of the dead."

Navujieip may mean soul or dream. Every human being is born with a dream that he retains through life unless he is robbed of it. One appears in the shape of one's *Navujieip* and still one may regard it as another being, a guardian spirit.[45]

The Ewe have a dreamland in which the soul enters in the dreams. Dreaming is called "seeing the shadows." Many people go back to their homes in the dream.[46]

The Bakairi think that the soul travels about in one's dreams and it is dangerous to wake a sleeper suddenly because the wandering soul may have no time to return.[46a]

The Malay idea of the human soul is that of a kind of "thumbling," a thin, insubstantial human image or mannikin which is temporarily absent from the body in sleep, trance or disease, and permanently absent after death. "The mannikin is usually invisible, but is supposed to be about as big as the thumb. It corresponds exactly in shape, proportion, and even in complexion to its embodiment or casing, i.e., the body in which it has its residence. . . . As the mannikin is in every way the exact reproduction of its bodily counterpart and *is the cause of life and thought in the individual it animates, it may readily be endowed with quasi-human feelings.*"[47]

Like the phallos in dreams the soul also appears in the form of a child. Frazer collected data on "the soul as a mannikin."[48] There are transitions between the soul as a child and the soul as a bird—another frequent form in which the *flying* means the same things as in the dream. In Greek vase paintings the soul is a tiny human figure, winged, naked, but sometimes clothed and armed.[49] We see the soul as a small child carried away by *seirenes*, winged demons of a maternal type.[50] The psyche or soul is a tiny winged figure hovering around the grave.[51] The word

45 Hultkrantz, A., "The Concept of the Soul Held by the Wind River Shoshone," *Ethnos*, XVI, 1951, pp. 30–32.
46 Spieth, J., *Die Ewe Stämme*, Berlin, 1906, p. 564.
46a Steiner, K. von, *Unter den Naturvölkern Zentral-Brasiliens*, Berlin, 1897, p. 295.
47 Skeet, W. W., *Malay Magic*, London, 1900, p. 47.
48 Frazer, J. G., *Taboo and the Perils of the Soul*, London, 1911, p. 26.
49 *Ibid.*, p. 29, f.n.
50 Rohde, E., *Psyche*, Tübingen, 1907, I, p. 244.
51 Kerenyi, K., *Hermes der Seelenführer*, Zürich, 1944, p. 85.

for butterfly is ψνκή and one kind that flies at night is called φαλλαινα, the female form of φαλλος.[52] An amphora of the sixth century B.C. bears the picture of a bearded man bent forward and blowing the flute. The phallos is erect and drops of semen fall on the magnified image of a butterfly.[53]

Pukutiwara, the famous chief of the Pitjentara, related the following dream:

I saw the soul of a man. It came like an eaglehawk. It had wings, but also a penis like a man. With the penis as a hook it pulled my soul out by the hair. My soul hung down from the eagle's penis and we flew first toward the east. It was sunrise and the eaglehawk man made a great fire. In this he roasted my soul. My penis became quite hot and he pulled the skin off. Then he took me out of the fire and brought me into the camp. Many sorcerers were there but they were only bones like the spikes of a porcupine.[54]

Then we went to the west and the eaglehawk man opened me. He took out my lungs and liver and only left my heart. We went further to the west and saw a small child. It was a demon. I saw the child and wanted to throw the *nankara* (magical) stones at it. But my testicles hung down and instead of the stones a man came out of the testicles and his soul stood behind my back. He had very long *kalu katiti* [the skin hanging down on both sides of the subincised penis] with which he killed the demon child. He gave it to me and I ate it.[55]

It is quite evident that we have here the typical erection and flying dream with castration anxiety and the formation of a series of doubles.

Another striking confirmation of our theory of the dream-body as a phallos comes from Northwest-Australia. Some of the tribes near Kimberley believe that in the dream the soul emerges from *the genital organ* as a finely spun thread and sees things that are not revealed in waking life.[56]

Every human being in the Aranda tribe leads a dual existence. He is a *rella ndurpa* or real person and a *rella altjera* or mythological person. The *altjera* is also called *ngantja* (double), or, rather, the distinction between *ngantja* and *altjera* is uncertain.

The mythical ancestors or *altjiranga mitjina* end their lives by be-

---

[52] Weicker, G., *Der Seelenvogel in der alten Literatur und Kunst*, Leipzig, 1902, p. 7.

[53] *Ibid.*, p. 2.

[54] This dream is his initiation dream as a medicine man.

[55] Published in *The Riddle of the Sphinx*, pp. 37, 38. Cf. *infra* the chapter on "Dreamers and Shamans."

[56] Petri, H. E. and Schulz, A. S., "Felsgravierungen aus Nordwest-Australien," *Zeitschrift für Ethnologie*, LXXVI, 1951, p. 88.

coming *tjurunga,* i.e., the stone or wooden sacred objects kept in the totemic caves. This is the myth, but nevertheless actual belief attributes a kind of existence to them *in the caves* or in the other world that is a kind of extension of those caves. When the ancestor throws his *tjurunga* at a woman and the child is incarnated, a third person arises who is neither the ancestor nor the human being. This is the *ngantja,* meaning "the hidden one." Just as the human being grows in its mother's womb, the "hidden one" grows in the mythological womb, i.e., the cave of the totem. On the other hand, the person who appears to the woman in her dream of conception, previously declared to be the *altjirangamitjina,* i.e., the ancestor, is also called the *ngantja.* It is perhaps more correct to say that the "eternal ones of the dream" (*altjirangamitjina*) end their mythological career by becoming *tjurunga* but continue to live as *ngantja.*

According to Aldinga of the Ngatatara tribe, the *ngantja* and the real human being emanate from the *tjurunga.* What does the *ngantja* look like? Just like his human double when the latter is decorated for the ceremony. Songs and new ceremonies are given by this supernatural double who shows these things to a human being in his dreams. As a group they are called *iruntarinia*—the people of the cold. This is because they have no fires of their own in their subterranean abode. They come to the fires of human beings to warm themselves. They are also called *arambaranga,* i.e., "mouth clean," because they have no beard. They are like young people. All their time they spend chasing women, hunting and performing ceremonies.[57]

The Ngantja of the Aranda is the Yalmuru of the Kakadu. When a man dies his spirit part, the Yalmuru, watches over the bones. After a time, however, it divides into two, the original Yalmuru and a second spirit called Iwaiyu. The two are distinct and have somewhat the same relationship to one another as a man and his shadow. For a long time they remain together but when the Yalmuru desires to undergo reincarnation they go forth together, the Iwaiyu in the lead, the Yalmuru behind. The Yalmuru takes the Iwaiyu and puts it in the shape of a small frog into some food that the man is searching for. As soon as he has secured the fish or whatever food it may be, the frog jumps out. It is caught by the Yalmuru and together the two return to their camp. The food in which the Iwaiyu was placed will be the child's totem. At night time the Iwaiyu and the Yalmuru come back to the camp and watch the people. The Iwaiyu is again in the shape of a little frog.

[57] Abstract of data given in Róheim, "Primitive High Gods," *Psychoanalytic Quarterly Supplement,* 1934, pp. 101–104.

When all are asleep the two spirits come up to the camp and enter the hut where the man and his wife are sleeping. The Iwaiyu goes up and smells the man to find out whether it is the right father. Then he does the same with the woman. The Iwaiyu says "these are my mother's breasts." "This is my mother." Finally it comes down from the breasts and goes into the woman. The Yalmuru returns to the old camp. "When it is evident that the woman is going to have a child *the Yalmuru comes up to the camp at night time* and tells the father that the child is there and also tells him about its totem."[58]

When a child is young the Yalmuru watches over it. If it strays away from camp and gets lost in the bush the Yalmuru guides it back and later on, when the child has grown into a man the Yalmuru still helps it. If the Yalmuru is not vigilant some hostile tribe may work evil magic against the individual. When the individual grows old the Yalmuru comes at night and whispers in his ear, "Iwaiyu, you look after a child, my backbone and thighs are no good, my eyes are no good and sore, you look after the totem." The Yalmuru is now worn out and the Iwaiyu that is the spirit within the man must provide for a new child and also take care of the totem. "The Iwaiyu is the new Yalmuru."

Spencer says: "It is really rather like a very crude forerunner of the theory of the continuity of the germ plasm. The old Yalmuru splits, as it were, into two; one half, the Iwaiyu, persists, the other finally disappears. In its turn the former becomes transformed into a Yalmuru which again splits, one half remains and the other perishes, but there is an actual spiritual continuity from generation to generation."[59]

These theories about the fission of the personality taking place at birth might, of course, be interpreted as reverberations of the birth trauma. But I think it is more complicated than that. In real life the dual unity of mother and child evolves slowly, that is, the duality or the perception of the other person develops gradually. In our sleep we tend to restore the intrauterine situation. But in the dream we create a sort of dual unity, a kind of fission, because it is our own body that forms the basis both of the subject and the object; that is, the dreamer moves in a space that is also created out of his own body. In thus being able to re-create the dual unity without another person man has acquired a trait that may lead to a complete break with reality *or* to a self-created world which in the course of time molds and influences reality itself.

The Egyptian Ka and the Roman genius are very similar in structure to the Yalmuru.

[58] Spencer, *Native Tribes of the Northern Territory of Australia*, London, 1914, pp. 270–272.
[59] *Ibid.*, pp. 273–274.

Moret thinks of the *ka* united with the corpse *zet* as a divine being that lives in the sky and manifests itself only after death.

The spells for "spiritualization" prove that while Horus purifies the body in the basin of the Hyena, the *ka* is purified in the basin of the sunrise. To die, in the texts of the Ancient Empire, is "to join one's *ka.*" According to other texts, there is an "essential" or supreme *ka* in the sky. *Ka* is the father who endows with life and also the spirit that protects the king against the fear of death.[60] He also presides over food, he gives life and strength.[61] The body united with the *ka* is like the gods, separated from it, it remains incomplete and subject to destruction. The root *ka* is certainly an expression of the power of generation used with the sign of the phallos. *Ka* when written means bull, a symbol of male potency. In the female form *ka.t* it means cow's vulva, and also cow in the plural, food as the life-giving substance. *Ka* with the hieroglyph of a man who talks means thought, intelligence, etc. In the late period we are told that the king and the gods have fourteen *ka,* such as magic power, physical strength, riches, health, nobility, forethought, sight, etc.[62] Writing about the Archaic period, Loret identifies the *ka* with the god Horus, the falcon as totem of the royal clan incarnated in the person of the king.[63] Loret also gives "to procreate" as the etymology of the word.[64]

Frankfort does not accept the traditional translation of *Ka* as the double. It is rather "vitality" or "vital force."[65] Yet when Frankfort describes the *Ka* of the king it clearly appears as a kind of double or second person.

"In the following text the *Ka* appears with typical features which the twin assumes in folklore: it repeats the actions of the king. . . .

> Wash thyself, and thy Ka washes itself.
> Thy Ka seats itself and eats bread with thee
> Without surcease, throughout eternity.

"The *Ka* also fulfils other functions which the twin sometimes fulfils in folk-tales. For instance, it goes to announce the king to the gods in heaven. . . . At Deir el Bahri there is a series of square pillars showing Queen Hatshepsut in the protective embrace of varying divine couples;

[60] Moret, A., "Le Nil et la Civilisation Egyptienne," *L'Evolution de l'Humanité,* Paris, 1926, p. 212.

[61] *Ibid.,* p. 416.

[62] *Ibid.,* p. 416.

[63] Loret, V., "L'Egypte au Temps du Totemisme," *Annales du Musee Guimet,* XIX, 1906, pp. 179, 180.

[64] Loret, in *Revue Egyptologique,* XI, 1904, p. 87.

[65] Frankfort, H., *Kingship and the Gods,* Chicago, 1948, p. 63.

and one pair consists of the king of the gods, Ammon, and the queen's own *Ka*."⁶⁶

"In the Middle Kingdom tomb at Dahshur a large wooden statue of the king was found bearing the *Ka* sign. More common is a rendering in relief already known in the Old Kingdom. . . . On either side we see the king and behind him a small figure characterized as a divinity by its 'false beard.' This figure bears the *Ka* symbol on its head, and between the arms of the sign appears the king's Horus name, the name which marks the king most directly as a deity. After Tuthomosis I this name regularly contains the epithet 'Strong Bull,' which is clearly appropriate for a personification of vital force."⁶⁷

"The notion 'twin' prevails only in the rendering of the birth scenes of Hatshepsut and Amenhotep III. The god Khnum is shown making two identical *homunculi* on his potter's wheel, while the goddess Hathor, the mother of Horus, appropriately gives them 'life.' One is the future king, the other is his *Ka*."⁶⁸ Further, Ammon commands that not only the queen but also her *Ka* be nursed.⁶⁹ In a pyramid text in which the king's survival is insured by identifying parts of his body with various deities, we find:

"Thy members are the twin children of Atum,
O imperishable one.
Thou dost not perish;
Thy *Ka* does not perish,
Thou art *Ka* [Pyr. 149c, d]."

"Very significant is another pyramid text, a self-contained exuberant poem. . . . . The opening phrases vigorously assert that the old sacred city of Pe is one of those hallowed spots where life throbs more powerfully than elsewhere, a place that stands in a peculiarly intimate rapport with the hidden forces of nature." King Teti, because he is buried at Pe, survives the crisis of death. His vitality (or *Ka*) is compared with two abstract phenomena which are most intensely alive, the burning flame and the beetle god of the rising sun. The text refers to the connection between vital force and food, and ends with an appeal to an anonymous goddess to let the gods love and honor Teti. "It is possible that the term 'love' must be taken here with sexual implications as the culminating expression of vitality which the spell glorifies:

"*Ka's* are in Pe; *Ka's* were always in Pe; *Ka's* will be in Pe, and
Teti's *Ka* is in Pe,
Red like a flame, alive like the beetle-god.

⁶⁶ *Ibid.*, pp. 69, 70.
⁶⁷ *Ibid.*, p. 72.
⁶⁸ *Ibid.*, p. 73.
⁶⁹ *Ibid.*, p. 74.

Be gay! Be gay! A meal for me, ye servants!

Now you should put, My Lady, the love for Teti and the respect
for Teti,
Now you should put, My Lady, the honor of Teti and the
charm of Teti
In the body of the gods! [Pyr. 561–62.]"[70]

In a building at Tahraqua at Karnak, we find, according to Frankfort,
a very unusual form of the *Ka*. Here the *Ka* appears with the hieroglyphs
for "life" and "ithyphallic."[71]

In the teaching of Ptahhotep this meaning of the Ka is also emphasized. When he adjures the listener to treat his son well if he proves worthy,
he says, "He is thy son, whom thy *Ka* has begotten for thee, separate not
thine heart from him."[72]

Jung quotes Preisigke showing that Pharao is regarded as conceived
by the Queen Mother with *Ka-mutef* as the procreating principle. Thus
it became quite easy for the Egyptians of latter days to identify the *Ka* and
the Holy Ghost. In the Coptic *Pistis Sophia* (third century) Jesus appears
with the Holy Ghost as his double, i.e., just like the *Ka*. In Egyptian
dogma, father and son are one, united by the procreating principle of
Ka-mutef, i.e., the *Ka* who is the bull of his mother.[73] But "bull of his
mother" is an attribute of the ithyphallic god Min. The sun god is also his
mother's husband, procreating himself in a series of procreations.[74] Eternity is here symbolized by the unachievable, oedipal wishes eternally ful-
filled. Horus (and all Egyptian gods were Horus-es or falcons) is the god
"who has his phallos," "the bull of his mother," "the avenger of his
father."[75]

The resemblance between the Australian doubles and the Egyptian
Ka is quite striking.

(a) Both are phallic in origin and active in procreation.

(b) Both appear on the scene as doubles.

(c) Both are companions of the individual and at the same time are
denizens of a supernatural world.

(d) The eternally juvenile is a trait both of the *ngantja* and the *Ka*.

[70] *Ibid.*, pp. 75, 76.
[71] *Ibid.*, p. 365.
[72] *Ibid.*, p. 67.
[73] Jung, C. G., *Symbolik des Geistes,* Zürich, 1948, pp. 331, 332, quotes Preisigke,
"Die Gotteskraft der frühchristlichen Zeit," *Papyrus Institut Heidelberg,* Schr. 6 *Pistis
Sophia,* translated by C. Schmidt (Geburtstag im Altertum, 1925) 121, 20 ff, p. 89;
H. Jacobsohn, "Die dogmatische Stellung des Königs bei den alten Aegyptern," *Aegyptische Forschungen A. Scharff,* 8, 1939, p. 17.
[74] Erman, A., *Die Aegyptische Religion,* Berlin, 1909, pp. 17, 18.
[75] Roeder, G., *Urkunden zur Religion des alten Aegypten,* Berlin, 1915, p. 93.

(e) Both also represent sublimation. The *ngantja* in so far as it inspires songs and ritual, the *Ka* as a source of insight.

One trait of the *Ka*, which we do not find in Central Australia, is its solar affinity. Frankfort writes, "There is a dramatic quality in the following pyramid text which reveals that Re is the king's *Ka*. It opens with an emphatic warning of the dangers of the journey into the Beyond. In Egypt as in Babylonia and in many other countries, the Hereafter is separated from the living by an expanse of treacherous water. The king's vital force has left his body and is summoning him. And it is now revealed to him that this vital force was no other than the god who begot him.

> "Messages of thy *Ka* come from thee;
> Messages of thy father come for thee;
> Messages of Re come for thee."[76]

From Egypt to Rome, the genius is similar to the *ngantja* and the *Ka* in so far as in a sense it is identical with the soul and yet different from it.

At birth every human being receives a *genius*—"nec incongrue dicuntur *genii* quia cum unus quisque genitus fuerit ei statim observatores deputantur."[77]

It seems that every human being has both a genius and a soul. It is interesting to note, however, that a woman's genius is a *iuno*, the same as the supreme goddess of the Roman pantheon.[78] The word *genius* is certainly derived from the verb *gignere,* to procreate, i.e., the procreator, but it can also mean he who endows with the power to procreate. Considering these phallic origins, the *genius* naturally appears in the shape of a serpent.

This procreative genius is specifically the protector of *marriage*. The bed of the married couple is *lectus genialis. Nuptiis sternitur in honorem genii.* (Festi epit 94. *Servius ad Aen.* 6. 603.) Lovers invoke his aid. From the genital, the meaning of the word becomes broadened to signify personality as such. It is the *genius* that makes a person industrious or lazy and decides whether life will be happy or unhappy. More specifically, however, the *genius* represents the pleasure principle, the desire and ability to enjoy life. *Genio suo bona facere* means to eat well. Birthdays were festivals of the *genius natalis;* they were celebrated with dances, cakes, wine and incense.[79] *Genium suum defraudare* means to be a miser, not to

---

[76] Frankfort, *op. cit.,* pp. 77, 78.

[77] *Servius ad Aen.* 6. 743. Quoted from *Roscher's Lexikon:* "Genius."

[78] Juno is now generally derived from *iuvenis*. Shields, E. L. "Juno, a Study in early Roman Religion," *Smith College Classical Studies,* No. 7, 1926, p. 9. Cf. the juvenile character of other *doubles* such as the *ka,* the *ngantja*. Norden, E., *Aeneis,* Buch VI, Leipzig, 1916, p. 33.

[79] Schmidt, W., "Geburtstag im Altertum," *Religionsgeschichtliche Vorarbeiten und Versuche,* Leipzig, 1908, p. 23.

enjoy things. *Genium indemnatum habeo*—"I can enjoy life." But the soul, properly speaking, i.e., the souls of the dead, appear under various names as *lemures* or *larvae* or also *genii*. Ovid describing the rites dedicated to the spirits says,

> "Hunc morem Aeneas, pietatis idoneus auctor
> Attulit in terras, iuste Latine, tuas
> Ille patris Genio sollemnia dona ferebat
> Hinc populi ritus edidicere pios."
> (Ovidius, *Fastorum*. Lib. II, 542–546.)

The home was protected by the *lar domesticus* and also by the *penates* —propagation and fertility was the function of the genius. Since the genius is obviously the phallos in snake form, the *genius loci* or localized snake demon must be secondary.[80]

The *ngantja* and the *genius* and the *Ka* are all more or less specialized representatives of the general soul concept. In a book published in 1930, I came to the conclusion that belief in the soul really represented the pleasure ego with the personified penis as the nucleus of the concept.[81]

The difference between what I had to say then and what I have to say now is this: *sleep is the prototype of death, it is uterine regression, and the phallic double or eroticized body image originates in the dream as a defense.*

This is Hermes. Among the many forms in which he appears the youthful image predominates. Characteristic attributes of the god are his shoes (which give him the ability to fly), his staff, which is that of a herald, of a shepherd, and finally a serpent staff.[82]

Hermes is both the psychopompos who leads the ghosts on their journey to the other world and the god of sleep and dreams. In the Odyssey he leads the batlike souls of the suitors killed by Odysseus to the other world.[83] The staff of Hermes has the power to put people to sleep and to awaken them. Again in the Odyssey, the Phaeacians pour out the last libation to Hermes as the god of sleep. Furthermore, representations of Hypnos and Hermes show a marked similarity.[84] Apollodoros relates that images of the god were fixed to the beds so as to ensure quiet sleep and good dreams. Adjectives like ἡγήτωο ὀνείρων or in Latin, *somniorum*

---

[80] Cf. besides the articles in *Roscher's Lexikon*, Róheim, *Animism, Magic and the Divine King*, London, 1930, pp. 17, 18.

[81] *Animism, Magic and the Divine King*, p. 104.

[82] *Roscher's Lexikon*, "Hermes," pp. 2403–2437. "Hermes as Agathos Daimon was once merely a phallos, that he was also once merely a snake is, I think, a safe conjecture." Harrison, J. E., *Themis*, Cambridge, 1927, p. 297.

[83] Roscher, W. H., *Hermes der Windgott*, Leipzig, 1878, p. 66.

[84] *Ibid.*, pp. 69, 70, 71. Cf. also Eisler, I., "Beiträge zur Traumdeutung," *Internationale Zeitschrift für ärztliche Psychoanalyse*, V, 1919, p. 295.

dator or *comes,* indicate that Hermes leads both the soul's sleep and dreams.[85]

What is the origin of this god? Roscher writes: *"The oldest form in which the god was represented was the phallos."* In Kyllene Pausanias says there is a temple dedicated to Asklepios, one to Aphrodite. Hermes is also one of their gods. They represent him as an erect phallos.[86] The stone piles or pillars called ἑρμαι are a second form in which the god appears. Finally, we have wooden or stone pillars with a phallos added to them— the ithyphallic Hermes.[87] Eros appears as a herm "very near akin to the rude Pelasgian Hermes himself, own brother to the Priapos of the Hellespont and Asia Minor."[88]

The phallic god is also animistic. Etruscan grave stones are phallic.[89] Kerényi interprets Hermes as the equivalent of Eros or the "male origin of life." The phallic milestone is a stabilized representation of the male principle and Kerényi regards both cult and image as originating in the mysteries of Samothrake. The square-shaped pillar is originally a gravestone. (See footnote above.)

Then what is Hermes? *He himself is a flying dream with his phallic form, his magic rod, his serpent staff and flying shoes.*[90]

Hermes is the god of movement, of transition of the passage in ‚and out.[91] When he conducts Priamos through the hostile Greek camp (*Ilias* 24, 343), the doorkeeper falls asleep. He himself is the "god of the door" (προπυλαιος) but also the "coachman" ('Αρμαιεν̄ς). Otto regards him as the god of the night. I would add, "of seeing at night" (νυκτὸς ὀπωπητήρ) or "the good seer" (εὔσκοπος). The god of the dream is also the god of the *primal scene.* Indeed, he himself recounts how his father Zeus *while Hera was asleep* left the assembly of Olympic gods and found the nymph Maia, and they were united, hidden from the gods and mortals in a cave.[92] Another more complicated reference to the primal scene is contained in the myth of Argos Panoptes. Hera asks Argos to guard Io, to prevent the amorous advances of Zeus. Argo Panoptes has many eyes some of which he closes alternately and thus is both asleep and awake at the same time. Io has been changed into a cow and Zeus the bull god is enamoured

85 *Ibid.,* pp. 70, 71. Cf. Siecke, E., *Hermes der Mondgott,* Leipzig, 1908, p. 3.

86 *Pausanias,* 6, 26, 5.

87 *Roscher's Lexikon,* "Hermes," p. 2393.

88 Harrison, J. E., *Prologemena to the Study of Greek Religion,* Cambridge, 1908, p. 630.

89 Kerényi, K., *Hermes der Seelenführer,* Zürich, 1944, p. 83.

90 On the intrinsic relationship "soul" and "flying" cf. Holland, R., "Zur Typik der Himmelfahrt," *Archiv für Religionswissenschaft,* XXIII, 1925, pp. 207–220.

91 Otto, W. F., *Die Götter Griechenlands,* Bonn, 1929, pp. 145, 146.

92 Kerényi, *op. cit.,* p. 27.

of her. Hermes as the messenger of Zeus lulls Argos to sleep with his rod or kills and blinds him with the sickle.[93] We must assume that Argos is another Zeus, his many eyes the stars of heaven. He liberates Arkadia from a devastating bull and then dons the hide of the bull himself. As a bull he is the guardian of the cow, but only in the *conscious dream content*. This would be a reversal of the latent dream content: as a bull Argos (Zeus) is cohabiting with the cow (Hera and Io). The all-seeing eye is again displaced; it is the child or sleeper who sees the primal scene which interrupts his sleep—i.e., the lulling to sleep motive is again displaced from the son to the father, from the sleeper to the vision of the primal scene. And the blinding? It is really the punishment of Oedipus again, but reflected in a dream.

And what is the first adventure of this god?[94] The very day of his birth he stole the cattle of his brother Apollo. "As he crossed the threshold of the cave on Mount Cyllene in Arcadia where his mother lived, he found a tortoise. Realizing at once the use to which he could put this find, he fashioned it into a lyre, thus becoming the inventor of the tortoise-shell lyre. After accompanying himself on his new instrument in a song about the love of Zeus and Maia—by which he was begotten—he left the lyre in his cradle and, feeling hungry, proceeded on his way after the cattle of Apollo." He then stole the cattle and warned the one man who *saw him* doing it not to tell on him. Upon reaching the ford across the Alpheus, he foddered the cattle and *put them away in a cave*. At the same time when he put the cattle into the cave he crawled back into his cradle through a keyhole and nestled down into the cradle.[95]

I think we have here the dream of an infant whose sleep is threatened by hunger and in his dream he gets back into the womb—represented as a cave for the cattle and as a cradle for the baby. Another disturber of sleep intervenes: the primal scene which, however, is transformed into a lullaby or the song of the lyre.[96]

Cave worship is regularly associated with him.[97] Originally, it was not because he was a pastoral god but a dream god. He is one of the Chtonians, that is to say, a soul himself, and also the phallic god. "His name φάλης at Kyllene was derived from the φαλλος."[98] As καταιβαῖς "the Descender" he would be very familiar to us from what we have called the "basic

[93] *Roscher's Lexikon:* "Argos."

[94] Cf. Radermacher, L., *Der homerische Hermeshymnus*, Vienna, 1933, and Allen, T. W., Halliday, W. R., and Sikes, E. E., *The Homeric Hymns*, Oxford, 1936, both quoted by Brown, N. O., *Hermes the Thief*, Madison, 1937, Chapter V.

[95] Brown, O. Norman, *Hermes the Thief*, Wisconsin, 1947, pp. 66, 67.

[96] Cf. *infra* the chapter "The Song of the Sirens and the Isles of the Blessed."

[97] Farnell, L. R., *The Cults of the Greek States*, V, Oxford, 1909, p. 10.

[98] *Ibid.*, p. 11.

dream."[99] Even more significant is his connection with doors—the god who stands by the gate of the house, guarding the entrance and the exit.[100] And the door in classical literature symbolizes the vagina.[101]

Hermes is also something of a culture hero.

> "Mercuri facunde nepos Atlantis
> qui feros cultus hominum recentum
> voce formasti catus et decorae, more palestrae
> Te canam, magni Jovis et deorum nuntium. . . ."[102]

"The phallus is so closely identified with magic in Roman religion that the word *fascinum,* meaning 'enchantment,' 'witchcraft' (cf. fascinate), is one of the standard Latin terms for the phallus, no better evidence for the appropriateness of the emblem for Hermes as magician. When Greek craftsmen hung images of ithyphallic demons over their workshops, it is clear that to them the phallus symbolized not fertility but magic skill at craftsmanship."[103]

When the dream re-creates the world out of the dreamer's body on a libidinal basis, this is magic. And the trickery? Is it not implicit in all dreams by their hidden meaning? But why the words, why the whispering?

What is whispered is a charm, especially a love charm. "One epithet, 'the whisperer,' which was shared by Hermes, Aphrodite, and Eros, underlines the connection between Hermes, the master of love magic, and Hermes, the master of magic words. The epithet implies that a special virtue is attached to *whispered* words. In Theocritus' second *Idyll* a woman chants a spell to bring back her lover, it is expressly stated that the magic words are 'crooned softly.' "[104] Persuasion, whispering, magic and love all go together. And therefore also the great *culture hero Eros* (Hermes is actually the father of Eros).

And what about the athlete, the *palaestra?* Is it because he is the *ephebos,* youth personified? Or is it because in the dream, especially in the flying dream—just as in athletics—the body is eroticized?

[99] *Ibid.,* p. 15.
[100] *Ibid.,* p. 19.
[101] Haight, E. H., *The Symbolism of the House Door in Classical Poetry,* New York, 1950, p. 40.
[102] Horace, *Carminum,* I:10.
[103] Brown, *op. cit.,* pp. 35, 36.
[104] *Ibid.,* pp. 14, 15.

III

DREAMERS AND SHAMANS

In dreams, as we saw before, the soul is supposed to wander about and to re-enter the body only when a person awakes. A frequent theory of sickness is that it is caused by the temporary absence of the soul. The link would be that sickness and sleep are both connected with death as forerunners or symbolic equivalents.

Among the Kiwai, the souls of sick people are in danger of being abducted by malevolent spirits or otherwise leaving the body. *A sick person is not allowed to sleep too much* for he might never wake, and for that reason they rouse him at short intervals.

The soul of a man in dangerous illness sometimes passes out of the body and may even go away forever. At night his friends light a fire outside of his house and watch the road which the spirits are supposed to take. Sometimes they see how the soul of a man is met by the spirit of his dead father who drives it back, saying, "The time has not come yet." When the soul re-enters the body the patient is awake and safe for the time being. But sometimes the dead father *wants* his son and comes to fetch him. Medicine men may bring these souls back, but if they fail to "catch" the soul, the man dies. Little children especially must be protected against departed relatives, particularly the grandparents who will come at night and carry away the babies' souls[1]—i.e., little children often have anxiety dreams.

Some men can send out their own souls to catch the departing soul of somebody dying. In this case, they swallow the juice of a certain plant which makes them unconscious and then their soul takes the form of a bird and flies after the departed soul.[2] The spirit of a person killed by a crocodile comes out of the water at night in search of some soul of the opposite sex and they have intercourse.[3]

In Mota (Banks Islands), the soul may have been captured by a ghost. In that case, the medicine man undertakes to bring it back. He makes a potion of leaves and drinks it before he goes to sleep. In his sleep

[1] Landtman, G., *The Kiwai Papuans of British New Guinea*, London, 1927, pp. 270, 271.
[2] *Ibid.*, p. 272.
[3] *Ibid.*, p. 274.

he dreams, which indicates that his soul has left his body to go in search of the ghost. Sometimes he is successful, sometimes he announces that he has failed when he awakes the next morning. "If he succeeds, the soul is brought back to the village and returned to the sick person. While the medicine man is asleep, no one must disturb him, for even if his soul has succeeded in bringing the soul of the sick man back as far as the village, the awakening of the medicine man would make his soul relax its grasp on the soul of the sick person and the latter might slip away."[4]

This sounds like the familiar experience of the dream slipping away at the moment of awakening.

The fundamental mechanism of the dream is the formation of a double, the dream image or the soul.

A dream recorded in Alor is one step advanced from this double formation—the double is duplicated.

"My familiar spirit and my soul went single file to Lemia which is the dwelling place of an evil spirit. My familiar took his sword and killed the evil spirit. Then its soul followed up. My familiar has good eyes and legs; he ran. Thereupon my soul hid under a rock. It took a thorny weed and covered up the entrance. I was very much afraid."

It should be noted that the man is really blind in one eye and crippled.[5] Therefore, the soul, the likeness of the body, is the same. But a duplicate is formed, an idealized version of the individual. It tries to eliminate anxiety, although in this case it does not succeed. *The medicine man now plays the role of this double or soul or second double.*

Shirokogoroff describes various forms of sleep disturbances among the Tungus. The general theory is that during sleep the soul is absent. However, it is usually assumed that during sleep only one of the components of the soul is absent because the absence of the total soul would be dangerous. On the other hand spirits may enter the body during sleep. There are three cases: (1) the soul is absent and travels elsewhere; (2) the soul is absent and the spirit enters the body; (3) the soul is present, but is overpowered by spirits.

"In all these cases there would be the phenomenon of speaking, singing, even moving in the state of sleep.

"Among the Tungus one can frequently observe these cases. About the same ages and sexes are affected as in the case of possession by the spirits.

"The subject affected by this condition may sing during the sleep or speak for himself or on behalf of the spirit. The Tungus sometimes

[4] Rivers, W. H. R., *The History of Melanesian Society,* Cambridge, 1914, I, pp. 165, 166.

[5] Du Bois, C., *The People of Alor,* Minneapolis, 1944, p. 284.

speak foreign languages, i.e., Buriat, Russian, Manchu, Chinese. In some cases they speak these languages only in the sleeping state, while they cannot speak them when awake. This constitutes one of the great puzzles for the Tungus who have only one possible explanation, namely the spirits are speaking."

Shirokogoroff remarks: "This phenomenon is very interesting and thus I have used all possible occasions for observing it in sleeping persons and *especially in shamans during the performance which as will be shown is not very far in nature from the condition here discussed.*"[6] [My italics.]

"The occurrence of speaking and in general of expressing oneself in sleep. There are three cases: (1) the soul is absent and travels elsewhere; disapproved, and when the subject knows that such an act is impossible as well as in the cases *when the subject is too shy for figuring, half consciously, as possessed by the spirit.*"[7] [My italics.]

Tungus, Manchu and other groups have a pluralistic soul theory. The Birarcea have a "reproductive soul" (*omi*) and a "life soul" (*erga*). It is the absence of the *omi* that causes fear.[8] The soul may be temporarily absent without causing death, for instance in loss of consciousness or dreams.[9]

It is significant that in his *ecstasy* the shaman is supposed to be *asleep.* Shirokogoroff describes one performance among the Manchus as follows: "The shamanizing began after eight o'clock in the evening. The shaman put on his full dress. As usual he was supposed to bring himself into ecstasy. The assistants as well as other people repeated the refrains. The spirit entered the shaman, he trembled, his forehead was covered with perspiration. The shaman then fell asleep. This is a somewhat theoretical sleep since the people continued to chat while the shaman was allegedly asleep."[10]

The dream is a journey of the soul and the main activity of the shaman consists in a journey to the Upper or the Lower World.

But in the case of many Siberian groups the matter is complicated by the sacrifice. Whereas in the original form it must have been the shaman's soul or the shaman himself chasing the soul of the sick person, a new motive is introduced if the aim of the journey is to carry the soul of the sacrificial animal to the gods or spirits who are thus placated.

The journey to the nether-world involves the sacrifice of a reindeer.

6 Shirokogoroff, S. M., *Psychomental Complex of the Tungus,* London, 1935, p. 256.
7 *Ibid.,* p. 257.
8 *Ibid.,* p. 53.
9 *Ibid.,* pp. 134, 135.
10 *Ibid.,* p. 313.

A receptacle for the shaman's guardian spirit is put on the back of the reindeer before it is sacrificed. The reindeer is led round the hut four times and each time it must step over a log. (We omit other details of the sacrifice.)

The shaman must send out his soul and take the immaterial substance of the sacrifice to the lower world. In this journey he has help from various manifestations of his spirits, bears, fishes, boars, anthropomorphic spirits, etc. On his way he meets with various difficulties on the road such as the attacks of other unmastered spirits, sometimes those sent by other shamans. His guardian spirit is carrying the intestines and the blood of the sacrificed animal and is helping the shaman.[11]

The shaman sits drumming and singing. He rises, hands the drum to the assistant and takes up the reindeer staffs. He takes a big cup of vodka, several pipes of tobacco and finally sings and jumps himself into an ecstasy. When this happens he falls down[12] on the raft and remains without moving. (Compare the "falling" sensation in falling asleep.) Now the drumming is slow and the singing stops. If the shaman remains motionless for too long a time he is sprinkled with blood three times (i.e., they suspect he is dead). If there is no effect he is recalled by singing. Then he begins to reply in a weak voice to questions asked by the people around him. Now he rises. This evolution is repeated four times in the same order. The falling down on the raft means that *the shaman* (*naturally his soul*) takes a rest. When the shamanizing is over the clansmen walk from west to east around the fire place (the shaman's journey was toward the west). Everyone hands a portion of the intestines to the shaman who hangs them on the figure that represents his guardian spirit. When the clansmen pass in front of the shaman he lies down and they step over his body. Finally the shaman throws himself down on the reindeer skin and for a long time remains motionless.

Light drumming and singing continues. Then the people begin to call back the shaman. If he does not reply they sprinkle blood on him and direct sparks of fire produced by flint and steel at him. If there is no effect the people become very nervous for the shaman may stay in the lower world, i.e., he may die.

When the shaman's consciousness returns the people lift him up. The people express their joy that he has returned from the lower world.[13]

Other forms of this journey can take place without an elaborate

---

[11] The Buryat put the fell of an ermine on a birch to carry the soul of the sacrificed horse to the sky. Sandschejew, G., "Weltanschauung und Schamanismus der Alaren Burjaten," *Anthropos*, XXIII, 1928, p. 546.

[12] The soul of a sleeper if suddenly frightened "falls down," Shirokogoroff, *op. cit.*, p. 208.

[13] *Ibid.*, pp. 304–306.

ceremony. The soul is captured, the shaman goes to the lower world to fetch it. A sacrifice is made to the guardian spirit. He goes through a mountain range in a northwestern direction where he may have to fight the spirits of other shamans. On his *way he has to go through a small hole near which the spirits and other shamans may capture his soul.* For protection he covers himself with the magic mirror or drum to avoid the arrows shot by the spirits. On his arrival in the lower world the shaman has to cross three rivers. When he enters the world of darkness his assistants strike a spark to light his way "like lightning." He finds the soul and after negotiations or a fight he brings it back.[14] Among the paraphernalia used for the ascent of the shaman to the upper world two are of importance. The "nine birch trees" for which larch may be substituted and the wooden ducks. The former evidently symbolize the world tree or the ascent of the shaman and the ducks are there to help him fly to the sky.

The paraphernalia are in multiples of nine. The sacrificial animal may be a sheep or a white horse.[15]

The journey to the other world is frequently connected with a fight that may take place at the frontiers of the nether-world. Fighting is, in general, one of the characteristic features of Siberian shamanism.

Among the Reindeer Tungus of Manchuria the shamans were continuously fighting among themselves and with the Kumarcen shamans. The fighting shamans are especially dangerous to other shamans whose souls they catch on their way back from the lower world. When the shamans are fighting they establish a system of spies—various animals— to look after the enemy shaman who cannot guess into which animal the other shaman enters. The most inoffensive bird or insect may be used by a shaman.

"The battles in a form of competition in art and murder usually take place at night—*in dreams*—but battles and murder may also occur in a wakening state.

"One night the shaman was hunting on the salt-marsh sitting there he saw a glittering fire. He pulled out his knife. The fire descended lower. Then he went home and said: 'Sanguni has come!' [Name of another shaman.] 'Keep quiet and let me fall asleep.' Then he fell asleep *and became a shaman.* While he was sleeping he followed Sanguni and reached his hut. Sanguni was sitting at the entrance. He scolded him: 'You see, I nearly caught you when you were asleep. You are a bad man. Why did you come in the form of fire.' "[16]

14 *Ibid.*, pp. 306, 307.
15 *Ibid.*, pp. 310, 311.
16 *Ibid.*, pp. 371, 372.

These data given by Shirokogoroff in his monograph on the Tungus are most significant. They confirm the hypothesis that the shamanistic trance is an imitation of the going to sleep and dreaming sequence. In the trance the shaman is allegedly asleep. Shirokogoroff's observation about the tendency of the Tungus to half-sleep or half-dreamy states in which they sing or talk or walk while yet asleep supplies the link between the dream proper and the shamanistic performance. Some people are too shy and stay at this stage, others go one step further and become real shamans. The belief that dreams are due to the wanderings of the soul is practically universal; the disease theory adds one other trait to this, disease is caused by the abduction of the soul. Wherever the soul is the shaman must go after it. That is, he repeats the soul journey. Since the journey is an ascent to the sky or a descent to the lower world, we see that the dream in question is the flying dream or rather our *basic dream*. Why the basic dream? It is the narrow entrance to the lower world which looks like the entrance to the uterus. The observation made by Eliade that the journey of the shaman is a journey to the center of the world, the *mandala*, and that the tree he uses for ascent is the world tree, is correct.[17] The world tree is connected with the idea of a milk-lake or milk-giving goddess. In their flight to the sky god, the shamans of the Altay reach the milk-white sea from which all life originates and human beings are born.[18]

The ancestor of the Yakuts is called "The Lonely Man." He lives in the center of a plain in a palace with four silver-gleaming corners, forty windows, seven storeys, etc. When he comes out of his house he sees the tree of life. Its roots reach down to Hades, its crown pierces the seven heavens. From under its roots foams "eternal water." Cattle and game drink or lick the sap which drips from the trees' branches and their youth and strength are restored. The spirit of the tree is a white-haired aged goddess with breasts as large as leather bags. When she leaves the tree it grows smaller, when she re-enters it it regains its former size.[19] This milk-breasted goddess of the tree is actually the mother of the First Man.[20] The milk-lake itself is personified by the Altai Tatars as Milk-Lake Mother.[21] The tree is also identical with the world pillar[22] and in a sense also with the

---

[17] Eliade, M., "Psychologie et Histoire des Religions," *Eranos*, XIX, 1951, pp. 270, 271; *Idem, Le Chamanisme et les Techniques Archaiques de l'Extase*, Paris, 1951, p. 237; cf. Holmberg, U., "Der Baum des Lebens," *Acta Soc. Scient. Fenn.*, XV, 1922/1923.

[18] Radloff, W., *Aus Sibirien*, Leipzig, 1893, II, pp. 11, 23, 24.

[19] Holmberg, *Mythology of all Races*, IV, pp. 353, 354. Middendorff, A. T., *Reise in den äussersten Norden und Osten Sibiriens*, III, 1 and IV, 2, Petersburg, 1851, 1875. (III, p. 79.)

[20] Middendorff, *op. cit.*, III, pp. 1, 87 (Holmberg, p. 359).

[21] Holmberg, *loc. cit.*, p. 413.

[22] *Ibid.*, p. 333.

shaman's drum because in his trance caused by beating the drum he climbs the world tree.[23] The images on the drum reveal another symbolic equation,[24] the drum is the universe. But these uterine symbols are also phallic symbols because they symbolize or bring about ecstasies, the phallic flying of the soul.

As for the tree or pillar we note that "Sources of the eighteenth century speak of a pillar or beam which the Lapps used to put on the place where the 'man of the universe' or 'ruler of the universe,' was worshiped. This pillar was called 'support of the universe,' and its function was to prevent the vault of the heaven from falling down. It seems that this column was a representation of the axis around which the world moves. Now vaerelden olmai [Lappish for the "man of the universe"] *in whose honor the genitalia of reindeer bucks were sacrificed* [my italics] and the 'support of the universe' was smeared with blood, seems to be identical with the Scandinavian fertility god, Frey, whom the Old Norsemen called *'veraldar* god,' the god of the universe."[25] But Frey himself is originally represented in the form of the phallos.[26] Then again the drum itself or the drumstick is identified with the animals on which the shaman flies to the land of the hereafter.[27] The horse or bird usually carries the shaman to the other world but he may also invoke his own phallos.[28]

The ecstasy is phallic, the goal uterine (*mandala*). Naturally so, since the whole is patterned on the dream. We have quoted a case above from Shirokogoroff where the text says that *the shaman becomes a shaman,* i.e., he dreams. In a Samoyed story the shaman cannot sleep because his guardian spirits have hidden his "heaven-tree" (i.e., his drum).[29]

The meaning of the trance, and of the shaman's performance in general, is now quite clear, it is a flying dream and flying is erection. The Teleut shaman in his sky flight sings:

> I have a white cap
> I have a collar with shiny buttons,
> My staff is like a horse's penis

[23] Emsheimer, E., "Schamanentrommel und Trommelbaum," *Ethnos* IV, 1946, pp. 166–181.

[24] Radloff, *op. cit.,* II, p. 18.

[25] Collinder, B., *The Lapps,* New York, 1949, p. 170. On the Thor-cult of the Lapps cf. Scheffer, J., *History of Lapland,* Oxford, 1674, p. 42.

[26] Meyer, R. M., *Altgermanische Religionsgeschichte.* Leipzig, 1910, p. 198.

[27] Priklonski, W. J., "Über das Schamanentum bei den Jakuten," in Bastian, A., *Allerlei aus Volks- und Menschenkunde,* Berlin, 1884. Krauss, F. S., "Das Schamanentum bei den Jakuten," *Mitteilungen der anthropologischen Geselschaft in Wien,* XVIII, 1888, p. 172.

[28] Ohlmarks, A., *Studien zum Problem des Schamanismus,* Lund, 1939, p. 175.

[29] Castrén, M. A. and Lehtisalo, T., "Samojedische Volksdichtung," *Mem. Soc. Finno Ou.* LXXXIII, 1940, pp. 304, 350.

When I descend from Ak Ulhan
I descend slowly like white cloth
I descend slowly like blue cloth.
Crossing the river Kemak I came
Impregnating the women of Kemak
Like a bird with blue legs
I have a penis that goes around
The young ones asked for it
But I won't give them the penis
Like a bird with red feet
I have a trembling penis
The girls asked for it
But I won't give them the penis
I came over the Abakhan and the Ssahaj
Impregnating the girls of Abakhan
The young girls have a vulva like a thimble
The old women have a vulva like the opening of a sack.

There is a birch in the tent with rungs fixed on it. While he is singing he mounts and descends this "ladder." He gesticulates wildly and hits the drum with the drumstick. He touches each of the male onlookers with his drum giving them added masculinity. Before he starts the shaman performance or flying he sacrifices a horse. He then appears with a mask and with a large wooden phallos between his legs, and he calls upon the "holy clan," that is, the mask to stick it in and cause "itching" (i.e., sexual desire). He says he has a hairy phallos which he compares to the neck of a horse while the mask itself is called *white stallion.* Wooden testicles are attached to the wooden phallos. Somebody knocks these and this puts the shaman into a trance, it makes him run and jump about.[30]

This description confirms not only the sexual interpretation of the flying shaman but shows a close connection between the sacrificed animal and the shaman.

Flying or climbing a tree; without these the essence of Siberian shamanism would be missing. Bird and tree go together. The Finnish shamans are sons of Ukko Aija (heaven god) and Ajy is the Yakut word for eagle. The birch is the tree on which the eagle descends and is therefore not chopped down by Väi-nä-möinen.[31] The Yakut shamans have trees with rungs for their performances. On these rungs they ascend to the sky. On the top of the tree there is a two-headed eagle as lord of all birds.[32] Among the Buryat the eagle is the prototype of shamans among the

30 Zelenin, D., "Ein erotischer Ritus in den Opferungen altaischer Türken," *Internationales Archiv für Ethnographie,* XXIX, 1928, pp. 88, 91.

31 Sternberg, L., "Der Adlerkult bei den Völkern Sibiriens," *Archiv für Religionswissenschaft,* XXVIII, 1930, pp. 133, 134.

32 *Ibid.,* p. 130.

Yenissei Ostyak the two-headed eagle is the first shaman.[33] The Gilyaks
use the same word for eagle and shaman and the Teleut call the eagle the
shaman bird because it helps them to fly into the sky.[34]

According to the Golds there is one world tree in heaven with duck-
lings surrounding it. These are the souls of unborn infants. On earth
there is the birch and this is where the shaman gets his paraphernalia.[35]
In some of the narratives about shamans the female character of the world
tree is clearly emphasized.[36] But the Tungus shaman's soul ascends on a
tree called *tuura* = *to stand* "and as he climbs the tree the *tree grows of
itself*."[37] The phallic and maternal symbolism of the tree explain all the
anxiety images connected with the activity of the shaman.

In the ritual as described by Shirokogoroff we can note the following
parallel traits (a) the reindeer steps over a log four times, (b) the clansmen step over the shaman's body.

When the shaman throws himself on the reindeer skin and stays
motionless, he is evidently identifying with the dead reindeer.

We have seen that the shaman passes through a hole to the other
world.

"At last the shaman jumps off the reindeer skin, cuts off two legs and
throws them with the *sêva*[38] in a northwestward direction making a hole
in the wigwam cover" (p. 306). If we remember that the seva is the supernatural representative of the shaman, that the shaman's journey is in a
northwestward direction, and that he passes through a hole, the symbolic
identity of the sacrificed reindeer and the shaman become obvious. Moreover the shaman goes to the lower world in a reindeer costume (to the
upper world in a duck costume).[39] Then what is the function of this parallelism? It is explained by our remarks about the basic dream. If sleep is
equated with death, going to sleep and dreaming have two aspects; it is
both death and coitus. The reindeer dies in reality, the shaman mimics
death and is revived.

The Chukchee have the theory of soul abduction as the cause of disease.[40]

"The shaman's search for the soul was formerly effected in a shaman-

[33] *Ibid.*, pp. 142, 143.
[34] *Ibid.*, p. 144.
[35] *Ibid.*, p. 146.
[36] Lehtisalo, "Tod und Wiedergeburt," *Journal de la Societe Finno Ougrienne,*
XLVIII, 1937, p. 30.
[37] *Ibid.*, p. 32.
[38] The figure that represents the shaman's guardian spirit.
[39] Shirokogoroff, *op. cit.*, pp. 288, 289.
[40] Bogoras, W., "The Chukchee," *Jesup North Pacific Expedition,* VII, Religion,
1907, p. II, 333.

istic trance which nowadays is replaced by the usual sleep over night *since dreams are considered by the Chukchee one of the best means of communicating with spirits* [My italics]. When the search is successful the shaman returns bringing the soul."[41] The restored soul is called "little fellow."[42] The spirits start communicating with the future shaman in dreams. Hysterical phenomena follow in the case of the really great shamans, who are supposed to sweat blood.

"The preparatory period is compared by the Chukchee to a long severe illness and the acquirement of inspiration to a recovery. With weaker shamans and with women the preparatory period is less painful and the call to inspiration comes mainly in dreams."[43] A famous shaman who was also the grandson of a great shaman heard a voice when he was quite a young lad. "Go into the wilderness, there you will find a tiny drum." He found the drum and started beating it. Then he saw all the world. After that he ascended to the sky and pitched his tent on the ground of the clouds.[44] This dream ascent into the sky is the beginning of his career as a shaman. The drum is called a canoe and in ecstasy "he sinks" meaning that in this state the shaman visits the underworld.[45]

In folk tales the shaman sinks into the other world to find one of the missing souls of the patient. In important cases, especially with a rich patient, the shamans will at least pretend to have sunk into unconsciousness.

It began in the dark, but when he suddenly stopped beating the drum, the lamp was again lighted, and the face of the shaman immediately was covered with a piece of cloth. He lay under the cloth and then suddenly awoke, took the drum from his wife and started to beat it.[46]

Possession by the spirits is more important here than the sending out of the soul. The shaman's trance is produced by consuming the fly-agaric. The spirits of this mushroom are very strong and when growing up they lift upon their soft heads the heavy trunks of trees and split them in two (this is probably a description of the shaman's sensations when under the influence of the fly-agaric). *Mushrooms appear to be intoxicated men* in strange forms, somewhat related to their real shapes. One of them has one hand and one foot, another a shapeless body. *The number of them seen depends on the number of mushrooms consumed.* The mushroom people grasp the shaman under his arm showing him the entire world and also things unreal. They follow intricate paths and delight in visiting the places where the dead live. Excrement appears as a boastful old man in a garment of sleek brown fur.[47] The "ground spirits" who in dreams and

41 *Ibid.*, p. 463.
43 *Ibid.*, p. 421.
45 *Ibid.*, p. 432.
42 *Ibid.*, p. 465.
44 *Ibid.*, p. 426.
46 Bogoras, *op. cit.*, p. 441.
47 *Ibid.*, pp. 282, 283.

visions appear as a group of black beings[48] are probably derived from these excrement spirits.

"The chief of the beings of the sea is called Keretkun. He feeds on the bodies of drowned men but he gives very efficient help against other spirits. In the incantation his house is called a 'shield against *kelet*' (spirits). Its door is a mouth. Every kelet who dares to *enter is eaten up and later thrown out as excrement. He then becomes an excrement spirit.*"[49] [My italics.]

Most of the means of defense against spirits are connected with waking. This does not apply to the spoon which derives its efficacy from its use in the blood sacrifice. But it does apply to the snow beater because it rattles all the time. Considering what we know about urethral awakening dreams the following passage is significant:[50]

"The spirits fear the chamber vessel, most of all human urine poured over a spirit's head will immediately drive him back. Urine freezes on a 'spirit's' clothes and turns to ice or frost. Therefore a spirit is sometimes said to have ice-covered clothes. The oil dripping from a lamp also wards off the spirits."[51]

Lamps and noise mean awakening like urine. We have commented above on the "obstacle flight" or magic flight motive. One thing that characterizes this motive is *"small stimulus and disproportionate representation,"* a feature that is characteristic of dreams. The shamanistic spirits are described as very small but their voices are very strong. They are supposed to be subject to sudden changes of size and able in case of need to grow to giant proportions. An ermine invoked as a shamanistic "spirit" or as a guardian spirit of an ordinary man may assume the shape of a polar bear. *A pebble will appear as a mountain.* A small wooden finger representing a supernatural dog will increase in size till it is a bear.[52]

The spirits of disease are kept out of the house by the following means. Several lines were drawn in the snow near the tent and these *were supposed to transform themselves into a large river and high inaccessible cliffs on the route of the disease spirits.*[53]

These ideas which I definitely regard as derived from dreams are acted out in ritual.

[48] *Ibid.*, p. 293.
[49] *Ibid.*, p. 317.
[50] Cf. the chapter "Vesical Dreams and Myths" *infra.*
[51] *Ibid.*, p. 298.
[52] *Ibid.*, p. 301.
[53] *Ibid.*, pp. 441, 476.

When returning home after disposing of the body "the fortifier"[54] and the chief of the cortège, who now close the rear, perform several incantations all of which belong to the cycle of the "magic flight" tales.

The chief of the cortège traces a line across the road where they have passed with a snow beater. This line is to be transformed into a chasm or a deep river. The "fortifying" person will leave one or two small stones behind, these will become steep mountains. He will bring along a small cup and a bunch of grass which served for washing the corpse and will hide these in the snow on the return journey. The cup will transform itself into a sea and the grass into a dense forest.[55] On one occasion an old man urinated at the head of the corpse. His purpose was to create a river between the corpse and himself.[56]

The Koryak perform a very similar ritual. After burning the corpse, when the flames were dying away, the grandfather of a dead girl "broke some twigs from the alder and willow bushes that were growing nearby and strewed them around the pyre. These twigs represented a dense forest which was supposed to surround the burning place. Before leaving the pyre he drew with his stick a line on the snow, jumped across it and shook himself. The others followed his example. The line represented the river which separated the village from the burning place."[57]

The dead ascend to heaven in the smoke of the funeral pyre. In one tale a shaman every time he wishes to ascend to the upper world is killed and burned on this pyre and then ascends in the smoke. He comes back in a whirlwind.[58]

However, Chukchee shamanism places more emphasis on the spirit going into the shaman than on the shaman's journeys. Possession is marked with a change in the manner of beating the drum, but chiefly by new sounds produced by the spirit. The shaman shakes his head violently, shouts hysterically or imitates the cries of animals and birds.

The Chukchee ventriloquists exhibit great skill. The "separate voices" of their calling come from all sides of the room creating a complete illusion. The voices would at first be faint as if coming from afar, then they would gradually approach, increase in volume, rush into the room, seem to go underground, etc.[59]

---

[54] A special magician to protect the living against the influences of the dead.
[55] Bogoras, *op. cit.*, p. 528.
[56] *Ibid.*, p. 531.
[57] Jochelson, W., "The Koryak," *Jesup North Pacific Expedition*, Vol. VI, Part I, Religion, 1905, p. 42.
[58] Bogoras, *op. cit.*, p. 334.
[59] *Ibid.*, p. 435.

After having entered the spirit usually offers "to try his breath," that is, he beats the drum for a while singing a tune in the special harsh voice belonging to spirits. The spirit declares that his breath is ebbing away. Now he begins to talk or takes his departure with a quivering sound like the buzzing of a fly.[60]

We are not advocating a theory according to which shamanism as a whole can be derived from the dream. It is evident from these and similar data that we have here to do with a conscious performance of ventriloquism. Moreover, reading these and other anthropologists' reports about the onset of shamanism among certain tribes compels a comparison with schizophrenia. If we confine ourselves to the two main traits, i.e., the journey of the soul and possession by spirits, it is evident that the former is more obviously linked to the dream than the latter. Yet if we look into the matter somewhat more closely we remember that the sleeper or dreamer actually withdraws into his own body—and the spirits are in the drum or in the shaman. Some of the spirits are the shaman's guardian spirits or helpers, i.e., the ego ideal or other aspects of the dreamer. Others may represent the father or mother imago. Moreover, we have commented on another aspect of the dream; the dreamer may represent himself as identified with food, excrements, or urine that pass through him, while his body is the space in which the dream takes place. The house of Keretkun with a mouth as a door and through which the spirits pass and become excrements is a case of this type of dream.

Among the Chukchee there is still a kind of link that unites sacrifice and the performance of the shaman. In the case of wolves and black bears after the sacrifice the master of the house takes the skin of the sacrificed animal and puts it on in such a way that his head is covered with the skin of the animal's head and the rest of the skin dangles behind. The master of the house dressed in the wolf skin performs the thanksgiving ceremony, sings and dances and beats the drum. From time to time he howls as if the wolf spirit had entered into his body.[61]

Among the Koryak the role that Big Raven plays in shamanism indicates that originally the flying dream must have been more significant in the shamanistic proceeding.

Big Raven is the first man and also the father and protector of the Koryak, but also a powerful shaman. He is supposed to be present at every shamanistic performance. When the sick are treated they go through the drama of how Big Raven treated his children in which case the shaman represents Big Raven and the patient is the child. When the shamans of the Maritime Koryak commence their incantations they say "Big Raven

---

[60] *Ibid.*, p. 437.   [61] *Ibid.*, p. 387.

is crossing." According to the Reindeer Koryak a raven or a sea gull comes flying into the house.[62]

In old times when Big Raven lived rain was pouring incessantly. He said to his eldest son "Universe" must be doing something. They put on their raven coats and flew up. There they found Universe beating a drum and his wife, Raven Woman sitting next to him. In order to produce rain he cut off his wife's vulva and hung it on the drum. Then he cut off his own penis and used it instead of an ordinary drum stick. When he beat the drum the water squirted out of the vulva which caused rain on earth. When he saw Big Raven and his son enter his house he stopped beating the drum, when they went out he started again, and it poured again. Big Raven now put Universe and Rain Woman to sleep. Then he stole the drum and stick and basted them over the fire until they were dry and crisp. He put them back into their former places and removed the sleeping spell. Universe and Rain Woman awoke. They beat the drum again but the more they beat it the finer the weather became. Finally they went to bed again but now the world was starving because Universe was sleeping.[63]

When Big Raven is in the house Universe does not beat his drum. Since the story is told about a periodically sleeping Universe this justifies the attempt to interpret the whole as a dream. In this case it would make sense if we regard Big Raven and Universe as the same person. Then we should reconstruct the nucleus of the story as follows. First flying, then drum beating as symbolizing coitus or masturbation and finally "being in the house," i.e., in the womb.

The Koryak call the Supreme Being "Universe" or "World" or "Supervisor," sometimes "Thunderman." His wife is "Supervisor Woman" or "Rain Woman" or "Dampness Woman."[64]

Between the remote and sublimated figure of Universe and the trickster hero Big Raven there is a link.

Big Raven's wife Miti was thrown down on earth by her father Master on High (i.e., Universe) during a thunderstorm. According to this version she is then the daughter of Dampness or Rain Woman who is the wife of Universe. In another story she is the daughter of the master of the sea or Big Raven finds her in a water hole.[65]

It is not going too far to regard the daughter as a duplicate of the mother. Since we also have a story in which Big Raven enters his wife's anus as if it were a house,[66] I think we can say that our interpretation is confirmed.

62 Jochelson, op. cit., p. 18.
64 Ibid., p. 20.
66 Ibid., p. 25.
63 Ibid., pp. 142, 143.
65 Ibid., p. 20.

In one of the songs of the Yurak Samoyeds the experience of becoming a shaman is told as a dream:[67]

> In the days when I became a shaman
> I heard in my dreams
> The noise made by the wings
> Of twice seven cutting spirits
> On the tent pole one sits[68]
> If one wants to go a bit further
> One goes to the heavenly tube road
> Of my mistress in the sky.[69]

In the third song he has taken the form of an iron pike.

> The water spirit, my grandfather
> Said, poor little one, where do you come from?
> I said I only came
> To have a look at the road,
> The mistress of the water, my girl friend
> Makes a bed ready for me
> They put "water stones" on me to weigh me down
> I snore seven days
> I jump up
> The stones of the water fall off me,
> And I say, Mistress of the Water, my girl friend, hurry
> I come to an iron dam
> The Spirit of Death, in the shape of an iron bull.
> I make my wings howl! (i.e., fly so quickly)
> My twice seven mistresses
> Start to embrace their children
> Saying, verily you go, which country are you trying to reach
> Seven times stopping with my foot
> I said, let me breathe
> I said: Long have I waited for you
> After snoring seven days
> I jumped up
> My twice seven widows came along
> I flew forward in the shape of an iron reindeer bull!!
> There was an iron road
> I reached its end
> I stopped running
> Got out of my iron shape
> O, fairy of the peninsular mountain of clouds
> My iron shape, I left it there
> In the shape of the Minlei[70]

[67] Lehtisalo, "Juraksamojedische Volksdichtung," *Mem. Soc. Finno Ougrienne*, LXXVI, 1947, pp. 427–477.

[68] Tent pole = world tree.

[69] The vaginal significance of the tube is now evident.

[70] The gigantic bird on the world tree. The same bird figures in the story quoted above.

I passed through an iron dam
Through the opening of his net.[71]

Lehtisalo publishes an account of the shamanistic performance among the Yurak Samoyeds. The handle of the magic drum symbolizes the world pillar. We also find rings on the drum, possibly representing the navel of the world. When the shaman returns from his journey, he awakes from the trance and throws the drum away.[72]

A story relates how a shaman was initiated. A man went to chop wood in the forest. Suddenly he felt that he was on the back of a mythical bird (this is where the dream starts). He saw a hole and crawled through it. He was falling toward the earth. He thought, now I am going to die *and he fell asleep.* He was back on what he thought was the earth. He saw four giants, they were playing. They cut themselves into two halves, now their number was doubled. Then the parts reunited. They did the same things to the human being (fission in dreams), then he came to other demons who also cut people into pieces and stuck them together again. The same thing happened to him. He arrived at a small hut. There was an old man there and seven beds. The old man told him to sit in the first bed but he *sank in it* as if it were a tube or shaft. From above he heard the voice of the old man. "Guess whose bed you are in," and he guessed the name of the disease represented by the bed. After the third guess he could not guess and that is why death eats human beings. The old man led him back to the earth in another tube and he became a great shaman.[73]

It is evident that we have here the basic dream with the flying sinking mechanism and the passage through the vagina.

In this poem the dream character is quite conscious. Flight and passage through the vagina we find here again, but there is also the oedipal element, the father imagos and the mistresses (also present in the person of the giants and the old man of the story).

Beside the journey of the soul another trait that especially characterizes Siberian and North American shamanism is the battle, particularly the aerial battle or the battle in animal shape.

Two Eskimo shamans fought. One became a polar bear, the other a musk ox. The ox strove to pierce the bear with its horns. Finally the bear managed to hit the ox, but the ox ripped the bear's flank open with its horn. The ox said, let us change back into human beings.[74]

71 *Ibid.,* pp. 481–484.
72 Lehtisalo, "Entwurf einer Mythologie der Jurak Samojeden," *Mem. Soc. F. Ou.* VIII, Helsinki, 1924, pp. 149–153.
73 *Ibid.,* pp. 46–48.
74 Jenness, D., "Report of the Canadian Arctic Expedition 1913–1918," Vol. XIII, *Eskimo Folk Lore,* Ottawa, 1924, 85 A.

Among the Netsilik Eskimos two shamans in bird form fought in the air.[75] Yukaghir shamans fight each other. In day shape they dig down into the earth, as storks they fly up.[76] Penobscot shamans or their guardian spirits fight in the water, one is a big eel, the other a big snake.[77]

Among the Tungus the fighting nature of the shaman is well known. Two shamans appeared in the shape of a bear and a tiger and they fought each other in the presence of the people. Physically they were separated by a great distance. One of these great fighters might turn into a "cart with horses." A Tungus shaman saw a great Yakut who was approaching in the shape of a cloud. He took the form of a cloud and rose above the Yakut shaman and killed him.[78]

Once a year when the snow melts and the earth is black the animals in which the Yakut shamans hide their souls, the ie-kuya (mother animals) arise from their hiding places and begin to wander about. They hold orgies of fighting and noise making. Great shamans become bulls, stallions, black bears and the weaker ones become dogs. Shamans whose souls are incarnated in the shape of these animals are very unfortunate because these animals are insatiable, however much the shaman may provide for them. The dog is especially bad; he gnaws the shaman's heart with his teeth, tears his body into pieces, etc. These fights of shaman animals take place when the shaman is in ecstasy.[79] Lapp shamans fight each other in the shape of reindeer bulls, the one whose bull is killed, dies. They also send out their "soul animals" as lights. These lights fight each other, and that is the Aurora Borealis. A terrible noise is heard when these duels are going on.[80]

The shaman also may fight spirits; in principle there is not much difference. In a Buryat story Thousand Eyes steals the cattle of a shaman. (It is not clear whether this is a spirit or another shaman.)

The old shaman went home, made tarasun (= kumis, alcoholic beverage made of horse milk) and drank it. Then he went to the corner of the room, got his axe and put it under the pillow on his bed, tied his horse to a post in the tent and lay down saying to his wife:

[75] Rasmussen, K., "The Netsilik Eskimos," Report of Vth Thule Expedition, Copenhagen, 1931, VIII, p. 299.

[76] Jochelson, "The Yukaghir and Yukaghirized Tungus," Am. Mus. Nat. Hist. XIII, 1926, p. 213.

[77] Speck, F. G., "Penobscot Shamanism," Mem. Am. Anthr. Assoc. VI, 1919, p. 282. Cf. also Lowie, R. H., "The Religion of the Crow Indians," Anthr. Papers, Am. Mus. Nat. Hist. XXV, Part 2, 1927, p. 344.

[78] Shirokogoroff, op. cit., pp. 371, 372.

[79] Mikhailovski, V., "Shamanism in Siberia and European Russia," Journal of the Royal Anthropological Institute, XXIV, 1894, p. 133. Czaplicka, M. A., Aboriginal Siberia. Oxford, 1914, pp. 182, 183.

[80] Holmberg, "The Mythology of all Races," IV, Finno Ugric, 1927, pp. 288, 287.

"Do not let my horse out and do not waken me." *Soon he and his horse were sound asleep.* [My italics.] But they were not asleep, it was only their bodies that were so quiet.

(What follows now is the dream narrative.)

In reality the shaman was riding swiftly. He came to a mountain, he saw that Thousand Eyes had made a bridge across the river and was beginning to drive his cattle over it. Half the bridge was silver, half of it gold.

The shaman turned himself into a bee, made his axe equally small, flew under the bridge and hewed the pillars so that the bridge broke in two. All the cattle fell into the river, also a woman who was riding one of the oxen.

Thousand Eyes on his gray stallion floated in the water. The shaman made a terrible rain and wind and finally compelled his opponent to surrender.[81]

Another story is about a shaman and a Lama. The shaman did not like the Lama so he turned himself into a gray wolf and went to the house at night. The Lama saw the wolf and cried out "he has come to kill me." But the wolf was invisible to everyone else except the Lama. It stayed there all night, ready to spring at him. At daylight, it disappeared.[82]

The dream origin of this story is quite obvious. The aerial flight, the battle and the animal metamorphosis are often combined.

In Hungarian witches trials we find the following data: In 1725 at Debrecen Mrs. Bartos, accused of witchcraft, protests that she is a *táltos* (shaman), not a witch. The court asks her: What is the function of the *táltos? They fight in the sky for the nation,* is her answer. How do they get there? God gives them wings like a bird has. Where was the fight? At Hortobágy near a mound,[83] etc.

Ilona Borsi confesses that when she was seven years old a man and a woman *táltos* came to fetch her. They mounted their horses and flew to Székesfehérvár where they met three times a year. When they dismounted the two *táltos* tethered their horses to trees and then undressed. Now they were completely naked, they took the shape of bulls and fought each other. She was lying on the ground when one of the horses spoke to her, "Don't be afraid of what you have seen, you bastard. *Go to sleep,* nobody will hurt you. The two *táltos* became human again and asked her what she had seen. She said, *lightning* but also that she was not afraid because the horse reassured her. But she also saw that the male *táltos* wounded

---

81 Curtin, J., *A Journey in Southern Siberia,* London, 1909, pp. 111, 112.
82 *Ibid.,* p. 109.
83 Komaromy, A., *Magyarországi boszorkányperek Oklevéltára* (Acta of Hungarian Witches' Trials), Budapest, 1910, p. 362.

the female on the left nipple. This happened several times but the female *táltos* always healed her own wounds.[84]

Go to sleep, i.e., what we have here is a dream. The latent content of the dream is evident, *it is the primal scene,* the struggle of the male and female, the wound (displaced upward). Flying is the erotic reaction of the dreamer to the primal scene.

The Samoyeds tell the following story: Two shamans lived at the same place. One of them was called the *ngannuun kurjutsi* shaman, the other *lampai* shaman. The *lampai* challenged the other one. First each shaman became a wolf and they ate the oxen of their opponent. This was not decisive, they got ready for another battle.

The *lampai* man had broad horns (this is what *lampai* means) and his opponent had one small crooked horn bent inward toward his other horn. Therefore he was the weaker one. He slipped and the *lampai* sorcerer dragged him to the edge of the sky. Here the one with the crooked horns grabbed a tree trunk and the other one could not drag him any further. The *lampai* then pulled him back again to the other end of the sky. In it, however, there was a hole and the *lampai* fell into it. The *ngannuun kurjutsi* knocked him on the head, it sounded like bells in the sky. Next morning the *lampai* shaman's children said—"Father is still asleep," but then they saw that he was dead.[85]

From the children's point of view the aerial battle with the hole would be the primal scene. The dream becomes a myth, the sorcerer is dead.

In Hungarian accounts of the táltos the spectacular nature of the battle scene is especially emphasized. The fight is usually between a young lad who is on trial, i.e., being initiated and an old táltos. In one case the lad becomes a white bull. He drives the black bull back into the clouds. If the black bull is victorious the lad disappears in the clouds with the shamans. This is not desirable because then everything will be destroyed by hail. The young táltos who is on trial may ask relatives to help him. This may be done by throwing a wet canvas on his back to refresh him. But the usual thing is to hit the toenail and the testicles of the big bull with a pitchfork.[86]

We shall now devote some space to describing the shamanism of the Voguls and Ostyaks.

---

[84] Lehoczky, T., *Bereg Varmegye Monographiája* (Monograph of County Bereg) II, Budapest, 1881, p. 250. Cf. Róheim, G., "Hungarian Shamanism," *Psychoanalysis and the Social Sciences,* III, 1951, p. 145.

[85] Lehtisalo, *op. cit.,* pp. 130, 121.

[86] Bartha, C. N., *Magyar Néphagyományok* (Hungarian Traditions) Debrecen, 1931, pp. 60–63.

The activity of the shaman consists in calling upon the god to appear as being possessed by the god.

The typical phrase is *tarem reine, pupi reine joxtawa* (god's heat, the idol's heat took possession of him). In Northern Ostyak the word for ecstasis is "the heat of the idol comes." Munkácsi distinguishes several phases in the proceeding.

I. The spirit introduces himself or relates his origin. For instance, they say, "We the seven demons coming from the forest above Golden One (i.e., the sky god) magically made us of yore on the holy land which is ours,"[87] etc.

The Ostyak's shaman induces several spirits to appear. The idol says:

From the source of the river Paset
I took a long step like a wood spirit
From my far away house
I came on the merry road of guests
I came on the merry road of those invited to a marriage, etc.
Then another idol comes:
From the end of the earth
From the end of the opening of the sea
From my seven hills that look like a bride
I, the little son of a forest idol came
I came on a sledge for two
I came on the road meant for many guests.
[This is the Old One of the mountain.]

Several other spirits appear and talk in the same style and then the shaman says to the idol called Pazet Aged One

Thou who guardest the source of the river Pazet
Forest devil prince with locks
Didst thou howl in the essence
With the essence of the reindeer bull?
Of this thy prince hero
Of this thy word-knowing hero prince
Of this thy incantation-knowing hero prince
Into the goose-inhabited lake of the underworld
Into the duck-inhabited lake of the underworld.[88]

This is an incantation to bring back the patient's stolen soul by making a clay puppet. The shaman is evidently asking the spirit whether he did it. "Shouting the spirit down to the lake of the underworld" is killing the patient. "The prince hero who knows incantation is the honorific title given to the patient."

87 Munkácsi, B., *Vogul Népköltési Gyüjtemény* (Thesaurus of Vogul Folklore), Budapest, 1896, IV, pp. 0381, 0382.

88 Pápay, I., "Osztják népköltési gyüjtemény" (Collection of Ostyak folklore), *Third Asiatic Journey of Count Zichy*, Budapest, 1905, V, pp. 273, 274.

The soul of the patient is identified with a reindeer bull. The idol replies that he is not responsible for what happened and he cannot help, but he suggests another god who will be able to rescue the patient.[89]

If a child is sick the shaman calls upon the Mother Goddess Kaltés:

> Goddess of midnight to whom we sacrifice food
> Goddess of Dawn to whom we sacrifice blood
> Magic Kaltés, wrathful goddess
> The little son who is in thy power
> The little infant whom thou hast caught
> Thou goddess who givest strength of back
> Thou goddess who givest power of chest
> How did they eating idols, drinking idols
> Thy many sons catch him?

Kaltés thus called upon *gets into a trance* and says she is not responsible for what has happened.[90] The point is that the spirit called upon by the shaman is now in a trance. The next step is that the spirit asks why they have invoked him. The shaman tells him or her what the trouble is and asks for help. Usually the spirit is evasive; some other spirit is responsible. The shaman thinks the spirit is fooling him and finally compels him to go to a superior spirit who then tells the shaman what sacrifice would be appropriate. The spirit and the shaman cannot agree. The spirit tortures the shaman. This is why he is tied hand and foot. If he were not tied he would run away and that would be his death. The spirit suggests some other spirits. These may again say they are not competent, till finally the right one appears. One spirit evokes the other the same way the shaman evokes the first one. Finally the right one is found. He tells them what sacrifice is demanded and says farewell.[91] In the myths the god often complains, "Why did you call upon me with such terrific strength, why did he have to come in such haste?" In one case the World Inspector Prince *turned round and round* because the incantation was so powerful.[92] The god comes like lightning, like rain, like the wind or "falls down."[93]

Karjalainen reports that sickness is due to soul abduction. The shaman descends to the nether world or sends his guardian spirit. If the soul has been abducted by a ghost, the shaman's guardian spirit takes the shape of a ghost and visits the other ghost. While they are having a friendly chat, a bear spirit jumps out of the first spirit. The ghost is so frightened that he drops the soul. If the soul is already in the nether

[89] *Ibid.,* pp. 375, 376.
[90] *Ibid.,* pp. 268, 269.
[91] Munkácsi, *op. cit.,* IV, pp. 0382–0394.
[92] *Ibid.,* IV, p. 0351, II, p. CCXL.
[93] *Ibid.,* IV, p. 0378.

world the task is more difficult and the shaman has to go himself. His net is made of human hair and he fishes the soul out of the dams of the underworld river. As soon as he has got hold of the soul he flies into the sky in the shape of a swan. There he deposits the rescued soul to *sleep* first in a lake in the sky then in a seven storied house in the forest. After having slept there for two weeks or a month, the soul is returned to its original owner.[94]

In my opinion Karjalainen is quite right when he emphasizes that both the seer and the dreamer are the forerunners of the shaman if by shaman we mean the trance experience.[95] After having taken fly-agaric the shaman first sleeps. This may be calculated to evoke a dream, but does not increase the power of the fly-agaric in the trance.[96]

We shall now note how the shaman himself is projected in the beliefs about a supernatural being and how this supernatural being confirms our views about the origins of shamanism.

We have observed that the shaman, when he returns with the soul, assumes the shape of a swan.

The Milky Way and the water fowl who leave for the south in the fall and return in spring are focal points of Ugrian mythology. They symbolize the departure and return of the soul or sleep and awakening.

The god we are concerned with is the Gander Chief of the Voguls. Like the shaman he is concerned with healing. Like a shaman he uses the fly-agaric to get into a trance.[97] He is in fact initiated as a shaman and he received his white horse at his initiation.[98]

The Gander Chief is the leader of migrating birds, ducks, geese, swans, cranes, etc. Many shamans have the duck costume, i.e., the shaman's garment is supposed to resemble a duck and the shaman is supposed to fly into the sky in the shape of a duck.[99]

Every Samoyed clan has a holy bird, frequently duck, goose or loon. This bird helps the shaman to fly and the clan spirit appears in the shape of this bird.[100] Among the Ket (Yenisei Ostyak) duck, goose, migrating water fowl in general, and the eagle, are the most important shaman

94 Karjalainen, "Die Religion der Jugra Völker," *F. F. Communications* No. 41, Porvoo, 1921, I, pp. 83–85, F.F.C. 63, III, pp. 305–308.

95 *Ibid.,* F.F.C. 63, III, 1927, p. 280.

96 *Ibid.,* p. 316.

97 Munkácsi, *op. cit.,* II, pp. 0106, 0109.

98 Tshernetshov, "Fratrialnoje ustrojstvo obsko-jugorskovo obshteshtva," *Sovjetskaja, Etnografia,* II, 1939, p. 36.

99 Holmberg, "The Shaman Costume and its Significance," *Annales Universitatis Feunical Arboensis,* Series B, Tom. I, No. 2, Turku, 1922.

100 Lehtisalo, "Entwurf einer Mythologie der Jurak-Samojeden," *Mem. Soc. F. Ou.,* LIII, 1924, p. 69.

birds.[101] According to the Samoyed shaman, Djuchadit, the frame of the shaman's drum is cut out of the world tree and this drum enables the shaman to fly away with the migrating birds.[102]

The Gander Chief, like the shaman, flies to visit other worlds. He arrives at the edge of the world where the sky and earth meet. There is a rock with a hole in it. He puts on his hawk skin (i.e., like the shaman costume) but the entrance is guarded by an old man who covers the hole with a sevenfold birds' net. But the Gander Chief changes his shape and swims through in the form of an iron pike.[103]

He flies to the land of migrating birds in the shape of a Gander, weds the Golden Swan woman and brings all sorts of waterfowl as a dowry for mankind.

The god has gone to sleep after having dined and feasted with his aunt Kaltesh. He awakes at the edge of the pine grove which is also the edge of the world. It is spring now, flocks of birds are returning from the south. A solitary goose is flying, he flies up as a gander, they live together as man and wife. They have a daughter. Spring comes back once more. Now he thinks of his horse, the horse that used to fly with him all over the world. He sleeps and sleeps and it is spring again. Ducks and other water fowl fly back. His wife, the Golden Woman, has lost her two children. She thinks he is dead, but he is lying on the ground and hears what she says. He vows vengeance. He thinks of the winged horse and the song says, "If my story should make headway, if my story goes on like a drop of rain from above, like a little wind from above, you would be here." He falls into a deep sleep and when he awakes the winged horse is stroking his face. He gallops to the bird land, the Golden Woman of the South. His wife is there, but the children are lost. He tells his horse, "Now descend on her so that her bones and flesh should be torn to pieces and hurled into the remotest parts of the earth."

Golden Woman says to her maid: "The hero, the Golden Chief, who is going to be my husband, is descending. When the horse descends prepare four silver cups for the four feet." He descends and the horse rips her to pieces. The little son and daughter are alive again and fly in the shape of geese.[104] The four cups are based on ritual, this is how the shaman invokes the World Surveyor who descends on his horse. In the myth his wife regards the descent of the horse as her bridal night. Actually it is her death.

[101] Shimkin, N., "A sketch of the Ket or Yenissei Ostyak," *Ethnos*, IV, 1939, pp. 160, 161.

[102] Lehtisalo, ". . . Mythologie der Jurak-Samojeden," p. 173.

[103] Munkácsi, *op. cit.*, I, pp. 25, 27, 28.

[104] *Ibid.*, I, pp. 53–64.

The important thing in all this is that the plot really unfolds itself to the sleeping Gander Chief. His sleep and periodic awakening is connected with the reappearance of spring and of the birds. He sleeps and dreams. It is a flying dream with a magic white horse. The Golden Woman is his wife but also his mother because he identifies himself with her dead children. They have been swept off her lap, they are dead. For to sleep is to die, or at least to die partially. In the flying dream life comes back with the erection, followed by birth, the young birds flying up again.

A part of the mythology of this shaman-god is developed from dreaming. This is just the part in which he shows himself as being closest to shamanism. We assume that the dream flight of the soul is the real nucleus of shamanism.[105]

The Eskimo have many beliefs and narratives about the journey of the shaman to the Mother of Sea Animals,[106] or to the Moon.

According to Iglulinmuit Eskimo, Aviliajog is the mother of sea animals. Sometimes she confines all the sea animals in her house. In this case the shaman has to pay her a visit and cut the animals off her hands. If deprived of her nails, the bears obtain their freedom, the first joint of the finger liberates one kind of seal and the second joint the other. Should the knuckles be detached whole herds of walrus rise to the surface and if he succeeds in cutting through the lower joint of the metacarpal bones, whales are liberated. *The door of her dwelling is a long passage* guarded by a fierce dog *which has no tail.* [My italics.] Aviliajog is very tall and has but *one eye,* which is the left, the place of the other is covered with a lot of black hair. Eskimo women usually wear two pigtails, she has only one, but this is so huge, *that a man can scarcely grasp it with both hands.* It is exactly twice the length of her arm and reaches down to her knee. Her father has but one arm and the hand is covered by a large mitten of bearskin. He is not larger than a boy of ten. This male spirit has a very nice house, but on account of the bears and walrus that surround it, nobody can go there. He is the patron of terrestrial animals and he withholds these from the Eskimo from time to time.[107]

Another name for the mother of sea animals is Old Woman. She sits in her house in front of a lamp. Under the lamp we find a vessel and the oil flows from the lamp into the vessel. *From this vessel or from the dark*

105 Cf. my two papers "Hungarian Shamanism" and "Hungarian and Vogul Mythology" in Vols. III and IV of *Psychoanalysis and the Social Sciences.*

106 Cf. Róheim, "Die Sednasage," *Imago* X, 1924, pp. 159–177. *Idem, War, Crime and the Covenant,* Journal of Clinical Psychopathology, Monograph Series No. 1, Monticello, N.Y., 1945, pp. 110–119.

107 Boas, F., *The Central Eskimo,* Bureau of American Ethnology, Report VI, 1884/85, Washington, D.C., pp. 585, 586.

interior of her house she sends out the animals which serve for food. Sometimes she withholds them. This is due to a kind of parasite that have fastened themselves around her head. They are called *agdlerutit,* i.e., abortions or stillborn children. It was the task of the shaman to deliver her from these and to induce her to send out the animals. In going down to her he would pass through the dwelling of the happy dead and then pass an abyss in which there was a *constantly revolving wheel*[108] as slippery as ice, and then having safely got past a boiling kettle with seals in it, he arrived at her house. The guardians of the house are sometimes described as seals, sometimes as dogs. Within the house passage he had to cross an abyss by means of a bridge as narrow as a knife edge.[109]

The great annual ceremony of the Eskimo is connected with the idea that this is the time when Sedna visits the people. If they have behaved properly, she gives them food in abundance. They try to divine the future through their shamans. All the people gather in one of the houses with the three shamans who are to visit Sedna.

"Now the people keep perfectly quiet. One of the *angakut* (shaman) holds the harpoon and line such as are used in their kayaks. When Sedna is near enough he throws his harpoon at her. Then she slides back to her abode. The people try to accelerate her return by exchanging wives. The soul of one of the shamans follows Sedna and stabs her with a large knife. His *soul returns to the body and the people cry for light.* The lamps are ablaze, the knife, the harpoon, and the floor are covered with blood. There will be plenty of food that year. Sedna feels kindly toward the people if they have succeeded in cutting her. The cutting makes Sedna feel better. It is like giving a thirsty person drink." Boas thinks the object may be to cut off the transgressions that are attached to her.[110]

However, according to other versions a regular battle takes place in the underworld. Sedna tears her hair and foams at the mouth, the shaman must fight her and then he can delouse and comb her. Her hands are the size of the fin of a whale and if she manages to strike the shaman, he is done for.[111]

Egede adds an important detail to the description of the journey; live seals are being boiled in the kettle.[112] The idea of the journey to Sedna and of summoning Sedna, or being possessed by Sedna, seem to be inter-

108 Cf. *The Revolving Castle infra.*

109 Rink, H., *Tales and Traditions of the Eskimo,* London, 1885, p. 40.

110 Boas, F., "The Eskimo of Baffin Land and Hudson Bay," *Bull. Am. Mus. Nat. Hist.,* XV, 1901, p. 139.

111 Nansen, F., *Eskimoleben,* 1903, pp. 221, 222 (references).

112 Egede, P., *Nachrichten von Grönland,* Copenhagen, 1790, p. 130; Ethnological Sketch of the Angmasalik Eskimo Meddedelser on Grönland XXXIX. p. 83, Cranz, D., *Historie von Grönland,* 1770, p. 264.

changeable. The Copper Eskimo call Sedna "Annahaphaluk." *She lives in a little bubble with her husband and child.*[113]

If taboos are broken she takes the soul out of women's sewing things and out of men's work which simply means that the women will not be able to sew and the men to work. They make a hole and summon her. She comes up through the hole and takes possession of the shaman's body.

He writhes and moans with pain. As long as the sins of the people are not confessed her hair is in the wildest disorder.[114]

The Iglulik Eskimo call Sedna "Takanakapsaluk." The shaman who makes the journey is called "one who drops down to the bottom of the sea." He is supposed to bore his way through a hollow in the floor where the water collects. There are obstacles on the way; three large rolling stones but he passes between them. A dog is stretched over the passage of the hut. When he comes back he blows like a seal.[115]

The journey to the other world and the journey to the moon are variations of the same theme—especially since Sedna is the ruler or one of the rulers of the other world.[116] Illness is caused by the absence of the soul. A shaman woman sent her soul down to the nether world to recover the absent soul. The way led through a ravine down which a great waterfall poured down under the earth. The ravine widened out suddenly. She caught the soul of the sick woman and brought it back.[117]

A mighty shaman who had a bear for his guardian spirit decided to pay a visit to the moon. The guardian spirit carried him rapidly through the air to the moon. The moon was a house covered with white deer skins which the man in the moon used to dry near it. On each side of the entrance was the upper portion of the body of an enormous walrus which threatened to tear the intruder into pieces. He saw a beautiful woman, the sun, who sat beside her lamp. The shaman passed, protected by his guardian spirit. The moon man came and then his wife. She carried an oblong vessel with a knife in it. The moon man warned him that he should not laugh. If he does, she will slit his belly open and cut out his intestines. *She put the vessel down on the floor, stooped forward and turned the vessel like a whirligig. Then the two of them danced, etc.*

113 A patient whose husband had left for Europe on a business trip expressed her desire not to meet anybody in order to keep out of the way of temptation. She dreamed, "Everybody lives in something like bubbles, but they are in pairs, male and female." The bubble is the womb.

114 Rasmussen, K., "Intellectual Culture of the Copper Eskimo," *Report of the Fifth Thule Expedition*, IX, Copenhagen, 1932, p. 24.

115 *Idem*, "Intellectual Culture of the Iglulik Eskimos," *Fifth Thule Expedition*, VII, 1929, No. 1, pp. 124–127.

116 Boas, *The Central Eskimo*, pp. 584, 588.

117 Rasmussen, K., *The People of the Polar North*, Philadelphia, 1908, p. 110.

The moon man let him look through a small building near the entrance. There he saw a vast plain with large herds of deer. He chose one animal, immediately it fell through a hole to the earth. In another building he saw many seals swimming in an ocean.

"During his visit to the moon his body lay motionless and soulless, but now it revived. He felt almost exhausted but when the lamps were re-lighted he told the crowd what he had seen in the moon."[118]

On the Yukon the moon is inhabited by a great manlike being who controls all the animals found on earth. When a season of scarcity comes the shamans go up and make offerings to him, and then he lets the animals loose. One shaman used to fly up like a bird. On the lower Yukon there are other ways of getting to the moon. They would slip a noose round his neck and drag him in the hut till he is dead. Then he goes up to the moon but he comes back again.[119]

The following account of a moon journey makes the dream origin of the narrative very clear.

A shaman was catching seals. He gazed up at the full moon. It came to him. "*Close your eyes* and sit on my sledge,"—it said. *At once the sledge began to move,* he could feel the swish and the sweep. He peered through his eyelids—there was a tremendous abyss, he almost fell off the sledge. There was a dog barring the way at the entrance of the house. The inside of the house was moving in and out like tent walls flapping in the wind. *The passage contracted and expanded like a mouth that was chewing* but he got through safely. In one room there was a pretty young woman with a child, she invited him to sit down but he refused because he was afraid that he would forget to go home.

He hurried away letting himself slide down toward the earth. *He arrived at exactly the same place where the moon had carried him away.*[120]

A Nunivak story follows the same pattern only we have the Northern Lights instead of the moon.

A poor boy *woke up* one cold winter night. He wanted to relieve himself (urethral). It was bright moonlight. He noticed somebody beside him who picked him up and flew with him toward the sky. While they were flying he tried to fall down but that person would not let him. He saw a lot of walrus. They were the northern lights.[121]

Men who die on the sea and women who die in childbirth go to the

118 Boas, *op. cit.,* pp. 598, 599.

119 Nelson, E. W., "The Eskimo about Bering Strait," XVIII, *Annual Report, Bureau Am. Ethn.,* 1899, pp. 430, 431.

120 Rasmussen, "The Netsilik Eskimos," *Report of the Fifth Thule Expedition,* 1921–1924, Copenhagen, 1931, VIII, p. 236.

121 Lantis, M., "The Social Culture of the Nunivak Eskimo," *Am. Phil. Soc.,* New Series, Vol. XXXV, Part 3, 1946, p. 272.

moon. If a woman is barren the moon man comes down from the sky and makes her pregnant.[122]

Another shaman journey is reported by Rasmussen. There was a famous shaman who was crawling into his house with a load on his back. He fell backwards and tumbled down through the very thing he was carrying. Down he went toward the inside of the earth. There was a swish and a roar round him. He saw the spirits of the dead with their chins grown fast to their breasts. Then he went further down to another underworld. There he saw a tent with a small hole and a little pup crawling through it.

Then he found another hole. He spat through this hole and jumped on his own spittle. He was back in the world of mortals. Then he turned himself into a gull and flew through the air.[123]

This story is only slightly re-edited from the dream prototype. The turning inward, the fall and the flight upward are typical of the basic dream. The flight is the erection, the fall the uterine regression. (Falling in the dream may also be an orgasm.) To make this quite clear we have a tent and a hole with a puppy crawling through and the dead with their chins grown to their breasts in the embryo position. The part about the spittle could not occur in a dream; this is literature. But what could occur would be an urethral waking stimulus, the dreamer might swim out of a cave, carried by a flood.

Another account of the journey is given by Bogoras. "They were about to go to sleep. They called the walrus spirit. Many walrus came, they were as numerous as sand. The walrus carried him away and made him sleep on the sea ice. The walrus dived to the bottom of the sea to the Polar Star. He is told by them: 'When you are overtaken by sleep roar like a walrus'—and he became a walrus."[124] This is about the clearest possible evidence for the dream origin of the shaman's performance—the metamorphosis in a dream,[125] and the journey in a dream.

Primitives have the practically universal dream theory that in the dream the soul leaves the body and wanders to a land unknown. In a sense sleep is turning inwards, and the sleeper's body (and in fantasy the maternal womb) are the elements that are used in building up the dream scenario—"being possessed" alternates with going out "toward," with wandering.

[122] Rasmussen, "Intellectual Culture of the Iglulik Eskimo" *Fifth Thule Expedition,* Vol. VII. No. 1, 1929, pp. 124–129.

[123] *Idem,* "The Netsilik Eskimo," *Report of the Fifth Thule Expedition 1921–1924,* Copenhagen, 1931, Vol. VIII, p. 317.

[124] Bogoras, "Chukchee Mythology," *Am. Mus. Nat. Hist.,* XII, 1910, p. 7.

[125] Cf. Róheim, "Metamorphosis," *American Imago,* V, 1948, pp. 167–182.

Another version of the possession type of shamanism is given by the Copper Eskimo.

"The spirits of the air see the shamans as shining bodies. This makes them wish to go and live in them and give them their own strength. They went in by the navel of the shaman and found a place in the breast cavity."[126] The navel is a practically universal uterine symbol. The regressive trend, to go into the uterus, is projected from the shaman to the spirit.

Yakut shamans have a sun and a moon disc on their shaman's coat. In one of these discs there is a hole representing the hole through which the shaman descends to the lower world. He goes down through the hole and comes back by virtue of his coat.[127]

There is also direct evidence on shamanism as based on dreams for the Eskimo. The candidate goes up to the hills to sleep. In one case he is swallowed by a bear monster and then chewed and spat out.[128]

Among the Nunivak the shaman's supernatural power usually came in dreams. The supernaturals of the shaman were a kind of dwarf or the "half people." They would give the shaman a song in the dream. More often, however, he would make up songs to commemorate these dreams and he openly said so. He also carved masks to resemble the spirits seen in dreams.[129]

Among the Greenland Eskimo the candidate seeks to acquire a *tornak* or guardian spirit by fasting and staying in solitary places. Finally *tornarsuk* appeared and supplied the novice with a *tornak*. While this was happening the candidate became unconscious and on regaining consciousness, is supposed to have returned to mankind. The spirits come from caves or the shaman candidate goes into a cave or a dried out lake. *Tarneerunek* is the act of taking the soul out of the body. This may be achieved by dreams or by the power of the moon.[130]

The descent to Sedna is certainly based on a dream. But why the cutting? What is the meaning of the abortions clinging to Sedna and causing pain? What is the meaning of the struggle between the shaman and the goddess?

This is the myth of Sedna. Once upon a time there lived a man with his daughter. His wife had been dead for some time. She rejected all her suitors. Finally when spring came and the ice began to break up a *fulmar*

---

[126] Rasmussen, "Intellectual Culture of the Copper Eskimos," *Report of the Fifth Thule Expedition*, IX, Copenhagen, 1932, p. 28.

[127] Jochelson, "The Yakut," *Anthrop. Papers, Am. Mus. Nat. Hist.*, Vol. I, Part 2, 1933, p. 109.

[128] Rasmussen, *The People of the Polar North*, Philadelphia, 1908, pp. 147, 149.

[129] Lantis, *op. cit.*, pp. 205, 206.

[130] Rink, *op. cit.*, pp. 56, 58.

came and wooed Sedna with his song. "Come into the land of birds," he sang, "where there is never hunger, and my tent is made of the most beautiful skins." She went with him and when she arrived at the land of birds she discovered that she had been deceived. She suffered from cold and hunger. She sang, "O father! if you knew how wretched I am you would fetch me in your boat over the waters!"

Next spring he went to visit his daughter. He killed the *fulmar* and took Sedna into his boat. The other *fulmars* started in pursuit and made a heavy storm. In order to escape himself, the father threw Sedna overboard. She clung to the edge of the boat with a death grip. The cruel father then took a knife and cut off the first joints of her fingers. They fell into the sea and became whales. Sedna held on to the boat more tightly, the second finger joints fell away under the sharp knife and swam away as seals. Then he cut off the stumps and they became ground seals. The *fulmars* thought Sedna was drowned and the storm subsided. Her father let her come back into the boat. She swore revenge. After they had gone ashore she called her dogs and let them gnaw off the feet and hands of her father while he was asleep. He cursed himself, his daughter and the dogs that had maimed him. The earth opened and swallowed the hut, the father, the daughter and the dogs. They have lived since in the nether world of which Sedna is the mistress.

Another version handed down in a song, has father and brother as rescuers. Besides cutting off Sedna's fingers he also pierces her eyes and thus kills her. He covers the body with a dogskin. The flood comes and carries her away. She is much taller than a normal person, but in accordance with the second tradition she has only one eye and is scarcely able to move. Her father is also a cripple and appears to the dying whom he grasps with his right hand which has only three fingers.[131]

In one Cumberland Sound version of the same story, the woman later becomes Sedna. There are two animals, a dog and a petrel. A girl lived with her father and refused all suitors. There was a stone in the village speckled white and red. The stone transformed itself into a dog and married the girl. She lived on an island with her dog husband and the puppies. Every day she sent her husband to the mainland for food. She hung a pair of boots around his neck which her father filled with meat for them.

One day when the dog was gone for meat a tall good-looking man came in a boat to woo her. When she stepped out of the boat she noticed that he was quite a small man. It was the petrel. Her father came to fetch her while the husband (as in the other story) followed in pursuit. The

---

[131] Boas, *op. cit.*, pp. 584, 585; Rink, "Eskimo Tales and Songs," *Journal of American Folk-Lore*, II, p. 127.

same story follows with the storm, with Sedna in the water, finger joints cut off, origin of seals, etc.

The father took his steering oar and knocked out her left eye. She fell backward into the water and he paddled ashore. "Then he filled the boots that the dog was accustomed to carry with stones. The dog started to sink and he was drowned. A great noise was heard while he was drowning. The father took down his tent and went down to the beach at the time of low water. There he lay down and covered himself with the tent. The flood tide rose over him and when the waters receded he had disappeared.

"The woman became Sedna who lives in the lower world in her house built of stone and whale ribs. She has only one eye and she cannot walk, but slides along one leg bent under, the other stretched out. Her father lives with her in the house and lies there covered up with his tent. The dog lives at the entrance of the house."[132]

Another Cumberland Sound version has only the dog-husband without the bird.[133]

Saviquong (Man of the Knife) lived with his daughter ("Girl" or "She who wants no husband"). She falls in love with the dog Ijiquang (Powerful Eye). They have ten children, five dogs, five *adlets* (demons). The children are very voracious, they are put on an island. The father kills the dog husband by putting stones in the boots instead of meat. She incited her sons to bite and eat their grandfather. Cutting off her fingers and joints is her father's revenge and explains the origin of seals, etc.[134] Practically the same story is told on the West Coast of Hudson Bay. The woman who married a dog is Nuliayoq (Sedna) who lives under the ocean with her father and her dog.[135]

Oral motives play a considerable role. Sedna is called Food Dish.[136] In the Smith Sound version it is a girl who starts to eat her parents. Father takes her out on a boat and chops her fingers off because she will not marry anybody. The fingers give rise to various kinds of seals.[137] In the Nunivak version "Her father said to her, 'What is the matter with you that you don't get married and get a helper for us? You are no help to us. What kind of man do you want? Do you want to marry your dog?' *When*

[132] Boas, "The Eskimo of Baffin Land and Hudson Bay," *Bull. Am. Mus. Nat. Hist.*, XV, 1901, pp. 163–165.

[133] *Idem*, "Die religiösen Vorstellungen der zentralen Eskimo," *Petermann's Mitteilungen*, 1887, p. 302; *idem*, "The Eskimo," *Transactions of the Royal Society of Canada*, 1887, Section II, p. 35.

[134] Rink and Boas, "Eskimo Tales and Songs," *Journal of American Folk-Lore*, II, 1889, p. 125.

[135] Boas, *Baffin Land*, pp. 327, 328.

[136] Rasmussen, *op. cit.*, p. 151.

[137] Kroeber, F., "Tales of the Smith Sound Eskimo," *Journal of American Folk-Lore*, XII, p. 179.

he said this the dog woke up, turned over and looked around as if he had listened to what the father said. He got up and shook himself as dogs do when they get up from sleeping."[138]

The dog marriage motive is well known among the Indian tribes of North America. The Thompson River Indians tell the story about a girl who was frequently visited by her father's dog, she puts red paint on her hands and that is how they recognize the culprit.[139]

A chief called Alke had a daughter. She could not leave the room because she was menstruating and she was visited every night by her father's dog. She smears red paint on the dog (Heiltsuk). Here again the story ends with a storm and a sinking boat.[140] There is another group of stories similar to those of the marriage with the dog. The nocturnal visitor is the brother, brother and sister are both consumed in flames. Red paint leads to recognition.[141] In another myth brother and sister become Sun and Moon. The paint marks are the spots on the surface of the moon.[142] The Arekuna say the menstrual blood is visible in the spots on the surface of the moon.[143] In one of the Dené stories recorded by Petitot the sequel of the dog-marriage is incest of brother and sister.

Evening came and she went to bed with the stranger. She awoke and her husband had disappeared but she heard a dog gnawing bones.[144]

In another similar group of stories we have a hammer instead of the dog. In a myth of the Nunivak Eskimo:

"In the summer she went to her little house to play again. She cooked and slept. When she slept there she felt someone touching her behind

138 Lantis, *op. cit.,* XXXV, Part III, 1946, p. 267.

139 Teit, "Mythology of the Thompson River Indians," *Jesup North Pacific Expedition,* VIII, p. 354.

140 Boas, *Indianische Sagen von der Nord-Pazifischen Küste Amerikas,* 1895, pp. 263, 264; cf. p. 37.

141 Teit, "Traditions of the Lillooet Indians of British Columbia," *Journal of American Folk-Lore,* 1912, pp. 340, 341.

142 Cranz, D. L., *Historie von Grönland,* 1770, III, p. 295; Egede, *Nachrichten von Grönland,* 1790, p. 75; Nansen, *Eskimoleben,* p. 235; Rink, *Tales and Traditions,* p. 236; idem, "Die religiösen Vorstellungen der zentralen Eskimo," *Petermann's Mitteilungen,* 1887, p. 311; idem, *Baffin Land,* pp. 173, 306, 307; "The Central Eskimo," *Report of the Bur. of Am. Ethn.,* XI, pp. 597, 598; Holm, G. and Petersen, I., "Legends and Tales from Angmágsalik," *Meddedelser on Gronland,* XXXIX, 1914, p. 253; Nelson, "The Eskimo about Bering Strait," *XVIIIth Annual Report of the Bur. of Am. Ethn.,* pp. 481, 482; Turner, L. M., "Ethnology of the Ungava District," *Annual Report of the Bur. of Am. Ethn.,* XI, p. 264; Kroeber, "Tales of the Smith Sound Eskimo," *Journal of American Folk-Lore,* XII, p. 179; Boas, *Sagen,* pp. 30, 37; Krause, A., *Die Tlinkit Indianer,* Jena, 1885, p. 270; Mooney, I., "Myths of the Cherokee," *XIXth Report of the Bur. of Am. Ethn.,* pp. 256, 257; Ehrenreich, P., *Mythen und Legenden der süd-amerikanischen Urvölker,* 1903, p. 37; Unkel, C., "Religion der Apapocuva Guarano," *Zeitschrift für Ethnologie,* 1915, p. 282.

143 Koch Grünberg, T., *Vom Rorvima zum Orinoco,* 1916, II, pp. 54, 55.

144 Petitot, *Traditions Indiennes du Canada Nord-Ouest,* 1887, Alencon, p. 301.

her. When she really woke up she saw someone going out. Her boots were off. Even though she was barefoot she went out and looked. That person went up the cliff and disappeared. When she went down to her mother again she did not tell her parents about it."

Her mother told her, "You be careful. Women always have monthly periods. The first time you won't know it." (The girl starts to menstruate.) That girl stayed in her little house three days and three nights. Every evening her father came to see her how she was getting along. One night she awoke very afraid. *She felt there was someone behind her but it wasn't her father* (the negative in dreams!). It was a very young man without any beard. He did not look like her father. That young man said to her, "Do not be afraid. You will get your first-born baby. Do not let your father or mother see it. Even though your first-born baby is ugly you will keep it, but keep it in secret."

"In summer her stomach was getting big. Her mother said, 'If that baby wants to come out you will watch it.' Her mother put a lamp behind her. Something came out of her. She felt it and took it. It was round and hard. It had eyes and ears and lots of teeth. It was not a real baby. It had everything as on a person's face but it was like a stone hammer with a little handle. She hid it under the bench."[145]

Boas records an origin myth of the Koantel clan:

"The chief of the Koantel had a daughter. She did not want to marry. Once a man crawled into her bed and she did not refuse him. It was her father's hammer, in human shape. Before dawn he left her and became a hammer again. Next night another man came and slept with her. It was her father's dog also in the form of a man. She was delivered of puppies because the dog was stronger than the hammer. When her father saw this he was ashamed."[146]

It is quite clear therefore that both the dog and the hammer represent father's penis. They are related to mythical dogs of the Micmac who are no bigger than a finger but are able to assume gigantic proportions.[147]

Dog and father who live with Sedna in the underworld are originally the same person. One report says that the father is no bigger than a finger or a little boy but he can also be gigantic.[148] The Dakota call a person who commits incest a dog.[149]

If further proof were needed we have the Cumberland Sound story of

[145] Lantis, "The Social Culture of the Nunivak Eskimo," *Transactions of the American Philosophical Society,* Vol. XXXV, Part 3, 1946, p. 273.

[146] Boas, *Indianische Sagen,* pp. 24, 25; cf. also p. 41.

[147] Rand, T. S., *Legends of the Micmac,* 1894, p. 286.

[148] Cranz, *op. cit.,* p. 264; Egede, *op. cit.,* p. 75.

[149] Riggs, S. R., "Dakota Grammar, Texts and Ethnography," *Contributions to North American Ethnology,* IX, Washington, 1893, p. 147.

Akkolookjo and Omerneeto. They were the primal beings who established the laws the Eskimo observe today. Omerneeto used to wear her husband's *boots*. She did not fasten the upper strings properly but allowed the boot-leg to sag down and the boot strings to drag over the ground. One day the soul of an infant that was on the ground crept up the boot string and up into the womb. The child grew in the womb and finally was born. One day it told its parents how it had crawled into the womb. It continued: "There I was in a small house. Every night when you cohabited a *dog would come in* and vomit food for me to make me grow."[150]

The dog is the father's penis, the boots are the vagina and the meat the father puts into the boots also represent father's penis.

We also assume that like its European equivalent[151] this story of the Beauty and the Beast, or dog marriage is based upon a dream. The dog or hammer disappears at the approach of dawn, the stories mention sleep and awakening. But we can even go one step further. This is the dream of a menstruating woman, she dreams of having intercourse *with her father who is symbolized in the dream by a dog or hammer*.

I have always found that there is a strong tendency in menstruating women to dream about coitus with the father or the analyst. Many primitive people believe that the menstruating woman is the wife of the moon, or an ancestor or supernatural being.[152]

In the Cheyenne story the unknown nocturnal visitor has a white mantle, red marks identify him as father's dog.[153] In the Thompson River story "At last she noticed her father's dog go out with a red streak of ochre on each of his sides."[154] In the Frazer River story the dog is black, she smears her hands with grease and red ochre.[155] A further variation of the motive she greases her stomach to seduce the dog.[156] In one story the color is white,[157] yet we may safely assume that red is the original color and that the red color symbolizes menstrual blood. We do not know whether the North West American stories should be regarded as the original ones that migrated to the Eskimo or are the Eskimo stories independently invented.

150 Boas, *Baffin Land*, p. 483.

151 Tegethoff, E., *Studien zum Märchentypus von Amor und Psyche*, Bonn und Leipzig, 1922, Rheinische Beiträge und Hülfsbücher zur germanischen Philologie und Volkskunde, Vol. 4.

152 Cf. Róheim, *Mondmythologie und Mondreligion*, 1927, p. 83.

153 Kroeber, "Cheyenne Tales," *Journal of American Folk-Lore*, XIII, 1900, p. 181.

154 Teit, "Traditions of the Thompson River Indians of British Columbia," *Mem. Am. F. L. Soc.*, VI, 1898, p. 62.

155 Boas, *Indianische Sagen*, p. 27.

156 Teit, "Traditions of the Lillooet Indians," *Journal of American Folk-Lore*, 1912, p. 316.

157 Farrand, L., "Traditions of the Chilcotin," *Jesup North Pacific Expedition*, II, p. 7.

But we do know that the belief in the shaman's journey to the mythical woman is based on a man's dream, while the story of the dog marriage was obviously first dreamed by a menstruating woman. Due to something they have in common in the latent content the two are united in the Sedna complex. The objects that cling to Sedna are usually interpreted as still-born children, miscarriages that have not been confessed by the women.

"The souls of the sea mammals are endowed with greater powers than those of ordinary human beings. They can see the effects of contact with a corpse which causes objects touched by it to appear dark in color and they can see the effect of flowing human blood, from which a vapor arises that surrounds the bleeding person and is communicated to everyone and everything that comes in contact with such a person. This vapor and the dark color of death are exceedingly unpleasant to the souls of the sea animals that will not come near a hunter thus affected. The hunter must therefore avoid contact with people who have touched a body or with those who are bleeding, more particularly with *menstruating women or with those who have recently given birth. The hands of menstruating women appear red to the sea animals.* If anyone who has touched a body or who is bleeding should allow others to come in contact with him, he would cause them to become distasteful to *the seals and therefore to Sedna as well.* For this reason custom demands that every person must at once announce if he has touched a body and the women must make known when they are menstruating or when they have a miscarriage. If they do not do so they will bring ill luck to the hunters.[158] The filth that accumulates around Sedna's hair is really identical with the state menstruating women are in or women immediately after delivery.[159]

Certain customs and rites are observed in connection with the descent of the shaman. Let us first take an obviously related belief and custom of the Yukaghis. The drum is the lake through which the shaman descends to the nether world. First the shaman takes deep breaths, inhaling the souls of his ancestors. The soul of the patient has gone down to shadowland and he is going to fetch it back. After a time he stopped beating the drum and remained motionless lying on the reindeer skin. His soul has now gone down accompanied by his guardian spirits. There is a dog there and an old woman. When she talks he is not to answer her (otherwise he will not return). There is a river, a boat, he crosses to the other bank. He catches the truant soul and inhales it. Then he stuffs his ears to prevent the soul from escaping. He appeals to his "sun rays," that is, to the solar image or his shaman's coat to drag him out, and he comes back to the earth.

158 Boas, ". . . Baffin Land," pp. 120, 121.
159 Rasmussen, "Intellectual Culture of the Iglulik Eskimo," *Report of the Fifth Thule Expedition,* 1921–1924, VII, No. 1, Copenhagen, 1929, pp. 132–141.

Virgin girls must now rub his legs to help him to revive. These are the kind of girls into whom the male spirits love to enter.[160]

We take this like a footnote that explains the text, the shaman enters the nether world, the spirits enter the girls.

At Cumberland Sound when Sedna is near enough the shaman throws his harpoon at her. Then she slides back to her abode. *The people try to accelerate her return by exchanging wives.* The soul of the shaman goes down to stab Sedna, then he returns to his body.[161]

If a woman is barren the shaman flies to the moon. From the moon he throws a child down to make the woman pregnant. After this he has the right to have intercourse with her.[162] In the same ceremonial on the north shore of Hudson Strait masked beings called Ekko appear. They are created by the shaman. The Ekko does not speak but indicates by moans that someone has transgressed a taboo. One Ekko is male, the other female. The man wears a hood over his head, his eyes are covered with goggles and he has a conical mouthpiece. Straps pass from the shoulders down his sides and between his legs, and his long penis is tied up.[163]

The shaman performs a phallic journey to the mother of sea animals. He cuts parasites off her head, sea animals are released. In the myth, Sedna's father cuts her fingers or finger joints off; this is the origin of sea animals. Obviously the shaman is playing the role of the father of the goddess. It is true that in the belief the cutting is an act of kindness, in the myth, one of utmost cruelty. Clearly the attitude toward the Sedna image is ambivalent. Although the shaman's journey is supposed to benefit the goddess yet he is also supposed to fight her, risking his life.

The whole ritual evidently allays an anxiety both in the shaman and in the people.

"When a person becomes an *angakok,* a light covers his body. He can see supernatural things. The stronger the light is within him the deeper and farther he can see and the greater is his supernatural power. The light makes his whole body feel well. When the intensity of this light increases he feels a strong pressure and it seems to him as though a film were being removed from his eyes which prevented him in seeing clearly. The light is always with him. It enables him to see into the future and back into the past. When he dies the light leaves his body to the eyes of the shaman, the earth is but a thin shell, he can see everything that is under it [cf. the

160 Jochelson, "The Yukaghir and Yukaghirized Tungus," *Memoirs of the American Museum of Natural History,* XIII, 1926, pp. 195, 196.
161 Boas, *op. cit.,* p. 139.
162 Nansen, *Eskimoleben,* Leipzig, 1903, p. 249; cf. also Kroeber, "Tales of the Smith Sound Eskimo," *Journal of American Folk-Lore,* XII, p. 180; Thalbitzer, "The Ammassalik Eskimo," *Meddedelser om Grönland,* XXXIX, p. 289.
163 Boas, *op. cit.,* p. 491.

seeing and the descent]. He can also see inside persons. *While there is a great pressure of light on the angakok he visits Sedna.*"[164]

After each shaman performance the people must exchange wives. If any woman should refuse to go to the hut of the man to whom she is assigned she would be sure to get sick.[165]

After the ceremony a spirit called Quailertetang visits the tribe. She is a servant of Sedna. It is a man in a woman's costume wearing a mask of seal skin. She is a large woman of very heavy limbs who comes to make good weather and the souls of men calm like the sea.[166]

According to the Ponds Bay myth Sedna was married to a *red dog* who was the father of the white people, the dwarfs and the Eskimo.[167] According to another story one sister married a dog and became the ancestress of mankind, the other married a bird and she became Sedna.[168]

It is a dangerous dream, coitus with the menstruating mother. No wonder that we find castration anxiety connected with the Sedna complex, "When telling of Sedna, Conieossuk and his wife would clutch the top of the table from the side, then letting go the right hand would draw it edgewise over the fingers of the left, or she would hold both hands while she struck them with the edge of his."[169] Sedna has only one eye and she cannot walk.[170] Eskimo women have two pigtails, she has only one, but it is very long.[171] Nuliayoq has but one eye, transgressions make her eye sore.[172]

Tornarsuk, variously called the father, son or husband of Sedna, has only one arm but it is very big and looks awful.[173] Sedna's father is the one-armed Anguta, he grabs the dying with his one arm.[174]

Behind all this is something else. These hunters kill with guilt feelings and libido, the animals they have killed are unconsciously identified with Sedna, the mother goddess. Sedna herself must be a seal, they harpoon her[175] (cf. above).

A captured seal must be treated with great consideration. The harpoon must be taken into the hut and placed near the lamp. If the harpoon

[164] *Ibid.*, p. 133.
[165] *Ibid.*, p. 158.
[166] *Ibid.*, p. 140.
[167] *Ibid.*, p. 497.
[168] *Ibid.*, p. 496.
[169] Smith, H. J., "Notes on Eskimo Traditions," *Journal of American Folk-Lore*, VII, p. 210.
[170] Boas, *op. cit.*, p. 119.
[171] *Idem, Central Eskimo*, p. 586.
[172] *Idem, Baffin Land*, pp. 496, 497, 504.
[173] Egede, *op. cit.*, pp. 23, 237; Cranz, *op. cit.*, p. 264.
[174] Boas, *Central Eskimo*, p. 586.
[175] *Ibid.*, p. 604.

should be left outside the soul would become cold and if it should report this to Nuliayoq she would be displeased. It is said that long ago when a harpoon had been left outside, the seal's soul begged a woman to take it in. The woman refused, so instead of entering the hut the soul went into her body and was reborn as a child.[176] We have seen that the act of cutting the attachments off the goddess is compared to that of giving a person a drink.

"When a seal is brought into the snow house a piece of snow is dipped into the kettle and held over its mouth allowing the melting snow to drip into it. This signifies giving a drink to the seal and is intended to please Nuliayoq."[177]

The souls of seals, ground seals and whales are believed to come from her house. After one of these animals has been killed its soul stays with the body for three days. If during this time any "violation" (of taboos) should happen the violation becomes attached to the animal's soul and causes pain. The soul strives in vain to get rid of these attachments and it takes them down to Sedna. The attachments make her hands sore and she punishes people by sending sickness, bad weather and starvation.[178]

The identity of the dead seal and the goddess who is the mother of seals becomes perfectly evident. But if she is a seal, then the myth in which the finger joints are cut off the goddess and the belief that she will send the seals out of her house, if freed of the stillborn children that cling to her, simply means that by coitus the shaman (a) kills her, (b) compels her to deliver the embryo from her womb.

We have a description of what happens after the Sedna ceremony at Cumberland Sound.

On this day all the people have attached to their hoods a piece of skin of the animal which their mothers used when cleaning them when they were born. The skins of ptarmigan, golden plover, goose, owl, etc., are used for this purpose. If they should not wear this piece of skin they would get sick. Their souls would become light and would leave the body. It is said that if they wear this skin they are *made new*.

They run round the tents shouting "hoo hoo" till the owners come out to give them a small present, generally something to eat. Their cries cause their souls to stay longer in their bodies. Then they have a rope-pulling contest. Those born during the summer stand close to the water, those born in the winter stand inland. If the winter should win there will be plenty of food, if summer should win there will be a bad winter.

Then they place a tub near the Quailertetang (the female masked

176 Boas, *Baffin Land*, p. 500.   177 *Ibid.*, p. 148.
178 *Ibid.*, p. 120.

being appearing as the servant of Sedna). Everyone brings some water and empties it into the tub. Now one after another they all sip a little of the water and they say: "I was born in such and such a place during the season of . . ." whatever place or season it may be and then they wish for calm weather and that their souls may be calm like the weather.[179]

Among the Central Eskimo the same ceremony is described as follows: "They all stand as near the kettle as possible while the oldest man among them steps out first. He dips a cup of water from the vessel, sprinkles a few drops on the ground, turns his face toward the home of his youth and tells his name and the place of his birth. He is followed by an old woman who announces her name and home and then all the others do the same down to the young children who are represented by their mothers."[180]

The seals are born and the people are born. The use of the animal skin, first used by their mothers to wipe them, makes this quite clear. The tub symbolizes the mother both as womb and as breast. Lantis writes: "The annual cycle economically and ritually culminated in a great winter festival honoring the food animals especially seals [= Sedna]—a ceremony of tremendous emotional value. The old year's taboos were ended, new utensils were consecrated, new clothing displayed, new songs composed, everything was set right with the supernatural world."[181]

After the descent of flight of the shaman comes rebirth—a dream-derived sequence.

But there is another factor to consider in determining the content of the dream (aggression, cutting). Oral aggression must have been tremendously important among the Eskimo.

A woman who has an infant puts a small piece of meat to the child's mouth and then places it in a bag. This is believed to please the child's guardian spirit (*tornaq*). At night a piece of meat is placed in a dish near the child. If the child's guardian spirit should visit it at night, he would look for food and if he should not find any would eat first the mother's vital organs, then the father's, and then those of the other natives.[182]

Sedna or Nuliayoq who causes starvation is the talio aspect of the child's oral aggression. Each seal that is killed and eaten represents Sedna or the mother, the way to ward off her anger is to have intercourse with her, to break up the mother-child unity by introducing the male. Stillborn children cling to her with guilt (she killed the child) but children who are born leave her and grow up—both the seals and the Eskimo.

And now we can reflect on what may also be called the two gates of

179 *Ibid.*, pp. 140, 141.   180 *Idem, Central Eskimo*, p. 605.
181 Lantis, *Nunivak Eskimo*, p. 255.   182 Boas, *Baffin Land*, p. 160.

the dream. We have found that dreaming has a mechanism of its own, sleep is uterine regression, the dream is the formation of a libidinal double and the re-creation of the world on a libidinal basis. Many are the ramifications thereof in our beliefs, myths and rituals.

But the dream is also conditioned by conflicts or wishes of waking life. Oral aggression and talio anxiety or the primal scene are subjects of the dream but not derived from dreaming.

Thus, there are two gates, one through which waking life goes into the dream and one through which our dreams influence our waking life.

The dream interpretation of the Eskimo New Year ceremony can be confirmed on the basis of comparative ethnography. We have commented above on the New Year ceremony with the masked dancers going round shouting "hoo hoo" and receiving little presents "to keep their souls in their bodies."

The corresponding festival of the Iroquois and Hurons was called the Festival of Dreams. It would take place toward the end of February and last three or four days.

Men, women and children would rush about almost naked. Sometimes they would have masks or paint. In a state of frenzy they ran from hut to hut smashing and upsetting everything and pouring hot water or cold ashes on the people. Each of them had dreamed of something and he would not leave the house till somebody had guessed his dream and carried it out in practice. The person in question was bound to present the dreamer with the thing he had dreamed of for his life depended on obtaining it. But he would not state it in simple words, he would hint at it or indicate it by gestures.[183] Early settlers found this belief rather inconvenient. A demand made for tobacco had to be complied with because it was based on a dream. They believed that they would die if they did not execute their dreams. One of them tried to kill a Frenchman because he dreamed that this would cure him.[184]

Hewitt has more to say about this ritual than the ancient Jesuit writers: "The annual sacrifice of a white dog at the New Year ceremony by the Iroquois is in fulfilment of a dream of Teharonhiawagon. The date for the ceremony is on the fifth day of the new moon called Disgona (i.e., long moon), i.e., about a month after the winter solstice. Teharonhia-

---

183 Frazer, *Totemism and Exogamy*, 1910, 111, pp. 482, 483; *idem, The Scapegoat*, 1911, p. 127; *Relations des Jésuites*, 1656, pp. 26–29, Canadian Reprint, Quebec, 1858, *Lifitau Moeurs des sauvages américains*, Paris, 1724, I, pp. 367–369; Charlevoix, *Histoire de la nouvelle France*, Paris, 1744, VI, p. 82; Hennepin, L., *Description de la Louisiane*, Paris, 1683, p. 71; Randle, M. Champion, "Psychological Types from Iroquois Folk Tales," *Journal of American Folk-Lore*, LXV, 1952, p. 16.

184 The Jesuit Relations; V, Quebec, 1632 (Le Jeune), pp. 159, 161.

wagon is the god of spring or summer, his opponent is Tawiskaron, the winter god. Dreams being the recognized means through which tutelaries may reveal the objects for agencies to be employed for the recovery of health when ruined by sorcery it was assumed that Teharonhiawagon in view of his weakened power must have dreamed what would restore his life, the life in nature to its normal condition and the tutelaries of man, his father's clansmen revealed the fact that he has dreamed that a sacrificial victim is required to disenchant the life forces in man and nature. If the ceremony would not be performed, emigrating birds and fishes would not return, animals would continue to hibernate and all normal life would cease. He who seeks the fulfilment of his dream must chant his death song, the challenge song of his tutelary and for this reason Teharonhiawagon sings his death chant in midwinter for if his dream be disregarded and remain unsatisfied, the complete destruction of all life on earth would take place.

"The name given to this rite by all Iroquois tribes signifies 'it drives, urges or distracts one's brain,' " meaning the promptings of the soul inspired by the guardian spirit to seek something.

"With the close of the two fire rites the Dream festival or ceremony begins, this usually lasts three days. This rite is the renewal or rejuvenation of the personal tutelary of every person who possesses one by having its distinctive chant resung by the clansmen of the father of the owner with a drum or rattles. (2) The divining or seeking to guess the 'dream word' of those who have had specific dreams for the purpose of ascertaining the dreamer's guardian spirit. The dreamer is usually a child and what he receives is a small symbolic representation of his guardian spirit. Every clan appoints a man and a woman to hear these specific dreams from children and different persons in their clan and they relate these dreams to the chiefs whose duty it is to divine the guardian spirits for each dreamer.

"The dream ritual ends with the masked performers or False Face Society whose reception requires that the dream word of the eldest of these be divined."[185] If we regard Teharonhiawagon as the presiding spirit of this dream festival, certain interesting deductions follow almost automatically. This god is identical with Jouskeha, i.e., Sapling or the god who triumphs in spring over his adversary Tawiscaron (Flint, Winter). We shall see later that the dying and reviving gods of ancient civilizations (Tammuz, Osiris, etc.) were only projected upon a cosmic and annual scale, originally the descent to the underworld is what happens to every human being when he goes to sleep and the return is awakening. The

---

[185] Hewitt, J. N. B., "White Dog Sacrifice," *Handbook of American Indians*, II, 1910, pp. 939–944, Bureau of Am. Ethn. Bull., No. 30.

etymology of the name given by Hewitt is also of interest. It signifies "double"[186] and the formation of a double is certainly the essential trait of the dream. His myths show[187] that he is identical with the Thrown Away Boy of North American mythology, who, as we intend to show, represents the creative, the genital impulse, the ideal as opposed to reality, the soul as opposed to the body. His name means Sky Holder and therefore he must be regarded as a duplicate of the Sky Chief of these myths whose name means He the Earth Holder.

This chief, suspecting his pregnant wife of having conceived by someone else caused the tree of light to be uprooted and then cast his pregnant wife down through the abyss. In her fall or after her fall her daughter is born. While she was falling the best divers among the water animals brought up wet earth from the sea and thus created the earth.

This happened because none could find what was the matter with the Sky Chief, they could not "search his dream word."[188]

The etiological myth of the Dream Feast, therefore, is again what we called the basic dream, the moment of falling asleep, the myth of the earth-diver, the world that is created night by night.

North American shamanism tends to blend in some tribes with the concept of the guardian spirit. On the other hand there is no hard and fast line between a vision induced by fasting and a dream.

The Mohave had the same beliefs about dreams as the Yuma.[189] In the power-giving dream the dreamer's spirit went to Awikwame, the mountain of creation and there he spoke with Mastamho, or some other deity. Special powers were given and the spirit was taught a particular song. Dreams in later life were often regarded as repetitions of what the embryo dreamed in the womb. The son frequently "dreamed" the same dream his father had dreamt before.[190]

The Yuma (Kucan) believe that whatever one does can only be done on the basis of a dream. In Chapter I we have already discussed the qualifications of a medicine man who is supposed to dream about creation and the intrauterine situation. The dream creates a new world and the medicine man who is re-creating the patient dreams about creation. According to Forde the medicine man (shaman) in his dreams goes back to the mountain of creation, Awikwame. Furthermore, he also retraces

---

186 Cf. article Teharonhiawagon in *Handbook of American Indians*, II, p. 718.

187 Hewitt, J. N. B., "Iroquoian Cosmology," *Annual Report, Bureau Am. Ethn.*, XXI, 1903, p. 188.

188 Cf. Hewitt, article Teharonhiawagon.

189 Cf. Yuma dreams in the first chapter.

190 Wallace, W. J., "The Dream in Mohave Life," *Journal of American Folk-Lore*, LX, 1947, pp. 252, 253.

time in the sense that the original mourning ceremony (*karook*) for Koko-mat is still being held when he arrives.[191] According to the Maricopa supernatural power comes only in dreams. Dream and spirit are the same word *camag*. "The only way to express spirit is that it comes in dreams. The word for 'one who has power' is 'one who dreams.' The spirit takes the shadow out of the dreaming man but the spirit itself is a shadow. Therefore the dream is a meeting of shadows, the dream experience is both dream and spirit and spirits exist only in dreams."[192] The *matkwesha* (shadow) or *matchaau* (double) is what communicates with the shamans in their dreams. But it is also the same shadow or double that goes into the woman's womb and becomes a child. Or rather it is a particle of the father's soul, though at the same time the soul does not become reduced with the number of children procreated. The soul enters the woman in the sexual act. Dreaming about anything that can be brought in connection with the creation myth—as for instance clouds—gives medicine power. A gambler has to dream of gambling in order to be a successful gambler. A man named Topom dreamed that the king of the pack of cards came and told him: "I am here to tell you that I will help you," and he could always tell what cards his opponent had. In order to become crazy you must first dream it. If somebody desires victory in the pole game or in war very strongly he will dream about it and then it will come true. The Xanye[193] was a fire witch or fire dreamer and even nowadays frogs can swallow burning coal. If someone dreams about a frog he will be able to cure burns. The Coyote in a dream makes the dreamer bad, a thief or trickster. Some medicine men dream of the frog and they will kill people by burning their excrements.

Mail takeva (Coming together) says his medicine dream was about a lot of birds or bats and he would be able to sing their song. He tries to start the song but his resistance is too great, he refuses to go on with it.

About the dream he offers some remarks. "I was told to use a basket turned upside down instead of a rattle. They took me over there and put me in the middle of the desert where the Bat lives. You will sing about the wind and the clouds, you will be a singer of these songs"—they said.

"The Bat said the wind and the clouds are my *matchau* (spirit) and asked me whether I thought I could sing these. I said, 'Yes, I sang it in my dream,' and the Bat said, 'Yes, that is right you will be able to sing it.' Then the Bat said, 'That is all the powers I am going to give you.'

"The Bats are like persons like the Kuccan here, they tell me the

[191] Forde, C. D., "Ethnography of the Yuma Indians," University of California Publications, in *American Archeology and Ethnology*, XXVIII, 1931, pp. 203, 204.
[192] Spier, L., *Yuman Tribes of the Gila River*, Chicago, 1937, pp. 236, 237.
[193] The frog in the creation myth who by eating his excrements kills Kokomat.

dream started at Awikwame." The Bat who spoke to him was a tall young man—then he is very surprised to find that a dead relative looked like this [Block at this point]. All questions I ask he replies to by general statements, which mean nothing, but little by little further details emerge. A part of the song:

> I got there, when I got there they brought
> It shall be sung this way to take it,
> Pick it up and put it down.

The bats came flying in flocks to give him the dream song.

He thinks he had this dream when he was about ten years old. When the bats were flying he was scraping the basket with a stick. Women use these baskets for winnowing wheat. When they are finished they put it away upside down.[194]

Another man whose name is *Korel jexam* (Far pretty) says he learned something from his father. He *eshemaak* (dreamed) of creation time but he really means that his father did. He talks about the song as if it were a person who comes from the north. The song sings:

> My home I leave it, I am going
> My home I left, I saw, I related.

Then the song moves on to a different place. It comes to a mountain and stands opposite to it. This mountain is called Evixaruntat (Sharp-pointed). The song looks back from there to its original home, etc. (a long narrative about the wanderings of the song or child).

A brave man or warrior must have had a dream about a cougar (Xatakulj).

Use Kochmal (White Mud), a medicine man, relates the following dream.

I dreamed of a mountain that was not very high, it was yellow, not very high, it was gold. I put it into my pocket. There was a house, an old style Indian House. I went in. I thought these must be all dead people. I was afraid and came out again. There was a wagon. I rolled up my blankets and went north with it. I arrived at a house. It was as if I had come back. It was just bedtime. I did not go in because I was afraid my blankets were wet. When I saw the mountain in the dream I said to myself, "Nobody knows about this mountain, it is only mine." *When I go to sleep I always think of it and then I am there.* [Regressive character of hypnagogic fantasy.]

He mentions also another mountain he dreamed of. He knows he went there in his dream and everybody else fell off that mountain, he alone did not. This means that all the other men of his age are dead,

---

[194] I conjecture that the dream is a symbolic coitus: elements, the basket (female), the stick (male) and the flying bats (male).

he alone survives (exaggerated statement). Then he mentions another
dream:

> I saw a pretty woman, she held my hand and invited me to go with
> her northward. There was a nice house but I did not go in. The country
> looked good, green. It was a high mountain, northward. But I came back.
> People came and asked me, why did you come back? I said, I did not
> like it.

He explains what all this means. The dream has something to do with
a real experience. The name of this mountain is Ecoor (name of a bird).
The woman was short, fat, good looking, big eyes. He knows nobody who
looks like that. He said, he went to a mountain where he found a *crystal*
stone standing up from the ground right at the place where he dreamed
about the woman. The stone had three branches at the top, the Yuma call
it *stooc ceulk*, baby carrying; it represents a woman carrying her two
children.[195] He kicked the stone away. If you had this stone you would
be able to get any woman in the world, and you could win all pole games—
but it might also make you sick. Since then he has not been able to find it.
In the dream a woman showed me the place. Therefore I might have been
able to get women with the stone—but then the first woman would have
been jealous and she would have made me sick.[196]

Eating salt or meat might also make him sick.

Another name for this crystal is *Kwec humuuk* (bodies three). He says,
"*Estoulj*. This word means to have power bestowed upon me by the
crystal. If I did anything to displease the dream woman, she might hit my
face, it would be crooked, or my hand it would be swollen. It was very
hard for me to get women when I was young. I wondered where others obtained their power. Going north in the dream means to be happy."

Although these dreams are not the typical shaman's dreams, yet they
shed some light on the dream about Awikwame. The mountain of creation
to which they always go back, and his private mountain, which he always
decides he will go back to when he goes to sleep, are the same thing, the
breast. He rejects the magic stone, he is afraid of women, afraid of the
jealousy of the dream woman. Becoming a medicine man is evidently a
sublimated or regressive substitute for success with women. The blackbird
is a medicine bird, makes you a medicine man, but also gives you luck with
women. It is also of interest to observe that the mountain dream is really
a dream about going to sleep. He arrives at the house = womb, woman,
mountain, just at bedtime.

---

[195] His real name was Metel saw kuraw—which means some sort of crystal used
for hair powder. He did not like it and chose the other one.
[196] The point in this is that the woman in question does not even exist except
in the dream.

If we assume that the shaman is really simply the dream personified, i.e., absence and recall of the soul, we can understand this idea of dreaming in the womb as a symbolic expression of dreaming of the womb, i.e., the basic dream. The shaman regresses and dreams about the creation of the world of his own birth, i.e, he visualizes the process of sleeping and dreaming.

According to the Mohave every shaman has his first shamanistic or power dream while still in the womb. They also assume that a normal embryo starts thinking and dreaming when it is about five months old. They dream about their growth and the way of being born. Sometimes they are awake, sometimes asleep. They know when their mothers are asleep and generally fall asleep a short time after their mothers do. "There is a community of dreams between the mother and the unborn child, though neither of them originates these dreams which, like all other dreams, come from the outside. The child also follows all of its mother's actions. He will be her second self—or her second spirit—almost." Potential shamans *do not wish to be born,* hence they dream of killing their mothers and themselves by assuming a transversal position in the womb.[197]

One singer goes so far as to say that he dreamed the song *in utero* and if he had dreamed it later he would not remember it.[198] The Takelma distinguish the *goyo* who both inflicts and cures disease and the *somloholxa* who only cures disease. He would dream of the creation of all things and of all that was to be. "Rock Old Woman" or "Grandmother" was one of the guardian spirits of these dreamers.[199]

The Digueno of California are interesting in many respects. We have emphasized above that the process of dream formation has two aspects, (a) the dreamer goes back into the womb, (b) sleep means that the dreamer withdraws object cathexes from environment, goes back into himself. Thus in shamanism we have either the flight or descent of the shaman to the supernatural world or the shaman's body as a receptacle of the spirits.

Preoccupation with dreams in the Digueno tribe has actually led to developing a kind of shamanism that could be called a primitive psychoanalysis because the "dream doctor" uses dream interpretation, especially of incest dreams, to cure his patient. However, what concerns us here is that the highest degree of these dream doctors have the *erur,* or *circle*

---

[197] Devereux, G., "Mohave Pregnancy," *Acta Americana,* VI, 1948, p. 104; cf. also *idem,* "Mohave Indian Obstetrics," *American Imago,* V, No. 2; cf. D. Mac. Taylor, *The Black Carib of British Honduras,* Viking Fund. Publ. in Anthropology, No. 17, New York, 1951, p. 111.

[198] Kroeber, A. L., "Seven Mohave Myths," *Anthropological Records,* XI, Los Angeles, 1948, p. 37.

[199] Sapir, E., "Religious Ideas of the Takelma Indians," *Journal of American Folk-Lore,* XX, 1907, pp. 44, 45.

dream. He dreams of putting his arms round the world with his fingers touching, a symbol of all-embracing knowledge. A doctor who has the complete circle dream in which his fingers touch will be powerful and successful all his life. The circle represents the world full of animals and women (i.e., a full womb, but also a complete grasp of mother). A doctor who feels his powers and self-confidence waning goes to the hills to fast and concentrate on his magic rocks, hoping that the circle dream will come to him again to reinforce him.[200]

These dream shamans are initiated by administering *toloache* (Jimson weed, *Datura meteloides*). During the narcosis they are supposed to have several pattern dreams and the circle dream indicates the highest degree achieved. Another of these pattern dreams is the dream of Synioxan, "the hunter's grandmother," and the first woman in the world. She was present when the primal hunter gave the animals their markings and names. An attendant sings the songs narrating the cosmology and cosmogony of the tribe known only to witch doctors thereby suggesting the dream of Synioxan to the candidate.[201]

Among the Naskapi, Algonquian hunters of the north, to dream is a religious experience and the more a person dreams the better. All sorts of techniques are used to induce dreams, fasting, dancing, singing, drumming, rattling, the sweat bath, meditation, alcoholic drinks and drugs, etc.[202]

"Dreams take the place of prophecy, inspiration, laws, commandment and govern their enterprises in war and peace, in trade, fishing and hunting. This idea impresses on them a kind of necessity, believing that it is a kind of universal spirit that commands them so far even that if it orders them to kill a man or commit any other bad action they execute it at once."[203]

The Naskapi have the usual expressions for soul, like shadow or reflection but they also have one that is all their own, meaning "Great Man."

"This is the term by which the soul in its active state is referred to. Another customary circumlocution for the soul is 'my friend.' It may mean one's own soul or the spirit of a slain animal. When the hunter has performed an act of satisfaction to himself like ceremonial smoking or when in response to a dream he has been drumming, singing or feasting, he says, 'I wish to make my friend feel good.'[204] The Great Man is located in the

200 Toffelmeier, G., and Luomala, K., "Dreams and Dream Interpretation of the Digueno Indians of Southern California," *Psychoanalytic Quarterly,* V, 1936, p. 216.
201 *Idem,* p. 217.
202 Speck, F. G., *Naskapi, The Savage Hunters of the Labrador Peninsula,* Norman, 1935, pp. 180, 181.
203 *Ibid.,* p. 183.
204 Cf. under *genius* ("indulgere genio").

heart, it is the equivalent of the life embodied in human beings and survives after death.

"The Great Man reveals himself in dreams. Those who respond to their dreams by giving them serious attention, by thinking about them, by trying to interpret their meaning in secret and testing out their truth, can cultivate deeper communication with the Great Man. He then favors such a person with more dreams and the dreams improve in quality. The next obligation is for the individual to follow instructions given in dreams and to memorialize them in representations of art." On page 45 Speck reproduces the Great Man, the design is typical *mandala*. "The process of self study of dream cultivation and submission to dream control becomes a dominant idea in the inner life of these people."[204a]

The following dream is of interest because it contains a confirmation of our interpretation of the Sedna journey of the shaman.

"Once an old man and his son were very expert in hunting. And it happened that the son dreamed that he cohabited with the caribou. It seemed that he killed a great many caribou. Then he sang, 'The caribou walked along well like me. Then I walked as he was walking. Then I took his path. And then I walked like the caribou, my trail looking like a caribou trail when I saw my tracks. I indeed am Caribou Man, so I am called.'[205] The Caribou shaman here develops into a mythical being. Caribou Man was once an Indian but his dream made him live with the caribou. He consorts with the main caribou herd and has offspring by the does. He sleeps between the bodies of the animals to keep warm, he eats moss as they do, and when the animals are pursued he rides on a big black bull. He also allows only a certain portion to the hunters under conditions which he indicates.[206] The belief is connected with another belief; the periodic disappearance and reappearance of the caribou. In the interior between Ungava Bay and Hudson Bay there is a distant country where the caribou live. There are pure white mountains shaped like a house but not made of snow, they consist purely of caribou hair. The caribou enter and leave their kingdom each year passing through a valley between two high mountains," etc.

"A conjuror can visit the caribou house and find out what cause keeps the caribou from coming out to the hunters and then he can make them follow him."[207]

While we can here clearly see the close connection with Eskimo beliefs (which is also obvious from the geographical situation), what interests us even more is the parallelism. "Dream intercourse with a doe," = "Dream journey to the house of the caribou." Speck found out that the design on

204a *Ibid.*, pp. 41–44. *Mandala* is Jung's expression for circle or concentric circle. It does not mean what Jung thinks, but simply the uterus.
205 *Ibid.*, p. 83.
206 *Ibid.*, pp. 89, 90.
207 *Ibid.*, p. 84; cf. *ibid.*, Eskimo myth of shaman's journey, p. 88.

the pouches described as trees and flowers (at Lake St. John and Mistassini) or as celestial symbols (St. Marguerite, Moisie) are called "soul," "heart" of "Great Man" (Barren Ground and Ungava). A man whom Speck questioned about the meaning of the design said that the wavy lines near the border were *paths* and some of the smaller patterns flowers. He was reluctant to explain the meaning of the flower-like central figure—till finally he replied, "That indeed is my Great Man."[208] Embryo-like formations are found within the belly of slain animals. The hunters say that they are found frequently complete with hair and all either inside a male or female animal. These miniature forms are called "second within caribou," "second within hare," "second within beaver," according to the animal in which they are found and are regarded as powerful hunting charms.[209]

I assume that "the Great Man within" and the "second within" are essentially similar.

The pattern of shamanism is primarily the dream journey to the house of the supernatural being.

Chinook seers go to the ghosts to recover the wandering soul. Three of them will go and one with a strong guardian spirit is placed first, another with an equally strong one, is last.

"When the trail begins to be dangerous the one in front sings his song—if danger approaches from the rear then the one in the rear does it."[210]

The following lines are italicized to show the dream origin of the journey and the ceremony: *"In the evening when it begins to grow dark they commence the cure of the sick person. When the morning star rises they reach his soul."*

They reach a hole in the ground where the souls of the deceased always drink. If the soul has drunk that water he cannot get well.

When the ghosts carry away the soul the person faints immediately. The spirits of the seers reach the soul that was carried away and turn it round. If the soul has already been taken into the house of ghosts it cannot be brought back. When the ghosts are watching a soul (to take it away) the shaman makes a deer. The ghosts pursue it and leave the soul. Then the shaman has tricked them and returns with the soul (dream chase, obstacle flight). The evil shamans take the soul while the person is asleep.[211]

Lummi Indian medicine men assemble each year after the fishing of

208 Speck, *op. cit.*, pp. 215, 216.
209 *Ibid.*, p. 227.
210 Boas, Chinook Texts, *Smithsonian Institution Bureau of Ethnology,* Washington, 1894, p. 205.
211 *Ibid.*, pp. 206, 207. Cf. *infra* "The Way Back."

the sockeye salmon is over to discover whether any of the souls of the sick are in the land of the dead. "Let us take a trip to the soul world and we shall find out." One says, "I will use the spirit of the woodpecker to bore holes for us to look through." Another, "I will use my mouse spirit to cut all bowstrings in case of a fight." Still another, "I will take my magnetic spirit that he might draw the soul of our friends quickly." They take a rope of braided, shredded cedar bark to symbolize a canoe. Each medicine man takes a pole which he calls his cane and takes his position in the canoe just as if he were really paddling. The people have sticks and drums and they beat these and sing. When they approach the land of souls they sing, "Let us wait until they are *asleep*." Having obtained the soul they return. The return trip is brief because there is nothing to stop them. They relate their adventures and after a time they return the missing soul.[212] Among the Coast Salish the loss of the guardian spirit takes the place of the more usual loss of the soul. (It is the same thing; the ego ideal.) The guardian spirit is taken by the ghosts, if it is not regained soon the patient must die. The guardian spirit of a shaman travels in a canoe. He crosses two rivers to get to the Land of the Dead. The first river is very swift, it cannot be crossed in a canoe. The spirits walk across on a tree, the shaman demonstrates this by walking on a pole. The second river is crossed in an imaginary canoe, the poles now become paddles. There is a fight between the shaman's guardian spirit and the ghosts in which the shaman is victorious.[213]

According to the Bella Coola the deity who initiates shamans is called Laloiail. He lives in the woods. In his hand he carries a wooden wand wound with red cedar bark which he swings producing a singing noise. He plays in ponds in certain mountains. When a woman meets him she begins to menstruate, when a man does his nose begins to bleed. When initiating a shaman he touches his chest with his wand and points his face with the design of the rainbow. Then he swings his wand, this noise makes a person faint. He creates sexual desire in man and animals.

But the shaman's initiation is still closely connected with the journey to the underworld.

A shaman told Boas that when his soul had reached the country of the dead he saw his deceased relatives sitting in the house. While they were talking, the chief called all the ghosts into the dancing house of the ghosts. *The entrance to the door was over a narrow plank.* When he had just stepped on the plank he saw the shaman spirit with red cedar bark

---

[212] Stern, B. I., *The Lummi Indians of North West Washington,* New York, 1934, pp. 80, 81.

[213] Haeberlin, H. K., "Sbetetdah, a Shamanistic Performance of the Coast Salish," *Am. Anthr.,* XX, 1918, pp. 249–256.

and strips of black bear skin. The spirit took hold of him, turned him round and told him to return to his own country.[214]

This narrative sounds precisely like my own dream theory. To sleep is to die or to return to the womb (house) but this is counteracted by the spirit that initiates shamans with his wand, by the phallic personification of the libido.

Since the house of Myths of Bella Coola mythology is so intimately connected with the *kusiut,* the shamanistic masked performance, we may learn some more about shamanism from the Bella Coola.

In the upper heaven we find the house of "Our Woman," the supreme goddess. In order to reach it one must go up the river from the house of the gods in the lower heaven. According to another myth one had to pass through a rent in the sky—a characteristic feature of the soul journey—in order to get through from the lower to the upper heaven. The upper heaven is a prairie without trees. A gale is continually blowing there *driving everything toward the entrance to the house.* (Cf. the swish and wind in the description of the shaman's journey.) Near the house, everything is calm (sleep). In front of the house stands a post in the shape of a large winged monster and *its mouth is the entrance of the house* (oral regression into mother). In front of the house door there is a gravel of three colors—blue, black and white. Behind the house is the salt water pond in which the goddess bathes. In this pond we find also the *sisiutl,* the mythical two-headed snake. When this serpent descends to our world, rocks burst and slide down the sides of the mountains.[215]

This double-headed snake is a helper of the shamans in curing disease. It obtains its supernatural power from the fact that it bathes in the salt water in which the goddess washes her face. When a person sees one of these snakes he should throw sand at it and then he can catch it. Its skin is so hard that it cannot be pierced with a spear or knife. The leaf of a holly is the only thing that will cut its skin. The eye of the snake is a foot in diameter and as transparent as rock crystal. The snake must not be taken into the house but should be placed in a small box under stones or buried in a hole. It is potent for curing disease.

A piece of it is thrown into the water and kept in it for four days. If a person washes in this water he will live to an old age.[216]

In a Kwakiutl story the relative importance of the woman and the snake is reversed. The ancestors of the Koskimo were living at Winter

---

[214] Boas, "The Mythology of the Bella Coola Indians," *Mem. Am. Mus. Nat. Hist.,* II, 1898, p. 42.

[215] *Ibid.,* p. 28.

[216] Boas, *op. cit.,* pp. 44, 45. Cf. "The Uktena of the Cherokee," in J. Mooney, "Myths of the Cherokee," XIX, *Annual Report Bureau Am. Ethn.,* 1900, p. 297.

Place and they had a chief whose name was *Centre* (the *mandala* symbolism). He received half of everything that was caught. His daughter was called Woman Receiving Half and she called her father Pet. Her husband was called Born to be a Fool.

Once it happened that one man refused to give the regular tribute of halibut to the Chief. Centre went and broke all the canoes including those of Born to be a Fool. He got angry and killed his father-in-law. Woman Receiving Half wailed for her father for four days. Then she heard a voice, "I come to invite you to the Ghost Showing Mouth on Ground" (Centre Dwelling Place of the Ghosts). She goes from one mythical house to the other always invited by a man. Finally she comes to a house where she sees her father. She saw her father sitting on a mat. He had a double-headed serpent face for a back rest. Centre invites all the ghosts to come and restore his daughter to life. The ghosts bring their batons, beating boards and chamber vessels and sing. He took the chamber vessel and sprinkled her face with its contents. Then they sang and she was alive again ready to be taken back to this world. The song was taught to the tribe. This is the means of restoring life when people are touched by a ghost.[217]

The visit to the house of the supernaturals is typical of North American shamanism—reviving by means of the chamber vessel is probably derived from the urethral waking dream.

In the next heaven of the Bella Coola we find the house of the Gods or the House of Myths. Other names are "the house where man was created," "the house from which people come down," or "the house to which people go."

In this house live Sen the Sun (Our Father) and various other deities connected with the masked dances or *kusiut*. One goddess rocks the unborn children in her cradle and supervises the birth of all animal beings. Two goddesses intervene in favor of man when the principal deities threaten him with death or sickness. Their names are Snitsmana and Aialilaaxa. They wake man after sleep. Without their help nobody would wake from sleep. Aialilaaxa is also the guardian of the moon. Every month she restores it to full size and she cleans her face after an eclipse. At the time of the eclipse the moon performs one of the most sacred performances of the *kusiut* which are thought to be very dangerous to the performer. The black paint is a protection against these dangers. Aialilaaxa and Snitsmana also revive those who are killed by the dangerous performances of the *kusiut*.[218]

217 Boas, "Kwakiutl Tales," *Columbia University Contributions to Anthropology,* II, 1910, pp. 313–323.
218 Boas, *Bella Coola,* pp. 29–31.

Beside these there are nine brothers and a sister who are regarded as the special patron gods of the *kusiut*.[219] The brothers are variously painted with the designs of the full moon, half moon, stars and rainbow. Letsaapletana, the sister, is painted with the design of a seal lion bladder filled with grease. She wears rings of red and white cedar bark. Some shamans are also initiated by this spirit. She flies in the air. *She keeps turning round.* Songs come of all the parts of her body.[220]

Haida shamans obtained their power through supernatural beings who "possessed" them. By fasting the shaman became clean, transparent as glass, a fit abode for the supernatural beings. Canoe People, Ocean People, Forest People and Above People spoke through the shamans.[221]

Swanton publishes the experiences of people who became shamans: A man and his wife went into the woods to gather hemlock sap. When they reached home she said something that displeased her husband. He struck her, there was a flash of lightning in the house, the house was almost on fire. The woman fell down and lay there all night. In the morning she lay as though she were dead but her heart was still beating. After she had lain there for a while she began to call out like a shaman. She had obtained supernatural power from the Moon.[222] Some people almost became shamans. They went through some remarkable mental experience. One of them said, he felt good, better than he had ever felt in his life. He saw a number of shamans standing in the sea around a big crab which they were trying to throw upon him. If they had succeeded he would have become a shaman. He was afraid they would succeed.[223]

The shaman goes to recover the lost soul. He puts the soul back, then the patient revives and drinks a little water. After midnight the patient is allowed his first meal. First he eats the tail of the salmon, later on the chest of the salmon.[224]

According to the Lummi Indians a young man may become ill because his soul is being carried by a fish on a tour around the world. When the medicine man discovers this he finds out when the tour was started and when it will be completed. Knowing this he knows when the patient will recover. If proper ceremonies are made at the proper time to pacify the spirit of the fish the fish restores the soul of the patient. When the patient recovers he knows all about that particular fish his soul has traveled with, the time and place of spawning, the season and place in

219 On the *kusiut* cf. Boas, "The Social Organization and Secret Societies of the Kwakiutl Indians," *Report of the U. S. Nat'l Museum,* Washington, D. C., 1897, p. 698.
220 Boas, *Bella Coola,* pp. 33, 34, 44.
221 Swanton, "The Haida," *Jesup North Pacific Expedition,* V, p. 38.
222 *Ibid.,* pp. 39, 40.
223 *Ibid.,* pp. 39, 40.
224 *Ibid.,* pp. 42, 43.

which the fish are most easily caught and everything else that makes him a skilled fisherman.[225] The link between the salmon and twins is important since twins like the shaman are a kind of dramatic representation of animism.[226] Chief of the Ancients wanted to have salmon. Therefore he was in search of a wife who was a twin because the twin and salmon are identical. His aunt the Star Woman bade him go to the graves to look for a twin. He went from grave to grave till at last one of them answered, "I am a twin." He gathered the bones, sprinkled them with the water of life and the twin woman came to life. "Beware, Chief of the Ancients," she said. "Do me no harm!"

He took her home and she became his wife and she made plenty of salmon. She had only to put her finger into her mouth and dip it in the water and there was a salmon. The traps were full of salmon, they came leaping toward her. Once, however, when the backbone of the salmon caught in the chief's head he got angry and scolded the salmon. "You come from the ghosts and you catch me," he said. That made his wife Salmon Maker very sad. She said to the dried salmon, "Come my tribe— let us go back." They followed her and all went away into the water. Chief of the Ancients tried to stop her, putting his arm round his wife's body, but her body was like smoke and his arms went through her.[227] Frazer compares the story to that of Cupid and Psyche, the parallel is also valid for Orpheus and Eurydike,[228] especially if we consider that the vanishing wife is a ghost.

There is a close connection between salmon and shamanism although it may not be quite conscious in some tribes.

Among the people of Kasaan there was a young boy who was hungry. His mother gave him only a mouldy piece of salmon from near the head. He went bathing and kept moving toward the deep water, looking for something he wanted. He went and went till the water became too deep for him and he was drowned. Around his neck he had a copper necklace.

Then the Salmon people got hold of his soul and when they returned to their own country they took it with them. They came to a town on shore. It was inhabited by the souls of those salmon which appear to die in the river. Really, however, they return to their own country. The Salmon people called the eggs their "excrements." A woman told him to go behind the town where he would hear noise like children playing. She

225 Stern, *op. cit.,* p. 80.

226 Cf. the chapter "Castor and Pollux."

227 Boas, F., and G. Hunt, "Kwakiutl Texts," II, pp. 322–330, *Jesup North Pacific Expedition,* III.

228 Frazer, J. G., *Totemism and Exogamy,* London, 1910, III, p. 337. On Orpheus and Eurydike, see *infra* in the chapter "The Way Back."

told him to take one of these children out of the stream and cook it. The townspeople looked like people but those in the river looked like salmon. He can eat them, all he has to do is to pick up the bones and throw them back into the river and they are alive again. Finally he went back to his own people. He was there watching them fishing but all the people saw was a salmon. Another Salmon-man stood up and he seemed to jump like a Salmon. One kind of salmon is long and thin with a big head. This is called "salmon's canoe" and was what the other salmon sat in. He ran up the river with the other salmon. His mother used to stand on the beach cutting salmon and when he saw her, he jumped toward her. Before she could catch him he always fell back into the water. This was repeated many times. Once his mother had made a wall of rocks around herself. He jumped and was killed. She told her husband what had happened. He told her to cut off the fish's head and roast it at once. Then she saw there was a ring of copper around the salmon's neck and she remembered her son had worn such a ring. She put a mat on the top of the house and put the salmon into it. A human head began to come out from inside the salmon skin. His friends drank salt water for two days and he came out entirely.

Now he made a noise like a shaman whereupon they took a clean mat out, wrapped him in it and brought him in. They began to drink salt water again. Presently he got up and went round the fire performing like a shaman. He became a very great shaman.

When the salmon became old again and worthless there was one salmon among them who was fine looking and almost translucent. This one they could not catch.

One day the shaman himself went down to the deep place where this salmon used to be seen and killed it. At once he too dropped dead on the beach. He had told the people to put his body along with the shaman's outfit into the same water hole and when they did so it turned around four times and sank. Drum and batons sank also.[229] Shaman's souls go to a different nether world. It is an island with houses reaching deep down into the sea. The most powerful shamans live in the lowest houses.[230]

The salmon leaves and returns, the sleeper goes to sleep and awakes. The deeper he sleeps the further he is removed from the world. A shaman is characterized by these two "movements"—to sink and to revive. The salmon story told above starts with oral frustration and ends with various forms of uterine regression (children into water, shaman into mother's lap, sinking into sea).

In another story, "The Shaman Who Got Power from a Dog Salmon,"

229 Swanton, *Haida*, pp. 243–245.   230 *Ibid.*, p. 37.

it is the salmon who is revived by the shaman and this is how the shaman gets his power.[231]

The Kwakiutl also have a Salmon Society and a Salmon dance. The dancer imitates the leaping of the salmon and sings:

Many salmon are coming ashore with me
They are coming ashore to you the post of our heaven
They are dancing from the salmon's country to the shore
I come to dance before you at the right hand side of the world
Overtowering, outshining surpassing all; I the salmon.
Another song of the salmon dance is this:
The salmon came to search for a dancer
He came and put his supernatural power into him
You have supernatural power
Therefore the chief of the salmon came from beyond the ocean.

The salmon weir is regarded as the toy of the salmon and the salmon weir dancer is initiated by the salmon.

The dancer changes from one leg to the other and bends from one leg to the other. He probably represents the Chief of the Tide to whom he speaks: "Stand still, chief! You who make the tide rise, who causes whirl-pools where the tides meet, whose skirt of seaweed makes the tides rise."

Then the Chief of the tide also represented by the dancer replies: "Cry hap! supernatural one, cry hap!"[232]

The priest or formulist of the Californian Indians in the renewal ceremony may originally be a shaman. This is the Yurok "World Renewal Festival." The Doctor of the World or Dam Chief travels upstream to Saa. He calls a "medicine," a song supposed to cure the world while all human beings hide in their houses. They build the dam so made that the salmon cannot get through. They swim into traps in which they are caught.[233]

Erikson is right in interpreting the "Doctor of the World" as the person who saves the world. The mythical culture hero is the salmon and the Doctor of the World is the master of the weir who stops further wandering.[234] But in the incantation the priest also represents the lonely wanderer, i.e., the salmon. In this role, "On the trail he stood, he heard him downstream beginning to cry, still he stood there in the middle of the night, he felt like wind coming to his heart, soon he was the size of a

231 *Ibid.*, pp. 246, 247.

232 Boas, "The Social Organization and the Secret Societies of the Kwakiutl In-dians," *Report of the United States National Museum for 1895*, Washington, 1897, pp. 474, 475.

233 Erikson, "Observations on the Yurok: Childhood and World Image," *Univ. Cal. Publ. Am. Arch. Ethn.*, XXXV, 1943, p. 277.

234 *Ibid.*, p. 242.

baby, then larger at dawn, still larger and he began to escape. He said: 'Let me walk, let me go, I am the one who travels at night.' The one who was holding him said, 'Why do you constantly cry?' "[235] "The 'normal' salmon stores up a large supply of fat and protein before migrating into the river and before beginning the migrational fast which at one and the same time marks the *beginning of the salmon's sexual development and the beginning of the end of its life. For the first ten days of its migration* the salmon still draws on this capital, both for its vigorous activity of swimming and jumping upstream and for its sexual development."[236]

In the salmon adolescence and senescence are synonymous. Their mythical hero or god is a father figure who becomes "girl crazy." Just as the salmon gets caught in the dam, Wohpekumeu gets caught in the closed vagina of Skate Woman. For the first ten days of its migration the salmon does not eat, the World Doctor or Dam Chief eats only one meal a day for ten days.[237]

Kroeber remarks about the Karok equivalent of the Yurok ritual: The formula speaker began his 10 days rites in the waning moon, timed so as to conclude with its death.[238] The climax of the ten days is lighting the new fire. He sings all night and the people "help to keep him awake," by their jests and laughter. Among the Maidu a shaman caught the first salmon of the season.[239]

We have seen that in Siberia the shaman is related to the migrating water fowl. In North West America, he may originally have been more intimately connected with the migrating salmon.

The real pattern of North American mythology, however, is the "visit to the house of the supernatural being" and the dream origin of this mythical motive is quite clear.

This is a Blackfoot "medicine myth."

"Na-toia-mon fell asleep and dreamed that he was traveling along the plains. He discovered a large *tipi* in the distance and as he drew nearer saw that it was decorated. [The details of the pictures and decorations are given here.]

"While Na-toia-mon was contemplating these picture patterns he heard a voice saying, 'Who is it that walks around my *tipi!* Why do you

235 Waterman, T. T. and Kroeber, "The Kepel Fish Dam," *Univ. Cal. Publ. Am. Arch. and Ethn.*, XXXV, 1938, pp. 49–80; cf. Róheim, *Psychoanalysis and Anthropology,* 1950, pp. 270–290.

236 Erikson, *op. cit.,* p. 278.

237 Waterman and Kroeber, *op. cit.,* p. 56.

238 Kroeber, "Handbook of the Indians of California," *Bureau of Am. Ethn. Bulletin,* 78, 1925, pp. 102, 104.

239 *Ibid.,* p. 437; cf. now Kroeber, A. L. and Gifford, E. W., *World Renewal,* Anth. Records, Univ. Cal. Press, Berkeley, 1949.

not enter?' Lifting the door flap and entering he beheld a large and handsome man smoking alone in the lodge." [The details are again obviously derived from the ritual.] The spirit said: "I am Es-tonea pesta, the Maker of Cold and this is the Snow Tipi or Yellow Paint Lodge." [He gives him the Snow Tipi, the mink skin tobacco pouch and the black pipe as charms.]

"Na-toia-mon then awoke from his sleep. He saw that the snow was abating and knew that the North Man would keep his promise."[240]

Crow Eagle relates how they had abandoned him at his own request because he was so weak that he was ready to die.

"It was nearly daylight when I died and they left my body there just as I had requested.

"The sun was again setting when the spirit returned to my body, I was very weak but I raised my head to look around for I heard the sound of strange voices singing. I saw a flock of ravens standing in a circle of magpies. [The circle means the same thing as the hut or lodge, in other dreams of this type.] They carried small sticks in their bills and seemed to be trying to raise me from the ground, they helped me to sit up, etc." He does not regard this as a dream for he goes on to say that then he cooked the meat, ate it and lay down to sleep. "While I slept the ravens appeared to me in a dream and gave me a dance showing me the movements and manner of dressing and teaching me the songs to be used. They told me that if any sick person would make a vow to join the Raven Society he would recover. Before they left they endowed me with supernatural power."

The Tlingit base their crests on similar narratives. A man was out camping and saw a wolf coming toward him. There was a bone between its teeth. He took it out and the wolf walked away. Next day the man dreamed that he had come to a very fine town. It was a wolf town and the wolf he had helped came to him and made him lucky. That is how the wolf crest was acquired.[241] A man belonging to the frog clan had kicked a frog on the back. As soon as he had done this he lay motionless, unable to talk. They carried his body into the house and he lost his senses because the frogs had taken his soul. He was tied to a post in their house. Some wanted to let him starve there but others said they should fetch the chief Frightful Face. The chief came in a canoe, told him that he had disgraced himself by kicking a woman of his own clan (the frog) and then let him go.

As soon as he had left the frog's house his body lying at home came to.

240 McClintock, W. L., *The Old North Trail*, London, 1910, p. 136.

241 Swanton, "Tlingit Myths and Texts," *Bureau of Am. Ethn. Bull.*, XXXIX, Washington, 1909, p. 233.

He had thought all the time that his body was also lying in the house of the frogs. Then he got up and began to talk. Among the Yavapai the relationship between dreaming and the visit to the house of the guardian spirits or gods is very clear.

Semacha was the generic name for deities that lived in the east and visited shamans at night. Komwidapokuwia (Old Woman Medicine Power —the name was also applied to the shamans themselves) was one of these. One shaman at San Carlos reported his first shaman dream:

Old Woman Medicine Power took my soul to a house which looked like a white cloud in the west over the ocean. Then she took me to a house to the northeast of the morning star where she lives now. It was doomed. It was the rainbow. Inside there were four crescent moons, horns up. Rays like those of the sun came out of the house. In a little while it rained. She sang this song to make rain for human beings. Old Woman Medicine Power's hair hung to her knees and shone like stars. She gave the shaman another song to cure all illness.

"The world has turned different, has turned white. The world has turned white and is moving around," etc.

In another dream Skatakaamcha, the son of the Sun takes his soul away and shows him things. After various mythological scenes:

"Next appeared a transparent container in which was Skatakaamcha's heart vibrating from side to side. On the top of the container he saw himself sitting." Then the god's body appeared above the dreamer's body and talked to him through the air.

The god said, "I have made things good in this world having been around and around it. Where I go around under the heavens I'll be singing," etc. The notion of circular movement is very prominent in all his songs. The patron goddess came into existence through a grinding or weaving movement. "In the morning it wove and made heaven." Heaven was used for her body. "Abalone shell wove the stomach of the girl who came forth and sang," etc.

The shaman says, "This is the way the first man in the world (Skatakaamcha) talked and sang. His heart and my heart intertwined go into the heavens. I am the highest man, I am the greatest man. The heart of the first man in the world and my heart are with each other all the time." All the heaven is clouded. After a little time a white foggy mass appears in the heavens. That is what I step into and I go around. It seems that "his heart is a cloud which he makes for himself. He makes clouds like small children on both sides of his body."[242]

The visit of the house of the supernatural being is the basic dream. The emphasis on rotating movements is very prominent. We have seen

[242] Gifford, E. W., "Northeastern and Western Yavapai," *Univ. Cal. Publ. Am. Arch. and Ethn.*, XXXIV, 1936, pp. 311–314.

that this rotating sensation frequently indicates the moment of falling asleep. The container with the dreamer both inside and outside is exactly what we mean by the double vector of the dream process as uterine regression and as denial of this regression. The identity of the dreamer and of the god who manifests himself in the dream is obvious, also the dream creation of an environment made out of one's own body. The repeated episode of Navaho mythology, the visit to the abode of the gods is an offshoot of the same theme. A youngest son keeps saying that he is dreaming and therefore his brothers hate him and they go hunting without telling him. He is alone and on the rim of Rock Cave Canyon he goes to sleep.

"As soon as it got dark talking was heard below him—they say. From below him a row of beings came out extending to a point across the canyon, opposite him, etc. They are the Holy People, the Gods whom he sees in his dream."[243] "Power obtained through dreams and visions" as well as the expression "dream ceremonial" are common phrases.[244] In Guatemala they believe in beings called the "guardians of the mountains." They are really the patrons of the deer and therefore not so different from the Holy People. A man had had sexual relations with his wife and then shot a deer he saw grazing (taboo to have intercourse when hunting).

"When he looked about he was inside a mountain there he saw many deer, some with bells around their necks, lions, serpents, etc. The Guardian appeared and told him not to break the taboo any more when he went hunting. And when he opened his eyes he was back in the same spot again on the mountains."[245]

But the cornerstone of North American shamanism and indeed of North American religion in general is the concept of the guardian spirit. Ruth Benedict emphasizes that the vision obtained by fasting and not the dream is the basis of acquiring a guardian spirit.[246]

However, I think the dream is the real *fons et origo,* fast and vision are substitutes. According to Hewitt, Innutska was the name of a tutelary spirit (Creek Indians) which came upon a youth when fasting at puberty. It means "what comes to him in sleep." Guardian spirits are acquired in dreams.[247] The Shipaya shaman passes on his magical power called "his

243 Sapir, E., *Navaho Texts,* Special Publication of the Linguistic Society of America, Iowa, 1942, pp. 137–141.

244 Haile, B., "A Note on the Navaho Visionary," *Am. Anthr.,* XLII, 1940, p. 359.

245 Wagley, C., "The Social and Religious Life of a Guatemala Village," *Am. Anthr.,* LI, 1949, p. 57.

246 Benedict, R. Fulton, *The Concept of the Guardian Spirit in North America,* Memoirs of the American Anthropological Association, No. 29, 1923, p. 26.

247 Hewitt, "Notes of the Creek Indians," Smithsonian Institution, *Bureau Am. Ethn. Anthropological Papers,* No. 10, 1939, p. 154.

dream" to his pupil.[248] Among the Oglala an animal appears in a dream. It is really a human being who then teaches them the use of medicines.[249] The Penobscot shaman is a dreamer, a "man who seeks about in dreams." The shaman goes to sleep to see what will be in the future.[250]

The fasting itself is undergone in order to induce dreams. Radin quotes the words of an Ojibwa informant about the fasting experience.

"The first and second night I did not dream of anything but the third night a very rich man came to me and asked me to go along with him—telling me that he would give me all I wanted. I went along with him but I did not accept what he offered and returned to my wigwam. Then I looked in the direction in which . . . he was disappearing and I saw that he had changed into an owl and that the lodge I had visited with him was a hollow tree with holes." (Similar dreams are repeated several times). Then his grandmother gives him something to eat and tells him to accept the dream blessing only if it comes with a gush of wind. "A gush of wind came and above me I saw a very strong man. With this man I went toward the north and finally came to nine old men sitting around in a circle. In the center sat a very old man and this was the man who blessed me."[251]

A detailed interpretation of the dream is neither necessary nor (without associations) possible. But again we find the house or the circle.

The Choctaw believe that some children when they are two or three years old are often sick and wander away from home. The Kwanokasha is a little spirit—he is a full-formed man but no larger than a child of two or three. He lives in a cave under large rocks. These spirits seize the wandering children and take them to their dwelling places. When Kwanokasha and the child enter the spirit's home they are met by three other spirits, all very old with white hair. The first offers the child a knife, the second a bunch of poisonous herbs, the third herbs that contain good medicine. If he accepts one of the first two he will be a bad man, if the third a good doctor.[252]

This is a real dream, or rather a belief based on a real dream. The sick child goes into a cave—the basic dream. The Hermes of this dream is exactly the age of the child, but shaped like an adult—the ego ideal.

[248] Metraux, A., "Le chamanisme chez les Indiens de l'Amerique du Sud Tropicale," *Acta Americana*, II, 1944/45, p. 211.

[249] Weisler, "Societies and Ceremonial Associations of the Oglala," *Anthr. Papers of the Am. Mus. Nat. Hist. XI*, Part 1, 1912, p. 81.

[250] Speck, "Penobscot Shamanism," *Memoirs Am. Anthr. Assoc.*, VI, 1919, pp. 268, 269.

[251] Radin, P., "Religion of the North American Indians," *Journal of American Folk-Lore*, XXVII, 1914, p. 365.

[252] Bushnell, D. I., "The Choctaw of Bayou Lacomb," *Bureau Am. Ethn. Bulletin*, XLVIII, 1909, p. 30.

The Yokut and Mono shamans' source of supernatural power was a dream or rather the dream helper who would say to the dreamer "use me" or something similar, and would give him a song. Sometimes the dream helper was sought, by fasting, praying, taking a tobacco emetic, sometimes the dream would just come unsought. The shaman's power was merely a greater quantity of dream experiences.[253]

We are told that according to the Paiute the spirit appears to the individual in recurrent dreams and bestows power upon him. In these dreams a person may meet a spirit helper like chicken-hawk or water baby,[254] or gun and is instructed in the nature of the power he is to have. The spirit tells him to carry some object at all times and he teaches him a song, and if a shaman, some dances. If he does not carry out the instructions in every detail he looses his power or sickens or dies. Whiting observes that the dreams are not completely unsolicited, that is only a theoretical point of view. A shaman's son sees his father practice and the father instills upon him the idea that he will have a dream and become a doctor. There is constant pressure to dream and to remember dreams.[255] The Caddo call the guardian spirit "partner" and they say, "You have the same power as your partner." Wolf gives thieving power, the hoot owl the power to predict. One man hung a huge fox skin on a pole and his father used to visit him in the shape of a fox. Men who had the clouds as partner could make a mist and hide from the enemy or rain that would wash their tracks away. Magic songs are acquired in dreams. The trance is now infrequent but this is how it used to be.

"On going into a trance the dancer will leave the dance circle falling down. On coming to he will sing the song he may have dreamed."[256] The Kaska acquire supernatural power from animals in a vision or dream in which the animal in human shape talks to the dreamer.[257]

A shaman will die if his guardian spirit is destroyed or imprisoned. Similarly a person could be bewitched by taking hold of his soul or his medicine bag (the bag made out of the guardian spirit animal). Some men had "medicine places" where their guardians lived—as for instance the place of sunrise or sunset and when they bewitched a person by taking his soul they sent it to these places where it was kept captive by their guardian

---

253 Gayton, A. H., "Yokuts Mono Chiefs and Shamans," *Univ. Cal. Publ. Am. Arch.*, XXIV, 1930, pp. 388, 389.

254 Mythical dwarfs who dwell in caves near water holes.

255 Whiting, "Paiute Sorcery," *Viking Fund Publications in Anthropology*, 15, New York 1950, pp. 30, 31.

256 Parsons, E. C., "Notes on the Caddo," *Mem. Am. Anthr. Ass.*, No. 57, 1941, pp. 57–59.

257 Honigmann, J. J., "Culture and Ethos of Kaska Society," *Yale University Publications in Anthropology*, No. 40, 1949, p. 49.

spirit. In such cases the shaman had to put on his mask and, traveling in spirit to the place, attempted with the aid of his guardians to take back the soul forcibly from its captors. If he failed in his task he became sick himself and felt like a man who had received a severe thrashing. Among the Thompson Indians the situation is very similar. The guardian spirit varied with the profession. Shamans had moon, stars, the Milky Way, the Pleiades, the Morning Star, sunset, wind, rain, snow, ice, lake, cascade, etc. Some guardian spirits were useful for several professions. Water for shamans, warriors, hunters and fishers, the loon, all kinds of ducks, and nearly all kinds of fish for shamans and fishermen. The following guardian spirits belonged to shamans exclusively: night, fog, blue sky, east, west, woman, adolescent girl, child, hand of men, feet of men, privates of men, privates of women, the bat, the land of souls, ghosts, grave poles, cairns at graves, dead men's hair, teeth and bones.[258]

Teit writes: "It is evident from the above list that each person partook of the qualities with which his guardian spirit was endowed. For this reason certain guardian spirits were considered more powerful than others. Thus a man who had a grisly bear or thunder for his protector would become a much better and fiercer warrior than another who had a crow, a coyote or a fox.

"Only warriors whose guardian spirits gave them the mystery of the scalp would take or wear scalps. In order to obtain this mystery or, as it is expressed, in order to 'know' scalps and become proof against them, some warriors washed themselves in water in which arrowheads had been placed or prayed to the weapons for knowledge."[259]

Among the Shuswap a few men inherited guardian spirits from their father. Usually, however, they acquired the guardian spirit themselves and the spirit manifested itself in dreams. In some parts of the tribe the dog, coyote, and water were considered the most powerful guardian spirits. The dead, cannibal, fox, tobacco, grisly bear, wolf, eagle and pipe were also very potent. Tobacco, fox and pipe was a group of guardians acquired together. Coyote and cannibal were also associated. Women had a guardian called "singing woman." She was acquired in conjunction with deer and black bear.[260] Men sometimes had this guardian spirit. A young man dreamed of a woman whose face was painted with white and yellow stripes. She told him that she was the deer, that she would help him and make him great and that whenever he wanted her aid he was to paint his

258 Teit, "The Thompson River Indians of British Columbia," *Jesup North Pacific Expedition, Mem. Am. Mus. Nat. Hist.*, 1900, p. 354.
259 *Ibid.*, pp. 355, 356.
260 *Idem*, "The Shuswap," *The Jesup North Pacific Expedition, Mem. Am. Mus. Hist.*, 1909, pp. 605, 606.

face with white and yellow stripes like hers and then she would appear and help him. The black bear or deer woman (appearing in both shapes) was the spirit that gave help in gambling and love. Thunder, weapons, blood and scalp—these were the guardian spirits of warriors. The dead and the wolf were specially suited for shamans, also the lion, otter, pinto and white horse. The cannibal spirit was for warriors and shamans. *"Persons partook largely of the character of their guardians,"* for instance a man who had a goat as his guardian could travel on steep rocks better than other people. A man with a swan guardian could make snow fall by dancing with swans down on his head.[261]

Men painted their faces and bodies as they were told by their guardian spirits in dreams, they arranged their clothes, ornaments and hair in accordance with the directions they had received from their guardian spirits, that is, in accordance with their dreams.

Among the Lummi tribe the wolf spirit enables a man to be a great hunter, the salmon spirit a great fisherman. The beaver gives him the ability to build a house, the raven to acquire shrewdness in bargaining. If he has ashes as his guardian he can lay the foundations of a house, if he has birds he will be a great orator. "All the skills of later life are acquired while in training and the youth also receives through spirit experience such gifts as war clubs, spears, carving equipment, dancing sticks, designs for dancing costumes, spirit dances and songs, drum designs, and directions as how to become wealthy."[262]

These data give us interesting insight into the unconscious background of shamanism. For reviewing the list of spirits that belong to shamans only we see that they are either associated with the above or the hereafter, that is, with the soul flight of the shaman. Another group of spirits indicates the latent meaning of the soul flight. These are sexual organs, woman, etc. And finally the third group reveals the soul flight as taking place in dreamland; these were night, fog, and so on.

The Finn shaman invokes his own *luonto* (nature, personality).

> Awake my nature
> My clan from the depths of the earth
> Nature of my father, nature of my mother
> My own nature.

It goes without saying that in the concept of the ego ideal the parental imago and narcissistic libido are united. An incantation of a Finnish shaman woman:

> My nature is awakening
> My spirit starts to talk

[261] *Idem*, p. 607.   [262] Stern, *op. cit.*, p. 21.

My nature is as hard as a stone
My skin is like iron
Although I am a woman
With a woman's belt.[263]

Among the Salish we have guardian spirit abduction, but the point is that the guardian spirit is but a specialization of the soul. If the guardian spirit is not regained the person dies.[264] When the guardian spirit is restored the sick person rises and dances.[265] Among the East Greenland Esquimaux the missing soul is restored by the patient himself. He sings:

Souls I have lost!
My two souls
Come back of your free will
Come back into me, come back and stay there.[266]

The soul re-enters through the rectum. The South American shaman (Caraib of Guyana) may use his own double just like a guardian spirit. He may send his double out or call other spirits in.[267] The meaning of the guardian spirit is clearly stated by an Achumawi shaman. It is his own thought, he says.[268]

The dream origin of shamanism is clearly revealed by the fact that when Paviotso shamans get power, it is always from the night, and they are told to doctor only at night. There are two nights, the second one comes behind the night that everybody sees. When it comes it makes a person feel he is a shaman. Only shamans can see it, it is under the darkness.[269] It is not surprising, therefore, to learn that the power of the Paviotso shaman comes in dreams,[270] and that in search of such a dream they sleep in caves.[271] Among the Kiowa the owl is the bird of the shamans. This bird is connected with the spirits of the dead and it paralyzes persons who are asleep.[272]

The other conclusion that we can draw from this list of guardian

263 Krohn, G., *A Finnugor Népek Pogány Istentisztelete* (Heathen Cults of the Finno Ugrians), translated from the Finnish, Budapest, 1908, pp. 184, 185.
264 Haeberlin, H. K., "A Shamanistic Performance of the Coast Salish," *Am. Anthr.*, XX, 1918, p. 249.
265 *Ibid.*, p. 256.
266 Thalbitzer, W., "Les Magiciens Esquimaux," *Journal de la Societe des Americanistes de Paris*, N. S. XXII, 1930, p. 93.
267 Metraux, A., "Le chamanisme chez les Indiens de l'Amerique du Sud Tropicale," *Acta Americana*, II, 1944/45, p. 211.
268 Angulo, J., "La Psychologie religieuse des Achumawi," *Anthropos*, XXIII, 1928, p. 562.
269 Park, W. Z., "Shamanism in Western North America," *Northwestern University Studies in the Social Sciences*, No. 2, Chicago, 1938, p. 17.
270 *Ibid.*, p. 23.
271 *Ibid.*, p. 27.
272 Collier, D., "Conjuring among the Kiowa," *Primitive Man*, XVII, 1944, p. 46.

spirits is that the guardian spirit is the *ego ideal*. A person who wants to be a warrior will dream of the ferocious grisly bear or the warrior's guardian spirit and one who wants to be a shaman of things that are associated with shamanism.

It is, of course, true that today the dreams dreamed by the young men in search of a guardian spirit are conditioned by what they expect to dream. Yet—and this is the salient point—the belief in the guardian spirit is but a specialized form of the belief in the soul. As we have shown above this first form of self-idealization is clearly derived from the dream in which the dreamer can leave his body behind like a sheath, in which he can fly and do many other things that belong to dreamland alone. In creating this image man has warded off sleep which is death. At each awakening we experience the immortality of the soul. The friend or helper who in many dreams appears as a duplicate of the dreamer, welded possibly with the father or mother image, is but a specialized form of this soul concept.

In a Tlingit story we read about a boy who walked a long distance and lost his way in the woods. Finally when he was very tired he caught sight of water through the trees. He thought it was the ocean and ran quickly toward it. But it was only a lake. He remained there for some time living on roots. He continued his journey. Next day he again saw water through the woods. He again thought it was the ocean and was happy once more. But it turned out to be the same lake he had left. By this time he was very tired and he thought he might as well stay where he was. *He covered himself with moss and went to sleep.* Suddenly he was awakened by a voice saying, "Who is this boy?" He looked around but saw no one. He fell asleep again and again something said, "Who is this boy?" *He thought he was dreaming,* for when he looked around *he saw only a black duck out in the water.* He decided that now he would keep watch. *While his eyes were closed he heard the same voice again but he was not quite asleep and so he opened them quickly and saw the black duck on the beach.* (The dream transformed into a narrative of a real event.) The duck turned into a man, looked at him and said, "What are you doing here?" The boy explains how his mother kept crying, how he left her and wandered away because he wanted to get away from her. "Since that day I have not been home to see my mother."

Then the man took off his coat and gave it to the boy and said: "Put on this coat. As soon as you have done so, stretch out your arms and keep going like that. Don't think of me and don't think of the lake. Think of your uncle's house."

The boy did as he was told and it seemed to him that he was flying along very rapidly far above the trees. For a long time he thought of nothing else but his uncle's house and his uncle's village, but at length he remembered the lake and lo! he was there once more with the man standing before him in the same place. Then the man said:

"Didn't I tell you not to think of me or of the lake? Start over again. Think of nothing but your uncle's house and the village you are bound for!" So this time the boy tried very hard and all at once he came out back of his uncle's house where his mother was waiting and calling for him. The story is called *the duck helper*.[273]

This is a dream of a boy who is flying toward his mother. Ducks fly to the water; duck and water, as we have seen above are shamans' guardian spirits since water could easily symbolize the mother in dreams and the flying bird, an erection (cf. water fowl, shamans, soul in Siberia).

Personifications of the dreamer in the dream may also have a preconscious meaning. In a paper on sublimation I have shown how the ego ideal has a threefold meaning, conscious, preconscious and unconscious.[274]

The guardian spirit appears in the dream and confers those very qualities on the dreamer which he desires to possess—either consciously, or in the preconscious or in the unconscious.

In a Tlingit story a man who always wanted to be strong bathed in secret (the dream quest). Finally he heard a voice saying, "Come hither." So he went. When he got there the little man (Strength) and he wrestled and he was thrown down. Strength told him to bathe again, this time he almost threw Strength. So Strength said, "That is enough. You are sufficiently strong."[275] According to the Bella Coola the path of the Sun is protected by the Bears of the Sky. The Bears are warriors and it is they who give man the warrior spirit.[276] According to the Haida, Death by Violence makes people die a violent death, Slave power drives them into slavery, Riches Woman is the origin of all songs and the Spirit of Theft turns people into thieves. In mourning people paint their faces black and cut their hair, because they have seen the Spirit of Mourning and this is how the spirit behaves.[277] Among the Nez Percé the puberty quest with its cold baths and fasting was held in order to overcome Mawish, the spirit of fatigue.[278] The Delaware believe that sleepiness is caused by the spirit

[273] Swanton, *op. cit.*, pp. 208, 209.

[274] Róheim, "Sublimation," *Psychoanalytic Quarterly*, XII, 1943, p. 338.

[275] Swanton, *op. cit.*, p. 387.

[276] Boas, "The Mythology of the Bella Coola Indians," *Jesup North Pacific Expedition*, I, 1898, p. 35.

[277] Swanton, "Contributions to the Ethnology of the Haida," *Jesup North Pacific Expedition*, V, 1905, pp. 29–32.

[278] Chamblain, A. F., "A Note on the Personification of Fatigue among the Nez Percés, Kutenai and Other Tribes," *Am. Anthr.*, XIV, 1912, p. 163.

of Sleep.[279] The White Russians believe in a spirit called Spiesska Spariska (Quick Woman Hot). Workers invoke her and she increases their energy and gives speed to their work. Nobody knows what she is like but she must exist because people call on her and it is through her that their work is helped.[280] In Swichloca the Russians said that if someone is very sad or tired and groans "Och" the Och will appear. This is a little man with a beard and he will grant wishes to those who are not frightened of the apparition.[281]

In writing about shamanism most authors distinguish the medicine man who operates with a trance or similar pathological phenomena from the one who finds his spirits or sends out his soul in a dream. Thus Loeb describes the shaman of Niue who sends his gods (*tupua*) to look for the soul that has been abducted by a sea snake. He goes into a trance and accompanies the performance with incessant whistling.[282] The Mentawei shaman who ascends to heaven in a dream is a seer in Loeb's terminology, who rightly regards the seer as more primitive than the shaman.[283] However, the Mentawei medicine men sometimes dance and make their steps quicker and quicker and this is done in order to fall to the ground in a trance. The house in which the dance takes place is then the seer's boat or eagles have taken him up to the sky.[284] Apart from the fact that according to Loeb's definition this should be a shaman, I would call the seer, or rather we should say "the dreamer," the original form of the shaman. The Yurak Samoyeds have their "dream seers" or "seers" or "gazer into the hole of a root" who in his dream reveals the past and the future about the weather, hunting and sacrifices but leaves the difficult task of capturing lost souls to those who can fall into a trance.[285] Harva tells us that the Tsheremiss "dream seer" sends his soul out while asleep to find out anything they want to know about supernatural beings.[286]

Ohlmarks regards this as the survival or rudiment of the trance and soul quest.[287] Since all primitives believe that the soul leaves the body when dreaming *it is clear that the shaman is simply the dreamer only more*

---

[279] Loewenthal, I., *Die Religion der Ostalgonkin*, Berlin, 1913, pp. 30, 31.

[280] Federowski, N., *Lud bialoruski na Rusi Litavskiej*, I, 1897, p. 135. These data were quoted in my paper in Hungarian "Psychoanalysis es Ethnologia," *Ethnographia*, XXIX, 1918, pp. 88–90.

[281] Federowski, *loc. cit.*, and Cosquin, E., *Les Mongols et leur pretendu role dans la transmission des contes indiens*, Niort, 1913, p. 40.

[282] Loeb, E. M., "The Shaman of Niue," *Am. Anthr.*, XXVI, 1924, p. 397.

[283] *Idem*, "Shaman and Seer," *Am. Anthr.*, XXXI, 1929, p. 62.

[284] *Ibid.*, p. 78.

[285] Lehtisalo, *Entwurf einer Mythologie der Jurak Samojeden*, p. 145.

[286] Holmberg-Harva, U., "Die Religion der Tscheremissen," *F. F. C.*, No. 61, pp. 192–194.

[287] Ohlmarks, A., *Studien zum Problem des Schamanismus*, Lund, 1939, p. 91.

so while the trance is an autohypnotically induced sleep, i.e., a further step in specialization. It is evident, however, that in some cases the initiation to shamanism is a schizophrenic episode.

The *utukwasa* of the Xosa in South Africa, as described by Laubscher, is the onset of schizophrenia. In a case of schizophrenia the patient's sister says *utukwasa* is usual in the family. Grandmother and grandfather, father's sisters were all witch doctors. "My uncle lost his senses and afterwards became a fool. My great-grandfather had *utukwasa* and ran away to the mountains. He got lost in the bush. My own father was called to the bush and completely lost his senses."[288] Or to quote another case (schizophrenia, catatonic): The patient's great-grandfather had two children. The man lost his senses and remained that way till he died. The girl was *utukwasa,* recovered and became a witch doctor. (Several other cases of *utukwasa* in the family are mentioned.)[289] Another case of schizophrenia, paranoid type: Practically all the members of the family on the mother's side had *utukwasa* but they never became successful witch doctors because they were Christians.[290]

Some people who have *utukwasa* run into the hills where the ancestral spirits reveal the secrets of herbs. Others dream about insects, usually bees or wild beasts, lions, elephants. The *utukwasa* of the medicine man is that he is called to the River by the River People. He stays with them underneath the pools for ten or more days. When he returns they know he has been with the River People and is now a wise man. He is not questioned because were he to reveal anything he would be called again and then killed.

"When a member of a kraal appears listless, looks queer, roams aimlessly about, looks worried and anxious, ignores the questions addressed to him and fails to communicate with those around, they know the power of the River People is at work and he may at any time be called to the River. He is kept under observation and soon maybe he will stand looking about as if in a dream and then start to run straight for the River. They call him by name, try to catch him and throw stones in front of him to distract his attention. They may catch him and tie him up at home until the River People have claimed some animal sacrifice as a substitute but it happens at times that the one called will outstrip his pursuers and plunge straight into a deep pool." If anyone weeps he will be killed. If not the River People may accept cattle as a substitute and he returns as an *isanuse* or seer.[291]

The Chukchee shaman is obviously more than simply a dreamer. The

---

[288] Laubscher, B. J. F., *Sex, Custom and Psychopathology*, London, 1937, p. 323.
[289] *Ibid.*, p. 331.   [290] *Ibid.*, p. 333.
[291] *Ibid.*, pp. 1–4.

description given by Bogoras has become famous. "The shamanistic call begins to manifest itself in an early age in many cases during the critical period of transition from childhood to youth. . . . The shamans among the Chukchee with whom I conversed were as a rule extremely excitable, almost hysterical and not a few among them were half crazy."[292] The parents of young people "doomed to inspiration" frequently object and so do the young people themselves "But this is dangerous, people who are thwarted in becoming shamans may sicken or die or run away and become a shaman elsewhere."[293]

The "great dream" of the hebephrenic patient quoted in Chapter I might well be the dream of a shaman's initiation. Baynes's schizophrenic patient dreams that he is following his mother down stairs leading to the beach, but the steps end in space, he stops. Later he came down to the sea level and "skipped" a stone. It hit a wave, and roared into the air. He looked for another stone to skip. Then he found himself in deep water with a shadowy figure beside him. Catching sight of a flat stone at the bottom he dived twice to reach it. When he brought it to the surface it was a watch exactly like the one he had inherited from his father.[294]

In other words, *certain types of shamans* are people who have had a schizophrenic episode[295] but have managed to sublimate their regressive tendencies; they have become social (object-directed) and ego-syntonic. Whenever the death of the candidate is part of the initiation ritual (or dream) I would suspect schizophrenic trends.

It is not within the scope of this book to discuss this aspect of shamanism. It is sufficient for the present to refer to the dream of the schizophrenic patient quoted in the first chapter and to the intrinsic relatedness of dreaming and schizophrenia.

In some cases beliefs about sorcery are based on dreams dreamed about the "sorcerer," in other cases on dreams dreamed *by* the sorcerer. The former is essentially an anxiety dream, especially the primal scene relived in an anxiety dream.

The *enobeu* or seer of Normanby Island is based on dreams dreamed *by* the seer, but the *barau* or sorcerer on nightmares *about* the sorcerers.

Yakudi, a lame man of about thirty, is an *enobeu* of the village of Wairakeli, district of Kelologeia, Normanby Island.[296] *Eno beu* means

---

292 Bogoras, W., "The Chukchee," *Jesup North Pacific Expedition*, VII, New York, 1907, p. 415.

293 *Ibid.*, p. 419.

294 Baynes, H. G., *Mythology of the Soul*, London, 1949, p. 521.

295 Epilepsy or hysteria may also be involved.

296 The following data are based on my field notes. Some of the data on the *enobeu* have been published in my paper "Teiresias and Other Seers," *Psychoanalytic Review*, XXXIII, 1946, pp. 314–334, and the data on witches in "Witches of Normanby Island," *Oceania*, XVIII, 1948, pp. 279–308.

sleep fall and the essence of the *enobeu* is a dream in which he descends to the world of the dead. The *enobeu* is a seer or more precisely a seer of the dead (Hungarian folklore has a specific term for this *halottlátó* = dead seer).

Jarekeni says: "My mother died when I was a baby, father when I was a little older. After father's death my second mother died also and then my uncle with whom I lived. People told me that Matagogojoka (Bad Eye) was an *enobeu*. I went with him to Maretana (name of a village) because we wanted to learn his magic. We went to the water and he made our *esiwe* (swimming). He rubbed us in the water with leaves and he made magic into a sponge to rub our eyes and make us see the dead. After the bath he gave us a coconut and made magic into it. He made magic for good luck and then he scraped the shell and made magic to avert bad luck. Then we oiled our body, and fried the leaves. We inhaled the vapor and then we were lying down in our house to sleep. He covered the leaves with his magic talk and then he scratched our feet. We rubbed our eyes and then we slept. A wind came and the house was moving. [This is already the dream; note the wind as in North American and Siberian shamanism.] *We went down* with our whole outfit, our lime pots, our baskets and feathers. Sine Bomatu (Woman East Wind) the granddaughter of Kekewagei the woman who rules the other world blocked our way but Kekewagei said, 'Ho don't block their path.' There were many people there and we came to a village of a dead uncle of mine. My uncle sang for us.

> Soul walk straight on the bridge[297]
> Sine Bomatu welcomes you
> They cook beach creepers with oil
> The virgins of Bwebweso welcome you.

"Then we woke and were asked what we had seen in the dream. After relating this he tells me what he dreamed last night. He knew he was coming to see me. The dream was: I slept and then my shadow flew out. I came here. I stood beside the post and a dog wanted to bite me."

The associations reveal the meaning of the dog, castration anxiety. The next subject he talks about is Bwebweso, the happy other world. "If an old woman dies she will have breasts like a young girl and if a little girl dies she will have breasts like a young woman who has just given birth."

In other words all the spirits are at the sexually optimal period. There are also "the virgins of Bwebweso," female spirits that never were mortal who entertain the spirits of dead men. His feet were scratched before

[297] Do not fall off the bridge that connects this world with the hereafter.

going to sleep to prevent him from falling off the bridge and his eyes were rubbed so he should see well. People are careful not to make a noise in the house because the dreamer might break his neck if they were to wake him suddenly. An old woman called Semudu from Bunama district relates the origin myth of the art of *enobeu*.

Nima-upa (Hand-cut), a woman of Bwebwehuna went to swim with her grandmother. By swimming she means *esiwe*, learning magic in the water. The grandmother said, "Let us go. I'll make you sleep and take you to Bwebweso" (other world). They went to Bwebweso and walked about. Their fathers and mothers cooked for them. They ate.

The following incantation is based on this myth:

> The shadow of people eaten in war
> We went down from above
> Shadows of dead people
> We went from the road
> My shadow you go up (awake)
> You become awake
> My soul, you fetch it (i.e., the shadow)
> You shall make it, fetch it
> Spirits of my relatives,
> You fetch it,
> My shadow you wake it
> You make it awake.

Then she relates her own initiation. Her grandmother took her to a tree, made powder out of its leaves and rubbed her body with the powder. She felt how she was becoming numb upward from her foot[298] and how her soul went out of her head. The women of the other world got jealous and cut her. She made a song out of this dream:

> Little Parrot came to Bwebweso
> They blocked the road, they were jealous
> Her village was Ojahenare
> They kept asking.

Little Parrot is her totem, Ojahenare the old village from which the present village originated. "They kept asking" means the women in Bwebweso said, "Who are you? Go away!" They were jealous, she explains because of Tau Dimidimirere (Man Smooth Down).

Tau Dimidimirere is the same person as Tau Mudurere (Man Pubic Part). But this woman comes from the southern shore of the island where the other world beliefs are somewhat different.

In Sipupu, Boasitoroba, Duau, etc., there are two other worlds. Bwebweso (the name of a mountain on the north shore) is where the

---

298 I.e., sleep is induced by a kind of massage.

spirits go to live in eternal feasting and dancing and love making. The ruler of this realm is a woman called Kekewagei. Under the ground that is under the soil of each village is the land of the *numu,* the spirits of fertility. They live under the garden soil and they make their yams grow. Souls are brought down here but they do not live here. When they are brought to this realm they are taken down by the witches and they are eaten by Tau Mudurere who is the husband of all witches.

But in her belief the two other worlds are identical. Man Smooth Down is the chief of Bwebweso. He is the "master," the "root" of the other world. His body is white like that of the white man. (But she shows a piece of yellow calico to demonstrate what color she means.) There are also *gomabwaina* (pretty boys) in the other world. "We have intercourse with them," she says. These *gomabwaina* correspond to the *nuadeja* (virgins). The former are the wishes of the female, the latter of the male. She has been in the other world several times. Once to see her brother, then her husband and then her son. The women resented her presence (in the dream quoted above) because they were all the wives of Man Smooth Down.

Later on she related one of her *enobeu* dreams.

I went to Bwebweso, they were having a *sagari* [food distribution ceremony]. There was plenty of food and they were dividing a pig. In the dream I saw Man Smooth Down and his wife Sine Rau Tegege (Woman Walking Round). He was dancing, his wife was jumping around behind him and the dreamer was behind the wife. (All native dances are circular, it is therefore probably once more the rotating movement "falling asleep.")

An old man named Donagini from the village of Limahuja was a famous *enobeu*. He cried bitterly when he heard the gramophone. What is the matter, we asked him. I hear the voices of dead white men but I do not see them—he said. He rubs his eyes and then he goes down and sees all his relatives. All the natives said, "go down" although if their other world is Mount Bwebweso this would really be "go up." His father taught him to be an *enobeu*.

"The first person I saw there was my uncle Didida. I saw him killing a man, but he did not eat the man because they belong to the same totem. My mother told me, 'You will grow up and be a fighter like your uncle. He always told his wife to make good food for me.' He went down to the other world after his father's death. Father, the *enobeu*, had said, 'When you grow up you will follow my ways. You come down always and you shall see me with your mother.' They married again in the underworld"— he remarks.

Another time when he went down they were all sitting eating. They offered him food but he refused because if he ate their food he would have to stay in the underworld.

He corrects the statement about going down after his father's death. He tried to, but that time he failed. But when his mother died too he succeeded immediately and he found them there together.

Witches also go down to the underworld, but in this case the purpose is not merely a friendly visit to see relatives. Libwebweso was an old woman whose reputation as a witch was very great. When she goes to the *numu* she goes to visit her spirit husband. She takes a bath and oils her body, she is beautiful like a bird of paradise when she goes down. The witches descend to the netherworld on the trunk of a tree. Tau Mudurere kills people but his son Bokunopita gives them happiness. When the witch goes to Tau Mudurere people die but if she goes to Bokunopita they are happy. Witches also rub their eyes to see well. The witch takes the soul or shadow down to Tau Mudurere. It is chiefly the rich or famous people whose souls are sent down by the witches to Tau Mudurere. Their own mothers and sisters do it, or rather a mother or sister exchanges her son or brother for another witch's son or brother for the fatal descent. In one case the theory of *soul theft* was used to explain what was probably a case of schizophrenia. Doketa's brother[299] was reputed to be *uwauwa* (mad), nobody could talk to him and he refused to live in the village.

He was taken to their cave by the witches because he refused to marry one of them. There was a big snake in the cave and Doketa's brother was lying on it. At night the snake went out for its food. He saw the "trunk" (*kerena*) of Sanaroa island going right through the earth but he also saw other islands, they were like mats floating on the water. He also saw Yaboaine[300] but he was running up and down in the middle of the earth. He made thunder and lightning and said: people are all thieves, etc. The proceeding for the descent is the same in the case of the witch and the seer. Leaves, oiling and a mat are spread out. In fact there is only one road, only after a time it branches off in two directions, to the *numu* for the witches, to Bwebweso for the seer. How is the witch initiated? A young girl is initiated into witchcraft by her mother or grandmother. The mother goes up into the house, the girl thinks she is going in through the house door but it is really her mother's mouth. She comes out again through her mother's vagina. She asks her mother why is there no light? The mother replies, "I fell asleep, the fire went out. Go and get some fire." The daughter does not know it, but she goes into her mother again

299 On Doketa cf. Róheim, "Psychoanalysis of Primitive Cultural Types," *Int. Journal of Psa.*, XIII, 1932, pp. 151–174.

300 Cf. Róheim, "Yaboaine, a War God of Normanby Island," *Oceania*, XVI, 1946.

and fetches the *kaya* (light). Then she is again swallowed and fetches, this time, poisonous leaves.

The shaman's initiation and his shamanistic activity frequently follow the same pattern. I believe we can use this analogy here, the journey to the other world, or the world under the ground, or the cave is really a journey into the mother, *the basic dream.*

It seems very likely that the fabled initiation was really based on this dream descent—only it is not the mother who is asleep, it is the daughter. This would be like Väinämöinen descending into the stomach of the sleeping great sorcerer, Antero Vipunen, for new magic to complete his boat (Kalevala XVII, Runo).

The *kaya* mentioned above is the mysterious light that leaves the witch's vagina *while she is asleep* and goes about the village burning people. Another version of how the young witch is initiated reverts the situation. Instead of the girl going into the witch, the mysterious objects are taken from the inside of the witch and thrust into the girl.

It seems then that these "descents"—now, of course, following a conscious pattern—originated in the past from what we have called the basic dream of uterine regression. Witch lore is largely concerned with the flying of the witch, the flying dream being the first genital countermove that follows uterine regression. The *enobeu* usually visits his relatives in the other world when they are eating, possibly the infant's eating dream as a fundamental form of return to life from sleep-death is involved. Father and mother together and anxiety in the dream would be the primal scene.

The primal scene is the outstanding thing in the activity of the *barau* or sorcerer.

The real nature of the *barau* was revealed through Doketa's dream. This great chief of Duau, my special friend and namesake, was certainly a great *barau* although as a nominal Christian he would have denied this.

People who roam about at night are either after girls or they are *barau*. Doketa's father and his uncle Kauanamo used to go on their *barau* expeditions together. They would kill a person, take his blood vessels out and then dry them. This is the famous *bona,* the bait used for catching fish or girls. When the *barau* cuts the veins out of people and revives them this is evidently something that takes place in a dream. Malinowski reports from Mailu that the *barau* comes at night and kills a sleeping man but then restores him to life again only to let him die later. When a *barau* is about to kill a man he always first has connection with some female member of the family—his wife, his sister or daughter *in her sleep.* The man bewitched by the *barau* does not remember what happened *after he awakes*—but she knows who had intercourse with her at night, i.e., in her dream.[301] In the Trobriand Islands the nocturnal escapades of young men after girls are compared to the clandestine expeditions of sorcerers.[302] The Normanby Islanders say to *barau* someone, metaphorically, this means the activity of the male in coitus. I have published the dreams of Kauanamo, himself a famous *barau,* and I quote one of his dreams.[303]

I walk about in the bush and Guy people come to chase me. "Why do you come," they ask. "I come for betel nuts," I reply. A man called Napiyeni leads them, they chase me, I run, I jump into a gully they want to kill me. I protest I came only for nuts, they say. We planted our betel nuts. They are our property. You can have what grows in the bush. Finally they gave me some betel nuts, but they told me never to come back again.

Associations: The man in the dream is his brother's son (rabaraba). Napiyeni calls him "father." Napiyeni is always joking. Whenever he sees a woman he says that is my wife, we had intercourse before. He really went once to Napiyeni for betel nuts. He is dutiful in real life and gives Kauanamo betel nuts. The gully into which he jumps is Kekura gully, the place of Matakapotaiataia, the Duau Oedipus. The footsteps of Mataka-potaiataia are visible there.

Something like the dream happened in real life. He visited an uncle of his and was chased although he meant no harm at all. The same thing also happened to this uncle. He walked into a strange village at night. The men held him. He said, "I came for the single girls." They said we thought you came for married women or *barau.* The words in the dream "we planted our betel nuts, they are ours, take whatever you can find in the bush," are what the old men usually say to the young men. Kauanamo himself has frequently said the same words "What I planted is mine. Let me chew it; when I die it will be yours."

The sentence means more than appears on the surface because the young men want the betel nuts so that they can give them to the girls and thus persuade them to spend the night together.

We see that in the dream his chief antagonist is a man whom he calls "son" and who calls him "father." But the roles are reversed. In the dream he is a young man (actually he must be about sixty-five) who is after betel nuts, i.e., girls. If he jumps into the gully of Matakapotaiataia, the hero

301 Malinowski, "The Natives of Mailu," *Transactions and Proceedings of the Royal Society of South Australia,* XXXIX, Adelaide, 1915, pp. 649, 650.

302 *Idem, The Sexual Life of Savages,* London, 1929, p. 223.

303 Cf. Róheim, "Dream Analysis and Field Work in Anthropology," *Psychoanalysis and the Social Sciences,* I, 1947, p. 93.

who kills the giant and has intercourse with his mother, then he is Mataka-potaiataia.

Sauaitoja (Bebe) finally admits that he is a *barau*. When the *baraus* go on their nocturnal prowls they wash and dress as if they were going for girls. The *barau* hides in the bush and throws a miniature and invisible spear at his victim. It flies back into the hands of the thrower who is himself hidden in the bush. If the man attacked is also a *barau* he feels the spear and throws it back. If not he dies in two or three days.

When the *barau* have killed a man they cut out one testicle and use the juice for hunting or fishing. This is a bait *(bona)*. Sometimes they cut out a man's tongue or his penis and make a pseudo tongue or penis grow in its place. This is done so that the people should not notice the absence of the real organ when they bury the man.

Bulema was another famous *barau*. He was always afraid of *baraus*, that is, he had nightmares. One of his early dreams:

The *baraus* surround me when I go for a walk. They order me to climb a betel-nut tree (this is what the *barau* is always supposed to do). I fall, I break my leg. Please don't put me into the grave, I say. My women (those of his clan) say, you should not let them make incantations against you.

The women in the dream are his nieces. They are pretty and young and like him. When they were orphaned they lived with him and he took care of their marriage. What about climbing trees? I ask him. I always told my sons to do that—he says, meaning that they should have the betel nuts. However, telling a person to climb a tree is just what the *barau* does when he wants to kill him. One of the *baraus* who was trying to kill him was his *tamana* (father). Not his real father but the man who took care of him after his father's death.

The dream *baraus* who kill him are "fathers," the women who protect him rejuvenated representatives of the mother imago.

This is the origin myth of the art of *barau*.

At Soija there was a man who came out of a tree. Children were playing there and he killed them, one after the other, by magic. Finally, someone came and asked, What is going on here? One of the surviving children said, "Father! where did he come from, this person who kills by magic?" "Perhaps he came out of that tree," the father said. The *barau* was hidden in the tree. A crowd gathered, they felled the tree. They chopped it into little bits. He kept hiding, jumping from one bit into the other. Finally, when they had got to the crown of the tree he jumped out and said, "Don't kill me, I will give you magic." They learned the *barau* incantations and the man disappeared into another tree. The two outstanding features of this story are that a *barau* is someone who disappears and that it is an adult killing children. They chop a tree trying to kill him. *Kaiwe* (tree) means also leaf and poisonous or magic substance derived from the leaf by the *barau*. In our story we see two groups of people and two single *dramatis personae*. The groups are children who are being killed and pupils of the *barau* art. The two single actors are the *barau* and the father, i.e., the bad and the good father. Actually people learn *barau* from their fathers or uncle—therefore we can condense the *pupil* and the *children* group into one unit. The *barau* pupil proves himself by trying to kill his teacher (father, uncle)—thus revealing the oedipal content of the *barau* complex. Actually nothing happens, it is all in incantations and not poisoning and both teacher and pupil survive proving themselves to be real masters of the *barau* art.

Bulema, the great *barau,* describes the nightmares he has been subject to since his childhood. He was always afraid that the *barau* were trying to kill him.

The *barau* is the father, his nocturnal performances are the child's sadistic version of the primal scene.

The dreams about *barau* are always ended by the sleeper calling out the *barau's* name, i.e., the dreamer is awake. The dream itself was a nightmare in which the dreamer took the mother's passive role. Nightmares of this type have helped to shape the form of beliefs about the male sorcerer.

The nightmare must also be regarded as the source of the belief in sorcerers inflicting invisible wounds on their victims who later sicken or die in consequence of the assault.

The Wiimbaio thought that medicine men of hostile tribes could sneak into the camp at night and with a net garotte one of the tribe. Then they would drag him a hundred yards or so from the camp, make an oblique cut in the abdomen, take out the kidney and caul fat and stuff grass and sand into the wound. The victim dies in three days. It is the Wotjobaluk, a neighboring tribe, who do these things. They sneak up on the victim *when he is asleep.* As soon as the sorcerer is near enough to see his man by the light of the fire he swings the *yulo* (bone) round his head and launches it at him. It penetrates into the man in an invisible shape and compels him to leave the camp and follow the sorcerer who throws him over his shoulder and takes him to a convenient spot.[304] What is described here is evidently a nightmare. If the man is acquainted with his victim he shares his camp and pretends to be asleep. Then he waits till his host is sound asleep and proceeds as described. Evidently these nightmares must be connected with sleep walking because the victim on awaken-

---

304 Howitt, A. W., *Native Tribes of South East Australia,* London, 1904, p. 368.

ing wonders as to how he came to be sleeping at the place where he finds himself.[305]

"The charming is generally performed upon a person asleep. Therefore when several tribes are encamped near each other there is always one keeping watch that they may not be charmed by any of the other tribes. Should a man have an enemy whom he wishes to enchant and he can steal upon him while sleeping without being discovered, he thinks to throw him into a sounder sleep by striking the air before his face as though in the act of sprinkling it with a tuft of emu feathers which have been previously moistened in the liquid from a putrid corpse."[306]

I have emphasized the nightmare character of these beliefs in my book on *Animism, Magic and the Divine King*, 1930, p. 60. For instance, when somebody dies without apparent cause they say a *marallya*, a man of hostile tribe in the shape of a bird must have pounced upon him, squeezed his ribs and caused him to die a lingering death. These birds attack their victims in their sleep.[307] The magic weapon may also be the property of a mythical being. Wyungarre pulled himself up into heaven by means of a line attached to his spear. He sits up there and fishes for men with his fishing spear and when they start in their sleep it is because he touches them with the point of his weapon.[308]

The Hunter River Tribe called this nightmare being Koin. "Sometimes when the blacks are asleep he makes his appearance, seizes upon one of them and carries him off. The person seized endeavors in vain to cry out, being almost strangled. At daylight, however, Koin disappears and the man finds himself safely convoyed to his own fireside. The demon is here a sort of personification of the nightmare—a vision to which natives from their habit of gorging themselves to the utmost when they obtain a supply of food, must be very subject."[309]

Kurnai wizards make the victim of their spells rise from his camp and walk to them like in sleep. His tongue was cut out and he was sent home to die.[310] In some accounts of this proceeding the victim is supposed

[305] *Ibid.*, p. 369.

[306] Taplin, G., *The Narrinyeri, an Account of the Tribes of South Australian Aborigines*, 1878, p. 27.

[307] Angas, G. F., *Savage Life and Scenes in Australia and New Zealand*, London, 1847, I, p. 110; Wilhelmi, C., *Manners and Customs of the Australian Natives*, Adelaide, 1862, p. 30.

[308] Meyer, H. E. A., "Manners and Customs of the Aborigines of the Encounter Boy Tribes," in J. D. Woods, *Native Tribes of South Australia*, Adelaide, 1879, pp. 205, 206; Taplin, *op. cit.*, pp. 56–58.

[309] Howitt, *op. cit.*, p. 377.

[310] Hale, H., *United States Exploring Expedition*, 1846, p. 111; Threlkeld, E., *An Australian Language as Spoken by the Awabakal*, 1897, p. 47; Braim, T., *History of New South Wales*, 1846, p. 248; Howitt, *op. cit.*, p. 496.

to faint. Since the cutting would be obviously impossible without awakening the person I must regard this as a mythical exaggeration of the sleeping situation. According to a myth of the Marind anim, the Mambara-anim (sorcerers) do something to their victim which makes him faint. Then they cut the body from the inside under the skin without leaving a wound that can be seen. The man awakes after having swooned but he does not know what has happened. In a few hours, however, he feels the pain and in a few days he is dead.[311] Again the Thonga in South Africa refer to the wizard as *mpfulo* = opening. One of them may possess charms to open a kraal and take the oxen out during the night. He comes into the village with the tail of a hyena in his hand. Waving the hyena tail he throws all the inhabitants of the village into a deep sleep. While they were asleep he would steal the cattle. Another kind of opening is opening a hut. The wizard puts the husband to sleep and has intercourse with the wife. What the "opening of a man" is remains unexplored but it is probably similar to what we know from Australia.[312] One of the techniques used by Kavirondon wizards is described as follows: He leaves his hut in the middle of the night when there is no moon and people are fast asleep in their huts. He goes completely naked and rubs his body all over with ashes from his wife's fire place. He dances up and down before his victim's hut and ends the dance by suddenly pointing his buttocks at his victim's door.[313]

This looks very much like something a man in the hut might have dreamed. We can always ask the question do people dream these things because such forms of sorcery actually exist? Or are the rites themselves dramatized dreams? In one case I am certain that the custom is practiced and yet the whole thing might easily be a dream of the sleeping victim. I quote the account of the pointing bone type of magic as given by my informants Wapiti and Mulda of the Ngatatara tribe (West and North of Hermannsburg).

When a man has been boned a dream or rather several dreams show him what has happened. He sees a crack in his dream, an opening in the ground. The next dream shows two or three men walking toward him in the crack. When they come near him they draw the bone out of their own body. It emanates from behind the penis between the scrotum and the rectum. But before a person actually bones the other he makes him fall asleep by taking semen from his own penis or excrements from his anus. He throws these toward the victim, they spread in the air like sand and

311 Wirz, P., *Die Marind-anim von Holländisch Süd Neu Guinea*, Hamburg, 1922, I, Part 2, p. 69.

312 Junod, *The Life of a South African Tribe*, 1913, II, pp. 469, 470.

313 Wagner, G., *The Bantu of North Kavirondo*, I, 1949, p. 113.

behind this cloud the sorcerer keeps his anonymity. The bone is endowed with a soul that goes into the victim.[314]

I should say that this was a passive homosexual anxiety dream. The crack in the ground makes the dreamer a female. What penetrates into him is the "anal penis" of the sorcerer. To be a woman is to be castrated, to be castrated is to be killed. Reassurance must be obtained from the dream-sorcerer, then a cure is possible. The successive stages of the boning were shown to me and I have a series of photos that illustrate the stages of the proceeding. I also had a very brief "analysis" with Yirramba kurka, an Aranda, who believed that he had been "boned" and refused to do anything. It was a paranoid episode which was relieved simply by abreactions. The third day he dreamed he went hunting with his cousin Yirramba kurka (same name as his own). They ascended a very high steep rock, his cousin walking behind him and holding him from behind. The other man kept holding him back. He could not move and shouted. They were hunting kangaroo but could not find any. He dug a yam out and ate it.

The day residue is the following: Old Wapiti and Intjirilaka, both yam men, said that somebody was talking against him and his brother. He asked them to stop talking, he does not want to fight.

His cousin is a quiet man, has nothing to do with women. He is too young. The eating of a yam in the dream means that a yam man is boning him.

The dreamer eats the yam, that is, there is an unconscious tendency to eat the person who is boning him. He eats the yam, i.e., the yam goes into him.[315] The persecutor of his other dream is in this case his own double. The ascent of the cliff and the cousin holding him from behind indicate the homosexual situation. (The cousin does not care for women, cliff = penis.) He cannot move, he shouts = anxiety. He used to walk like that with his beloved grandfather who treated him like a father.[316] The sorcerer as "boner" is evidently the "bad" father imago of the dream. Yet, as I said before, there can be no doubt about the fact that "boning" is actually performed by the natives. Arguing from our knowledge of Bulema and his nightmare and his fame as a sorcerer, it would seem probable that the act of sorcery is originally the dramatization of a dream. In doing this a kind of self-cure is effected, i.e., the transition is made from passivity to activity. I believe that this principle applies also to other forms of ritual.

In these dreams, in this magic we see destruction followed by something like restitution. They are comparable to the initiation dream (ritual)

---

[314] Cf. Róheim, *Psychoanalysis and Anthropology*, 1950, p. 129; cf. also *idem*, "The Pointing Bone," *Journal of the Royal Anthr. Inst.*, LIV, 1925, p. 90.

[315] This is to be compared with Wapiti's initiation dream *infra*.

[316] Róheim, *War, Crime and the Covenant*, Monticello, 1945, pp. 124, 125.

of the medicine man where, however, the restitution phase is emphasized.

The Berndt couple give the following description of the initiation of a *kinkin* (medicine man) in the Ooldea region: The candidate leaves the camp accompanied by two medicine men. He is taken to a water hole where he is to receive the power called *daramara*, i.e., "cutting up." They go to a water hole inhabited by the mythical serpent "Wonambi." The serpent swallows the candidate, the medicine men return to the camp. After an undefined period the medicine men go back and offer a kangaroo rat to the water serpent. The Wonambi then vomits the candidate who comes out at a nearby rockhole. When he comes out he is no longer a man but a baby. Large fires are made in a circle, they act as an incubator, the "baby" is placed in the midst of these and it grows up rapidly to achieve the size of a grown man. The medicine man now knows Wonambi because *he has been inside his stomach,* he and Wonambi are "friends."

After a period of seclusion in the bush he lies down full length before the fires. He is now called "a dead man." The head medicine man dislocates his wrists, his joints, knees, ankles. His neck is also broken. A black stone is used to cut up his body. Then into each portion that has been cut the initiator inserts a pearl shell which revives the limb. The shells are put into his ears so that he can hear and understand everything. They are placed in his ear, so that he can hear the spirits, into his forehead so that he can see through everything into his stomach which gives him a renewed life and invulnerability. Then they "sing" him, he is revived and sits up.[317]

Among the Ilpirra and the Northern Aranda the medicine man is initiated at a cave near Alice Springs. This cave is occupied by the Iruntarinia, the *spirit doubles* of each individual and of the mythical heroes whose reincarnation the man is.

When any man feels that he is capable of becoming a medicine man he wanders away from the camp quite alone until he comes to the mouth of the cave. Here with considerable trepidation, *he lies down to sleep,* not venturing to go inside, lest he should, instead of being endowed with magic power, be spirited away altogether. At break of day, one of the Iruntarinia comes to the mouth of the cave and, finding the man asleep, throws an invisible lance at him which pierces the neck from behind, passes through the tongue, making therein a large hole, and then comes out through the mouth. A second lance thrown by the Iruntarinia pierces the head from ear to ear and the victim falls dead. He is carried into the depths of the cave which is also the happy other world of the Iruntarinia.

317 Berndt, R. and C., "A Preliminary Report of Field Work in the Ooldea Region, Western South Australia," *Oceania,* XIV, 1943, pp. 58–60.

There the spirit removes all the internal organs and provides the man with a completely new set. After this he comes to life again but stays in a sort of stupefied condition for several days. Besides the new set of organs the spirit also inserts magic stones into his inside. With the aid of these stones he can withstand all evil influences.[318] The whole thing has always been regarded as somewhat of a mystery by anthropologists. But it becomes quite clear if we assume, as the text really implies, that we have here stereotyped dreams. Of course, a hole could not be made in the tongue in a dream, but after the neophyte had dreamed what he was expected to dream the operation would then be performed by another medicine man with the usual combination of belief and fraud that is so characteristic of the whole complex.

Wapiti of the Ngatatara tribe was a medicine man. He was initiated as follows. He tells the whole thing *as a dream* which is undoubtedly correct. "The *altjira*[319] Wapiti (means yam) came to me holding a yam in his hand. He thrust the yam under my nail and the *nankara* stone (magic stone) went right in from there. It spread right through my flesh and came out through the nails of the other hand."

He had to prepare for this dream by regularly eating the yam that is his own totem.[320] Every time he ate it he felt a stitch inside[321] till finally he was "made" by the *altjira* in the dream.

When he woke up after the dream he was deranged and continually talking. He saw a stump and taking it to be a man he said,

"Scolding talk, bad word"
(*Warkinyi wanga kujanga*),

which means that the man is cursing him. Then he sees two men and keeps protecting against their curses. Now he understands the language of all animals and he knows why infants at play laugh or smile. He can see right through people and also pull things that cause disease out of them.

The outstanding feature of this story is the part played in it by the mythological Wapiti, i.e., his supernatural father. His mother conceived him from a *tjurunga* thrown by the ancestor which becomes an infant in her womb. The parallel to the *tjurunga* of the yam totem is the yam itself, which he receives through the mouth and which permeates his whole body. The dream that makes him a medicine man is really the primal scene in which he replaces the mother.

[318] Spencer, B. and Gillen, F. I., *The Arunta,* London, 1927, II, pp. 391–393.
[319] Spirit, ancestor, double.
[320] This is perhaps the only really authentic case of a totem sacrament in the strict sense of the word.
[321] Normally he is supposed to eat of it only sparingly and only at the fertility ceremony.

The state in which he finds himself after the dream is a paranoid or schizophrenic episode. Central Australian curses always refer to the sex organs.

Asked whom the spirit reminds him of, he says of his father. But then why two of them? This might be either a denial of the implicit parricide (eating the yam) or a compromise with his mother in passive sex gratification (one father for each). Spencer and Gillen record a similar case among the Warramunga. The future medicine man sees two spirits, he is just about to throw a spear at them when they say, "Don't kill us we are your father and brother."[322]

After having told me that he was initiated by the ancestral spirits in a dream he goes on to recount what is evidently a second dream and a second initiation.

The *marali* (eagle hawk demon) comes from the west and flies away with the soul. The demon looks like a man with *narkapala* (charcoal paint) on his breast but with the head and wings of an eagle hawk. The demon eagle hawk takes the soul to a great sea. Then he flies into a big mountain with it and then brings it back again.

The *marali* really take all the souls to an old woman who lives in the far west. She is the *mother of* all *maralis*. She makes a bed of gum leaves for the souls and they sit up there.

This *marali* endows the candidate with the magic stones. But he is chief of all the medicine men and he can take the stones back again.

This is what happened to him at Merino:[323]

It was daytime and yet everything felt like dark. He went to sleep and felt something coming upon him like a bird. He was frightened and all the stones ran out of his body. They came out through his nose. However, while I was inquiring about these matters his magic stones were restored in another dream. "A Kukurpa came and embraced me. Then he put the magic stones back again."

Kukurpa is the same as *marali*. He woke in a dazed state like drunk. The *Kukurpa* looked like a spotted dog, in fact like the writer's fox terrier. I visited him in his hut, the evening before he had this dream and the dog came with me. It is clear that this is a transference dream with latent homosexual content and that he owes the restoration of his magical stones to the feeling of increased importance due to the fact that I am interested in the things he can tell me.

Pukuti wara's dreams are all more or less initiation dreams.

The best way to understand the nature of a Central Australian medi-

---

[322] Spencer and Gillen, *The Northern Tribes of Central Australia*, London, 1904, p. 482.

[323] Name of a mountain, in his own tribal lands.

cine man is through the dreams of medicine men with whom we are personally acquainted, especially because most of these dreams are dreams
of the medicine man's initiation or dreams in which he practices his art.
Some of these dreams have already been discussed as dreams of individuals, others I have reserved for this chapter.

Dream 1: My *kurunpa* (soul) was in the shape of a *wamulu* (eagle-
hawk-down) and the wind blew it to the west. The feather rolled over,
disappeared in the sand and went right in under the ground. Then the
kurunpa looked like myself and came out of the ground on top of a high
hill. Then I flew up to the *tjukal* (milky way). There was a camp there
but no people in it. Paper was lying about the camp. There was a black
hill there and the place was called *Talarara* (Hill Standing Up). This is
where the souls always fly to when they go up to the sky.

Then I flew to Mount Gillen near Alice Springs and there I saw a
house.

Then I flew northeast to an unknown country where all the creeks
ran toward the northeast.

There were camps there and I sat down. The rocks were shining
like fire. The rocks stopped. I flew away again up to *tjukal* into the
tjukal eri (point of the *tjukal*). There was a lot of *ilin*[324] on the point.
Then I flew south from the hill and I saw chips of *mulga* like those used
for making a *mandagi* (bull roarer). Then I went along the *tjukal eri* and
I saw many from *mamu* coming out of earth and looking at me. Then I
came to another place. My own *wami* (snake) was frightened by the frog
and it became a *waninga* on my head. The snake pressed my neck down
I could not see. But my *nankara bone* was on my neck and that held it up.

I went south to Kurkno; there were many Kurunpa people there. I
saw their paint marks; they were shining on the breast like gum.

Then I flew north and I heard two *iti-iti* (*ratapa*) spirit children. I
looked and I thought they were in the earth but they were in a hollow
tree. The two babies were twins and their mother stood beside the tree.
I killed both children with my penis. First I stood up as if I were throwing my testicle and my testicle became like a stone—the children were
frightened and then my *kalu* (penis) killed them. Then I roasted them
using my forehead instead of a stick to hold them into the fire. I hid them
in a hole in the hard ground so that nobody should take them away.

Tonight I will eat them, I shall find the place where I left them.

Then I went on. My snake came right out and fell down. My soul was
full of *nankara* stones, they were sticking right out like the spines of a
porcupine. Then I chased the snake along, following the Milky Way, for
all this happened at the point of the Milky Way.

I went on always following the *tjukal* (Milky Way). The snake came
back into my body and I flew back. I saw many white men's houses and
there was light everywhere, I came down when it was beginning to get
light on the Milky Way, I had been flying from one point of the Milky
Way to the other.

In the sky earth I saw a mole in a good sand hill. At daylight when

---

324 (*lyanpa A*) Shavings dipped in blood used for ceremonial purposes as head dress.

the point of the *Tjukal* is above us I came back into my body. When I flew back I saw the fire I had made before I was transformed into a feather. The fire was covered with *matati* (pubic tassels).

Pukuti-wara's dreams are somewhat different from those of others— and so is Pukuti-wara himself. The amount of nonrepressed sexual elements is far greater and they are also exceedingly rich in "magico-religious" symbolism. Penis and testicles are part of his stock-in-trade as a medicine man for he has been initiated by having one testicle removed. His dreams are decidedly of a psychotic type and so is his personality. He stops in the middle of a narrative on the lookout for imaginary hostile attacks—a thing I have never seen another native doing in broad daylight. He is stiff and rigid and has an angry scowl on his face. He will sit and brood without a word for a long time. He is proud of his dignity both as hereditary *atunari*[325] of the Pitjentara's and as medicine man of no mean standing. The white settlers like him, they say he has never taken any of their cattle. He would not stoop to do something which might put him in the power of the white man and prefers to roam about in the arid country.

The *basic dream* or moment of falling asleep in the shape of the rolling feather, the descent underground, and the rolling rocks is followed by the *genital countermove*, "the hill called *standing up*, flying upward, etc."

The woman with the two babies, was like Dori. She is the wife of a native from the northern country who is now employed by a white man. She is here in the camp now, with her husband. One of the children is like her son, the other looks like his own son Jankitji.

Now in the dream text he has called the two children twins. But if Dori is the mother of Jankitji then she is *ipso facto* Pukuti-wara's wife. Dori is one of the women of the "mother" type for through her connection with a white man she is in the position to give him a little flour or something of that kind. Pukuti-wara is so deeply imbued with the beliefs and myths of his tribe that I think I am justified in using these in order to explain his dreams even if he did not mention them in this connection. Now there is one period in life at which a Central Australian native thinks that he might kill his own child. That is if he has *intercourse with the pregnant mother*. Iti-iti like *ratapa* means an unborn child, a "spirit child" in the ancestral cave, an embryo in the womb and also a baby. But in this case he thinks he hears the voices from the inside of the earth and then they are in a hollow tree—that is, he is really cohabiting with a pregnant woman, a mother, and killing his own children in the womb with his penis.

[325] Chief.

In connection with the snake we get some data about various medical specialists. The snake is the mother of the *nankara* stones. Some medicine men have only the snake or only the bone or only the stone. Pukuti-wara has all three kinds. A man with a snake pulls it out with his finger. The man who has a bone inside uses only one finger, the *tarka* (bone) finger. He thrusts it in to the afflicted part whereupon the bone comes out of the finger and pushes the pain out. The man who has the stone uses his mouth and sucks the trouble out of his patient. At any rate he calls his own snake a mother and part of his aerial flight consists of flying after this snake. What can the transformation of the snake into a *waninga* mean? We shall understand this after having gone through the whole material of associations.

This side of the sky is the *tjukal* (milky way) lying there like a rainbow. But on the other side of the sky, the side which we cannot see from the earth, there is another *tjukal*.[326] This *tjukal* is like a *kuntanka* and this is where he walks in his dream. *This is nice and smooth like the subincision hole.* If it is not like this but rough the *kurunpa* cannot get back for it may get stuck there. Only a man's *kurunpa* who has one testicle can go up to the *tjukal*. When he goes under the earth he makes a hole with the penis. The penis gets very long and the soul goes out. When the *kurunpa* emerges from the testicle it also sucks the marrow out of the bones and puts a *kunti* (little club, *tjutinpa* or *kupulu* in Pitjentara) into the bone instead of the marrow.

A flood of light on a number of important points! The aerial flight of the medicine man symbolizes an *erection* for it commences by the penis becoming very long and boring a hole in the earth. The dreamer thinks that the children are in the earth; thereby our interpretation is proved and the infanticide in the dream is revealed as a foeticide with the penis.

Aggression intervenes in the uterine regressive trend; he does not go into the hollow tree but kills the twins he finds there. But when he goes under the earth he opens the way with his penis. Very characteristic for dream psychology is the goal of the dream journey, the Milky Way is his own subincision hole. But the subincision opening symbolizes the vagina. Therefore the dream shows very obviously both the uterine regression and the dreamer (sleeper) going back into his own body.

The dreamer's forehead figures as a spit for roasting the two children. The glans penis is called "forehead" and here we have the whole body as a symbol of the penis. Perhaps the two shining rocks can also be explained in this way. The rolling rock would be the birth of a child,

---

[326] Cf. *infra* "The Other Night" in the initiation of the Parriotso Shaman.

caused by the dreamer's "foot" and its shining quality might be derived from the intrauterine fire.

We are now compelled to go beyond the association material and to quote a group of myths connected with the Milky Way. According to these myths the Milky Way is a woman and a young boy who are stuck together in coitus and appear on the sky as a *kuntanka* or *waninga*.[327]

If the medicine man's flight is an erection and the goal of this flight a phenomenon in nature that represents the primal scene, the latent content of the dream is evidently the sexual desire of the child as witness of the primal scene. The snake in Pukuti-wara is transformed into a *waninga* because the *waninga* itself symbolizes the primal scene. His neck is held down by the same snake or *waninga* so that he cannot see, that is, the primal scene fantasy cannot become conscious. Regarding this fantasy itself the two main trends may be described in the terms of the dream itself. The dreamer is chasing the snake, i.e., the mother. Or, the snake mother is in the dreamer. When the child witnessed the primal scene he had an erection wishing to thrust his penis into the mother (earth) and to let his *wamulu* (sperm) go flying. But it must be a dangerous thing to enter the maternal vagina, for if the subincision hole (*tjukal*) is rough, the "soul" (penis) might get stuck and never return into the body. What does the Milky Way represent? A young man who after circumcision got stuck in a woman in coitus. That would mean a loss of the penis (soul). A *nankara* man can fly up to the *tjukal* and come back again; he is bisexual, his subincision wound (vulva) is the Milky Way.

It is, of course, castration anxiety which conditions the opposite trend of fantasies. The snake mother is in the dreamer or rather he is in the snake mother when the father approaches with his penis. These two fantasies both representing the past are condensed in one that stands nearer to the present tense. Having desired to kill the father in the act of coitus and also to be in the womb when his penis approaches, these two fantasies are woven into one. The adult Pukuti-wara desires to kill his son (retribution anxiety) when the latter is in the mother's womb (identification with the son and uterine regression). In the dream the infantile and the adult repressed material appears in the guise of his profession, i.e., of the mythology of the *nankara* man.

The starting point of the dream is the present situation. They are now (1929) having an initiation ceremony in the presence of a white man. The situation is not completely new. He has been to Alice Springs and was received in a friendly manner by the missionary Mr. Kramer. He re-

---

[327] Cf. Róheim, *The Riddle of the Sphinx*, 1934, pp. 70, 71. *Waninga* are crossed sticks supporting a rhomboid pattern of threads.

members that they camped at Mount Gillen when they went to Alice Springs and they sang a *ngallunga* song there. They are doing the same thing at present. The place to the northeast reminds him of Palm Paddock near the mission, a place he passed through on the same trip.

At the basis of the dream we have the oedipus complex with the primal scene as correlated trauma. The latent content comprises all kinds of fantasies with more or less secondary elaboration based on this content. The whole complex is revived by the analogous latent content of the initiation ritual which is going on at present and slightly colored by the presence of a white man. The latter factor is probably responsible for the appearance of Dori in the dream as she is also associated with a white man.

An additional feature in the dream content is the sight of the pregnant mother, provoking feelings of rage against the brother in the womb, represented in the dream by the son. Many details, however, still remain unexplained, though we can form a guess as to the meaning of some of them. The *nankara* bone which makes his neck stiff when he ought not to look probably means an erection. The fire from which he emerges and to which he returns is covered by the *matati,* which in real life is used for covering the penis. The *nankara* stones of which his body is full are testicle symbols, the fact that they are compared to the spines of a porcupine may perhaps be explained by the legendary connection of the porcupine with castration. The things seen at the *tjukal eri* are chips of the *mandagi,* or bull roarer, used for love magic. Why the *lyanpa* should be found at the same place we do not know nor can we ascertain the significance of the frog demon.

Dream 2: I dreamed of a woman who had only one leg, one arm, and one breast. She came to my camp from the west and sat turning her back to me. We flew to the sky together and there we found another earth. There was a little fire smouldering there and she stood beside the fire. Then she *kurkararingu* (became a *kurkara,* i.e., desert oak tree), I stood on the other side of the fire and also became a desert oak tree. I was a shorter tree but very straight.

Then we became human beings again and came down to this earth. We killed two *wanka* (*iwupa*) and sucked their marrow fat out. Then we came to a place called Ili-piti (fig-tree hole). Women were gathering figs there and we saw their tracks. We came to Untiri (Open) on the Pando (Lake Amadeus) and frightened some *indorida* birds there (a kind of pigeon). Then we went to a place called Inderapiti (Bandicoot hole). This is where they *make* the bandicoots. We came to a place called Ngatu-ngunanyi (Crooked stand up) a place where an emu ancestor stood up. Then we came to a cave called Kunanpiri (Bird excrement). Near the cave there was a camp with very many children's bones. Their mothers had eaten them all, because they were very thin. Then we went to Mulara (nose place). There was a big crowd there making *ngallunga*.

The *kunka mamu* (Woman devil) led me and I followed her. We came to a *mamu* place with many bones, the *mamu* had eaten the souls. She told me that this was her place. This place was Witapi-wara (Backbone-long).[328] Then we came to Wawilja (fire-stick used for love magic). But it was not the place on earth called Wawilja; it was a strange place. There were many Kuna-tarka-tara men there ("Anus bone with": another name for the demon called Karpirinyi). They are the *mamus* who make the *nankara* man. They held me in their arm and then they threw me into the fire. They put fresh bones into my head and body and also *ulkurungu* (hot stones or fire). Then we came to the home of the *tunta mutu* (one leg) people. They were all like the woman who led me. She took me to a big hole and said: See that! The hole was full of the *ngambu* (testicles) they had taken out. They put one into my hand and said: "That is yours." Then I went with the *tunta mutu* people to a frog place. Many frogs were sitting there in a row. This is how we sat (drawing in sand)

0[329]

330—   —   —   0

0

0

0

Then the *tunta mutus* introduced the frogs and said: "They are men not frogs." Then we came to a place called Watan-gulunyguluny (Frightened frightened). There were many *watan-gulunyguluny mamus* there, men with curly hair. They ran when they saw the *tunta mutus*. Some of the *mamus* were transformed into grass, others into sticks and others became *kuntanka* (*kuntaringu*). These *kuntanka* were like *mandagi*.[331] At night I went into the bush with the *kunka mamu* and I saw some of the *mamu* making marks on the *Kuntanka anangu*. They said this *kuntanka* was called *rupi-inpa* this being their word for *reru-reru* (bull-roarer). Then I came back with the demon woman. The *tunta mutu* all became frogs and went into the earth. We came to a place called Warupi (Kangaroo tail). All my friends were there. Then we came to Nankavil (Spiders web) and saw the track of a *muruntu* (mythical serpent). We chased that *muruntu*, caught him and put him back into his hole again. Then we came to Aputuleri (Turning round). An ancestor who was running after a kangaroo turned back at this place. We went to Ngataultul, this being the place where an ancestor had cut a damper into two halves (*ngata* = half).

Then we came to Nuninta (Tail standing up) where a *wallaby* ancestor had been standing with the tail pointing upward. There was no water there, only the track of a wild dog who had been digging for water. When we came to my camp the woman became a whirlwind with a fire in the middle and disappeared.

There is an obvious parallelism in the dream episodes. (1) Pukuti-wara and the demon woman eat *wanka* (worms). (2) Mothers eat their chil-

---

328 Meaning the "backbone" of a hill.
329 Frogs.
330 *Tunta mutu.*
331 *Kuntanka* = Aranda *tjurunga*, *mandagi* = bull-roarer.

dren, bones lying about. (3) Demons eat souls, bones lying about. (4) The hole in the custody of the *tunta mutu*, testicles lying about.

The *tunta mutu* is a being who has only one of every organ that should be a pair, but so is Pukuti-wara himself, he has only one testicle. In the dream he wanders with the *tunta mutu* woman and then with the group of *tunta mutu*. In the case of a Pitjentara medicine man who has had one testicle cut out, castration anxiety has a very realistic basis. Hence the identification of the male with a woman who symbolizes the castration complex. The demon woman of the dream is like Kunpala, Pukuti-wara's sister. There is a series of *equivalent activities* in the dream. The *wanka* (A iwupa) are one of the forms in which the ancestors travel when they are after a woman through whom they intend to be reborn.

They suck the marrow out of the bones of the *wanka,* a thing that is always done in reality in the case of children whom they eat, but cannot possibly be done with a caterpillar. Hence *wanka* = child = soul = testicle. On the other hand the destroyers are Pukuti-wara = sister = "the mothers" = one foot demons = frogs. The castrated male identifies himself with the dangerous mother of his infancy whose cannibalistic practices were a matter of actual experience. Four out of eight children had been killed and eaten by Pukuti-wara and his wife; it is hardly likely that the custom should not have been observed in Pukuti-wara's infancy. Pukuti-wara is always castrating others and eating children's souls in his dreams and fantasies, having been castrated himself.[332] He has identified himself with the mother as castrator. The men who in the dream throw him on the fire and thrust long bones and hot stones in his head and body, that is the demon initiators of the medicine man, would then be the representatives of the father imago. Their name itself suggests anal coitus (anus with bone) the bone symbolizing the penis.

Pukuti-wara has really lost one testicle, he is evidently trying to make up for the loss in the dream for the *tunta mutu* show him the lost object. After the one foot and frog demons our wanderer meets the demons called "frightened," that is, the representative of anxiety. He and his demon sister then witness a sight which the child is not permitted to see, the making of a *tjurunga* or more exactly the making of the incisions in the "body" of the *tjurunga*.

We have had several dream analyses in which "making a *tjurunga*" was revealed as the representative of the primal scene. The dream we are considering contains innumerable references to mythology and has probably a series of overdetermining elements. We had not time to get all the

---

[332] We do not know whether the operation he talked about was real or simply a dream. He may have had an undescended testicle.

myths, for each place has, of course, a myth of its own. So I asked him to choose and tell me one of the myths. He thereupon related the wild cat myth of Kinkinkura. The essential features of the story are the supernaturally large *double penes* of the wild cat men, the conflict of the group and the Old Wild-cat and finally a coitus scene, in which the young wild cats have intercourse and the old men sing as they look on.

We should therefore say that the primal scene of infancy with the correlated castration anxiety is again the latent content of the dream. In the great shock which constitutes the initiation of the medicine man this castration anxiety was abreacted and realized. He can do things that are beyond the powers of ordinary mortals, this is his boastful claim, for the worst he has already endured. Yet such a heavy loss can never be compensated but in his dreams he is always trying to compensate for it by castrating others, killing children and hunting for his own testicle. Even though he has only one testicle he will go to the hole where all testicles are in safekeeping (maternal womb). Perhaps the frog demon in this connection means the same thing as the frog in European folklore, viz., the womb. Then we could understand Pukuti-wara's drawing, the semi-castrated males trying to enter the mother's womb.

Dream 3: It is really difficult to know what is dream material and what is reality in this narrative. For one testicle is really missing.

I was asleep and I saw a man's *kurunpa* come like a *walauru* (eaglehawk). It had wings but it had a penis like a man. It caught my soul with the penis and drew it out of my hair. My soul was hanging down from the penis and the eaglehawk flew first west, then to the east. He took me to a far away country. Then we flew southnorth and again to the west. It was just before dawn and the eaglehawk man had made a big fire into which he threw my soul. Then my penis became all hot and he pulled the skin right off. He took me out of the fire again and took me to a camp. There were many *nankara* men there standing in a group. They were all bones like the spines of the porcupine. He threw me on top of these bones and all the bones entered my body.

Then we went west and the eaglehawk man split me open. He took out the lungs, the liver and left only the heart. Now I have only the heart.

Then we went further west and I saw a little baby. It was a *mamu,* I saw the child and lifted my hand to throw the *nankara* stone. My testicles were hanging down and they flew out instead of *nankara* stones. A man came out of one of the *ngambu* and this *kurunpa* stood behind me. This man had a very long *kalu katiti* (the two sides of the subincised penis) and he hit the *mamu* child dead with it. Then he gave it to me and I ate it. After that both *kurunpa* went into my body.

This dream is of great interest because it confirms our interpretation of the soul, of the dream flight, of the spines or bones that enter the dreamer's body of the "split body" and of the extraction of vital parts.

He says that the eaglehawk man looked like himself; therefore the dream flight with the soul hanging on his own penis would be a masturbation fantasy. Compensation and projection appear on the scene; the testicle he has lost becomes an additional soul and a source of power and a means of killing children, i.e., genital symbols. That the child really symbolizes the testicle and in a generalized way the whole genital is confirmed by the rest of the data. When he sleeps in a camp the *tjitji mamu* (baby demon) jumps out of his leg and then it jumps on the foreheads of all the men who are lying in the camp. He sees him jumping out of his leg and coming back into it again. It is probably this *mamu* whom he credits with taking out the *ngambu* of all the people in the camp. This, of course, is only Pukuti-wara's dream and that explains why they are not angry when he shows them the *ngambu* he has extracted. The trauma is reflected in the dream for something goes out of his "leg", the wish fulfillment is that it returns again, while the connection of all this with the operation he has undergone is shown by his *mamu* extracting the testicles of others. This *mamu* is called *tjitji ngan garpa* (child mad) and it urinates all over his face. That is why he has such a long beard just as the urine flowed down. Urine comes from the penis child who is also responsible in some cases for conception. The children born after it has gone into a woman are "half demons." When he was initiated he had three *kurunpas,* now he has two for he has given one to another man. But he always gets new *kurunpas* from the children he eats and the child demon that comes out of his leg is also one that he has eaten.

Dream 4: I dreamed that the earth heaved up first from the west and then from the east. It was like a wall, then it came from the south and from the north as if it would cover me. Beside me the spines of the porcupine were sticking out of the earth. The earth covered me till I was lying on the top of those spines. An eaglehawk *kurunpa* came and ate my *kurunpa.* It was a man with wings like an eaglehawk.

He was a small boy when he dreamed this. It was a long time before he was initiated as a medicine man. He used to go about with his father hunting kangaroos or with his mother digging for witchetty and ants in the earth.

The earth symbolizes the mother as in Dreams 1 and 2. Now we know that there is a typical situation of great traumatic importance in the life of these natives. It is the custom of the mother to lie on top of her son and the repressed memory of this situation is projected in the *alknarintja,* the woman who sits on the sleeper's penis and thus reverses the normal position of male and female. In the dream the spines of the porcupine, which figure so conspicuously in the symbolism of the *nankara* man, penetrate into the child's body form underneath. At the same time his soul is "eaten" by a male *kurunpa,* the significance of which we already know from Dream 14.

This dream of his childhood reveals the importance of the inverted oedipus complex as basis of the *nankara* sublimation. For both the porcupine and the eaglehawk are definitely parts of the *nankara* symbolism and he either knew this as a child[333] and dreaming in this symbolism indicated the adequate form of sublimation or he has added these features to the dream afterward—because of the link that connects it in the unconscious with the art of the medicine man.

Pukuti-wara is certainly the typical medicine man of anthropological books. There is something verging on the psychotic in his whole behavior. But Wapiti, Aldinga, Urantukutu, Leliltukutu are very different. They are absolutely normal in the native sense of the word and their medical craft is just one more accomplishment like their hunting or ceremonial knowledge. But every medicine man stresses the importance of initiation and practices his art as a repetition of what was done to him when he was a neophyte.

In many "initiation dreams" (rites) we see this "going down" which is so characteristic of the shaman in a trance. The Kabi in Queensland believed that the Rainbow serpent lived in unfathomable water holes in the mountains. When he is visible in the shape of the rainbow he is passing from one water hole into the other. He is also responsible for stealing children and replacing them with changelings.

"A man's power in the occult art would appear to be proportioned to his vitality and the vitality depended upon the number of sacred pebbles and the rope he carried within him. One kind of sacred pebble was called *kundir* and the man who had many of them was *kundir bonggan* (pebbles many). The rope was obtained as follows: *a man would go to sleep* near a water hole. He would then become dimly conscious of a prickly sensation in his limbs. *Dhakkan* (Rainbow) *would take him down into his domain* and extract from his body the crystals giving in exchange rope, a kind of magical rope that medicine men are believed to possess within their bodies and that confers great powers. The man is then laid against the edge of the water hole and when he awakes again he is *mangurngur,* i.e., full of life and power."[334] The Wirdadthuri medicine man does not dive into a pool

333 Father, mother, grandfather were all *nankaras.*

334 Mathew, I., *Two Representative Tribes of Queensland,* 1910, p. 171; Curr, E. M., *The Australian Race,* 1886, III, p. 177; Mathew, *Eaglehawk and Crow,* 1899, p. 146; cf. also Roth, W. E., "Superstition, Magic and Medicine," *Bulletin of North Queensland Ethnography,* V, 1903, pp. 10, 30; Mathews, R. A., *Ethnological Notes on the Aboriginal Tribes of New South Wales and Victoria,* 1905, p. 162.

but he is initiated by Baiamai who lives "on the other side of the sea." Baiamai intimated in a dream given to the father or grandfather of the candidate that he was to be initiated as a medicine man. Baiamai came up to the candidate saying, "I will make you." Then he brought forth from his own body the sacred water called *kali* that was within him. This water had great power and was said by some to be liquefied quartz crystal. The liquid emanated from either side of Baiamai as he moved his head from side to side and fell upon the neophyte or neophytes. This was the *kurmi*, "the going into them." The *kali* falling upon the postulant would spread completely over him, his body absorbing every particle, not a drop falling to the ground; it would run over the man but on falling would be absorbed immediately by his body. Some little time afterward when the fluid had entered every portion of his body, feathers emerged from his arms so that they resembled the wings of a bird.[335] After this Baiamai teaches him how to fly.

The next scene is in the camp once more. Baiamai took a thick sinew cord about twenty yards in length! He placed the cord round each neophyte in such a position that the two ends rested one on each foot, in a U-shaped position up the legs of the candidate and crossed below the chest. Baiamai then "sang" the cord into the candidate's body so that it disappeared. This cord called *maulwe* was used by the medicine men for many purposes *as a spider uses his webbing thread.*[336]

In another version of the initiation rite the candidate went to a wombat hole and began to dig. He had dug only a little way when by looking into the hole he could see a *goana* moving. He put his arm into the hole but instead of catching the *goana* something caught him. When he came to the end of the tunnel he was in the country "on the other side of the sea."

Follows the time spent with Baiame (as above) and then he is brought back to the exit of Baiame's cave and under the tunnel through the sea again.[337]

Later we are told about the medicine men exhibiting their magic power. They "sang out" their *"buru maulwe"*, i.e., *testes cord,* in the same manner as does the spider and began climbing up using both hands one after the other so that the top of the tree was reached. Then they sent their cords to the next tree and walked across the air.[338] Another account about the medicine men showing what they can do is this:

[335] Berndt, R. M., "Wuradjeri Magic and 'Clever Men,'" *Oceania,* XVII, 1947, p. 335.

[336] *Ibid.,* p. 336.
[337] *Ibid.,* p. 338.
[338] *Ibid.,* p. 340.

"While all the men were watching him, he lay down on his back near the butt of the tree, he kept his arms close to his body and stretching out his legs, opened them fairly widely, keeping them suspended above the ground. He then sang to himself and his *maulwe* cord gradually came out of his testes and went directly upward, he climbed up this and reached the top of the tree where there was a nest about forty feet from the ground."

When he came back the cord could be seen coming down and re-entering the testes.[339]

How much of this is illusion and how much juggling does not concern us here. What we are interested in is the dreamlike character of the situation and the analogy with our Pitjentara data.

There the shaman is carried up to the sky by an eaglehawk by means of his penis, his testicles fly out, a double is projected out of his scrotum, etc. Here a rope emanates from the testes and he uses it for climbing up a tree. On the Forrest River District the rainbow water serpent is the source of the medicine man's power. An old medicine man takes the candidate up into the sky. First, however, he puts him into a pouch he carries, having reduced him to the size of a very small child. The ascent is made on the rainbow serpent which he uses as a *rope* (cf. the testes cord rope above. On the phallic aspects of the rainbow serpent cf. Róheim, *The Eternal Ones of the Dream*, 1945, pp. 132, 264) sitting astride the serpent at the same time, when near the top he throws the candidate out of the pouch onto the sky. Now he is "dead." If he sees the rainbow serpent near a water hole he enters the water and obtains various magical objects from the rainbow serpent. He is brought back again, regains his normal size and keeps practicing the sky flight on the rainbow serpent.[340]

The women of the Kimberley district are initiated into the art of medicine women in a similar manner. She is visited by the ghosts *taken away in her sleep* and then returned to the camp where for a few days she may be in a stupefied state "a little bit mad." Later she bathes in a pool where Kaleru dwells and magical objects are inserted into her. She can see the dead and uses a string to go up into the sky.[341]

Kaleru is the rainbow serpent, all spirit children come from him, he made them in the mythical period out of his semen and put them in the water holes where the husband finds them.[342] We note the phallic nature

339 *Ibid.*, pp. 341, 342.

340 Brown, R., "The Rainbow Serpent Myth of Australia," *Journ. Roy. Anthr. Inst.*, LVI, 1926, p. 20; Elkin, A. P., "The Rainbow Serpent Myth in Northwest Australia," *Oceania*, I, 1931, pp. 349, 350.

341 Eaberry, P. M., *Aboriginal Woman*, Philadelphia, 1929, p. 251.

342 *Ibid.*, p. 42.

of the rainbow serpent who initiates the shaman and the fact that the whole thing takes place while the shaman is asleep.

The Caribe shaman of Dutch Guiana go up to Grandfather Vulture. They ascend by means of a *revolving ladder*. Then they meet a beautiful woman, the spirit of the water. They plunge into the river and from her they learn charms, magic. They arrive at a place called "Life and Death." Now they can choose, do they want to go to the "Land without Dawn," or the "Land without Sunset." Suddenly they are back on earth.[343] (Reveals dream origin.) The account given by Lehtisalo of the initiation of the Siberian shaman is extremely interesting. It contains all the traits we have been discussing, the descent (diving), flying, death and resurrection, birth and also some of the primal scene type and oedipal content.

A Yakut shaman describes how he became a shaman while yet in the womb when he was five months old. (This is a parallel to the Yuma; cf. above, first chapter). His mother married the Smallpox Spirit in her sleep and this is how he became a shaman. At the age of three he was dead for several days. (The following is evidently a combination of a childhood schizophrenic episode and dreams.)

"During this period I dived under the ocean. A voice said, Your shaman name will be *diver*."[344] The following sentence proves that the diving into the ocean is really diving into the womb because what now follows is the way out and up. He wanders, climbs up a hill and is suckled by a spirit woman. Then he sees the Master of the Netherworld and the Spirits of Smallpox eating each other. (The Smallpox Spirit was his supernatural father.) He comes to the land of shamans. There are nine seas there, in one of them there is an island with the world tree growing on it. In each sea a kind of duck or swan or falcon is swimming with their young.[345]

Out of the world tree he makes a drum and now he learns to fly with the birds. He crosses a swamp, led by his guardian spirits a mouse and an ermine. There he sees two women with hair and antlers like reindeer. While he looks on, they are just delivered of the two kinds of reindeer that can be used for sacrifices.[346]

It is noteworthy that all this is told in mythical style and regarded as prototypical of customs already practiced—another parallel to Yuma

[343] Metraux, "Le chamanisme chez les Indiens de l'Amerique du Sud Tropicale," *Acta Americana,* 1944/45, II, p. 207; Friedrich, A. B., "Die Himmelsreise der caraibischen Medizinmänner," *Zeitschrift für Ethnologie,* LXX, 1939.

[344] Lehtisalo, J., "Tod und Wiedergeburt des künftigen Schamanen," *Journal de la Societe Finno Ougrienne,* XLVIII, 1937, p. 3.

[345] Lehtisalo, *op. cit.,* p. 5.

[346] *Ibid.,* p. 6.

and Mohave, because beside dating shamanism from the womb he also goes back to cosmic beginnings.

Then he relates how he crawled through a gap (birth), was cut to pieces and then restored. Finally, "I awoke and I was in my own tent beside father and mother."[347]

In another Yakut account each shaman has a mythical bird with an iron beak and claws as mother animal. She cuts him to bits and restores him again. The mother animal takes his soul away and it grows on a branch of a pine in the nether world. Again the narrative ends, "I awoke and was again as before." According to another account the future shaman acts like crazy during the daytime, at night, when he is asleep, his soul is in the house of the nether world or ghosts.[348]

If we attempt to summarize the main features of the initiation of the shaman we find (a) that it is often said to take place in a dream; (b) the characteristic features are descent, frequently under the water, rebirth symbolism, death and revival, sky flight emphasizing the phallic aspect of this flight. The striking parallelism with the *basic dream* is quite evident. Sleeping is unconsciously equated with death and therefore awakening with revival, rebirth. The Achomawi word for soul is *delamdzi* and *delalamdzi* is dawn.[349] Sinking is the moment of falling asleep, or uterine regression. Uterine regression and genitality are the same or the genital aspect is the countermove to uterine regression.

However, if we did not know that the dream environment is shaped out of the dreamer's body, that therefore in the dream the dreamer is in a sense both active and passive, we would be at a loss to explain the type of shamanism in which the spirit goes into, takes possession of the shaman. Or rather we could not explain it on basis of the dream theory. However, since we know that the spirit *is* the shaman it is easy to grasp on this basis, *how he possesses himself in the dream.* We are told that the soul of the Yaruro shaman goes to the land of Kuma and then his body is empty, ready for the supernatural beings to occupy. We note that this Kuma is the woman who created all things, from whom all things emanate and that she lives in the far west beyond the ocean.[350] The medicine men of the Taulipang drink tobacco juice and that makes them ascend to the sky. There they consult the souls of dead medicine men about the sick man. When the tobacco juice gets dry in the body the soul must come back but

[347] *Ibid.,* p. 12.
[348] *Ibid.,* p. 15.
[349] Angulo, J. de, "La psychologie religieuse des Achumawi," *Anthropos.,* XXIII, 1928, p. 575.
[350] Petrullo, V., "The Yaruros of the Capanaparo River, Venezuela," Smithsonian Institution, *Bureau Am. Ethn. Anthr. Papers,* No. 11, 1939, p. 249.

with it come the souls of his dead colleagues to take possession of the body.[351] Metraux says that the shaman sends his soul to the gods whereupon his body becomes the receptacle of the spirits.[352]

Thalbitzer writes about the shaman in East Greenland. When the lamps have been extinguished his movements get wilder and wilder. The drum rocks or stands erect on the floor, it springs up on the shaman's forehead, knocking frantically in restless agitation. His inner vision is "dawning," his soul is about to "pass over into the other world," he sinks down into the depths of the earth in mingled despair and ecstasy. He rises (or his soul does) and he sinks like a man about to drown. The spirit comes and goes through the anus.[353] *"His body is like a house that changes tenants."* Sometimes his own spirit is in it, sometimes others. The attendant spirits are called "they who cause to flee."[354]

In the ritual of the shaking tent the tent is simply an extension of the shaman's body.[355]

We have noted dreams in which the dreamer becomes identified with the feces or urine that pass through his body. I have emphasized the excremental significance of the magic quartz crystal as early as 1914[356] and we have now discussed the rope as the phallic symbol in the shaman's body.

Animism is the child of the dream, not of a pseudo-rational theory to explain dreams, but of the very deepest unconscious trends (double vector of the id, uterine regression and genital cathexis) that shape the dream. And the shaman is animism dramatized.

ADDENDUM

THE REVOLVING CASTLE

In the eleventh century *Voyage of Mael Duin,* the voyagers arrive at the thirty-second island. It has a fiery rampart around it. "And this rampart used to revolve around the island. There was an open doorway in the side

351 *Ibid.,* p. 249.

352 Metraux, "Le chamanisme chez les Indiens de l'Amerique du Sud Tropicale," *Acta Americana,* II, 1944/45, p. 322.

353 Hence probably the well-nigh universal significance of *wind* in shamanistic performances.

354 Thalbitzer, W., "The Heathen Priests of East Greenland," *Verhandlungen des XVI. Internationalen Amerikanisten Kongresses,* Wien, 1910. Part 2, p. 458.

355 Cf. Hallowell, I. A., "The Role of Conjuring in Saulteux Society," *Publ. Phil. Anthr. Soc.,* II, Philadelphia, 1942, p. 36; Burgesse, I. A., "The Spirit Wigwam," *Primitive Man,* XVI, 1943, p. 51; Flannery, R., "The Gros Ventre, Shaking Tent," *Primitive Man,* XVII, 1944, p. 54; Cooper, J. M., "The Shaking Tent Rite among Plains and Forest Algonquin," *ibid.,* p. 62.

356 Róheim, A varázserö Fogalmának eredete (Origin of the Mana Concept), Budapest, 1919.

of the rampart. Now, whenever the doorway would come in its revolution opposite to them they used to see the whole island and all that was therein and all its indwellers, even human beings, beautiful, abundant, wearing adorned garments and feasting with golden vessels in their hands. And the wanderers heard all their music."

In another island was a dun (fort) with a brazen door. When they went up the bridge they fell backwards. A woman came out with a pail in her hand. They struck the brazen door—sweet soothing music sent them to sleep. Another island; a maiden gives them a liquor that sends them to sleep for three days and three nights. When they awoke on the third day they were in their boat at sea. Nowhere did they see their island or their maiden.[1]

Professor Brown writes: "Very often in the romances the hero comes first to the tower of the dead. In the second story from Andreas Capellanus outlined above (p. 346) the hero comes first to a round palace with no apparent entrance from which emerges a giant carrying a copper club. Afterwards the hero comes to the square-cornered Castle of the *fées*. In *Perlesvans* Perceval rides through a turning castle to reach the isle of Elephants where he slays the Knight of the Dragon and frees the Queen of The Golden Circlet. Afterwards he comes to the Grail Castle. In La Mule sanz Frain Gawain rides into the revolving castle, cuts off an opponent's head and later rescues a queen."[2] When Parzival approaches the Grail castle (Chretien AB) he comes first to a tower shaped as if turned in a lathe. Unless an enemy flew in or was borne in by the wind it could not be stormed.[3]

The underworld castle harassed by Pwyll and Pryderi has a number of names, one of them is Caer Sidi, the Revolving Castle. In the Taliesin poems of the fourteenth century the bard says:

> Perfect is my chair in Caer Sidi
> Plague and age hurt him not who is in it
> They know, Manawydan and Pryderi
> Three organs round afire sit before it
> And about its points are ocean's streams
> And the abundant well above it
> Sweeter than white wine the drink in it.[4]

In the Welsh Seint Greal Peredur rides into the revolving castle. "And they rode through the wild forests and from one forest to an-

---

[1] Brown, Arthur C. L., *The Origin of the Grail Legend,* Cambridge, 1943, pp. 272–275. Quotes Stokes, *Rev. celt.* IX, 1888, pp. 447–495; X, 1889, pp. 50–95.

[2] *Ibid.,* p. 356.

[3] *Ibid.,* pp. 356, 357.

[4] Rhys, J., *Studies in the Arthurian Legend,* 1891, pp. 300, 301.

other they arrived on clear ground outside the forest. And when they beheld a castle coming within their view on level ground in the middle of a meadow; and around the castle flowed a large river and inside the castle they beheld large spacious halls with windows large and fair. They drew nearer toward the castle and they perceived the castle turning with greater speed than the fastest wind they had ever known" (etc.). Rhys concludes: "One would probably not greatly err in regarding the Turning Castle as a form of the abode of the king of the dead and the swiftness of its revolution would explain such a name as that of the Isle of the Active or Strenuous Door."[5]

In Russian folk tales the real owner of the revolving hut is the Baba Yaga. She lies stretched out from one end to the other, her iron nose passes through the roof. When the proper words are addressed to it the hut stops revolving so that its back is turned toward the forest and its entrance toward the speaker. The hut revolves on a fowl's legs.[6] She is a hideous old woman, very tall, very bony with an iron nose, pendant breasts and sharp teeth. The fence around her dwelling is made of the bones of the people she has eaten and tipped with their skulls. "The upright of the gates are human legs, the bolts are human arms and 'instead of a lock there is a mouth with sharp teeth.' " She flies in an iron mortar. She propels this with a pestle. According to the White Russians, Death gives the dead to the Baba Yaga and her subordinate witches feed on the souls of people.[7] The hut revolves on fowls' legs. "Hut, hut, look me in the face and turn your back to the forest," the heroine says.[8] In a Hungarian folk tale from Kalotaszeg, the hero who descends to the nether world (Bear's son type) finds a castle owned by a dragon and revolving on a cock's foot. By throwing the water fairies ring at it, he can make it stop.[9] In another folk tale we have a castle of diamond revolving on the foot of an elster. "Stop!" says the hero. "Only if my owner tells me to," says the castle. The hero shoots at the leg and by hitting it makes the castle stop.[10] The owner of the castle is the seven- or nine- or twelve-headed dragon but in the castle is the fairy princess or queen. The castle is personified. "Stop castle, I'll kill you if you don't," says the hero, Johny Sheeps Son. Once the dragon kills the hero but his mother the black sheep revives him. He asks, "Mother,

[5] *Ibid.*, p. 302. Cf. Macculoch, *The Religion of the Ancient Celts,* Edinburgh, 1911, p. 368.

[6] Ralston, W. R. S., *Russian Folk Tales,* 1873, p. 138.

[7] *Idem, The Songs of the Russian People,* 1872, pp. 161–163.

[8] Afanassjev, M., *Russische Volksmärchen,* Wien, 1906, p. 60.

[9] Kovács, A., *Kalotaszegi népmesék* (Folktales from Kalotaszeg), Budapest, n.d., p. 102.

[10] Ortutay, G., *Nyiri és rétközi parasztmesék* (Peasants' stories of Nyir and Retköz), Gyoma, n.d., p. 70.

where did you come from?" "*I dreamed such a beautiful dream in the lap of the three queens.*"[11] In a southern German folk tale the hero has to leave the castle by midnight because by that time everything starts revolving in the castle.[12]

Solymossy believes that this motive is originally Ural-Altaic. In the Hungarian folk tales it occurs very frequently and most of the cases belong to the Beowulf or Bear's Son type, but with one exception they are all connected with the other world. Solymossy derives the motive from shamanism.[13] He emphasizes the frequency of the duck and the goose as the birds whose foot supports the castle but he does not see that this is an argument that supports his thesis since the shaman is regularly associated with migrating water fowl. The shaman in his trance is supposed to ascend the world tree and the world tree[14] is a kind of pillar that supports a revolving universe.

The revolving universe,[15] however, is not the origin of the revolving hut or castle. We have (a) the revolving shaman, (b) the revolving hut, and (c) the revolving universe. In the Vogul myth the seven sons of Numi Tarem run round the world in one second,[16] and when he invokes the World Surveyor Chief this god who is himself the prototype of shamanism, starts revolving.[17]

In Vogul mythology we find this motive usually connected with the World Surveyor Chief. In the course of his wanderings he arrives at the river Ob. He sees three birch trees revolving on a wall. One of them has a gold leaf, it revolves so rapidly that it is hardly visible. But the hero hits it with his arrow. As soon as he has done this he falls asleep. He dreams. A woman is talking to him.

Is this the way to behave for young people; they go around the world and shoot holes into my cloak!

When he awakes it seems he has dreamed this while seated on his horse. He is at the entrance of a house. His aunt, the Kaltesh woman, is talking to him and gives him various instructions that all refer to the future shamanistic activities of the hero god.[18]

---

11 Kálmány, L., *Hagyományok* (Traditions), n.d., Szeged, pp. 1–12.

12 Zingerle, I. and J., *Kinder- und Hausmärchen aus Süddeutschland*, Regensburg, 1884, quoted in Siuts, H., *Jenseitsmotive im deutschen Volksmärchen*, Leipzig, 1911, p. 228.

13 Solymossy, S., "Magyar ösvallási elemek népmeseinkben" (Hungarian Heathen Traits in Our Folk Tales), *Ethnographia*, XXI, 1929, pp. 134–150.

14 Cf. Holmberg, V., "Der Baum des Lebens," *Acta Societatis Scientiarum Fennicae*, XVI, 1922/1923.

15 Munkácsi, *Vogul Népköltési Gyüj-temény* (Thesaurus of Vogul Folklore), I, CCXXXII, "The sky revolving like a hoop."

16 *Ibid.*, II, p. 117.   17 *Ibid.*, II, p. 0351.

18 *Ibid.*, I, p. 7; II, p. 077.

The other instance of a revolving house is also connected with Kaltesh and the World Surveyor Hero. The hero and his friend arrive at a house that is standing in the water and it is revolving in water like a whirlpool. An old man and an old woman live in the house. The old man *is asleep,* she stabs him with a knife to *wake* him. He puts his snow shoes on, jumps into his mother's mouth (here the old woman seems to be his mother) and disappears. She yawns, he is back again falling out of her mouth. He has brought an elk to feed the guests. The old man has a daughter, the hero marries her. This daughter is the Kaltesh woman.[19]

We can be sure, therefore, that the idea of revolving has really something to do with shamanism. That it also has something to do with the Kaltesh woman and with dreaming is evident. But let us take shamanism first.

What revolves is not so much the universe as the shaman himself. The dance of the Buryat shaman is circular, clockwise.[20] About the Eskimo we are told that the drum rocks, it springs up, knocks the shaman on the head, he jumps about in restless agitation.[21] The Yakut call a humming top a wooden shaman[22]—obviously it suggests to them what the shaman does. The Khirgiz Baksha revolve around themselves to get into a trance.[23] I have witnessed the whirling dance of the dervishes myself in Constantinople; they whirled round till they collapsed, some of them foaming at the mouth. "Each dervish moves around himself as a central point and all move together round the sheikh who stands in the middle."[24] It is very likely that the famous praying wheels of Tibet are only substitutes for the whirling shaman. "The Lamas with these articles came in and squatted down in a row like sitting Buddhas and a wild gust of sound ushered in the dancers who came along dancing and whirling." After dancing in a circle for a short time, going round with the right shoulder to the center which is the same turn as the Praying Wheel goes round they retired.[25] The ascent of the Carib shaman to the sky is symbolized by his rapid dance. Then he is placed on a platform that is revolved by the aid of ropes.[26] The

---

[19] *Ibid.,* I, pp. 294–310.

[20] Sandschejew, G., "Weltanschauung und Schamanentum der Burjaten." *Anthropos.,* XXIII, 1928, p. 554.

[21] Thalbitzer, W., "The Heathen Priests of East Greenland," *Verhandlungen des XVI. Internationalen Amerikanisten Kongresses,* Wien, 1910, p. 458.

[22] Jochelson, W., "The Yakut Anthropological Papers," *Am. Mus. Nat. Hist.* XXXIII, Part 2, 1933, p. 105.

[23] Castagne, J., "Magic et exorcisme chez les Kazak Kirghis," *Revue des Etudes Islamiques,* IV, 1930, p. 58.

[24] Simpson, W., *The Buddhist Praying Wheel,* London, 1896, p. 139.

[25] *Ibid.,* p. 31.

[26] Metraux, A., "Le shamanisme chez les Indiens de l'Amérique du Sud Tropicale," *Acta Americana,* II, 1944/45, p. 209.

"shaking tent" ritual[27] of the Algonquins may be regarded as a body extension of the shaking shaman.

It is therefore obvious that the whirling movement is used by the shaman in his journey to the other world, that is, it is a means of falling into a trance.

In the first chapter we have seen that patients report this whirling sensation as the transition from the waking state to sleep, i.e., the journey to the other world. We contend that the trance pattern is unconsciously based on the sleep pattern. Vogul mythology holds the key to the interpretation. Just as the Baba Yaga is really identical with her own whirling jut, the whirling tree or hut is identical with the Kaltesh woman mother (foster mother) and wife of the shaman hero god. After shooting the arrow at the whirling leaf *he falls asleep* and dreams of the Kaltesh woman. In the other mythical episode the old man who lives in the whirling house is asleep—and he descends into the inside of his "woman mother"—as the Vogul text says, i.e., we have the basic dream. That the basic dream is also genital is clearly shown by the marriage of our hero to the Kaltesh, i.e., to the mistress of the revolving hut. The environment in the dream is made out of the dreamer's body—the dreamer at the same time as he enters the mother enters into himself—and the revolving dreamer becomes a revolving hut, a revolving woman, a shaking tent.

The Eastern European versions of the story make the hut revolve on a fowl's leg, especially a water fowl's. We have noted the symbolization of the Ural-Altaic shaman in the migrating water fowl. The shaman trees, as we have also seen above, frequently end in a carved duck. But in our story we have the duck's leg under the hut. Sinking and rising in the basic dream are identical. The Udehe shamans' trees are carved with the root upward and the root is regarded as the hair of a human being. Sometimes two are erected or one with a double human face.[28] This is the double vector in the id and the identity in the basic dream of sinking and rising. However, we do not assume that all revolving castles must be derived from the ritual of the shaman. The myth may also be, as in the Celtic versions, directly derived from the sensation of falling asleep. But the revolving castle is also identical with the heroine or witch and the revolving is not merely a functional representation of the moment of falling asleep but also a condensed symbolization of coitus and uterine regression.

The same patient with hysterectomy whose dreams are quoted in the

27 Cf. Flauneny, R., "The Gros Ventre Shaking Tent," *Primitive Man*, XVII, 1944, p. 54; Cooper, M., "The Shaking Tent Rite among the Plains and Forest Algonquins," *ibid.*, p. 67.

28 Kagarow, E., "Der umgekehrte Schamanenbaum," *Archiv für Religionswissenschaft*, XXVI, 1929, pp. 183, 184.

first chapter reports the following dream. The situation is one of a new beginning of anxiety.

It is raining. I am going somewhere with my sister. There is a man who invites us to sit on the ferris-wheel. The wheel is encased in glass.

The associations point to the uterus and coitus. The man who offers her the wheel is the analyst.[29]

---

[29] Cf. a case published previously. Róheim, "The Story of the Light that Disappeared," *Samiksa*, I, 1947, p. 61.

IV

DESCENSUS AVERNO

If we regard the soul as a concept derived from the dream, it follows that our ideas about the other world must also be based on our dreams. Let us take the following two dreams of Leliltukutu, dreamed in the same night.

Dream 1: Devil women were coming. They had teeth like dogs and eyes popping out. They looked like Akiti, his elder sister, who played a kind of maternal role in his life.
Dream 2: A whole crowd of men on the warpath (blood avengers) were coming. They had their spears aimed at him. Then he flew up a tree and from there he flew up to the sky. There was a hill there, he fell down and rolled down to the earth. He was dead. Frightened, he woke up and was reassured to find he was alive.[1]

In this dream we see the *vagina dentata*, the *phallic mother* (eyes popping out), then the father with the spear (the men), flying (i.e., an erection), then rolling down, i.e., falling asleep (the basic dream) as dying. The sequence of events has been rearranged by the secondary elaboration: first, rolling down, then episodes one and two.

The bridge and the narrow passage, so often found in our dreams, are also characteristic of the *passage to the other world*. In the following description of a Samoan's journey to the other world, we clearly see what we have called the *basic dream*.

Near the west end of Savaii, there were two circular openings among the rocks on the beach where the souls of the departed were supposed to find an entrance to the world of spirits, away under the ocean. The chiefs *went down* by the larger of the two and the common people used the smaller one. They took a straight course through the bush westward. There is a stone at the west end of Upolu called "the leaping stone" from which spirits *in their course leaped into the sea,* swam to Manono, leaped from a stone on that island again, and at last arrived at the entrance of Hades. There was a coconut tree near the entrance of Hades. This was the tree of the *Watcher*. If a spirit struck against it, that soul went back to its body.[2]

In stories of people who returned we see clear evidence of dreams

[1] Author's field notes on Central Australia, copybook VII, p. 136.
[2] Turner, G., *Samoa, A Hundred Years Ago,* London, 1884, pp. 257, 258.

probably dreamed by those who were really sick or even in a critical state. The body is not separated from the psyche, the usual dream journey or basic dream is perceived as a sign of mortal danger and the return often hailed as the turning point of the disease for the better.

For the assumption that the state of the body is also in the unconscious, I quote a dream of my own. I had virus and double pneumonia. As the doctors later told me, my life was really hanging in the balance for a week or two. Every evening, my wife took my temperature, but she always told me that the fever was many degrees lower than it really was.

Dream: My wife comes into the room walking in a slow-measured step on *kothurnoi* like in a Greek tragedy. She holds the thermometer very high as if it were the Grail. I murmur in the dream, Lachesis, Klotho, Atropos.

Interpretation: Mentioning the three Moirai, the third being the inevitable (Atropos) death, shows my knowledge of what is happening and my resignation. The Grail vessel borne by my wife is too high. I shall die, no more coitus (grail = vagina). Holding the thermometer high and walking on the *kothurnus* shows that unconsciously I know that the temperature is much higher.

Returning to Samoa we notice that another name for the hereafter is "Hollow Pit" and a curse, "May you go rumbling down the hollow pit." At the bottom there was a running stream. On this the spirits floated away to the nether world. When they touched the water they were not to look right or left, nor could they come back as the current made that impossible. *They drifted along in a semiconscious state* (this would be the dream state) until they came to a bathing place called Water of Life, where they bathed and all became young again.[3]

At Bougainville, the place a ghost goes to is called *Tataupra,* and a ghost is an *orar.* It is in the thick bush at a place where there is a hole with white paint. The other ghosts paint him white, and then they put out his eyes with a stick. *The dead man climbs a tree and jumps off into the sea.* Then he goes back to the place where he died. After the burial rites he goes back once more to spirit land.

In the following story we see the dreamlike character of the other world.

There was a little child. His mother died. The child went and went till he came to the place belonging to the ghosts. He stopped at the edge of the water and sat down. He saw a stretch of sand, it was quite clear. He made a hole in the sand big enough for himself. He went inside, he hid in the hole. He covered his head with the leaves of the wild banana, but he

3 *Ibid.,* p. 289.

did not cover his eyes and he saw the ghosts coming. Finally, he saw his mother. He took hold of her hand. "I am so sad about you, that is why I have come," he said. The child wanted to stay with its mother, but the mother said, "If you come with me now, what will you eat?" "I will eat the same food as you eat." The mother said, "All of us here eat feces." The mother hid him from the other ghosts. The mother lay down and the child put his head in her lap. The mother went to sleep. Her skin came off and the child was lying against her bones. Next day she brought the child back to the village, but she would not partake of *taro,* the food of the living. The mother went back to the other world, and the next day the child died.[4]

At Maavo, in the New Hebrides, they think that the departed soul mounts a tree in which there is a bird's nest fern, and laughs and mocks at the people who are making great lamentations. "What are they crying for? Here am I!" The real thing is the soul which leaves the body just as a man throws off his clothes. The soul is like the yolk of the egg. The soul goes along through his gardens and along his customary paths and finally leaves the place. He runs along till he reaches the end of the island, and here he comes to the place of recollection, *the stone of thought.* If there he remembers his child or his wife or anything that belongs to him, he will run back and come to life again. In the same place, there are two rocks with a deep ravine between them. If the ghost clears this as he leaps across he is forever dead, but if one fails he returns to life. The ghost who has got through the rocks runs to the end of the island and there in the sea the other ghosts welcome him. Another path of the ghosts takes them to the northern point of Maavo where there is a deep gully and three leaping places, one for men, one for women and one for ulcerous persons. It is a curse to wish a man may fall down; if a man falls in leaping he is smashed to pieces. Here is the mouth of a hollow which leads to the other world. There is a huge pig on the way which devours all those who have not planted *pandanus* from which mats are made.[5]

At Alor, people who die *go down* a slope and come to a level place where there is a big *ravine with a bridge across it.* The feet of those who cross becomes slippery. The young and the swift get across and arrive at Hamintuku. Those who fall arrive at Karfehava's village. If Karfehava does not like them, he spits into their mouths instead of inviting them up into the veranda. He orders them to follow the river down to the sea. There they turn into salt and lime rock. "When lime bites our tongues, we say this is our dead forebears turned into lime."[6]

4 Blackwood, B., *Both Sides of the Buka Passage,* Oxford, 1935, pp. 506, 511.
5 Codrington, R. H., *The Melanesians,* Oxford, 1891, pp. 279, 280.
6 Hose, C. and McDougall, W., *The Pagan Tribes of Borneo,* London, 1912, II, p. 41.

According to the Kayans, the ghosts must cross a river by means of a bridge consisting of a single large log suspended from bank to bank. *The log is constantly agitated* by a guardian called Maligang. If the ghost during his life on earth has taken a head, he crosses the bridge without difficulty but if not he *falls below* and is consumed by maggots or by a large fish.[7] The Malanau call the guardian of the bridge "Maiwiang." It tries to frighten the soul by throwing ashes at it while it passes the bridge. This spirit is really a two-headed dog: it has to be propitiated by a valuable bead. This bead is fastened to the right arm of the corpse before the coffin is closed.[8]

Layard writes that the being the natives of Malekula dread most is called "Le-hev-vev." "It is something that pulls us down to swallow us." Layard tells us that in matrilineal areas this being is male and in patrilineal areas female. But he also remarks that the name given to old men who are very important is a variation of the name of the doorkeeper of the other world. Layard asked the informant, "Does he swallow you with his teeth?" The answer was no, since he has no body. He (or it) is a ghost. "It is to protect ourselves from Le-hev-vev that we perform rites and sacrifice pigs."[9] Everybody must also have a live pig with curved tusks that protects him when he encounters the doorman of the hereafter. The pig is killed when he dies and is received by the doorman of the other world as payment. When he comes to the *cave of the dead* the evil spirit pulls him back, but there is also a good spirit, Tagar or Tagar-lavo, who also receives a pig and who permits him to go on. He wanders on until he arrives at the shore. He lights a fire to attract the attention of the ferryman of ghostland and plucks a kind of grass. He is ferried over on a piece of bark of the banana tree to a great volcano called "Origin of Fire." They also talk about a "path of fire" which seems to mean "going into the volcano."[10]

In another version of the journey of the dead, the being at the gate is definitely female, the grandmother of ten petrified brothers. In this district, a staff of bamboo exactly the length of the dead man is put into the grave. A hen eaten by the mourners is also supposed to go with him. He carries the spirit on the end of his staff. Now he walks to the "cave of the dead." A magical fruit tree called *nu-wi-men-men* grows here. Then the dead man starts eating the fruit of this tree or chewing its bark, the

7 *Ibid.*

8 *Ibid.*, p. 45.

9 Layard, J., "Der Mythos der Totenfahrt auf Malekula," *Eranos Jahrbücher,* Zürich, 1937, pp. 254, 255. Cf. also *idem*, "The Journey of the Dead," in *Essays Presented to C. G. Seligman,* London, 1939, p. 113.

10 Layard, "Der Mythos . . .," pp. 256–261.

mourners know it and now they know that he has *left for good*. He comes
to a river. Now we see what the staff is for. He touches the river, the waters separate and he passes unharmed. The "nose-eating stone" would eat
his nose if it were not for the hen he carries at the end of the staff and
which he offers as a sacrifice. The next meeting is with a spirit called Le
saw who lives in a stone in the ocean. The stone is also a shark and a bird
is seated on the stone. The bird lures the dead to approach and if he has
no pig to offer he will be eaten by the bird. But if he has a pig, he offers
it as a sacrifice and escapes unharmed. In the mortuary ritual, this spirit
is represented by a mask about twenty feet high. The men shoot at the
mask, the women cry. The mask is decorated with drawings of a human
face, of a shark, of a bird, of the new moon and a pentagram.[11] A man
called Mel-teg-to introduced an innovation by erecting a big stone mauso-
leum for himself decorated in a fashion that resembled fins. Thereby he
believed that after death he would be a stone shark that enters the spirit
shark.[12]

Deacon, discussing the same area, gives us a somewhat different version of the journey of the dead. At the boundary between Seniang and
Mewun there lies in the sea a rock called Lembwil Song. The Land of the
Dead is situated on the parkland behind this rock and is just a short distance underground. When anyone in Seniang dies, the ghost travels north-
ward until it comes to a channel called Niew, which leads to the lagoon.
This it must cross just as a living person traveling in the same direction
would cross it, but whereas to a live man it is some thirty to forty feet wide
it seems but a ribbon or a rivulet over which the ghost steps with ease.
As the ghost passes on its way, the landscape, though it is the same as that
which it knew when it was alive, appears *subtly changed; the hills and
valleys are distorted as in a dream.*

After crossing the channel, the ghost sees the rock Lembwil Song and
before the rock the female ghost Temes Savsap. Before her traced in the
sand is a geometrical figure called "Nahal" (the path). The route along
which the ghost must go lies between the two halves of the figure. As the
ghost approaches, Temes Savsap wipes out half the tracing and tells the
traveler that before he goes on he must complete the picture correctly.
Most men during their lifetime have learned how to make this and other
geometrical figures and so they pass safely on their way. But if a man fails
the test Temes Savsap seizes him and devours him so that he can never
reach the land of Wies. However, some two generations ago a famous
warrior died. He failed in the test but escaped the clutches of the ogress.
He came back to his body, entered it, and asked for his bow and arrows.

---

[11] *Ibid.*, pp. 261–266.   [12] *Ibid.*, p. 266.

Without more ado, he went back, shot her and passed unobstructed. Women never learn these geometrical figures. How they get past the ogress is not recorded. Then the ghosts come to two trees, one for the men and one for the women. They leap from these trees and then swim across to the other world.[13]

According to another version, the female ghost herself is represented by the geometrical figure called "the path."[14]

What we have here is simply our basic dream, the moment of falling asleep, but with considerable anxiety. The basic dream is represented in several versions, such as being swallowed, entering a female ghost, the passage through the cave or the waters, climbing trees and leaping down, etc. The staff that cleaves the waters is the length of the dead man's body, i.e., the ghost is the body as phallos. The so-called maze patterns are variations of the *mandala* or the Central Australian concentric circle, in other words, of the vulva and uterus. The riddle he has to solve or the drawings he has to make is the typical examination dream—and the middle road he is to pass is the road into the female body. The ogress and the pattern are the same, like the Sphinx and the riddle of the Sphinx.[14a] The hero solves the problem by male aggression with bow and arrow. "Much of the information about the life of ghosts was obtained from a man who had actually visited the Land of the Dead and returned thence alive."[15] In other words, it is based on a dream.

To make it quite clear that the passage is also coitus, we quote the Trobriands version of the journey to the other world.

The spirit that obstructs the way is called Topileta. He lives with his daughters. If the spirit is a female, Topileta copulates with her, if a male his daughters do the same. Then they can pass on. Once in the other world the spirit copulates with one of the hostess-spirits in the open while the others look on or, stimulated by this sight, do likewise.[16]

The passage here is more coital than uterine regression, and the first thing that happens in the other world is a dream of the primal scene.

The "sleep" motive reappears in the Rossel Islands. When a man gets old, his friends tell him that he smells and that his time has come. They lead him down to the ocean and tell him to walk straight on. He

---

[13] Deacon, A. B., *Malekula*, London, 1934, pp. 552–556, 580.

[14] *Ibid.*, p. 585.

[14a] Cf. Róheim, *The Riddle of the Sphinx*, London, 1934.

[15] Deacon, *op. cit.*, p. 556. Cf. also Deacon, "Geometrical Drawings from Islands of the New Hebrides," *Journal of the Royal Anthropological Institute*, LXIV, 1934, pp. 129–147; Layard, John, "The Making of Man in Malekula," *Eranos Jahrbücher*, XVII, 1948, pp. 203–283; *idem*, "Labyrinth Ritual in South India," *Folklore*, XLVIII, 1937, pp. 115–183.

[16] Malinowski, B., *The Sexual Life of Savages*, London, 1929, pp. 363, 364.

disappears into the sea and turns into a huge fish *which sleeps for a few days and then dies*. The Lord of the Other World (Kangö) was the first person killed by violence. Since he was a person of rank, they did not want to eat him and they stretched him out on the beach. A small boy remained with the corpse. While they waited, the anus of the dead man grew larger and the small boy looked inside. Given a kick by the others he disappeared into the dead man's anus, whereupon the dead man got up and became the first ruler of the dead. Here death is connected with entering a body, though in a homosexual and anal version.

It is interesting to note that this boy who entered his anus becomes the soul of the Lord of the Dead and leaves his body at night, re-entering it in the morning when the Lord of the Dead awakes.[17]

The following myth of Ceram again contains the spiral entrance to the other world.

A man called Ameta (*meta* = night) got himself a daughter from a coco palm. Her name was Hainuwele, which is derived from *nuwele* (coco nut palm) and *hai* (branch or leg). In three days she grew to be a young girl. But she was not like ordinary human beings. When she defecated it was not excrements but Chinese plates and gongs, and thus her father became very rich.

A great *maro* dance (explained below) was being held and they danced in the great ninefold spiral. Hainuwele stood in the middle of the dancers and gave them *sirih* and *pinang* to chew. Nine nights they danced and Hainuwele was always in the middle. And each night she gave the dancers, instead of the things they usually got to chew, more and more valuable things. People were very jealous because she was so rich and they decided to kill her.

In the ninth night of the dance when she was standing in the middle again, they dug a deep ditch near to where she stood. They danced in a spiral, closing in upon her. Finally, they pushed her into the ditch and covered her with earth. When the spiral dance had ended and Hainuwele had not yet come home, her father knew that she had been murdered where they danced the *maro* dance. He took nine leaves and went to the place where the dance was usually held. He stuck the leaves into the earth and when he pulled the ninth leaf back, hair and blood of Hainuwele were stuck to it. He dug her corpse out and all the parts of her body became objects of great value. Her stomach became a big pot, still kept in the middle of the village as a sacred object. Her lungs became a certain fruit, her breasts another fruit, her eyes again another plant and her vulva a plant that has a nice smell and a good taste. Another plant originated from

[17] Armstrong, W. E., *Rossel Island*, Cambridge, 1928, p. 119.

her buttocks and another from her ears. Her feet, thighs and head all gave rise to a variety of plants.

Her father cursed all human beings for this murder. A woman called Mutua Satene then built a great gate at the place where the dance took place. The gate consisted of a ninefold spiral, just like the *maro* dance. She stood at one end holding the chopped-off arms of Hainuwele in her hands. She assembled all human beings at one side of the gate. "I am leaving you because you have committed murder. Now you must all pass through this gate and those who pass will stay human, those who don't will have something else happen to them."

This is how many animals and spirits came into being. First they were all human. Those who went through the spiral gate came to her. Some went to the right, some to the left. Each passer-by she hit with one arm of Hainuwele. Those who went to the right became Patalima, those who went to the left the Patasiwa (two moieties). When people die, they go through the ninefold spiral to Satene.[18]

There are many ramifications to this story, both within Ceram and in other Pacific areas. We note that the coconut girl has a duplicate figure in the death goddess. Furthermore, we have a myth in which the first woman comes from a coconut and therefore coitus is also derived from a coconut. Then we find that this goddess of death is the moon and that the first girl who menstruated became the moon.[19]

We can certainly arrive at two conclusions from these myths. One, that the path into the other world is the road to the vagina, and two, that the vagina is a dangerous menstruating vagina.[20]

However, the aggression starts from the males. They kill Hainuwele because of the things that come out of her excrements. The connection of the coconut with the pig and also the excremental origin of valuables shows that the story is related to the myths of the *kune* cycle.[21]

The anal is hereby clearly indicated and that confirms our previous assumption of the spiral as representing the intestines. But as the woman is the moon, i.e., the menstruating vagina, the dangerous path may very well also symbolize the vaginal entrance. In the primary process these "meanings" certainly do not exclude each other.

The following dream might well be a myth of the soul's journey.

[18] Jensen, A. E., and Niggemeyer, H., "Hainuwele," *Veröffentlichungen des Forschungsinstitutes für Kulturmorphologie,* Frankfurt a. M., 1939, pp. 59–63.

[19] *Ibid.,* p. 45.

[20] *Ibid.,* pp. 53–55.

[21] Cf. Róheim, *Psychoanalysis and Anthropology,* pp. 184–192; *idem,* "Psychoanalysis of Primitive Cultural Types," *International Journal of Psycho-Analysis,* XIII, 1932, p. 121, Tauhau and the Mwadare.

A patient, who is being analyzed by Miss Lillian Gordon, dreams:

I am running in an alley way toward a place where my parents used to live. Or perhaps it is another place where my first girl friend Mary lived. *I go past a revolving house, people go in there but don't come out.*
In the second scene, a middle-aged man, like his boss' husband (the boss is a woman) but also like an analyst he knows, is wheeling a baby in a perambulator. He says, the baby is to be wheeled into a garage. The garage looks like an insane asylum in Switzerland. He has something to say about the revolving house. It is like a circular house he saw when he was in the country with his girl friend. At that time she was pregnant.

It is clear that the revolving house is the womb (other world, where people go but do not return) and also the moment of falling asleep. The middle-aged man is the father imago, and he is the reborn baby in the perambulator, wanting to regress again (garage, mental hospital). Regression into the womb is equated with insanity.

After a quarrel with his wife a patient (anal character) dreams:

I am with Peter whom I kiss and fondle. We go into a big dark house. It turns out to be the Metropolitan Opera as if I had a dressing room there. I think it is the opera *Fledermaus* [Bat]. We wander through a labyrinthine passage; a door. The doorman (must be the analyst) gives me a key to a room. I refuse to take it. We wander on. There is a little room we are about to go in when suddenly an uncanny-looking little old woman is in the entrance. She opens her wings, it is a bat [*Fledermaus*]. Then my mother comes into the room but she is a young girl. I awake.

His constipation and his sexual difficulties are closely connected with each other. The labyrinthine path is his own intestinal tract. The little old woman, of course, the *uncanny mother*. The bat gets into your hair, castration anxiety.

According to the Lushei Pupawla, the first man who died shoots at those who die after him with a big pellet bow. But there are some he cannot shoot at, those who have killed men, sacrificed certain wild animals, or those who have had three virgins or seven women who are not virgins; women he always shoots at. Those he hits with his bow cannot cross the river.[22]

Is this idea of only men entering the netherworld really based on male superiority? In my opinion, it has nothing to do with it. These beliefs are based on dreams in which the dreamer's body (even if the dreamer is a woman) is phallic, while the house or gate (or pool) represents the vagina or uterus.

The Toradja ghost must pass a pig which may bite it and the corpse

[22] Shakespeare, J., *The Lushei Kubi Clans*, London, 1912, p. 63.

of a child gets a nut to throw at him. Langkoda, the examining ghost, lames those who have not married and have not killed an enemy. The way to pass him is to recount one's conquests in love and in battle so cleverly that he laughs, then his great underlip covers his eyes and the soul can pass unobserved.[23] The counterphobic attitude in the dream, as in all these dreams is phallic power opposed to the biting vagina. In other words, the "basic dream" may in its manifest content show more of the wish element or more anxiety. According to the Wathathi and other tribes of New South Wales, the soul reaches a pathway divided into two roads. The first is a clean road and it leads to a young and beautiful woman. But the ghost has to travel the other road. This is full of brambles and he has to jump over a flaming chasm. Two women try to trip him with a rope. One woman tries to seduce him and the other who is blind tries to trip him. Finally, he comes to the father-god Tha Tha pulli who gives him a spear to show him how he can spear emus. Since in this region the emu is the usual mother symbol, the interplay of phallic pride and castration anxiety is quite obvious.[24]

The path of the souls is a very complicated journey at Fiji. First, the soul arrives at a certain pandanus tree which he must hit with the whale tooth that was placed in his grave. If he hits the tree, it is all right, for this proves that his friends are strangling his wives for him and they will come with him to the other world.[25]

What is the connection between strangling wives and throwing a whale tooth at a tree? If we take both tooth and tree symbolically as penis and woman, it is evident why strangling wives means a passage to the other world. It shows his potency. This is confirmed when we consider that a bachelor ghost has no chance at all to get there.[26] According to Thomson, the shade arrives at a bridge that is really a monstrous eel. While a shade is crossing it, it writhes as a sign to the shade to go quickly because his wives are being strangled to follow. The wriggling eel is again the penis and it is only by phallic power that the dreamer conquers his anxieties.

If a man has no wives at all, he is sure to be killed on the way by the Great Woman. Another spirit hides behind the reeds and challenges the

[23] Moss, R., *The Life after Death in Oceania and the Malay Archipelago*, London, 1925, p. 279; Kruijt, A. C., *Het Animisme in den Indischen Archipel*, Hague, 1906, p. 350.

[24] Cf. Róheim, *Animism, Magic and the Divine King*, London, 1930, p. 51; *idem, Australian Totemism*, London, 1930, p. 205; Cameron, A. L. P., "Notes on Some Tribes of New South Wales," *Journal of the Royal Anthropological Institute*, XIV, 1884, p. 364; *idem*, "Traditions and Folklore of the Aborigines of New South Wales," *Science of Man*, 1903, p. 46.

[25] Williams, T., *Fiji and the Fijians*, London, 1858, I, p. 239.

[26] Thomson, B., *The Fijians*, London, 1908, pp. 120, 121.

spirit to battle. "Who are you and where do you come from?" If the ghost lies and pretends that he is of vast importance, he is killed by this spirit. If he is killed in the fight, he will be cooked and eaten by the spirit.

The path to the other world ends *abruptly at the brink of a precipice,* the base of which is washed by a deep lake. In the lake we find the Fijian Charon, either the god Ndengei himself or his deputy. We come to the cross-questioning again. If the ghost answers, "I am a great chief. I had great wealth, many wives and I ruled over a powerful people, I have slain many in war," the ferryman replies, "Take a seat on the broad part of the oar and refresh yourself in the breeze." But as soon as he is seated, the handle of the oar is lifted and he *is thrown down headlong into the deep waters* through which he passes to the other world.[27]

In Normanby Island, we can obtain detailed information about the hereafter. I knew several of those who had made the journey and returned, consequently these data are based on firsthand information.

Yakudi, a lame man of the village of Wairakeli, told me how he became a seer. A seer is *enobeu* (that is, "fall asleep"). He found an *enobeu* to teach him. Finally, he said, "We rubbed our eyes and went to sleep." His teacher also had to scratch his feet before they slept. Their feet are scratched in order that they be able to walk over the gully to the other world, and their eyes are rubbed in order that they see well. "We went down with our whole outfit.[28] A wind came and the house was moving. Sine Bomatu (Woman East Wind) blocked our way. But Kekevagei (her granddaughter, the ruler of the other world) told her, 'Don't stop them.' When he arrived there, his uncle said he had been expecting him and he made the following song for him.

> "The soul walks straight on the bridge
> Sine Bomatu says, Welcome!
> I cook beach creeper with oil
> O! virgins of Bwebweso."

The virgins of Bwebweso are ready to give themselves to the soul. These virgins are spirits; they never were human beings. Their feet are scratched in order to enable them to walk over the gully that separates the two worlds and their eyes are rubbed in order that they see well.

"If an old woman dies, she will have breasts like a young girl. If a little girl dies, her breasts will also be like a young woman's who is just after delivery.

"The emphasis on the breast of the virgins in the other world is

---

27 Williams, *op. cit.,* pp. 245–247.

28 The sensation of going down is significant because the other world is on Mount Bwebweso.

significant; it also implies that the *enobeu* or the sleeper or the ghost is a newborn infant."

"When we came back from the other world, it was daybreak," he says.

Kekevagei is the ruler of the other world. Her body is pretty, her skirts are short. Her skin looks like pink unripe coconut. Her hair is long and nicely oiled. The skirt is like the Trobriand women's skirt and Boyowa (Trobriand) means just about what Paris means in America.

The other one, Sine Bomatu (Woman East Wind), is an old woman who looks like a grandmother. If a widow remarries, it is not a real marriage because her first husband is still waiting for her at Bwebweso.

They have everything there that we have on earth. Fishing, gardening, dancing, the *kune*.[29] They fight for women, but there are no cannibal raids. After the fight, they are not angry. Everything is flat, there are no hills. The distinction between one village and another ceases.

Bwebweso is inside the earth.[30] When a man dies, they put up a *spirit ladder* and the dead person goes down. After the ladder there is an abyss underground. The bridge is very smooth, but all the spirits pass. Sine Bomatu is very smooth, but all the spirits pass. Sine Bomatu is the only obstruction. The gully is not very deep; when it rains there is water in it. When the ghosts go to Koiwaga hill[31] there is a spring with "oily water" there.[32]

There was a man called Dukoja (Waves going hillwards). He had quarreled with his wife and now he wanted to commit suicide by falling into the gully of Bwebweso. But he found a woman in a cave; her name was Oiwaga. "O, what a beautiful woman," he said. "I wish she were my wife." He went back home and told his wife he would start next morning for the other world. They slept till morning, and she cooked two yams for him to eat on his way to Bwebweso. But instead he went to Oiwaga, the woman in the cave. They got married and she was always well supplied with yams. "I am not like human beings," she said, "my garden is invisible." In the meanwhile, the children in the village reproached their mother because she drove their father to suicide. Finally, he returned to his own village.

The *fall* or basic dream element may be represented just as in dreams by the falling, not of the dreamer but of something else that represents the soul.

Among the Wamira in British New Guinea, "when a man dies, the

---

[29] Trade expedition. Cf. Róheim, *Psychoanalysis and Anthropology*, New York, 1950.

[30] This notwithstanding the fact that it is actually a mountain.

[31] One of the hills that form part of the great mountain Bwebweso.

[32] To oil the body is important in all sorts of love magic.

spirits of the other world know of the death by the falling of something called *obu* from a tree. . . . When the spirit comes it passes up the Uruam, the further river into the mountains."[33]

This is an account of the journey of the spirit to the other world given by a Winnebago informant to Paul Radin.

"Now the very first thing you will encounter will be this. You will come upon a ravine. It will be quite unpassable. It will extend to both ends of the earth right into the water. But what did my grandfather say when I asked, How will I get through? Did you not think that he said 'Plunge right through.' "[34]

The point in accumulating all these data, and many more of course could be given, is this; if the moment of passing from this to the other world is *falling asleep*, then our concept of the other world is unconsciously modeled on that of sleeping or dreaming. Once more we return to Lewin's theory of "sleep is oral" and "to be eaten up" is an id wish. What we find is precisely the opposite. "Oral" means object-directed; sleep is primarily narcissistic. The concept of "being eaten" certainly occurs in eschatological beliefs, but far from being an id wish it represents oral aggression turned inward and figures as the main *obstacle* in reaching the happy other world.

The first great epic ever recorded, the story of Gilgamesh the most valiant king of Erek, throws some light upon the meaning of these stories.

Eabani, the friend of Gilgamesh, is dead. First, Gilgamesh perceives his friend's death as a horrible kind of sleep. Finally, when he understands what has happened he goes mad with fear and anguish. He then decides to visit his ancestor Utnapishtim who has been rescued from the flood and become immortal to ask him to reveal the secret that conquers death. He passes through the *Gate of the Sun* which is guarded by the two scorpion giants. Gilgamesh is following the sun and the gate is the western horizon. At the end of the world Sabitu, the beautiful goddess and protectress of life tries to prevent him from the futile attempt to find immortality. "The life you are in search of you will not find; immortality is for the gods only, death is for mankind." At the edge of the world where the waters of death encircle the world he meets Sursu, the messenger of Ut-Napishtim "the distant one." He is ferried across the waters of death. Either the mast breaks or something else happens, but it seems that Gilgamesh is in danger. Finally he speaks to Ut-Napishtim who tells him the story of the flood. Ut-Napishtim tells him that he can conquer death by

33 Seligmann, A. G., *The Melanesians of British New Guinea,* Cambridge, 1910, p. 658.

34 Radin, P., "The Culture of the Winnebago as Described by Themselves," *Special Publications of the Bollingen Foundation,* No. 1, 1947, p. 69.

staying awake seven days and seven nights. They are brought in great haste but too late. Ut-Napishtim's wife brings him seven loaves of bread to keep him awake. He dozed off for a second and thereby forfeited his right to immortality. But he is given a bath that restores his youth and strength and is clad in garments that will not wear off *till he comes back to his home city.* Again the wife of Ut-Napishtim helps him. She tells him where to find sweet water and the "plant that rejuvenates human beings. He dives to the bottom of the pool and comes up with the plant. But a few days later he finds another pool, bathes in it and while he is in the water a snake steals the plant of immortality."[35]

This is strictly speaking not a myth of the "descensus Averno" type, but closely related to it. If we take the whole thing as the dream of Gilgamesh, we should say that he plunges into the pool of the dream to get the plant that rejuvenates. His dream proper is of the oedipal type. The ancestor who does not wish to grant him immortality and the mother imago trying to rescue him with her loaves (breast). There are two pools of water, one with the penis that rejuvenates and the other with the penis that kills (serpent). If it were not for castration anxiety man might be immortal.

T. H. Gaster has published newly discovered Canaanïte texts that deal with the well-known pattern of the Seasonal Combat of the God of Light or Thunder (Jahve, Marduk) against the ocean, chaos or night. We shall now quote one of these myths. The title of this particular myth or dream is: *Baal is lured into the Nether World.*

Mot, the God of the Nether World, invites Baal the mighty, the wielder of thunder and lightning, to be his guest at a banquet. He is in a state of terror at having to go. The nether world is described as follows:

> "Its one lip is stretched upward to the sky
> its other downward to the netherworld;
> Baal will descend into its maw,
> go down into its mouth,
> like a canape of olive,
> like a herb or a piece of fruit!
> Verily, Baal Puissant is frightened,
> terror-stricken is the Rider on the Clouds."[36]

But evidently there is nothing to do but accept the invitation. The goddess Anat advises him to take with him all his equipment and appurtenances of office. In addition, he is advised to copulate with a cow in order to provide himself with a bull-like strength and also to leave issue

[35] Jensen, R., *Das Gilgamesh Epos in der Weltliteratur*, Berlin, 1906, pp. 1–49. Ungnad, A. and Gressmann, *Das Gilgamesh Epos*, Göttingen, 1911, pp. 135–144.
[36] Gaster, T. H., *Thespis*, New York, 1950, p. 189.

upon earth should he fail to return. He mounts a young cow eighty-eight times; it conceives and bears offspring.

> "And come, take thou thy clouds, thy winds, thy
>   buckets, thy rains:
> and two goddesses, one of them the Dew nymph.
> Straightway turn thy face toward the cavernous
>   mountain,
> Raise the mountain on thy hands,
>   the holt upon thy palms,
> and go down into the corruption of the nether world,
> be counted among them that go down into the earth,
> and thou wilt experience nothingness,
> for thou wilt have become as one who has died!"

Messengers report the disappearance of Baal to El. The Supreme God thereupon mourns for Baal and for his posterity, i.e., his descendants. Anat, Baal's beloved, decides to do more than this, she will enter the nether world to fetch her lord.

> "With her goes down the sun, that torch of the gods.
> The while she is sated with weeping,
>   drinking in tears like wine,
> loudly calls she to the sun, that torch of the gods:
> 'Load upon me Baal Puissant!' "

Finally the Sun Goddess finds Baal, places him on the shoulder of Anat and he is duly buried. Ashtar is named as a successor to Baal, but he proves too weak for this position. Anat again goes in search of Baal who although duly buried has not returned to life yet. Mot refuses to restore Baal to life.

> " 'I place him like a lamb in my mouth,
> like a kid in the . . . of my . . . is he crushed!
> Why, 'tis at the whim of the godling Mot
> that the sun, that torch of the gods, scorches,
> that the heavens flash!' "[37]

The Virgin Anat is still searching for Baal, "like the heart of a cow for her calf, like the heart of a ewe for her lamb." Then she seizes Mot; she rips him up with a sword, she scatters him in a sieve, she burns him in a fire, she grinds him in a mill so that the birds may eat his remains.

Now Anat reports to El a dream that portends the return of Baal. She says:

> "In my dream, O gentle-hearted El,
> in my vision, O Creator of all Creatures,
> the skies were raining fatness,
> the wadies were running with honey.

[37] *Ibid.*, p. 199.

So I know that Baal Puissant is alive,
that his Highness, the lord of the earth still exists!"

Again the Sun finds Baal, the lord of the earth who now ascends his throne and conquers Mot.[38]

In a parallel Hittite version of the "seasonal drama" the god who has disappeared is called Telipinu. All the gods do their best to bring him back because in his absence the earth and the gods themselves will perish of hunger.

> The Queen-goddess says to the Weather-god:
> " 'Do something!
> Thyself, O Weather-god, go see Telipinu!'
> So the Weather-god conducted a search for Telipinu.
> In his city he knocked at the gate, but could not get it opened;
> He but smashed his hammer on the door."[39]

Then they look for Telipinu in the darkling swirl of the waters, in the forests, but they cannot find him. Finally the bee finds him and by its sting *awakens* the god. "While I am *sleeping* and nursing a grievance you all come disturbing me," Telipinu says.[40]

The reader should follow Gaster in his careful and learned exposition of the *seasonal drama* theory. This is the essence of the proceedings. The ceremony takes place on a crucial calendar date, often coincident with solstice or equinox, which marks the beginning of a new season or year.

1. It opens with a series of public rites like fasts, lents and other austerities.

2. Follows a "vacant" period marking the interval between the old and the new period. Frequently the customary order of society is reversed and customary activities suspended.

3. The next period is characterized by rites to expel evil, either as scapegoats or exorcised demons.

4. Now the positive side of the ceremony begins. A battle is staged between the forces of Life and Death. The battle ends with the victory of the Life Force. Magical rites to stimulate vegetation, rites of sexual license.

5. The end of the series is a joyous celebration of the new-won life.[41]

The eclipse of the old life and the renewal of the new took the form of the god's descent into the nether world and his return.[42]

When Baal descends into the "jaws of Mot" he copulates with a cow. If this is a dream the two experiences would be identical. Mot refuses to restore Baal to life. The goddess Anat comes to the rescue. She grinds Mot in a mill, she scatters him in a sieve. *Anat then dreams* that rain will fall

[38] *Ibid.*, pp. 189–224.
[40] *Ibid.*, pp. 361–367.
[42] *Ibid.*, p. 37.
[39] *Ibid.*, p. 363.
[41] *Ibid.*, pp. 34–35.

again and Baal will be revived. This is what actually happens. If we interpret the whole as the dream of Baal we should say that the descent (or basic dream) is represented also by the coitus with the cow. Anat rescues Baal and grinds Mot in a mill. Since a person in the dream is frequently represented by other or even opposing images, we might say that the goddess is both the castrator (the grinding mill) and the rescuer, the rain that falls from the sky. The rain is the urethral pressure, the awakening dream. This alternation of night and day explains also the role of the Sun.

In the parallel myth we have quoted, it is expressly stated that Teli-pinu is asleep, and the house which the hammer of the weather god cannot open might be the *sleep womb* itself. But even if someone does not accept our dream theory, where do we have in human life the obvious prototype of this seasonal ritual of death and resurrection? In going to sleep and awakening in the morning.

The oldest myth of descent to the other world and returning is that of Ishtar (Sumerian Innimi).

Ishtar must descend to the nether world because the king Tammuz is dead.

> "The lord Idin-Dagan sleeps,
> And the gardens of themselves restrain their growth.
> The city weeps for Ishme-Dagan, who slumbers,
> And the gardens of themselves withhold their fruit.
> The city weeps for Lipit-Ishtar, who sleeps.
> The city weeps for Or-Ninurta, who sleeps.
> The city weeps for Bur-Sin, who sleeps.
> The sturdy youth is in the land of weeping."[43]

We know that the death of the divine king is called sleep,[44] yet the myth may also have another meaning or origin.

Ishtar (Innini) puts on all her royal splendor. She adorns herself with stones of lapis lazuli, etc. A band of birthstones she girded on her loins. Innini appeals to her father the Water God:

> "O father Amanki, wise lord . . .
> The plant of life thou knowest,[45] the water
> of life thou knowest.
> This one restore to life for me."
>
>   .   .   .
>
> . Innini to the splendid palace of the underworld
> drew night

[43] Langdon, S. H., *The Mythology of All Races: Semitic,* Boston, 1931, pp. 326, 327.
[44] Róheim, *Animism, Magic and the Divine King,* p. 251.
[45] The analogy with the Gilgamesh epic where Ut-Napishtim, the one who has survived the flood, has the plant of life is quite striking.

> The door of the underworld harshly she . . .
> 'Open the house, O watchman, open the house . . .
> Open the house that I may enter.' "

Upon being questioned by the watchman, she replies:

> "I am the queen where the sun rises,
> Why comest thou? to the lower world
> On the road where he who journeys returns not."

Finally she is admitted through the gate, or rather gates; one of her ornaments or garments is taken away from her at each one till she is quite naked. Nevertheless, when she descends to the land of no return, Ereshkigal trembles before her.

> "After Ishtar the queen had descended to the
>   lower world,
> The bull mounted not the cow, the ass impregnated
>   not the she-ass.
> The strong man impregnated not the maid in the
>   highway.
> The strong man slept in his chamber.
> The maid slept beside him."

The Sun God reports to Ea what has happened. *Ea forms an image in his mind* and creates a person whose name is "His Coming Forth is Brilliant." This person is described as a eunuch, and is offered to the Goddess of the nether world as a substitute for Ishtar.[46]

Ereshkigal then sends her messenger to knock at the palace of the Annunaki (the gods of the ocean) and stamp on its threshold of coral. "Cause them to ascend," etc.

According to this passage the gods who dwell in the nether sea of fresh water have their abode below Arallu, the land of the dead.

Ishtar is washed with the water of life and conducted back through the seven gates upward. At each gate she gets one of her garments or ornaments back. How Tammuz ascends to the upper world is not explained.

> "Tammuz the husband of her youth
> Wash with clean water, anoint with fine oil.
> With a dazzling garment clothe him, let him
>   play the flute of the lapis lazuli.
> May the harlots appease his soul."[47]

In the Babylonian version, seven demons assist the goddess in her efforts to arouse Tammuz from the sleep of death. Since he is symbolized as a lamb and Ishtar as a ewe, they seek him in the sheepfolds.

---

[46] Ishtar is the patroness of eunuchs. Langdon, *op. cit.*, p. 332.
[47] *Ibid.*, p. 334.

" 'Tammuz the lord slumbers,' in woe they sigh much.
'The sacred consort of the heavenly queen, the
 lord, slumbers,' in woe they sigh much."

This liturgy ends with the following lines:

"Innini to her sacred women cried:
 'In heaven there is light, on earth there is light.'
 In the bosom of his mother, in his childhood she
 gave him rest.
 In his childhood the mother, mother compassionate,
 compassion spoke.
 In her bosom his sister, sister compassionate, com-
 passion spoke.
 In her bosom his wife Innini gave him rest."[48]

There is no doubt about the ritual background of all these myths. We know that the dying god was represented by the divine king, that the sacred marriage of the divine king to the goddess was enacted in ritual, and we know also the seasonal significance of the whole complex.

To quote Frazer, "For although men now attributed the annual cycle of change primarily to corresponding changes in their deities, they still thought that by performing certain magical rites, they could aid the god who was the principle of life in his struggle with the opposing principle of death. They imagined that they could recruit his failing energies and even raise him from the dead. The ceremonies which they observed for this purpose were in substance a dramatic representation of the natural processes which they wished to facilitate. They set forth the fruitful union of the powers of fertility, the sad death of one at least of the divine partner and his joyful resurrection."[49]

If the change of the seasons is dramatized by this symbolism, there must be some unconscious reason why this should be the case. In my book *Animism, Magic and the Divine King,* I showed the oedipal background of these myths. I now suggest another formative factor, that the myths on the descent to the other world and the return are based on the basic dream mechanism and probably on a dream actually dreamed by someone and then told and retold. The descent is coitus and death and also sleep (the gradual undressing of Ishtar). The ascent is rejoining the mother, sister, wife, the object world being born and awakening. But the descent is also going to the mother, for in Ereshkigal we have the sister, i.e., the doublette, of Innini or Ishtar.[50]

The descending hero (Tammuz, Gilgamesh) travels the path of the

48 Langdon, S., *Tammuz and Ishtar,* Oxford, 1914, pp. 20–22.
49 Frazer, J. G., *Adonis, Attis, Osiris,* London, 1907, p. 4.
50 Ereshkigal, the goddess of darkness, doom and death.

Sun (Shamash) and the Sun, like human beings, goes down in the evening to return in the morning.

In a Sumerian prayer addressed to the Sun God Utu we read, "As the light broke forth, as the horizon grew bright, as Utu came forth."[51]

The Sumerian myth shows quite clearly the association between the descent of the goddess to the nether world and coitus. Nunbarshegunu, the "old" woman of Nippur, instructs her daughter Ninlil (—Innini, Ishtar) on how to win the love of Enlil.

> In those days the mother, her begetter gave
> 　　advice to the maid,
> Nunbarshegunu gave advice to Ninlil:
> "At the pure river, O maid, at the pure river
> 　　wash thyself,
> O Ninlil, walk along the bank of Idnunbirdu,
> The bright-eyed, the lord, the bright-eyed,
> The 'great mountain,' father Enlil, the bright-eyed,
> 　　will see thee,
> The shepherd . . . who decrees the fates, the bright-eyed,
> 　　will see thee,
> He will . . . , he will kiss thee."

"Ninlil follows her mother's instructions and as a consequence is impregnated by 'the water' of Enlil and conceives the moon-god Nanna. Enlil then departs from Nippur in the direction of the nether world, but is followed by Ninlil. As he leaves the gate he instructs the 'man of the gate' to give the inquisitive Ninlil no information of his whereabouts. Enlil takes the form of the 'man of the gate' and cohabits with the goddess and impregnates her. As a result she conceives Meslamtea (Nergal) the king of the nether world. Coitus is described as 'the water' (i.e., semen) going into the goddess. Enlil then impersonates the 'man of the river, the man-devouring river,' and as such cohabits with Ninlil. Finally, he is the 'man of the boat' and in this role he cohabits with Ninlil."[52]

A rather peculiar feature of these descent myths is that they are interrelated with flood myths—as in the case of Gilgamesh or when the gods of the waters ascend into the nether world and thereby initiate the return of Ishtar (Innini). The flood myth is a urethral myth of awakening and this means the return of Ishtar. In some variants of these myths the path goes upward.

Tammuz and Ningiszida (Gilgamesh) stand at the *gates of heaven.* Adapa, a mortal, stands at the gates clad in a mourner's garb because of the two gods who have disappeared from earth. They offer him "bread and

---

[51] Kramer, S., *Sumerian Mythology*, Philadelphia, 1944, p. 42.
[52] *Ibid.*, pp. 44–47.

water of eternal life" which he rejects. The "plant of life" is probably identical with the "plant of begetting."[53]

We now come to the famous passage of Virgil from which this book takes its title. As we have noticed already in these oriental myths of the "journey to the dead and return" types, gates figure prominently in all these beliefs of the world above and the world below.

> "Sunt geminae somni portae; quarum altera fertur
> cornea, qua veris facilis datur exitus umbris.
> altera candenti perfecta nitens elephanto,
> sed falsa ad caelum mittunt insomnia Manes."[54]

While the general meaning of these lines of the great Latin poet are quite clear, the details are somewhat puzzling. What is essential from our point of view is that (a) ghosts and dreams are practically identical, and (b) dreams come out of gates—in other words, the dreamer goes into a gate, passes through a gate, a vagina.

The distinction between the two gates is far from clear. That the shining or ivory gate is the one of false dreams while the gate of horn is that of real ones might perhaps mean that anything that shines is an illusion. But why should Anchises after having shown his son the glorious future of Rome lead him back through the gate of illusions—thereby invalidating the prophecy of Rome's future greatness?

The lines of Virgil are based on Homer, *Odyssey*, XIX, lines 562–567.[55]

There is a play upon the words κέρας (horn) and κραίνω (to fulfil) and upon ἐλέφας (ivory) and ἐλεφαίρομαι (to deceive).[56] Knight, in discussing Virgil and Homer,[57] i.e., Aeneas and Odysseus, emphasizes that the dead either enter a cave or pass through water and are ferried over to the other world. In the Aeneid there is what seems to be an unnecessary delay, the visit to the Cumaean Sybil. Before descending to the nether world Aeneas seeks the abode of the Cumaean Sybil, the priestess of Apollo. Virgil then gives a detailed description of the temple made by Daedalos, the designer of the famous labyrinth of Minotaurus. The labyrinth itself with its endless, unwinding passages

> "Excisum Euboicae latus ingens rupis in antrum,
> quo lati ducunt aditus centum, ostia centum,
> unde ruunt totidem voces, responsa Sibyllae."
> (*Aeneid*, VI, pp. 43–45.)

53 Langdon, *Tammuz and Ishtar*, p. 33.
54 Virgil, *Aeneid*, VI, pp. 893–896.
55 Cf. Norden, E., *P. Vergilius Maro Aeneis*, Leipzig, 1916, VI, pp. 47, 348.
56 Cf. Murray, A. T., *Homer, The Odyssey*, Cambridge, Mass., 1946, II, p. 269.
57 Knight, J. N. F., *Roman Vergil*, London, 1914, p. 176.

The Sybil hastens Aeneas to approach Apollo, and thus he prays to the patron god of Ilion,

> "Phoebe gravis Troiae semper miserate labores
> Dardana qui Paridis direxti tela manusque . . ."
>   (*Aeneid,* VI, pp. 56, 57.)

Apollo responds to the prayer. He possesses his priestess and she prophesies the future. But Aeneas is not satisfied with this; he must seek advice from his father Anchises. The Sybil now tells him the only way in which a mortal can enter the realm of shades.

> "Latet arbore opaca
> aureus et foliis et lento vimine ramus,
> Junoni infernae dictus sacer; hunc tegit omnis
> lucus et obscuris claudunt convallibus umbrae
> Sed non ante datur telluris operta subire,
> auricomos quam qui decerpserit arbore fetus."
>   (*Aeneid,* VI, pp. 136–141.)

Two doves, the birds of Venus his goddess mother show Aeneas the way to the Golden Bough:

> Inde ubi venere ad fauces grave olentis Averni,
> tollunt se celeres liquidumque per aera lapsae
> sedibus optatis gemina super arbore sidunt,
> discolor unde auri per ramos aura refulsit.
> Quale solet silvis brumali frigore viscum
> fronde virere nova, quod non sua seminat arbos,
> et croceo fetu teretis circumdare truncos:
> talis erat species auri frondentis opaca
> ilice, sic leni crepitabat brattea vento.
> Corripit Aeneas extemplo avidusque refringit
> cunctantem, et vatis portat sub tecta Sibyllae.
>   (*Aeneid,* VI, pp. 200–211.)

Once in the cave or entrance to the hereafter, Sybilla encourages Aeneas:

> "*tuque invade viam vaginaque eripe ferrum:*
> *Aenea,*
> *nunc animis opus, nunc pectore firmo.*"
>   (*Aeneid,* VI, pp. 261–262.)

There follows a description of a vast elm, clinging to which are the *vana somnia* or *false dreams.*

> In medio ramos annosaque bracchia pandit
> ulmus opaca, ingens, quam sedem Somnia volgo
> vana tenere ferunt, foliisque sub omnibus haerent.
> Multaque praeterea variarum monstra ferarum,

Centauri in foribus stabulant Scyllaeque biformes
et centumgeminus Briareus ac belua Lernae,
horrendum stridens, flammisque armata Chimaera,
Gorgones Harpyiaeque et forma tricorporis umbrae.

Aeneas wants to grasp his sword but the prophetess explains that the sword can accomplish nothing here because these *vana somnia,* shadows, dreams, do not yield to steel (*Aeneid,* VI, pp. 282–290).

This is a good introduction to the dream interpretation of classical mythology, and it seems obvious that *vana somnia* simply means *dreams,* and all the monsters hanging on the "dream tree" are thereby characterized as beings that originate in dreams. Horace says the same thing in *De Arte Poetica* (11, 1–9):

Humano capiti cervicem pictor equinam
iungere si velit, et varias inducere plumas
Undique collatis membris, ut turpiter atrum
desinat in piscem, mulier formosa superne
spectatum admissi, risum teneatis amici
credite, Pisones, isti tabulae fore librum
persimilem, cuius velut aegri somnia, vanae
fingentur species, ut nec pes, nec caput uni
reddatur formae.

As Knight suggests, "*Much of the Sixth Aeneid may be dreamland.*"[58]

Highbarger discusses the entire classical and oriental literature.[59] "In early antiquity no hard and fast line was drawn between life and death, hence dreams and ghosts could be perceived in the same forms; for it was believed that the soul left the body temporarily at night in the case of the dream, and this was not greatly different from its final and complete desertion of the body when death occurred. The close association here of Θανατος, Ψυχή and ὗπνος (or ονειρος) indicates the close bond of their mutual relations. Hermes conducts the souls of the dead suitors through the Gates of the Sun.

"This passage clearly identifies the (western) Gate of the Sun as the abode of dreams and the home of the souls of suffering men. In Homer's view the Gate of the Sun was the gate through which the souls of the deceased passed, and it was located in the West, by the Ocean. It was also the 'Gate of Dreams' since it is said to give admission both to dreams and the souls of the dead.

"In Hesiod, Sleep and Death are the sons of Night, but dreams are also the children of Night. Therefore Sleep, Death and Dreams were all

---

58 Knight, *Roman Vergil,* p. 176.

59 Highbarger, E. L., *The Gates of Dreams,* Johns Hopkins University Studies in Archeology, No. 30, Baltimore, 1940.

regarded as the Children of Night and were said to be found in the dreadful abode."[60]

Highbarger emphasizes the oriental background of these Greek and Roman concepts stressing especially the solar aspect of the gate.

The most striking representation of the Gate of Horn in Mesopotamia is a beautiful cylindrical seal of the Sargon period (2500 B.C.). Here the sun appears between two broad pillars disappearing over the mountains. His head is human but he has two curving horns and rays ending in stars, obviously the setting sun.[61] The Gate of the West, however, is frequently represented as extremely narrow and sometimes the bull is not the sun, but the guardian of the passage.[62]

The assumption is that the common solar element means that the Greek myth is influenced by the Orient, Egypt or Assyria. This is hardly tenable. Since the sinking sun means sleep and sleep means death, the belief of the soul following the sun can occur anywhere.[63] Highbarger also compares the Aeneid with one of the myths of Plato.

Er, a Pamphylian, has lost his life in battle. The corpses of fallen warriors lay on the field rotting. On the twelfth day after his death, Er was miraculously restored and became a living man again. Since his apparent death, his soul had undergone strange experiences. The soul came to a meadow where countless other ghosts were assembled. Here there were two openings in the earth close together and directly above them two corresponding openings leading to the sky.[64]

There are several reasons for assuming that these gates or openings really mean the *mouth*. At Cumae the cave was called the mouth of Avernus.[65] In the above-mentioned account of the other world by Plato besides the holes that serve as entrances to the other world we find also judges, and whenever an unworthy soul attempted to pass through the opening it *bellowed*. The verb used means both the groaning of heavy gates in their sockets and the bellowing of a bull.[66] Virgil himself describes the cave as a mouth (*fauces Orci*).[67] The explanation given by Servius is very interesting. According to the Roman scholar, the *porta cornea* signifies the *eyes* because of the color suggested by *cornu* and because the eyes are harder than other parts of the body, while the *porta eburnea* represents

---

60 *Ibid.*, p. 6.
61 *Ibid.*, p. 16.
62 *Ibid.*, p. 21.
63 Cf. Frobenius, L., "Die Seelen-Sonnenbahn . . . in Oceanien," *Weltanschauung der Naturvölker,* Weimar, 1898, p. 134.
64 Highbarger, *op. cit.*, p. 60.   65 *Ibid.*, p. 72.
66 *Ibid.*, p. 64, and cf. Appendix, p. 118.
67 *Ibid.*, p. 72.

the mouth from the character of the teeth.[68] Although this is probably only a "free association" of Servius, we should yet see what value it has from a psychological point of view.

There are enough arguments in favor of the view that one meaning of the gate is a wide-open jaw.

Kerberos, the gate keeper, would perhaps confirm this view. On a sarcophagus of Klasomene we see two dogs as guardians of the descent. The dogs are really bitches. Between the two bitches we see a young man (the soul) with two cocks in his hand evidently to be sacrificed to the bitches. Besides, he has either two clumps of rice or two kidneys as means of keeping the bitches from biting him. The dead are usually supplied with honey cakes so that the dog should eat the cake instead of the dead.[69]

The watchdog of Hades who guards the gate is Kerberos, and I have no reason to assume that he has replaced a bull.[70]

The dog with its threatening teeth is an appropriate doorkeeper of Hades. It is interesting to note that Charon and Kerberos are those who receive the sacrifice, one to carry the soul and the other not to prevent the entrance. But Charon sometimes appears in animal shape. "The Etruscan Hades wear a *wolf's skin* or a *bear's head*."[71] The Etruscan Charon was the Greek Hades, the god of death. Here personified Charon drags the soul from the world on horseback, accompanied by black dogs, in the shape of a skeleton with fire in his eyes.[72]

The Nordic nether world is guarded by two dogs, Gifr and Gess. They take turns sleeping and watching the gate.[73] The Nordic hell has two dogs, Kerberos has two heads.

In the Rigveda, we have two dogs standing guard to keep the departed souls out of bliss. "Run past straightway the two four-eyed dogs, the spotted and the dark, the brood of Sarama; enter in among the propitious fathers who hold high feast with Yama."[74] They also appear among men to deprive them of their lives. "The two brown, broad-nosed messengers of Yama, life robbing wander among men." In the Atharvaveda, "the two

68 *Ibid.*, fn., p. 4.
69 Rohde, E.: *Psyche.* Tübingen, 1907, I, p. 305. Cf. "Kerberos," in *Roscher's Lexikon.*
70 Highbarger, *op. cit.*, p. 45.
71 Carpenter, R., *Folk Tale, Fiction and Saga in the Homeric Epics*, New York, 1946, p. 134.
72 Róheim, "Charon and the Obolos," *Psychiatric Quarterly*, 1946, p. 19; Schmidt, B., "Totengebräuche und Gräberkultus im heutigen Griechenland," *Archiv für Religionswissenschaft*, XXIV, 1926, p. 281.
73 Simrock, *Die Edda.* Pp. 117, 118. Cf. Patch, H. R., *The Other World*, Cambridge, 1950, pp. 74 *et seq.*
74 Bloomfield, M., *Cerberus, the Dog of Hades*, London, 1905, p. 5.

THE GATES OF THE DREAM

dogs of Yama, the dark and the spotted, that guard the road shall not go after thee." We are not surprised to find the two dogs in the role of guides of the soul to heaven.[75]

In the Avesta (*Vendidad,* XIII, 8, 9), killing of dogs is forbidden because the soul of the slayer "when passing to the other world shall fly amidst louder howling and fiercer pursuit than the sheep does when the wolf rushes upon it in the lofty forest. No soul will come and meet his departing soul through the howls and pursuit in the other world. Nor will the dogs that keep the Cinvad bridge help his departing soul."[76] The aggressor seems to be the mortal, the biting dogs are guilt feelings—*Gewissensbisse.*

Following Wolff, it is not a dog at all but a porcupine.[77] According to a fragmentary myth (*Iliad,* V, 1. p. 397), Herakles fights Hades at the pillars that are the gate of the netherworld.[78] Presumably, Kerberos and Hades are mythologically identical. There is, moreover, good reason to assume that the gaping mouth of the hell-hound and the gates of hell are the same thing.[79]

This might suggest an interpretation in Lewin's sense—the oral triad of sleep, of eating and being eaten.[80] It is interesting to compare the other sacrifices offered to the dead—the obolos.[81] These coins are used either for covering the eyes or the mouth of the dead and thus severing the connection between the living and the dead. Rumanians in Transylvania put bread and money in the coffin[82]—or (in Szilágy) a silver coin under the tongue of the dead to pay the ferryman of the river that separates this world from the next.[83] In the Retyezát, two pennies are used for each eye, and one is put under the dead man's tongue.[84]

In Rumania proper, a wax candle and money are put into the hand of the corpse. There are obstacles between this world and the next, towels and pieces of cloth are put into the coffin. These are called "bridges" and in the other world they become bridges to carry the dead man over thresh-

[75] *Ibid.,* p. 16.

[76] *Ibid.,* pp. 28, 29. Cf. Hovelaque, A., *Le Chien dans l'Avesta,* Paris, 1876.

[77] Wolff, F., *Avesta.* Strassburg, 1910, p. 396.

[78] Highbarger, *op. cit.,* p. 115.

[79] *Ibid.,* pp. 63, 64. Cf. also, Landau, M., *Hölle und Fegefeuer in Volksglaube, Dichtung und Kirchenlehre.* Heidelberg, 1909, pp. 70–77.

[80] Lewin, B. D., *Psychoanalysis of Elation,* New York, 1951.

[81] Cf. for the following and other data Róheim, "Charon and the Obolos," *Psychiatric Quarterly,* Supplement, XX, 1946, pp. 160–196.

[82] Matuska, L., "Rumanian Superstition," *Ethnographia,* X, 1899, p. 299.

[83] Petri, M., *Szilágy Vármegye Monographiaja* (Monograph of County Szilagy), I, p. 203.

[84] Téglás, G., "A Retyezát videke" (The country around the Retyezát) *Földrajzi Közlemények,* XVI, Budapest, 1896, p. 466.

olds or ditches. The money is also used for those who died before—in order that they not resent the newcomer. At the gates of Paradise the dead encounter the most dreaded obstacles. The dead have to cross a bridge not thicker than a nail and not broader than a knife. Under the bridge there is a bottomless lake with dragons and serpents. A cat attacks the soul and tries to drive it off the bridge. With the money, the dead man can hire a person to drive away the cat.[85]

The worst curse is, "May there be nobody to close your eyes." If a dead person opens his eyes it means famine in the house, or it means that *he has slept too much during his lifetime*—and that *another death will occur soon in the family*. If only one eye is open it is said that the closed eye sees the path to the other world, *the open one* is looking around in the house for someone to take along.[86]

In Bánát the dead person receives nine pennies for there are nine gates to pass through. The survivors are very careful to *cover eyes, ears and mouth* to prevent the dead from haunting the living.[87]

The Tshuvash stuff ears, mouth and nostrils with pieces of silk and they cover the eyes with two little pieces of silk. The reason given is this: The chief of the cemetery will ask the ghost, "Are there still people on earth (i.e., people whom he could fetch for the cemetery)?" Then the dead says, "I saw nothing, they covered my eyes." The chief of the cemetery then asks, "Did you hear anything?" "No, they closed my ears." "Did you smell anything?" "They closed my nostrils." "Why didn't you ask?" "They also closed my mouth."[88]

In general we may assume that eyes and mouth must be closed or otherwise the dead will take a living person with them to the other world.[89]

But how do the dead, according to the well-nigh universal animistic belief, fetch the living? *They appear in a dream*. If their eyes are not open they cannot dream—since the dream consists of visual images. Moreover, the open mouth means the primary object relationship, that is, the element in the dream which can be regarded as a defense against sleep, i.e., death. The man-eating animals at the gate we regard therefore not as proofs of a primary desire to be "eaten up" (Lewin), but (a) as the talio anxiety for primary object relationship (eating the mother), and (b) as the

[85] Flacks, R., *Rumänische Hochzeits- und Totengebräuche*, Berlin, 1899, pp. 47, 58–60; Moldovan, G., "Birds in Rumanian Folklore," *Erdelyi Museum Egylet*, V, 1888, p. 293.

[86] Moldovan, G., *A magyarországi románok* (Rumanians in Hungary), Budapest, 1913, pp. 185, 187.

[87] *Ibid.*, p. 3.

[88] Mészáros, Gy., *A csuvas ösvallás* (Tshuvash Heathenism), Berlin, 1909, pp. 219–220.

[89] Sartori, P., *Sitte und Brauch*, Leipzig, 1910, I, pp. 131, 132.

vagina represented as a mouth, i.e., the *vagina dentata* or castration anxiety.

When the Altai shaman starts on his journey to the Prince of the Underworld, he meets the nine daughters of the Prince of Darkness. They try to seduce the shaman and get from him the presents that are really meant for their father. They are described as voluptuous females with big genital organs—but also sometimes as black serpents.[90] Returning now to the Kerberos image discussed above, we notice that the dogs are both female and the sacrifice they receive is eminently male: kidney and cock. Moreover, a frog is certainly a female symbol.[91] Further, Kerberos is also associated with a birth cave—the birth cave of Zeus.[92] The body of Kerberos is encircled by serpents like the head of the Medusa or a dog with a snake as a tail.[93] This would suggest a vaginal entrance to the other world with the snake (phallos) in the vagina as the danger on the path.

It is to be noted that in the Aeneid the Golden Bough opens the path to the other world. I think the identification of the *fatale ramum* with the mistletoe is perfectly valid.

The mistletoe or the mountain ash (another parasite) in Sweden shows where wealth lies hidden in the earth. The treasure seeker places the rod on the ground after sundown and when it rests directly above the treasure it begins to move as if it were alive.[94]

The *Aeneid* describes the golden light spread by the mistletoe,[95] and in Shropshire it was believed that the oak tree blossoms at Midsummer Eve and the blossom withers before daylight. A maiden who wishes to know her lot in marriage spreads a white cloth under the tree at night and in the morning she will find a little dust on it fallen from the flower. If she puts the pinch of dust under her pillow her future husband will appear to her in her dream.[96] We should not forget that Aeneas is led to the tree by two doves, symbols of his mother, the goddess of love.

Moreover, notwithstanding all the supernatural protection given by the *fatale ramum,* the Sybil tells Aeneas to *draw his sword* when he is in the cave.

According to Pliny, the Druids believed in the fertilizing power of the mistletoe. A priest clad in a white robe climbs the tree with a golden

---

90 Harva, U., "Die religiösen Vorstellungen der altaischen Völker," *F. F. Communications* No. 125, 1938, pp. 352, 353.

91 Cf. *Roscher's Lexikon,* "Kerberos."

92 Antoninus Liberalis, 19, quoted by Jung, C. G., and Kerenyi, C., *Essays on a Science of Mythology,* New York, 1949, p. 85.

93 *Roscher's Lexikon,* "Kerberos."

94 Frazer, J. G., *Balder the Beautiful,* London, 1913, II, p. 69.

95 Quoted above.

96 Burne, G. S., and Jackson, G. F., *Shropshire Folk-lore,* London, 1883, p. 242.

sickle and cuts the mistletoe. A potion made from the mistletoe will make barren animals bring forth.[97]

Why is the labyrinth engraved on the Cumaean temple of Apollo, the place that marks the descent of the Trojan hero to the shades?

According to Knight, "The Trojans on their Pilgrim's progress, looking for a new city of the gods, reached the middle of their course when they came to the western land. There is a rich symbolism in any western land that is a journey's end. So it is at Cumae for it is a western land of death and new birth that is reached. Aeneas goes to the temple of Apollo and on the gate of it there is a picture of Attica and Crete and the labyrinth with the Minotaur inside to which the Attic boys were sent. The problem is to find the poetry and meaning in the pictured gate and see how it colors and fixes the poetic world of The Aeneid."[98]

The labyrinth motive occurs once more in the Aeneid.

> Hinc via, Tartarei quae fert Acherontis ad undas
> Turbidus hic caeno vastaque voragine gurges
> aestuat.
>
> (*Aeneid*, VI, pp. 295–297.)

"The pattern of a labyrinth is the pattern of a maze. Frequently a labyrinth is a maze pattern rendered by brick or stone; but the words labyrinth or maze can without much danger be used interchangeably to indicate the pattern. . . . There is an area with the inside and an outside sharply distinguished. There is a long path from the outside to the inside which is usually called the nucleus. Sometimes the path has turnings, so that a wrong turning not leading to the nucleus might be taken by one who does not know the way. Sometimes there are no turnings which lead wrong, but only a very long path from the outside to the inside, a path which can bend in many different shapes, but cannot possibly be straight. With alternatives, the pattern is 'multicursal,' without them 'unicursal.' The description shows the meaning and purpose implicit in the shape. There are two opposite objects; exclusion from the nucleus and admission to it. Mazes and labyrinths provide correlative obstruction to those who would enter the middle point of a certain area and at the same time a conditional penetration to that point. They serve in fact the purpose of gates, giving entrance on certain terms."[99]

All over Europe we find games and dances in this labyrinthian or

[97] Pliny, *Natural History*, XVI, 249–251; Frazer, *Balder*, II, p. 77. Cf. also pp. 78–79, 85–86, 291.

[98] Jackson Knight, F. W., *The Cumaean Gates*, Oxford, 1936, p. 2. Cf. also Kerényi, K., *Labyrinth Studien*, Zürich, 1950.

[99] Knight, *op. cit.*, pp. 59, 60.

Trojan style, but in the Aeneid they are performed as mortuary games for one of the dead Trojans. All sorts of convolutions are performed on horse-back.

> et nunc terga fuga nudant, nunc spicula vertunt
> infensi, facta pariter nunc pace feruntur.
> Ut quondam Creta fertur Labyrinthus in alta
> parietibus textum caecis iter ancipitemque
> mille viis habuisse dolum, qua signa sequendi
> frangeret indeprensus et inremeabilis error:
> Haud alio Teucrum nati vestigia cursu
> impediunt texuntque fugas et proelia ludo.
>   *(Aeneid,* V, 586–593.)

The game was called the Trojan game and was carried over from Troy to Rome.

It is even more surprising to note that all over Europe we have Troy dances and mazes called Trojan. In Italy the Truia or Trojan game was labyrinthine in its movements. A kind of cavalry was called *trossuli* from *troare, redantruare,* to ride up and down or around. *Redantruare* is a technical word also used in the Salian dance.

All over Europe we find this notion of Troy as a city or maze or labyrinthine dance. In old Welsh literature the city of Troy is styled Caer Droica and the same word is also used for a labyrinth.[100]

The country folk believe that these were places where games were held. A virgin sat in the middle and the young men ran around trying to get near to her. Some labyrinths were simply concentric circles, others had two outlets, one leading out of the labyrinth and not to the center. These mazes were always near the ocean, so that they seemed to have something to do with seafaring.[101] Knight believes that the mazes are not called Troy because they have anything to do with Troy as a real city but because Troy itself is a maze, a labyrinthine city.[102]

The other name of Troy is Ilion. The easiest derivation is from a root *wal* or *wel,* ϝαλ or ϝελ. There is a digamma in the root and in Ilios also. Related to Ilios we have the verb ϝείλα, to roll up tight, to pen in a narrow space, and also, to wind, turn around.

Another important fact has to be added. Some years ago, Babylonian tablets (1000 B.C.) were discovered marked with maze patterns. The patterns mean the intestines of animals used for entrail divination. One inscription reads, "Palace of the intestines."[103] Knight adds, "This conjecture can be strengthened by the further comparison of the word *Taroisa*

---

100 *Ibid.,* p. 112.
101 Krause, E., *Die Trojaburgen Nordeuropa,* Glogau, 1893, pp. 19, 20.
102 Knight, *op. cit.,* p. 114.
103 *Ibid.,* pp. 115, 129.

and the root of *Troare* in Italy. The appearances of the root in Italy are bewildering in their variety, from *porca troia,* a pregnant sow, to *redantruare,* to repay a kindness, and *trulla,* a cooking pot."[104]

According to Knight, the Descensus Averno is the moment when Virgil himself is descending into the dream lands of the "unconscious."

The underworld is the abode of Sleep and Dreams, of Death and Fears.[105] "Virgil's Elysium, that is to say, is the spiritual equivalent both of a tomb, wherein Dardanus' 'dead' Troy awaits 'resurrection,'" and of a womb, wherein a 'reconceived' Troy awaits 'rebirth;' this Elysian tomb-womb having its material counterpart in that cinerary urn, shaped to resemble the Romulean beehive hut symbol of Rome's birth."[106]

One of the conditions for establishing the new Troy is the sacrifice of the sow.

> Ecce autem subitum atque oculis mirabile monstrum
> Procubuit viridique in litore conspicitur sus
> quam pius Aeneas tibi enim, tibi maxima Juno
> Mactat sacra ferens et cum grege sistit ad aram.[107]

Crutwell then goes on to show that the word *Tros* means *going round* and probably, in the dialect that was Virgil's mother tongue, also means *sow.*[108]

Tros means "going around" or manliness or cavalry operations. Therefore a Tros is somebody who is qualified to penetrate entrances.[109]

We assume that the dangerous or winding path is the vagina or the entrails and the sow a symbol of the female.

Homer mentions Penelope as slumbering softly in the "Gates of Dreams."[110] The souls pass through the Gate of the Sun, the abode of dreams and ghosts.[111]

Charon expresses it quite clearly, the other world is the world of dreams.

> quisquis es, armatus qui nostra ad flumina tendis
> Fare age, quid venias, iam istinc, et comprime gressum
> Umbrarum hic locus est, Somni Noctisque soporae.
> (*Aeneid,* VI, 387–390.)

Knight's argument is both ingenious and learned. He calls our attention to the fact that Cassandra, Helena and Athena are really the city of

104 *Ibid.,* p. 117.
105 *Ibid.,* p. 165.
106 *Ibid.,* p. 169.
107 Virgil, *Aeneid* VIII, lines 81–85.
108 Crutwell, R. W., *Virgil's Mind at Work,* Oxford, 1946, pp. 174–178.
109 *Ibid.,* p. 179.
110 Homer, *Odyssey,* IV, 1, p. 808.
111 Highbarger, *op. cit.,* p. 3.

Troy itself. He regards Cassandra as both an actual human girl in Troy and as a sibyl, a prophetess of Apollo at the entrance of a cave.[112] However, the city is the maiden, and Knight quotes Müller: "proinde ut virgo nuptiarum die 'cingulo' ligabatur, quod vir solvere solebat sequenti nocte, ita urbs condendi die cingulo (fossa) ligabatur, cuius rei ritus condendi etruscus, quem Romani denuo asciverunt, praeclarum testimonium est. Quae ei respondet conclusio, scilicet urbis tali rite 'ligatae' expugnationem antiquis idem fuisse atque *violationem virginis*," etc.[113]

Knight's opinion is that Virgil consciously represented the initiation to the Eleusian mysteries in the sixth book of the Aeneid and he regards the parallel with Malekula (quoted above) as most important.[114] The labyrinth is the entrance to the other world and the other world is the Earth Mother.

While the labyrinthine rites are performed in honor of the dead Anchises, Palinurus at the helm of the leading boat of the entire fleet *falls asleep*. In the dream he sees a god in the semblance of Phorbas who tells him to go to sleep, that he will take care of the helm. But Palinurus is suspicious and decides to stay awake—"mene hui confidere monstro?" **But** what can he do against a god?

> ecce deus ramum Lethaeo rore madentem
> vique soporatum Stygia super utraque quassat
> tempora, cunctantique natantia lumina solvit.

Now he is asleep. Lethe and Styx, the water of forgetting and of death, are equally active in inducing sleep. What happens? He falls into the water—the basic dream—and the helm and part of the stern are torn away = castration anxiety. (Virgil, *Aeneid*, V, 835–871.)

In the dreams and fantasies quoted in the first section of this book, we have found that the patient on the couch feels a whirling movement when about to fall asleep. The infant in the process of being born turns around. The maze has two exits, one leads to sleep, death, the womb; the other, which takes the person out again, signifies awakening. What I suggest is that the ritual of the labyrinth originates in the process of falling asleep—which may perhaps be a repetition of being born in reverse. This would be a second interpretation of the labyrinth besides that of the descent of the excrements in the intestines.

A third aspect of the spiral or maze is functional but equally important. Imre Hermann has noticed that if the patient really associates the way he should on the couch, the association is not completely free but

112 Knight, *op. cit.*, p. 96.
113 Müller, *Mnemosyne* III, pp. 186, 187, in Knight, *op. cit.*, p. 126.
114 Knight, *op. cit.*, p. 127.

sort of circulates round the original word from which it has started out. To patients who absolutely refused to associate he gave a maze toy and one of them declared that the toy was like analysis—it came nearer to the goal and then away and back again.[115]

According to Hermann, primitive animals and the young of some animal species do not move in a straight line but in a kind of peculiar circular motion. In general, he regards the straight line as belonging properly to the ego, while the spiral is the id or primary process.[116]

It is of importance to note what Bender says about schizophrenic children from infancy to puberty: "Rotating and whirling motor play in all planes make up a large part of their activity. It finds expression in their dreams and all other forms of fantasies, and in the nucleus of many of their psychological problems, such as fear of or preoccupation with losing their limbs, inability to determine the periphery of their own bodies, or boundaries of their personalities or 'ego boundaries,' their relationship to the reality of the outer world, to determine their own center of gravity, to relate themselves to time and space, or even be sure of their own identity."[117]

The straight line represents the ego, whirling or spiral is the primary process. The functional and the "content" symbol do not exclude each other.

If the whirling or spiral movement is the process of falling asleep, the ego merging into the id, we can understand why the Gates of the Underworld are labyrinthine.

We now turn to Theseus, the real hero of the labyrinth. Theseus, the son of the ocean god, Poseidon, undertakes to end the periodic sacrifice of Athenian youths and maidens to the Minotauros. This monster, half human and half bull, is the son of Minos who seems to be another Zeus. Theseus penetrates the labyrinth and kills the bull monster. But nobody can return from that maze except with the aid of Ariadne. It is her thread that makes it possible for Theseus to find the way back. The labyrinth symbolizes the Underworld from which nobody comes back alive. According to Pherekydes (Schol. Homer, *Od.* 11, 320) Ariadne gives Theseus the advice that if he finds *Minotaurus asleep* he should first cut the locks of his forehead and then offer him as a sacrifice to Poseidon. Emerging from the maze, he dances the labyrinthine dance with the maidens and youngsters who were to be sacrificed to the Minotaurus.

115 Hermann, Imre, "Das Unbewusste und die Triebe vom Standpunkte einer Wirbeltheorie," *Imago*, XXI, 1935, pp. 415–418.

116 *Ibid.*, pp. 419–428.

117 Bender, L., "Childhood Schizophrenia," *American Journal of Orthopsychiatry*, XVII, 1947, p. 43.

The meaning of Ariadne is unclear. She seems to be identified with Aphrodite and is the spouse of Dionysos who too makes the journey to the nether world. Theseus' leaving her while she is asleep is again a remnant of the dream origin of the whole myth.[118] On a bowl from Corneto and on a vase in the Louvre, Ariadne is seen with a coiling thread. It seems to start from the top of her chest.[119] The thread may either be the intestines or the umbilical cord. Ariadne is supposed to have been pregnant when left behind by Theseus and to have died with the embryo in her womb. At her festival in the month of Gorpaion (about August) a young man imitated the birth pangs of Ariadne.[120] We see therefore that the nucleus of the myth is a dream. The dreamer goes through the maze, i.e., falls asleep and in his dream he kills the father bull.[121] He awakes again, i.e., is reborn with the aid of the thread (navel cord or intestines) given him by the mother imago.

Theseus is also the hero of a real (i.e., undisguised) *descensus Averno*. With Peirithous he descends to Hades to abduct Persephone herself after they had captured the partly mortal Helen of Troy.[122]

We believe that the myths of descending to the other world and returning are based on dreams. On the other hand antiquity evidently regarded dreaming as a descent to the nether world and awakening as a cure.

The temple of Asklepios in Epidauros was built like a concentric circle, and water may have been flowing between the walls.[123] This is where the dreamer lies.

The dreamer at the cave of Trophonios is swaddled like an infant, then descends on a ladder to a cave, then crawls through a narrow passage where he can barely squeeze through and is finally drawn in as if it were into a whirlpool.[124] And the whole dream oracle or incubation is a *Katabasis*, a descent like the descent to the nether world.

With this we leave the classic world, in order to mention some primitive journeys to the nether world.

A Winnebago story sounds like a dream. The narrative is of the Orpheus and Eurydike type.

"Here all around this little knoll the country was beautiful. 'In yonder very beautiful spot I would like to die,' he thought to himself. So he

---

[118] *Roscher's Lexikon,* "Ariadne," "Theseus."

[119] Knight, *op. cit.,* p. 138.

[120] *Roscher's Lexikon,* "Ariadne," p. 543.

[121] On the Minotaur, cf. Highbarger, *op. cit.,* p. 27.

[122] Cf. *Roscher's Lexikon.*

[123] Meier, C. A., *Antike Inkubation und moderne Psychotherapie,* Zürich, 1949, p. 71.

[124] *Ibid.,* p. 92.

rolled over the best he could and *moving and crawling,* finally attained his wish and got there. Arrived there he awaited his death.

"He lay there with his eyes closed when to his surprise he heard a man speaking. 'Let us go home, I live here,' the voice said. Then he opened his eyes and to his surprise there stood a man. 'Come on,' this man said, so he jumped up. Then he followed him, *walked around* a lodge that stood there and finally entered it."

The spirit tells him that he will have to cross a stream and that he must do so by jumping across.

He arrived at a very wide stream. The water actually *whirled in a turbulent fashion* (the whirlpool or spiral) and he was afraid to jump. However, he closed his eyes and jumped, when *he looked back* there was nothing but a very little creek.[125]

Opler says there is a general pattern (among the Chiricahua Apache) for these stories about visits to the underworld. A person who is very rich finds himself *sliding down* a mound of sand to the underworld. A relative guides him to the camp where his dead ancestors dwell. It is apparently not time for him to stay there and he is warned against eating food offered to him. He *refuses the food* and finds himself in the world above recovering from his illness. He relates his adventures to those about him.[126]

The "sliding down" is the basic dream and this pattern really summarizes our whole theory.

In the place where the Chiricahua go after death everything goes on like in the world above. There is a trap door with tall grass. When this opens a mountain of sand is there and you step on this and *go down*.

Once at Fort Sill one old woman said that a boy and a girl appeared to her and they said, "You are wanted in the other world." She went with them a little way. The door opened and she slid down. Shortly after this she died. If you go, as this woman did, and eat some food there you cannot come back.

A Chiricahua woman was very sick. She said that her ghost had gone from her body and come to a high bluff. Below there was darkness. She jumped off and landed on a great cone of sand. When she landed the sand began to move and she went further down. She visited her dead relatives. Two relatives warned her not to accept any food at her father's camp if she wished to come back to earth again.[127]

125 Radin, P., *The Culture of the Winnebago as Described by Themselves,* Special Publications of the Bollingen Foundation, No. 1, Berkeley, 1949, pp. 52, 53.

126 Opler, M. E., "Myths and Tales of the Chiricahua Apache Indians," *Memoirs of the American Folklore Society,* 1942, p. 82.

127 *Ibid.,* p. 83.

The Lipan Apache tell similar tales. A woman fell off a horse and was knocked senseless. She was dead, she started toward the other world. She came to the edge of the world and looked down. People were sitting there in a circle. She wanted to go down, but she was afraid. The earth crumbled and carried her downward. They told her where the camp of her mother was. Her father told her to go back, it was not time for her to come yet. She saw a light in the distance (awakening). She saw something red. It was the buckskin dress she had worn in the hunt. She came to her body and entered it. She woke up.[128]

If they are really dead, the old woman of the underworld gives them prickly pears to eat. In another story it is again the earth that crumbles under the dreamer.

"The people down there offer you something, fruit or a smoke if you are really dead and come to their world. The men in the circle would have offered their fellow a smoke if he had been really dead."[129]

In a story from the Yukon, the "food" motive assumes the typical qualities of a nightmare.

A young woman goes down to the other world and she comes to a house. Two men tell her to go in and take her place in the middle of a room. An old woman objects to her presence and makes passes over her with a wand. Someone starts a fire in the house and she is nearly *choked* by the stifling atmosphere. (Choking is a characteristic nightmare sensation; cf. *infra*.) The sticks in the fire move about by themselves. She runs to the fire and pokes the sticks together. The flame leaps up and a voice at her side says, "Why are you doing that? You are burning me!" When she hears that she looks closely and sees the outlines of the figure of an old man sitting by the fire. The two young men come and invite her to eat fish with them, but she is *nauseated* by the sight of the food and its odor, and she will neither eat nor drink the water they offer her. This is repeated day by day, and day by day she refuses the food.

Because she has had no food, she feels weaker and weaker until one day she feels she is about to die. *She thinks of the clear water she used to drink at home, and it seems to her as though there is nothing else in the world that would taste so good.* She lifts her face and she is delighted to see at her side a bowl of water and beside it another bowl filled with mashed blueberries and the best kind of dried fish.

The winter draws near and the people start for the winter hunt. The trail leads up a steep precipice, but although all the others go up easily she cannot do so. An old woman takes care of her. She tells the girl that

128 Opler, M. E., *Myths and Legends of the Lipan Apache Indians*, XXXVI, 1940, p. 99.

129 *Ibid.*, pp. 101–105.

the men will come and kill her, and then she can go up easily. But if she wants to go back to her own people she can do so. *The old woman digs out a great hole in the path by which they came and makes the girl get into it.* There she is concealed until spring when she can go back to her own people. Finally, in the spring she gets back to her mother, first in the shape of a bird and then in her own shape.[130]

In this story the usual motive of *refusing food in the underworld* is combined with nightmare elements (nausea, choking) and inability to move (*Hemmungstraum*). The hole in which she hides is the intrauterine situation and the bird shape would be the flying dream. What interests us here especially, however, is the dream rhythm of *down and up* extended over a whole year, i.e., winter is night, spring is awakening.

In a Coos story we find the usual motive of *food refused*. The huckleberries they offer him are really lice. When he offers them eels, that is, good food, they are frightened. Finally, he gets back to his own people. He had been asleep for five days. He filled the river with flounders for them. That man did not age. He always looked like a young man.[131]

This is a hero-god in the making—the hero of the *descensus Averno* becomes a kind of immortal.

The descent myth of the Luiseño reveals the basic dream very clearly. A medicine man went to a spring. He had a stick in his hand and he dropped it into the water. It sank so deep he could not get it. So he went down after the stick and under the water there was another world. He returned, but because he told his adventures he died in a short time.

The people burned his body and buried his ashes. There was no water in the place before, but a spring of water bubbled up there and is still visible.[132]

Here again we have an incipient attempt to make the hero of the descent myth a giver of fertility or life.

An Oraibi story very definitely states the dream character of the journey to the other world and also connects the descent and ascent theme with the sun.

A young man was always thinking about the graveyard. "Is it true that people live there?" he thought. He prayed to the Sun and the Sun promised to let him see for himself. The Sun handed him something. "When you

130 Chapman, John W., "The Happy Hunting Ground of the Tena," *Journal of American Folk-Lore*, XXV, 1912, pp. 66–71. Cf. *idem*, "Tena Texts and Tales," *Publications of the American Ethnological Society*, VI, 1914, pp. 12–19.

131 Frachtenberg, L. J., "Coos Texts," *Columbia University Contributions to Anthropology*, I, 1913, pp. 139–149.

132 DuBois, C. G., "The Religion of the Luiseno Indians of Southern California," *University of California Publications in American Archaeology and Ethnology*, VIII, 1908, p. 155.

sleep in the evening, eat a little of this," he said. The young man told his parents. "Yes, as soon as I shall sleep in the night, I shall not wake up quickly. Hence as soon as the Sun is risen and high up, you must work on me and then maybe I shall wake up." He ate a little of the medicine, and then he descended. (The details of the other world in this story we can omit.) When the Sun was high up, he awoke once more.[133]

The Kiwai, a tribe in New Guinea with a very interesting mythology, tell the following stories about people who returned from the Land of the Hereafter.

Once a Mawata man named Asai who had died returned and told his friends about Adiri (the other world). A newly deceased person arrives at Adiri *in a canoe* and is welcomed there by his father or some other relative. A mat is spread for him and then the spirits dance to make him "cranky" so that he shall not want to go back.[134] While he watched the dancers, Asai thought, "This is a good place. I ought to stop here all the time." The ruler of the nether world is a woman called Dirivo. She called the spirits, and his father told him to go into the house. He was afraid, but his father persuaded him to go in. At the door two heavy spears were standing and Sido[135] who was in the house told them to enter between these spears. They sprang in and the two spears closed behind them with a clack. Now Asai thought, "I can never go back again." In the house there was a young girl with round breasts and Sido bade Asai cohabit with her. If a man does this, he forgets about the world of the living and stays in the nether world forever. But Asai *did not cohabit with* the girl, so they decided to take him back. The two spears lifted themselves up. Asai was not given any canoe this time, but Sido kicked him from behind and he flew up and landed at his own place where *he woke up*. He was among his own people. They told him, "You died yesterday."[136]

The visit to the other world is in a dream. The passage, as in many beliefs, and myths takes place by canoe. The posts of the house are significant. They keep clashing together, thus making it difficult to pass through.[137] Coitus with the supernatural being is not actually carried out. Instead, we have the "flying dream." Coitus in the nether world would have the same significance as eating in other texts.

A Mawata woman went through these clashing posts in her dream. The ghosts were dancing for her as usual, but just before sunset her hus-

[133] Voth, H. R., "Traditions of the Hopi," *Field Columbian Museum, Anthropological Series,* VIII, 1905, pp. 109–114. Cf. also the following story.

[134] Lethe!

[135] Cf. *infra.*

[136] Landtman, G., "The Folk Tales of the Kiwai Papuans," *Acta Fennicae,* XLVII, Helsingfors, 1917, p. 167.

[137] *Ibid.,* p. 168.

band who died before her said, "You go back. Your time has not come yet." Her husband told her that if she had eaten the food of the underworld she would have had to stay there forever. She told the people about Adiri where everything comes of itself, the gardens bring forth without anyone cultivating them, the coconuts plant themselves, the fish just come out of themselves, and everything is light, has no weight.[138]

These visits to the other world, although the main element in them is what we have called the basic dream, i.e., the moment of falling asleep, contain also other familiar or typical dream elements.

A man named Gibuma went in his dream, like Aeneas, to visit his father in the nether world. A man named Miria who had died long before welcomed him. Two armed men came from the bush and attacked him, trying to spear him. He tried to run but *he could not move*. He managed to roll into the water. *But then his arms would not move, he could not swim*. At the moment when his pursuers were upon him, he opened his eyes, screaming.[139]

The latent meaning of the dream can be guessed from what Freud says about this type of dream, that it is a sexual wish and at the same time the negation of this desire.[140] In this case then it must be the female ruler of the nether world as representing the mother.

Other dream elements enter into the following journey to the nether world. A spirit in the underworld sent a cassowary to fetch a man called Wioburi. He seized his bow and arrow and shot at the bird, but although it was not far, he missed it. This happens sometimes; the arrow just misses the mark. The bird jumps and the arrow passes under it. They both ran until they came to a river. The bird swam across and the man followed. Finally they came to the nether world. The bird went down into the men's house and the man *fell down* close to the *ladder* in a faint. A female spirit came and rubbed his eyes with the string of her grass skirt and he came to. They gave him water and food and all the spirit girls claimed him as their husband. He chose two wives with nice breasts and they bore him a son and a daughter. He feels homesick for his mother and her place. The children were offered food and water, but would not take anything. The two mothers came and put them to their breasts, but the children went on crying.

Then the spirits decided that they all have to go back home. "The spirits took a small mat and a pelican's feather and put them on the water and they became a canoe. The same was done with more feathers and

---

[138] Cf. in the Aeneid, "accipit alveo *ingentem* Aenean," *Aeneis,* VI, p. 412; cf. Norden, E., *Aeneis,* Buch VI, Leipzig, 1916, pp. 236, 237.

[139] Landtman, *op. cit.,* p. 170.

[140] Freud, S., *Gesammelte Schriften,* II, pp. 332, 333.

there were more canoes floating on the water. Wioburi refused all the canoes; they were all too slow. A cassowary feather is transformed into a canoe, but he thinks there is not enough room there. Finally, he decides to go by a bamboo. The bamboo stretched itself high up from the ground and bending down their tops, reached his home in the same minute.

The people heard the sound at night and woke at the noise. Wiobari alighted and sent the bamboo back to the other world. He saw *his mother sleeping* and said, "Poor mother, she looks like the cassowary."[141]

Here we have a dream with erection (bow and arrow, bamboo), incest (mother—cassowary) as the latent content. The motive of food or coitus or breast refused, is displaced from the hero to his children.

Duobe's spirit went down and he saw many people making a garden. This was the land of the spirits, but he refused to eat their food. A man came with legs and a nose like a pig, and he asked Duobe whether he wanted that kind of a nose. He refused. The spirit took his nose off and underneath there was a skull. The other spirits sent him home saying that otherwise he would be killed by the man with the skull. They showed him a small canoe which would take him home. *But he is not allowed to turn back.* He just pushed the canoe and the canoe went back on its own. Just as his spirit entered his body, he woke up shrieking.[142]

I assume that the stuff out of which the *dying god* was made was this type of dream. The dream vision of the self is the body cathected with libido; each dreamer sees himself in the dream, i.e., he dreams because he is afraid to die (sleep). *This is how the self becomes idealized, how we acquire an ego ideal, and animism is the background of all idealism.* But if the death aspect of sleep becomes conscious and the dreamer "returns from the nether world," we have the starting point for a hero or hero-god. Now, among the Kiwai, we actually have something similar in the person of Sido, the culture hero of the Kiwai.

One day, his father smoothed the ground, moulding it into the vulva of a woman. He had intercourse with the ground every day, and a child sprang up with supernatural rapidity. Later, however, Sido does have a mother, though it is not explained how. "The mother took off her grass skirt and sat down with her legs apart, and when a fly settled on her vulva she caught it." From this she made love medicine for her son's drum.

At Yasa there was a beautiful girl called Sagaru, and this is how Sido found her. At night when his mother and father were asleep, he got up and heard the sound of drums. "He took his navel cord which his mother had kept since his birth and tying one end of it to the corner post of the house, he threw the other end out. The navel cord went right out and extended

141 Landtmann, *op. cit.*, pp. 165–167.   142 *Ibid.*, pp. 171, 172.

itself till it reached the men's house." This is how he finds Sagaru. He has intercourse with her under the house and in the morning he is back with his navel cord following. This certainly sounds like a dream. *While his father and mother are asleep,* he has intercourse with a woman to whom he is tied by the navel cord, i.e., who is his mother, and by the time they are awake he is back again.[143]

Later he quarrels with his wife Sagaru. She leaves him, goes to a rival. Sido and the other person fight, Sido is killed. His spirit goes through various adventures, mostly of a sexual nature, wandering westward all the time. Finally, he comes to Adiri, the land of the hereafter, at the extreme western border of the world where the sun and the moon go down.

The way he got there is significant. He entered the stomach of a big "rockfish" which swam away with him inside and at last reached the point of Adiri, the other world.

Two men, called Adiri and Dirivo, were spearing fish when the rockfish arrived. They cut the fish up and dried it in the sun because they had no fire. The intestines were opened by a girl belonging to one of the men. She took Sido as her husband. He brought fire to the other world by taking out his teeth and rubbing them against a piece of wood. While the other men were asleep, he took the girl and had intercourse with her. He had a very large penis, and when he withdrew it his semen flowed all over the place making all sorts of vegetable. That is how taro, sweet potato and everything else originated.[144]

The journey to the west is in a fish[145]—uterine regression in sleep. But it is followed by a genital trend—fire, coitus, fertility.

This story is very close to a folk tale of Bugotu, Isabel Island. Kamakaju wades into the ocean in the morning and is swallowed by a big kingfish. It went off with him eastward toward the rising sun. The fish landed on a beach, and he cut himself out of the belly of the fish with an obsidian knife. He sat down and wondered where he was. "So up rose the Sun with a bang and rolling from side to side. . . . And he drew aside till the Sun rose away and then he followed." They arrived at the village of the Sun's children. He remained there and showed them fire and they ate cooked food. Then he sees a hole in the sky and is homesick for his village. He refused the food they offered him—and so they let him down into his village.[146]

Sido ought to be a returning hero, and he is nearly that. The house of

143 *Ibid.,* pp. 93–100.
144 *Ibid.,* pp. 100–114.
145 Cf. for this motive Frobenius, L., *Das Zeitalter des Sonnengottes,* Berlin, 1904; Schmidt, H., *Iona,* Göttingen, 1907.
146 Codrington, R. H., *The Melanesians,* Oxford, 1891, pp. 365, 366.

the underworld is divided into two parts, the one ruled over by Adiri is for those who come to stay, the other ruled by Sido is for the souls who come down but are sent back to life.[147]

Herakles, the son of Zeus and Alkmene, was cheated of his birthright to become the most powerful of men. Hera induces Zeus to swear that whoever was born that day would become the lord of men. Then she flies from Olympos to Argos and Eurystheus is born prematurely in the seventh month and thus becomes ruler of Argos and master of Herakles.

Herakles killed his own children and those of his brother in a fit of madness sent by Hera. To expiate his crime he was made to serve Eurystheus. He went to Tiryns bearing the arms the gods had given him, the sword of Hermes, the bow of Apollo, a robe of Athena, a breastplate of Hephaistos, and a great club he had cut for himself in Nemea.

Some of the well-known labors he had to perform in the service of Eurystheus bear a striking similarity to his descent to Hades. Near the river of Okeanos, that is, the end of the world, was a monster called Geryoneus, son of Chrysaor and the nymph Calliroe. He had three bodies, and a famous herd of red cattle guarded by Eurytion, and the two-headed dog Orthos, *a brother of the hell-hound Kerberos.* Crossing Europe, Herakles came to the straits between Europe and Africa and erected two pillars in memory of his journey. Helios here beat so hotly upon his head that he shot an arrow at him. Helios was not angry, but gave him a *golden cup* in which he crossed Okeanos and reached the island and accomplished his task. Herakles also makes war on the sons of Minos like Theseus and the Minotauros. Finally, he was dispatched by Eurystheus to Hades to fetch the two-headed Kerberos. On his way to Tainairon, at this spacious entry to the nether world, Herakles halted at Eleusis and after Eumolpos had purified him from the blood of the Kentaurs, he descended to Hades. He first released Theseus from his bonds and overpowered Menoites, the herdsman of Hades' kine, till Persephone begged for his life. Protected by the impenetrable lion's skin and the breastplate of Hephaistos, he grabbed Kerberos and forced him to submit to be led away. He made his ascent by the grotto at Troisen, and when he had shown the dog to Eurystheus took it back to Hades.[148]

Philochoros relates a myth in which Peirithous, another wanderer to the nether world who wanted to elope with the daughter of Hades was thrown to Kerberos to be devoured.[149]

Herakles *with the gigantic club* is the only hero who can master the

[147] Landtman, *op. cit.*, p. 115.

[148] Fox, W. Sherwood, *The Mythology of All Races, I: Greek and Roman,* Boston, 1916, pp. 76–93.

[149] Dietrich, A., *Nekyia,* Leipzig, 1893, p. 49.

two-headed beast—and if Kerberos were not a matter of belief but only a narrative the story would end there. The phallic hero conquers, the vagina dentata is removed, the passage to women is open—this would be the story of a North American culture hero. According to Usener, the name means "the young, dear hero," i.e., the hero of heroes.[150]

J. E. Harrison observes that Hermes and Herakles are linked to each other because they are both herms. The club of Herakles is originally a green bough. In an Orphic hymn, Herakles is addressed:

> "Come Blessed One, bring spells for all diseases
> Drive out ill fates, wave in thy hand thy bough
> With magic shafts banish the noisome Keres."[151]

As one of the Idean Daktyls, he is certainly phallic.[152]

We have seen above how the dream character of the soul makes it also solar; like the sun, man goes to sleep in the evening and awakens in the morning.

Harrison writes, "In much of his mythology that cannot be explained here, Herakles is but the humanized double of Helios. It is from the sun he gets his tireless energy. As the young sun he fights with Hades, the setting sun, at Pylos. As again the rising sun, he rescues Alkestes from the shades," and finally he travels in the golden cup of the sun.[153]

In reading the adventures of Herakles one is struck by the frequency with which he conquers someone who obstructs the passage of the traveler —the passage to the world below or into the vagina.

Herakles is both a hero and a god. Again Pausanias: "They say that Phaistos when he came to Sikyon found them devoting offerings to Herakles as to a hero. But Phaistos would nothing of the kind but would offer burnt offerings as to a god."[154] Leaving the question as to what is a god unanswered, we may ask, "What is a hero?" Or, rather, in Greek, "What is the *heros*?"

The *heros* is a dead man or woman or, to put it differently, the soul.

On one of the Spartan grave reliefs a seated man holds in the right hand a great Kantharos, in the left a pomegranate. A large snake in his left hand marks his *daimon* character, but he is an actual dead man Timokles. A hero-feast is dedicated to *Kudrogenes hero,* or to *Lais heroine.* In the archaic grave reliefs of Sparta the dead man is represented as a hero.[155]

---

150 Usener, H., *Sintflutchsagen*, Bonn, 1899, p. 58.
151 Harrison, Jane, *Themis*, Cambridge, 1928, pp. 364–366.
152 Kaibel, "Daktyloi Idaioi," *Nachrichten der königlichen Gesellschaft der Wissenschaften zu Göttingen*, phil. hist. Kl., 1901, p. 506.
153 Harrison, *op. cit.*, p. 70.
154 Pausanias, II, 10, 1.
155 Harrison, *op. cit.*, pp. 313, 314.

In a sense, everybody is a hero: he goes to sleep, i.e., enters Hades every night, and then he becomes a visual image, a soul, an *eidolon*, a phallic serpent. He dreams and he awakens.

But when human beings actually sleep their last sleep, this "coming back" is still represented by motives both oral and genital (banquet, snake), yet it is not the same as the real *coming back, a resurrection,* an awakening after death. Herakles, the hero of heroes, accomplishes this feat. For does he not carry the *great club* which threatens even the gods? To quote the Sybill:

> sate sanguine divum,
> Tros Anchisiade, facilis descensus Averno
> Noctes atque dies patet atri ianua Ditis
> sed revocare gradum superasque evadere ad auras
> Hoc opus, hic labor est, pauci quos aequus amavit
> Juppiter aut ardens evexit ad aethera virtus
> dis geniti potuere.
> *(Aeneis, VI, pp. 125–130.)*

The sleeper awakens, the hero returns.

The princess Deinareia complains that she is visited every night by the river god Acheloos. He appears in the shape of a bull or as a snake, or as a man with bull's head. Laistner correctly interprets this as a dream, and Herakles as in all dreams of the nightmare type wrestles with his Protean adversary and wins.[156]

What we add to Laistner is that it must be the dream of Herakles who represents himself as the sleeping Deinareia, and in the dream he is both passive as Deinareia and active as Herakles. Instead of being castrated he castrates his opponent represented as the dreamer breaking off one of the horns of his bull adversary. Herakles is there rightly called "he who chokes the nightmare"—Ἡρακλῆς Ἠπιάλτα πνίγων—[157] the dreamer himself is idealized.

"He the greatest Kouros swings his *klados,* his branch from the tree of life against a pygmy *ker* (nightmare demon with shrunken body and distorted face). He the greatest Kouros lifts his *klados* to slay the shrivelling ugly figure and inscribed as γῆρας, Old Age.

> "We blossom like the leaves that come in spring
> What time the sun begins to flame and glow
> And in the brief span of youths gladdening
> Nor good nor evil from the gods we know

[156] Laistner, L., *Das Rätsel der Sphinx,* I, p. 166.

[157] *Ibid.,* I, p. 167 (quoting Sophron). Deinareia is a warlike woman. The antagonists of Herakles are the bull Acheloos and the Kentaur Eurytion (*Roscher's Lexikon,* "Deianaeira") typical nightmare beings.

But always at the goal black Keres stand
Holding one grievous Age, one Death within her hand."
(*Mimnermos*, 2.)[158]

Thus will mankind dream great dreams, hoping to conquer Hades the invincible. There must be someone who can do it—the great phallic hero Herakles.

First we must assume that the typical or basic dream was remembered by certain individuals who experienced these dreams in a state of increased anxiety, i.e., sickness. The dream heralded their recovery. Many times they must have told this experience to their family or friends until they became incipient heroes themselves. But the dream movement "up" from Hades is an erection, the returning hero may become typified as a spirit of fertility. With the hero, spring is back again—the dawn of another year.

If the myths about the other world are based on dreams, can the motive of "refused food" be interpreted in the sense of Lewin as proving the "sleep is oral"?[159]

The Egyptian ritual performed over Osiris was really meant for each and all of the dead who are supposed to repeat the fate of their great prototype Osiris. The most important ceremony in the revival of Osiris is the ritual of the "opening of the mouth." "Horus hath pressed for thee thy mouth, he hath weighed (or balanced) thy mouth against thy bones (i.e., teeth). Horus hath opened for thee thy mouth. Behold thy son loveth these,"[160] etc. During the mortuary ceremony the mouth of the deceased was touched, i.e., opened by Horus who employed the same instrument he had used to open the mouth of his father Osiris. He then pressed the sides into their natural position during life and "balanced" the mouth, and after this the deceased was able to speak and breathe and eat and drink, and his members could perform all their natural functions once more.[161]

The opening of the mouth is the sucking activity of an infant. If, as Budge tells us, the dead were buried in the antenatal position of a child,[162] we might assume that "opening of the mouth" means that he is to start his life again in the other world. Just as in the dream, the oral element means escape from sleep (i.e., death). If the dead dream their dreams in the other world, they are not likely to molest the living. Closing the mouth of the corpse with a coin[163] means the same thing: do not live here in the world

158 Harrison, *Themis*, p. 380.
159 Cf. *supra* in the chapter "The Basic Dream."
160 Budge, E. Wallace, *Osiris and the Egyptian Resurrection*, London, 1911, I, p. 76.
161 *Ibid.*, p. 102.
162 Budge, E. Wallace, *Egyptian Ideas of the Future Life*, London, 1900, p. 162.
163 Cf. *infra The Song of Sirens and the Isles of the Blessed*, p. 697.

of the living (the oral as beginning of object relatedness), go to the other world. But if the soul *eats* in the other world, then that is where he lives and belongs.

It is obvious that people or tribes who already have a belief in a land of the hereafter will dream in terms of this belief. Our hypothesis is different, it implies that *this belief itself originates from the basic dream,* especially the basic dream as dreamed by those who are really ill and on their way to recovery, surmounting a crisis.[164]

The belief in the soul does not *necessarily* lead to a belief in another world.

In Ontong Java "as soon as a baby can crawl about it receives its *kipua* (spirit). In appearance it resembles the person to whom it is attached, growing old with him and being subject to other changes also. Thus if a person limps the spirit will also limp. There is no land to which the *kipua* go after the death of their owner but certain spots are regarded as dangerous because the spirits live there.[165]

Sleep is periodical uterine regression. Uterine regression has two aspects, desire and anxiety. The anxiety is due to the fact that it involves relinquishing all object cathexes. This anxiety is warded off by creating a double, a genitalized, immortal dream-body. In the basic dream we have a "return of the repressed" or something analogous to it. The dream image descends (or ascends) into a symbolic uterus thus giving rise to a belief in a land of souls. All this is not simply a survival of intrauterine engrams, it is due to the conflict generated by sleep and wakefulness, regression and the object-directed trend. The peculiar nature of these our deepest trends is that they are both antithetical and identical at the same time.

In one version of the *descensus Averno* type the hero fails to return. Naturally so, since the hero is here the prototype of human mortality, and the story explains the origin of death. This is the story of Maui and his great ancestress Hine-nui-te-po (Great Mother Night).

"His great ancestress Hine-nui-te-po is what you may see flashing opening and shutting where the horizon meets the sky." He arrives at her dwelling place in the *evening* and finds her fast asleep. He is accompanied on this trip by little birds. Maui tells them not to laugh when they see him going into his ancestress, but they may do so when they see him coming out of her mouth. However, they laugh when he goes in, the old woman awakes

---

164 Cf. for instance Seligmann, C. G., *The Melanesians of British New Guinea,* Cambridge, 1910, p. 734.

165 Hogbin, J. J., "Spirits and the Healing of the Sick in Ontong Java," *Oceania,* I, 1930, pp. 148, 149.

and kills Maui.[166] Tylor adds that the author has omitted an important detail of the story.

"I have to thank Sir G. Grey for a more explicit and mythologically more consistent translation of the story of Maui's entrance into the womb of Hine-nui-te-po and her crushing him to death between her thighs than is given in the English version."[167]

In another New Zealand version Maui sees that Sun and Moon are renewed because they bathe in the Wai Ora Tane, the water of life. He wanted to kill Hine-nui-te-po and carry off her heart. Hine drowns all in her womb, none may return. Maui tells the birds not to laugh. His head and shoulders are already in the womb when one of the birds laughs. Night awoke, closed her portals, Maui died.[168]

If we change one trait we can reconstruct the basic dream. It is Maui who when he goes to sleep enters the womb of his mother, Night, and who returns to life when the birds sing, and he is awake alive. This must have been the original story, a myth derived from a dream. When the story became a mythical explanation of the origin of death two motives became displaced (sleep from the hero to Hine, awakening noise from rescue to danger), and we have the present form of the narrative.[169]

In the Beowulf story and allied mythological material the dream origin of the "descent" is quite clear, but it is complicated by other dream-derived motives. The Eddic voyage of Thor to Utgardloki has traits in common with the Beowulf epic. Thor, Thialfi and Loki are on their way to Jötunheim or Giantsland. They had wandered the whole day and at dusk were in a big forest. Finally, they found something like a hut and there they *went to sleep*. Around midnight they heard a terrific noise. The hut was shaking and it was like an earthquake. The noise lasted until daybreak. Thor then went out and he saw a giant snoring. This was a giant called Skrymir. They decided to wander together. Next evening, Skrymir *went to sleep* before Thor and his companions and started snoring immediately. Thor got so furious that he hit him on the head with a hammer. Skrymir awoke and said that a leaf must have dropped on his head. The next night the same thing is repeated; this time the giant thinks it is an acorn that has hit him. The third time when Thor swings the hammer with his full might against the temple, the sleeping giant thinks it must be

---

166 Grey, G., *Polynesian Mythology,* London, 1855, pp. 16–32.

167 Tylor, E. B., *Primitive Culture,* London, 1903, II, p. 336.

168 Taylor, R., *Te ika a Maui of New Zealand,* London, 1855, pp. 30, 31. Cf. Shortland, E., *Traditions and Superstitions of the New Zealanders,* London, 1854, pp. 45, 46.

169 Cf. also Róheim, "The Garden of Eden," *Psychoanalytic Review,* XXXII, 1940, pp. 184–193; Luomala, K., "Maui of a Thousand Tricks," *Bernice P. Bishop Museum Bulletin* 198, Honolulu, 1949, pp. 50 *et passim.*

the birds defecating from the branches. The giant then shows them the way to Utgard's castle. In the presence of Utgardloki, the giant asks, "How can this little fellow be the famous Thor?" He asks them what they can do. Loki said that nobody could eat his food quicker than he could, but Logi beat him in this match. Thialfi was beaten in racing.

Thor offered to compete in drinking. They brought him a horn and Utgardloki said, "A really good drinker would quaff this off at once, a medium drinker might empty it in two gulps, but even the worst ones can do it in three." Thor drank with all his might, but the giant made fun of him; the great Asathor could do no better than that.

Thor suggested wrestling. A big grey cat was brought into the room. Thor thought this would be easy, but he could not lift the cat. Finally, he made it lift one leg. Then Utgardloki said Thor should wrestle with his old nurse Elli. The harder Thor pushed, the harder she resisted. Asathor the Invincible is finally half-kneeling.

Next day, Utgardloki[170] took him out of the castle and bade him farewell. Thor felt embarrassed at his defeat. Utgardloki said, "Now I shall tell you the truth, but you shall never get into my fortress again. All this was magic, illusion. When you hit me with the hammer as I slept there was a rock between my head and your hammer but you could not see it. Loki could not possibly compete with Logi since Logi was a prairie fire. Thialfi could not outrun Hugi because Hugi was my thought. When you drank we were all frightened to death; the end of the horn was in the ocean and we thought you would drink up the whole ocean. The result was the ebb. Do you know who the cat was? It was the Mitgard serpent,[171] and you nearly lifted it to the sky. Nobody could have won against Elli; her name is Age. But now we must part company, and you shall never see my castle again." Thor lifted his hammer to strike, but, lo and behold, Utgardloki was there no more.[172]

This beautiful allegory has its origin in the inversion of a well-known dream motive; a very small stimulus is magnified to colossal proportions. If we assume that the sleeping giant (Skrymir and Utgardloki are the same person) and Thor are identical, we come to the conclusion that this is a thirst dream, and the thirsty dreamer imagines that he is emptying the whole ocean. Thirst dreams are very often also urethral, and the combination of fire and water may indicate just this. The cat is the typical form the nightmare takes in medieval European folklore.[173] Thor, the hero,

170 Utgard really means "castle at the end of the world." Loki is the same as the Loki who accompanies Thor.

171 The serpent that encompasses the earth.

172 Simrock, Karl, *Die Edda*, Stuttgart, 1896, pp. 278–284.

173 Róheim, *Adalékok a magyar nephithez* (Contributions to Hungarian Folk Beliefs), Budapest, 1920, p. 73.

wrestles with the cat-nurse (mother imago) but even he cannot conquer age. The duplication technique which is so very characteristic of dreams is marked in this myth, Thor and his two hypostases, the giant and his duplicates, finally even the identity of Thor and the sleeping giant.

We find the same duplicate formation in the hero and his companions combined with the journey to the other world in the folk tale of the Bear's son, i.e., in the epic of Beowulf.

Hrodgar, king of Denmark, has built a beautiful castle. But no one can *sleep* in the castle. The demon Grendel comes from the ocean every night and kills the sleepers. Finally, he encounters Beowulf. They struggle all night. Grendel notices that Beowulf is stronger and tries to flee. He manages at a price: his arm and armpit remain in Beowulf's hand. The blood tracks point toward the sea.

Grendel's Mother appears as avenger, and the killing of the sleeping warriors starts again. Beowulf *dives* into the ocean to kill the she-demon. Just when he is about to strike, his sword breaks. But a colossal sword appears ready for his use, and he cuts the she-demon's head off.[174]

Again, we must regard Beowulf and the other sleepers as the same person. To sleep is to die or at least to have a nightmare. As if the sleeping position were not enough, the dream's character or origin is re-emphasized by the statement that the demon must disappear by daybreak.[175]

The content of the anxiety is also quite clear; the arm torn out of its socket, the broken sword, mean castration anxiety, and the fact that it is the demon's arm and not the sleeper's does not make much difference. But what is the diving into the ocean and the struggle with the mother imago? We shall answer this question after analyzing the folk tale.

The type of folk tale we are discussing is usually known as the Bear's Son. The hero whose father or mother may be a bear (or some other animal; horse, cow, etc.) goes through a series of adventures. The first of these shows some similarity to the haunted mill.[176]

The Hungarian story is of "the son of a white horse." A white mare is delivered of a son and suckles it for fourteen years. He wanders in the world and acquires three companions, Tree-tearer, Stone-breaker and Iron-breaker, by wrestling with them and conquering them. One evening they made a hut, and the next day White Horse's Son said to Tree-tearer, "You boil some porridge while we go hunting." Tree-tearer boiled the porridge, and a devil came who was very small but his beard was very long. "My name is Hétszünyü Kapanyányimonyók, and if you don't give me porridge, I shall eat it on your back."

[174] Panzer, F., *Studien zur germanischen Sagengeschichte*, Munich, 1910, I, pp. 249–294.

[175] *Ibid.*, p. 261.   [176] Cf. *infra* under *Feralis exercitus*.

Hétszünyü does not mean anything, but a parallel version shows that it is really Hét-sing, "seven ells," which is the length of his beard. Kapany-ányimonyók is a condensed word. *Kappany* is *capon, anyányi* means belonging to the mother and *monyók* is *mony,* testicles. The name shows (a) the phallic nature of the dwarf, (b) the castration anxiety (capon), and (c) the mother, i.e., the oedipus complex.

Tree-tearer gave him the porridge and when he had eaten it he left. There was nothing left to eat for the others.

Stone-tearer does not give up the porridge so easily. They wrestle, but anyway the dwarf eats it with Stone-tearer lying on his back and the porridge on his stomach.

The same happens with Iron-grinder. The fourth time it is the Son of the White Mare. He ties the dwarf by his beard to the tree and wants to show him to his friends. But by the time they get to the tree, the dwarf has pulled the tree out by its roots and disappeared through a hole.[177]

In another Hungarian version, we have the same situation, but the dwarf is called Beard-seven-ells-long-penis-like-a-hoe. An added episode: when the guardians offer him some porridge, instead of using a spoon, he just grabs it with his hand. White Horse Peter is so furious that he grabs the dwarf and sticks his head into the porridge.[178]

In the Kalotszeg story, the hero's father is a white horse. The dwarf is a small Jew with a very long beard.[179] In another version, the hero wedges the dwarf's tremendous moustache into a tree.[180] Or the hero's name is Cow's Johnny and the dwarf Long Beard, with the wedging episode.[181] In a Szeged version, the hero is the son of an ewe, and he pulls the beard of Seven Ell Beard through a gap in a tree which he makes with his war club.[182]

The usual situation is that the demon or dwarf appears the day *after* they have slept a night in the hut. The dwarf is thumb sized and his beard is very long. The Serbs call him Yard-high-forehead-and-span-long-beard.[183] The small stature and long beard are equally significant.[184]

The situation is very similar to the haunted mill. The food and the demon's paws reaching into the food as well as the "wedged in" motive in-

177 Arany, L., *Magyar Népmesegyüjtémeny,* Budapest, 1911, p. 131.

178 Ortutay, G., *Nyiri es rétközi parasztmesék* (Folktales from Nyir and Rétköz), Gyoma, n.d., p. 61.

179 Kovács, Agnes, *Kalotaszegi népmesék* (Folktales from Kalotzeg), Budapest, n.d., II, p. 109.

180 Bánó, Stephen, *Baranyai népmesék* (Folktales from Baranya), Budapest, n.d., pp. 164, 168.

181 Nagy, John Berze, *Baranyai Magyar Néphagyományok,* (Folk Traditions from Baranya), Pecs, 1940, II, p. 72.

182 Kálmány, Lajos, *Hagyományok,* Szeged, n.d., II, p. 1.

183 Panzer, *op. cit.,* I, p. 81.   184 *Ibid.,* p. 78.

crease the similarity of the two situations. After this, we shall not be astonished to find the Miller and the Waterspirit among the hero's companions. Another interesting feature of our stories is this. There are two introductions to the story of the bear's son. One is about the house in the forest and the dwarf. The second goes along these lines:

Once upon a time, there was a king who had twelve sons. He had a garden and in the garden there was a tree. That tree grew one apple a year and that one was of gold. But the king could not get the apple. A seven-headed serpent always got hold of it. He told his oldest son to guard the tree with a sword, but before the fruit got ripe at eleven o'clock he was *asleep*. At midnight, therefore, the apple was plucked by the serpent just as usual. All the others went to sleep too, except for the youngest one who stayed awake and chopped the snake's head off.[185]

In a story from Sicily, the king's two elder sons fall asleep; the youngest one is awake and when a giant's arm reaches over the high wall to pluck the fruit he cuts it off with a sabre.[186]

Returning now to the scene in the forest house, we can safely assume that it is a dream. The next assumption is that the dwarf is the penis; he is openly called so in two Hungarian versions. The hero and his companions are duplicate figures of the same person, originally the dreamer. Some of these duplicate figures are represented as sleeping, another as doing something. This is the sleeper's dream. In the dwarf situation, the dwarf with whom the sleeper wrestles is a masturbation dream, and the hot porridge on his stomach is evidently the semen pouring out. But what about the hero, the third? There is no hot porridge there, but castration anxiety represented as the wedged-in beard of the demon. The demon has now disappeared, usually leaving drops of blood behind him that lead to a hole.

We are now at the edge of the underworld where Alice goes down the rabbit hole, or, in other words, what we have called the *basic dream*.

In an Icelandic version, following the demon and the drops of his blood they come to the opening of a cave. Stairs lead into the unknown. One of them goes four steps down, then he is afraid and returns. Finally, the hero goes right down to the bottom of the cave.[187]

In a Hungarian story quoted above we read:

"They arrived at a big hole. This is where Seven Ell Capon Testicles went down to the other world." The others are afraid; finally, the hero is let down in a basket on a rope to the other world.[188]

185 Ilg, B., *Maltesische Märchen und Schwänke,* Leipzig, 1906, I, p. 40.
186 Gozenbach, L., *Sicilianische Märchen,* Leipzig, 1870, II, pp. 49, 50.
187 Rittershaus, A., *Neuisländische Volksmärchen,* Halle, 1902, p. 104.
188 Arany, *op. cit.,* p. 135.

In a related Hungarian story we read that *the hero falls asleep and dreams that one can descend to the other world. Two men let him down on a rope.*[189] In the Vogul story, he meets a noseless man who hears the beautiful song of the girls of the nether world and that induces him to be let down into the ditch.[190]

The hero frequently finds the wounded demon, or the dragons who own the girls, asleep in the other world.[191] The entrance to the nether world is a *well* in most cases.[192] The gate or door of the house, in which the hero subsequently finds the princesses, is especially emphasized[193] (the gates of the dream).

The gist of the adventure in the dream world is the fight with the three dragons and the rescue of the three princesses.

In the Greek version, the hero lifts a marble stone and sees a dark well under it. Hot steam rises from the well. He screams, "Fire! fire!" while passing through this region, but he had instructed his brothers not to pull him back. Besides, they refrain from pulling him up out of treachery in order to get rid of him.

Finally, he comes to a beautiful castle with a big garden. The whole castle seems uninhabited. He finds the princess and she tells him that she is the captive of the dragon and the dragon turns out to be the same demon he has wounded in the world above.

The princess says, "He is lying in that chamber, and if his eyes are open he is sleeping. If they are closed he is awake. At his head there is a bottle of water, at his feet another one; the two should be exchanged. There are many sabres who will say, "Take me!" Do not touch them, but take a rusty one in behind the door." He awakens the sleeping dragon and kills him.[194]

In the Russian story of the Norka, the prince finds an inscription on a white stone. "Then only will you overcome me when you enter here" (i.e., into the other world). The prince is lowered down by his brothers into the other world. He finally finds the Norka *sleeping in the middle of the sea,* and when he snores the water is agitated seven versts around. The prince kills the sleeping Norka.[195]

In a Bohemian story the events in the underworld take place as follows: "Thereupon the door flew open unexpectedly and into the room

189 Ortutay, *op. cit.,* p. 44.

190 Munkacsi, *Vogul Népköltési Gyüjtemény* (Thesaurus of Vogul Folklore), Budapest, 1896, p. 358.

191 Panzer, *op. cit.,* pp. 131–135.

192 *Ibid.,* p. 116.

193 *Ibid.,* p. 125.

194 von Hahn, J. G., *Griechische und albanesische Märchen,* Leipzig, 1864, II, p. 53.

195 Ralston, W. R. S., *Russian Folk Tales,* London, 1873, p. 76.

came the wizard, a bent old man in a long black garb with a bald head, a grey beard down to his knees, and three iron hoops instead of a girdle. By the hand he led a beautiful girl with a crown of pearls on her head, but she was pale and sad as if she had risen from the grave." The wizard said, "If you can keep her in sight for three nights so that she does not vanish from you, you can have her." But after a time the prince and his companions all began to nod, fell asleep and slept the whole night *just as if the wizard had thrown them into water.*[196]

The other world is sleep or the intrauterine situation. Why does the fight with the father imago take place in the other world? Because the falling down into the well or water is the *basic dream,* and the content of the dream itself is the oedipus complex.

But now let us see how our hero comes back from the other world.

There are complications about the ascent. The two companions or brothers who show treachery in letting him down repeat it in the ascent. He sends the three princesses up in the basket. The fourth time he is suspicious and puts a stone in the basket. They let it down with a crash.[197]

Son of a White Horse wandering disconsolately around in the other world finds little gryphons in a nest and covers them with his overcoat. The mother gryphon is full of gratitude. He asks her to bring him up to the world above. But she needs an enormous amount of supplies in flesh and bacon. They were just about to make it when all the supplies were gone. The hero perched on the gryphon's back, gives the animal first his arm, then his leg. When they arrive and the gryphon sees that he has neither arms nor legs, she gives him a magic bottle which restores everything.[198]

In the Greek story, he kills the snakes and rescues the young eagles. After the battle with the snake he is *sleeping,* exhausted. While he sleeps, the eagle mother wants to eat him. The young eagles tell her that he is the man who rescued them. As a reward he is carried up to the upper world. The same thing happens again. He has to feed the eagle with his own flesh which is then restored to him.[199]

In the Esthonian version, he shields the young eagles in a storm.[200] In the Tshuvash story, an old woman tells him that there is no water in the country because a snake is withholding it. He kills the snake, but an-

[196] Wratislaw, *Sixty Folk Tales from Exclusively Slavonic Sources,* London, 1889, p. 10.

[197] Ortutay, *op. cit.,* pp. 72, 73. On the treachery of the companions or brothers, cf. Panzer, *op. cit.,* pp. 173, 174.

[198] Arany, *op. cit.,* pp. 140, 141.

[199] von Hahn, *op. cit.,* II, p. 58.

[200] Kallas, O., "80 Märchen der Ljutziner Esten," *Verhandlungen der gelehrten estnischen Gesellschaft,* XX, 1900, p. 121.

other one threatens the little gryphons. He makes a wall of sods and sits in the nest himself with the young birds. The ascent to the upper world is as usual.[201]

If we now take the story as a whole, the maternal role of the bird is quite obvious. The hero sits among the young birds, rescues them and finally is carried by the mother bird. In this journey it is the oral element that is the most important. The child feeds the mother with its own flesh, the integrity of which is then restored. This is reality, only veiled by inversion. The mother feeds the child with its breast and the breast is still there.

In analyzing the dream myth and then the epic of Beowulf,[202] we find that only the episode of the masturbation dream with castration anxiety and an ejaculation in the dream preceded our basic dream, i.e., *the moment of falling asleep.* Is this a displacement? I hardly think so. The dreamer probably awakes after the ejaculation and then has another dream in which the moment of falling asleep appears as descent into the womb (well, nether world). What follows is the oedipal dream. Awakening, i.e., returning to this world, is then symbolized as oral; hunger ends the dream.

Addendum

I omitted the all too familiar reference to Freud who interpreted the Minoan labyrinth as the intestines.[203] This has been confirmed by the discovery of the Babylonian "Palace of Entrails."[204] In this case it is clear that the dreamer is in his own "male womb," awakening through the rectum and being both Theseus and Ariadne.

201 G. Mészáros, *Csuvas Népköltési Gyüjtemény,* Budapest, 1912, pp. 375–377.
202 Also the Esthonian Kalevipoeg.
203 Freud, S., *Gesammelte Werke.* London, 1940, XV, p. 26, *Neue Folge der Vorlesungen zur Einführung in die Psychoanalyse,* Wien, 1933, p. 35.
204 Weidner, F., "Zur babylonischen Eingeweideschau." *Orientalische Studien, Fritz Hommel zum 60 Geburtstag.* Vol. I, Leipzig, 1917.

V

THE SONG OF THE SIRENS AND THE ISLES OF THE BLESSED

XXX (Song)[1]

Weird women we! by dale and down
We dwell, afar from tower and town
We stem the flood, we ride the blast
On wandering knights our spell we cast;

While viewless minster touch the string
'Tis thus our charmed rhymes we sing
She sung, and still a harp unseen
Fill'd up the symphony between

XXXI (Song)

Soldier, rest! Thy warfare o'er
Sleep the sleep that knows not breaking
Dream of battled fields no more
Days of danger, nights of waking
In our isle's enchanted hall
Hands unseen thy couch are strewing
Fairy strains of music fall
Every sense in slumber dewing.

In the chapter on shamanism we have seen how frequently the activity of the shaman is identified with diving or canoeing. The other world from which they bring back the soul is beyond a river, or under the water or on an işland and the ecstasy of the shaman may be represented as flying, climbing or rowing. On the way back from the other world (cf. the Chapter The Way Back) the frontier between the supernaturals and reality is again set by water. The dead of Egypt arrived at the frontier of the land of the Hereafter at Gizeh. There were two paths, through land or through water. Either way the soul has to pass through a gate of fire. The land of the blessed is an island with water flowing around it. The dead get a canoe of clay in their graves. This is to take them over the water. The gods are nourished by the tree of life and the goddess Nut suckles the dead accepting him (or her) as her child. The two mothers,

---

[1] Sir Walter Scott, "The Lady of the Lake," Songs XXX and XXXI. *The Poetical Works of Sir Walter Scott*, edited by I. L. Robertson, London, 1926, pp. 215–216.

the vultures with long hair and swelling breasts, give him their breast, so that he lives again as a child. Some are carried over the water in the boat of the Sun, others are ferried over by an Egyptian Charon whose name means, "He who looks behind and turns his face." He ferries both the gods and the dead to the other shore.[2]

The sun passed through the Tuat, the world of darkness from sunset to sunrise. As the sun passed through the Tuat large numbers of souls made their way into his boat and they were renewed to life and light as the boat passed into the light of day.[3]

Beyond the water lies the field of peace, sometimes identified with Heaven, sometimes with a fertile region of the Earth, the Elysium of the Egyptians, *Sekhet Aaru* = Field of Reeds, is one of the names of this happy land. In the Papyrus of Nebseni this Land of the Hereafter is described as follows:

(1) Nebseni, the scribe and artist of the Temple of Ptah with his arms hanging by his sides entering the Elysian fields.

(2) Nebseni making an offering of incense to the "great company of the gods."

(3) Nebseni seated in a boat paddling; above the boats are three symbols for "city."

(4) Nebseni addressing a bearded mummied figure.

(5) Three pools or lakes.

(6) Nebseni reaping in Elysium.

(7) Nebseni grasping the Bennu bird,[4] in front are three Kau and three Khu (various reduplications of the soul).

(8) Nebseni seated and smelling a flower. The text says, "Thousands of all good and pure things to the Ka of Nebseni."

(9) A table of offerings.

(10) Four mythical pools or lakes.

(11) Nebseni ploughing with oxen by the side of a stream. The stream is one thousand measures in length, the width is beyond measure, there are neither fish nor worms in it.

(12) Nebseni ploughing with oxen on an island, "the length of which is the length of heaven."

(13) A division shaped like a bowl, in which is inscribed "the birth place of the god of the city of Kuenquentet Nebt."

(14) An island whereupon are four gods and a flight of steps. It says "the great company of the gods who are in Sakhet hetep."

(15) The boat Tchetetfet with eight oars, four at the bow and four

---

[2] Erman, A., *Die ägyptische Religion*, Berlin, 1909, pp. 109–110, 131.

[3] Wallis Budge, E. A., *The Gods of the Egyptians*, I, London, 1904, pp. 172–173.

[4] The Phoenix, symbol of rebirth of the rising sun. Wallis Budge, *op. cit.*, II, p. 96.

at the stern, floating at the end of a canal; in it is a flight of steps. The place is called The Domain of Neth.

(16) Two pools.

The papyrus of Ani is a variation of the same themes.[5]

The mood is one of repose and peace. "Beatus ille qui procul negotiis, paterna rura bobus exercet suis" (Ovid). The region is that of infancy or birth or rebirth, the passage is through water. Again we find the symbol of the ladder. It is noteworthy that the sky goddess Nut was identified with the coffin. The dead by being put into the coffin were put into the body of the goddess. The following inscription has been found on the lid of the coffin of Teti. "Nut, the shining one, the great one sayeth this is my son N.N. to whom I have given birth." Nut, the great vulture declares, "This is my beloved N.N., my son. I have given him the two horizons that he may grow powerful in them like Haruchte [the infant Horus]."[6] At the same time the dead are also having intercourse with the goddess.[7]

One would certainly incline to interpret the passage through the water as the passage into the womb since we find them as alternative forms of the other world. The passage in the boat of night is also self-explanatory in the light of the general thesis of this book.

According to the Malays of Sarawak the dead wanders first to a river named "Biraie tanggalan" which he crosses in a canoe. Then he climbs up a mountain, then there is another river and another mountain. Then he comes to the Valley of Tears, he meets several men and women and children to whom he gives clothes. After other obstacles he again comes to a river watched by a man named Tamai Patakloeng to whom he must give the barbules which grow round the mouth of a kind of fish. A woman is there, stamping rice, she tries to persuade him to stay there. He must avoid her and go on. There is a fire in the middle of the road. Having passed this there is another woman with ears so big that he might take shelter under them. He passes other stations and finally a very narrow road. Finally there is a river where he takes a bath.[8]

We assume that this is a series of dream images, though by no means the simple reproduction of an actual dream.

The Dayak believe that there is a borderland between this world and the next, the inhabitants of which can communicate either way.

5 Idem, Egyptian Ideas of the Future Life, London, 1900, pp. 176–183. Cf. idem, Gods, I, p. 437, Hathor and the dead.

6 Rusch, H., "Die Entwicklung der Himmelsgöttin Nut zu einer Totengottheit," Mitteilungen der vorderasiatischen Gesellschaft, XXVII, 1922, p. 13, cf. pp. 19, 28.

7 Ibid., pp. 38, 59.

8 Roth, H. L., The Natives of Sarawak and British North Borneo, London, 1896, I, pp. 220, 221.

A man called Kadawa was a great cock fighter. Having suffered several defeats he decided to go and fetch a mythical cock. Aided by this bird he could defeat all opponents. He arrived at the borderland in search of the bird and then he came to Hades. Among the dead he saw his own wife. He got his cock, sword and spear and rushed to join her. She repelled him but in vain. At length they came to a stygian lake and found a boat lying on the shore, he embarks in the boat with the ghosts. He wants to join his wife even if he has to stay dead. This can be done, she says, if he eats of their sugarcane. *He jumped out of the boat and as soon as his feet touched the rock, boat and people and lake vanished and he found himself standing at his own doorstep.*[9]

The dream character of this whole complex of other world beliefs could not be expressed any more clearly than this. If the ghost falls into the water when passing the bridge *it wakes up* and goes back home again.[10]

The Kayan shape their coffins somewhat like a boat. Figurines added to the coffin are supposed to row the boat to the Land of Souls.[11] They have also something like a Charon.[12]

The Ewe in Southern Togo also have a mountain and a river on the way to the other world. *Kauris* are put into the grave, part of this the ghost uses for food and part for toll money to the Ewe Charon. The shores of the river are fraught with great anxiety. Death sends the ferryman, named Kutsiame, to row them across. He is very cruel. He asks many questions (examination in dream!).[13] Human beings are preformed in the other world. The passage from the other world into this world is also replete with dangers and obstacles and the soul or embryo can only enter the mother when it has passed all these dangers.[14]

We assume that the two roads or rivers, viz., that of being born and that of dying, are identical. This all the more so as one of the Ewe tribes, the Ho, represents the journey into the other world as follows:

The dead comes to a woman who has a big wound. She asks him where he wants to go. He answers to the land of the dead. He also has to tell her what he did in this world. After this he licks her wound and then he can pass. Some say he also has to pass through a river.[15]

[9] *Ibid.*, I, p. 212.
[10] *Ibid.*
[11] Hose, C. and McDougall, W., *The Pagan Tribes of Borneo,* London, 1912, II, p. 34. Cf. Evans, I. H. N., "Folk Stories of the Tempassuk and Tuaran Districts," *Journ. Royal Anthr. Inst.,* 1913, p. 427.
[12] Hose and McDougall, *op. cit.,* II, p. 41.
[13] Spieth, I., *Die Religion der Eweer in Süd Togo,* Leipzig, 1911, p. 249.
[14] *Ibid.,* p. 228.
[15] *Idem, Die Ewe Stämme,* Berlin, 1906, p. 258.

In Melanesia the ghosts of Florida go to the Vanabo being conveyed there in the ship of the dead. On arrival there the door keeper asks them if they have come to stay or not. (This must refer to people who have fainted or to dreams). In San Cristoval and Ulawa the ghosts swim to the "Three Sisters" Islands where they are examined to see if their ears have been pierced and after a short stay there they swim to Malapa. According to the people of Bugotu the first person who died is the lord of the other world or Tulikagi. A pool called the "pool of quicksands" guards the entrance. A post is erected on each side of the pool and the ghosts cross by means of a tree laid on the two posts. There are two guardians of the other world, one for the male, one for the female ghosts. When the ghost arrives and calls the guardian appears and the ghost is asked, "Where are your credentials for asking for a light?" Then the ghost shows the frigate bird tatoo on hands and forehead. The iron-wood crossing is put down and the ghost passes to safety and life. But if the mark is missing, they put down the soft-wood crossing and the ghost falls into the pool and ends there.[16]

In Fiji we again find Charon combined with the "motive" of the "Exam" (dream of questioning, of examination).

On the road to Nai Thombo thombo (other world) there is a solitary hill. Here the spirit throws the spirit of a whale's tooth which was placed in the hands of the corpse at burial at a spiritual pandams, having succeeded in hitting this he ascends the hill and waits for the spirits of his strangled wives. If the ghost is a bachelor he has to avoid the Great Woman who is out to destroy him and a male spirit Nangganangga, the god of high tide. The spirit tries to arrive at low tide and hopes that a local spirit will ferry him to the other shore. Nangganangga sits by the fatal stone and he *laughs* at their vain efforts to escape. Do they think the tide will never flow again? And at high tide he destroys them.

The path of the husband leads straight forward. Like Aeneas he advances to the Fijian Charon (Nai Thombo Thombo) and club in hand boards the canoe which carries spirits to meet their examiner. The highway to Mbulu lies through Nambanggatai *which, it seems is at once a real and unreal town,* the visible part being occupied by ordinary mortals while in the unseen portion dwells the family who hold the inquest on departed spirits. All doorways are built opposite to each other because spirits can only proceed in a straight line. A demon who tries to kill souls opposes the spirit. The spirit, if he has the courage, raises his club in defiance. The questioning starts, "Who are you and where do you come

[16] Ivens, W., "The Diversity of Culture in Melanesia," *Journ. Roy. Anthr. Inst.,* LXIV, 1934, pp. 48, 49.

from?" the demon asks. If the spirit tries to boast and lie he is felled to the ground.

Those who escape the club of the soul destroyer walk on to Naindelinde, one of the highest peaks of the Kauvandra mountains. Here the path ends abruptly in a precipice the base of which is washed by a deep lake. Beyond the precipice projects a large steering oar in the keeping of an old man and his son who act under the command of the great god Ndengei or in the keeping of Ndengei himself. "These accost the coming spirit thus, "Under what circumstances do you come to us? How did you conduct yourself in the other world?" If the ghost is one of rank he answers:

"I am a great Chief. I lived as a Chief and my conduct was that of a Chief. I had great wealth, many wives and ruled over a powerful people. I have destroyed many towns and slain many in war." To this the reply is "Good, good. Take a seat on the broad part of this oar, and refresh yourself in the cool breeze." No sooner is he seated than they lift the handle of the oar which lies inland and he is thus thrown headlong into the deep waters below through which he passes to Murimuria (other world). Those who are specially favored by Ndengei are told not to sit on the oar but to sit near those who hold it and after a short repose are sent back to the place whence they came to be deified.[17]

According to the beliefs of the people of Buin a gigantic banyan tree grows on the road to the other world. The souls of people live on this tree in bird form. The birds sit on the leaves of the tree as long as a man is healthy, the leaves are green, if he gets sick they wilt. If the leaf falls from the tree a human being dies. But the leaf falls for a reason. The bird that contains the soul of a human being makes it fall. The soul of the sleeper visits the tree while the body is asleep. The guardian of the tree shows the soul the leaf, the soul wants to see whether it is in good condition. The soul that is the *ura* also visits the tree when a man is sick. *Ura* means reflection, dream, shadow. The *ura* flies like a bird but only those can see it who are about to die.

Three or four days after the mortuary rites are concluded the guardian of each human being starts on the journey to the other world accompanied by the soul. The soul wakes the keeper of the gate by knocking at the threshold and he hands him the string money that permits him to enter. When the gate has been opened there are two lakes, one to the right, one to the left. The one to the left is as black as the skin of a human being. The souls of those who have not died a violent death bathe in this lake and rid themselves of ashes, dirt and sickness. The red lake is for those who died a "bloody" death, i.e., they were killed in battle or fell from a

[17] Williams, T., *Fiji and the Fijians*, Vol. I, London, 1858, pp. 243–247.

tree (because this is regarded as due to sorcery). The chief of the other world is called Kugui. If somebody is about to die, Kugui makes a house for him in the world of the hereafter. If somebody sleeps a lot, he will die soon.[18]

In both these accounts of the journey to the other world the traces of their origin in dreams is quite clear. In the Fiji version we have the motive of an exam and we know that dreams about repeating classes or exams express doubts about potency. The dreamer who has had wives and killed people will manage to get into the Land of the Hereafter—that is, the libidinal and aggressive triumphs in the basic dream against anxiety as represented by the father imago. Father and son figure in the role of a Fijian Charon and combined with the quieter form of transition as represented by the boat gliding on the water we have the sudden fall of the basic dream—i.e., falling asleep.

In the Buin version we have two other characteristic dream traits. The chief makes a house for the soul who is about to arrive; *falling asleep means going into a house*. Then there are the two lakes, they correspond to the bodies of the two kinds of dead who go into them—another trait that is obviously derived from the dream.

Grotjahn reports a dream of a patient that is not very different from these other-world beliefs. The diagnosis is oral character neurosis and this is the dream:

I found myself on the grounds of a very elaborate estate, one of the big palaces of Europe—a swimming pool with a lake like sailboats and with coves and all kinds of things. I had the feeling of trespassing—as if I had sneaked in there to defecate. A man approached me rowing in a canoe or rowboat. I decided that I should leave before I was thrown out. I came to a staircase which was cleverly constructed so that it collapsed under your feet when you wanted to go down. In this way I came down and admired the construction. I met at the bottom of the stairs, in a kind of basement, the mistress of the estate. She said, "Yes, this construction is expensive." I told her how I admired her estate and she replied that she used to entertain 200 guests at a time with all her servants. The palace had 500 rooms of which she now occupies only one room. I thought, how interesting it would be to tell my wife about it. I put my coat around the woman to keep her warm. I thought it would be wonderful to get acquainted with her and all her friends. No sex thoughts entered my mind. She got away and returned later.

In the house there were some other people. She talked to a small man of slight build with a goatee, intelligent looking. He was supposed to be her adviser or guardian. He estimated the value of the house as close to $97,000.00; or that is the amount it would cost to redecorate the house.

18 Thurnwald, R., *Forschungen auf den Salomo Inseln und dem Bismarck Archipel*, Berlin, 1912, I, pp. 316–318.

There has been a tragedy. Her husband had died recently (or been murdered?).

Grotjahn explains the dream as follows: "It was remarkable that this vivid and pleasant dream was dreamed in a situation of depression and hypochondriacal fear of illness. In his associations the patient revealed his anxiety and depression after his return from a vacation which he grudgingly admitted had been 'the best vacation in all my life.' Now, however, a few days after his return he feared that he had an ulcer of the stomach, intestinal bleeding and possibly a carcinoma. The night before he had this dream he started to have sexual relations with his wife but did not finish because he was disgusted with her lack of response. He attempted it again during the night and in spite of her lack of interest, finished the act.

"The associations, the dreams and previous material could be used to give the patient an interpretation that his manifest dream content pictured a happy life after death. This regressive patient felt persecuted and unloved even by his own body. In the last analysis his death anxiety was an orally regressive wish to be born again, this time by a better mother and into a happier environment."[19]

The elaborate estate is the other world and as such is also identical with its mistress. "I shall tell my wife," i.e., I shall go back to my wife and wake up. "I am trespassing"—it is not time to die yet. Expensive estate—you have to give up life to get here. The old man with the goatee and the man who has been murdered = the oedipus complex.

He puts his own coat round the woman to keep her warm—we might say, of course he does this since the image of the woman is a regression in terms of time coinciding with an introversion in space and the fantasied mother is also his own body. The sensation of falling (staircase = coitus) and the water with the boats characterize the state of sleep.

Aristophanes was the first to mention the Greek custom of inserting two *obols* into the mouth of the dead. This was to pay Charon, the ferryman of the underworld (Aristophanes, Ran 139, 270). Rohde explains the rite as a survival of an earlier custom—that whatever the dead owned was to be buried with him. By inserting two *obols* in his mouth, the property was symbolically bought by the survivors.[20]

B. Schmidt tells us that although Charon in modern Greece appears mostly as Death personified and usually on horseback, we also find the

---

[19] Grotjahn, M., "About the Representation of Death in the Art of Antiquity and in the Unconscious of Modern Men," *Psychoanalysis and Culture,* New York, 1951, p. 419.

[20] Rohde, E., *Psyche, Seelencult und Unsterblichkeitsglaube der Griechen,* 4th Edition, Tübingen, 1900, I, pp. 306, 307.

belief in the ferryman of the underworld and in the toll which is his due for the voyage.

According to a book written by Protodikos and published in Athens in 1860 (Περιτης παρ 'Νμιν Ταφης) the Greeks in Asia Minor inserted a Περατικιον, i.e., toll money into the mouth of the dead person for Charon. In Mariais (Zakynthos) a *gasta* (Venetian copper coin) was put into the corpse's mouth and a key into his or her bosom. The key was to open the gates of paradise. Schmidt reports that in his time, in another village of Zakynthos, the coin was put into the bosom of the dead with a key and an old comb, "so he could comb himself properly." At Arachoba on the Parnasos the money inserted into the mouth of the dead is not for a ferryman, but is for toll money on a bridge and, as Schmidt suggests, this must be due to Turkish influence.[21] In Thrace, a coin was put into the mouth of the dead to give to the angel as a fare for carrying it across a legendary bridge of hair, a wicked soul would fall off into the Danube. Dawson comments on the significant fact that often it is not a coin that is put into the mouth of the dead but a potsherd with the *pentalpha* scratched on it.[22] In Macedonia the duty of *closing the eyes and mouth of the deceased* devolves upon the nearest relatives. In some districts, Charon's penny is still put under the tongue or in the lap of the deceased.[23]

In Rumania, there were several variations of the custom. Rumanians in Transylvania put bread and money in the coffin.[24] In the Hungarian county of Szilágy, the Rumanians put a silver coin under the tongue of the dead to pay the ferryman of the river that separates this world from the next.[25] In the Retyezát (mountains in Transylvania), two pennies are used to keep each eyelid closed, and one penny is put under the dead man's tongue "for Charon."[26] At Nagyszeben, a wax candle is put into the hands of the dead, so that he can light it on the bridge to heaven. Then money is put into his hand for the ferryman who rows him over the waters of death.[27]

In Rumania proper, a wax candle and money are put into the hands

21 Schmidt, B., *Das Volksleben der Neugriechen,* Leipzig, 1871, I, pp. 236–240.
22 Dawkins, R. M., "Soul and Body in the Folklore of Modern Greece," *Folk Lore,* LIII, 1942, pp. 139, 142.
23 Abbott, G. F., *Macedonian Folklore,* Cambridge, 1903, p. 193.
24 Matuska, L., "Román babonák" (Rumanian Superstitions), *Ethnographia,* X, 1899, p. 299.
25 Petri, M., *Szilágy vármegye monographiaja* (Monograph of County Szilagy), I, p. 203.
26 Téglas, G., *A Retyezát vidéke* (The Retyezát country), Földrajzi Közleméneyek (Geographic Publications), XVI, 1896, p. 466.
27 Pacala, V., "Nagyszeben vidéki resinárok" (The Resinar people near Nagyszeben), *Földrajzi Közleméneyek,* XXXIII, 1913, p. 319.

of the dead. The money is for the ferryman or for the customs at the frontier of the other world.[28] There are innumerable obstacles between this world and the next. Therefore, towels and pieces of cloth are put into the coffin. These are called "bridges," and they become bridges in the other world which take the dead over every threshold, ditch or bridge.[29] Another purpose of the money is that other dead persons should not resent the newcomer; he is paying for his quarters.[30]

The most dreaded obstacle is at the gates of paradise. The dead person has to cross a bridge not thicker than a nail and not broader than a knife. There is a bottomless lake with dragons and serpents under the bridge. A cat attacks the soul as it is crossing the bridge and tries to push it off, a dog comes to the rescue. With the money, the dead man can hire a person to chase the cat.[31] Another way to overcome difficulty in obtaining entrance to the other world is by sacrificing a hen. The hen will then open the way for the souls as if they were her chicks.[32] At the last minute, someone must close the eyes of the dead and tie his jaws with a handkerchief. The worst curse is "May there be nobody to close your eyes."[33] If the dead person opens his eyes, it means great famine in the house, or it means that he slept too much during his lifetime. It is also assumed that another death will occur soon in the family. If only one eye is open, it is said that the closed eye sees the path to the other world, the open one is looking around in the house for someone it could take along. If the mouth is open, this means that the dead man wants to say something, to ask the survivors for forgiveness or to ask for alms.[34] At Naszód a little honeycake is inserted between the three fingers which, during a person's lifetime, hold the cross, also a small cross with a copper, silver or gold coin attached to it for the ferryman who rows him over to the other world. In Bánát, the dead person receives nine pennies, there are nine gates where he has to pay toll. A piece of wood is put into the coffin, and the coin is inserted into this piece of wood. The survivors are very careful to cover eyes, ears and mouth to prevent the dead from haunting the living. For the same purpose, the midwife would also stick something through the dead man's skull.[35] If an infant dies, mother's milk is put into the coffin; if a baby dies who has

---

28 Flachs, R., *Rumänische Hochzeits- und Totengebräuche*, Berlin, 1899, p. 47.
29 *Ibid.*, pp. 58, 59.
30 *Ibid.*, p. 60.
31 *Loc. cit.*
32 Moldován, G., "A szárnyasok a román nép eszmevilágában" (Poultry in Rumanian Folklore), *Erdélyi Muzeum Egylet* (Museum Association of Transylvania), Budapest, 1888, p. 293.
33 *Idem, A magyaroszági románok* (Rumanians in Hungary), Budapest, 1913, p. 185.
34 *Ibid.*, p. 187.
35 *Ibid.*, p. 188.

already been weaned, rolls or pancakes. If it is a mother, as many dolls are put into the grave as there are surviving children.[36] Furtwängler shows that Charon must have been part of ancient Greek folklore since remote times, and the fact that he is not connected with the Olympians is no proof against his antiquity. The problem in all these representations seems to be that of *transition*, the boat is too small for all the ghosts, some have to wait, and those who have not been buried regularly cannot pass.[37] Everywhere, from Pausanias to Dante, Charon is an old man—sometimes an object of fear. The Charon of the Etruscans has a long nose, or a beak, or feet and wings like the spurs of a cock, and a winding serpent in his hands.[38]

This takes us back to the scene itself, as described in the Aeneid. Aeneas is on his way to the underworld to visit his father Anchises. His reception by Charon is anything but friendly:

> Quisquis es, armatus qui nostra ad litora tendis
> Fare age, quid venias, iam istinc et comprime gressum
> *(Aeneis,* VI, pp. 388, 389.)

He compares the visit of Aeneas to that of Theseus and Pirithous, the one who chained the dog, Kerberos[39] and the other who tried to steal the wife of Hades himself. Sybilla, who patronizes Aeneas in his journey to the other world, disclaims any such intention of her protegée.

> Troius Aeneas, pietate insignis et armis
> Ad genitorem imas erebi descendit ad undas
> Si te nulla movet tantae pietatis imago
> Ac ramum hunc adgnoscas
> *(Aeneis,* VI, pp. 403, 405.)

And she shows him the mistletoe. Luckily for Aeneas, Charon has not read Frazer's "Golden Bough"; otherwise, he could hardly have regarded the *fatale ramum* as proof of the piety of our hero. "Within the sanctuary at Nemi, grew a certain tree of which no branch might be broken. Only a runaway slave was allowed, if he could, to break off one of its boughs. Success in the attempt entitled him to fight the priest in single combat;

---

36 *Ibid.,* p. 198.

37 Furtwängler, A., "Charon," *Archiv für Religionswissenschaft,* VIII, 1905, pp. 191–202.

38 Landau, M., *Hölle und Fegefeuer in Volksglaube, Dichtung und Kirchenlehre,* Heidelberg, 1909, pp. 46–54.

39 Cf., on the oral meaning of the obolos, a parallel to the obolos for Charon is the honeycake for Kerberos. Rohde, E., *Psyche,* Fourth edition, Tübingen, 1907, I, p. 305. "The Etruscan Hades wears a wolf's skin, or a bear's head," Carpenter, R., *Folk Tale, Fiction and Saga in the Homeric Epics,* 1946, p. 134. Cf. also de Ruyt, F., "Le Thanatos d'Euripide, et le Charun etrusque," *L'Antiquite Classique,* I, 1932, p. 71 (I owe this reference to Prof. K. Marót).

and if he slew him, he reigned in his stead with the title of King of the
Wood (*Rex Nemorensis*). According to the public opinion of the ancients,
the fateful branch was that Golden Bough which at the Sybil's bidding
Aeneas plucked before he essayed the perilous journey to the world of the
dead.[40] We know, of course, that the successor was "the priest who slew
the slayer and shall himself be slain," i.e., that he was liable to be challenged and killed his predecessor. Since the king is obviously the father,
the ritual king-killing is parricide. But what is the symbolic meaning of
this specific "king," the *Rex Nemorensis?* As he is the guardian of the
sanctuary of *Diana Nemorensis,* his nature can probably be inferred from
that of the goddess. Her function was to grant expectant mothers easy
delivery. Models of the organs of generation, both male and female, have
been found in her sanctuary, as well as those of couples seated side by side
and those of pregnant women. Frazer has collected a few parallels to Pliny's
report on the Druids in which a decoction made of mistletoe is supposed
to make barren animals bring forth young.[41] This is supposed to be a
master key to open all locks, and it also functions as divining rod.[42] The
phallic significance of the golden bough or mistletoe is therefore pretty
obvious,[43] and the meaning of the ritual at Nemi would be that *the priest
of the goddess of generation is challenged to fight by a symbolic castration
threat.* The angry retort of Charon, therefore, seems like the last rudiment
of a fight, the gesture of the Sybilla (the mother, or Diana) proclaims
Aeneas as the challenger. And Charon is the "Father Imago" from whom
Aeneas must obtain the images of the future (Anchises), i.e., whom he must
vanquish in order to succeed in his mission. The other world can be the
other shore of a river or an island.

Procopius describes the island other world off the coast of Brittany.
They say that the souls of men who die are always conveyed to this place.
The men say that the conduct of the souls is laid upon them in turn.
And at a late hour of the night they are conscious of a knocking at
their doors. They hear a voice calling them.[44] They rise from their beds,
and walk to the shore not knowing why they do it but doing it nevertheless.
There they find skiffs in readiness. They are not their own boats but of a

---

[40] Frazer, I. G., *The Magic Art,* London, 1911, I, p. 11.

[41] Frazer, *ibid.,* I, p. 171, pp. 1–12, quoting *Bulletins dell' Inst. di Corrisp. Archeo-
logica,* 1885, p. 183; *Notizie degli Scavi,* 1885, pp. 160, 254. *Idem,* 1895, p. 424; Rossbach,
A., *In Verhandlungen der vierzigsten Versammlung deutscher Philologen und Schul-
männer in Görlitz,* Leipzig 1890, p. 160; Wallis, G. H., *Illustrated Catalogue of Classical
Antiquities from the Site of the Temple of Diana, Nemi, Italy,* 1893, pp. 4, 15, 17.

[42] Frazer, *Balder the Beautiful,* II, pp. 77, 78, 79.

[43] Kuhn, A., *Die Herabkunft des Feuers und des Göttertranks,* Gütersloh, 1886,
p. 206.

[44] Abbreviated.

different kind. They embark and start rowing. They see no one, but they are aware of passengers. After an hour's rowing they arrive at Brittia. The same trip would take them a night and a day in their own boats. They do not see anybody in the boat but they hear a voice from the island announcing the names of the passengers to those who take them in charge.[45]

The dreamlike character of this narrative is supported by further evidence. At Noirmontier a mysterious empty ship is seen and a voice heard "Embark, embark! We are going to Galloway." At Morbian the spirits called Bolbiguanclet force travelers to enter their black barge. When it is full it disappears as rapidly as an arrow to an unknown island. The souls arrive at their destination, and the human being who has been rowing the boat, finds next morning that he is back on the earth, asleep.[46] "This is the story of the voyage of Bran, son of Febal. T'was fifty quatrains the woman from unknown lands sang on the floor of the house to Bran, son of Febal when the royal house was full of kings *who knew not whence the woman had come* [*my italics*], since the ramparts were closed.

"One day in the neighborhood of his stronghold Bran went about alone and he heard music behind him. At last he *fell asleep* at the music, such was its sweetness. When he awoke from his sleep he saw close beside him a branch of silver with white blossoms." Going home with a branch in his hand he finds a woman in strange raiment. She sang:

> A branch of the apple tree from Emain
> I bring like those one knows
> Twigs of white silver are on it
> Crystal brows with blossoms
> There is a distant isle
> Around which sea horses glisten
> A fair course around the white swelling surge
> Four feet uphold it, etc.

He embarks to find this Happy Other World. After a journey of two days he sees Mannanan Mac Ler, the god, approaching. Mannanan says:

> What is a clear sea
> For the trowed skiff in which Bran is
> That is a happy plain (Mag Mell)
> With a profession of flowers
> To me from the Chariot of two wheels
> Speckled salmon leap from the womb
> Of the white sea, on which thou lookest
> They are calves, they are coloured lambs,
> With friendliness, without mutual slaughter.

[45] Procopius, *History of the Wars,* VIII, XX, pp. 48–56, "The Gothic War," IV, p. 20; Patch, *The Other World,* New York, 1950, p. 28.
[46] Sebillot, P., *Le Folk-Lore de France,* Paris, 1905, II, pp. 148, 149.

Finally they reach the Land of Women. The chief of the women invited him to land, but he is afraid. She threw a ball of thread, his hand clave to the ball and she pulled him ashore in his coracle. They went into a large house where there was a bed for every couple. The food that was put on every dish did not diminish. When they came back to Ireland, Bran collapsed like a heap of ashes, for many hundred years had elapsed since they left home.[47]

We do not assume that these stories in their elaborate form are based on dreams really dreamed. But at the beginning we find sleep or dream mentioned. The hero who *awakes* has now really started to tell his dream in which we find the crossing of water, the Land of Women, the inexhaustible food as the backbone of the plot. Anxiety is represented by his reluctance to land, coitus by the "stuck together" motive. The first narrative must once have been a dream about crossing the waters to be received by the Queen of the Other World. In the Voyage of Maelduin a maiden comes to meet them, brings them on land and gives them food and also liquor. They drink out of a little vessel and they sleep three days and three nights. When they awake they are at sea, island and maiden have vanished. The next island has a fortress with a brazen door and a bridge of glass. A woman comes out of the fortress, pail in hand to get water, "housekeeper for Maelduin," his friends say. When they strike the brazen door it makes a sweet music and sends them to sleep till tomorrow. Three days and three nights they sleep.

"On the fourth day she comes, beautiful verily, wearing a white mantle with a circlet of gold round her hair, a brooch of silver with studs of gold in her mantle and a film silken smock next to her white skin." She refuses to go to bed with Maelduin. When they awake they are in their boat on a crag, island, fortress and lady have all disappeared.[48] In the Morte Arthur the motive is inverted, "And when they were at the water side even fast by the bank hoved a little barge with many fair ladies in it and among them all was a queen and they all had black hoods and all wept and shrieked when they saw King Arthur." And Arthur says, "For I will unto the vale of Avilion to heal me of my grievous wound."[49]

On a more primitive level we have the Murngin of Arnhem land whose souls emerge from the totemic pool or well and return to the same. "The most unifying concept in the whole of clan ideology is that of the sacred waterhole in which reposes the spiritual unity of clan life. It is the fundamental symbol of clan solidarity. From it come all the eternal quali-

[47] Meyer, K. and Nutt, A., *The Voyage of Bran, Son of Febal,* London, 1895, I, pp. 2–4.

[48] *Ibid.,* pp. 165, 166.

[49] Malory, *Le Morte D'Arthur,* 1912, II, Chapter V, p. 389.

ties and to it those qualities return when they have been lived or used by members of the clan."[50] The aim of the mortuary song is to make the soul such a perfect character that he will find his ancestors and go straight to his totem well.[51] According to the beliefs of the Western Aranda the place of the ghosts is an island far north in the ocean. Trees are peculiar in this ghost land, they grow in semicircles so that their branches touch the earth. Everything is white; trees, birds, animals and the ghosts themselves. The ghosts dance at night and sleep during the daytime (i.e., they dance when people dream about them).[52] In some of the myths I have collected, the heroes of the "Dream Time" go back to the ocean whence they come instead of sinking into the totemic caves.

In ancient Greece Elysium corresponds to the Isle of the Blessed. The inhabitants of Elysium are not dead.

"But for thyself Menelaus, fostered of Zeus, it is not ordained that thou shouldst die and meet thy fate in horse pasturing Argos, but of the Elysian plains, and the bounds of the earth will the immortals convey thee where dwells fair haired Rhadamanthys thus and where life is easiest for men. No snow is there, nor heavy storm, nor even rain, but ever does Ocean send up blasts of the shrill-blowing West Wind that they may give cooling to men; for thou hast Helen to wife and art in their eyes the husband of the daughter of Zeus" (Odyssey, IV, 560–569, p. 149).

This is said, sorely against his will by Proteus, the Old Man of the Sea.

But how can he be made to speak? This is revealed to Menelaus by Eidothea, the daughter of Proteus. "When the sun hath reached mid-heaven, the unerring old man of the sea is wont to come forth from the brine, at the breath of the West Wind, hidden by the dark ripple. And when he is come forth he lies down to sleep in the hollow caves, and around him the seals, the brood of the fair daughters of the sea. Thither will I lead thee at break of day and lay you all in a row. Now, as soon as you see him laid to rest hereafter let your hearts be filled with strength and courage and do you hold him there despite his striving and struggling to escape" (Odyssey IV, 400–422, p. 137). Proteus turns himself into a lion, a serpent, a leopard, a huge boar, flowing water and a leafy tree (Odyssey IV, 456–460, p. 141). But finally he speaks. The Protean transformation and the struggle are one of the motives claimed by Laistner for the nightmare theme. Elysion, the Island of the Blessed is really a second Olympos for demi-gods who once were mortal. Hesiod, after describing death as the end of all human beings, says:

[50] Warner, W. Lloyd, *A Black Civilization*, New York, 1937, p. 19.
[51] *Ibid.*, p. 414.
[52] Strehlow, C., *Die Aranda und Loritjastaemme*, I, p. 15.

"But to the others father Zeus, the son of Cronos, gave a living and an abode apart from men and made them dwell at the ends of the earth. And they lived untouched by sorrow in the lands of the blessed along the shore of deep swirling Ocean, happy heroes for whom the grain-giving earth bears honey, sweet fruit flourishing thrice a year, far from the deathless gods for Cronos rules over them; for the father of men and gods released him from his bonds. And these last equally have honor and glory" (Hesiod, *Works and Days*, 166 sq., translation by Hugh G. Evelyn-White, Hesiod, I, p. 15, Harvard University Press). Elysium where there is no snow, no storm, no rain (Odyssey IV, pp. 565, 566) is in a sense a parallel to Olympos, the abode of the gods, that is not shaken by winds or rain or snow (Odyssey VI, pp. 44, 45). The mortals who are conveyed there by the gods are not dead like those in Hades, they are there with their bodies and live in this land of undisturbed bliss.[53] Telogonos, son of Odysseus by Kirke unwittingly killed his father. Kirke reanimates them all and on the isle of Aea, Penelope lives, is wedded to Telogonos, and Kirke herself to Telemachos[54]—a very thinly veiled representation of oedipal wish fulfillment, especially as all reference to Odysseus is omitted. Heroes and heroines live there more than human yet less than divine as eternal glorified images of themselves.[55] The Land of the Phaeacians is another kind of Elysium. While Odysseus is swimming among the breakers, pursued by the wrath of Poseidon, Athene comes to the rescue.

"But Athene, daughter of Zeus, took other counsel. She stayed the paths of the other winds and bade them all cease and be lulled to rest but she roused the swift North Wind and broke the waves before him, to the end that Zeus born Odysseus might come among the Phaeacians *lovers of the oar escaping from death and the fates*" (Odyssey V, pp. 382–387).

Again we find a people on the borderline between mortals and immortals, a race of divine ferrymen on an island. And how does Odysseus arrive at this place, and may we ask also, how does he leave it?

And as a man hides a brand beneath the dark embers in an outlying farm, a man who has no neighbors, and so saves a seed of fire, that he may not have to kindle it from other source, so Odysseus covered himself with leaves. And Athene shed sleep upon his eyes that it might enfold his lids and speedily free him from toilsome weariness (Odyssey V, pp. 488–493). He is conveyed back by the Phaecian oarsmen asleep on their boat *"and he awoke out of his sleep in his native land"* (Odyssey XIII, pp. 187, 188). And the divine Nausikaa? She was but a dream. But the images of this

53 Rohde, *op. cit.*, I, p. 70.
54 *Ibid.*, pp. 87, 88.
55 Capelle, P., "Elysium und Inseln der Seligen," *Archiv für Religionswissenschaft*, XXV, pp. 245–265 and XXXI, pp. 17–40.

dream world are not always so free of anxiety. They may be alluring but dangerous.

The Wikmunkan say that the ghost girls come up out of the water and sit on the logs of the lagoon sunning themselves. They play in the water and sing. There is a big lagoon in which the male ghosts live and a smaller one for the female ghosts.[56]

The male water spirits of the Kiwai have large genitalia, the women wear no petticoats. A drum is hidden at the bottom of one of their lakes.[57] An Eskimo shaman told Thalbitzer, "No singing is so lovely as the singing of the spirits."[58] The far-famed Mousai of Greek mythology are spirits of the water.[59] In Wales we are told about a whirlpool frequented by a lovely lady who lured youths attracted by her beauty into a whirlpool where they perished.[60]

The Vends believe that if little children look into the well the Nix sings and hums something. It sticks its big head out of the water. The children are so enchanted by the song that they too start to sing. Then they fall asleep, whereupon the water spirit drags them to the bottom of the well. There it lives in a beautiful palace.[61]

Water spirits have a predilection for singing. Hungarians at Szigetvár talk about sea maidens whose upper halves are like girls, the lower like fishes. All songs come from them, and their song brings or magically influences the future.[62] The Ukrainians have practically the same belief. The ladies of the sea are girls with fishtails. In fine weather they come out of the sea and sing. Men listen to them and write the songs in books; that is why there are so many songs. Who on earth could invent so many songs if they were not aided by the sea-ladies?[63] The White Russians say that all songs come from the Ludzie Morskie, the people of the sea.

The "water queens" swim on the surface of the water, and what they sing is the origin of all songs.[64] Slovak coachmen passing the river Garam hear an irresistible song; the fairies of the river are singing and luring

56 McConnell, U., "The Wik Munkan Tribe," Oceania, I, 1930, pp. 198, 199.

57 Landtman, G., The Kiwai Papuans of British New Guinea, London, 1927, p. 307.

58 Thalbitzer, W., "The Heathen Priests of East Greenland," Verhandlungen des XVI. Int. Amerikanisten Kongresses, Wien, 1910, p. II, 463.

59 Roscher's Lexikon.

60 Trevelyan, Folk Lore and Folk Stories of Wales, London, 1909, p. 9.

61 Veckenstadt, E., Wendische Sagen, Märchen und abergläubische Gebraeuche, Graz, Leuschner und Lubensky, 1880, p. 185.

62 Mátyás, L., "A szigetvári néphitböl" (Folk Beliefs of Szigetvar), Ethnographia, V, 336, 1894. Kiéneklik a jövendöt ("they sing the future out").

63 Hnatjuk, V., Znadobi do Halicko Ruskoji Demonologii, Lemberg, 1901, II, p. 197.

64 Federovski, Lud bialoruski na Rusi Litevskiej, I, 1897, pp. 108–09.

them to their deaths.[65] At Teplitz, the water spirit is seated on the shore of the lake. He is sewing, mending his clothes and shoes. At the same time he sings:

> I sew, I sew my shoes
> For land and water
> Light moon, light
> My thread, may it sew
> Thursday today, Friday tomorrow
> I sew, I sew a little coat.
> At Zlivice he sings: Give light, I'll light for you
> Too if you help me sew my boots.[66]

In Silesia, at Zittau, the beautiful song becomes a noise. The waterman's cloak consists of little patches. He keeps counting these in the moonlight and clapping his hands and slapping his legs. Inquisitive persons are attracted by this noise and they try to interrupt him by doing what he does, counting and clapping their hands. If they do this he plunges into the water. Then people hear this counting and clapping every night. He keeps at it until they are so angry that they do the same thing themselves. Then they hear a loud laugh and the nightly visitation ceases.[67]

The male water spirits of the Russians are also given to singing and to combing their hair.[68] Fisherfolk are reluctant to use torches at night or to dip their nets very deep lest they disturb the *sleeping* water spirits who might then take revenge by capsizing the boat. Their hoarse laughter is a very characteristic feature.[69] The Slovenian water spirit is a huge old man who emerges from the water on moonlight nights and makes a noise splashing around. In his rage he may raise a storm that shakes the crowns of the trees. If a river or creek is dry, it is because the *vodnik* is marrying. He drinks too much at the wedding and when he gets drunk he plays around till he splashes all the water out of the lake, breaks the dam, or destroys the bridge.[70]

Modern Greek Nereids are famous for the beauty of their song. If a girl is famous for her singing it is said that she sings like a Nereid.[71] Their irresistible love of dance music and song is a feature which they have in common with all water spirits. In a story found at Euboa a Nereid dances until she collapses. At night in particular do they visit the barn, dancing

---

[65] Benkóczy, E., "Garammenti mondák" (Legends of the Garam), *Ethnographia,* 1908, p. 165.

[66] Kostal, "Vodnik v. Podani lidu ceskeho" (Water beings in Czech folk beliefs), *Cesky Lid.,* I, 1901, pp. 247–248.

[67] Kuehnau, R., *Schlesische Sagen,* 1911, II, pp. 215, 216.

[68] Ralston, W. R. S., *The Songs of the Russian People,* London, 1872, p. 153.

[69] Zvonkov, *Ethnograficeskoje Obozrjenie,* Moscow, 1889, pp. 72–75.

[70] Machal, L., *Bajeslove Slovanske* (Slavic Mythology), Prague, 1907, p. 107.

[71] Schmidt, B., *Das Volksleben der Neugriechen,* Leipzig, 1871, p. 106.

and singing. At the millpond at Lerna, the Nereid appears in daytime. She has green hair with pearls and corals in it, and she is drying her linen. At night, Nereids dance on the sea. Like Pan, the devil nowadays plays the violin for them when they dance. Sometimes it is a human shepherd who plays. In Crete a man says that he sees them at night and they ask him to play the lyre and sing.[72]

Perhaps the most outstanding feature of German water spirits is their irresistible song. In Mecklenburg the water-mothers (*Watermome*) sing on moonlight nights at midnight. They come out of the lakes. Their song is so beautiful and irresistible that anyone hearing it must go in the direction of the song and thus get *drowned in the lake*.[73]

In Oldenburg the sea women are very beautiful; they have lovely long hair and lovely full breasts. Their song is supremely beautiful. They sing, they look and they call the fisherman who cannot resist the lure of their eyes.[74]

A place on the river Main is called Hulda's bathing place. An old man tells the story of how *he fell asleep at noon*. He heard some splashing, and, when he looked, he saw three women with long golden locks of marvelous beauty. They were covered by the water up to their waists. He tried to go nearer but a twig cracked under him—and lo and behold, they had disappeared,[75] i.e., he was awake.

At Nidden the story is told about a girl who comes out of the water and by her beautiful song she entices the wanderer to swim to her island. But when he tries to do this he drowns in the sea.[76] Water or the water spirits pull those in who get drowned. A water spirit went to the butcher in Zittau. While chopping the meat for her he happened to chop her finger off. "I shall be revenged for that," she said. Many months later he had to cross a ditch and there was just a little water in it. She grabbed him, dove with him and he was drowned.[77] The next story tells us that the pull of the water-beings is a dream. At Striegau a woman fell asleep at noon near a little lake. She felt that something was dragging her down into the lake.

[72] *Ibid.*, pp. 107–111.

[73] Bartsch, K., *Sagen, Märchen und Gebräuche aus Mecklenburg*, Wien, 1879, I, p. 394.

[74] Strackerjan, L., *Aberglaube und Sagen aus dem Herzogtum Oldenburg*, Oldenburg, 1909, I, p. 514.

[75] Fries, A., "Sagen aus Unterfranken," *Zeitschrift für deutsche Mythologie und Sittenkunde*, 1853, I, p. 25.

[76] Tettau und Temme, *Die Volkssagen Ostpreussens, Litauens und Westpreussens*, Berlin, p. 172; H. Bertsch, *Weltanschauung, Volkssage und Volksbrauch*, Dortmund, 1910, p. 132.

[77] Kühnau, R., "Schlesische Sagen II," *Elben, Dämonen und Teufelssagen*, Leipzig, 1911, p. 219, cf. p. 224.

She struggled hard and managed to save her life.[78] A girl in Frankenstein saw a little grey woman carrying a heavy parcel on her back. The woman said, "I have far to go," and suddenly with a shrill laughter she dove her head foremost into the lake.[79] The dream starts as a nightmare (the heavy parcel) and ends with the basic dream. An invisible rope (umbilical cord) pulls little children down into the water.[80] In France we still hear about the water fairy, the Mari Morgan who seduces young men and they disappear under the water and are never seen again.[81]

"Then Sir Bedivere departed and went to the sword and lightly took it up and went to the water side, and there he bound the girdle about the hilts and then he threw the sword as far into the water as he might and there came an arm and a hand above the water and met it and caught it and so shook it thrice and brandished and then vanished away the hand with the sword in the water.

"And when they were at the water side even fast by the bank hoved a little barge with many fair ladies in it and among them all was a queen and they all had hoods and they all went and shrieked when they saw King Arthur. Now put me into the barge, said the king. And so he did softly, and there received him three queens with great mourning and so they set them down *and in one of their laps King Arthur put his* head. And then that queen said: Ah dear brother, why have you tarried so long from me?"[82]

The dream is a nightmare or a dream about the primal scene. It ends with the descent into the water, return to the womb (lap of sister), the basic dream. Since we regard the basic dream as symbolizing the moment of falling asleep it should be the beginning, not the end. In other cases that is true. But we must consider that dreaming in a sense is staying half awake and then we understand the technique of dream images (castration, nightmare, coitus, etc.) that delay the moment of falling asleep, i.e., dying.

In a story from Carinthia a young man falls asleep and then hears the song of the beautiful water spirits.[83] A fisherman and his wife went out in a boat on the lake. While the boat was being rocked by the waves they started to make love. One of the water-elves approached and beheld the scene with amazement and curiosity. The following night the fisherman was alone in his boat. He heard a marvelous song, he listened with

[78] *Ibid.*, II, p. 230.
[79] *Ibid.*, II, pp. 232, 233.
[80] *Ibid.*, II, p. 247.
[81] Sebillot, *op. cit.*, p. 35.
[82] Malory, T., *Le Morte d'Arthur,* Book XXI, Chapter V, Everyman's Library, Vol. VI, p. 389.
[83] Graber, G., *Sagen aus Kärnten,* Leipzig, 1914, p. 5.

breathless attention. A beautiful woman emerged from the water and they made love.[84]

The Rumanian "jele" are nine beautiful girls who dance and sing in the air on moonlight nights. A shepherd leads them and after being with them for nine years they give him a flute, the tunes of which are irresistible.[85] The water spirits of the gypsies dance on moonlight nights. They can be wooed and may become good wives if deprived of their red shoes[86] (phallic symbols).

Fairies are not quite water spirits, but they have many features in common with their mermaid sisters. And fairy music is certainly a characteristic feature of fairyland. This is from the story of a woman in Glamorganshire who is trying to get her child back from fairyland.

"At last she began to hear the sweet sound of music approaching from afar nearer and nearer, and the sweet sound continued to come and she listened to it with rapt attention. Ere long it was close at hand and she perceived that it was a procession of the *Bendith y Mamau* going somewhere or other."[87] Among them she sees her own child. The fairy who takes Condla in her boat of glass to the island realm of the Everliving (other world) sings in praise of that country.[88] In the other-world journey of Maelduin, after the apparition of the fairy queen, a sweet and soothing music is heard which sends them to sleep till the morrow.[89] The concept of the other world is regularly associated with music in Irish lore. Mider, wooing Etain to leave her mortal husband and join him in the other world, sings: "Woman of the white skin, wilt thou come with me to the wonderland where reigns sweet blended song, there primrose blossoms on the hair, snowfair the bodies from top to toe."[90]

Music, dancing at night and fairies go together in Wales. The fairies dance and sing in their rings.[91]

It is the same in Scotland: "Angus Mor was a shepherd on a farm near Tomnahurich, in Inverness. On a wet misty evening, he was returning from compassing the hill, he thought he heard coming out of a rock beside the path on which he was traveling—a voice like that of a young maiden whom he was going to marry that very night." He peeps into the

84 *Ibid.*, p. 1.
85 Moldován, *A magyarországi románok* (Rumanians in Hungary), Budapest, 1913, p. 326.
86 von Wlislocki, H., *Volksglaube und religiöser Brauch der Zigeuner*, Muenster i. W., 1891, p. 32.
87 Rhys, J., *Celtic Folklore, Welsh and Manx*, London, 1901, I, pp. 265, 266.
88 *Ibid.*, II, p. 667. Meyer and Nutt, *op. cit.*, I, p. 190.
89 *Ibid.*, I, p. 165.
90 *Ibid.*, I, p. 176.
91 MacDougall, J., *Folk Tales and Fairy Lore*, Edinburgh, 1910, p. 133.

Fairy Knoll and sees "fairy men and women wheeling and dancing with mad energy." Then again the music may come from the fairy as a changeling. The shepherd's wife had a baby who was difficult to nurse. It was really a changeling, a little old gray-headed man. Music came from the cradle and the infant sang as follows:

> Hush! Oranan, Hush, Oranan
> Hush! Oranan, Hush, Ohee
> Long is the lassie of coming
> To give the Canaan a wee
> Hush! Oranan, etc.

He kept playing this tune until he heard the woman coming; then the music ceased and he was again a little child.[92]

There are also fairy musicians or minstrels. They come out of the fairy mound with a musical instrument in their hands and whoever hears this music at once falls asleep.[93]

Now suppose we ask the question: Who are the supernatural beings, fairies, mermaids and all these beings of another world? We can hardly fail to recognize them as projections of the mother imago. Welsh fairies are called *Bendith y Mamau*,[94] "the mother blessing"—probably in an euphemistic sense. In Russian folklore children cursed by their mothers before they were born become water-fairies Rusalkas.[95] According to the narrative of Jean d'Arras (1357), King Helmas married a fay named Pressina whom he found singing beside a fountain. She became his wife but under the condition that he was never to visit her when she was lying in. He broke the oath and saw her bathing with her three newborn daughters. A separation followed, and one of the daughters, Melusina, avenged her mother by imprisoning her father. Indignant at this unfilial conduct, her mother cursed Melusina. She was to spend every Sabbath in semifish form. Her husband was never to pry upon her privacy on Saturday. He looked through the keyhole and to his dismay saw her in the water, her lower extremities changed into the tail of a fish or serpent.[96]

The stories of the mother and the daughter follow each other like two scenes of the same dream: The son is not to see where babies come

[92] *Ibid.*, p. 155. To the song of the *side* compare the death song of Norse ghosts from the burial mound. Chadwick, N. F., "Norse ghosts," *Folk Lore*, 1946, p. 106.

[93] Evan Wentz, W. Y., *The Fairy Faith in Celtic Countries*, Oxford University Press, 1911, pp. 289, 340.

[94] Rhys, *op. cit.*, I, p. 174.

[95] Ralston, W. R. S., *The Songs of the Russian People*, London, 1872, p. 145.

[96] Baring Gould, J., *Curious Myths of the Middle Ages*, London, 1873, pp. 471–483. Cf. Kohler, J., *Der Ursprung der Melusinensage*, Leipzig, 1895; Nowack M., *Die Melusinensage*, Zürich, 1886; Fraenkel, L., "Altes und Neues zur Melusinensage," *Zeitschrift des Vereins für Volkskunde*, 1894, IV, p. 387.

from, and, when he looks, his fantasy distorts reality, instead of the vagina, he sees a penis (fishtail, snake). The *Martes* of French folklore are big brown women who live among the rocks of the seashore. Their breasts and arms are naked, and their long breasts hang down to their knees. They inspire great terror because they run after people and throw their long breasts over the men's shoulders.[97] When Melusina disappeared, the nurses of her children beheld a glimmering white figure which took the little ones to her breast and suckled them.[98] But if the song of the Lorelei is just a fairy mother's lullaby,[99] then why the fatal connotation of the song?

Psychoanalytic theory has always held that the parallelism of sleep and death is no mere figure of speech.[100] In death all object cathexes are relinquished, in sleep they are temporarily withdrawn.[101] Falling asleep may be described as an irresistible force, but, except in the case of neurotic sleeplessness, it will hardly be connected with anxiety. One explanation, of course, would be that the anxiety is a break-through of reality. Death has been represented as falling asleep in mother's arms, but behind all this we know that it is really the end.

This explanation still fails to account for all the details of the story.

> First to the Sirens shalt thou sail who all men
> do beguile
> Whoso unwitting draws anigh, by magic of their wile
> They lure him with their singing, nor doth he reach
> his home
> Nor sees his dear wife and his babes, ajoy that he is
> come
> For they, the Sirens, lull him with murmur of sweet
> sound
> Crouching within the meadow about them is a mound
> Of men that rot in death their skin wasting the
> bones around.[102]

Thus the beautiful Circe advised Odysseus about the Sirens. Odysseus' men have their ears stopped with wax, so they cannot hear the fatal song and can continue to row. But Odysseus himself is to hear the beautiful song. Lest he should be tempted to make a move in the direction of the fatal maidens, his men are to tie him to the mast where he should *stand erect*;[103] and if he begs or orders them to untie him, they must pull

97 Sebillot, *op. cit.*, I, p. 315.
98 Baring Gould, *op. cit.*, p. 478.
99 MacDougall, *op. cit.*, pp. 105–115. (Fairy lullabies.)
100 Cf. Jekels, L., "A Bioanalytic Contribution to the Problem of Sleep and Wakefulness," *Psychoanalytic Quarterly*, XIV, 1945, p. 149.
101 Deutsch, F., "Euthanasia," *Psychoanalytic Quarterly*, V, pp. 347–349.
102 Od. XII, 39 et seq.
103 Od., XII, 162.

the cords even tighter. And when he arrives he hears the song of the Sirens:

> Hither, far famed Odysseus come hither thou the
> boast
> Of all Achaean men, beach thou thy bark upon our
> coast
> And harken to our singing for never but did stay
> A hero in his black ship and listened to the lay
> Of our sweet lips, full many a thing he knew and
> sailed away
> For we knew all things whatsoever in Troy's land
> had birth
> And we knew all things that shall be upon the
> fruitful earth.[104]

The real song of the Sirens is the lure of the past, the future only in so far as it is the part projected to return.

An Attic amphora represents Odysseus tied to the mast very erect looking upward with the sirens hovering above him, their bosoms emphasized.[105]

Now we know a type of dream that is characterized by the feeling of wanting to move but not being able to, and this is exactly the situation of Odysseus tied to the mast. In these dreams, just as in the Odyssey, a desire is expressed and also inhibited. The figure of Odysseus tied to the mast suggests the penis in erection.

Harrison comments as follows: "The artist's desire for a balanced design has made him draw two islands on each of which a Siren is perched. Over the head of one is inscribed 'lovely voiced.' A third Siren flies or rather falls headlong down to the ship. The drawing of the eye of this Siren should be noted. The eye is indicated by two strokes only without the pupil; this is the regular method of representing the sightless eyes, i.e., the eye in death or sleep or blindness. The third Siren is dying, she has hurled herself from the rock in despair at the fortitude of Odysseus."[106]

The suicide of the Siren, the leap into the sea is like the leap of the Sphinx, *again the basic dream* and Odysseus, the wily, is another Oedipus, the man who can solve riddles.

Crusius published the representation of a siren, a female with considerable sex appeal, with wings and human legs spread out, but with claws, descending upon a shepherd who is asleep and lying on his back.

---

[104] Od. XII, 184 et seq. Both translations are as given by Harrison, I. E., *Prolegomena to the Study of Greek Religion*, Cambridge, 1908, p. 198.

[105] Weicker, G., *Der Seelenvogel*, Leipzig, 1902, p. 165.

[106] Harrison, *op. cit.*, p. 201.

Evidently this is the representation of a dream, the content of the dream is coitus, more specifically *coitus inversus*.[107]

In connection with a passage of Suidas on dreams Crusius goes even further and interprets the siren scene as a dream with seminal ejaculation.[108] It is significant that on the same page Crusius also mentions the bearded siren and notes that the siren is really in the male position in the dream scene.

Crusius also quotes mythographers according to whom the sirens are girls who died as virgins and who are now seeking attainment of their unfulfilled sexual wishes in their attacks upon sleeping men. Philostratus (*Vit. Apollon,* IV, p. 25) relates a story in which an apparition is seen at night by a young man. It takes the shape of a beautiful woman who sings enticing songs. Thus the siren appears as practically equivalent with the *Lamia, Empusa, Gello* and other nightmare demons.[109] The *Lamia of the Sea* in modern Greek folklore is the same thing as the sirens of Odysseus. The *Lamia* engulfs ships in a whirlwind or whirlpool. The countryfolk at Parnassus believe that if a shapely young man approaches the sea at midday or midnight and plays his flute the *Lamia* will emerge from the water and try to persuade him to marry her. If he refuses she kills him. In a folk song, the shepherd, *disregarding the warning of his mother,* plays the flute on the beach. The *Lamia of the Sea* appears and the shepherd and the *Lamia* make a wager. If he can outplay her, i.e., if she gets tired of dancing first, he can have her as a wife; but if she can outdance him, all his herd is hers. The mortal loses the bet and all his strength and his sheep into the bargain.[110] The motif of music is displaced to the dreamer or mortal, he is playing his flute (masturbating) while the *Lamia* ("bad mother") is dancing. Seafarers hear the enticing song of the *Lamia* in the storm. Hoping for rescue, they steer their boat in the direction of the sound and the nearer they go, the further the song recedes until they perish in the storm.[111]

The sirens are birds with human heads or rather with female heads and a strong emphasis on femaleness in general. In some cases they appear

---

107 Crusius, O., "Die Epiphanié der Sirene," *Philologus* 50:93; Roscher, W. H. R., *Ephialtes XX,* Abh. der phil.-hist. Cl. Koenigl. Sächs. Gesellschaft der Wissenschaften, 1900, No. II, pp. 36, 37.

108 Crusius, *op. cit.,* p. 102.

109 Crusius, O., *op. cit.,* 50:99, 1891. Scyllia is also associated with water and Hekate is the mother of Scylla. All these beings are part of the *Hekatés komos* and responsible for nocturnal anxieties. Cf. Rohde, *op. cit.,* II, pp. 410–411. Cf. also on the Sirens attributes, Bunker, H. A., "The Voice as (Female) Phallus," *Psychoanalytic Quarterly,* III, 1934, p. 411.

110 Schmidt, B., *Das Volksleben der Neugriechen,* Leipzig, 1871, p. 131.

111 *Ibid.,* p. 132.

as positively maternal figures, carrying the child-soul into the other world; in other cases, there is a naked man, lying on his back, trying to ward off the attacks of the sirens.[112] The song of the sirens is the same as that of all sorts of other supernatural beings: of the nymphs, the harpies, Empousa, and Circe.[113] The name "siren," according to the etymology given by Weicker in the article in *Roscher's Lexikon* means "the one who chokes." The siren would, therefore, be the same figure as the Sphinx; and both are represented, in particular, as attacking from above youthful male figures who seem to be dying and at the same time are recumbent, passive and female.[114]

The bird form, through flying, would symbolize the erotic content of these beings, while beak and claws indicate castration anxiety. A demon of the Maya is called "the female deceiver." Her home is under shady bowers in the forest, and the ardent hunter sees her there, combing her beautiful hair with a large comb. She runs so as to invite pursuit. When the man clasps her, the body changes into a thorny bush, the feet become claws. In a few days the hunter succumbs to fever.[115]

Odysseus is tied to the mast, *erect* while his men are rowing. In a dream, the dreamer may be represented by several figures. The men are also Odysseus, they move while he is tied. The dream, in the first layer, must be of coitus with the mother. Her voice is irresistible, it means "go to sleep and dream of having intercourse with the sirens." And the song of the siren is a mother's lullaby. Pliny believed the sirens lived in India and lulled people to sleep by their beautiful song, then tore them to pieces.[116]

Anxiety transforms the siren-dream into a nightmare; the dreamer would like to move but he cannot, he would like to scream with anxiety —but his scream becomes the beautiful song of the sirens or of the Lorelei.

Modern European narratives about water spirits show an obvious affinity with dreams, especially with nightmares.

In Oldenburg the *Waldriderske* (nightmare spirits) are very beautiful and they sing a wondrous song. They arrive on the water from England (*Engelland* = angel land) in a milk-sieve with cows' ribs as their oars.[117]

At Striegau (Silesia) one finds a story about a water spirit that sounds just like a nightmare. A woman was *lying down* for a rest near a lake at noon.[118] She felt a mighty pull toward the lake. She dug her fingers into

[112] Weicker, *op. cit.*, p. 7.   [113] *Ibid.*, pp. 18, 19.

[114] Cf. article "Sphinx" in *Roscher's Lexikon*, p. 1370.

[115] Brinton, D. G., *Essays of an Americanist*, Philadelphia, 1890, p. 178.

[116] de Gubernatis, A.: *Die Thiere in der indogermansichen Mythologie*. Leipzig, 1874, p. 499.

[117] Strackerjan, *op. cit.*, p. 466.

[118] Laistner, L., *Das Rätsel der Sphinx*, I, Chapter 1, 1889.

the ground with all her might and thus managed to keep immobilized for an hour. At the end of that time the pulling ceased,[119] i.e., after what seemed to be an hour in the dream, she was awake. The water spirit attaches himself to lonely female wanderers and plagues them with questions (sphinx motif). He wrestles with them (nightmare) they hear his huffing and puffing[120] (heavy breathing of the dreamer). The spirit jumps on people near the lake and makes them carry him. The *Rusalkas* of Russian folklore, usually beautiful women in white garments, and with beautiful breasts, appear in a real nightmare shape in the Saratoff district. There, they are hideous, humpbacked hairy creatures with sharp claws and an iron hook with which they try to seize passersby. If the mortal does not give the right answer to their question, they tickle him till he foams at the mouth and drag him to the bottom of the lake.[121] Not only the drowned but also those who are choked or strangled are liable to become *Rusalkas*[122] (nightmare). The water spirit will jump on a horse and ride it to death.[123]

The *djedushka vodjanoj* (grandfather of the waters) loves to ride cattle and horses; and, when he gallops on these, the dead sink even lower in the water.[124] The water spirits of the Kreuzensee in Oldenburg dance on the lake. Horses catch sight of them and they cannot move from the spot—like Odysseus. When the clock strikes midnight the spirits disappear in the lake and the horses can move again.[125]

Now the horse for some reason is both eminently the nightmare animal and (with the bull) the animal representative of the water spirit.

Water bulls and water horses are characteristic male personifications of the water in Celtic folklore. On the Isle of Man, the water horse was supposed to make away with men, children and even domestic horses, carrying or dragging them down beneath the waters of the river which it haunted.[126]

The water horse tempts the unwary traveler to mount him, then soars over river and mountain and suddenly melts away and throws his rider to destruction. "Suddenly the traveler became anxious at the speed because the horse went like lightning. At moonrise he found himself thrown on the slope of a hill."[127] In this case, we have a flying dream with anxiety.

119 Kuehnau, *op. cit.*, II, p. 230.
120 Kuehnau, *op. cit.*, II, pp. 245, 246, 251.
121 Ralston, *loc. cit.*, p. 146.
122 *Ibid.*, p. 145.   123 *Ibid.*, p. 153.
124 *Machal*, *op. cit.*, p. 107.
125 Bartsch, K., *Sagen, Märchen und Gebräuche aus Mecklenburg*, Vienna, 1879, pp. 395, 396.
126 McKay, I. G., "Gaelic Folklore," *Folk-Lore*, 1925, XXXVI, p. 169.
127 Trevelyan, M., *Folk-Lore and Folk Stories of Wales*, London, 1909, pp. 59, 60.

But frequently, we have the typical nightmare narrative. The water horse in the shape of a frog leaps upon people and grasps them in a fiendish embrace or crushes them with its superhuman weight. In some instances, it appears in goat shape. Or again it may take the shape of a squirrel and, leaping between a man's shoulders, clasp his neck so as to make him gasp for breath.[128] Men who ride water horses are drowned or have narrow escapes.[129] At Lichterwelde (Austria) the water horse rises in the evening from the earth and is high in the air in a terrific storm.[130] Or a black horse with fiery eyes jumps on people from the rear and lifts them up in the air.[131] At Mummelsee a brown bull comes out of the lake and joins the herd of cows. These bulls are called *Seebulle,* i.e., bulls of the lake. When the bull appears from the lake it goes straight to the cows.[132]

In ancient Greece the ocean god Poseidon is a horse. According to Fick's conjecture the word means "sweller" in the sense of the penis in erection. Poseidon and his consort Demeter cause earthquakes, probably when the goddess yields to the advances of the amorous god.[133] The month *Poseidon* (December) is his because of the frequent storms in that month. Mythology has a lot to say about Poseidon's marriages and his wives, the Nereids.[134]

The male water spirit of the Czechs (called *hastrman-Wassermann*) appears at weddings, causes storms, lures people into the water and chokes them. He neighs like a horse and then he jumps into the water. He asks for a ride; and when he jumps off the wagon he says: "Do you know whom you were carrying? The *hastrman.*" The coachman sees that water is dripping from his passenger's left side and that his foot is a horse's foot. The farmer notices a white horse. He would like to mount it. The horse's lower lip is missing, however. "It is lucky for you, you did not sit on me or I would have drowned you," the water spirit says.[135] At Rugawa, the water beings are horses; but their lower jaws are made of wood. They also men-

128 *Ibid.,* pp. 63, 64.

129 Campbell, I. F., *Popular Tales of the West Highlands* (London, 1893), IV, p. 302.

130 Vernaleken, T., *Mythen und Braeuche des Volkes in Oesterreich* (Wien, 1859), p. 185.

131 Bertsch, *Weltanschauung, Volkssage und Volksbrauch* (1910), p. 327. Schambach, G., und Müller, N., *Niedersächsische Sagen und Maerchen* (Göttingen, 1855), p. 117.

132 *Ibid.,* pp. 303, 304.

133 Gruppe, O., *Griechische Mythologie und Religionsgeschichte,* II, 1906, pp. 1137–1140.

134 Meyer, E. H., "Poseidon," *Roscher's Lexikon,* 1902–1909, VII, pp. 2, 2802 referring to Ficks, in *Kuhn's Zeitschrift* XXI, p. 462, and *Vergleichendes Wörterbuch,* I, p. 507.

135 Kostal, L., *Vodnik v. podani lidu ceskeho* (Water Beings in Czech Folklore), Ceskylid, I, pp. 52–53.

ace grazing horses.[136] In Sweden, a dapple-gray horse rises from the water with its prey. In German chronicles a huge black horse comes out of the water. The farmer uses the horse for ploughing; but finally, farmer and plough are dragged into the lake.[137]

The word "nightmare," as the name of a well-known type of anxiety dream, clearly indicates the notion that a mare causes the dream. Spirit horses roam on the meadow, it is dangerous to go there at night. A spirit horse creeps through the keyhole and puts a front hoof on the dreamer's chest. In Pomerania the *Mahrt* or nightmare jumps on mortals and makes them carry her. She takes the form of a gray horse. The miller's wife at Bamberg wants to seduce the miller's apprentice. She comes into his room every night in the shape of a horse and takes all his strength.[138] In a Croatian narrative a man is plagued at night by his own horse. A tailor notices a horse's hair on him at night, he cuts it with his scissors, the horse is found dead in the stable.[139] The nightmare fiend will ride the horses all night in the stables, this is why they are covered with perspiration in the morning.[140]

Why should the horse rather than any other animal give its name to the nightmare experience? Every psychoanalyst knows the answer; riding in a dream symbolizes coitus, it is the male riding on a female. In one type of narrative about witches we find the motif of the farmer's wife who rides to the witches' Sabbath every night on the young lad who works for the farmer, after having transformed the boy into a horse. Finally he turns the tables on the witch and throws the bridle over her head and mounts her.[141] *The nightmare is a coitus dream and if dreamed by a man, it is a dream of coitus inversus, with the woman on top.* The change of position is due to anxiety or, more specifically, to castration anxiety. This would explain the presence of the horse in nightmare beliefs, but how does the horse get connected with water? Ernest Jones suggests that the role of the horse in various beliefs is due to the interest in the stream of urine produced by

[136] Vernaleken, *op. cit.,* p. 185.

[137] Grimm, J., *Deutsche Mythologie,* Guetersloh, 1875, I, p. 1875.

[138] Laistner, *op. cit.,* I, p. 172 (with references). Jones, E., *Nightmare, Witches and Devils,* London, 1931, p. 256.

[139] Krauss, F. S., *Slavische Volksforschungen,* Wien, 1908, pp. 152–153.

[140] Strackerjan, *op. cit.,* I, p. 467; Wuttke, A., *Der deutsche Volksaberglaube der Gegenwart,* Berlin, 1900, p. 451; Frison, I., "Contes et legendes de Basse Bretagne," *Revue des Traditions Populaires,* XXV, 1910, p. 320.

[141] Hansen, *Quellen und Untersuchungen zur Geschichte des Hexenwahns,* 1901; Index "Nachfahrten" Alpenburg, *Deutsche Alpensagen,* 1861, p. 148; Kuehnau, *op. cit.,* III, p. 27; Krauss, *op. cit.,* p. 40; Laistner, *op. cit.,* I, p. 171; Strackerjan, *op. cit.,* I, p. 471; von Schulenburg, W., *Wendische Volkssagen und Gebräuche,* Berlin, 1880, p. 162; Jones, *op. cit.,* p. 204.

the animal.[142] "Even more frequently than by the growth of vegetation is the trampling of horses followed by the issuing of springs. No better symbol of reproduction could be found, for this represents both the pouring out of the male principle (semen, urine) and the birth itself (uterine water)." Jones mentions Pegasus (from *pege* = spring) giving rise to a spring, and other instances.[143] Horses, rivers and the idea of something that is fiery and glistening, lightning, sunshine are specifically associated,[144] and any combination of water and fire is likely to indicate urethral symbolism.

Since our mythical material definitely shows traces of having gone through a dream stage,[145] perhaps we can apply this key to unlock the mystery of water spirits in horse form. There is a type of dream, well known to every psychoanalyst, which is a reaction to urethral pressure experienced by the dreamer. The dream is an awakening dream or rather a dream designed to delay awakening for a few moments. In its simplest form it is that the dreamer is urinating. Further complications: He (or she) is urinating, but what comes out is not urine, it is a river. The dreamer is trying to find the toilet, all sorts of delaying motifs occur, other people appear who are urinating or pouring water or wine or milk. Or the volume of water grows from a puddle on the ground to a lake or ocean, representing the increasing pressure of the urine.[146]

Sometimes the motif of the fluid is omitted or appears merely as an erotic chase or running. A patient dreamed that he was chasing a girl called Pearl N. She was dressed in the hourglass style. He ran after her from one room to another—finally he awakened and had to urinate. About Pearl N., he remarked that he once tried to have an affair with this girl, but failed. Pearls: imitation jewelry, rhinestone, *Lorelei*—then hourglass: time runs short, one drop falling after the other (i.e., he must get out of the bed to urinate). Hourglass—the fashion in mother's time, big bosom.

A story told by Apuleius confirms our interpretation of the siren as a urethral anxiety dream. After having escaped the lure of a witch, the hero has a big meal and falls asleep. The door opens and two women enter. One of them has a lamp in her hand, the other, his girl friend, a sword and a sponge. They slaughter him like an animal for sacrifice, his blood

142 *Ibid.*, p. 318.
143 *Ibid.*, p. 298.
144 *Ibid.*, p. 318.
145 "A handsome Puruma boy while steering a canoe was seen by an *oboubi* (water spirit) girl who came to him the next night when he was sleeping in the canoe." Landtman, G., *The Kiwai Papuans of British New Guinea*, London, 1927, p. 305.
146 Cf. the chapter "Vesical Dreams and Myths."

runs into a goatskin bag to the last drop. His wound closes after the women have put the sponge on it with the following incantation: *Spongia cave in mari nata per fluviam transeas.* Then the women (like the sirens in the drawing of the relief shown by Crusius) sat on his face: *Vesicam exonerant quoad me urinae spurcissimae madore perluerunt.* The dreamer tells his friend that he has been slaughtered; he is told not to worry, it was only a dream. But the next day, when he is about to drink from a river, his wound opens and he falls down dead.[147]

The urethral basis of the dream is here made obvious by its ending. The urethral pressure is transformed into an erotic experience (one of the women is his girl friend), and this in its turn becomes castration (death). The flowing blood means that urine is symbolized by blood while the girl, who collects it in a bag, shows the coitus symbolism of the whole scene. The sequel—death when drinking water—signifies the oral-aggressive basis of castration anxiety and indicates the link between dream apparition and the water spirits.

In a Hungarian story a man goes to the witches' meeting place and sees them jumping about as horses. He mounts one of the horses and the others shout "He is riding on Aunt Kate." The horse gallops away and finally *throws him into a lake.*[148]

In a Silesian story the farmer's fingers have been cut off by the water spirit (castration motif). In order to make them grow again he has to find a certain number of gold pieces and throw them into the water. But he cannot find the right number; and, therefore, a finger starts bleeding and every drop of blood becomes water—so much water that it fills buckets, then inundates the house. Tables, chairs and everything float in the water until the peasant shouts to God for help.[149]

We have mentioned the Czech belief to the effect that one recognizes the water spirit because water is dripping from his left side. In dream language it is not the dreamer who has to urinate but someone else. A boy is dancing with a girl (Silesia); when she disappears, he notices a puddle of water where they had been standing.[150] A peasant hears something splash-

---

147 Apuleius, I:6. Quoted by Crusius, *op. cit.,* p. 100.

148 Molnár, I., "Adalékok az alföldi magyar nép hiedelemvilágához" (Contributions to the Beliefs of Hungarians in the Lowlands), *Ethnographia,* LIV, 1943, p. 69.

149 Weinhold, K., "Beiträge zur Nixenkunde auf Grund schlesischer Sagen," *Zeitschrift des Vereins für Volkskunde,* 1895, p. 133. (God does not help him, a saw cuts his body into two.)

150 Kuehnau, *Schlesische Sagen,* II, 1911, p. 237. In Ibsen's *Die Frau vom Meere,* Lynstrand wishes to make a sculpture representing the faithless wife of a seaman. The seaman, drowned after a shipwreck, appears in her dreams with water dripping from him. Ibsen, H., *Die Frau vom Meere,* Sämtliche Werke, VIII, Berlin, n.d., p. 134.

ing and shouts: "Wash my apron too!" The next minute he is drenched by a breaking wave.[151]

Another apparition is a woman who washes linen all the time. She seduces men and has a big knife.[152]

The hair of the *Rusalka* must be wet, otherwise she is lost. But she can always produce a flood of water by combing her hair.[153] The women of the well (*Brunnenfrauen*) are human down to the waist and then end in fishtails: "She had long blond hair and breasts white as snow and nobody had ever seen a more beautiful woman." There is a widely known story in German folklore about water fairies who come to dance in the village. They stay beyond their time, i.e., midnight. Wailing and bemoaning their fate, they tell their human swains that if, on their return to the lake, milk flows from the lake, it will show that their father has forgiven them, but if the flow is blood, it will mean their deaths.[154] In a Hungarian story, the "little water man" can always be recognized because of the water that drips from his sleeve.[155]

The frequent ending of these narratives in which the horse or girl or spirit of the water rushes or dives back into the lake would be easily understandable as a urethral awakening dream, *somebody else* than the dreamer must rush to urinate.

I think the assumption that the core of these narratives is a dream is very plausible. This dream must then be a reaction to a definite somatic stimulus, i.e., to the need to urinate. This becomes a dripping wet being, male or female, a lake or river. We also know, however, that the dreamer frequently transforms this bladder pressure situation into a coitus dream. This would certainly explain the well-known amorous inclination of all water spirits while the fact that all dreams invariably regress,[156] explains the maternal lure of the sirens and the phallic-paternal nature of Poseidon and other water horses and bulls. But what about the nightmare quality? The wish is transformed into a nightmare because of the oedipal content. In the only clinical nightmare case published so far by a psychoanalyst, Schoenberger traces the nightmares of his patient to the *primal scene*.[157] In 1934, I wrote, "It seems that the nucleus of the nightmare is

151 Kuehnau, *op. cit.*, II, p. 238. Cf. Bayard, S. P., "The 'Johnny Collins' Version of Lady Alice," *J. Am. Folklore*, 1945, 58:73–103.

152 Proehle, H., *Unterharzische Sagen*, O. Fokke, Aschersleben, 1856, pp. 80–81.

153 Ralston, *op. cit.*, p. 141.

154 Wolf, I. W., *Beiträge zur deutschen Mythologie*, Goettingen, 1852, II, pp. 282, 283.

155 Ipolyi, A., *Magyar Mythologia*, Budapest, 1854, p. 56.

156 Cf. the song of the sirens; they know what has happened to the hero in the past.

157 Schoenberger, S., "A Clinical Contribution to the Analysis of the Nightmare Syndrome," *Psychoanalytic Revue*, XXXIII, 1946, p. 46.

the desire to replace one of the parents in the primal scene. But the desire is transformed into a punishment through castration-anxiety, and the male sleeper appears in the passive role. If a man puts a woman's cap on before going to bed the elves will come and lie on him at night."[158] Since then, I have found this confirmed in many clinical cases.

Behind the nightmare content, we expect to find the primal scene.

The water spirit and his wife appear in all sorts of shapes. Dreamers see him as a soldier, his wife as a mare. He mounts her and they gallop into the water.[159] According to the Slovaks, the water spirits are always fighting for each other's wives. A peasant gets a reward for telling the water spirit that another water spirit has eloped with his wife.[160] According to the Votjaks in the districts of Glasov and Sarapul, the water spirits celebrate their marriages twice a year by rollicking and shouting in the water. When the water breaks through the dam, the water spirits are celebrating their marriages.[161] According to Russian belief a girl who drowns becomes a *Rusalka* (water fairy) and marries a *vodvanoy* (water spirit). At these occasions they indulge in such revels and pranks that the waters are wildly agitated.[162] If a river is dry, that is also because the water spirit is marrying.[163] Elves appear at a wedding in Carinthia and disappear in the well.[164] In another narrative of the same area (already cited), the roles are inverted. Human beings make love, the water spirit is amazed by the sight and sings. A bull emerges at certain times from a marsh in southern Saxony and is seen mounting the cows.[165]

It is here, of course, that the *voyeur* element enters the picture.

Water fairies in Silesia are very beautiful, and are naked. Anyone who catches sight of them must die.[166] Or anyone who looks at them will be sick all his life.[167] The wanderer must beware of looking in the direction where he may expect to see the Nereids,[168] and a girl who is descended from the Nereids is remarkable for her beautiful eyes.[169] While the Lorelei as such, is purely an invention of Brentano, subsequently de-

[158] Róheim, *The Riddle of the Sphinx*, p. 56.

[159] Kuehnau, *op. cit.*, II, p. 270.

[160] Dobsinsky, P., *Prostonarodnie obycaje povery a Hry Slovenske*, Prague, 1880, p. 117.

[161] Holmberg, U., *Die Wassergottheiten der finnisch-ugrischen Völker*, Helsingfors, 1913, p. 65.

[162] Ralston, *op. cit.*, pp. 149, 150.

[163] Machal, *op. cit.*, p. 107.

[164] Graber, *op. cit.*, p. 4.

[165] Grimm, *op. cit.*, I, p. 406.

[166] Kuehnau, *op. cit.*, II, p. 229.

[167] *Ibid.*, II, p. 232.

[168] Schmidt, B., *Das Volksleben der Neugriechen*, 1871, p. 121.

[169] *Ibid.*, p. 103.

veloped by other poets and cast in its final mold by Heine, the name itself or rather *lur,* the root of the word, certainly belongs in this context.

Hertz tells us that *lur* or *lure* means "to gaze, to look through half-closed eyelids." In the Swiss dialects *loren, luren,* is to look intently; also to blink. In Danish *lure* means to look out for something. In Scottish, or English dialect, to "glower" is to look intensely, to stare. In contemporary German, *lauern* is to peep, spy from an ambush. The word also means to cheat, also to gaze in a sleepy fashion as if a person were just going to fall asleep and was trying to keep awake.[170] In French, *lorgner* is to peep.[171]

The latent content of the dream (primal scene) is what the child is not supposed to see. Other taboos against voyeurism enter into the picture, the taboo against seeing mother naked, seeing her vagina, seeing the fantasied maternal penis (fishtail), which is the cover memory for the vagina and the abbreviated symbol of the primal scene. The *Nivashi* or water fairies of the gypsies have six fingers, and blood taken from the sixth finger cures blindness.[172] It is really the mortal who is the *lure,* in the sense of being the voyeur, but his desire to see becomes the *lure* of the supernatural being. In the dream narrative already cited from Apuleius, one of the women who enters the room comes with a lamp—obviously a hint at the visual background of the whole scene. On several vases of the archaic period, the body of the siren is represented as if it were a big eye.[173] With Crusius, Seligmann also assumes that we have amulets here to ward off the evil eye. The Etruscan *Lasa* (Nemesis) is represented with big eyes on her wings. One of these figures has a bull's head on her breast.[174] The siren occurs as an amulet in combination with the winged seahorse in modern Italy. The female figure, or siren, wears a crown and ends in two fishtails or is seated on two seahorses.[175]

One of the things the child always notices in the primal scene is the increased breathing activity. The water spirit who is heard huffing and puffing while chasing mortals[176] is the father in the primal scene. Just as the urethral pressure becomes magnified in the dream into a river or lake, increased breathing and sexual excitement become a raging tempest or whirlwind.

[170] Hertz, R., *Gesammelte Abhandlungen,* Stuttgart, 1905, p. 473.

[171] *Ibid.,* p. 490.

[172] von Wlislocki, H., *Volksglaube und religiöser Brauch der Zigeuner,* Muenster i. W., 1891, p. 31.

[173] Crusius, *op. cit.,* p. 101; Weicker, G., *Der Seelenvogel,* Leipzig, 1902, pp. 155, 156.

[174] Seligmann, S., *Der böse Blick und Verwandtes,* Berlin, 1910, II, p. 148.

[175] *Ibid.,* II, p. 310.

[176] Kuehnau, *op. cit.,* II, p. 252.

From here we get back once more to the irresistible song of the water beings. It is first, as we have seen, the mother's lullaby, then, also, the noise made by the parents in the primal scene.

A patient who suffered greatly from nightmares in his childhood (feeling of suffocation and of a swelling of his limbs) remembers that he was always trying to recapture a certain *melody* he had forgotten. Analysis makes it clear that what he means is the noise made by the parents in the primal scene.

One suspects that the sirens' song is also the scream of anxiety of the dreamer trying to awaken. We have noticed several times that the water beings are characterized by certain activities. Patching their clothes, or sewing, or counting, or spinning, is important, but the paramount feature is combing the hair, which seems just as important as the singing. Now we know that the dream images are frequently projections of what the dreamer himself is doing, that the dream world in a sense is formed out of the dreamer's body. We suspect, therefore, that the water spirit's long tresses are the dreamer's pubic hair and that all the spirits' activities—combing, sewing, patching, counting—represent masturbation.[177]

It has been pointed out in the foregoing that the oedipal content of the dream changes it into an anxiety dream or nightmare. In other words, the transformation is effected by the *superego*. These beings of the water *devour* their victims (superego = German: *Gewissensbisse*, biting). In a French song, when the diver is drowned, his mistress sings:

> There were neither fish nor carp
> Who did not cry,
> Only the sirens,
> They kept on singing;
> Sing, sing, sirens
> It is easy for you to sing
> You have the ocean to drink
> And my love to eat.[178]

Taken together with the motifs of milk or blood from the lake, of the white breast and the devouring teeth, claws or beak (sirens) we are reminded of the oral significance of the primal scene and of the possible interpretation of these man-eating beings as the infant's oral aggression in *talio* form, with the irresistible song as the flow of milk, or as nothing more or less than the truly insatiable hunger of an infant.[179] We assume

---

177 Róheim, *Mondmythologie und Mondreligion*, Wien, 1927. Cf. Chapter IX.

178 Sebillot (*op. cit.*, II, p. 33), quoting Bujeaud, J., *Chansons populaires de l'Ouest*, II, pp. 161, 162.

179 This unconscious content appears in the comedy writers; what the Sirens promise Odysseus and his men is a good meal (Weicker, *Der Seelenvogel*, p. 53). Food, especially cake, appears in the stories of these water beings. The cake brought by the

that these narratives have been evolved on the basis of dreams, the nature
of which we can reconstruct from the texts.

1. The water or water spirit is derived from the basic dream or a urethral dream of awakening or both combined.

2. Urethral dreams of this type are always coitus dreams.

3. Anxiety transforms the coitus with the mother (*mutatis mutandis,*
father) into a nightmare.

4. The nightmare is a repetition of the primal scene, with the
dreamer in the passive role.

5. The irresistible song of the water fairies is both a mother's lullaby
and the noise made by the parents in the primal scene. Voyeuristic impulses enter into the picture, the dreamer sees the mother's breast or
vagina (penis).

6. The water fairy combs her beautiful hair; the dreamer is masturbating.

Now, quite apart from the admittedly conjectural nature of these
"steps" in forming the dream, other questions, more in the field of folklore,
must be asked. Must everybody who has these beliefs, or all European
peasants who imagine they have seen these spirits, have actually dreamed
this kind of dream? Certainly not. They receive these beliefs ready-made
in tradition and the beliefs appeal to them because of their unconscious
content. Then why assume the dream stage, since the unconscious would
contain the same elements, even without dreams? But the dream theory
explains not only identity in content but also in structure and sequence.
Must we then assume that the original dream was dreamed by one person
in a definite locality, was accepted as a real experience and that, hence,
the belief spread by migration? This is hardly likely. Many have dreamed
such dreams, they shaped the narrative form in many centers, became traditional, then merged and influenced each other in the course of history.
Our oldest dreams are with us forever.

The belief in the fatal power of water spirits to lure human beings
and the representation of this lure as a sexual attraction are not based on
dream material. It is the stories we are trying to explain, the sequence of
motifs, by the assumption that this is based on dreams. If we believe with
Ferenczi in the possibility of unconscious phylogenetic experiences surviving through the ages in beliefs, this, of course, would be an obvious
instance of "*thalassal regression.*"[180] Ellida, Ibsen's heroine in the play

---

water being should be eaten up completely and yet left intact. A mother loses a child
in the water. A friendly old man from the lake had given such good food to the
child as it had never had before. The mother finds the child, but in a few days it
dies. Lohre, H., *Märkische Sagen,* Leipzig, 1921, pp. 44, 45.

[180] Cf. Ferenczi, S., *Versuch einer Genitaltheorie,* Wien, 1924.

Die Frau vom Meere, expresses something like this: Human beings would have been much better, if they could have grown up in the sea, and their depressions are due to their remorse on this account (third act). However, it is not necessary to make this assumption in order to explain water spirit beliefs. A patient of the writer, an eminently narcissistic and infantile girl, was carrying on two affairs at the same time. The one was with a man who was potent and also masculine in character. The other was with a neurotic; his potency was uncertain; and she rarely had an orgasm with him. But she and he kept finding similar traits in each other, in their appearance, background, mannerisms, etc., so that it seemed to her as if she were having intercourse with herself. This affair satisfied a craving in her that was somehow different from the sexual. The same girl also described her "oceanic feeling" (Freud), her desire to commit suicide by drowning in the lake of her native city, to become one with the water, etc.

Bunker has commented on the myth of Narcissus:[181] "A certain youth the loveliest of young men became enamored of his reflection in a pool beside which he remained until he died of starvation." Bunker quotes Freud[182] to explain the myth: "It seems that an accumulation of narcissistic libido over and above a certain level becomes intolerable. We might well imagine that it was this that first led to the cathexis of objects—that the ego was obliged to send forth its libido in order not to fall ill of an excessive accumulation of it." In some versions of the story, however, Narcissus does not die at the edge of the pool but drowns himself in it.[183] *Narkissos* certainly symbolizes regression, and the withdrawal of object cathexis means both regression to the mother and to the narcissistic state.[184] Parallel myths to *Narkissos* are related about Eutelidas and Hylas. The latter is drawn into the depths by the dryads,[185] or by the nymphs of the spring. His mother is a nymph, and the nymphs are in love with him. *Narkissos* is also beloved by the water nymphs, and his mother is one of the nymphs.[186] Sleep and the dream are both withdrawal into the mother and into oneself.

In Brittany the spirit lures women and children into the depth through mirrors floating in the water.[187] The lure is the universal human

---

181 Bunker, H. A., "Narcissus," in *Psychoanalysis and the Social Sciences,* 1947, I, p. 159.

182 Freud, *Introductory Lectures on Psychoanalysis,* London, 1929, p. 351.

183 *Roscher's Lexikon,* "Narkissos."

184 This is the interpretation I gave in *Spiegelzauber,* 1919, p. 118.

185 Zielinski, T., "Hermes und die Hermetik," *Archiv für Religionswissenschaft,* VIII, p. 327.

186 Cf. Seliger, "Hylas," in *Roscher's Lexicon,* p. 2794; and Greve, in *Roscher's Lexicon;* Ovidius, *Metamorphosis,* III, 456.

187 Sebillot, *op. cit.,* II, p. 417.

tendency of regression: regression from life or from the genital oedipal stage toward the dual-unity phase, i.e., an oral organization in which the differentiation of child and mother, of subject and object was none too clear.[188] The latest theory of the *extraject*[189] amounts practically to the same thing. Weiss's theory is best illustrated by a Koryak myth.

·   The Koryak creator-hero Raven slept in the house of the Mouse people. They tell him, "You will come to a stream on your way. You will surely be thirsty. Drink some water out of it." (They had painted his face.) When he reached the stream he stopped to take a drink. He saw a painted face in the water and cried: "Ah! Many-Colored Woman, you are here? Here I am letting down a stone hammer for you." He dropped the stone hammer, bent over to drink and fell into the water. The current carried him down to the mouth of the stream. He came out of the water and turned into a raven.[190] Raven thus takes his own reflection for a woman whom he wants to marry. First he throws his stone hammer in, then himself. The water carries him away, he sinks down and dies.[191] The "narcissistic choice of object"[192] or extraject is obvious. The stone hammer he first throws in is his penis. The withdrawal of cathexis from the object world is death.

The narcissistic and the functional aspect would explain existence of the water spirit as a child, i.e., the path of regression goes toward the child in us. At Reinshausen people show children their own faces in the water, and then they tell them the face is the *Haekelmann* who will pull them into the well if they go too near.[193] Water spirits (*Nixe*) look like little children; that is why they like bright, red colors and wear green caps. But the mothers are afraid of them because they steal little children and lure the bigger ones into the sea.[194] The water spirit of the Vends is a *little black man* with a red cap. He is lurking just under the surface to catch little children.[195] The Slovaks talk about the "boys of the water" (*vodni*

188 For the dual-unity theory, cf. Herrmann, I., "Sich Anklammern, Auf Suche Gehn," *Int. Zeitschrift für Psychoanalyse*, XXII, 1936, p. 338, and many other papers. Cf. also Róheim, *War, Crime and the Covenant*, 1945, J. Clin. Psychopathol. Monograph Series No. 1, Part I.

189 Weiss, E., "Projection, Extrajection and Objectivation," *Psychoanalytic Quarterly*, XVI, 1947, p. 357.

190 Jochelson, W., *The Koryak, Religion and Myth*, The Jesup North Pacific Expedition, Mem. Am. Mus. Nat. Hist., VI, 1905, p. 264.

191 *Ibid.*, p. 326.

192 Freud, "Zur Einführung des Narcissmus," *Gesammelte Schriften*, VI, p. 155.

193 Schambach, G. and Mueller, W., *Niedersächsiche Sagen und Märchen*, Goettingen, 1855, p. 65.

194 Lohre, H., *Märkische Sagen*, Brandenburg, 1921, p. 43.

195 Veckenstedt, E., *Wendische Sagen, Märchen und abergläubische Gebräuche*, 1880, p. 185.

klapni).[196] The *Rusalkas* (water spirits) steal the souls of unbaptized children and these become water spirits. The same thing happens to infants who have been cursed by their mothers before they were born or before baptism.[197] On the other hand, water spirits are especially inclined to steal children and substitute changelings.[198] "The water spirit is a child" means that the child extrajects itself into the water, i.e., the mother. "Water spirits steal children" means that there is a trend in the child toward reunion with the mother. The uterine significance of the water in these themes is undeniable.

Bonaparte believes that stagnant lakes and ponds attract the imagination of men by their immobility and silence, the attributes of living bodies when death has stiffened them. Thus death is combined with the universal mother symbolism of water.[199]

Human midwives are sought after especially by the water fairies. Gervase of Tilbury in the thirteenth century relates what happened at the banks of the Rhone. A woman was washing clothes near the river. A wooden bowl floated by her and trying to grasp it she was dragged down under the water. She was made nurse to a child of a Drac, i.e., water spirit.[200] In Germany a midwife is summoned to aid a woman in labor. She goes under the water, it is the wife of the water spirit. The woman is in labor. She says, "I am a Christian woman as well as you and I was carried off by a waterman. When my husband offers you money take no more than you usually get or he will twist your neck."[201] A Vend story is the same, water-women must have human midwives.[202] In another Vend story the water spirit meets a pregnant woman. He takes her along to his house under the water. He strikes the surface of the water with his wand, it makes a passage. When the time of delivery comes he gets a midwife for her.[203] In Hessen two horsemen appear and summon a midwife. They *wake her* but she refuses to go with them. They use force and gallop away with her under the sea. The queen of water spirits was in labor. She saw many marvelous things there, palaces, treasures. They brought her back *at night*.[204]

196 Dobsinsky, *op. cit.*, p. 117.

197 Ralston, *op. cit.*, pp. 144, 145.

198 Sebillot, *op. cit.*, I, pp. 439–442; Wlislocki, Mrs., "A gyermek a magyar néphit-ben" (The child in Hungarian Folk Belief), *Ethnographia*, IV, pp. 209, 210; Seyfarth, K., *Aberglaube und Zauberei in der Volksmedizin Sachsens*, 1913, p. 15; Abbott, G. F., *Macedonian Folklore*, 1903, p. 128; Ploss-Renz, *Das Kind*, 1911, I, p. 114.

199 Bonaparte, M., "The Legend of Unfathomable Waters," *Am. Imago*, IV, 1946, pp. 29, 30.

200 Hartland, E. S., *The Science of Fairy Tales*, London, 1891, pp. 64, 65.

201 *Ibid.*, p. 48.

202 Veckenstedt, *op. cit.*, p. 194.

203 Schulenburg, W. von, *Wendisches Volkstum*, Berlin, 1882, p. 58.

204 Grimm, *Deutsche Sagen*, München, n.d., No. 58, p. 59.

A midwife in Halle tells the following story. Her gate was open and a man fetched her at night. The water opened and they sank down into a beautiful palace. She helped a young woman in delivering her child. Luckily on her way back she held on to Dosten and Dorant (origanum vulg and Marribium vulg) as the woman had advised, otherwise the waterman, the woman's husband would have killed her. In another story the water spirit appears to a mortal woman in labor.[205] At Calbe a girl calls on a famous midwife at night and calls her to a woman in labor. The gates of the city are closed at night. They will be open, the visitor says. They go to a hill which opens and find a tiny woman in labor, etc.[206] In a parallel version of this story the way is down under the river. Instead of the gates, it is the water that opens.[207] The nocturnal descent and the opening gates point to the basic dream. In Silesia the story goes that the local midwife knew that the water fairy was about to be delivered. The husband came to fetch her, he said she should not be anxious but she must not look. They descend through the water that opens when struck by the water spirit.[208] At Giebichenstein the water spirit fetches a midwife. His palace is all gold and silver and jewels.[209] In the Vogtland we have the same legends, sometimes the water spirit dwells in the cellar of the house, thus showing that the descent is the essential feature of the story.[210] A midwife lived at Corwrion (Wales). One of the fairies called her to attend his wife. "Off she went with him, and she was astonished to be taken into a splendid palace. There she continued to go night and morning to dress the baby for some time. One day the husband asked her to rub her eyes with a certain ointment he offered her. *She did so and found herself sitting on a tuft of rushes,* not in a palace. There was no baby, all had disappeared."[211]

"An old woman of Garth Dorwen was in the habit of putting women to bed and she was in great request far and wide. A gentleman came to her on horseback one night when the moon was full and there was a slight rain and just a little mist to fetch the old woman to his wife. When they reached the spot they entered a large cave and they went into a room where the wife lay in her bed. It was the finest woman she had ever seen."[212]

If we regard the human heroine of the story, the midwife, as the

---

[205] *Ibid.,* I, No. 65, pp. 66, 67.

[206] *Ibid.,* No. 68, p. 70.

[207] *Ibid.,* No. 69, I, pp. 71, 72. Cf. also No. 49, I, p. 50.

[208] Kühnau, *op. cit.,* II, pp. 224, 225.

[209] Sommer, E., *Sagen, Märchen und Gebräuche aus Sachsen und Thüringen,* Halle, 1846, p. 41.

[210] Köhler, A. E., *Volksbrauch, Aberglauben, Sagen und andere Ueberlieferungen im Vogtland,* 1867, p. 472.

[211] Rhys, *op. cit.,* I, p. 63.

[212] *Ibid.,* I, pp. 212, 213.

dreamer we can see the dream technique quite clearly. The basic dream is *sinking under the water*; inverted, giving birth. Countermove, the galloping horse, the flying dream.

There is another clear proof of the intrauterine significance of the subaquatic world in these stories, *viz.*, the souls in a pot. In the palace of the water spirit there are many pots and in the pots the souls of those who were drowned.[213] At Leobschütz in Silesia stairs take the lad down under the lake. The pots with the souls are under the oven. He opens them and then runs for dear life. When he turns around the lake and everything has disappeared.[214] The water spirit lures the lad into the water in the shape of floating wood that keeps sinking and reappearing. The lad liberates all the souls from their pots.[215] The midwife who is called to deliver the baby also takes the lid off the pot.[216]

In a Flemish story the souls of the drowned, before they are liberated from their pots, sing in praise of a beautiful woman.[217] In Austria, a peasant went to swim in a brook. Something was constantly pulling him always deeper down. He felt that he was going through a hole and then he awoke. He saw a beautiful palace, but the floor was covered with fish eyes. The water spirit said, "Don't be afraid, your time has not come yet." He showed him the pots. Some were covered, some uncovered. The covered ones contained the souls of the drowned, the open ones were ready for those who were going to be drowned.[218] Mac Culloch believes that the island Elysium of the Celts and the world under the water are the same thing "over-sea and under-waves are often synonymous."[219]

It is difficult to decide whether we have really an engram of the amniotic fluid. It is true that the intrauterine symbolism is obvious but in some cases it is too obvious to be really "deep" unconscious. One alternative would be that mother is fluid because mother is milk, the other would be the amorous disposition of all water dwellers.[220] The water into which the human being sinks is the lubricated vagina. A third alternative would be the urethral dream. The water derived from the bladder becomes a lake, but the dreamer also identifies with his own urine that flows in his own body and he is born, i.e., he awakes. But the association of sleep,

213 Grimm, *Deutsche Volkssagen*, I, No. 52, p. 55.
214 Kühnau, *op. cit.*, I, pp. 258, 259.
215 *Ibid.*, II, p. 278.
216 *Ibid.*, II, p. 342.
217 Goyert, G. and Wolter, K., *Vlämische Sagen*, Jena, 1917, p. 122.
218 Vernaleken, Th., *Mythen und Bräuche des Volkes in Oesterreich*, Wien, 1859, p. 382.
219 Mac Culloch, I. A., *The Religion of the Ancient Celts*, Edinburgh, 1911, p. 371.
220 Cf. for instance, von Schroeder, L., *Griechische Götter und Heroen, Aphrodite, Eros und Hephaestos*, Berlin, 1887. "Nymphen," in *Roscher's Lexikon*, III, pp. 514, 515.

water and birth or death is so constant that these hypotheses seem inadequate as an explanation. There must be some deep unconscious engram of the embryo in the floating state which is restimulated everywhere by the sight of water. Fluid is also associated with coitus (semen and vaginal fluid) and coitus like sleep with uterine regression. Coitus plus castration anxiety is the Song of the Sirens and postcoital relaxation or uterine regression is Elysium.[221]

[221] *Acknowledgment*: In this chapter parts of two papers—"Charon and the Obolos" (*Psychiatric Quarterly Supplement*, 20, 1946) and "The Song of the Sirens" (*Psychiatric Quarterly*, 22, 1948) are reprinted with the permission of the Editor. I have also reprinted my paper "The Bear in the Haunted Mill" (*American Imago*, V, 1948) with the permission of the Editor of the *American Imago*. The essay on "Mondmythologie und Mondreligion" (*Imago*, XIII, 1927) has been partly translated, partly amplified and modified with the permission of the quondam Editor of the *Imago*. The same is valid for the paper "Die wilde Jagd" (*Imago*, XII, 1926).

VI

THE NATURE OF OGRES

The folktale of the three Hairs of the Devil is in many ways a parallel to the Epic of Gilgamesh.

A great king got lost in the forest. He spent the night in the house of a woodsman whose wife was about to be delivered. The next day the wood-chopper promised to show him the way out of the forest. At night the boy was born. Three women clad in white came to his cradle. The first one said: Bad luck for this child! The second: I shall give him something to ward off disaster. The third: He shall marry the king's daughter who is being born at the same moment. The king, lying awake in the next room, heard all this and decided that the child should be killed. The servant put the baby in a basket and let it float on the river. Fishermen rescue the child and call it "Nameless." The king finds out what has happened and sends the young man, now aged twenty, to the queen with a letter. The letter said, "This young man should be killed." On the way, however, he happens to go through a forest where a woman in white invites him to come into her hut. He goes to sleep and while he is asleep she finds the letter. On awakening he finds himself in the royal palace. The woman in the forest had substituted another letter, and in accordance with this second message he was married to the princess. The woman in the forest was an Urme (Fate) and she had protected the child. The king returns and wants to get rid of his unwelcome son-in-law. He therefore sends him to get *three golden hairs of the Sun King.* He is ferried over the black water. A king whom he tells where he is going tells him to ask the Sun what has happened to the spring of youth which ceased to flow in his town twenty years ago.

Another question an old man wants to know is this: twenty years ago a tree bore golden apples and anyone who tasted those apples was reju-venated. Now there are no more golden apples. Finally he sees a big house. The mother of the Sun King tells him that the Sun, an aged man, comes home every evening and falls asleep on his mother's lap. *She hides the young man in a big barrel of water* and while her son is asleep she pulls a hair out and he awakes. "Mother, why don't you let me sleep?" The mother says, "I dreamed about a city with a tree and golden apples" (as above). The Sun answers, "They should kill the snake that is gnawing at the roots of the tree!" The same is repeated with another hair and the answer is, "A great toad is blocking the opening of the spring." The third question is about the man in the boat on the black water. "If he can put the oar into another man's hand he is free and the other takes his place." Nameless returns home with the three hairs of the Sun King. The old king who tries to imitate him gets caught with the oar in hand and becomes the Charon of the black water.[1]

The Grimm version of the story is called "The Devil and the Three Gold Hairs." The questions are: wine flowing out of a well, tree with golden apples, and the ferryman rowing hither and thither. The mortal is changed into an ant and hidden in the plaits of the skin of the devil's mother. The devil on coming home says, "I smell human flesh."[2]

A common trait of all these stories is the fact that the young hero overhears a dialogue between a male and a female supernatural being. What is it about? In some versions we find the wafers of the Holy Communion, in many a toad; in a Vend story the dragon comes home and says, "I smell the blood of a Christian." His wife awakens him and says, "I dreamed that a miller's daughter used to be beautiful and after the first communion she became so ugly that nobody could look at her." The dragon says, "The minister dropped the wafer and the wafer was swallowed by a toad. If they take the wafer out of the toad, the miller's daughter will regain her beauty." Again in the same story a well is muddy on account of a toad.[3] In another story of the same people the toad is obstructing the source. What is the matter with the tree? A girl has killed her child and buried it under the tree; the tree will bear fruit again when the child is dug out.[4] In a French story the hero calls himself "Messager du Diable et le Carillon d'Enfer." He has made two daughters of the Emperor of Russia pregnant, the third one is sick. She has vomited "la Sainte Hostie," which was then swallowed by a toad. The toad is in a hole. It must be dug out and boiled. When the princess drinks this water, she will be cured.[5] In a Hungarian story the water is blocked because of the immoral life led by the daughters of the Emperor.[6] The problem is evidently: Where do

---

[1] Wlislocki, H. von, *Märchen und Sagen der Transsylvanischen Zigeuner*, Berlin, 1886, pp. 16–21.

[2] Grimm, *Kinder und Hausmärchen*, No. 29.

[3] Veckenstedt, E., *Wendische Sagen, Märchen und abergläubische Gebräuche*, Graz, 1880, pp. 237–240.

[4] *Ibid.*, pp. 76–77.

[5] Luzel, F. M., *Contes Populaires des Basse-Bretagne*, Paris, 1887, I, p. 132.

[6] Kriza—Orbán—Benedek, Székely földi gyüjtés (Folklore of the Szekelys), *Magyar Nepkoltesi Gyujtemeny*, III, 1882, p. 319; Sklarek, E., *Ungarische Volksmärchen*, Leipzig, 1901, p. 33; *Magyar Nyeloör*, X, 1881, p. 40.

babies come from? and this is expressed in various symbolic forms. The toad especially may symbolize both the embryo and the womb.[7] The child is hearing the answer to the age-old problem: Where do babies come from? It is well known, however, that when children ask the age-old question it is merely a cover-up for sexual curiosity. We surmise that the hidden hero is the child witnessing the primal scene. In a Norwegian version the queen has lost her golden keys. The Dragon says, "Oh, she'll find them soon enough if she looks among the bushes where she lay that time she wots of."[8] In Icelandic versions the primal scene element is even clearer. It is the giant (devil, ogre, dragon) who spends the night at the feet of the young couple.[9] If we come to the conclusion that we have to do with a story derived from the primal scene we must also take the next step: the nucleus of the story is a *dream of the primal scene*. All the problems are represented as *dreamed by the ogre's wife,* and the ogre himself is represented as sleeping. It is easy to see the secondary rearranging of roles, the primal scene which reappears in the *dream of the child observer*.[10] Again we notice a kind of blending of the primal scene and the intrauterine motive or basic dream. The hero is hidden in a barrel of water, or in the skirt of the ogre's wife, or under the bed.

In a Slovak story of this type called, "The Journey to the Sun," the Sun says, "Every morning I am delivered again by my mother as a youth and every evening I am an aged man whom she buries." At the end of the story the hero clearly identifies himself with the Sun. He dons the *Sun-garment* (which the Sun has given him hidden in a nutshell) and by doing so obtains the bride.[11] The *descent* and *ascent* is clearly the basic dream element, superimposed on which, we find the primal scene. The meaning of these hiding places is quite clear in the following story. Four men of the Yuchi tribe kill their wives. Then they decide to fetch them. They go to where the Creator is. They go westward to a place where there is a great cave. There is a cloud swaying up and down at the entrance. Three decide to become animals; they pass. The fourth one says that he will be a man; the cloud falls on his head and crushes him. Inside the cave the three men take their natural shapes as men. They climb up a black cloud and they come to an old woman. She is the Sun. They tell her they have come to fetch their wives. She invites them to stay for a dance. A panther

---

7 On the womb symbolism of the toad in European folklore, cf. Róheim, *Addálé-kok a magyar néphit hez* (Contributions to Hungarian Folk Beliefs), Budapest, 1920, pp. 219, 220.

8 Webbe Dasent, G., *Popular Tales from the Norse*, Edinburgh, 1903, p. 210.

9 Rittenhaus, A., *Neuisländische Volksmärchen*, 1902, p. 5.

10 Cf. for previous discussions of this folk tale, Róheim, "Charon and the Obolos," *Psychiatric Quarterly Supplement*, XX, 1946, pp. 160–196.

11 Wenzig, J., *Westslawischer Märchenschatz*, Leipzig, 1857, pp. 36–40.

monster comes and they are very much afraid. The old woman lifts her dress and tells the men to go under it. When the great monster comes near, it says, "I smell people," but the old woman says, "You smell me." The monster goes away and she gives them their wives in the shape of four gourds. She says to them: "*Now lie down and sleep*. When you wake up you will be back to earth. Don't open the gourds before you take them to a dance." One man disobeys and opens the gourd; the wind takes his wife away. The other three have their wives again.[12]

The descent to the cave or other world itself is the same thing as hiding under the skirt of the mother figure. Opening the gourd, like Pandora's box or like Orpheus, is the forbidden vision. It is a dream, they sleep, awake and they are back to earth.

The ogre in the story of "Jack and the Beanstalk"[13] is a sky-dweller. Once upon a time there was a poor widow who had an only son named Jack, and a cow named Milky White. They have no money so they decide to sell Milky White. Jack sells the cow for five beans. His enraged mother throws the beans into the garden and refuses to give Jack any supper. He goes up to his little room and falls asleep. When he awakes the room looks funny. The sun is shining into part of it and yet the rest of the room looks dark. He sees that the beans have grown into a big beanstalk which goes up and up till it reaches the sky. He climbs up to the sky and comes to a big house. On the doorstep of the big house, he finds a great big tall woman. He tells her that he is hungry, and she gives him breakfast. When the ogre, her husband, comes she hides Jack in an oven. The ogre says:

> Fee, fo, fum
> I smell the blood of an Englishman.
> Be he alive or be he dead,
> I'll have his bones to grind my bread

The wife tells the ogre, as usual in these cases, that he is completely mistaken. She hides Jack in the oven. When the ogre falls asleep after his breakfast, Jack bolts with one of the ogre's bags of gold. He climbs back to his mother's garden on the beanstalk, and gives her the gold. The same episode is repeated: this time he steals a hen that lays golden eggs. The third time it is a golden harp, but the harp, upon being carried away, calls out, "Master, Master," and the ogre wakes up just in time to see Jack running off with his harp. Jack climbs down the beanstalk followed closely by the ogre. When he comes quite near his home, he cries out, "Mother!

---

[12] Speck, F. G., *Ethnology of the Yuchi Indians*, University of Pennsylvania, Anthropological Publications, I, No. 1, Philadelphia, 1909, pp. 44–146.

[13] Cf. Desmonde, W. H., "Jack and the Beanstalk," *American Imago*, VIII, 1951, p. 287.

mother! bring me an axe." His mother comes to the beanstalk with an axe; she stands stock still with fright, for there she sees the ogre with his legs just through the clouds. Jack cuts the beanstalk in two. "The ogre felt the beanstalk shake and quiver, so he stopped to see what was the matter. Then Jack gave another chop with the axe and the beanstalk was cut in two, and toppled over. Then the ogre fell down and broke his crown and the beanstalk came toppling after."

Jack and his mother were rich. He marries a great princess and they live happily ever afterward.

In another version we are told that the treasures were stolen by the ogre from Jack's father.[14] This addition is not merely a moralistic note, as Jacobs thinks, but it clearly shows that the ogre is identical with Jack's father. Jack sells Milky White, the mother symbol, and falls asleep hungry, i.e., deprived of mother. Frustrated in his dream, he has an erection—the beanstalk, and climbs over his own penis. The dream origin of the myth becomes quite clear in the sleeping ogre from whom Jack steals various objects, into the detailed symbolic meaning of which we need not go. On the way back, the beanstalk is both Jack's penis and father's penis. When it is cut, the ogre dies.

We find other stories too in which the dream origin of the peastalk motive is made quite clear. A Russian peasant says to his wife, "Wife, wife, I say, I shall climb up into heaven and see what's going on there!" So he climbs up and there he finds a large wooden house. He enters it and sees a stove garnished with suckling pigs and geese and pies, "and everything which the soul could desire." But the stove is guarded by the seven-eyed goat. The *moujik* charms six of the eyes to sleep but overlooks the seventh. The seventh eye sees him eat and drink and then fall asleep. The owner of the house arrives and the intruder runs out. He descends on a cord made of cobwebs (the beanstalk has disappeared) but it does not reach down to earth. He jumps, lands in a swamp, etc.[15]

The repetitious *motive of sleeping* shows that we have a dream of climbing and falling.

The Eddic gods were in need of a fortress to protect them against their enemies, the giants (*iötun* = eaters). A mason appears who is willing to build Midgard. The price is the Sun and the Moon and the goddess, Freyja. But there is a condition: it must be completed before the first day of summer dawns. The mason works with his horse, Swadlfari, and the horse does most of the work. The gods are alarmed at the speed with

14 Jacobs, J., *English Fairy Tales*, London, 1907, p. 235; Hartland, E. S., *English Folk and Fairy Tales*, Camelot Series, p. 35.

15 Ralston, W. R. S., *Russian Folktales*, London, 1873, p. 295. Includes several other versions.

which he builds, the price they have to pay if he succeeds is too high. It was Loki's advice to permit the presence of the horse, now he must come to the rescue. Loki becomes a mare and the stallion runs after the mare, thereby preventing its master from completing the work. When he saw how he had been tricked, the giant showed his wrath. Now the gods knew who their mason was, and disregarding their oaths, called upon Thor for rescue. As usual in these situations, Thor smashes the giant and ends his activities as a builder.[16]

In a Christian version of the same story, King St. Olaf, the first Christian king, is about to build a church and accepts the offer of a giant (troll) who is willing to build it within a given time, but for his work he wants St. Olaf himself, or Sun and Moon. The deal would be void if Olaf could guess his name. The church was nearly complete, and Olaf was afraid that he might be held to his bargain. Wandering in the hills he hears a child crying, and its mother saying, "Don't cry, your father, Wind and Weather, will be home tomorrow and will bring Sun and Moon and St. Olaf." He goes home and when the troll is about to put the spire on the church, he says, "Wind and Weather, the spire is crooked." The demon falls off the church and crumbles.[17] The typical form of the popular legend is that a giant or the devil promises to build a castle or church in a very short time, or the building gets bigger and bigger with supernatural speed. In order to cheat the ogre or devil of his due, the human being, with whom he has made his contract, makes a cock crow before dawn—and that is the end of the ogre.[18] It seems to be a general attribute of giants in German folklore that daylight petrifies them and ends their existence.[19] Why beings of the order of giants should be intent on building churches is far from clear[20]—unless we use the key of interpreting the myth as an actual dream. The peasants of Oberndorf say that the devil demanded a part of the earth from God. The reply was that he could have what he could surround by a wall before the cock crowed. But just when he wanted to put the last stone in his wall, the cock crowed—the wall was unfinished and the devil got nothing at all.[21]

We know that the day stimulus of the dream is the unfinished task.

[16] Simrock, K., Die Edda, 1896, pp. 275–277, Gylfaginning, 42.

[17] Grimm, Deutsche Mythologie, I, 1875, p. 454.

[18] Leyen, Friedrich von der, Die Götter und Göttersagen der Germanen, München, 1909, I, p. 186.

[19] Grimm, op. cit., p. 457.

[20] Zingerle, I., Sagen aus Tirol, 1891, pp. 125, 126.

[21] Grimm, Deutsche Sagen, I, n.d., No. 188, p. 218, cf. Weinhold, K., "Die Riesen des germanischen Mythus," Sitzungsberichte der Philosophisch-Historischen Classe der Kaiserlichen Akademie der Wissenschaften, XLVI, 1888, pp. 225–306. Weinhold attempts to explain the giant as derived from natural phenomena.

In the Eddic myth this unfinished task becomes projected to the father, the giant, and at the same time becomes cathected with libido—it is the primal scene: the stallion chasing the mare. Thus the superego-conditioned, unfinished task becomes the child dreamer's wish—to interrupt the primal scene. The trait of *rapid growth* (erection) of the building also indicates the erotic transformation of the unfinished task. But why this craving of our giants, ogres, etc., for the Sun and the Moon, that is, the light?[22] We should not forget that Samson, who in the original story must have been the ogre and not the hero, is blinded like Polyphemos.[23]

In a story of the Dithmarschen quoted by Laistner, we are told that a one-eyed giant haunts the cornbin every night and steals the peasant's corn. The peasant catches him, tears his one eye out and restores it only on condition that the giant will be his helper.[24] The Lorg, a kind of nightmare demon of Tyrol is a one-eyed giant.[25] The Gascogne people talk about one-eyed giants living in caves and eating whomever they can catch.[26] The Tartaro of the Basques, like the Cyclops, has one eye in the middle of his head and eats those who go astray in the forest.[27] The Spillalutsche in Silesia is one of those demons who haunt lazy spinners at night. She looks through each little hole and crag to see whether the spinning has been done. She has terrible eyes and teeth like a wild boar's tusks.[28] The "Fänsmutter" with fiery eyes is also one of the demons of the nightmare group.[29] The Hungarian Liderc, admittedly a demon of the nightmare type, radiates light like a lamp.[30] A dog with eyes of fire is another demon of this kind.[31] All demons of the night probably originate in dreams. The vouivre in the French Comté is a tall man with a single eye of fire.[32] A spirit of Westfalia which acts as a nightmare has one glaring eye in the middle of the forehead.[33] A story of Dithmarschen again reveals the dream origin of these one-eyed beings. A mysterious being steals wheat every night. The youngest stays awake, catches the one-eyed giant and tears his eye out.[34] The Hottentots tell of an ogre with

---

[22] Stucken, E., *Astralmythen*, 1907, p. 294; Goldzieher, J., *Der Mythos bei den Hebräern*, 1876, p. 133.

[23] Cf. *infra*.

[24] Laistner, L., *Das Räthsel der Sphinx*, II, p. 59.

[25] Zingerle, *op. cit.*, p. 2.

[26] Sebillot, P., *Le Folklore de France*, 1904, I, p. 434.

[27] Sebillot, *l.c.*, I, p. 295.

[28] Kühnau, R., *Schlesische Sagen*, II, 1911, p. 57.

[29] *Ibid.*, II, p. 121.

[30] Róheim, *Magyar Néphit és Népszokasok*, 1925, pp. 93–98.

[31] Rakovsky, L., *Babonás Történetek* (Superstitious Stories), *Ethnographia*, 1910, p. 30.

[32] Amersbach, K., *Licht und Nebelgeister*, Baden-Baden, 1901, p. 27.

[33] Laistner, *Das Räthsel der Sphinx*, 1889, II, p. 49.

[34] *Ibid.*, p. 51.

a very curious displacement of the eye: it is on the instep of the foot. It looks like a human being but its sight is directed toward the sky. They hunt human beings whom they consider to be zebras, and whom they tear to pieces with their toenails.[35]

In a folktale from Athens the prince sets out to get the magic wand of the famous Drakos.

He sat down under a tree and *fell asleep*. When he woke he saw an old woman sifting flour into a great baking pan. But the flour dropped to the ground, not into the pan for she was blind. He helps her and in return she says, she is to go near the great cave.

Draw near, if thou hear sounds of snoring thou wilt know that the Drakos is asleep within.

Tied to his beard is a golden key. Cut the beard and key with these scissors.[36]

In the oldest representation of Polyphemos the Aristonophos-Vase we see the eye in the middle of the forehead. Besides we have also the normal eyes, but they are closed as if he were asleep.[37]

Odysseus relates his encounter with Polyphemos. When he describes the cave of the giant he says:

"There a monstrous man was wont to sleep, who shepherded his flocks alone and afar." Odysseus gives the man-eating Cyclops some wine and he falls into a drunken sleep. Odysseus and his comrades thrust the red-hot stake into his eye and blind him. He wakes and cries in pain and cries so loud that the other giants assemble around the cave.

"What so sore distress is thine, Polyphemos, that thou criest out thus through the immortal night and makes us sleepless." The well-known answer is that Outis (the name given by Odysseus, i.e., Nobody, Noman) has done this to him. The others say if Noman is doing him any harm it is all right, and they go their way.

"As soon as early Dawn appeared, the rosy-fingered, then the males of the flock hastened forth to pasture." Odysseus ties himself and his comrade under the rams and thus they escape the giant and come out of the cave.[38]

In this story we have a cave, a sleeping giant, and the story ending with the dreamer coming out of the cave at dawn—carried again by an animal as in the story of the Bear's Son.

[35] Schultze, L., *Aus Namaland und Kalahari*, Jena, 1907, pp. 392, 393.
[36] Cook, A. B., *Zeus*, Vol. II, Cambridge, 1925, Part II, p. 991; Dawkins, R. M., *Modern Greek in Asia Minor*, Cambridge, 1916, p. 550.
[37] Hackman, O. (*Die Polyphemsage in der Weltliteratur*, 1904, p. 168), quotes Sauer, B., *Die Torso von Belvedere*, Giessen, 1894, p. 45.
[38] *Odyssey IX*, Translation by A. T. Murray, Cambridge, 1946, Vol. I, p. 303.

The trait of the sleeping giant, the sojourn in a cave, and coming out of the cave in the morning indicate the basic dream.

In a Kabyle version, the Eye of the Head Cyclops has the Kabyle Odysseus and his companions in his cave. But here it is the giant who thrusts the redhot iron into the eye of one man after another and then eats them. Finally, when only the hero is left, he says, "I will tell you a story." The ogre agrees: "All right, *if I fall asleep* first, you can do what you want with me. And if you fall asleep first I can do what I like with you."[39]

In a Transylvanian (Hungarian) version, the visitors to the giant's cave are herding their father's sheep. The blinded giant gives the hero a ring. As the ring directs the giant who is pursuing the hero and he cannot pull it off his finger, he cuts his finger off and throws it into a lake. The giant in hot pursuit gets drowned.[40]

In an Aramaic version of Abdin, the son of a prince serves a blind giant as a goatherd. He stabs the giant with a pin and then passes between the opened legs of the giant out of the cave. Then it turns out that he is the giant's son, and he regains the giant's eyes from a *she bear* who has stolen them.[41] Here we stand again on the borderline between *Sage* and *Märchen*. A Karinthian "saga" tells us how a place was haunted by a demon that was half horse, half human (the nightmare). The peasants have to scratch him till they collapse with fatigue. A priest advises the hero to scratch the demon with a heated hatchet and to say that his name is "Selbertan" (I did it myself).[42]

In Tyrol, the Fanggas hand gets caught in a wedge, and the human being is called "I did it myself."[43]

If the "lost eyesight" can be equated with the "caught in a wedge" motive, then I would assume that in both cases we have castration anxiety.

Just as in the "wedge" stories (quoted *infra*) the alleged aim is to teach the bear or demon how to play the violin, we find versions in which the one-eyed being wants to get a second eye and they pour fluid lead into the one eye he has.

In one Swedish version of Finland the barn is inhabited by a pixie (*Kobold* = more like a spirit of the house). The peasant brings him his food everyday. One day the hired lad brings him his food and he calls

39 Frobenius, L., *Atlantis, Volksmärchen der Kabylen,* Jena, 1922, II, pp. 26, 27.

40 Horger, A., *Hétfalusi csángó népmesék* (Csángó folktales from Hétfalu), Budapest, 1908, pp. 179–182.

41 Prym and Socin, *Der neuaramaeische Dialekt des Tur Abdin,* Göttingen, 1881, II, p. 115.

42 Graber, G., *Sagen aus Kärnten,* Leipzig, 1914, pp. 31, 32.

43 Zingerle, *op. cit.,* p. 134.

himself "Self." The pixie complains that his one eye is sore. The lad promises to cure it and pours hot lead into it. The cries of the brownie are heard by the peasant but when he says Self did it the peasant replies, if you have done it to yourself you may as well help yourself.[44] The peasant (father imago) seems here to be in alliance with the spirit against the lad.

The anxiety aspect of the sleep-cave is really castration anxiety, the female organ can be both the castrating vagina and the protecting womb.

The castration content hidden in the motive "blinding" reveals itself in some "deviant" variants; the giant is a female and the lead is poured into her vagina. In a Swedish version the "Earth woman" (vätte) lifts her skirt and tries to seduce the peasant. He says his name is "Self" and then pours whatever he is cooking into her vagina.[45] In another version the concave back of the sea-woman is substituted for the vagina. Finally in a third story the peasant is having an affair with the "woman of the forest" (*Waldfrau*) and he throws hot soot into her face to get rid of her. All these stories contain the "Self" motive.

In some versions of the story (as in the Hungarian version quoted above), the danger ends when the hero cuts his own finger off.

In an Italian version, there are two monks. They lose their way and come to a cave in which a monster was building a fire. The monks did not believe it was a monster, but said, "Let us go and rest there." They went in and saw the monster killing a sheep and eating it. The monster compels them to eat, although they are reluctant to do so. Finally they eat. Then he takes a sharp iron, heats it in the fire and sticks it in the throat of the larger of the two monks, roasts his body and makes the other monk help him eat it. In the night the monk takes the iron, heats it and plunges it into the monster's eyes. Then he slips into a sheepskin and in the morning escapes from the cave with the other sheep.[46]

In a story recorded by Grimm, the giant in the cave eats one of the wanderers every day, leaving the leader who was thinner than the others for the last day. He tells the giant that he is a doctor who will cure his eyesight if his life is spared. He pours hot oil into his eyes, blinding him completely. The giant jumps up roaring and chases him all over the place with a big club. Finally, he hides under the skin of a ram. It was the giant's custom to let all his sheep pass between his legs when they went out of the cave in the morning. The giant would grab them all and whichever was the fattest he would eat for his breakfast. He grabs the hero, but the latter slips out of his hands several times so the giant

---

[44] Hackman, O., *Die Polyphemsage in der Volksüberlieferung*, Helsingfors, 1904, pp. 151, 152.

[45] *Ibid.*, pp. 120–122.

[46] Crane, T. F., *Italian Popular Tales*, London, 1885, p. 89.

says angrily, "Go to the wolves!" Once outside, he throws off his skin
and shouts back, "I have fooled you!" The giant throws him a golden
ring as a present, and he puts the ring on his finger. The ring keeps
shouting, "Here I am," so that the blind giant can follow him. He cannot pull the ring off, so that the only way he can escape is to bite his
finger off.[47]

The Ostyaks tell a tale about a man whom nothing could frighten.
He wanders about to learn fear. Another man who also wants to learn
fear joins him. They find a little hut in the forest and enter. A cannibal
comes and says, "What a pity that there are only two of them!" The
cannibal goes to sleep and the first fearless man also goes to sleep amid
the sheep. He is still not afraid. In the morning the cannibal throws his
sheep out of the hut, one by one. He also throws the man out. The
fearless man now catches sight of an axe with a golden haft wedged in
a tree. He is pleased and goes there to get it. But when he holds it in
his hand, he can't let go, or it won't let him go, and he hears the cannibal coming. He is so frightened that he cuts his own hand off with
a knife. Now he knows the meaning of fear.[48]

Now we can attempt an interpretation. We have assumed that this
is a dream: (a) it takes place in a cave, (b) one or several of the *dramatis
personae* are represented as sleeping, and (c) the end of the myth like
that of many of our basic dreams is coming out of a cave or passing
through the legs of a giant, i.e., birth. Besides the *basic dream,* we have
something else. The giant says *nobody* or the giant says *myself.* Naturally we suspect that he is right and that the two, giant and human being, are in a sense one person.

In the Osset story, the giant first tries to drive the spit into Urysmag,
but when the giant is asleep Urysmag shoves it into his eye.[49]

The masturbation is also revealed in the cutting off of the finger
or hand or in the hand being glued to the weapon.

But masturbation goes with castration anxiety. Freud has explained
the essential problem of the boy. On seeing the vagina, the libido it
evokes and the absence of the penis imply the threat of castration for
masturbation, i.e., for sexuality in general. The boy has two choices: to
accept the threat and renounce gratification, or to deny reality (i.e., the
castrating father) and go on masturbating. This can only be achieved
at the expense of the unity of the ego.

47 Bolte, J. and Polivka, G., *Anmerkungen zu den Kinder- und Hausmärchen,* Leipzig, 1918, III, pp. 371, 372.
48 Polivka, "Nachträge zur Polyphemsage," *Archiv für Religionswissenschaft,* I,
1898, p. 326.
49 *Ibid.,* I, pp. 310, 311.

Freud then quotes the case of a child of three who saw the female organ and then started to masturbate. His solution was that the
girl would have a penis, only it had not grown yet.

However, in some cases when castration is threatened, he actually
gives up masturbation. The next step is that a "fetish" is evolved that
serves as a substitute for a penis.

He now continues his masturbation, but at the same time he is
afraid of the castrating father. This fear of the father as castrator is not
expressed directly, but by regression to the oral phase as a fear of being eaten by father.[50]

I believe that these statements by Freud contain the whole explanation of the Polyphemos myth. The hero goes to sleep in the cave.
He masturbates in his dream and is afraid that father will castrate him
(eat him) in consequence. But while the companions who also stand for
the dreamer are eaten, the hero himself inverts the situation and castrates the castrator, i.e., the giant, the representative of the father imago.
Since in the masturbation fantasy on the oedipal level, the son identifies
himself with the father, we can say that the giant is both the cannibal
Cyclops and *myself*, the dreamer—Odysseus of many wiles.

An animal story recorded by Mannhardt as a parallel to the Polyphemos episode is hardly a parallel at all, we mention it only because
of its obvious dream origin. In the Norwegian version *a hen falls asleep*
on an oak. She dreams that the world will end if she does not get to the
Dovrefjeld. The hen awakes, starts on the journey and on her way
collects other fowl (cock, duck, goose). The fox waylays them into his
cave. Goose and duck *fall asleep,* the fox gets the goose and starts roasting it. The hen *keeps awakening and the fox keeps telling her to go to
sleep again.* Finally hen and cock escape being eaten by *flying out of the
chimney.*[51]

Seeing has to do with the dream and with awakening. In the folk
tale on the "Light That Disappeared,"[52] we shall see how the reappearance of sun, moon and the stars signifies awakening. Therefore the
demon beings of the night, the gigantic parental images are trying to do
their best to prevent awakening, to steal sun, moon and the heavenly
light. They are beings of the night, they disappear when the cock crows.
If they steal the light they prevent awakening and prolong their own
existence. But the eye that glares at the mortal so ominously must be a

---

[50] Freud, "Die Ichspaltung im Abwehrvorgang," *Internationale Zeitschrift für
Psychoanalyse und Imago*, XXV, 1940, p. 244.

[51] Mannhardt, W., "Ulysses in Germanien," *Zeitschrift für deutsche Mythologie
und Sittenkunde*, IV, 1859, pp. 93–102.

[52] Cf. the Chapter, "Vesical Dreams and Myths."

punishment for what the eye of the mortal did, for seeing the primal scene. Another aspect of many ogres has always puzzled me. Frobenius summarizes the mythological situation as follows: The wandering god has arrived in the home of the ogres. He finds a woman who warns him of impending danger, and hides him. The ogre comes home and starts sniffing. "I smell human flesh," he says.[53] In a Russian story the old woman says, "Pfui, pfui, till now I have never smelt a Russian bone and now here it is, all of a sudden."[54] In a Hungarian story the dragon says to his wife who stumbles: "May dogs drink your blood." "What is the matter with you? Do you smell the smell of Szépmezöszárnya (Beautiful Hero of the Meadow)?"[55] The dragon says, "Woman, I smell the smell of a stranger." His wife answers: "You always say that when you come home."[56] In a Tartar story when the "Seven-headed Yelbegen" finds the hero in his house, he says, "I smell the smell of human beings."[57] In a Zulu story the cannibal woman, Lungtoo, comes home. Her daughters have hidden their lover in a pit. "Eh, eh," she says, "In my house here today there is a delicious odor. My children, what have you done, whence comes this odor?"[58]

I think the key to the meaning of the *smell* motive is contained in the fact that the ogres (or *some* of them) are really dogs. The kala are the man-eating demons of the Koryak. In one story a kala appears with a human face and a dog's body. He asks a woman: "Does your boy play late at night?" The dead have sent him to kill the boys who play late at night; their eyes are sore, they can't get any sleep.[59] These spirits really behave like dogs. They not only smell humans, they lap them.[60] The following episode is decidedly dreamlike. A cannibal spirit called Gormandiser eats human beings. He says, "It smells of human flesh here." He eats a woman.[61] Jochelson relates how, "She found herself in the underground world (lit on the other side). There she found all her relatives and all the other people whom Gormandiser had killed. She said to them: 'Hurry back before the sides of the road come together.' "[62]

[53] Frobenius, *Das Zeitalter des Sonnengottes*, Berlin, 1904, p. 388.

[54] Afanssjew, A., and Meyer, A., *Russische Volksmärchen*, Wien, 1906, I, p. 213.

[55] The name of the folk tale hero. Horger, A., *Hétfalusiodángó mesék* (Csángo Folk Tales from Hétfalu), 1908, p. 409.

[56] Kálmány, L., *Hagyomanyok* (Traditions), Szeged, n.d., p. 7.

[57] Radloff, W., *Proben der Volksliteratur der Türkischen Stämme Süd Sibiriens*, I, 1866, p. 307.

[58] Callaway, H., *Nursery Tales, Traditions and Histories of the Zulus*, Vol. I, part 1, 1866, p. 49.

[59] Jochelson, W., "The Koryak," *Jesup North Pacific Expedition*, VI, 1906, p. 191.

[60] *Ibid.*

[61] Petitot, E., *Traditions Indiennes du Canada Nord Ouest*, Alencon, 1887, p. 49.

[62] Jochelson, *op. cit.*, p. 303.

Athapaskan tribes also have traditions of human-like beings with dog faces or partly canine bodies.[63]

The Norwegians and Swedes have stories of beings which are called "Trynetyrk" or "Hundetyrk" and so have the Lapps and Finns. The Lapps call them "Baednag-njadne," i.e., dog's nose, and the Finns "Koi-ran-Kuolainen" which means the same. These monsters were men who had noses like dogs and so could track men by their scent. They were said to be enormously large and to have had one eye in the middle of the forehead, and were cannibals. In a Lapp story it is again the wife of the dog monster who tries to hide the stranger.[64] The Fomorians or giants of Irish mythology are dogheads.[65] The mountain elves of the Eskimo *smell* the coast people.[66] The Eskimo also talk about people whose upper limbs were human but below the waist they were shaped like dogs. They had bows and arrows, and they could catch the scent of man and beast.[67] The Erinyes of the Greeks are not only ghosts but they are ghosts in dog form.[68]

In Hungarian folklore we have the dog-headed giant or the dog-headed Tartar.[69] The Slovenes regarded the Huns or the Avars as dog-headed giants, later the Pecheneges or the "Calvinists" (i.e., Hungarians) took over the role of the dog-headed ogre.[70] The story of Polyphemos is told about a giant who is called "One-eyed Dog-head."[71] In Ceram we again find the traits of cannibal spirits, dogs, and smelling human flesh in close connection. The hero of a folk tale finds a beautiful woman in the forest. She hides him because of her mother. The mother comes home with seven dogs. "I smell human flesh," she claims. The daughter induces her mother to refrain from eating the guest and finally she elopes with him. The mother and the seven dogs die.[72] In another story the

---

[63] Boas, F., "Traditions of the Ts'ets'aut," *Journal of American Folk-Lore*, X, 1897, p. 44; Petitot, *op. cit.*, p. 49.

[64] Jones, H. W. W. and Knopf, L. L., *The Folk Tales of the Magyars*, Publications of the Folk-Lore Society, XIII, 1889, p. 340.

[65] Brown, A. C. L., *The Origin of the Grail Legend*, Cambridge, pp. 20, 84. On dog people cf. Liebrecht, F., *Zur Volkskunde*, Heilbronn, 1879, pp. 19, 20.

[66] Rink, H., *Tales and Traditions of the Eskimo*, 1875, p. 218.

[67] *Ibid.*, p. 207.

[68] Roscher, W. H. R., *Das von der Kynanthropie handelnde Fragment des Marcellus von Side*, Abh. d. phil. hist. cl. der Königl. Sächs. Ges. d. Wiss., XVII, Leipzig, 1896, p. 49.

[69] Kozma, F., *Mythologiai elemek a Székely Nep Költészet és Népéletben* (Mythological Traits in Szekely Folk Poetry and Customs), Budapest, 1882, p. 11. The anthropological explanation of the dog-headed Tartar given by Bartucz has nothing to do with this; cf. Bartucz, L., "A Kutya fejü tatár" (Dog-headed Tartar), *Magyarnyelvor*, LVII, 1928, p. 93.

[70] Copeland, F. J., "Slovene Folklore," *Folk-Lore*, XLII, 1931, pp. 441, 442.

[71] *Ibid.*, p. 437.

[72] Jensen, A. E., *Hainuwele*, Frankfurt am Main, 1939, pp. 192, 198.

cannibal woman has iron hips and dogs. The iron hips are like spears. Again we find the trait of smelling the flesh of a human being,[73] and the elopement.[74] In these stories the cannibal mother and her daughter are but two aspects of the same person. The mother figure means anxiety, the daughter libido. An old spirit woman kills her prey with an iron tail by sitting on them. She has fifty dogs and of course smells human flesh.[75] In another story it is really the dogs who smell the human being, or rather, bees temporarily changed into dogs.[76] Dogs figure also in nightmare beliefs. In stories of the Tyrol a monster (*Unthier*) comes into the hut at midnight in the form of a gigantic shaggy dog. The animal weighs on the sleeper and grabs his hand down with vulture claws. "Jesus Maria, it is tearing my hand off!" the sleeper exclaims, and the animal disappears, i.e., he is awake.[77] A black poodle wrestles in a haunted castle at night with the sleeper.[78] We find these dog nightmares in a specific form, of almost totemic character in the *Dorfthier* of German folklore.

Wettlingen is haunted by a big village poodle, the spirit of a suicide. It is big and black with eyes that light the night.[79] A black "Dorfhund" at Tegerfelden jumps on people who walk about at New Year's Eve and pushes them about. He jumps on the night watchman who then has to carry him[80] (nightmare).

In Silesia the story is about a poodle who jumps onto the wanderer's back and has to be carried, with the wanderer panting under the weight of the poodle till the next crossroad.[81]

While these stories with the weight to be carried are evidently nightmares, the folk tales of ogres show their dream origin by other traits. But the ogre's sniff, the giant and the dog, perhaps, are really identical or rather the smell motive in the dream myth is really the last trait of the canine shape of the hero's adversary.

We can now combine the motive of the hero's visit to the Sun or devil[82] with the well-known "Fee fo fum!" Three golden hairs of the ogre devil are torn out by the hero, aided by the ogre's mother, wife, etc. Here it is evidently the father imago who is castrated. On the other hand

---

[73] *Ibid.*, pp. 200, 201.
[74] *Ibid.*, pp. 202, 203.
[75] *Ibid.*, pp. 262, 263.
[76] *Ibid.*, p. 386.
[77] Zingerle, *op. cit.*, p. 205.
[78] *Ibid.*, p. 200.
[79] Rochholz, E. L., *Schweizersagen aus dem Aargau*, 1867, II, p. 32.
[80] *Ibid.*, II, p. 37.
[81] Kühnau, R., *Schlesische Sagen*, I, 1910, p. 520.
[82] By the way, L. Frobenius is completely wrong in assuming that the sun is never cast in the role of the ogre. Frobenius, L., *Zeitalter des Sonnengottes*, 1904, p. 384.

the ogre is a dog, and a dog phobia in clinical analysis always means castration anxiety.

It is noticeable that in all ogre stories the ogre's wife, mother, etc., is on the hero's side.

This is the story of Samson whose name means "little sun." In Gaza the Hebrew hero sleeps with a whore and the Philistines lie in wait for him all night expecting to kill him in the morning. But he leaves before dawn, and in going, he grabs the gates of the city and carries them on his shoulder to Mount Hebron. Later he falls in love with a woman named Delilah, one of the Philistines, the enemies of his people. And the chiefs of the Philistines prevailed upon her to give the secret away: What is the source of Samson's terrible strength. Samson said: "If they bind me with seven green withes that were never dried then shall I become weak and be as another man." This happens and Delilah shouts, "The Philistines be upon thee, Samson." He, of course, breaks the withes. The next answer is "seven new ropes which have never been worked on." Again the Philistines fail. Finally, he says, "If thou weavest the seven locks of my hair with the web and makest the whole fast with the pin, then shall I become weak and like any other man. *And Delilah makes him sleep;* she weaves the seven locks of his head with the web and fastens it with a pin, saying, "The Philistines be upon thee Samson!" He awakens and plucks away the pin and the web. Finally, as is usual in these stories, he tells her that his strength lies in his hair. When shorn of his hair, he falls into the captivity of the Philistines and Delilah.[83] The solar aspects of this myth have been emphasized by older writers.[84] Stucken noticed that the rôles of hero and ogre had been inverted; Samson is the ogre betrayed by his wife to the young hero. Therefore it must be a story originally told by the Philistines, and later adapted by the Hebrews.[85] The solar aspect of the myth is supported not only by the hero's name which means "little sun" but also by place names like Beth-Shemesh, "House of the Sun."[86] If we reread our text, the dream quality of the myth becomes quite clear. This is a dream dominated by castration anxiety (hair, blindness). The feeling of being tied or unable to move is well known in dreams. There is a repetition of the waking motive, "The Philistines." Finally it is even openly stated that the hero is asleep. And this is the origin of the "solar" myth. The hero who awakens becomes the sun rising on the horizon.

The ogre is definitely the father imago. In a Deccan story, while a

[83] Judges: 16.
[84] Goldzieher, J., *Der Mythos bei den Hebräern*, Leipzig, 1876, pp. 160, 187.
[85] Stucken, E., *Astralmythen*, Leipzig, 1907, 294.
[86] Frazer, *Folk-Lore in the Old Testament*, II, 1919, p. 482.

princess is rocking the cradle with her baby, a mysterious Fakeer, who is really a wicked magician, takes the princess away in the shape of a little dog. The little boy grows up and sets out to find his uncle's father and mother (the uncle and the father had been turned to stone by the same magician). After traveling many hundreds of miles, he arrives at his place of destination. The magician's wife, as usual, decides to help him and he is dressed up as a young girl (her daughter). In this disguise, which ensures his safety, he finds his mother imprisoned in a tower by the magician. At his advice, she seemingly agrees to marry the magician. After this she asks him: "And do tell me, are you quite immortal? Can death never touch you? Are you too great an enchanter even to feel human suffering?" He replies: "Why do you ask?" "Because," she says, "if I am to be your wife, I would fain know all about you, in order, if any calamity threatens you, to avert it!" The magician answers:

"Far, far away, hundreds of thousands of miles from this, there lies a desolate country covered with thick jungle. In the midst of the jungle grows a circle of palm trees and in the center of the circle stand six chattees full of water, piled one above another; below the sixth chattee is a small cage which contains the life of a green parrot; on the life of the parrot depends my life. If the parrot is killed, I must die."

The prince sets out to kill the parrot. Being very tired, he sits down under a tree and *falls asleep*. He is awakened by a rustling sound. He sees a snake that is threatening to kill two young eagles in the nest. He draws his sword and kills the serpent. The two old eagles fly home and are grateful to him for having saved the little ones who henceforth become his servants. The two young eagles carry him to his place of destination. It is noon and the heat is great. *All around the trees were genii fast asleep*. The eagles carry the prince through; he overthrows the six chattees of water and seizes the parrot. *As he mounts up into the air again the genii awake*.

He returns to the magician. When he tears off the parrot's right wing, the magician's right arm falls off, and with the second wing, the left arm. Finally when he wrings the bird's neck, the magician dies.[87] We note the ending of the story. The prince *falls asleep* and then comes the familiar eagle-rescue episode, then the *flight*, and the *sleeping genii*. Then again, awakening of the genii and flight.

In a Panjab story, the Princess as usual wants to elicit the secret of the Jinn's invulnerability. "The Jinn who was more than half asleep and quite tired of being cross questioned, answered drowsily:

'In front of the house lies a heap of bones and in front of the dog, a

[87] Frere, M., *Old Deccan Days*, London, 1898, p. 1–12.

heap of grass. Whoever takes a long stick and changes the heaps, so that the house has grass and the dog bones will have no difficulty in passing . . . (and find the soul which is in a starling in a golden cage, etc.).' "[88]

The situation is the same as we have seen in previous *ogre* stories. The child hero is hidden and a dialogue takes place between mother and father. There is a further parallel with the "Three golden hairs of the devil." The ogre's wife elicits a secret from the ogre. Furthermore, if we look at the matter somewhat closer, the secrets are the same: the embryo in the womb, or the toad in the well, and the egg incapsulated in a number of animals—where the babies come from, or the Riddle of the Sphinx—the primal scene. The young hero, whose castration anxiety is dealt with by castrating the cannibal father, at the same time projects his sleep regression into the womb to the ogre or father figure. When the egg is broken, the demons of the night disappear—*the hero is awake*.

We have seen above that the cannibal ogre or dog is really the castration complex and "to be eaten" means to be castrated by the father or to play the female role, the negative oedipus complex.

In Greek mythology, we have Uranos, Kronos and Zeus. According to Hesiodos, Kronos, the youngest child of Uranos, hates his father because Uranos, afraid of his Titan sons as pretenders to his throne, pushes them all back into their mother's womb. When Uranos at night approaches Gaia, Kronos, who is in hiding, castrates his father. We have here the primal scene motive as in the "Three hairs of the devil" and the castrated father figure. Besides we have also the regression into the womb as in the External Soul motive. Gaia tells Kronos that he in turn will be killed by his son. He therefore *eats all his sons* till finally Rhea gives him a stone to swallow instead of Zeus. How he is vanquished by Zeus is not recorded exactly except that he and the other Titans are relegated to Tartaros.

Why is the sickle the instrument of castration? The god who is mowed down by a sickle is the harvest. In the Ras Shamra texts, Anat the goddess seized Mot (Death), the divine son. With a cutting blade, she cuts him. With the winnowing sickle, she winnows him. With fire, she roasts him. In the fields, she scatters his flesh for the birds to eat. It is the corn god who is mowed down with a sickle, winnowed with a shovel, etc.[89] Kronos, who wields the sickle, seems to have been con-

88 In a Kabyl story the external soul motive is paralleled by that of a beautiful maiden taken out of the inside of the ogress. Frobenius, L., *Atlantis*, II, München, 1922, p. 115.

89 Eisler, R., "The Passion of the Flax," *Folk-Lore*, LXI, 1950, p. 123.

nected with the harvest.[90] On the other hand in Orphic tradition, Kronos, the ogre, is castrated by his son, Zeus.[91] The Egyptians also wailed for the death of the corn (Maneros), and the personified chief of corn or corn god is identified with Osiris.[92] The identification of Osiris with the corn and the phallic aspect of the god are equally prominent. "The festival (of Osiris) opened on the twelfth day of Choiak with a ceremony of ploughing and sowing." At the resurrection, Osiris is again the corn god. "Here we see the dead body of Osiris with stalks of corn springing from it while a priest waters the stalks from a pitcher which he holds in his hand. The accompanying inscription sets forth that, 'this is the form of him whom one may not name, Osiris of the mysteries, who springs from the returning waters.' "[93]

We have also numerous ithyphallic representations of the resurrection of Osiris,[94] thus leaving no doubt that Hornblower[95] correctly interprets Osiris as a phallic god. Returning again to Hellenic religion, we find that certain aspects of the cult of Zeus make him look very much like Kronos, a kind of deified ogre. Greek religion is of special interest because of the alternating "motives" of castration and cannibalism. Hesiod in his Theogony says, "But afterwards she (Gaia) lay with Uranos (Heaven) and bore deep-swirling Okeanos, Koeus, and Krios and Hyperion and Japetos, etc., . . . after them was born Kronos, the wily youngest and most terrible of her children, and he hated his lusty sire.

"And again she bore the Kyklops, overbearing in spirit Brontes and Steropes and stubborn-hearted Arges,[96] who gave Zeus the thunder and made the thunderbolt. In all else they were like the gods, but one eye was set in the midst of their foreheads.

"And again three other sons were born of Earth and Heaven, great and doughty beyond telling: Kottos, Briàrcos, and Gyes. From their shoulders sprang a hundred arms not to be approached and each had fifty heads upon his shoulders on their strong limb.

"For of all the children that were born of Heaven and Earth, these were the most terrible and they were hated by their own father from the first. And he used to hide them all away in a secret place of the Earth so soon as each was born and would not suffer them to come up into the light. And Heaven rejoiced in his evil doing. But vast Earth

---

[90] Article in *Roscher's Lexikon,* p. 1518; Farnell, L. R., *The Cults of the Greek States,* Oxford, 1896, I, pp. 27–30.

[91] Usener, H., *Götternamen,* Bonn, 1896, p. 26; *Roscher's Lexikon,* p. 1470.

[92] Eisler, *op. cit.,* p. 124.

[93] Frazer, *Adonis, Attis, Osiris,* 1907, pp. 321, 323 (with references).

[94] Wallis Budge, E. A., *The Gods of the Egyptians,* 1904, II, pp. 132, 136, 137.

[95] Hornblower, G. D., "Osiris and the Fertility Rite," *Man,* 1941. XLI. Pg. 71.

[96] Brontes—The Thunderer; Steropes—The Lightener; Arges—The Vivid One.

groaned within, being straightened, and she thought a crafty and an evil wile. Forthwith she made the elements of grey flint and shaped a great sickle and told her plan to her dear sons: 'My children gotten of a sinful father, if you will obey me we should punish the vile outrage of your father; for he first thought of doing shameful things." And Kronos is the one who volunteers to carry out Gaia's designs.

"And Heaven came, bringing on night and longing for love, and lay about Earth, spreading himself full upon her. Then the son, from his ambush, stretched forth his left hand and in his right took the great long sickle with jagged teeth and swiftly lopped off his own father's members and cast them away to fall behind him.

"The Erinyes, the Giants, the Nymphs called Meliae and Aphrodite originate from the severed phallos.[97]

"But Rhea was subject in love to Kronos and bore splendid children . . . and wise Zeus, father of gods and men by whose thunder the whole earth is shaken. These great Kronos swallowed as each came forth from the womb to his mother's knees.

"But when she was about to bear Zeus, the father of gods and men, then she besought her own dear parents, Earth and starry Heaven to devise some plan with her that the birth of her dear child might be concealed and that retribution might overtake great, crafty Kronos for his own father and also for the children whom he had swallowed down."[98]

Kronos is given a stone to swallow instead of Zeus. On a tomb painting discovered on the road from Ostia to Laurentium we see Kronos and Rhea both veiled. Kronos bends forward to seize a naked boy who flings up his arms in a gesture of frantic supplication. But the ogre, with grim face and horrible wide mouth, has him by hair and hand and leg. In the nick of time a handmaid rushes forward to present Kronos with a stone.[99]

If the stone swallowed by Kronos instead of Zeus was a pillar[100] the difference between the swallowing and the castration is not so great for these pillars are well-known phallic symbols in Greece. Retributions and the castration complex are carried over from one generation to the other.[101]

The sickle used by Kronos to mutilate Uranos is also used by Zeus to mutilate Kronos. According to the Rhapsodic Theogony of the Orphists, Zeus, at the advice of the Nyx, made Kronos drunk with honey

---

[97] Hesiod Theogony, pp. 132–190. Hesiod translations by Hugh G. Evelyn White, 1943, Harvard University Press, pp. 88–93.

[98] Idem, 454–473, pp. 113, 114.

[99] Cook, A. B., Zeus, A Study in Greek Religion, III, Part I, 1940, p. 935.

[100] Cook, op. cit., II, 1925, Part I, p. 447.

[101] Cf. "Uranos" in Roscher's Lexikon, p. 112.

and then bound him beneath the tall oaks and gelded him on the spot.[102]

The oak is not without reason, for since Frazer we know that it is the symbol of the sky-god and the tree under which one divine king kills the other and succeeds to royalty.

We do not expect to find Zeus, the father of gods and men in the role of an ogre yet there is plenty of evidence to support the conclusion that this is an aspect of his personality that he has shed, but which, not too well marked, is still here in myth and ritual.

Cook compares the data given by Pliny, St. Augustine, and Pausanias. From these it appears that a child was sacrificed by the Arcadians to Zeus Lykaios, i.e., Zeus Wolf. The person who first tasted the sacrifice became a wolf and for ten years remained a wolf. He is also supposed to have won at Olympia.[103] The infant is sacrificed by Lykaon, i.e., by Zeus as wolf king. But Zeus is also identical with the sacrificed child.

Pelops was chopped to pieces by his father Tantalos and dished up to the gods to test their omniscience. Pelops established the Olympic games in honoring Olympian Zeus.[104] Pausanias tells us that the temenos of Pelops at Olympia was between the temple of Zeus and Hera and also that he was regarded as pre-eminent among heroes like Zeus among gods.[105] Tantalos is probably identical with Atlas and Kronos[106]—so that here we have the same *theme* as in the Kronos-Zeus myth.

Cook is right in regarding the Kyklops as an older form of Zeus. The mere fact that these ogres own the thunder proves this hypothesis. Cook remarks that the three-eyed Kyklops of Sicily bears a striking resemblance to an archaic statue of Zeus with three eyes.[107] Zeus is also threatened by successors. According to the prophecy the son he procreates from Metis (wisdom, magic) will oust him. Instead of mating with her he swallows her. In Orphic mythology, Metis is identified with Phanes. Zeus leapt upon Phanes and swallowed him whole (Orph. fragment 63).[108]

This interlocking of the phallic or castration theme with that of the cannibal ogre reappears in Central Australia.

What we have to go by in this case are both the general belief in demons of the man-eating type and a large collection of folk tales about these demons. Demons in Central Australian beliefs and folk tales are

---

102 Cook, *Zeus*, Vol. II, Part I, 1925, p. 448.

103 Cook, *op. cit.*, I, 1914, pp. 72–78.

104 Pelops in *Roscher's Lexikon*.

105 Pausanias, XIII, 1, 8.

106 Cf. Marót, K., "Ατλσόλοοφρων," *Philologische Wochenschrift*, 1926, p. 588; *Idem, Kronos und die Titanen*, Studi materiali di storia delle religioni, Rome, 1932.

107 Cook, *Zeus*, I, 1914, p. 320, quoting Panofka, T., and Grimm, W., who also regarded Zeus as another Kyklops.

108 Cook, *op. cit.*, Vol. III, 1940, Part I, p. 745.

characterized by their large genital organs, their cannibalism, frequently their distorted shape and their association with caves.

My Ngatatara informants told me about the *patiri* demons with long teeth. They go into the baby with the mother's milk and bite the child with their long teeth when they are inside. This demon looks like a cat. It takes the baby from the mother and eats it; the mother cries in vain. Although up to this point we would assume that the demon is the "bad mother," we are told that they come from the other side of Wallungara (a big lake) and it is the males who come into this country and eat the children.

The Tangara are very curious cannibal demons because they eat themselves or rather their arms and legs, but another limb grows immediately to replace the one they have eaten. They live in caves and when a real man comes into their country, they give him a kangaroo to eat and then they eat him. The Yumu and Pindupi are also acquainted with these gentlemen. The Tangara is like a man but has only one leg. He kills human beings by throwing his club and then he eats them. If he happens to be hungry, he cuts a piece out of his own leg and eats it. These demons live in the limestone.

Another demon of the Yumu and Pindupi has long ears, long hair and the shape of a cat. It bites people and penetrates into their bodies.

A widespread type of demon is called *kukurpa*. This comes from (or is) the body of a real man. The man shakes *kuntanka nguampa* (like a tjurunga); that is, he performs the *alknantama*. Feathers grow from his arms and these develop into wings like an eaglehawk. His nose becomes a beak, his feet are now talons. He flies to other countries and there he eats souls. The people whose souls he has eaten die. The interesting trait in this demon is the phallic significance of the act of becoming a demon and the parallelism with the ritual.[109]

Another kind are the demon-eaters (mamu kurata) who specialize in eating Kukurpa demons and babies. They are very thin, shaped like a pole, have straight thin heads, and have no anus. They have many wives. Face, arms, fingers, penis or vagina—everything is very long. A group of them sitting on a long string and flying through the air are called "ngaluru punguta," i.e., stuck together. In this case, they look like dogs and are connected with each other by the penis and the tail. One dog's penis and tail is stuck right into the anus of the other dog. They are stuck together in married couples. When they bite, they bite right through so that a person falls into two halves.

The following data are obtained from Lelil-tukutu and represent real Pindupi demon-lore (not mixed with Yumu). Men, women and chil-

109 Róheim, *The Riddle of the Sphinx*, pp. 137–148.

dren will become demons. A man has been hunting all day and returns home empty-handed. He is hungry and he rolls about like a dog, and in his dog form, he catches a kangaroo. Then he becomes a man again. A child may also turn into a dog for the same reason. Or a real dog may become a man in shape, i.e., a dog demon. The man who has become a dog may now become the dog of his former dog. The mamu kurata digs a man's eyes out and pulls his ears off when he is asleep.

Another mamu (demon) developed from a human being is the *child demon*. This is really a man with his son on his shoulders. When he sees another man or woman, the child jumps off his father's shoulders and kills the other person with a club. Then father and son eat their victim together; they cook it for a long time till the head is soft. This is the part they like best. The child demon looks like a child when it is sucked out of people by the medicine man. The Matuntara talk about a dog demon that goes into the human body and bites people. Dog demons are very frequent. The Mularatara variety is of this type. Several men are assembled in a group talking in the camp. One of them feels a shivering sensation in his back, then he sees a dog demon coming nearer and nearer. It disappears in the sand. It is like a dog but has no ears and has a tail like a kunnia (wild cat, Dasyurus Geoffryi). He lies down beside the camp, bites the babies and then disappears into a hole. Another kind of demon is called, "karpirin-pa," i.e., "hair tied up." It looks like a man with his hair tied up. Besides being the initiators of medicine men, they eat babies. First they play with the child's soul, then they tickle the child, and then they kill him. The ghost demon comes from a corpse that has not been buried properly. An old woman who died the other day at Wotturka turned into a demon in her lifetime, i.e., she was "cranky." A *mamu* (demon) went into her anus and that is how she became a *mamu* herself.

There is also a kind called *mamu nyungura (erintja arunkulta* in Aranda), i.e., devil evil magic. If a man does not get the woman who has been promised to him and she goes with other men, he cuts his beard and hair and makes a string. He calls the string by the name of the man or woman he wishes to injure. He passes it to another man who comes from the west and carries it *meritnja* (dancing). The second passes it to a third and he carries it on his knees till he gets to the *mamu piti* (devil hole). The last man can approach the hole; the newly created demon would bite the others. The dog demon goes in through the anus of the sender and comes out through his mouth. Then it goes to the *papa kumuli,* i.e., the urinating place of dogs, a little water hole where all the dogs go to drink and urinate. *The water tells him:* "There he is!" the *mamu* runs straight at him, bites and kills him.

It was Tjintje wara[110] who first told me that all male demons have a huge phallos, and all female demons a huge vagina. Later on this was confirmed by other authorities. The Pindupi compared the size of a demon's penis to a desert oak. The women have a huge vagina and when they cohabit, they open it wide (*lalpintaranyi*). Their breasts are the size of pumpkins.

A demon belief shared by each subgroup is that of the *erkurindja* or "dogs" stuck together flying in the air. I have discussed these double demons in *The Riddle of the Sphinx*. Among the Aranda they are called *erkurindja;* among the Ngatatara, *tjintjirata;* and among the Yuma and Pindupi, *ngalura punguta* (joined together). They look like a pair of dogs permanently connected by the male dog's penis and tail which are permanently fixed in the bitch's anus. They are thus a married couple. When they bite, their victim is immediately cut in halves. According to the Matuntara, the male dog is called *mamara*, "like the father" and the bitch, *jakura*, i.e., like the mother.[111]

Interpretation may be attempted after we have briefly surveyed the material as embodied in the *tukurpa* or *altjira*, i.e., folktale. These stories are more like European folktales in their whole structure than those of any other primitive group that I am acquainted with. The fundamental theme is how the *entuta* (i.e., normal human being) conquers a whole crowd of *bankalangas* or *nananas* (other names for *mamu*, i.e., demon, ogre) gets initiated (or marries) and *stays always* (*kutu nyinanyi*), i.e., "They lived happily ever afterward."[112] We get another surprise through linguistics. The western tribes (Luritja) call a folk tale, *tukurpa;* the Aranda call it *altjira*. *Both words mean dream*. There is, as we should expect, no lack of reference to sleeping and dreaming in these stories.

In one of the stories a younger brother (human) goes to find something to eat (No. 7 of my collection):

"He saw a demon with a body like a man's and feathers like an emu lying near the fire. The demon was sleeping on gum tree leaves. As he came nearer he saw men cut in halves, and the bones of the men the demon had eaten. Then he saw his red eyes which were like the *moon*, and he knew it was a demon. He speared the demon in the backbone. They had a fight; sometimes the demon knocked him down; sometimes he knocked the demon down. The demon had a cave nearby where he had his axe. He managed to drag him into the cave where he killed him with the axe. Then he cooked and ate him.

---

[110] Cf. Róheim, "Dreams of Women in Central Australia," *Psychiatric Quarterly Supplement*, XXIV, 1950, pp. 35–64.

[111] Róheim, *Riddle of the Sphinx*, pp. 28, 29.

[112] Cf. Róheim, "Myth and Folk Tale," *American Imago*, II, pp. 266–279.

"The second part of the story is the same but with a happy ending. The older brother goes the same way and he kills the demon."

In both cases we have a nightmare with a happy ending. After "several times" the hero wins. "Several times" is an unconscious technical device—mounting anxiety and finally happy end evolved out of the same nightmare nucleus.

Story No. 82 further illustrates the dream origin. A mingalpindji[113] woman found two entutas *asleep* in one camp. She picked up a stone and hit them through the nose and ate them in her camp. This she repeated many times. But once they had a dream, and they saw what she was about to do. "Eh, that is the one of the dream," they said, and they speared and burnt her. They went back to a big camp and stayed there ever afterward.

The following is No. 79 in my collection, a Pindupi *tukurpa*. A bird man was a demon, and he always went to sleeping people and tied their legs up to their arms with a string. Then he pulled their beard and hair out, lifted them on his shoulder, carried them to his cave where he finally killed them and put their bodies in the cave. It was always sleeping men he put in the cave. Finally one of them awoke, got his spear and killed the ogre. He burned his body. He then went to a big camp and stayed there ever afterward. This is a urethral and phallic awakening. The dream has the same structure as this story. The anxiety aspect of the nightmare is repeated several times; the solution is represented by the awakening, and the spear comes as a *dénouement* of the situation. The dream in the story, seemingly a technical device, is really a return of the repressed origin.

In story No. 96 we are told: "One woman dreamed (*tukurp mana nanji*)[114] that a *nananana* (demon) came up. Then she saw him coming. He sat down at their fire[115] and asked, 'Where do you come from?' They did not answer. The Kuna-tai-tai went to sleep and snored. One put her yamstick through his heart, another through his ribs, and the third across his nose. They burned his body and went to a big camp."

Another story, No. 15, relates how the *manataitai* comes when the girls are asleep and carries them away in a wooden cradle or bed.

If the folk tales of this type or some of them are derived from dreams, they are certainly nightmares. What is the content of these nightmares? Let us take our story No. 45 as an example (told by Tjintjewara):

There was a *ltata* (nonsacred dance) of the *nananana*. The mother of all *nanananas* was standing aside and dancing alone. She sang: "O my

---

113 The species of bird is called *konkatakata* in Pindupi.
114 The same word is used for dream and story.
115 In reality there seem to have been several women.

star, the man standing here." She was nursing a dog like a child[116] and dancing. Everybody was glaring at her. When she had finished her dance, she threw the dog at the people. The dog bit and killed everyone of them and the *nananana* ate them. She went to another camp where she picked up all the children and nursed them. She said that she was their grandmother. On one arm she had a child, on another a dog. *Before daybreak* she let the dog go and it killed them all. After this was repeated several times, finally one *indatoa* (hero, normal person) kills the dog at daybreak and spears the old woman and all the demons. *They burn all the bodies* and stay there forever.

In Northern Australia near the Roper River a myth has been recorded that illustrates both the close connection between ogres and castration and the dream origin of the ogres themselves.

There was an old woman called Mumuna or Kunapipi, she had two daughters called Mungamunga.

She would make a large fire at Minima and heap green boughs on it to make plenty of smoke, in this way she attracted two men to the camp who thought they would get food there. She gave them food, and then offered them her two daughters for coitus. She herself went behind a boulder pretending to sleep. The men would "play" sexually with the girls till at last they would be exhausted and fall asleep. Then she would kill them by dropping a large stone on their chest. The old woman cooked and ate the bodies but she always left for her daughters the two heads, the hands and feet and the penes. This is repeated several times. The girls feel sorry for the men. "We are sorry for those penes," they said to each other. "We've had them inside us copulating. Look there are still our vaginal juices and traces of semen on them." And turning to their mother they would say, "Why did you leave those penes for us?" "That is good beef," she would reply. "Those penes are big and fat with plenty of meat." (This can mean both the penis as food and the penis in the vagina.) Finally the men noticed what was happening. Two of them approached the girls while the others watched. They saw the Old Woman come out and bend over the sleeping couples and pick up a stone to kill them. She dropped the stone, killing one man but at that moment the Eaglehawk (one of the men) jumped up, for he was a light sleeper and the others rushed in. The Eaglehawk killed the old cannibal woman.[117]

If we take the old woman and her daughters as offshoots of the same image we can call this an anxiety dream in which the male dreamer is devoured by the *vagina dentata*. The Eaglehawk, the symbol of flying or erection finally provides the happy end version of the dream.

116 This is an actual custom of the natives.
117 Berndt, R. M., *Kunapipi,* New York, 1951, pp. 148–151.

Several elements seem to be the stable structure of these stories: (1) the anxiety of being devoured; (2) the antithesis of a human being and gigantic beings, male or female; (3) the happy end or awakening based on two elements: the spearing of the demon (phallic), and burning its body. The *nanananas* and *bankalangas* are never buried or eaten;[118] they are always burned. Our knowledge of the symbolic meaning of fire makes us suspect a urethral waking dream.

The Uitoto relate a story about an old demon woman who is alternately called ghost (*hanai*) and *taife* (full moon).

The children were joking; they said there might be a ghost at the end of this hole, come and visit us!

An old woman ghost came limping on a stick she used as a crutch. Her eyes were ugly, red, her hands enormous and she had claws like spoons.

She tells the children to make a fire and then she goes to sleep in a hammock above the fire. She also instructs the children not to tell their mothers anything about the nocturnal guest. The children are puzzled, how is it that the "aunty" talks about father in her sleep. When the fathers and mothers come back the children have to hit the old hag's legs to wake her. She disappears.

The mothers reproach the children for having used up all the firewood. The old hag comes again and says, "I must have a fire, I have not warmed my body since ages." She warns the children not to touch her stick. This arouses their curiosity, they chew a little of it, it tastes good. Finally they confess all to their mothers. Their mothers tell them, "Cut the stick into pieces." They make many dents into the stick with shells and when the old woman wants to get up from the hammock, leaning on her staff, it collapses and rolls away.

A whole tribe called "Hurama of dawn or origins" eat the staff. The old woman comes back, and the children tell her what has happened. She drives with the thistles till she drives them all into a basket where they die.

One of the children escapes and tells the fathers what has happened. The fathers light a fire round the cave or basket into which the children have disappeared. The ghosts had eaten the children. The fathers killed the ghosts by burning them.[119]

The persistency of the mythical motive "cannibals are burned to death" is certainly remarkable. This dream myth operates with displace-

---

[118] The latter occurs in some versions probably owing to faulty memory of the narrator.

[119] Preuss, K. T., *Religion und Mythologie der Uitoto*, Göttingen, 1921, I, pp. 78, 79; 345–353.

ment, instead of saying that the children are asleep it is the being who appears in the dream who is asleep. Fire always means urine and a urethral dream is a waking dream. This is strikingly confirmed in our narrative, the people who eat the stick are the people of dawn. The "eating" motive probably also belongs to the awakening factors of the dream. Hunger, cold, the vesical pressure all tend toward awakening. The old woman with the stick is the phallic mother. But as in other cases her phallos is also the breast, that is why it is good to eat and why the "people of origins" eat it. Then the cannibalism of the witch woman is clearly the infant's cannibalism in reverse.[120] Finally there is one sentence which seemingly has nothing to do with the rest of the story. "Why does the 'aunty' mention father in her dream," reveals the "aunty" as a projection of the "bad mother."

The Kiwai tell the following story about a cannibal old woman.

This old woman used to entertain people in order to get victims to satisfy her cannibal appetite. When anybody had to *defecate* she told them where to go. There they would be transfixed by an arrow while defecating and she ate the dead.

"After a number of women had disappeared the people began to suspect that something was wrong. *One night the truth was disclosed to one of them in a dream inspired* by the spirits of the women who had been killed. The next morning when the hag was lying in the house unable to move after eating so much flesh the people set fire to the house.[121] The same thing happens to the cannibal demon woman in Ceram.[122]

The following story was obtained from Uran-tukutu (Yumu). A girl lived alone in a camp. It was the rainy season and she made a hut for protection against the rains. She came out of the hut and when the water ran down the creek, she danced beside the water and sang: "Porcupine grass to the shore run about." Then she slept. Next morning she went for putaia (a small marsupial). When the rain stopped, she went out again singing as before. At night the flood washed her and her hut away, and she was never seen afterward (story No. 98).

From the same informant, another flood story: A big girl lived with her little brother. They went to get white ants for food. The little boy would not go back into the hut with his sister; he camped in the ant hole. Then a heavy rain came and she ran into a cave, but the little boy refused to follow her; he stayed in the ant hole. A heavy rain came and

[120] Cf. Róheim, "Aphrodite or the Woman with the Penis," *Psychoanalytic Quarterly*, XIV, 1945, pp. 350–390.

[121] Landtman, G., "The Folk Tales of Kiwai Papuans," *Acta Societatis Scientiarum Fennicae*, XLVII, 1917, pp. 241, 242.

[122] Jensen, A. E., *Hainuwele*, Frankfurt am Main, 1939, p. 285.

flooded the ant hole and washed the boy and the anthill away. She went to a big camp, told the story, and stayed there always.

Urethral awakening dreams frequently contain an intrauterine or birth element here represented by the cave and the ant hole. The mechanism of the story would be somewhat like that of the former dream of the governess; it is the little boy who is washed away by the urethral flood, the big sister is saved.

The following story is number forty-four in my collection, contributed by Mulda of the Ngatatara tribe. A *bankalanga* lived with his wife. They had one little *kunindjatu* (human) boy whom they had stolen. They made a hut with a partition inside and the *bankalanga* slept on the top of the partition. The man was hidden so that the little boy never knew that he existed. The woman sent one child for rats and gave this meat to the *bankalanga*. The boy was wet; he thought it was rain that had come through the roof but it was the *bankalanga* urinating. The old woman said, "You make a big fire and then you will be dry." But next morning she smelled the wet sand and said, "That is not water, it is urine." She saw the *bankalanga* coming away from the top of the hut. He went for a fire stick and set fire to the hut. The *bankalanga* was burned in the hut. The old woman carried one burned body to a big camp, crying. There the *kunindjatus* killed the old woman, burned both bodies, and then they initiated the young boy.

As a urethral awakening dream this would mean that the urge to urinate is displaced from the boy to the *bankalanga* or paternal ogre and also an identification of urine with semen, i.e., the traumatic reaction to the primal scene. The ogres are always burned and the urethral symbolism of fire is well known. The vesical dream in this case includes the erected penis as a waking stimulus, hence the *tukurpa* ends when the demon is speared and his body is burned. But the gist of the story is a nightmare with the cannibal parental ogre. A difficulty arises at this point. Among some of the tribes who tell these stories the cannibal parent is a reality.

I quote the data on the custom from *Psychoanalysis and Anthropology:*

"In general as far as my own experience goes, there are two forms of teknophagy. The Yumu, Pindupi, and Nambutji eat small children when they are hungry without considering any ceremonial or animistic motives. The southern tribes—Matuntara, Mularatara, Pitjentara—eat every second child and believe that by doing so the strength of every first child will be doubled. But even in these southern tribes the custom presents different aspects when we get our information from the men and when we talk to the women. The men do a thing on principle, the women do it because they are hungry. A unique aspect of Central Australian cannibalism is that of procuring an abortion for the purpose of eating the embryo. Patjili, a Ngali woman told us that the Ngalis and Yumus eat their own children or procure an abortion out of "meat hunger." They pull the child out by the head, then they burn the placenta, roast the child and eat it. The infant is eaten by the mother and the other siblings. The other children are supposed to eat it so they may grow bigger, the mother does it because she is hungry. Iwana of the Maturtara tribe says that a small baby would be killed by the mother but a bigger one by the father. The father knocks it on the head and goes away. Then he comes back and keeps knocking it till it dies. The father does not eat of the child but he gives it to the mother and other children. Twana says that they might eat a child like Aldinga (age three). They eat the head first, then the arms, feet and finally the body. Tankitji Ulura and Aldinga (Pukutiwaras' sons) have all eaten their siblings."[123] However in the south, on the Nullarbor plains, the custom takes other forms. According to Daisy Bates:

"Baby cannibalism was rife among these western central people as it is west of the border in Central Australia. In one group east of the Murchison and Gascogne Rivers every woman who had had a baby had killed and eaten it, dividing it with her sisters, who in turn killed their children at birth and returned the gift of food, so that the group had not preserved a single living child for some years. When the frightful hunger for baby meat overcame the mother before or at birth of the baby it was killed and cooked regardless of sex. But the mother never ate a child she had allowed to live at the beginning."[124]

Here we have the "bad mother" or cannibal mother of the pre-oedipal phase in real life. We cannot say that she is *only* a projection of infantile aggression; we must admit that the child is not so wrong in projecting what the mothers of these tribes really do, and what pregnant women in our society dream, i.e., both have hostility to the unborn child and the infant.

A being called the mother of all the demons does figure in our stories. In story No. 39, we are told:

"Then he (the boy) saw a huge woman who was the mother of all *bankalangas* and *nanananas*. She came with a dead body on her shoulder."

In story No. 55, we have the same situation. There is a boy and a girl; they are near a waterhole. The boy is hiding behind the Yaja (plants, etc., all part of slime that covers the water). He made a little hole in the Yaja

---

123 Róheim, *Psychoanalysis and Anthropology*, p. 61.
124 Bates, D., *The Passing of the Aborigines*, 1938, p. 107.

which was just large enough for his eyes. He looked out and then he saw one old woman who was very large. She was the mother of all demons and she was approaching with a dead body. She said, "Is anybody here? What is the matter?" Her dog came to drink and the boy killed it with his boomerang. She looked everywhere. She saw the boy's eyes looking out of the water. She put the meat down (i.e., the corpses) got a big rod and hurled it at the boy. She missed him and then he came out of the water and cut her head off.

The next story (No. 53) represents a phase in the process of growing up with change of roles, i.e., frightening the cannibal mother (number 52):

An old woman demon lived with a normal boy; she said she was his grandmother. There was a steady rain and they killed and ate rats as they went along. One day the boy adorned himself with the feathers of a dead kurkur (a kind of bird). The old woman was frightened at the feathered thing and ran away. She shouted, "Boy, where are you? Is that you?" He gave no answer, and she kept saying, "Yurai" (rain), and running away. She always came right around and when she saw the feathered figure, she screamed, "Yurai," and ran. The boy finally came out of the hut, threw a stick at her neck, killed her and burned the body. The next morning he went to a big camp. He was made a young man and stayed there always.

The looking and the anxiety probably refer originally to the boy in connection with mother's vagina. But in growing up, roles are inverted; the woman is afraid of the penis (feathered thing, rain). In the men's ritual, they cover their body with bird's down, and any woman who approaches the place reserved for the ceremonies is killed. Characteristically, the story ends with the initiation of the young man.

The generally accepted theory regarding the origin of the demon-women's child-eating propensities is that they represent the child's oral aggression in *talio form*.

Story No. 95: Two women from a big camp were on a road eating seeds. When they rubbed the seed, they saw a little boy coming from a sandhill walking on all fours toward them. Then they nursed him, and both gave him their breasts. When he had had enough, he walked away on all fours again and went back into the hill. The two women went away. Then they got seed again, and when they rubbed it, they saw about ten boys coming on all fours. They gave them milk and then the boys went back into the sandhill, walking like frogs. They said, "Ata, ata." They came to another camp and there was a large number of children there and they said, "Come along, ata, ata." The two women gave them their breasts and when they had finished the milk they ate the breast and then the whole woman. They were mamus. The child demon (*tjitji mamu*) went back into the hill and stayed there forever. (A curious feature of this story was the laughter of the audience on hearing how the child ate the breast and the woman.)

We might therefore assume that in these stories of the mother of all man-eating ogres, we find the talio aspect of the child's oral aggression. According to Bergler, the infant reaches a transitory stage between object love and infantile megalomania in which a compromise is accepted by the child. "Everything 'good' stems from himself, everything 'bad' (refusal) comes from the Giantess, making her cruel, refusing, dangerous."[125]

Oral hatred and aggression directed against the mother become guilt and anxiety.[126]

In European folklore we find parallels. In Silesia we are told that children who have been weaned and then are suckled again develop into nightmare-demons (*Alp*).[127] The nightmare demon gets children by grabbing them by their lips.[128] Slovenian folklore makes the nightmare demon suck the breasts of its victims.[129]

A demon woman in Tirol is called *die Langtüttin* (she of the long breasts). She pursues children and there is milk in one of her breasts and urine in the other. Having suckled a little boy she lured him into her beautiful little room and kept him there for a few days. Finally he pretended that he had to urinate and this way he escaped.[130]

The dream character of this narrative is quite evident. First the breast, then the womb, and then the awakening vesical dream.

In the area of these western Central Australian tribes, the women actually do what other mothers merely wish (consciously or unconsciously), they kill and eat their children. Why do mothers have this fantasy at all? Primarily because the mother-child situation is a repetition of the child-mother situation. But at any rate we must assume that wherever these "maternal" emotions are actually acted out, anxiety increases and the stories in which youth triumphs over ogress and ogre have a definite functional significance.[131]

Another aspect of the "ogre" woman or bad mother imago should be mentioned here. According to Hermann, memories of the large size of the mother's pelvic region are not infrequent, especially in men. These recol-

[125] Bergler, E., *Neurotic Counterfeit Sex*, New York, 1951, p. 45.
[126] Klein, M., *The Psycho-Analysis of Children*, London, 1937, pp. 25, 26.
[127] Kühnau, R., *Schlesische Sagen*, III, 1911, p. 146.
[128] *Ibid.*, p. 149.
[129] Krauss, F. S., *Slavische Volksforschungen*, 1908, pp. 146, 147.
[130] Zingerle, I. V., *Sagen aus Tirol*, Innsbruck, 1891, pp. 110, 111.
[131] Cf. Róheim, "Myth and Folk Tale," *American Imago*, II, 1941, pp. 266–279.

lections may concern either the mother herself or a mother substitute. It is a short step from here to the assumption of huge genital organs as belonging to the mother. In obscene talk, huge genitals are attributed to women who are particularly desirable sexually. The image of the mother emerging from behind these memories corresponds to the first sculpture of the paleolithic age: huge breasts, a huge pelvis, and huge external genital organs. In one case a rather small woman emerges from the childhood memories of her son as a big woman with huge thighs; he dreams of a woman whose external genitals protrude in the form of a prepuce or piece of bowel.

Thus we get a glimpse of how the fantasy of the so-called phallic mother is developed. Lying by the side of the mother the child feels exactly that the mother has no penis but another kind of genital organ, the presence of which is betrayed by touch and smell. When, later, the picture that represents the maternal body is repressed, the image of a giant mother continues to live in the unconscious. The huge genital organ in being in this memory suffers an illusionary misinterpretation due to incest prohibitions and castration fear. What happens is not simply the creation of an imagined penis or that of a picture of a displaced mamma, neither—in the case of the boys—does a conclusion *per analogiam* take place but the actual picture of huge external female genitals is interpreted as a penis and complemented suitably.[132]

In an Eskimo story of Baffin Land, a giantess asks a man to become her husband. She goes to sleep and says, "Place a stone beside me if you see a bear and strike my head till I wake up!" He does this, but she says, "This is only a little fox (although it was a bear)." Finally a gigantic animal comes which she kills. Her husband is afraid that he will drop into her vagina. She tells him to hold on by the hairs. But nevertheless he fell in and was never seen after that.[133]

A quotation from my first field report shows that there is plenty of opportunity for observation of the huge genital organ: "One of the Ngatatara women who used to come and tell me their dreams told me that in her dream she had been chased by her brother. When she woke up from the incest dream, she was lying on her son Nyiki. After this, I began to make further inquiries and I soon found that this was the typical way for a mother to lie on her child. They even added, to make things clearer, that she lies on the child like the male on the female in coitus."[134]

132 Hermann, I., "The Giant Mother," *Psychoanalytic Review*, XXXVI, 1949, pp. 302, 303.

133 Boas, F., "The Eskimo of Baffin Land and Hudson Bay," *Bulletin of the American Museum of Natural History*, XV, 1901, pp. 196, 197.

134 Róheim, "Sexual Life in Central Australia," *International Journal of Psycho-Analysis*, XIII, p. 54.

When discussing official dream interpretations, I was told that if a man dreamed about an *alknarintja* woman (who always appears in the dream under the guise of a *njurpma*, i.e., forbidden incestuous woman known to the dreamer) he must awake speedily. The reason given was that the *alknarintja* woman would sit on a man's penis, thus playing the role of the male and transforming the man into a female.[135]

It is of interest in this connection that the beauty ideal of these tribes emphasizes that *everything should be big*. The Pindupi as represented by Lelil-tukutu regard a woman with big eyes, big buttocks, a pointed nose, big breasts, a lot of pubic hair, a big mons veneris, and fat legs as beautiful. Note the emphasis placed upon size, pubic hair and the prominent parts: nose, mons veneris, etc. An Aranda woman should have small eyes, not too wide open, big cheeks, a pointed nose, round breasts, big buttocks, plenty of pubic hair and a fat mons pubis. And all the other tribes defined beauty in nearly the same words. On the other hand, to say to somebody, "big vulva" or "big penis" is a curse which implies also the accusation that the person is very desirous sexually. The phallic character of the mythical *alknarintja* is stated in that they are supposed to have had three penises (clitoris and labia now).

I could get very few dreams from children. Sometimes they reported a nightmare; they had been frightened by a *mamu* (demon). They would draw this demon with a huge phallos and would usually associate, and would comment that they had cursed their mother or grandmother before falling asleep.

In assuming that the female cannibal demon and the *alknarintja*, i.e., refusing woman, originate from the same infantile sleeping situation, we are not overlooking the fact that whereas the former is an object of anxiety, the latter is the virgin who is ultimately always subdued. It is only a question of degrees of anxiety or admixture of libido and anxiety.

We have also a mythical being who is a kind of transition; she is both *alknarintja* and demon woman. The *allaparinja* (or *labarindja*), according to our Aranda informants, is another kind of *alknarintja* with this difference—they have *arunkulta* (i.e., poison, magic) in their vulva. Anybody who would have intercourse with them would die.

However, there is no doubt about the fact that the emphasis in the whole *bankalanga* mythology is on the phallic and aggressive aspect of the ogre.

The *malpakara* are a special category of beings in these tales. They are "half *mamu*," that is, partly demons, and partly human beings. There are only male *malpakara* and they are characterized by their incessant sex

135 *Ibid.*, p. 53.

drive and lack of skill in hunting. The *malpakara* are always young men and they either have an erection and lack a woman, or are actually cohabiting.

Two *malpakara* were wandering. They saw the tracks of an *entuta* (normal man-being) with two women. They camped together. When the man went far away from the camp they caught the wrists of the two women and tried to rope them. But the two women embraced each other and stuck together. When the *malpakara* dragged them apart they each held fast to a tree.[136] The *malkaparas* were unable to pull them away. The man felt something in his abdomen. One of the *malpakara* let the woman go and hid behind a bush. The man returned and killed them both with his spear. *They burned the bodies and stayed at a big place forever.* This means that the *malpakara* were demons which is then also definitely stated.

The aggression manifested by these demons or ogres is a combination of the oral and the phallic.

Story No. 54: Two *bankalangas* came from the west. On the plain they saw a man and his wife cooking a kangaroo. The two *bankalangas* sneaked up and speared the man right through the back. The woman tried to run away but they killed her too. Then one of the *bankalangas* inserted his finger into her vagina in an attempt to extract the young ones (like they do with the kangaroo). First the two *bankalangas* ate the kangaroo and then they ate the man and the woman. This is repeated several times till finally they are surrounded by a big group of humans, speared and burned.

The following story again shows the symbolic equation, spear-phallos, and rape as the essential trait in the make-up of the ogre.

An old woman lived with her daughter.[137] The old woman followed an emu she had speared. There was a *nananana* sitting on a hill, and when he saw the woman coming his penis became erect. Then he thought it was a man and got ready to kill her with his spear. When she came nearer, he saw she had a vagina and put his spear down. She came through a gap and he had intercourse with her from behind.[138]

The primal scene situation with the ogre in the father role is quite frequent in these stories, as might be expected from what we have said about their beliefs. (Cf. *The Riddle of the Sphinx,* pp. 28, 29.)

In order to understand the situation completely we have to add

136 Up to this point their behavior is no different from that of a young man who wants to get married.

137 Old woman simply means adult not necessarily old in our sense.

138 A characteristic trait of these stories: the gap through which she passes symbolizes her own vagina. The *coitus a tergo* infrequently practiced by the natives seems to be a specially "fiendish" performance of the ogres.

what the women believe. For according to the beliefs of the women, what the men call *ngantja* (double) is really the *mamu* (demon), i.e., each man exists (a) as a human being, and (b) as a supernatural being, a demon whose one and only occupation is to chase the women.

Can we say that sadism (or aggression) just migrates through all the erogenous zones from the oral to the phallic?

In a story of the natives of Ooldea Old Man Tulina is a giant ancestral being who lives at a waterhole with his wife and two children. Hunting for *mamu* children, he gives them to his children to eat. His wife who is also a *mamu* recognizes her sister's child in one of the demon children she has killed. Therefore she leaves him. He gives *mamu* meat to his children to eat and then his breasts grow and he suckles them as a mother would. He comes to a cave where all the demons live. He pokes his spear into the entrance of the cave and a mob of demons rush out. They break his spear and swarm all over the giant like ants. Then the lame *mamu* demands his penis and testes. The others pull these organs out of the giant and give them to him, etc.[139]

Here we certainly have a being with both breast and penis. Nevertheless I would not say that aggression originates in the oral stage and is then carried over to the phallic, but we should rather consider that it is essentially a part of male sexuality. When women have visions of the men or dream about them, the men are always *mamu;* that is, they are chasing the women.

Although I was one of the first to apply insight derived from psychoanalytic theory and practice to the data of anthropology, now we see that there is such a thing as a too one-sided application of a point of view, and that in making statements that are supposed to be valid for mankind in general, the practicing psychoanalyst should also know something about biology and anthropology.

Bergler believes that the oedipus complex is merely a "rescue attempt from an oral danger."[140] "The latest of these rescue attempts, and a denial of passivity in the boy, is the famous oedipus complex. What it practically amounts to is borrowed strength from the father; the boy wants to act the father's part and to demote the 'dangerous' mother to a passive being: at bottom, to an image of his own self. The reversal of the roles is perfect here; mother is passively penetrated (as once the child was oral-anally penetrated); the active penetrating is done by the child. A perfect setting for an alibi.[141]

139 Berndt, C. and R., "Preliminary Report of the Field Work in the Ooldea Region," *Oceania,* XIV, 1943, p. 155.

140 Bergler, E., *The Basic Neurosis,* New York, 1949, p. 70.

141 *Ibid.,* p. 16.

"The psychological situation pushing the child into the oedipal stage is more important than the banal fact of 'digesting' a reality situation; the father is present and proves to be a powerful competitor for the mother's attention and love.

"The oedipus complex is generally misunderstood by the laity [I must comment that the laity here includes Freud and nearly all other psychoanalysts excepting Bergler] as meaning the boy desires the mother sexually. What is freely and naïvely misunderstood is the fact that the oedipus complex has a prehistory full of fright, terror, massive passivity, etc."[142]

In other words the activity or aggression of the male is a mask for passivity.

Since Freud we understand that in our development there is such a thing as a transition from passivity to activity. It happens that I described this transition from passivity to sadism in Central Australia many years ago. In the Alknarintja situation (habitual sleep posture) the boy is lying under his mother in a combination of oedipal seduction and passivity. As a reaction formation we find sadistic handling of the woman in the rape custom (*mbanja*) and a patriarchal society in which women are excluded from ritual.[143]

Bergler overlooks several important factors: (a) The fact of growth; genitality has actually made great strides from age one to age three. The situation is actually different. (b) Activity is not only a defense, it is also a fact, a developing mastery of locomotion, etc., by the ego. (c) The father as a rival is far from being just a "banal negligible factor"—the woman is actually divided between wife and mother, genitality and suckling.

Finally, and this is the decisive factor, *aggression and male sexuality* go together as part of our biological heritage, and not merely as a defense mechanism.[144]

According to Ford and Beach, "The fact that many human societies implicitly recognize a connection between sexual excitement and the infliction of pain upon one's partner is particularly interesting in view of the fact that fighting and mating are so closely related in a large number of vertebrate species. It is not an exaggeration to state that physically aggressive behavior forms an integral part of the sexual pattern for vertebrates of every major phyletic class, although it does not follow that this is true of every species.

[142] *Ibid.*, p. 50.
[143] Róheim, "Psychoanalysis of Primitive Cultural Types," *International Journal of Psycho-Analysis,* XIII, 1932, pp. 93, 119.
[144] The biological factors are recognized by Bergler in a footnote, *op. cit.,* p. 67, but he goes on discussing the subject as if they did not exist.

"A male jewelfish that is ready to breed assumes possession of a small territory and defends it against all comers. If a second male intrudes, the resident promptly launches an attack, nipping at the newcomer and striking him with the tail.

"When a fertile female enters into the territory of a breeding male she is accorded the same treatment as a member of his own sex. The female, however, neither retreats nor attempts to return the attack. The male's aggressive reactions become less and less intense until finally they shift from the fighting pattern to the one of courtship and spawning occurs."[145]

"Male shrews, bats, and rabbits mount the female from the rear and during copulation they seize the skin or fur of her neck or back in their teeth. Biting and holding the female's neckskin is an indispensable part in the coital patterns of some species.

"This description might appear to justify application of the term rape to copulation in these animals . . . the violent behavior has an important biological function. Many males refuse to mate with females that are too compliant and therefore fail to offer the normal amount of resistance. If coition takes place without the usual conflict, conception rarely occurs.

"The functional importance of the aggressive encounter is further emphasized by the fact that some minks have been known to ovulate *without copulating* after they have engaged in a protracted struggle with an active male.[146]

"Numerous avian species exhibit aggressive behavior which is apparently conditioned by testicular hormones. . . . In describing the elimination of fighting in the female short-tailed shrew during estrus, the possibility was suggested that estrogen may exert an inhibitive effect and a similar situation obtains in the case of the lizard Anolis carolinensis, according to the observations of Evans. Injections of androgen produce increased aggressiveness."[147]

"In sexual play and premating activity (of the chimpanzee) the male tends to be more aggressive, threatening and commanding than the female. . . . The total picture of mating almost invariably indicates a measure of masculine dominance."[148]

Zuckerman writes about baboons: "In addition to mating with her, he often followed her round the cage, biting her, usually in the scruff

[145] Ford, C. S., and Beach, F. S., *Patterns of Sexual Behavior,* New York, 1951, pp. 57–58.
[146] *Ibid.,* pp. 58–60.
[147] Beach, F. A., *Hormones and Behavior,* New York, 1948, p. 100.
[148] Yerkes, Robert M., *Chimpanzees,* New Haven, 1943, pp. 70, 71.

of the neck. These attacks were carried out without noise from either animal."[149]

A Central Australian native (Kanakana) of the Mularatara tribe, one day when I was inquiring about a friend of his, remarked in an offhand manner, "He is a tame prick! He has never killed a man!" and thus showed real insight into the essence of maleness. This, and not tender love, is the male, whether we like it or not.

In *Man and Superman,* Shaw expresses the same truth. Tanner, representing maleness and destruction says, "I am afraid I am too feminine to see any sense in destruction."

Euripides in his *Electra* tells the same truth, perhaps with more eloquence. Electra, referring to her brother Orestes, says, "His father slew Troy's thousands in their pride; He hath but one to kill . . . O God, but one! Is he a man, and Agamemnon's son?"[150]

What bearing have these data on the belief in ogres or stories about ogres? Is the man-eating male giant merely a cover figure for the witch-mother and is aggression displaced from the oral to the genital? If we see that the phallic activity of the male is *per se* perceived as aggression (and correctly perceived) we must admit the validity of the usual or classical psychoanalytic interpretations, *viz.,* that the fear of being eaten is the fear of being attacked sexually, i.e., turned into a female, castrated.

Anxiety over being eaten or being bitten, as Fenichel says, may be a disguise for castration anxiety. "In such a case the castration fear has become distorted in a regressive way; that is, by choosing as a substitute an archaic autonomous fear. The regression may be a partial one and frequently we see manifestations of anxiety that contain elements both of being eaten and of being castrated."[151]

Freud clearly interprets the famous case of the wolf-phobia as a negative oedipus complex, and being eaten by the wolf as being castrated by the father, and of replacing the mother in the primal scene.[152]

As we have seen before in discussing Greek mythology, being eaten by the father or being castrated are closely parallel contents. On Normanby Island, where I worked in 1930, the people have a childhood trauma that looks like the paternal ogre in real life:

"The father who is officially called the to-sapwara or petter (i.e., he is supposed to play a lot with children of both sexes) stimulates them

149 Zuckerman, S., *The Social Life of Monkeys and Apes,* London, 1932, pp. 243, 244.

150 Translated by G. Murray. Cooper, L., *Fifteen Greek Plays,* Oxford University Press, 1943, p. 361.

151 Fenichel, O., *The Psychoanalytic Theory of Neurosis,* New York, 1945, pp. 199, 200.

152 Freud, S., *Gesammelte Schriften,* VIII, pp. 464–485; *Hemmung, Symptom und Angst,* Wien, 1926, pp. 33, 34.

sexually at a very early period while they are still being carried (genital trauma in the oral stage). He playfully smells the vagina or sucks it with his mouth; with the boys he playfully bites the penis. The children are tickled; they laugh. The native informant continued: 'Therefore, when they get a little older, they imitate what their father did to them. The girls insert their fingers into their vagina and the boys pull their penis up and down.' The difference in emphasis is worth noting. The father kisses or smells the vagina; he bites the penis. There is ample evidence to show that the male sorcerer (barau) represents the father, and 'they will barau you' is the typical threat for disobedience."[153]

In the mythical world, Tokedukeketai is the typical projection of the paternal ogre.

Tokedukeketai (eater of men) was very big like a tree. His head was like a stone, his hair was long and thick; eyes, nose, mouth—everything was big. Some say he had only one eye, some say he had one in the front and one in the back of his head. He had a stone club and his spear was like a post. His penis was big and long. Tokedukeketai[154] married and his wife gave birth to children. He ate the children. Finally she hid her children in a book, and these children went down to the netherworld and brought up fertility magic for their village.

People persisted in stealing Tokedukeketai's cocoanuts. He caught them, put them in his long basket and ate them; finally they gathered round him and burned him.

In the long myth of Tokedukeketai,[155] the Giant aided by Grunting Pig eats all the people. A pregnant woman hides in a cave, and her son, Matakapotaiataia (who has two eyes in front and two in the back of his head), kills the giant. He has two assistants, an eagle and a dog. He had intercourse with his mother who then gave birth to the eagle and the dog. In the battle in which the giant is vanquished, the eagle scratched his eyes off and the dog bites off his testicles.

According to one curious piece of information, Matakapotaiataia himself, although he has four eyes, has no penis and no testicles.

The mythical figure of the man-eating ogre is here clearly oedipal and the anxiety is castration anxiety.

But the belief in the witch, i.e., the female counterpart of the ogre is more important than the mythical Tokedukeketai. The outstanding traits of witchcraft are their man-eating or corpse-eating habits, their connection with oral frustration and their phallic attributes.

153 Róheim, *Psychoanalysis and Anthropology*, p. 160.
154 Story told in Sipupu—field notes.
155 Published in Róheim, *The Riddle of the Sphinx*, pp. 179–182.

It should be observed that the *werabana* in this area may be a supernatural being or may be a real person.

The information I got through Sopadaba about the neighboring island of Tubetube[156] certainly indicates supernatural beings. There are good and bad *werabana*. Sometimes they live under the water, sometimes in a cave. The tall black ones are good. The brown ones eat the dead. Their faces are narrow because they live in caves. They have the bones of their victims in their hair. But he mentions a real woman called Susu Kaikaigeda (Breast one) who used to dance at night in the village and who was one of the corpse-eating witches. What he describes may be a vision or perhaps a dream.

According to Duau beliefs there are two kinds of witches though they seem to differ in degree only. The corpse-eating witches first revive the corpse and then they kill it and eat it.[157] The corpse-eating witches have things in their inside that are lacking in the other witches. These are (1) *kwahaguana* (firefly), (2) *diadia* (flying fox), (3) *mwehiki* (a little bird), and (4) *kosio kosia* (another little bird); (1) and (2) come out of the witch's vagina at night, (3) and (4) in the daytime.

Any trouble with the mouth is pre-eminently due to witchcraft. Gimwagimware ya remembers that when she was a girl of about seven, she could not eat, and her saliva dropped out of her mouth. A witch had put a fish hook into her mouth. Her grandmother, who was a witch herself, cured it. A woman of Sigasiga says that the witches make people sick if they refuse to give them food.

The beautiful witches also eat human beings but they do it more indirectly. They do not actually eat the corpse but they take it down to the land of the Numu (spirits) where it is eaten by Tau Mudurere (Man Pubic Part Tattooed). Tau Mudurere divides magic among them; he gives them new boats or new kinds of yams as a reward for the souls which he eats. The witches call these their pigs. The witches comb their victims first to make them look pretty. If they are not pretty, Tau Mudurere refuses to eat them. The witches who go down to the underworld, oil themselves and make magic, just like the *enobeu* (sleep-fall) the seers *who send their souls to Bwebweso* (other world). Tau Mudurere also rewards the witches for their efforts by having intercourse with them for he is the "husband of all witches." The parallel with the *enoben* means that the descent to the underworld occurs in a dream[158] and one is tempted to ask how much of the belief in man-eating witches in general is due to dreams.

156 Anthropologically a *terra incognita*.

157 For what follows cf. Róheim, "Witches of Normanby Island," *Oceania*, XVIII, p. 404.

158 Cf. Róheim, "Teiresias and other Seers," *Psychoanalytic Review*, XXXIII, 1946, p. 328.

A witch, when questioned about her dreams, told me, "No, I have no dreams, only a witch will dream"—a statement that is a denial of her being a witch but at the same time shows an intimate tie-up of dreams and witchcraft.

Loyawesi relates the following dream: "I saw Nesebo, my former wife. She came to the river and pushed me into it with her foot. She said, 'I want bananas as pay because my son got hurt. If I don't get it I will make you sick.' Nesebo always scolded him for going after other women. Finally he left her. When he left her and married another woman, people told him she was a witch. She killed her own brother by sucking his body when he was asleep."

The following stories about witches might easily be derived from dreams: There was a little boy who had a *gatura* (kind of fish). His father and mother took his fish and ate it. He cried from morning till evening. They loaded their canoes with food and they left the child *while he was asleep*. They left and a witch came. She ate all the food; then she took her vulva off and closed the door of the house with it (the witch's vulva is a savage animal that bites). When the boy saw this, *he went back to sleep* in an old house overgrown with creepers. The witch said to her vulva: "Eat that man." He took a stone, heated it and threw it into the witch's vulva. The witch died.

The sleeping boy has an anxiety dream. In its milder form—"The parents leave me"; anxiety increases—"a witch comes to eat me." But the boy is sleeping, that is, he is inside the witch-mother (i.e., old house). It is not on the way out that the vulva would bite him but on the way in. Why bite? This is the talio anxiety for his oral-phallic desire to penetrate the mother. And the hot stone? Probably anal-urethral awakening from the dream.

The following story again might very well be a dream: A young boy was walking about and came to a river. There he saw a stone like a house. *So he went in and slept in the stone.* Then he asks his mother to prove that she is a witch by carrying the stone. She made an incantation and the stone came along very quickly toward the village. But one of the witches flatulated and the others laughed. The stone immediately became heavy and she could not carry it.

The boy is in the mother again but he is also rapidly moving with the mother. Flatus awakens him. We have indicated the phallic nature of the flying dream. The flying witch is a phallic witch.

Dedi, a young boy at Dauwada dreamed: "Wadanoi came at night and chased me. I had wings and flew. I fell to the ground and was covered with flies and ants. They washed me with hot water and I awoke."

Wadanoi is his grandmother and she used to fondle him a lot when he was a baby. Later she would sometimes come at night and reproach him for not giving her food. She would chase him if his mother refused to give her food. The dream is like what happened to his younger brother. He climbed a tree in the garden and he fell and they found him covered with ants. People thought the old witch had done it.

The meaning of the dream is clear. It repeats the accident that happened to his younger brother. We assume guilt feelings. The guilt would be connected with the flying, a dream that invariably means coitus. If we substitute mother for grandmother, the whole thing is clear. The next step would be the assumption that the flying witch originates in flying dreams.

Wadanoi was also a flying witch. These flying witches are frequently connected with the sea. The Sebulu-Igwana (string sing), with hair white like a string, have their haunts in caves at Nadinadia and Dobu and elsewhere. Their canoe is made of stone. When one of them gets into the canoe it is very short but as they keep moving to make room for the next one it becomes longer. It is a man with his wives sailing on a stone. They go out to fight. The geraboi are similar to these. They are women dressed as men. They are also called Toke-kewa-kewa (door flying-flying). They tie two trees together with a string. One of these trees may be in Duau, the other in the Trobriands. They ride on the string and pull it. The people see a falling star and they say, "The witch flew away." It is the string that makes the light on the sky. The string is really fire that comes out of the witch's vagina. At Dobu a gigantic testicle comes out of the witch's body at night and becomes visible as a ball of fire passing through the air.[159]

Phallic attributes of mythical mothers are widely known and they may or may not be connected with flying. The Baba Yaga with a leg of bones comes every day to suck the milk out of the breasts of the Princess.[160] According to Ralston, the Baba Yaga is a hideous old woman, very tall of stature, very bony of limb, with an excessively long nose and dishevelled hair. Her nose is of iron, and also her long pendant breasts, and her strong sharp teeth. As she lies in her hut, "she stretches from one corner to the other and her nose goes right through the ceiling." Frequently she lives in a cottage that revolves on fowl's legs. The gates of her castle are sometimes human legs and instead of a lock there is a mouth with sharp teeth.[161]

She flies in an iron mortar which she propells with a pestle. The

---

159 Fortune, R., *Sorcerers of Dobu*, New York, 1932, p. 297.
160 Afanassjev, A. N., and Meyer, A., *Russishe Volksmärchen*, Wien, 1910, p. 25.
161 Ralston, W. R. S., *The Songs of the Russian People*, 1872, p. 161.

White Russians see her in the sky in a fiery mortar which she urges on with a burning broom.

While the phallic aspect of the witch is certainly emphasized when she is identified with a fiery snake, on the other hand, she is also said to suck the white breasts of beautiful women.[162]

I have published other cases of phallic witches in European folklore in 1945 and previously in 1920.[163] As I have shown in the paper on Aphrodite, the phallic woman is really the woman with the breast, the mother.

"The male child first reacts to the separation trauma (withdrawal of breast) by identifying his own genitals with the maternal source of pleasure, and thus having obtained a guarantee against deprivation, goes through the same process again in the opposite direction. "First, it is not true that I am deprived of pleasure (mamma), since I have my penis; second, it is not true that something is missing there (at sight of maternal vagina). My mother has the same pleasure organ that I have, (phallos; originally nipple)."[164]

If we emphasize the *cannibal* witch, the picture becomes somewhat more complicated. First we have the oral aggression of the infant. In reverse form; the sucking witch or cannibal female being (ogre). Next we have the male aggression of the boy (phallos). In reverse form; the phallic mother. But since "phallic" also means having an orgasm, and since the phallic witch is frequently seen in a voyeur ritual (cf. paper on Aphrodite quoted above), "to be eaten" may also be a symbolic expression of the genital act, or of orgasm, as in the case of the male ogre. However, we should also emphasize the fact that the opponent of the ogre or cannibal is always the hero with his sword, or in Australia, with his spear. Since the sword (etc.) is obviously phallic, the opponent, even when appearing in a male form, must derive some of his aggression from the oral in reverse, i.e., the projected "bad mother" image. The many heads of the ogre in the European folk tale might be interpreted as mother plus siblings as targets of aggression, and therefore, causes of anxiety.

In a Tartar folk tale of the Caucasus, we are told how the hero meets a colossal giantess whose breasts are thrown back over her shoulders. He touches her breasts, and by this gesture, he becomes her adopted son. "What a pity," says the ogress, "that you have become my son so quickly. You would have been a dainty morsel for my jaws." The hero

162 *Ibid.*, pp. 162, 163.

163 Róheim, "Aphrodite or the Woman with a Penis," *Psychoanalytic Quarterly,* XIX, 1945, p. 362; *Idem, Adalékokamagyar nephithez* (Contributions to Hungarian Folklore), Budapest, 1920, pp. 235, 236.

164 Róheim, "Aphrodite," *Psychoanalytic Quarterly,* XIV, 1945, p. 372.

replies, "What a pity that you have become my mother so quickly. You would have been a dainty morsel for my sword."[165] The phallic answer to oral *talio* anxiety.

The question remains unanswered; are all these beliefs based on dreams? Or all the narratives? Or some of the narratives?

The children in Central Australia rarely admitted having dreamed something but when they did the dream was always an anxiety dream about demons. Berndt and Berndt write: "Most of the aborigines dream from time to time of *mamu* (demons). And sometimes a boy or a young man will awaken at night and disturb the whole camp with his fear. At such times wood is piled on the fires to keep away any *mamu* who might be loitering nearby."[166]

This latter trait reminds one of the fact that all folk tales end with the demon being burned. We have also good reasons to assume that a narrative that ends with fire or water is a urethral dream.[167]

In a Kiwai story about a cannibal witch we are told that: "One night the truth was disclosed to some of them in a dream inspired by the spirits of the women who had been killed. The next morning when the hag was lying in the house unable to move after eating so much flesh, the people set fire to her house."[168]

Here again the dream is indicated in the text and the demon ends her life in flames.

The ogres of India are the Râkshasa. The word means the "harmer" or "destroyer." *They go about at night,* haunt cemeteries, animate dead bodies and devour human beings. In folk tales the Râkshasa has a pretty daughter who protects the hero. Her father comes in with the cry of "Manash gandha" which is the equivalent of the "Fee, fo, fum, I smell the blood of an Englishman." When Hanuman entered the city of Lanka, in the form of a cat, to reconnoitre, he saw the Râkshasas *who slept in the house* were of every shape and form. Some had long arms and frightful shapes, some were dwarfs, some giants. Demons with one eye or one ear. Some had monstrous bellies, hanging breasts, long projecting teeth and crooked thighs. Others were very beautiful. Some had heads of serpents, asses or elephants. Ravana, the leader of the Râkshasa has twenty arms, teeth as bright as the moon. He may look like a thick cloud or mountain or like the god of death with open mouth. Like all demons,

165 Dumezil, G., *Légendes sur les Nartes,* Bibliothèque de l'Institut Français de Leningrad, XI, 1930, p. 128.

166 Berndt, R. and C., "Field Work in Western South Australia," *Oceania,* XIV, 1943, p. 153.

167 Cf. passim in this book.

168 Landtman, G., "The Folk Tales of the Kiwai Papuans," *Acta Societatis Scientiarum Fennicae,* XLVII, Helsingfors, 1917, pp. 241, 242.

they are scared by light, and the lamp is called, "the destroyer of the Râkshasas."[169]

Names vary but the substance of the belief is unchanged since Vedic times. The names Raksha and Yatu vary. The Raksha is a spirit emitted by the evil sorcerer. The incantation against the Raksha says, "Eat the one who sent you, eat your own flesh."

Night is the time of the Raksha. They disappear at sunrise. The demons are called, "the eaters." They slip into the body through the mouth; into women through the vagina, and they change the sex of the embryo from male to female.[170] Some of the narratives of male or female Rakshasha are decidedly dreamlike:

"There he suddenly woke up in the night and beheld that the woman had slain Nishthuraka and was devouring his flesh with the utmost delight. He rose up and drew his sword, and the woman assumed the terrible shape of a Rákshasi (female Rákshasa) and he was about to slay her. . . . Nishthuraka rose up again alive without a scratch on his body."[171]

If we interpret the hero of the story and his friend as the same person, the dreamlike character of the narrative becomes evident. Moreover, the changing forms, the nightly character and the disappearance of the ogres at dawn strongly indicate an origin in dreams. In a Punjab story the Prince creeps into the garden while the man-eating Juni is sleeping. Moreover, sleep seems to be the chief preoccupation of this particular ogre.[172]

In a Coos text we have the two motives of a dream in the text and of the giant woman perishing by fire.

The Giantess was all the time enslaving people. Whenever she saw a man she would say, "Come here, my husband." She would take the valuables off the necks of the children and out of the graves. She would put them in a basket and carry them home. *In her house she had a hole as a door.* In the morning the two usually slept, in the evenings they would sit up. One brother dreamed about the house of the giant woman (or rather the two giant women) who had stolen his brother and sister. Then he went with his father and set fire to their house and burned the two giant women.[173]

[169] Crooke, W., *The Popular Religion and Folk-Lore of Northern India,* I, 1896, p. 247.

[170] Oldenberg, H., *Die Religion des Veda,* Berlin, 1894, pp. 268–272.

[171] Tawney, C. H., *The Kathasarit Sagara or Ocean of the Streams Story,* Calcutta, 1880, I, p. 60.

[172] Steel, F. A. and Temple, R. C., *Wide Awake Stories,* London, 1884, pp. 169–177.

[173] Frachtenberg, L. I., "Coos Texts," *Columbia University Contributions to Anthropology,* I, 1913, pp. 71–77.

On the whole I would assume that most of the stories, myths, etc., were based on dreams, and the others, freely invented because the dream stories were already being told and thus stimulated fantasy.

The question whether the distorted fear-inspiring images of human beings themselves, witches or ogres, are derived from dreams is hard to answer. It is possible but not certain.

I have interpreted the Central Australian folk tale as a narrative that deals with the problem of growing up. The hero is always juvenile, the ogre always old. There is always a happy ending, the hero's marriage or initiation.[174]

In general I suspect that there are two sources of mythology. The dream is the one we are discussing in this book, the other would be the problem of growing up. The altjira or tukurpa is certainly based on both these elements.

In one of the long stories that are typical of Yuma folklore (field notes, 1931, Yuma, Arizona) we have the phallic giant or ogre, the primal scene and the growing up or victory of the young hero.

Kujuu (Giant)

There was an old woman called Akoj Metshtexexethuuk (Old Woman Picking Up). She was called this because being a giantess she had a huge basket on her back and she used to pick the people up and put them in it. She lived with her grandson who was a small baby in a cradle. She left him in the middle of the house and went to look for food. She went to look for *imjeilk,* a worm living in stumps. While she was in the woods she sang *Enyee enyee* (crying) "somebody eat, I would like to taste it" (wants to eat someone). As she sang this in the woods the baby boy got out of his cradle and was playing before the door. He saw a group of birds coming very near to him. While he was watching these birds he knew his own mind like a grownup. And as he hears what the old woman sang he knocked the birds on the head, made a great pile of them and went back into his cradle. When the old woman comes home she says; I wonder who knows that I want to eat—and she got angry and threw the birds away. When the baby saw her do this he cried and the grandmother would not pacify him. Then she wondered what she had done to make him cry like that. So she went out and picked up the birds she had thrown away. The boy continued to grow and she went out again singing the same song. When he heard this song he asked her to give him a small bow and arrow and he would go and get food for her. She refused telling him he was too small to have a bow and arrow. Again he cried. She

174 Róheim, "Myth and Folktale," *American Imago*, II, 1940, pp. 266–279.

asked him what he will do with it. He said, he would go hunting. As he kept it up she made him a very small bow and arrow. The boy went out and saw the ears of rabbits and came back crying to the old woman. What are you crying for? I saw something long and pink and was afraid of it. She explains they were rabbits. The boy stopped crying and said he was going out to kill the rabbit. You can't do it, you are too small! she said. She told him it was difficult even for grownups. But he went out. But he found his bow and arrow were too small so he came back and asked for a bigger one. She said, hardly anybody can kill it, how do you think you will be able to! But he persisted and went out again. He shot two or three and as they were too heavy for him to carry he dragged them home. She said, Somebody must have killed them and you picked them up! She threw them out, he cried. So she picked them up again and they baked and ate them. This made the boy very happy. He went a little further and saw somewhat larger ears. The animal got on his hind legs, he was frightened and told the grandmother what he saw. She asked, what did it look like? He explained and she explained it was a jack rabbit and hardly anyone could kill it. He said he could kill one and asked for a bigger bow and arrow. Again he brought two or three home throwing out eating as before. Again he went out, this time a deer looked back at him. Again description and he gets a bigger bow and arrow. The boy shot a deer, it was too heavy for him to bring home, so he ran home, told his grandmother. The old woman refused to help, he could not have killed a deer! But he begged and finally she went out and got some meat. He was very happy. This time he went further than he had ever been and he saw the (giant) Kujuu who was getting a drink at a well. When the little boy saw him, he went up to him and said, "Kujuu, move on; I want to wash my hands!" The giant was sitting and his penis was hanging into the well in the way where the little boy wanted to drink. The giant said in a gruff voice, "What little boy are you that you know me." The boy again asked him to move so he could wash his hands. The gaint refused, so the child said, I will go home, get my bow and arrow, and shoot you! You are too small to kill me! He ran home to get the bow and arrow and tell the grandmother. When the boy got home he told his grandmother what had happened. She told him he could not do this and tried to keep him back, but the boy went. When the boy got there he started shooting at the giant's penis. But all the arrows could not penetrate and just fell off the giant's skin. The giant had a sharp stick and when the boy finished shooting he pierced him through the stomach with it and carried him home. The giant flew up with the boy into the air and went up to the fourth sky. When they came there, there were two wives waiting for him.

He told them to make a big fire and have the earth hot to bake the boy so he should be ready for him to eat when he comes back in the evening. When they started the fire he wondered what it was for. One of the women told him it was to bake him. They boy said, "All right," but by his magic he made rain and put the fire out. This happened four times. By the fourth time the giant came home and they told him what happened. The next day the giant told his wives, "Don't fail this time!" They said, "We have tried and failed but we will try again!" Again the boy made rain and put the fire out. As it was getting late, the women made a stew (*ashuvi*) of dried human flesh for the giant's supper. Four kettles of this were ready. The boy reached to the four quarters and drew from them four *ahque* (stone knives) which went into the kettle by magic. He comes back in the evening and asks if they have got the boy baked. "We have tried and we have failed," they said, "but we have something else for you." He took the first kettle, swallowed with a gulp. He felt the knife in his throat and said, "The gravy is very hot." Then he ate the second kettle with the same remark. Then the third—the same. The last kettle had the knife which came from the south. Again he said the same thing but this knife cut his throat, and he fell over dead. When the giant died the boy got up and danced with happiness. Then one woman asked the other, Did this boy kill the giant? The other said, yes. Then the two danced with happiness and they were his wives. And all the dry flesh and skulls and bones danced too. The boy grew happier every minute that he danced till he took hold of the giant's leg and shook the bones out of the body. Then he put on the giant's skin and danced with it on. The girls embraced him and danced with him. For four days they danced like this and then he told the girls that he was going back to his own country. The girls were in love with him and asked to be taken with him. He refused them and they cried with grief till he told them he would take them. He was wondering who would take him back to his own country. He goes out of the house, sits down and thinks. A caw comes there and he pretends not to see it till it passes. Then it turns round, looks at him and asks him who he is and how he came to the country. So the boy told him about the giant and how he killed him and how he wants to go home. When the caw heard this he promised to take him but he was to get something for him to eat before he could take him. Then the boy went for deer to feed the caw. I will take you down, the caw said, but when you arrive at your grandmother's house you are not to open your eyes for four days. The boy consented. The caw flew in a circle and brought him down to the next sky. When he brought him here he told him, I will leave you here but I will change you into something so you can go on to the next sky and someone else will tell you there what to do. So he changed him into a white flower bud and in this shape he went down to the next sky. There he changes into a very heavy rock (*eljuxaj*), also by the wishes of the caw, because in the other form it took him very long to get down. He goes down to the third sky in this form and here he is turned into an arrow without feathers (*ipaxhasheet* = featherless arrow, doesn't go straight, they think the lightning is such an arrow and it occurs in legends).

In the form of an arrow he lands at the back of his grandmother's house and sticks in the ground. For four days he sticks in the ground in the form of an arrow and every night all the birds and animals came to the grandmother and had intercourse with her. He saw all that was going on but he did not dare to open his eyes. In the daytime the birds and animals went away but at night they would come back again. On the fourth day he changed into his own form and looked down through the smoke hole. While looking down through the hole he pitied his grand-mother and cried. There was a Coyote cohabiting with the grandmother when the tears dropped on him and the boy was wondering how he would be revenged on these people for what they had done to his grandmother. The Coyote feels this, thought it was raining and went out to see. The boy by his magic causes the house to fall down and kill all the birds and animals that were having intercourse with his grandmother. But the grandmother he pulls out from under the house. They had the same house built up again and cried for joy at seeing each other. All her skirt was torn but she had a new one made for herself. The grandmother asked him what he had been doing and when he tells her of his trip and how he killed the giant she did not believe him. The boy said to her, You have told me about things, that you thought I could not kill but I have killed them! There is a man who lives to the north and I am going to kill him! It is impossible for you to do that because he is a giant and a great medicine man! But the boy said he would do it. The boy went out to the house of Methar kwackwat (Penis striking with) and while he was away the grandmother cried and thought whether he is a human being or a ghost. But she consoled herself with the thought that if he were a ghost she would hear the ghosts at night. When he came to this giant he said "Növii" (Uncle) and the giant said, What child are you that you should call me uncle? Don't you know me, it is I? So the giant looked at him and said, I am going to kill you! The boy said, You shall not kill me! and turned himself into gravel. It was the giant's custom to kill people by striking them with his penis but he hit so hard at the gravel that he killed himself and fell down dead. He was dying on the ground. The boy stepped on his neck to make sure to kill him. The boy sent his shadow home to make the old woman believe that he was dead instead of the giant. When she heard the shadow round the house she cried because she thought her grandson was dead. The boy said, I never brought anything home to prove to my grandmother that I killed the other giant. So he took hold of the leg and shook the bones out. And then he covered himself with the skin and danced all the way home with it. When he was near the house she heard him dancing and singing so she began to dance too. So they were both dancing together. When she saw him with the skin she was happy to know he had told the truth, so she took the skin away from the boy, put it on herself and danced. I think I have killed the most dangerous person in this part of the country, the boy said, and I don't think there are any left to harm the country. This is clearly a story of growing up. The grandmother keeps saying he is too small and he keeps getting bigger and bigger weapons. Then he identifies with the phallic paternal ogre by donning its skin. The primal scene motive is also clearly indicated.

The story of King Arthur's victory over the giant is somewhat parallel to this Yuma folk tale.

"Then came to him a husbandman of the country and told him how there was in the country of Constantine, beside Brittany, a great giant which had slain, murdered and devoured many people of the country and had been sustained seven years with the children of the commons of that land insomuch as that all the children be all slain and destroyed, and now late he hath taken the Duchess of Brittany as she rode with her meyne [retinue] and hath led her to his lodging which is in a mountain for to ravish and lie by her to her life's end." An army set out to rescue her but they failed. "They left her shrieking and crying lamentably wherefore I suppose that he has slain her in fulfilling his foul lust of lechery. Arthur challenges the giant. 'Therefore arise and dress thee, thou glutton, for this day shalt thou die of my hand.' Then the glutton anon started up and took a great club in his hand and smote at the king that his coronal fell to the earth. And the king hit him again that he carve his belly *and cut off his genytours*" (genital organ).[175]

The "glutton" is originally the child in *talio* form, the mother, then the father who is also the castrator. The hero, however, is the growing son who turns anxiety into victory.

175 Malory, T., "Le Morte D'Arthur," Book V, Chapter V, *Everyman's Library*, I, London, 1912, pp. 135–139.

VII

THE WAY BACK

In one of Campbell's West Highland Tales the giant takes a liking to the king's son and rears him as his own son. He falls in love with the giant's youngest daughter.

The giant is angry and imposes several tasks on his would-be son-in-law.

"Before thou getst her thou must do the three things that I ask thee to do." The giant takes him to a byre.

"Now," says the giant, "the dung of a hundred cattle is here and it has not been cleansed for seven years. I am going from home today and if this byre is not cleaned before night comes, *so clean that a golden apple will run from one end to the other end of it,* not only thou shalt not get my daughter but 'tis a drink of thy blood that will quench my thirst this night."

The prince has given up all hope when the giant's daughter appears on the scene. He was so tired that he *fell asleep* beside her. When he awoke the giant's daughter was not to be seen but the byre was so well cleaned that a golden apple would run from end to end of it. The next task is to thatch the byre with birds' down which is solved in a similar way. Then he must bring magpie's eggs for the giant's breakfast; finally the giant consents and they get married. When they went to bed his wife said:

"Now," says she, "sleep not or else thou diest. We must fly quick, quick or for certain my father will kill thee."

She cut an *apple* into nine shares and placed them all over the house.

The giant awoke and said, *"Are you asleep?"* *"We are not yet,"* said the apple that was at the head of the bed. And so it goes on with all the pieces of the apple. The giant's daughter and the hero are escaping on horseback. "Put thy hand quick," said she, "in the ear of the gray filly and whatever thou findest in it throw it behind thee." What he finds is a twig of the shoe tree, and when he throws it back, it becomes a black thorn wood. The giant came headlong and there he was with his head and neck in the thorns. The giant went back to get his big axe. Then they throw a splinter of gray stone to detain the pursuer. It becomes a

406

rock and the giant again breaks through. The third time he threw a bladder of water behind and it became a fresh water loch twenty miles in length, the giant went under and rose no more.[1] In another version of this story the apple figures again. The giant's daughter gives the hero a *golden apple,* he is to throw it back at the vulnerable spot on the giant and that will kill the giant instantly.[2] In a third version, she tells the king's son to put the apple under the filly's foot. When the horse smashed the apple the giant fell over dead for his heart was in the apple.[3] In another version the flight is described as follows:

"She put a wooden bench in the bed of the king's son, two wooden benches in her own bed. She spat at the front of her own bed, she spat at the front of the giant's bed, she spat at the passage door and she set two apples above the giant's bed."

The giant *awoke* and shouted, "Rise daughter and bring me a drink of the blood of the king's son." "I will arise," said the spittle in front of his bed *and one of the apples fell and struck him between the two shoulders and he slept.* (This motive is repeated.) At the mouth of day the daughter said, "I feel my father's breath burning me between the two shoulders," and the king's son took a drop of water from the filly's right ear and threw it over his shoulder. It became a lake which the giant could not cross.[4]

In Grimm's story No. 79, "The Water-Sprite," a boy and a girl are captured by the water spirit. When they escape she throws a brush behind her and it becomes a mountain of brushes with a thousand thorns. The boy throws a comb, it is a mountain of combs with many spikes. Finally the girl throws a mirror, it becomes a slippery mountain of mirrors and he cannot get through. The water spirit goes back into the well.

In a story from Iceland the giantess has stolen the only cow of the peasant. The lad finds the cow but is pursued by a giantess. Obstacles made by the cow; lake, flames, mountain. The giant woman gets stuck in a narrow passage in the mountain.[5]

In a Greek story the king orders his son to be killed because he dreamed that the king left his throne and his son occupied it. They cut his little finger off and take this and the blood of a dove to the king. The wandering prince is adopted as son by a dragon. While the dragon is *asleep* the prince finds the golden steed that helps him escape. The dragon

[1] Campbell, I. F., *Popular Tales of the West Highlands,* 1890, I, pp. 30–34.
[2] *Ibid.,* p. 48.
[3] *Ibid.,* p. 51.
[4] *Ibid.,* p. 56; cf. p. 60.
[5] Rittershaus, A., *Neuisländische Volksmärchen,* Berlin, 1902, p. 190.

awakes and the usual chase follows. The last object thrown back is salt. It becomes an ocean which the dragon cannot wade through.[6]

In a Hungarian story from Egyházaskér (Southern Hungary) the hero has stolen the golden duck of the Devilish Old Woman. She sees what has happened in her *dream* and now the usual obstacle flight with the hero on horseback and various objects connected with the horse thrown behind and all turning into dense forests.[7]

The oldest version of the magical flight is contained in Japanese mythology (the Kojiki dates back to 712 A.D.).

Izanagi and Izanami are brother and sister. The gods tell them to create the world and give them the Jewel Spear of Heaven. Hirata, the commentator, says that this was shaped like the Wo-bashira, the phallic pillars that are still used in the cult. The god and the goddess stood on the bridge of heaven[8] and started creating by stirring the primeval waters with the Jewel Spear. A circumambulation of the spear is the marriage. They have intercourse and their first child is born. The last of their children is the fire god who kills his mother by burning her vulva. Izanagi cuts the fire god into pieces with his sword. He follows his sister-wife into the underworld through the clapping door, intending to fetch her back to life. "What a pity you did not come earlier. I have now eaten the food of the underworld." She nevertheless makes an attempt to follow him in his upward path. "Don't look back," she says. But he disobeys her and lights one tooth of his comb to see her. This was again the "male pillar." He now sees that she is becoming putrid and her body is full of worms; on her head there is the Great Thunder, on her breast the Fire Thunder, in her stomach the Black Thunder, in her vagina the Splitting Thunder, in her left hand the Young Thunder, in the right the Earth Thunder, in her left foot Rolling Thunder, in her right foot Lying Thunder. Izanagi recoils in horror from this sight and Izanami says, "You have now made me ashamed," and she sends the "frowning women of the netherworld" to chase him. He takes the black ornaments from his hair,[9] and throws them back behind. They become grapes and while the women of the netherworld eat the grapes Izanagi gained time but they were still after him. He threw down his many-toothed comb and this became changed into bamboo shoots. They tore them out and ate them and were still in

---

[6] von Hahn, J. G., *Griechische und albanesische Märchen*, Leipzig, 1864, II, pp. 259, 260.

[7] Kálmány, *Hagyományok* (Traditions), no date and no place of publication, II, p. 64.

[8] Bridges are now built over lakes that lead to the shrine. Izanagi is said to have built the sky bridge, but he fell off it while *asleep*.

[9] F. Florenz remarks that it is difficult to understand what could be meant by black ornaments (*Die historischen Quellen der Shinto Religion*, Leipzig, 1919, p. 23).

hot pursuit of our hero. The Ugly Females (or the Thundergods) continued their pursuit. On reaching the Even Pass of Yomi (Underworld) he gathered three peaches and smote his pursuers with them; they all had to flee. This is the origin of the custom of using peaches in exorcism. At the Even Pass of Yomi, Izanagi was overtaken by Izanami herself. He took a great rock and blocked up the pass with it at the same time pronouncing the formula of divorce—namely, "Our relationship is severed."

His sister arrived and said, "If you do this I shall kill one thousand mortals every day." "If you do this," he replied, "I shall cause one thousand five hundred to be born every day."[10]

Izanagi, who is defiled by the dirt of the underworld, now goes through a ritual of purification which is regarded as the prototype of all such rituals. The ritual, like the myth, consists in throwing things away. The stick he throws away becomes a god called "Erect standing go no further place." He throws his girdle away. The name of this god was "The Long Distance of the Road." He threw away another piece of garment worn around the hips; this god was "To untie, to put down." Another garment thrown away became the god "Master of Suffering and Sickness." He threw his trousers away and this became the God of Crossways. In ritual this god appears in two shapes, Male and Female, with genitalia emphasized and turned toward each other.[11]

In another version of this myth Izanagi urinates, the urine becomes a river and this prevents his sister from following him.[12]

Like other heroes of the underworld journey Izanagi is forbidden to look back. Unlike other versions of the "obstacle flight" story in this case pursued and pursuer are man and wife. The sexual import of the visual taboo is very clear, because light is spread by a phallic object. Moreover, Izanami also dies of giving birth to the fire god and she becomes the ruler of the underworld. She dies a second time when her husband (brother) lights the tooth of his comb; the male is the phallos, or fire, his journey to or from the underworld kills the female.[13] What he is not supposed to see is the awesome sight of the female genital organ "crawling with maggots or thunder gods." Desire is transformed into anxiety; a *running after* or coitus becomes a *running away from*. Among the objects thrown behind we find the phallic stick and the peach, the symbol of the vagina. Aston explains that the Sahe no-kame, the Preventive deities of the purification ritual are all connected with Izanagi's

10 Florenz, *op. cit.*, pp. 11–25; Aston, W. G., *Shinto,* London, 1905, pp. 89–94.
11 *Ibid.*, p. 26.
12 Cf. Aarne, A., "Die magische Flucht," *Folklore Fellows Communication,* XCII, 1930, p. 6, quoting Florenz, *Geschichte der japanischen Literatur,* 1906, pp. 4, 10, 56.
13 Cf. the myth of Maui in the chapter "Vesical Dreams and Myths."

descent to the netherworld. The third of these gods is the Kunado, the phallos, Izanagi's staff. "Like the apricot in India and the pomegranate in ancient Greece the peach in China and Japan is the acknowledged representative of the *kteis* as the pestle and the mushroom are of the phallos."[14] Anxiety has transformed the female into a representative of death. In the ending of the story, the contest between the phallos and the vagina, the genital nature of the myth is again emphasized.

The taboo on looking back connects the myth of Izanagi and Izanami with Orpheus and Eurydike.

Eurydike has been bitten by a serpent and dies. Orpheus descends to the other world to fetch her back. But he looks back *before dawn* and she disappears.[15] In a myth of the Telumni Yokuts, the Land of the Dead lies in the west. A big river has to be crossed and there is a bridge that moves up and down, when a person crosses. When the traveler has arrived on the other side the bridge stops. A man loved his wife very much, she died and was buried. He wants to bring her back and sleeps on her grave. On the second night, just before dawn he sees her rising. She walked, but she staggered, as if she were drunk. She talked to her husband, "You can't cross the bridge, you'll fall off and become a fish." But he has eagle-feather down with him. He flies over the bridge and arrives on the other shore. The ghosts were dancing a round dance. Everyone spoke of the newcomer's bad smell—because the living smell *is* bad for the dead. The ghosts offer him food, but he does not take it. He can return with his wife on one condition, viz., if he stays awake all night. He falls asleep just before dawn and awakes with a log in his arms (instead of his wife). This happens twice.[16] The Miwok have the same story: the land of the dead is the land where newborn babies come from. The water is enormous. A frail bridge spans it; those who fall off become pikes.[17]

The dream origin of the story could not be clearer. The river, the moving bridge, the circular dance are all typical other-world motives. The bridge is the phallic way of entering sleep land, the river is the water or uterine world and the rotating dance the rotating sensation of falling asleep.

The Tlingit tell the story of a young man who was very sad because his wife died. He stayed awake all night. When she was buried he walked to the land of the dead. He saw a lake. On the other side of the lake there

14 Aston, *op. cit.*, p. 189.

15 Gruppe, "Orpheus," in *Roscher's Lexikon*, p. 1157.

16 Gayton, A. H., "The Orpheus Myth in North America," *Journal of American Folk-Lore*, XLVIII, 1935, pp. 267, 268.

17 *Ibid.*, p. 269; Barrett, S. A., "Pomo Myths," *Bull. of the Public Museum of the City of Milwaukee*, XV, 1933, p. 347.

were people but they did not see him. He shouted, "Come over and get me!" But they did not hear. However, when he whispered to himself they heard him. "A person has come up from dreamland," they said. They carry him across in a canoe and he finds his wife. She warns him not to take the food they offer. They are taken back in the Ghost's canoe. He takes her home but she is only a shadow.

"During the day the woman was very quiet, but all night long the two could be heard playing. The boy's father was resentful because she kept them *awake* all night. A young man who had been in love with her before spied on them just in the moment when she would regain her earthly form and cease being a shadow. In the moment when the young man thought of lifting the curtain, a rattling of bones was heard. They both went back to Ghost Land."[18] In a Thompson Indian story two young men are in search of their dead mother. They cross a river or a lake in a canoe. As they went on it *grew darker and darker and then lighter and lighter*. One of them returned to the land of the living, the other stayed with their mother.[19]

All these narratives show traces of their originating in dreams. When the dead say a person has come from dreamland, that by the usual process of inversion can only mean one thing; not the land of the living but the land of the dead is dreamland.

The descent into the underworld is a descent into mother (uterus), the basic dream. Gruppe conjectures that in the original form of the Orpheus-Eurydike myth, Eurydike or Agriope is really another Persephone, the personified netherworld. "To bring back the wife," is a secondary trait introduced probably into the original dream in a realistic situation; the wife is dead, his longing for her is the libido, and the libido or life impulse is also awakening. The path downward is fraught with anxiety, (a) because sleep is death, (b) because it is uterine regression (desire and anxiety mixed), (c) because it means coitus with mother. The seeing taboo which we find so frequently in these myths has to do with their origin; the dream itself is a vision, it is seen and it disappears.

In a Zuni story the husband and the dead wife start to go westward to the land of the dead. Each night the dead wife becomes visible; *at dawn she disappears*. The typical obstacles may be placed on the downward passage instead of the way back. Thus they pass through lava beds, a cactus patch, a chasm. By means of a ladder they descend to the bottom of a large lake.

[18] Swanton, J. R., *Tlingit Myths and Texts,* Smithsonian Institution, Bureau of American Ethnology Bulletin 39, 1909, pp. 249, 250.
[19] Teit, I., *Traditions of the Thompson River Indians of British Columbia,* Mem. Am. F. L. Soc., VI, 1898, pp. 84, 85.

Here the owl pities him and brings her back—but on the fourth day he kisses the sleeping girl and she disappears instantly.[20]

In a Yuchi myth four Yuchi kill their wives. "There is no such thing as death," they say. "Now we shall bring them back." They decide to travel westward and find Creator. They came to a place where there was a great cave. Before its mouth swayed a great cloud in such a manner that they could not get in or around it, for it was moving up and down. One man says, "I'll be a deer," the second, "I'll be a panther," the third, "I'll be a bear!" These three get through. The fourth says, "I'll be a man." The cloud fell on his head and crushed him. The three take their human shape again in the other world. They meet an old woman, the sun.

They tell her what they came for. She says, "You can stay for the dance and then you will see them." A panther monster came up and they were very much afraid. The old woman *hides them under her dress.*

When the dance started, they said, "We can hear but we cannot see."

The old woman said to them, *"If you cannot see, lie down and go to sleep."*

While they are asleep she puts the women in four large gourds, telling them to carry these back but not to open them until they reach home. Three disregard this and only the fourth one keeps his wife.[21]

Beside the motive "sleep," we have in this story the meaning of the journey to the underworld, which is under the skirt of the old woman.[22] In other stories there are at least rudiments of the dream origin.

In a Southern Okanagon myth, Coyote crosses the water and attracts the attention of the dead by *yawning.* He sleeps beside his dead wife, but on the fifth night he breaks the taboo by having intercourse with her. She disappears.[23]

The version in which the woman disappears, because the continence taboo is broken, simply means that she was taboo in the first place, and if in the dream coitus appears as the dreamer's intention; she disappears—the image is blotted out. Practically all Orpheus stories lack a happy ending. The one told by the Akikuyu is an exception:

Wangiru was a girl who was sacrificed in order to bring rain but there was a young warrior who loved her and wanted to bring her back. "Where has she gone? I want to go to the same place." He took his sword

[20] Cushing, F. M., *Zuni Folk Tales,* New York, 1901, pp. 18–33.

[21] Speck, F. G., *Ethnology of the Yuchi,* Univ. Penn. Anthr. Publ., Vol. I, No. 1, 1909, pp. 144–146. Cf. also Moones, I., *Myths of the Cherokee,* Bureau of Am. Ethn., XIX, Annual Report, 1900, p. 253.

[22] That is, the inside of the old woman is the underworld.

[23] Gayton, "The Orpheus Myth," *Journal of American Folk-Lore,* XLVIII, 1935, p. 278; cf. also for continence taboo, p. 271.

and spear and shield. As the dark fell he came to the place where she had vanished. His feet began to sink, and he sank lower and lower till the ground closed over him and he went by a long road under the earth till he found her. He takes her on his back like a child and at nightfall introduces her into his mother's house.[24]

The fugitive usually does not look back but he (or she) always throws objects behind him (or her) to delay the pursuer. The objects thrown back are remarkably uniform, a stone, a comb and water (oil). The last is probably the most significant and the most widespread. In an Armenian story of this type the jug of water gives rise to a flood.[25]

The Heiltsuk tell the following story. A girl ran into the forest because her parents were always scolding her. She saw a house. In this house there lived an old woman with a gigantic mouth and also big hands and feet. She gave the girl a basket, some fish oil, a whetstone, and a needle. The husband of the old woman was Root. He came home and ordered her to louse him. His lice are frogs and she only pretends to eat them but really hides them under her cloak. He goes fishing and orders his *night chamber to report* if the girl should try to escape. The old woman fills the girl's basket with all sorts of things and tells her how to use comb and whetstone and oil. The girl ran. But the night chamber warned Root and he pursued her at once. She threw the whetstone back, it became a steep hill; then the comb which became a dense forest. Then the oil, it became a lake with a fog covering it. Before he could get through this she had reached her father's house.[26] In another story we have a man called Noakaua and his four sons. Against their father's warning ("Dreadnaught" motive; Stith Thompson) they go to the house of red smoke. They notice that they are in a house inhabited by cannibals and run for their lives. The cannibal ("He who first ate human flesh at the delta of the river") is after them. Whetstone becomes a hill, hair oil a big lake, and comb a thick forest. They arrive at their father's house; the cannibal demands to be let in. Their mother digs a deep ditch, makes a fire in it, and heats stones in the fire. The cannibal and his wife sit down at the edge of the ditch with a prop for their backs. The cannibal says to Noakaua, "You know how things happened *in the beginning*. Tell me something about it." Noakaua said:

"What shall I tell you about ancient times, grandchildren? A long time ago that hill was covered by a cloud. *Soon you shall sleep!* After he

[24] Routledge, W. S. and K., *With a Prehistoric People*, London, 1910, pp. 288, 289.

[25] Chalatianz, G., *Armenische Bibliothek*, IV, *Märchen und Sagen*, pp. 69, 70, quoted in Stucken, E., *Astralmythen*, Leipzig, 1907, p. 235.

[26] Boas, *Indianische Sagen aus der nord-pazifischen Küste Amerikas*, Berlin, 1895, pp. 267, 268.

had sung this four times, the cannibals were all fast asleep. Noakaua and his wife pulled the props away and they all fell into the ditch. This is how the cannibals died in the fire.[27] Here again we find the giant sleeping as in the European stories, only here it is at the end instead of the beginning. We see the characteristic end of all ogres; they are consumed by fire or water. Finally the fall into the hole (basic dream) is also displaced, it is at the *end of the dream*—but it is in consequence of an untold story about the *beginning of the world.*

In one of the Tlingit versions the bears who are pursuing the girl want to marry her. The objects she throws back are "devil's-club," thorn and rose bushes. But the water does come in at the end. There is a beach, the ocean, and a man in a canoe who consents to save her if she will become his wife.[28]

Then again it may be an old woman and a boy. One boy said to the other: "Look here, friend! Look at that moon. Don't you think the shape of the moon is the same as that of my mother's labret[29] and that the size is the same too?" The other answered, "Don't! You must not talk that way of the moon." Then suddenly it became very dark round them and the chief's son saw a ring round them like a rainbow. When it disappeared his companion was gone. He thought the moon must have gone up with him. That circular rainbow must have been the moon.

The youth felt very badly about the loss of his friend. He shot a chain of his arrows up to a star that was next to the moon.

Lying down under the arrow chain *he went to sleep.* After a while he awoke, found he had slept on a hill and instead of the arrows there was a ladder reaching right up into the sky. He ascends on this ladder and an old woman gives him a spruce cone, a rose bush, a piece of devil's club and a whetstone.

He heard his playmate screaming with pain in the moon's house. He pulled him out of the smoke hole and put in a spruce cone instead. He told the spruce cone to imitate the voice of his friend and the two ran away. The moon started in pursuit. The devil's club becomes a patch of devil's club, the rose bush a thicket of roses. The grindstone became a high cliff, which kept the moon rolling back. "It is on account of this cliff that people can say things about the moon nowadays with impunity."

The old woman gave them something to eat and when they were through she said to the rescuer, "Go and lie down at the place where you lay when you first came up. Don't think of anything but the playground

---

27 Boas, *op. cit.,* pp. 223, 224. Cf. also the story on p. 164.

28 Swanton, J. R., *Tlingit Myths and Texts,* Bureau of Am. Ethn. Bulletin, 39, 1909, p. 127.

29 A labret is an ornament worn in holes (that are) pierced through the lip.

you used to have." They went there and lay down but after some time the boy who had first been captured thought of the old woman's house and immediately they found themselves there. Then the old woman said, "Go back and do not think of me any more! Lie there and think of nothing but the place where you used to play." *They did so and, when they awoke they were lying on their playground at the foot of the ladder.*[30]

The end where the hero finds himself lying at the same place as in the beginning certainly suggests sleep and dreaming.

The Modoc tell the following story: A woman is pursuing a man who rejected her. He says, "Let her *sleep* till I reach the first house." He arrives at the house of two old sisters who immediately turn him into a baby. When the cannibal woman arrives they are fondling the baby. She suspects it must be her man, but they reply that he was born today. The two sisters have the power to make the ogress fall asleep from time to time while he runs on. When she awakes she runs after him. Finally he disappears into a hole under a woman.[31]

Here we certainly have the basic dream with the mother imago in several images, dangerous and protective and sleep displaced as usual to the pursuer.

Perhaps the most constant of the varying traits of the story is the death of the ogre or ogress. It is in water or fire.

In a Chippewayan story we have the Big Man or Tyrant and the young man called Caribou Footed who is escaping, helped by the moose. A clod of earth gives rise to great hills, a piece of moss to a great swamp, and a stone to rocky mountains. Finally they come to a river. The moose promises to carry the giant over the river. But he overturned him and down he swept through the swirling rapid.[32]

In a Cheyenne tale the husband finds that his wife has a lover, a water monster. He kills her and makes the children eat her flesh. Their mother's skull pursues them. Yellow porcupine quills become a great bed of high prickly pears, white quills turn into mulberry bushes and red quills into thorny rose bushes. With a stick they make a little furrow in the ground that becomes a big ravine filled with water and the skull falls into it.[33] In a similar Dakota story the woman is the mistress of the bears. After having had intercourse with them she kills them. Her husband compels her to eat her lovers' flesh and then kills her. He gives

[30] Swanton, *op. cit.*, 39, 1909, pp. 209–211.
[31] Curtin, J., *Myths of the Modocs*, Boston, 1912, pp. 20, 21.
[32] Bell, J. M., "The Fireside Stories of the Chippewayans," *Journal of American Folk-Lore*, XVI, 1903, pp. 80–82.
[33] Grinnel, G. B., "A Cheyenne Obstacle Myth," *Journal of American Folk-Lore*, XVI, 1903, pp. 108–110.

the children the skin of an oriole and a whetstone. Their mother's skull pursues them. Finally they come to a large river where they see a man in a canoe. He takes them into the canoe and kills the skull.[34]

The ogre or skull generally falls into a river even if it is not an obstacle flight story.

A man once had a *bad dream* (Maidu). He dreamed that he ate himself up. The next day while picking pine nuts his son accidentally hit him on the leg and his leg began to bleed. He licked his blood and it tasted so good that he ate himself all up except the skull. Then the skull began to eat other people till it finally fell into a river and that was the end.[35]

In another Modoc story an old woman is pursuing a man who has eloped with her daughter. Awls become a thorny thicket, *looking back* (cf. above) produces a ditch full of water. A looking glass thrown back turns into a lake. The old woman says: "I am not afraid because it is made by a harlot girl."

But she drowns and as she tries to drink the water her belly bursts.[36]

The water as ending has a definite significance. In a Quileute story the hero is escaping after having killed the chief of the wolves. A comb stuck in the beach becomes a headland, etc. Finally when the wolves had nearly caught up with him he urinated and made Ozetta Lake which they could not pass.[37]

In an Eskimo story a gigantic cannibal pursues a medicine man. By his magic he first creates berries and then a river. "How did you get across," the giant asks. "I drank all the water till I could wade through," he says. The giant drinks till he bursts and dies.[38]

The water ending is sometimes curiously displaced. In a Thompson River story a man steals a horse. The first obstacle is a river, the second a tract of mud, then thick timber and ice. Finally the pursuer gives up and goes home.

He goes to the mountains and dreams of a canoe and water. He makes the water, it reaches to the thief's village. He embarks on the canoe which has a prow like fire. The other man had changed his horse into a loon which was swimming on the water. He gave chase on the

[34] Wissler, C., "Some Dakota Myths," *Journal of American Folk-Lore*, XX, 1907, pp. 195, 196.

[35] Dixon, R. B., "Maidu Myths," *Bulletin American Museum of Natural History*, XVII, 1901, pp. 97, 98.

[36] Curtin, *op. cit.*, p. 90.

[37] Farrand, L., "Quileute Tales," *Journal of American Folk-Lore*, XXXII, 1919, p. 254.

[38] Boas, "The Eskimo of Baffin Land and Hudson Bay," *Bull. Am. Mus. Nat. Hist.*, XV, 1901, p. 77.

water. But his wife changed him and the canoe into a fish and married a Teal Duck.[39]

In some versions of the story fire ends the ogre's career, not water. In a Tahtlan story a father-in-law changes his daughter into a bear to kill her husband. He kills his wife and is pursued by the father-in-law. The inside of the bear-wife becomes a deep chasm with lakes. His stick turns into fire and that is how the pursuer perishes.[40] In another story of the same tribe a mother pursues her son who killed his step-father. Caribou hair becomes a herd of caribou, the tripe of the caribou a deep gulch. The bones become rocky ground. Finally fire stones thrown back become fire and that is the end of the ogress.[41]

The objects thrown backward are in some versions, parts of the body of the fugitive or of the body of an animal killed by the fugitive.

In a Thompson River Indian story the Coyote sent his two daughters to marry two hunters who lived in a distant country. A child was born to one of them. The child cried for his grandmother (i.e., Coyote's wife). The father sent them on their way home. He says:

"On your way back you will come to a parting of the trail. One of the trails that you will see is rough and narrow while the other is wide and smooth; the former is covered with red ochre, while the latter is covered with birds' down. Take the red trail . . . and avoid the other, as it will lead you over a wide prairie devoid of trees to a land where dead people live, monsters, and mysterious people."

They go on the wrong trail. Cannibal catches them. The boy cries: "Kill me first and put me in the bottom of the kettle." He killed him and *doubling him up* put him in the bottom of the kettle. Then he killed the two women, bending them also and putting them in the kettle. He then put the kettle on the fire to boil and sat by, waiting for his meal to cook. In the meantime the boy made *a hole in the bottom of the kettle and urinated through it on the fire underneath* so that the bottom of the kettle remained cool and the contents never boiled. Later they all got out of the kettle through a hole which the boy made by urinating.

Next morning the Cannibal gave chase. One of the women took *four hairs out from her pubes.* They turned into four trees—they climbed on one of them. As the Cannibal chopped down one tree they jumped to the next one. The boy urinated down the heart of the tree, it became soft and elastic and difficult for the Cannibal to chop.[42]

[39] Teit, I., "Traditions of the Thompson River Indians of British Columbia," *Memoirs of the American Folk-Lore Society,* VI, 1898, pp. 92, 93.
[40] *Idem,* "Tahtlan Tales," *Journal of American Folk-Lore,* 1921, XXXIV, p. 235.
[41] *Ibid.,* p. 90.
[42] *Ibid.,* pp. 34, 35.

We shall finish our survey of North American versions. Man Fond of Deer Meat (Wichita) cannot get any deer. His wife is therefore in danger of being eaten. Sparrow gives her a stick with a double ball, a handful of deer hair, bark from a dogwood tree and a bundle of reddish-colored pieces of fine stones for paint. The deer hairs become a lot of deer, the dogwood bark big bushes of dogwood, the colored stones a lot of stones. With her stick she makes a deep canyon. Finally she runs right into her father's lodge.

"There were a good many people inside of this place. *When it grew dark* they could hear Man Fond of Deer Meat talking outside of the lodge asking her that she might be turned out and saying that he wanted her. The woman's father said to her, "Let me tell you a story." He then commenced to tell her a story about a chief having a daughter who married and left home for the sake of keeping her husband when the old folks did not want her to keep her man. The chief told her the whole tale of her life while out by herself and with the man."

But Man Fond of Deer Meat was calling for his wife when the chief ended the story. He ended the story about his daughter's life, telling her what time she arrived at the village, that she was without her blanket, how she ran for her life to her father's grass lodge and what a crowd of men were waiting. *It was daylight when he completed the story. At the same time Man Fond of Deer Meat fell dead just outside the lodge.*[43]

The dream is in a sense a life history. By the time the dream is told, it is morning and the anxiety image is there no more.

What kind of a dream is this? We have good reason to assume that the *urethral awakening dream* is the most important dream factor. The Kojiki and the Quiute story end in the urethral flood and where the urine is not openly mentioned the end is water or fire—the well-known symbols of urine. The urethral dreams of our patients are frequently obstacle dreams in this sense that they want to urinate but find all bathrooms closed, etc. They also contain the motive of "increasing volume of water," here represented by a bladderful becoming a river, lake, etc. They always transform the somatic stimulus into a sexual situation, represented here by the chase. The hero who disappears in a hole under the woman, the fugitives in and out of the kettle represent the basic dream.

A comb, a stone, and oil (water) are the usual objects used in the obstacle flight.

In the Highland story we quoted above, the hero's first task is to clean the stables filled with dung *so that a golden apple will run through*

[43] Dorsey, G. A., *The Mythology of the Wichita*, Washington, D.C., 1904, pp. 234–239; cf. also No. 19, p. 130.

clean from one end to the other. We suspect that the apple that figures in these stories to detain the pursuer may be an excremental symbol.

In an allied situation, magic objects delay the pursuer by impersonating the fugitive. In a Kamtschadal myth, Kutka defecates all sort of berries to detain his pursuers.[44]

In a Tembé story a man is escaping from a skull. The excrements talk as if they were the fugitive.[45] In a Lillooet story the people decide to decamp and abandon a thief. They eased themselves in several places and after they were gone their excrements continued to whistle.[46]

In an excremental dream with the desire to prolong sleep and the pressure of the excrements as threat the excreta might easily become the enemy or a kind of pseudo enemy.

In another Lillooet story, Raven, while taking four women through enemy country, went ashore and defecated and urinated. He told his excrements to shout loudly as if they had been enemies.[47] In an Awikyenoq story Raven tells his excrements to shout as if they were a crowd of enemies; by this ruse he gets all the food.[48] As mentioned above, a comb, a stone, and oil are the typical objects of the magic flight. The oil is urine, the stone excrements. The third object thrown behind by the fugitive is a comb and the result is a forest.[49] The comb usually turns into a forest. The comb is substituted for hair, the hair for pubic hair[50] and finally pubic hair for the genital organ (cf. the story of Izanagi and Izanami).

In a parallel version the fugitives, instead of throwing objects behind them, transform themselves and thus delude the ogre or witch.

An Eskimo story combines the obstacle flight and the "fugitive transformed" type:

A male and a female bird were traveling and the female had a little bird "in her womb" (disregards the difference between birds and mammals). Whenever they see a hill on the tundra, she wants to lay the egg and he says, "If you lay an egg there the man will kill us." Finally she does lay her egg and a boy kills the father bird.

"When the wife found out that he was killed *while the people were asleep* she took her husband up to her nest." They bury the husband and

<hr />

44 Steller, G. W., *Beschreibung von Kamtschatka,* Frankfurt and Leipzig, 1774, p. 263.

45 Nimuendaju Unkel, Curt, "Sagen der Tembé Indianer," *Zeitschrift für Ethnologie,* XLVII, 1915, p. 291.

46 Teit, "Traditions of the Lillooet Indians," *Journal of American Folk-Lore,* XXV, 1921, p. 297.

47 *Ibid.,* p. 317.

48 Boas, *Indianersagen,* pp. 213, 233.

49 Aarne, "Die Magische Flucht," *F.F.C.* No. 92, 1930, p. 24.

50 Rank, O., Die Symbolschichtung im mythischen Denken, *Psychoanalytische Beiträge zur Mythenforschungen,* Wien, 1919, p. 144.

while she is doing this a ptarmigan says he will be her husband. She rejects this suitor and flies on with her daughter. The next suitor is a crane, also rejected. Then a man, also her suitor, flies away in the shape of a ptarmigan. Same episode repeated; man flies away as crane.

They come to an old man's house who wants to kill them. The daughter *wanted to defecate,* so they went out. They were tied with a rope but they tied the rope to some roots and flew away. The old man was after them. The mother bird invokes the aid of her grandmother. *High bushes* grew between them and the old man; then *tall grasses.* Then a river appears with tall trees floating on it. They crossed; he was after them. Big rocks grew up, but he cut them all with a sharp knife. Finally the last rock killed him.[51]

In a Hungarian folk tale the witch decides that she will boil her daughter Anyicska and the daughter's suitor Ráadó ("He who gives or puts on") in oil. She is happy at the prospect of how she will see them shrinking in hot oil in the tub. But the maid warns Anyicska, and she spits three times as a delaying action. The saliva answers, "I am coming," when the old witch calls. Finally when the witch has found out what has happened and she is about to catch up with them, Anyicska says, "I shall be a church and you an eremite, and when my mother asks, 'Have you seen a boy and girl escaping this way?' you shall answer 'Yes, it must have been about three hundred years ago.' "

Then the girl is a lake, the boy a duck. But in this transformation the old witch recognizes them. She is now an eagle swooping down on the duck. The duck dives under the water. She is a hunter but her bullet misses the duck. Finally she gets so furious she decides to drink the whole lake. She does this and flies home with it. Then she pours it out again (how is not explained) hoping to see her daughter drown in the water. But Ráadó has hidden her in a few drops of water under his wings. When she discovers this she gallops after them with a rake. The rake is in her daughter's hair but at the same moment they have passed the frontier of fairy land.[52]

In another Hungarian version from Baranya, the obstacle flight is combined with the transformation. The witch is in pursuit and her daughter is escaping with the prince. The comb she throws behind her becomes a forest and the army sent by the old witch cannot get through.

The second time they throw the horsewhip; it is a river. When the soldiers go back to the old witch she tells them that the river was her daughter and the bridge the prince. If they had hit either the river or the

51 Lantis, M., "The Social Culture of the Nunivak Eskimo," *Trans. Am. Phil. Soc.,* New Series, XXXV, Pt. III, 1946, pp. 293–295.

52 Arany, L., *Magyar Népmese Gyüjtemény,* Budapest, 1911, pp. 69–105.

bridge the real forms would have appeared. The girl then becomes a mill, the boy a miller. The story ends again with the frontier of fairy land.[53]

In a Mecklenburg version she becomes a rose bush, her lover a rose. Then she is a merry-go-round and he is the proprietor, finally she is a lake and he a duck. The old woman falls into the lake and is drowned.[54] In an Iceland story the ogress' stepmother wants to kill brother and sister. She *dreams* that they must be in some animal form. First they are two colts, then two singing birds, then she is a whale and he the fins of a whale.[55]

In some of the Finnish versions the transformation is to shepherd and cow or peasant and field. In a Danish version, it is *bull and cow*.[56] In many European versions quoted by Aarne, we find priest and church.[57] The American versions seem to be all recently imported. In a Micmac story the Otter is trailing the Rabbit. The fugitive first becomes an old man in a wigwam, then a gentleman in a house, and then a ship (survival of "water" motive).[58] In a Salish version there are three fugitives. The girl is a lake, her husband a duck, their child a duckling.[59] In one version of the transformation type, that may be of independent origin, the fugitive after assuming various shapes, meets an old Beaver woman who is making a boat because of an impending flood.[60]

Here we can stop for the time being. The "transformation" type is more uniform than the obstacle flight. In both types the story ends with water, no wonder it should be linked with the flood theme. In this case the urethral awakening dream (indicated in the Hungarian stories by the frontier of fairy land; dream and reality) is closer to the dreams in which coitus is represented as the whole person being in the woman. Priest and church, duck and lake, etc.—the mother imago undergoes a fission: the protecting young girl and the cannibal witch.

Deukalion [Little Aeus and Pyrrha (Red)], the daughter of Epimetheus, and Pandora float for nine days and nine nights in a box carried by the flood till they land on Parnassus. Through Hermes, Zeus tells them

53 Bánó, S., *Baranyai Népmesék* (Folk Tales of Baranya), Budapest, 1941, II, pp. 200, 201.

54 Bartsch, K., *Sagen Märchen und Gebräuche aus Mecklenburg*, Wien, 1879, I, p. 478.

55 Rittershaus, A., *Neuislandische Volksmärchen*, 1902, p. 139.

56 Aarne, *Die Magische Flucht*, p. 45.

57 *Ibid.*, p. 39.

58 Speck, F. G., "Some Micmac Tales from Cape Breton Island," *Journal of American Folk-Lore*, XXVIII, 1915, p. 65.

59 Teit, "Folk Tales of the Salishan and Sahaptin Tribes," *Mem. Am. F. L.*, 5, 1917, XI, p. 60.

60 Dorsey, I. O., "Abstracts of Omaha and Ponca Myths," *Journal of American Folk-Lore*, I, 1888, p. 205.

to create human beings by throwing their mothers' bones, i.e., stones (bones of Mother Earth) behind themselves. This is why people are called λαοι, from λαας = stone.[61]

The nine-day period in the box is reminiscent of the "obstacle flight" combined with the infantile birth theory of anal birth.

Mudjekeewis's brothers have stolen the wampum of Mishe Mokwa (the great bear-female). One of his guardian spirits, an old man, attempts to stop her. The old man has two magic clubs. First they are quite small and then they grow and are immense. The same happens to his two little dogs. He *strokes* them, they grow and fight the she-bear. The phallic nature of the growing clubs and dogs, furthermore of the whole flight and fight, is obvious. However, the she-bear wins the battle and Mudjekeewis and his brothers have to keep running. "I have another dream," says Mudjekeewis and immediately there is a lake with a canoe. The brothers are in the canoe. But the gigantic bear-woman is about to swallow the whole lake—Mudjekeewis raises his club, but she vomits it all out again and they are hurled to the opposite shore. Now comes his last *dream;* this is the skull of Jamo. Jamo lived with his sister but as she touched him with her blood he was burned to ashes. All that remained was his skull. The magic of the skull makes the she-bear faint and then the brothers kill her. The little bears of today are the pieces of her body.[62]

This is a coitus dream with plenty of anxiety. If we interpret Jamo's sister and the she-bear as one person, it would be coitus with the gigantic menstruating mother. Anxiety, urethral pressure (water, skull) complicate the imagery.

The two types of the "obstacle flight" motive are both awakening dream; bladder pressure and excremental pressure genitalized. In the second type, however, "he in her," the emphasis on genitality and probably also on a continued desire to sleep are stronger.[63]

[61] *Roscher's Lexikon,* p. 994, quoting Apollodoros, etc.
[62] Schoolcraft, H. R., *The Myth of Hiawatha,* Philadelphia, 1886, pp. 142–153.
[63] Cf. also Campbell, Joseph, *The Hero with a Thousand Faces,* Bollingen Series XVII, 1949, p. 196.

VIII

MYTHOLOGY

I. Creation Myth

The widespread myth of creation called the Earth-Diver is a striking illustration of the dream origin of mythology.

According to the Pomo, their culture hero, Coyote, is also the creator. There was nothing but water. Coyote swam around and tried to find some land where he might live. By and by, he found a little island upon which there was some dirt, etc.

In another version Coyote creates the Earth with the assistance of Spider. He had a small amount of earth wrapped up in some pendant moss. He first took a little of this earth and blew it out into the air. Then he lay down and went to sleep in order that *he might dream*. But he could not dream. He ordered the Spider to spin a web and when he had done so to look in the other direction. He then spread the remaining earth on the web and the earth stretched out.[1]

"Tribes of the southerly stocks very generally believed in primordial waters, the waters of chaos before the earth or the flood enveloping it. Above this certain beings dwell—the Coyote and the birds.

"In some versions they occupy a mountain peak that pierces the waves, and on this height they abide until the flood subsides; in others they float on a raft or a pole or a tree that rises above the waters. In the latter case the birds dive for soil from which to build the earth—it is the *Duck* that succeeds floating to the surface dead but with a bit of soil in its bill."[2]

The Blackfoot tell the story of creation as follows: "In the beginning all the land was covered with water, an Old Man and all the animals were floating around on a large raft. The beaver went down and was gone a long time, but he could not reach the bottom. Then the loon tried and the others and the water was too deep for them.

[1] Barrett, S. A., "Pomo Myths," *Bulletin of the Public Museum of the City of Milwaukee,* XV, 1933, p. 15.

[2] Alexander, H. B., *The Mythology of All Races, North American,* X, Boston, 1916, p. 217 and references cited.

"At last the muskrat dived and he was gone so long that they thought he had drowned but he finally came up, almost dead, and when they pulled him on the raft they found in one of his paws a little mud. With this the Old Man formed the world and afterwards he made the people."[3]

The Cherokee version is this: "The earth is a great island floating in a sea of water and suspended at each of the four cardinal points by a *cord* hanging down from the sky vault which is of solid rock. When the world grows old and worn out the cords will break and the people will die and the world will sink back into the ocean again. The Indians are afraid of this.

"When all was water, the animals were above in the sky-land above the arch, but it was very much crowded and they were *wanting more room*. They wondered what was below the water, and at last Beaver's Grandchild, the little Water-Beetle, offered to go and see. It darted in every direction over the surface of the water, but could find no firm place to rest. Then it dived to the bottom and came up with some soft mud which began to grow and spread on every side till it became the island we now call earth."[4]

We find the same creation myth in Siberia and among the people of the Ural.

In the Vogul version given by Munkácsi, an old man and an old woman lived together. They did not go out of their house, they did not know what the world outside was like. Suddenly they heard noises. It was an iron-diving bird flying down from the sky. It flew down to the bottom of the ocean several times, only a tiny bit of earth was on its back. Coming up it took a deep breath, a part of its throat burst. Next day when the old man and woman awoke an iron-*vöcsök* flew down from the sky, his head nearly burst with the deep breath he took, and he brought up some more earth. In the meanwhile, the earth keeps growing.[5]

Munkácsi explains that in Vogul the word for creation means "to let down" since all creation is imagined as something that is "let down" from the sky. The first bird is the Colymbus septentrionalis Linne, the second the colymbus auritus Pallas, a smaller black swamp bird called *luli* in Vogul.[6] It is noteworthy, however, that the birds in question are iron-birds and the bird costume of the shaman is an "iron-duck."

In another story, Tarem (Sky God, Creator) has let down an old man

3 Grinnell, G. B., *Blackfoot Lodge Tales*, London, 1893, p. 272.
4 Mooney, James, "Myths of the Cherokee," *19th Annual Report of the Bureau of American Ethnology*, 1897/1898, 1900, p. 239.
5 Munkacsi, *Vogul Nepköltési-Gyüjtemey*, I, Budapest, pp. 1–3. We omit the continuation of the story.
6 *Ibid.*, p. 178.

and an old woman to the earth. They pray to him for a little piece of earth big enough for a house to stand on. This happens. The woman is delivered of a child who then grows up. There is no room for the child. The old man mustering all his strength climbs up a ladder in mink form and asks for help. Numi Tarem gives the son a *diver-bird costume* (hence the iron) in which to dive to the bottom of the ocean. After several futile attempts the son finally manages to fetch earth from the bottom of the ocean.[7]

In another similar myth Xulater (the Devil) takes the form of a diving duck.[8] The contrast between God and the Devil (or really, Prince of death) is also expressed in the colour of the birds, the black diving duck or *luli* is also called Duck of Death.[9]

The Yenisei Ostiak version brings the story even closer to shamanism.

"The great shaman, Doh, hovered over the waters in the company of swans, loons and other water fowl. As he could nowhere else find a nesting place, he asked the diver bird to bring him a piece of earth from under the ocean. Of this he made an island in the sea—that is the earth."[10]

Other Asiatic variants can be found in Holmberg. One step further and we are in Europe. Since Dähnhardt, it has always been assumed that this is a case of diffusion from Europe through Asia to America. Many apocryphal Russian legends follow the dualistic type of creation. In one of these myths (Bulgarian) God creates Satan out of his own shadow.[11]

The Ukrainians in the Carpathian mountains sing this cosmogonic myth as one of their Kolyadki or Christmas songs:

> Once there was neither heaven nor earth
> Heaven nor earth, but only blue sea
> And in the midst of the sea two oaks
> There sat there two pigeons
> Two pigeons on the two oaks
> And began to take counsel among themselves
> To take counsel and to say
> How can we create the world
> Let us go to the bottom of the sea
> Let us bring thence fine sand. . . .[12]

A Russian version: God saw a diving bird and said, "Who are you?" The bird said, "I am God." "Then who am I?" God asked. "You are the

---

[7] *Ibid.*, pp. 135–148.

[8] *Ibid.*, p. 160.

[9] *Ibid.*, p. cciv.

[10] Holmberg, U., *The Mythology of All Races: Finno-Ugric, Siberian*, IV, Boston, 1927, p. 323.

[11] Dähnhardt, O., *Natursagen*, Leipzig, 1907, I, p. 44.

[12] Ralston, W. R. S., *The Songs of the Russian People*, London, 1872, p. 194.

God of Gods," the bird said. God said, "Where do you come from?" The bird said, "From the Depths." "And where do I come from?" God asked. "From above." God said, "Give me from the Deep." The diving bird brought up foam and mud, and from this mud God created the earth.[13] The Rumanians tell the following version of the Earth-Diver myth.

In the beginning there was water everywhere and only God and the Devil were wandering about above the water. After they had wandered for seven years God was tired and sent the Devil to the bottom of the water to find some seed out of which to make the Earth in God's name. Some earth remained under the devil's nails (abbreviated). God then took three grains of sand from under the Devil's nail and out of these he made the Earth.

The Devil tried to arrange that God should be drowned when he fell asleep so that he (the Devil) should remain the lord of the Earth. God knew what he was plotting *and pretended to sleep*. The Devil caught hold of his leg and tried to drag him into the water so that he might be drowned. Whenever the Devil gave a big pull the crust of the earth stretched itself out and so, as the Devil went on pulling in all directions, the earth extended itself and became as we now know it.[14]

Pulling the leg and extending it is probably a masturbation dream.

We shall not go into detail regarding the path of diffusion or whether we have to assume that originally there were one or two divine beings or birds. However, it seems that India has some of the oldest versions of the myth and might be considered its original home.

Zimmer and Campbell give the following rendering of one of the Puranas. Vishnu has decided to destroy the Universe, that is, to take it all back again into himself. "Vishnu sleeps. Like a spider that has climbed up the thread that once issued from its own organism, *drawing it back into itself*, the God has consumed again the web of the universe. Alone upon the immortal substance of the ocean, a giant figure, submerged partly, partly afloat, he takes delight in slumber."[15]

"Inside the god is the Cosmos, like an unborn babe within the mother; and here all is restored to its primal perfection. Though without there exists only darkness, within the divine dreamer an ideal vision thrives of what the universe should be."[16]

Now Markandeya comes upon the scene. . . . This is a mythical saint

13 Dähnhardt, *op. cit.*, I, p. 46.

14 Murgoci, A. and H. B., "The Devil in Roumanian Folklore," *Folk-Lore*, XL, 1929, pp. 135–137.

15 Zimmer, H., *Myths and Symbols in Indian Art and Civilization* (edited by Joseph Campbell), New York, 1945, p. 37. For other Indian versions, cf. Dähnhardt, O., *Natursagen*, Leipzig, 1907, I, pp. 16–20.

16 *Ibid.*, pp. 38, 39.

with unending life. He wanders through the interior of Vishnu's body where there are many countries, hermitages, etc.

The sturdy old man slips accidentally out of the mouth of the all-containing god. "Vishnu is sleeping with lips a little open, breathing with a deep sonorous rhythmical sound in the immense silence of the night of Brahma. And the astonished saint, falling from the sleeper's giant lips, *plunges headlong into the cosmic ocean.*

Because of Vishnu's Maya (i.e., illusion) the saint does not see the sleeping giant but only the endless ocean, the dark water. He begins to wonder. *Is it a dream?* An illusion? What has become of the earth?

He finally perceives the sleeping giant and swims nearer. The giant seized him, swallowed him, and he was again in the familiar landscape of the interior. Now we are told that Markandeya was really Vishnu's dream —but from Markandeya's point of view the whole story was Markandeya's dream. He sees a lonely little boy at play amidst the vast ocean. The little boy calls him a *child,* enraging him beyond measure. But the divine child said that he was the primeval cosmic man, Narayana.[17]

Narayana then swallows Markandeya. The saint is so happy that he does not even wander in the interior this time, but he seeks rest in a solitary place. There he remains and listens to "the song of the immortal gander." The gander is the animal mask of the immortal principle, identical with Brahma.[18] But the gander means also the inner self, the Atman.

"It is the nature of the Supreme Being to take delight in himself in the cosmic ocean. Presently out of his cosmic body he puts forth a single lotus with a thousand petals of pure gold and Brahma himself is seated in the centre of the Golden lotus. Thus came into being again out of the Maya power of the brooding god, the whole vast dream of the universe."[19]

However, the same theme has many versions. The next myth begins with the same situation: no universe, only water; the lifeless interval between dissolution and creation. Vishnu (as before) is floating on his own essence. In the form of a luminous giant he is recumbent on the ocean. Another being appears, Brahma the fashioner of the universe. Brahma says he is the progenitor of the universe. Vishnu says he is.

"The two mighty presences proceeded to contest each other's claims and to quarrel. And while they were arguing in the timeless void, they perceived rising out of the ocean a towering *lingam* crowned with flame." They regarded it with amazement not being able to measure its height nor its depth. Brahma, in the shape of a gander, flew upward. Vishnu,

17 *Ibid.,* pp. 39–44.
18 Cf. the Gander Chief of the Voguls.
19 Zimmer, *op. cit.,* p. 52.

as a boar, dove into the deep, but while they did this the phallos kept growing so that they could not find its end. Shiva steps out of the phallos declaring himself as the supreme power of the universe.[20]

We have assumed that there is such a thing as a *basic* dream. The dreamer falls into something, frequently a lake or a hole. We also have assumed that the dream is characterized by a *double vector* regression to the uterus, and the body as penis entering the vagina. If we assume the identity of the ageless Markandeya and of Vishnu, the first part of our myth is simple. The dreamer is withdrawn into himself, but out of his own body he also forms a womb (ocean, lotus, etc.). In the dream he actually recreates a world out of his own body—and that according to the myth is how the universe originates or reoriginates. The regressive-progressive character of the dream explains the two powers involved. And what is the flying? The higher they fly or the deeper they dive the greater the penis becomes—since flying in dreams or diving is an erection.

The core of the myth is a dream actually dreamed once upon a time by one person. Told and retold it became a myth, a creed even, and gave rise to gods or philosophies because it appealed to those who heard it. All had dreamed something similar; some had remembered these dreams, some had repressed them. What follows is history. How cultural influences spread from one people to another and are accepted is beyond the scope of this book. However, the unconscious somehow "knows" the dream origin of the myth. Here and there it would crop up in varying forms. We noted above in the Coyote myth that Coyote is dreaming when he creates. In the Vogul version, while the bird flies down or dives, the woman gives birth. The creation of a double by God in one of the Russian versions conforms to the well-known rules of the dream mechanism.

The Uitoto in Columbia relate the following myth of creation. "An illusion, there was nothing else the father touched. *Through a dream* father Nainuema (he who has an illusion or is an illusion) held it. There was no staff to hold it. He held the illusion *by means of a dream web* with his breath. The father held emptiness by means of a dream web. According to his dream he held it with a magical substance. Now he took possession of the illusory foundation (or soil) and stamped on it repeatedly."[21]

It is clear that this myth is independent of the main stream of mythology of the Earth-Diver, which probably spread from India. The myth itself is the basic dream with descent and stamping instead of fly-

[20] *Ibid.*, pp. 128–130.
[21] Preuss, K. T., *Religion und Mythologie der Uitoto*, I, Göttingen, 1921, pp. 166, 167.

ing. Whether this proves that the Earth-Diver myth itself may have originated at several centers of migration remains doubtful.[22]

Another trait that these Earth-Diver myths have in common is that of the *gradual growth of the earth*. In the Onondaga myth, Ataensic, who is pregnant with a daughter, called Gusts of the Wind is hurled down from the sky by her jealous husband.

"Without interruption the body of the woman being continued to fall." The animals see that the pregnant woman is falling and they come to the conclusion that solid Earth must be created to receive her. All the animals volunteer. Otter and Turtle fail, the Muskrat succeeds in placing the soil he has brought up on the carapace of the Turtle. "Now at this time the carapace began to grow and the earth with which they had covered it became Solid Land. On the growing earth Gusts of Wind is reborn and grows up."[23] The parallelism pregnant woman = growing masses of earth is not accidental.

A parallel is contained in the egg-born earth or cloacal creation. The following is the Betul version.

After laying their eggs on the face of the ocean the Singamali bird began to brood upon those eggs, and nine months and nine days she brooded. A boy and a girl were born from the egg.[24]

The myths about fetching the earth show certain peculiar traits. In the Lett version the earth brought up by the devil swells in his mouth so that it nearly tears his mouth. He cried to God to rescue him. As the devil ran along in his torment, earth began to drop out between his teeth and hills arose wherever it fell. The devil tries to keep his mouth shut to keep the earth for himself, but in vain, for the power of the swelling earth compels him to open it.[25]

If we substitute the rectum for the mouth the myth makes sense as an awakening dream conditioned by excremental pressure. This conjecture is confirmed by a Gadaba myth.

Larang devoured the world and nothing was left but water. When Mahaprabhu saw nothing but water he thought and thought. He made a crow from the dirt of his body and sent him out. The crow flew back and told Mahaprabhu what had happened. Mahaprabhu caught Larang

---

[22] Professor Earl Count is preparing a book about this myth.

[23] Alexander, H. B., *The Mythology of All Races: North American Mythology*, X, 1916, p. 36.

[24] Elwin, Verrier, *Myths of Middle India*, New York, 1949, p. 16. Cf. also on egg creation myths P. W. Schmidt, "Grundlinien einer Vergleichung der Religionen und Mythologien der Austronesischen Völker," *Denkschriften der kaiserlichen Akadamie in Wien Phil-Hist. Klasse*, Band LIII, Wien, 1910, pp. 18, 19; Muensterberger, W., *Ethnologische Studien an Indonesischen Sehöpfungsmythen*, Haag, 1939, p. 187.

[25] Dähnhardt, *Natursagen*, 1907, pp. 56, 57.

and squeezed his whole body so violently that not a bone remained unbroken. *From the earth that Larang excreted the earth was formed again.*[26]

As in the biblical narrative, Creation may start with daylight, i.e., *awakening.*

In the Tlingit myth all the beings that Raven had created existed in darkness and Raven was sorry for them. *He obtains light by being born*[27] (awakening). In the Tsimshian version this is how Giant (Raven) acquires daylight. He put on his Raven skin and flew upward. Finally he found the hole in the sky and he flew through it. The rest is again the story of his rebirth and acquiring light.[28] Here we have the characteristic dream trait of flying through a hole.

It seems very probable that creation myths, wherever they exist, are ultimately based on dreams. The category of creation myth, which is based on the idea of creating by wishing or thinking would agree very well with the restitutive function of our dream theory, as well as the type of creation myth in which the world is made out of the creators or first being's body.

We give only one example—a creation myth of the Gadaba in India.

Before this world was made there was born in the midst of the waters a potter. He came to the surface (awakening) and tried to find somewhere to live. He swam round and round visiting all the four quarters of the world until he was very tired. He was so tired that a stream of saliva trickled from his mouth. This spread on the surface of the water and slowly set and hardened until it had formed a crust over the ocean,[29] etc.

II. Castor and Pollux

Among a number of primitive tribes magical practices are associated with twins who are themselves regarded as supernatural or uncanny. The twins may be attributed to dual paternity. Thus among the Cross River people of Africa one of the twins has a human father, the other an evil spirit.[1] Father Cessou reports from the Golah in Liberia that the bush goat is taboo to them and to their children. This is explained by

[26] Elwin, *op. cit.,* p. 37; cf. also Muensterberger, *op. cit.,* p. 181.

[27] Swanton, John R., *Tlingit Myths and Texts,* Bureau of Amer. Ethnol. Bull. 39, Washington, 1909, pp. 80, 81.

[28] Boas, F., *Tsimshian Mythology,* Report of Bureau of Amer. Ethnol., XXXI, 1916, pp. 60, 61.

[29] Elwin, *op. cit.,* p. 35.

[1] Partridge, *Cross River Natives,* London, 1905, quoted by Harris, Reudel, *Boanerges,* Cambridge, 1913, p. 60.

saying that in old times twins found out in their dreams that the spirits of the dead appear in the form of bush goats.

When twins are born one of them may disappear in a mysterious fashion. The surviving twin must then be presented to another person who is a twin. He washes the child in a "medicine" (magical mixture) prepared in a white basin. Then he gives him a girdle of beads, etc. The infant twin is now brought back to the parents, saying, "You see we do not bring back your child empty-handed." Evidently the idea is that the child has to be compensated for the loss of its twin.

"Twins have the singular privilege of finding out things in dreams."[2] According to the Ewe all twins are born medicine men. Parents never beat them and people in general are always giving them presents to appease them.[3] Among the Bambara, if one of the twins dies early they make a little statue and give it the name of the dead and never give a present to the living twin without giving at least five Kauris to the statue.[4] According to the Kpelle a twin is a greater medicine man than any professional medicine man.

The informant says: "Twins are born with medicine, they are *taught by medicine men while in the womb* and when grown up are brought to a sandplayer (medicine man) to be his children. They are born with a little sack on their body which contains their magical power."[5]

The main features of the complex are (a) the dual parenthood of twins which makes one supernatural while one remains human, (b) the emphasis on duality, (c) the association of twins and dreams, (d) of twins and magic, (e) of twins and the intrauterine situation.

The Fon and the Yoruba have a cult of twins. The mother of new-born twins calls together the other mothers of twins and gives them two little pots of earthenware which are joined by an arm; this joint twin pot is the characteristic of the cult. With the twin pot, two cloths, four fowls and some colas and cowries, the women go into the bush calling on the spirits of dead twins. Dead twins live in the forest in the form of red monkeys. Two mounds are made and sacrifices are offered. Offerings of fowls and frequent libations of palm oil are made in these pots. The twins are now under the protection of the dead twins. A child that has lost its dead brother or sister wears a carved wooden doll tucked in front or back of his cloth. In some tribes these twin images are in the shape of a wooden phallos.[6]

2 Cessou, P. I. M., "A propos du Totemisme chez les Golahs, Nigeria," *Anthropos.*, VI, 1911, pp. 1037, 1038.

3 Westermann, D., *Die Kpelle, ein Negerstamm in Liberia*, Leipzig, 1921, p. 212.

4 Henry, J., "Les Bambara," *Bibliotheque Anthropos.*, I, Münster i. W., 1910, p. 98.

5 Westermann, *op. cit.*, p. 355.

6 Parrinder, G., *West African Religion*, London, 1949, p. 112.

We surmise that the unconscious meaning of the twin is that of the soul which, as we have seen above, is also sometimes called the twin or double. The Dinka of the White Nile have a peculiar series of totemic origin myths. Thus the elephant clan originated from a boy who was a twin, his twin brother being an elephant. The founder of the lion totem was the twin brother of a lion, etc. Among the Nuer the majority of clans derive their totems from animals born as twins with their human ancestors.[7]

Among the Shilluk we find the following myth: The ostrich and the crow and Den (name of a human ancestor) were split out of a gourd. All three were twins (i.e., there were two of each). These three are the parents of the people. The Shilluk say, "The ostrich and the crow are our family."[8]

These twin myths are really birth myths. In one Dinka group the animal origin myths are absent and instead we have the myths of the "river people." Long, long ago men and women of the river people would sometimes come out of the river and settle down in the neighboring villages. The description of the landing of one of the river people is like the description of birth. The river becomes agitated and the water rises up around a human being whose umbilicus is joined by a cord to a flat object beneath the water. The cord is cut, bullocks are killed and thrown into the river, etc.[9]

Among the Baganda we find a similar myth. The Kaita clan has the tortoise and the hippopotamus as totems. When Kaita was born his mother was delivered of a tortoise instead of the afterbirth. The tortoise was subsequently transformed into a hippopotamus. The lands of the clan bordered on a lake and their duties were connected with water like those of the Dinka crocodile men.[10]

In connection with these myths we are told that twins are associated with birds and with all animals that lay eggs. The bodies of twins are placed in a fork on a tree. Adult twins are placed on platforms and their spirits will fly up into the air because they are birds. Twins avoid birds, fishes, crocodiles, reptiles, all animals that lay eggs because these are all regarded as twins.[11]

Among the Acholi the umbilical cords of twins are buried near the hut. If they die young the bodies are put in a hut with the mouth well

[7] Seligmann, C. G., Report on Totemism and Religion of the Dinka of the White Nile, pp. 5–7.

[8] Westermann, D., The Shilluk People, Berlin, 1912, pp. 178, 179.

[9] Seligmann, op. cit., p. 9.

[10] Roscoe, J., The Baganda, London, 1911, p. 166. Cf. also Seligman, C. G., and Seligman, B. Z., Pagan Tribes of the Nilotic Sudan, London, 1932, p. 212.

[11] Seligman and Seligman, op. cit., p. 228.

closed, *and buried in the bed of some small stream.* If the house is moved
to another site the pot is dug up and again buried in a stream.[12]

Again in South Africa we find the belief that twins are supernatural.
Twins are animals but at the same time supernatural beings. Fighting
boys call upon a twin to ask for his opinion because his decision must be
right. A twin goes to a waterfall and listens to the fall of *the water in a
dreamy way.* Soon he begins to chant a song and when a wedding is held
he teaches the people the new song. A twin is consulted by grown-up
people as if he were a diviner.[13]

The best known of mythical twins are, of course, the Dioskouroi or
sons of Zeus. They are either the sons of a mortal father, Tyndareos or
of Zeus, perhaps they had originally two fathers, one mortal and one immortal. Their mother is Leda with whom Zeus cohabits in the shape of a
swan. Their sister, Helena, is born of an egg or they are born of an egg.
Kastor is mortal, Polydeukes immortal. They are the rescuers of those
who are in danger at sea; and later they are regarded as identical with
the phallic Kabiroi. Their oldest symbols are two vertical poles connected
by two horizontal ones. The two amphorai with snakes wound round
them are also one of their characteristic symbols; furthermore, the serpent alone or the cock. The pilon (peaked hat) and the horse are closely
associated with them.[14]

Other Dioskouroi like Picumnus and Pilumnus, Mutunus and Tu-
tunus[15] are openly phallic.

We do not believe with Jane Ellen Harrison that there is any real
contrast between the Dioskouroi as represented by the snake entwined am-
phorae and as the horsemen descending to the Theoxenia,[16] and we do
believe that we can answer the question, "Why did the twins go to sea."[17]
For the same reason that a person born with a caul will not drown—i.e.,
because they came from the sea, that is, the womb.

When we find that this duality appears as uncanny or magical to a
variety of people we must assume that it acquires this quality by representing repressed contents. We go through this experience of becoming
two every night in our dreams. Actually twins are in some places said to
be dreamers and hence, of course, diviners, sorcerers. The African association with egg-laying beings and the egg in the myth of the Dioskouroi can hardly be accidental. The soul or the double is a twin and the
Dioskouroi and some African twin images are obviously phallic like the

12 *Ibid.,* p. 121.
13 Kidd, D., *Savage Childhood,* London, 1905, pp. 45–49.
14 Furtwängler, "Dioskuren," article in *Roscher's Lexikon,* pp. 1154–1176.
15 Harris, Rendell, *The Cult of the Heavenly Twins,* Cambridge, 1906, p. 80.
16 Harrison, J. E., *Themis,* Cambridge, 1927, p. 307.
17 Harris, *Boanerges,* p. 195.

dream image of the body. If the twins unconsciously elicit basic dream material that would explain a large part of their mythology and beliefs. The Vedic counterparts of the Dioskouroi, the Asvins, are associated with the dawn[18] (like the Dioskouroi with stars), because that is the end of the night, the waking dream. There are some indications of the erstwhile horseshape of the twins with mares as their brides[19] which might be analogous to the medieval nightmare. The Asvins. the mythical twins of the Veda, are closely connected with horses and with the dawn or awakening. They are also called "the shining children of the night."[20] Like true "children of the dream" they fly with the birds.[21] The sacrificer recites his prayer in the position of a bird that is about to fly upwards.[22] According to Myriantheus the Asvins

(1) deliver from darkness;

(2) they are the authors of rejuvenescence (hence their help is sought by the aged and the emasculate);

(3) they protect in battle;

(4) they act as physicians;

(5) they are the patrons of the bride chamber, etc.[23]

Are they not a phallic waking dream with their duality symbolizing the testicles?

We frequently find a duality of heroes among primitive tribes.

The following is the initiation myth of the Nambutji: At Kuna-tari (With the vagina) an old man sat with erected penis. A woman had been urinating there, and the urine made a hole in the sand. It was an Ukura (demon woman). The penis went into the hole; it got bigger and bigger, and it coiled around. Then he pulled it out again, and he stopped where he was with his penis at a place called Watukari (Lying). The penis lay down there. He wound his penis back again and put it in a pouch like a kangaroo. Then he went to Pukapanti (Stink smell). He smelled his own penis there. Then he went to Tjiwiripanta (Lake sand). There is a lake there. He made a little hole for his penis and he camped in another hole. He went to Pulumpiri (*pulu*—penis, *piri*—to pull out). He tried to pull his penis out of the pouch but he could not. Then he went to Walkuru-walkuru (Tomahawk). A woman had left her tomahawk there, and he

[18] Oldenburg, H., *Die Religion des Veda,* Berlin, 1894, pp. 207–215.

[19] Eitrem, S., "Die göttlichen Zwillinge bei den Griechen," *Videnskabselskabets Skrifter,* II, Historisk-tilos Klasse, No. 2, Christiania, 1902, pp. 14, 15.

[20] Oldenburg, *op. cit.,* pp. 207–211.

[21] *Ibid.,* p. 212.

[22] Hillebrandt, A., *Vedische Mythologie,* III, Breslau, 1902, p. 395.

[23] Quoted by Harris, J. Rendell, *The Dioscuri in Christian Legends,* London, 1903, p. 15. On the problem of the weak and the strong twin in general, cf. Cook, A. B., *Zeus, A Study in Ancient Religion,* Cambridge, 1925, II, p. 843.

put his penis under it. When she came back she saw the penis there and cut it into pieces with a tomahawk. The woman was a demon (*onuntu*) woman from another place. The chips of the penis became stone (*puleringu*, i.e., became *tjurunga* there). There are *tjurunga* stones marked with a penis underneath.[24]

Part of the song refers to the actual initiation ritual. The women who dance for the boy and those who lie *irkapiri* (the Mothers and others united to the boy by sympathetic magic) sing this. These women are the equivalents of the mythical phallic women or *alknarintja*.

In these myths closely connected with the initiation ritual the women who occur are always demon women, because from the point of view of the circumcised neophyte, the women are demons, i.e., to be avoided. The colossal penis and the tendency to be *two* is a camouflage or a counterphobic attitude to *castration anxiety,* and of course the symbolic castration is the essence of the initiation. The phallic double in the dream is also connected with anxiety—of regressing through the *vagina dentata* into the womb, of death. The hero starts with an erected penis and ends in a hole. Another interesting feature of the myth is its narcissism (smelling own penis, putting it in one's own pouch—womb).

I give now an abstract of myths previously published. Culture hero myths of the Ngallunga ritual have two phallic culture heroes.

(1) The heroes are two kangaroos called Testicles and Semen.

(2) They come to a place called Teeth and take their teeth out.

(3) They come to a place called Heart.

(4) They come to a place called Red Ochre place (probably symbolizing the blood).

(5) They come to a place called Narrow where there is a narrow gap with water in it. (Birth anxiety, passage through the vagina.)

(6) They come to a place called Pubic Tassel where they put their pubic tassels on for the first time.

(7) At Excrement they defecate.

(8) At a place called Testicles they pull their Testicles out and put them back again.

(9) At a place called Penis they see each other's penis and they subincise each other.

(10) At a place called Mullatjitji they open each other's veins and stand soaked in blood.

(11) Water drips from their hair at a place called Hair.

(12) They come to a place called Tjiwiri-wiri (Noise made by urinating from the subincision hole), and they urinate from their subincision hole.

24 Róheim, *The Eternal Ones of the Dream,* pp. 34, 35.

(13) Finally, they go into a totemic cave, first putting the *kuntanka* in and then following and becoming *kuntanka*[25] themselves.

In a myth of the tribes of the Ooldea region, Njirana is the father and Yulana the son, and the latter is also the penis of the former. Berndt and Berndt write: "In some versions of the myth the two are treated as two persons with separate identities" even when Yulana is the penis. At a certain water hole Njira says to Yulana, "I want to be a man." So Yulana cuts the penis of Njira and then vice versa, and now they are men.[26]

The following myth has also been recorded by the same authors. Child pigeon and a small sand lizard wander together. *The child is lured from home by the lizard,* and is away for such a long time that the mother believes him dead. As the boy follows, the sand lizard grows bigger and bigger until it is a large iguana. The boy also grows into a young man. They come to a water hole and the lizard enters the hole. The child (or the child pigeon) pulls the iguanas out of the holes. He pulls several out, but they are none of them the right ones. Finally he gets the right one and pulls the tail of the iguana until the tail breaks. At that moment his foreskin falls off. He then returns as a man to his mother.[27]

The penis is the wanderer and the growing up is the wandering. The two form a unity: child (man) and penis. Growing up is connected with castration anxiety which is then *acted out* in the initiation ritual.

Culture heroes tend to show another type of duality; one is mortal and the other immortal, or one adjusts to reality and the other does not; one does the right thing, the other always does the wrong thing.

The Winnebago version is as follows: "This earth on which we live is the very last of the four earths created. The Twins were created even after the event. They killed all the evil spirits that were continually molesting and frightening the people. When man made his first appearance on earth there were many cannibals. Grasshoppers and toads were enormous in size and they ate human beings. All these the Twins killed and all the animals that had been in the habit of eating human beings were transformed into small ones. Today instead of eating us, they merely bite us."[28] But as Radin tells us, the twins are of opposing temperaments, one active and one passive, one a rebel; and one a conformer.

"The Twin cycle of the Winnebago begins with the father-in-law

---

25 *Kuntanka (tjurunga)*—penis symbol. Róheim, *Eternal Ones of the Dream,* p. 30.
26 Berndt, R. and C., *A Preliminary Report of Field Work in the Ooldea Region,* Sydney, 1945, p. 257.
27 *Ibid.,* p. 260.
28 Radin, Paul, "Hero Cycles, a Study in Aboriginal Literature," *Indiana University Publications in Anthropology and Linguistics,* 1948, p. 49.

killing his daughter-in-law. He flees from his sons' anger after having cut the Twins out of her womb. One of them he wrapped in something and put into the corner of the lodge next door, and the other he put into a hole at the bottom of a tree stump.

"When the father comes home he finds only the boy in the lodge. He then takes care of him. But while this little boy was playing, he heard a voice singing, 'You have a human father and therefore you eat only flesh. I, however, I have a little stump for a grandmother and therefore wild beans only I eat.'

"Flesh (the name of the Lodge Boy) plays with newly-found brother. However, when the father approaches home, the wild boy disappears in the lake like a meteor. Finally, they prevail upon him to stay, but the stranger was very mischievous. He trampled on everything within the lodge. Flesh was not able to cope with him. He was outclassed everywhere."

Flesh is always afraid to undertake an adventure. Father always forbids these adventures, but the adventurous spirit of Stump always triumphs in the end. When they see snakes, Stump calls them garfish and starts killing them. While they were fighting, Flesh got killed. His brother said, "Say, it is such great fun killing fish! *Why are you sleeping?* Get up," and he took him by the arm and made him stand. The snakes grew larger and larger and after a while Stump was killed. "Say, my younger brother, killing fish is such great fun—why are you sleeping?" said Flesh. This goes on in turns till finally the snakes give up.

"Indeed, he (Flesh) was really afraid of him, he was really being forced to do those things.

"Each adventure is accomplished against their father's will. Flesh would be willing to obey, but Stump always triumphs. Finally, their father flees from them in desperation."[29]

Radin gives the following interpretation: Here we have the first statement of the Winnebago conception of man's nature. "It consists of two parts, they contend, the rooted and the unattached. Originally, in the mother's womb both were united. At birth they are forced asunder. Since they belong together, however, they unite at the first opportunity. The new union is effected with considerable difficulties for the second child (the unattached) resists it strenuously. Alone, the first child is unable to seize and detain him. Only with the aid of his father is he successful."[30]

Radin writes, "Translated into Winnebago religious terms Flesh is the soul which inheres in living man and which dies when he dies, Stump

29 *Ibid.*, pp. 141–145.
30 *Ibid.*, pp. 51, 52.

is the soul that leaves upon death and which returns to spirit-land, in other words, to the universe at large."[31]

The official interpretation of Winnebago esoteric wisdom is nearly the same as the psychoanalytic interpretation. Stump (and his equivalents) would be the id, while Flesh (Lodge Boy) would be the ego ready to accept reality if aided by the Father Imago. This is actually how reality impresses itself upon the ego in the person of the forbidding father. At the end the two culture heroes retire to a hill in the east where they are still living.[32]

The id, the phallic element, that which pushes forward, conquers the fathers and monsters, is the real hero. The Wichita tell a similar story. A boy is cut out of his mother's womb. A fire stick was thrust into the afterbirth and it was thrown into the water. It grows up to be a child and plays with its human brother. The first boy finally tells the father that there is another boy of his age around who calls him brother. "He told him that the strange boy had a wonderful tail that looked like a stick used for a poker. When the father found out who the strange boy was, he turned himself into a firestick and was lying by the fireplace. The After-birth boy discovers the trick—the usual adventures follow. Spider Woman wants to boil them in a pot, After-birth Boy defecates and urinates into the pot. They find themselves in the power of Water Monster, and get out through the magic of After-Birth boy."[33]

In South American mythology we again find the weak and the strong brother. The Bakairi tell the story of Keri and Kame. They are cut out of their dead mother's womb. They kill and burn the Jaguar, their foster mother. The twins perish in the same fire, but each of them revives the other.

When they were burning their foster mother, Kame was hidden in a hole. He peeped out because he was curious, and he was burned to death. Keri blew upon him and resuscitated him.

The Fox owned the fire. He had it in his eyes. When he wanted to light the wood, he bit his own eyes and the sparks lit the wood for him. He had made a weir to catch fish. Keri became a long fish and Kame a snail. The Fox came to the weir, caught both and started to roast them. But they kept pouring water on the fire and eluding him until he was tired. The Fox ran away and they got the fire.

Kame gets swallowed by a fish. His brother cuts him out of the fish's stomach and he says: "I slept well." "You were not asleep, you

[31] *Ibid.*, p. 53.
[32] *Ibid.*, p. 151.
[33] Dorsey, G. A., *The Mythology of the Wichita*, Washington, D.C., 1904, pp. 88–102.

were dead," his brother says.[34] In the Yurakare version a tree becomes a man and is killed by a Jaguar. Reanimated by his wife, he says: "It seems that I have slept well."[35]

The strong and the weak brother are often identified with the Sun and the Moon.[36] In a sense, though in an inverted sense, this is true, for the Sun is day and the Moon is night. In our dream life we transcend reality and the immortal phallic double, the soul, moves freely in a libidinized space.

I am aware of the fact that this is a somewhat "mythological" statement since mankind is such an unhappy species that even when liberated from the restrictions imposed by reality there is always the superego to contend with.

III. Vesical Dreams and Myths

The basic dream is certainly not the only dream that has become a myth. We know that the desire to urinate, the bladder pressure and also the excremental pressure causes dreams of a certain type. In these the urine is projected into space as a lake or river or ocean and an element of anxiety is bound to occur. In dreams that combine fire and water, the urethral significance is quite certain. The dreamer is in conflict; by projecting these images into space he is trying to prolong the dream and delay awakening. These dreams evidently occur in light sleep, just before awakening. Moreover, they usually try to transform bladder pressure into an erotic scene (morning erections in men) or into birth or delivery. Both techniques are frequently combined. They are also another instance in which environment is formed out of the dreamer's own body.

The best known case of a urethral awakening dream has been called the "dream of a French governess." It consists of a series of pictures discovered in a Hungarian comic strip by Ferenczi, and communicated by him to Freud.

In the first picture we see the governess with the little boy. She is taking him to a place (or rather he is dragging her) where he can urinate.

Second picture; turned towards the wall, you can see the urine on the pavement.

[34] Steinen, Karl von den, *Unter den Naturvölkern Zentral-Braziliens,* Berlin, 1897, pp. 319–326.
[35] Koch-Grunberg, *Indianermärchen aus Südamerika,* 1920, pp. 275–282, quoted from A. d'Orbigny, *Voyage dans l'Amerique meridionale,* III, 1844.
[36] Metraux, A., "Twin Heroes in South American Mythology," *Journal of American Folk-Lore,* LIX, 1946, pp. 114–123.

Third picture; same situation but more urine and the street is now a canal.

Fourth picture; the canal is a river with a boat. Somebody rowing.

Fifth picture; the rowing boat is a big gondola.

Sixth picture; size of boat increases, sail boat.

Seventh picture; mail liner on ocean.

In the last picture she is awake. The child is really screaming because he wants to be put on the potty.[1]

It is the increasing bladder pressure that symbolizes itself in an increasing volume of water and finally compels the reluctant sleeper to awake.

The dream of old Yirramba of the Aranda tribe (Alice Springs group) is a typical vesical dream.

A flood came and the rushing water knocked me down. I was calling for help. The flood was coming always quicker. I was floating on the water and the water was reaching toward a big water hole. A man came, he reached into the water with a big stick and pulled me out. I was there —shivering. I made a fire and got dry. He carried me to a big camp, people were pleased to see me.

Associations and Interpretation: The man who pulls him out of the water is Ratarinja (his mother's real brother, his uncle). This man was a kind of second father to him and this is the socially determined role of the uncle. The place where he is pulled out of the water looks like Oltja. When he completed his initiation—that is, he was a novice at the *inkura* (rebirth ceremony)—they showed a totem ceremony of the fish totem of Oltja. He also says that the tents are like my tent.

The morning after this dream he came to our house very early for a cup of tea because it was a cold night and he was afraid of the cold and dying.[2] The increasing volume of water combined with the cold and the fire make it evident that we have to do with a vesical dream. He is pulled out of the water by the penis of a father substitute (probably myself). This is just what the *inkura* is, a symbolic rebirth from a male.

Rank has shown that the primary process regularly transforms this somatic stimuli in two directions, coitus and birth.[3]

The following dream is a good example; the patient is a young woman, her child is about four years old.

My friend Marion is waiting by the river's edge when I come back.

---

1 Freud, *Gesammelte Schriften,* III, p. 84.

2 Yirramba is a blind old man with a young half-caste wife.

3 Rank, O., "Die Symbolschichtung im Wecktraum und ihre Wiederkehr im mythischen Denken," *Jahrbuch für psychoanalytische Forschungen,* IV, 1912; *Psychoanalytische Beiträge zur Mythenforschung,* 1919, Chapter VII.

My sister is supposed to be taking her turn watching the boat but she has not come back. The three of us are evidently taking *a trip downstream* in a rowboat. When my sister returns I angrily point out that the boat has filled up because *she has failed to bail it out*. She starts a tirade against me, and I am surprised that I do not get upset.

I leave them behind and go to a fancy food store like Vendome. In the center of the store behind a glass counter a man is making fancy Easter eggs with children's names written on them. I walk to the right where toys are sold. I have come there to buy a toy for Tommy (her son). The salesman shows me a number of toys but they are all too expensive. I have five dollars. Finally he shows me a complicated contraption that is made partly of black rubber hose and jumps and bounces around. I decide to take it and then the salesman says, "That's $6.90 plus 10¢."

I say that is too expensive and walk out. The salesman has turned into Harry Truman.

I am down on a pier holding on to the rope used to moor the boat. I keep pulling the boat closer to the pier and it keeps drifting away. This worries me as the river is muddy and I am afraid that Tommy will fall into the space between the boat and the pier. I keep calling to Robert (husband) to help me, but he is busy talking to some people.

Then I am in the cabin of the boat which is now a large scow or barge. I am playing poker with Robert and John, who is drinking. I tell them it is time to cast off but they want to go on playing poker. I suggest they leave the cards and money on the table and come back after the boat has started off.

The boat is now a sailing vessel—a ketch or yawl. John is the Captain. There are a number of other women and children on board whose faces I don't see. We are sailing down near the river's mouth. John then tells me that *we can't go out to the ocean because of all the children aboard*. I say the children will be all right. He then says that we can't go *because of the cat which is resting on the railing*. I think angrily to myself that he shouldn't have brought the cat. He says we can sail as far as X.[4] and that we will then have lunch.

Associations: "Marion is a high-school friend of mine. She had a postpartum psychosis after the birth of her second child. My sister is in her ninth month now. Mother always said she was the healthiest one, but she had a three-day labor with her first child while I had a supposedly difficult birth delivery in only seven hours. Sister has never been analyzed. The boat and the river would seem to me to be birth and this part of the dream to show fears about having a second child.

"The Easter eggs would be pregnancy. Truman reminds me of my father (they both wore rimless glasses, and fought in World War I). The black rubber hose toy is a sort of mechanical penis. The $6.90 suggests *soixante-neuf* and the ten cents the dime-a-dance halls, both of which represent sex without biological fulfillment or conception. I

---

4 X. is a place where boats going seaward can just manage to squeeze through.

suspect that this is the sort of sex that my father had most of his life—that is, sex bought with money which involved no real relationship. The sixty-nine would represent my belief that he had a distinct problem of unconscious homosexuality. All my life I sided with my father against my mother. Maybe my feeling that the price of this toy is too expensive means that I feel a continued allegiance to him at the expense of lack of identification with my mother is too great a price to pay any longer. Or that hating my mother is a revenge and a luxury I can no longer afford.

"The part of the dream where I am on the pier calling to Robert happened in reverse recently. We went to Martha's Vineyard and I got off the boat with Tommy before Robert. Tom saw his father on the boat and started toward the end of the pier. Robert yelled at him to go back and then upbraided me for not watching him more carefully although I had my eye on him all along. But in the dream I worry instead. The worry of losing a child has certainly occurred recently when I had thought of becoming pregnant. Before my first pregnancy I was late several times by three weeks. One theory was that I might have miscarried in the very early stages.

"Then in the cabin of the boat I am playing cards. Robert and my father and I used to play cards and John reminds me of my father. Robert had an affair with John's wife before they were married and before we were married. When my father came to visit us I was always upset by his presence and felt guilty when I had intercourse when he was around. I felt he was hostile to my pregnancy and thought I should be sick or that I was not really pregnant.

"We actually went on a sailing trip once with John and I was dreadfully seasick at first. I never trusted his abilities as a seaman. In the dream I resent his taking on the duties. He is Captain simply because he has set himself up as such. He has a cat named Mary. My first analyst's name was Mary and Robert's first analyst was also Mary. The children on the boat must be mine with my father.

"Lunch at X. reminds me of a cartoon I was told about that was never published. The cartoon shows a man standing outside a delivery room talking to a nurse holding a baby. He says, 'Never mind wrapping it up. I'll eat it here.'[5] I remember too my father holding me over an alligator cage in Florida which terrified me. He had ulcers which I gathered came from eating nasty things and he lost his teeth early. He had a bad breath and was the only one in the family who ate fat. He ate voraciously and intensely and during his ulcer period he drank quantities of milk. Mother

[5] Cf. the chapter "Nature of Ogres" *supra*.

used to talk about his eating with disgust. I remember too that I was told that I was found in the garbage can."

On awakening the patient had to urinate. The typical features are the increasing size of the boat, the problem of bailing the water out, the trip toward the ocean, the child falling into the water and the Easter eggs, the narrow passage (birth canal), playing cards with father (incest). John represents the analyst who expressed doubts about the advisability of a second pregnancy at the present stage of the analysis.

It is interesting that, as in many of the myths we shall analyze, the paternal ogre appears on the scene in connection with an urethral dream.

The mechanism of flood myths and urethral dreams has been discussed by Rank. Perhaps we can add something to their understanding, notably to the reason why the vesical dream develops into birth or genital symbolism. Rank quotes the following dream:

"It started to rain and I say I must run because I shall get wet. I run and I am told in the dream to go and urinate before I come home."[6]

From Sharpe's book we quote the following dreams.

"I was in a room and suddenly the door opened and a flood of water came in."

Sharpe thinks the dream may represent the birth trauma. It was ascertained that the patient's birth was heralded by a sudden and unexpected bursting of the waters. This was not known to the patient at the time when the dream was dreamed.[7]

The flood of water may also be a vesical awakening dream.

In the next dream, the dreamer identified himself with his own urine.

"I was running one way on one side of the railing and a man in shorts was running the other way on the other side of the railing."

"I was running" in the dream meant a pictorial representation of bodily experience during urinating.[8]

In other words, the running person in the dream is really the urine "running" in the dreamer.

Since the dreamer or sleeper withdraws not only into the maternal uterus but into his or her own body, some common ground can be found here with Lewin's theory.

The identification of the self with the feces can be assumed in the following dream quoted from Sharpe:[9]

"I gave a ball of silver paper to old Dr. X."

6 Rank, O., *op. cit.*, p. 69.
7 Sharpe, E., *Dream Analysis,* London, 1937.
8 *Ibid.*, p. 86.   9 *Ibid.*, p. 52.

The patient (male) associates silver paper with coverings on chocolates. His mother used to eat the chocolates. The idea of Dr. X. was connected with nauseating smells.

The balls of silver would be himself represented by his own feces.

Sharpe reports the following dream:

"I was in a lift and suddenly it went down flop."

"This dream I found as a representation of fluid excreta rushing down and flopping on the floor."

Another dream of the same patient:

"I saw a marvelous thing happen. A 'car' went straight up a building on the outside somehow and got safely up to a garage."

The patient who is recommencing her analysis after the summer vacation complains that during the vacation she has been too excitable and that a new enterprise of hers, with which she intends to begin the year, might fail if she behaves this way. The dream is this:

A man tells me that I must go up on a narrow pathway to the top of a small mound. There I shall find a bear's head and then I should take medicine out of the bear's mouth that will make it possible to sleep a little longer. I go up the black hill and take it out of the bear's mouth. I am alarmed because the bear who is buried in the ground moves, it seems to be alive. But I get the pills, and I say "Their Royal Highnesses are ready," meaning the two daughters of King George VI. The pills are like what you would give a little dog to keep it quiet in the car.

Associations: The bear reminds her of Sitting Bull or of herself on the potty. It is Shitting Bull and that would be the black hill—the narrow path is her rectum. Evidently she is disturbed by the need to defecate and wants at the same time to prolong sleep (the medicine out of the bear's mouth). This dream shows an interaction of internal stimulus and environment formed out of the body, unfinished task and infantile desires (the English princess, etc.). The anus is much emphasized in her erotic life, the narrow path is her own rectum plus intestines; she is identified with her own excrements.

The association was the dentist chair going up and down, and herself as a child in the dentist chair. To car, she associated "ka-ka", i.e., the excrements in her own body.

A young woman analyzed mainly for a feeling of inferiority, dreams as follows:

My husband and another man (a priest? = the analyst) show me that the men can see the women seated on the toilet. How horrible—I think —and start going toward that toilet. I crawl on my belly in a narrow coal chute. I am wearing a sexy black chemise. Pieces of coal fall all over me and make me all dirty. I come to a platform, it obstructs the path. The crawling is at an end. I cannot reach the toilet.

The coal chute is her intestines. She herself sexy, black and dirty, that is, her own excrements wandering down toward the rectum. The platform; the function of the sphincters which makes it possible for her not to defecate immediately but to stay asleep. Corroborative, infantile material is brought by the patient on anal sex play combined with exhibitionism (the men can see the women on the toilet).

Her hysterectomy is what brought her to the analyst. After the operation she really felt inferior to others.

In the following dream several months later she is again "*in her own body.*" The day stimulus for the dream was the news that a friend of hers was pregnant.

I am in a beautiful pink room. But there is no light in the room. A mother comes in with two children. One of them touches my rectum and burns her hand. In my rectum the temperature is 102 or 140 degrees. I run about looking for a salve but I can't find the right kind. Music is heard. "Let dreams and trumpets sound, here comes the conquering hero!" I awake and have a bowel movement.

102: The association is *Hunter* College, Park Avenue. In that case she is still a college girl. 140 = one (her husband) and 40 = herself at the age of 40. Then people will really pity her because she has never had a child.

She must have been feverish but she did not take her temperature. This would be the burning sensation combined with the rectal pain that is caused by excremental pressure.

The beautiful inside is a way of denying the havoc caused by the operation. She is in it, her inside is cathected with libido. She can have a child, the excrement child. This is the conquering hero, while the drums and trumpets that herald its approach are flatus. Not the right kind of salve, she does not need the jelly any more because she cannot conceive.

This is where my dream theory meets with that of Lewin.

Since the dreamer not only regresses into the womb but at the same time supplies that womb, in his or her own body, he may be identified perhaps with the food but more with the excrements in his own intestines. There is no hard and fast line between the stomach or intestines or womb from the point of view of the unconscious as long as they are *inside.*

A young woman, hysterical type, dreams:

"I am on a train at home. The train is *on fire*. I get out at a place covered with gravel with my parents. I take a metal rod and point it at the flames. *Water* pours out of the rod and the flames are extinguished. Then the train goes on, in flames once more.

Associations: The place with gravel is the house in her home town where she was born. She then quotes from a book in which flame means intercourse at night. She remembers that her husband was with her at the beginning of the dream but he disappears. The rod is her penis envy; she has the penis and extinguishes the flame. The combination of fire and water is a nearly universal urethral symbol. The association to the fire at night and the presence of the parents is the primal scene, but what is significant here is the *birth* (out of the train, house where she was born). It means awakening, coming out of the dream, but it is pseudo awakening—the train is still in flames.

In these urethral dreams the pressure of the urine frequently appears as an increasing volume of water.

A middle-aged Navaho informant, married and father of several children, relates the following dream:

Four days ago I milked my cow, I was halfway finished when it began to move around. I tried to stop it. I had a rope around her neck. I jerked her with the rope two or three times. I looked at the cow's feet. It looked like a donkey, but it had a bag of milk here (shows stomach) that was easy milking, easier than a cow. The bag was red, I milked it pretty fast into a bucket. The burro was tame, stood still. I took the milk to feed it to the small calf. I was worried, the calf wouldn't take the milk. It smelt sour so I just threw it away. I went back, the cow wasn't there any more. Then while I was looking for the cow I found a big creek. It was very clean, like mountain water. I went into the water pulling up my pants. It was good, I saw little fish in the water. Couldn't catch one. I fell into water, that woke me up. (Had to urinate.)

Associations: Cow—*I dreamed* a lot about a bull. Red bull in a fence in alfalfa field. Walking through alfalfa, *bull looked at me* meanly. He walked toward me, chased me. I went through fence. He couldn't get through fence at me. I ran up hill. When I got near trees, it broke the fence. I climbed up a tree. *The bull did not see me.* He laid down under the tree *to rest*. I could not get off the tree. I thought the bull *might go to sleep* and then I could get down. The cow had a calf one year old. The calf had broken through a fence.

"Donkey—My father used to say donkeys are good things to have. They are gentle, you can ride them without rope or saddle, and it doesn't take much to feed one. They stay fat all the time, don't get poor. He can hold up better than a horse. He can stand a good load, he can go nearly any place. He can climb up a rock."

The dream ends, he feels cold and has to urinate. *We have here a urethral awakening dream.* Evidently the cow's udder symbolizes the scrotum. The sour, disgusting milk and the clear water (representation by the opposite) are both urine. Instead of the cow he finds a big creek—very characteristic of these urethral dreams. The general rule of these dreams is that the bladder pressure is represented as an erotic situation. In this case it is masturbation: (a) he jerks the cow's neck with the rope, and (b) the calf (his own infantile ego) is scared.

We have to explain the transformation of the cow into a donkey and then into a creek. In connection with the donkey, he repeats what his father said about donkeys. The mamma-penis equation[10] is behind this dream. The donkey has an udder like a cow. There was ambivalence in the oral phase, but everything goes smoothly in the omnipotence of masturbation (the bag is *red,* the burro stands still, he milks it pretty smoothly). The third transformation is into a creek; the urethral element predominates. The fish he is trying to catch in the water is again the penis.

The dream about the bull is told as an association. Yet, we can guess at least roughly at its latent content. The passage about the *bull looking at him,* the bull seeing him, indicates the *primal scene* in which the little boy (in fantasy) replaces mother. The bull *might go to sleep* is projected. The boy pretends to sleep but hears or sees the parents' intercourse.

These urethral dreams usually contain the motive of an increasing volume of water, of being in a boat and coming out of the boat.

A hysterical patient with penis envy as one of the prominent characteristics dreams:

I am in a rowing boat with John (her boy friend). He is seated *behind me* (position of the analyst). The passage becomes narrower and narrower, and there are other boats lined up near the shore. (Her mother had been talking about her previous boy friends in the presence of John.) I get wet in the boat—the river is flowing over. John gets out of the boat and pulls me with the boat. All this is in X-ville, the home of my maternal ancestors. It is raining. I shall have to change my clothes. John says he will look all right even if it rains.

The river, the overflow and the rain are all symbols of the urine. She gets wet means the same. Connected with it, however, is the narrow

10 Bergler, E., and Eidelberg, L., "Der Mammacomplex des Mannes," *Internationale Zeitschrift für Psychoanalyse,* XIX, 1933, p. 552.

passage (birth), being in a boat (womb), and the analyst who pulls her through the passage (rebirth in the analysis). She has been talking about her mother's personality being more feminine than hers.

Flood myths frequently represent the flood as urine, thereby revealing their dream origin.

In the New Hebrides we have the following myth:

Tabui Kor was a woman, Tilik and Tarai were her two sons. They lived near a sacred spring where they were making the land. While the men worked, she cooked their cabbage. Their food tasted nasty, so one of them decided to hide and watch the cooking. He saw that she urinated into their food, and put sea water into her own food. Then they exchanged the food and ate hers. She got angry and rolled away the stone which had hitherto kept the sea confined and the sea poured out in a great flood, and this was the origin of the sea.[11]

Buin tells a similar story. Atoto was the primeval woman. She had children but no husband. She had a son Kugui and a daughter. The son married the daughter and they had many children. Before that time there was no water. People roasted taro but could not boil it. But Atoto cooked the food by urinating into a pot and this was the food she gave her son. Then she changed this and had the urine ready all the time in a hole under her bed. One day he came home unexpectedly. He beat his mother when he saw what she was doing. He broke all the pots that contained the urine, the water poured out and flooded the land. This is how the ocean originated.[12]

The Narrinyeri told the story of Nurundere and his wives. The two women run away when he chases them. At a place called urine he urinates. Then he orders the Sea to rise and drown his two wives.[13]

In a Heiltsuk story two brothers lived with their sister. They made a small weir and caught a small fish and put it in the weir. They kept chasing bigger and bigger fish, and making bigger weirs. Every night the fish disappear from the weir. One of the brothers says, "Go to sleep" (meaning the other brother and the sister), *I shall stay awake* and see what happens." A big headless man with eyes on his chest takes the salmon. He shoots at him four times seemingly without hitting it. He follows the cannibal to his home, cures him of his wounds (made by his arrows) and marries the cannibal's daughter. He wants to take his wife

11 Brown, G., *Melanesians and Polynesians,* London, 1910, p. 357.

12 Thurnwald, R., *Forschungen auf den Salomo Inseln und dem Bismarck Archipel,* Berlin, 1912, II, pp. 347, 348.

13 Meyer, H. E. A., "Manners and Customs of the Aborigines of the Encounter Bay Tribe," in Words, J. D., *The Native Tribes of South Australia,* Adelaide, 1879, pp. 202–204.

home. She urinates and they go home in a boat on the river made by her urine.[14]

In a Pomo myth, this is how the deluge came about.

Coyote *dreamed* that water was about to cover up the world but nobody believed him. He said, "There is going to be water all over the world." It was raining and presently the water began to rise. The people climbed trees because there were no mountains on which they could escape. Coyote with a number of people was on a log. With the aid of Mole Coyote creates mountains and then the world was new and he created people.[15]

Thunder People lived in a village. They used to go to a spring. But one day a very large trout appeared in the spring. First they were afraid to eat these miraculous fish, but finally as there was nothing else to eat they did eat them. An old woman told her three grandchildren not to eat the miraculous fish.

Presently everyone went to bed as usual, but when the children awoke next morning there was nobody in the camp. They had all been transformed into deer. The children went to a very high mountain. The rain began to pour down. It rained very hard. The world was flooded and there was only a little bit of ground left. They asked an old man what he could do about the water. He said he did not know. But when night came the children went to sleep. The old man dug in the ground all night. In the morning he woke the children. The flood had disappeared and the world was a beautiful place.[16]

I emphasize the fact that sleeping occurs twice in this story. If we take it as the dream of Coyote (who is identical with the old man), the flood is the urethral flood. The fish in the water would be an attempt to transform the danger into the fantasy of being born. But only when he digs a deep hole (phallic) does the water disappear—that is, he awakes with an erection.

The next myth is about Gopher, a character in many ways similar to Coyote.[17]

"During the Deluge everyone except Gopher was killed. He saved himself by climbing on the top of Mt. Kanaktai. As the water rose, he saved himself by climbing to the top of Mt. Kanaktai. He climbed higher and higher, and just as the water was about to wash him off the top of the mountain it receded. Now he had no fire so he dug down into the

14 Boas, F., *Indianische Sagen von der Nord Pazifischen Küste Amerikas*, Berlin, 1895, pp. 237, 238.

15 Barrett, S. A., *Pomo Myths*, Bulletin of the Public Museum of the City of Milwaukee, XV, 1933, p. 130.

16 *Ibid.*, pp. 131–133.

17 I mean in the phallic significance.

mountain till he found fire inside. In this way he got fire again for the world."[18]

Fire and water as destroyers of the world frequently appear in the same myth or as sequels or substitutes. Coyote who destroys the world by a deluge also destroys it by fire.

Coyote lived with his two little boys whom he had got by deceit from one of the Wood-duck sisters. Everybody abuses his children so he decides to set the world on fire. He digs a tunnel at the *east end of the world,* fills it with fir bark and then lights it. He puts his two children into his hunting sack, ascends the roof of the dance house and expects the conflagration. Coyote calls for rescue from the sky. Spider descends from the sky with his web and Coyote jumps on Spider's belly. He is pulled up through the gates of the sky. He comes back again and finds everything roasted. He drinks too much water and gets sick. Kuksu as medicine man jumps on his belly, the water flows out and covers the land.[19]

Leaving out numerous variants of the same theme found in Pomo mythology, we quote the following version.

The young men of the village had killed Coyote's mother, they had choked her with a hot rock. When Coyote saw what had happened he cut open the breast of his mother and took out her heart. He took a stick and removed the bark and with the blood of his mother's heart he made four red bands around it. Just below each band he tied some down. Then he put a topknot of falcon feathers at the upper end of this wand. . . . At the lower end he suspended the heart of his mother. "Thus Coyote made a sleep-producing wand." He ties the wand to the center pole of the dance house. Everybody is asleep inside. He sets fire to the house and burns all the people. Then he becomes thirsty again (as above). He goes to Frog Woman. By pointing his arrows at her he compels her to show him the water she is sitting on. Then he returns to his mother's grave and revives her. She becomes a young and beautiful woman and Coyote acquires Falcon for his grandson[20]—which probably indicates incest with his mother.

If we take this as a waking dream of Coyote with the vesical pressure symbolized by fire and water and his "mother's heart" as representing sleep, we must regard Frog and Turtle who retain the water as symbols of his mother (retaining the water—preventing him from micturating and awakening) and the incest with mother as the erotic stimulation caused by the bladder pressure.

18 Barrett, *op. cit.,* p. 135.
19 *Ibid.,* p. 9.
20 *Ibid.,* p. 124.

While Frog denies that she has water, she keeps making baskets. One of these baskets she threw into the Blue Lake. "When a menstruating woman passes by these lakes she is very likely to see one of these baskets and to be made ill by it."[21]

The following story I quote is not a flood story, yet I think I should insert it here because of its connection with water and sleeping.

Tsuntia, the culture hero of the Lillooet, threw his mother into a lake because she would not tell him who his father was. She begat people by her intercourse with the lake. Her descendants were beautiful, especially the young women. The young men of the village would have liked to marry them, but on entering the houses of the "frog people" they were overcome by the smell of frog and *fell into a sleep in which they invariably died*. A young man went into the mountains and prepared his "medicine" for five years because he wanted to overcome the difficulty. He gained the desired knowledge of escaping death while having intercourse with the frog-eaters.[22]

When he went in, an elderly person said to him, "You are a young man and I would not like to see you die, therefore do not enter." He did not eat their food and they were astonished that he did not fall into a death sleep. He took to wife two of the prettiest maidens. He then persuaded some of them to eat deer and these became human beings.[23]

In another group of flood myths we find a different situation. The water is first in the inside of a living being.

According to the aboriginals of Lake Tyers all the water was contained in a huge frog and they did not know how to get water. They agreed that the way to do it was to make the frog laugh. Many animals danced without success. Finally the remarkable contortions of the eel produced the desired effect. The frog laughed and many were drowned in the flood.[24] In an Andamanese myth quoted by Andrew Lang the toad that contains the waters dances with the same result.[25]

I have shown the genital significance of this dancing and this, of course, is in context of the urethral meaning of these myths.[26] The Andamanese myths combine fire, water and the origin of animals. The Aka Jeru version is this, *the people were all asleep*. Sir Sea Eagle came and threw fire among them. They awoke in a fright and all ran in dif-

21 *Ibid.*, p. 201; cf. Index under *Frog.*

22 The people in the lake ate only frogs, and frog skins were their blankets.

23 Teit, J., "Traditions of the Thompson River Indians of British Columbia," *Memoirs of the American Folk-Lore Society*, VI, 1898, pp. 96, 97.

24 Brough Smyth, R., *The Aborigines of Victoria*, Melbourne, 1878.

25 Lang, A., *Myth, Ritual and Religion*, London, 1906, I, p. 44.

26 Cf. Róheim, *Australian Totemism*, London, 1925, p. 432.

ferent directions. Some ran into the sea and became fishes and turtles, others ran into the jungle and became birds.[27]

In a Jivaro story we have two young men who were companions. One of them tastes the flesh of a giant serpent. He is very thirsty and he starts to drink. "I shall burst from the water I drink," he said, "and be changed into a lake because I have eaten serpent flesh." He first became a frog, then a small alligator and finally a water serpent which kept growing. At the same time the water in the pool increased more and more and became a lake and then a very big lake which threatened to engulf the earth. All the people drowned except the friend of the youth who was turned into a serpent. He appeared to his friend *in a dream* and said, "Do not come near me or I am bound to swallow you."[28]

The Tahtlan relate how Raven wanted to make lakes but a man swallowed all the water and the whole lake was in his belly. *When the man sleeps* Snipe pushes his bill through the belly and the water runs out.[29]

The water in the belly of a living being condenses two dream motives, (a) the hero of the flood inside of something (inverted), (b) the urine in the bladder.

In the following Chippewayan myth the hero named Wis represents his dream by displacing the sleeping situation to his antagonist. A wolf man who is also a medicine man wants to be revenged on the water lynxes who have killed his nephew. He must first turn himself into a stump at the edge of the lake. *Frogs and snakes are sent to pull the stump down. Wis had a severe struggle to keep himself upright* (i.e., not asleep). The lynx, his suspicions now lulled to rest, lay down to sleep on the sand. Wis resumed his natural shape and although he had been warned to strike at the *shadow* of the lynx he forgot this and shot at the body. The second arrow, however, was aimed at the shadow and the wounded animal ran into the water. The river began to boil and rise and Wis escaped in his canoe. The water continued flowing until land, trees and hills were all covered (Follows the Earth Diver myth).[30]

The stump myth is also told about Nanibozhu. When transformed into a stump the serpent coiled himself round him till he nearly screamed with pain. Then the sea spirit came forth and soon all the monsters were

[27] Brown, A. R., *The Andaman Islander,* Cambridge, 1922, p. 207.

[28] Karsten, R., "The Head Hunters of Western Amazonas," *Societas Scientiarum Fennicae Commentationes Humaniarum Litterarum,* VII, I, Helsingfors, 1935, p. 534.

[29] Teit, J. E., "Tahtlan Tales," *Journal of American Folk-Lore,* XXXII, 1919, p. 219; cf. *idem,* "Kaska Tales," *ibid.,* XXX, 1917, p. 439.

[30] Frazer, J. G., *Folklore in the Old Testament,* London, 1919, I, pp. 229, 230; Hooper, W. H., *Ten Months among the Tents of the Tuski,* London, 1853, pp. 285–292. Other versions of the same myth are quoted by Frazer.

sleeping on the beach. Nainbozhu shot the sea spirit in the heart and then he fled, pursued by all the monsters and the waters. When he could no longer find dry land a canoe appeared and he was saved.[31] Another Wisaka myth reads exactly like a dream.

The people hurled fire into all the places where they thought Wisaka might be hiding. After the fire came the rain. Rivers rose, lakes overflowed, water ran over the land. The water followed him wherever he fled even to the top of the mountain. It pursued him up a lofty pine to the very topmost branch. He called on the pine to help him. A canoe slid off the top and he floated on the water with a paddle in his hand.[32]

The disturbed sleep of the sea is responsible for the flood in Tahiti. A fisherman let his hooks down and they became entangled *in the hair of the sleeping god.* The angry god came bubbling to the surface. When the sun set the waters of the ocean began to rise and the next morning only the tops of the mountains appeared above the sea.[33]

The Loucheux or Dene tell the story of a man who was the first person to build a canoe. He rocked the boat and this caused a flood. *He got into a gigantic hollow straw and caulked up the ends.* Finally he landed on a hill. The only living thing inside was a raven, who gorged with food *was fast asleep. He thrust the raven into a bag and dropped him in the bag,* so that he was dashed to pieces at the foot of the mountain.

The only living beings he found were a loach and a pike. He revived the raven and they went together to the beach *where the loach and the pike were still sleeping in the sun.* They bore holes into them and out of the pike came a crowd of men, out of the loach a crowd of women.[34]

The hero caulked in the straw, the sleeping animals all characterize sleep as such. The falling raven is the moment of falling asleep. The people coming out of the animal's inside—awakening.

We quote the story here because of the connection of motives: going into the mother, sleep and death. And the reverse side of the picture, water = mother, triumph of the libido.

In some of the flood myths the *duration is from evening to morning.*

"Once upon a time the whole world was flooded. All were drowned except one man and one woman who ran to the highest peak of a hill where they climbed up a tree and hid themselves among its branches. They intended to pass the night there. However, in the morning they

31 Chamberlain, A. F., "Nanibozhu amongst the Otchibwe, Missisagas and other Algonkian Tribes," *Journal of American Folk-Lore*, IX, 1891, p. 205.

32 Jones, W., "The Culture Hero Myth of the Sauks and Foxes," *Journal of American Folk-Lore*, XIV, 1896, p. 234.

33 Frazer, *op. cit.,* I, p. 234; Ellis, W., *Polynesian Researches*, I, pp. 389–391.

34 Petitot, E., *Traditions Indiennes du Canada Nord Ouest*, 1886, 13, 34–38.

found that they had become a tiger and a tigress. Pathiany (the supreme god) sent a man and a woman from a cave to re-people the earth.[35] From evening to morning the threat of flood is over.

In the Guiana version, the myth starts with cutting the world tree that contains the waters. The culture hero covers the stump with a closely woven basket. The monkey was sent by the culture hero to fetch water in an open basket—to keep him out of mischief. But he came back and out of curiosity lifted the basket from the tree trunk and the water poured forth.

The culture hero assembles all his people on the highest palm tree to rescue them from the rising waters. Those who could not climb he sealed up in a cave. He and his followers spent the night on the tree till finally the birds hailed the approach of the day.

One episode of this myth is the dismal cry of the monkey—the sleeper awakening from a nightmare.[36]

The flood ends with the approach of day—it is a dream. It begins with the *unfinished task* (like water in a sieve)[37] and continues with the voyeur element (tree trunk like Pandora's box, mother's vagina). Then the flood (urethral), the cave (uterine) and the climbing (genital).

One version of the Pima myth again contains the "sleep" motive. The sleeping prophet is warned three times by an eagle of the flood approaching but he pays no attention.[38]

The myths of world destruction by water and those of destruction by fire merge into each other.

In a Toba myth of the Great Fire, we are told that the *people were all sound asleep.* They awoke to see that the moon was being eaten by the jaguars—and the jaguars were the spirits of the dead. Fragments of the moon began to fall down on earth and started a big fire. The entire earth was on fire. They all ran to the lagoons covered with bull rushes.[39]

A typical urethral awakening dream projected into cosmic proportions.

In a Yokuts myth on the origin of fire the animals who are stealing the fire come to a place *where everybody is asleep.* Coyote took and covered the fire. Then he saw a baby asleep. He picked it up, put it in the hot ground where the fire had been and ran. The baby screamed and woke all the people. The chief picked the fastest runners and started

[35] Shakespear, J., *The Lushei Kuki Clans,* London, 1912, p. 177.

[36] Brett, W. H., *The Indian Tribes of Guiana,* London, 1868, pp. 378–382.

[37] Cf. below *The Danaids, Work and Punishment.*

[38] Bancroft, H. H., *The Native Races of the Pacific States,* New York, 1875, III, p. 78.

[39] Metraux, A., "Myths of the Toba and Pilaga Indians of the Gran Chaco," *Memoirs of the American Folklore Society,* XL, 1946, p. 33.

them after Coyote. Coyote dodged on one side, then the other, and as he ran the water followed his trail, and that is why the river is so crooked.[40]

If we *condense the personnel* of this story, we have the sleeper who dreams that he is a baby (rebirth) and owing to the bladder pressure he keeps running. Water and fire are the same thing. It is interesting to note that among the Lipan Apache, Coyote stories are bedtime stories.[41]

The dream origin of the flood myth is quite clear in the following Tsetsaut story.

A man and his wife went up the hills to hunt marmots. When they reached the top of the hill they saw that the water was still rising. They climbed higher and higher but the water rose steadily. Finally when the water was about to reach them they resolved to enclose their children in hollow trees. They supplied them with food and closed the cavities up with wooden covers.

But the water continued to rise and all the people were drowned.

Then the water began to retreat. *The children went to sleep and when they awoke one of the boys opened a hole and came out.*[42]

The Tsimshian relate the deluge as follows:

The waters of the Lake of the Beginning arose and a great whale came to the surface. When the whale went down the water subsided. One man went down to the bottom of the Lake of the Beginning to get supernatural power. Then the water rose again and the great whale came out. At the bottom of the lake there was a large house. The door opened suddenly, he entered.[43] (We omit the rest of the story.) The rising waters are here combined with the basic dream of falling asleep.

Boas gives a condensed version of all the Northwestern stories of *how Raven obtained water.*

Raven causes the owner of the water to go to sleep, makes him believe that he has soiled his bed, and by means of the threat that he will tell on him, Raven obtains permission to drink.

(The soiling in this case is excremental, but in many cases these two pressures go together.)

After he has thus obtained water, he creates the rivers. He spits them out, or he *makes the rivers by urinating.*

[40] Stewart, G. W., "Two Yokuts Traditions," *Journal of American Folk-Lore,* XXI, 1908, pp. 237, 238.

[41] Opler, M. E., "Myths and Legends of the Lipan Apache Indians," *Memoirs of the American Folklore Society,* XXXVI, 1940, p. 107.

[42] Boas, F., "Traditions of the Tsetsaut," *Journal of American Folk-Lore,* IX, 1896, p. 262.

[43] Boas, F., "Tsimshian Mythology," *Bureau of American Ethnology,* XXXI, Report, 1916, pp. 346, 347.

In one version, obtaining water and obtaining the sun are the same thing.

Raven becomes the lover of the daughter of the Sun-owner who also owns the water. He asks for a drink and *when the girl is asleep he flies away with the water basket.*[44]

The flood myth is frequently combined with others such as the fire or conflagration, the theft of the *sun and especially the Earth-Diver motive of the creation myth.*

In the Iroquoian myth (Onondaga version) quoted above, when the pregnant woman thrown down from the sky is floating toward the earth, there seemed to be a lake at the spot where she was falling. There she saw many ducks and other water fowl falling. The Loon shouted, "A woman is coming to the depths of the water, her body is floating hither." So recognizing that she needs earth to live on, they dive for the earth. After several failures, the Turtle gets the earth and he is also the one who carries it on his back.[45]

In a Kathlamet myth, Beaver floods the world with his tears. Bluejay dives, but his tail remains above the water. Then Otter tries in vain. Finally the muskrat dives and remains under the water a long time.

In a myth of the Potawatomi, after the world has been inundated, Messon sends a raven to build up another world. Everything was covered with water. The raven could not find any earth. The otter also returned without achieving anything. At last, the muskrat descended and brought back some earth.

In the Menominee version the same happens with Manabush. The animals are the Otter, the Beaver, the Mink, and finally the Muskrat. In another version, when the Muskrat reappears on the surface he is nearly dead and he has one single grain of sand in his paws. From this the world is remade by Great Hare who courses around it.[46]

Boas comes to the conclusion that the opening of the Raven and the Mink myths in North West American mythology is a deluge myth "which has been elaborated in different directions but presents in all these tales the beginning of the world. The loss of the deluge element in the Raven tales, of the Tsimshian and Newettee may be due to the occurrence of other deluge legends in these tribes. Among the Newettee the Mink tale not only contains the element of destruction of the world by fire, but refers also to the start of all vegetation which is brought up by diving

44 Boas, F., *op. cit.,* XXXI, 1916, pp. 651–652.

45 Hewitt, J. N. B., "Iroquoian Cosmology," *Annual Report of the Bureau of American Ethnology,* XXI, 1903, pp. 181, 182.

46 Alexander, H. B., *The Mythology of All Races, North American,* X, Boston, 1916, pp. 42, 43, with references.

animals the same way the new earth is created after the deluge by the eastern tribes.[47]

From the point of view of the dream nucleus of these myths, we have here a rather interesting situation. The flying, diving bird element is the basic dream, the transition from waking to sleeping. The deluge and world fire myth is the awakening urethral dream, the transition from sleeping to waking. The dream, in so far as it is "historical," i.e., personal, is left out, and the beginning of the world is the awakening of the sleeper. We quote Campbell who writes, "Dream is the personalized myth, myth is the depersonalized dream."[48]

The second half of this view is right or nearly right, but the first half can only be accepted if we believe in inherited symbols or "the collective unconscious."

To return, however, to our flood and creation myths. The diving dream is both regressive and libidinal. The moment of falling asleep is also awakening or rather in this case the resistance to awakening. The water as the origin of things is both the uterus and the pressure exerted by the bladder. Sin, guilt and anxiety are components of the flood myth; they are also found in all urethral waking dreams on a superficial level because by urinating the dreamer will mess the bed, and on a deeper level because of the magic aggressive elements implied in the dream of urine.

In some North American myths the flood is followed by the birds flying up to the sky.

In a Papago myth a baby deserted by its father and mother starts to cry. First the earth around the baby is moist, then there is a stream and then it is evident that a flood is coming that will destroy the world.

Older Brother made a pot out of greasewood to save himself in. Coyote did the same. Older Brother told the birds to hang on to the sky.[49]

We must substitute urine for tears and then the myth with its urethral, intrauterine (box) and genital symbolism becomes quite clear.

If we look at the biblical narrative closely we find the same equivalence of the creation and the deluge myth.

The Spirit of God soaring over the water (Genesis I, 1) is evidently a bird and when God says, Let there be light! that might well be the moment of awakening. As for the biblical narrative of the Flood, the ark of

47 Boas, F., op. cit., pp. 640, 641.

48 Campbell, J., The Hero With a Thousand Faces, New York, 1949, p. 19.

49 Kroeber, H. R., "Traditions of the Papago Indians," Journal of American Folk-Lore, XXV, 1912, p. 98.

Noah with the male and female couples in it already indicates the tendency to re-create (as in the dream) and the birds emitted one after the other from the ark (Genesis VI, 6–8) are obviously identical with the diving birds of our creation and deluge myths.[50] The Spirit of God above the waters usually appears in the shape of a dove.[51]

Offshoots of the biblical myth indicate the reaction of the unconscious to the meaning of the ark as symbolizing the womb.[52]

Numi Tarem (Sky God) wishes to kill Xulater, the prince of the underworld, by destroying the universe in a cataclysm of fire. Xulater is having an affair with the wife of the Vogul sky god and he gets into the ark by crawling into her stomach. In various other versions the devil abetted by Noah's wife crawls into the ark or bores a hole in the ark, in the shape of a serpent or a mouse.[53]

Greek myths of the hero rescued by the dolphin are parallel versions of the flood myth. The dolphin is δελφυς, the womb. Usener concludes that Phalantos, that is, the phallos, must have been one of the hero gods rescued by the dolphin.[54] Eros is actually represented on the back of the dolphin.[55]

Flood myths in which the "closed in" aspect of the rescuing boat is especially emphasized are probably derived from urethral awakening dreams combined with the intrauterine situation.

The people of Banks Island tell the flood myth about their culture hero Qat.

He made himself a large canoe and when he finished he collected all living creatures and shut himself in the canoe with them. A deluge of rain came and the canoe tore a channel for itself and disappeared.[56]

It is perhaps of interest that Qat is also the hero who brings Night and Daylight. Qat travels to Night who shows him how to sleep. He returns to his brothers with a knowledge of sleep and with birds that would awaken them in the morning.

"What is this coming out of the sea—they cried—that is night, sit down on both sides of the house and when you feel something in your eyes lie down and be quiet." When their eyes began to blink they said What is this? Shall we die? Shut your eyes and go to sleep, he said. When

50 I am not discussing primitive beliefs that are due to missionary influence.

51 Eisler, R., "Kuba-Kybele," *Philologus*, LXVIII, p. 180.

52 By offshoots, I do not mean modern missionary influence but archaic cultural traditions.

53 Dähnhardt, O., *Natursagen*, I, Leipzig, 1907, pp. 257–290.

54 Usener, H., *Die Sintflutsagen*, Bonn, 1899, p. 159.

55 *Ibid.*, p. 223; cf. on the fish symbolism also Eisler, R., *Orpheus—the Fisher*, London, 1921.

56 Codrington, R. H., *The Melanesians*, Oxford, 1891, p. 166.

night had lasted long enough the cock began to crow and the birds to twitter. Qat took a piece of red obsidian and cut the night with it, the light shone forth again and Qat's brothers awoke.[57]

In dreams of menstruating women we also find the same structure as in vesical dreams. The volume of the fluid increases, it is a flood.

Once upon a time (Toba myth) a woman was menstruating. Her mother and sister forgot to leave drinking water for her. So she went down to the lagoon to drink. It rained until all the people were drowned. All the corpses turned into birds and flew up (the flying dream). This is because Rainbow is angry when a menstruating woman goes near a lagoon.[58] A parallel version of this myth from the same tribe is interesting. The cataclysm is due to fire instead of water. Menstruation is not mentioned—but the moon has something to do with the cataclysm.

The people were all sound asleep. One of them awoke, the others slept. The moon is about to be eaten by an animal. The jaguars were eating the moon, they were really the spirits of the dead. Fragments of the moon fell on the earth and started a great fire. Everything was burned, even the lagoon of water. Birds flew up out of the corpses.[59]

The Wemale relate a flood story. Human beings were under the rule of a woman called Bouwa. She was the daughter of the sun god Tuwale. Tuwale floods the world and she ascends higher and higher escaping from the water. She reminds her father that he still owes mankind the purchase money for Rabie, his wife. In order to do so she covers her genitalia with a silver girdle. She wore this girdle for three days and since then women menstruate for three days. That ended the flood and mankind was rescued by the morning star[60] (awakening).

We find another flood myth based on menstruation in Arnhem Land.

According to Elkin and Berndt, the Wauwelak were two sisters who came from the interior of Arnhem Land. Following incest with a man belonging to their own moiety the elder sister gave birth to a child. The journey was continued while the afterbirth blood was still flowing and they approach a water hole belonging to a large, female, rock python, Julunggul. She smelled the blood and came out and made lightning and rain. The rain gradually washed some of the afterbirth blood into the pool. The female python gradually came nearer the "shade" in which the sisters sat. The dancing of the elder sister which caused her blood to

57 *Ibid.*, p. 157.
58 Metraux, *Myths of the Toba and Pilaga Indians of the Gran Chaco,* Philadelphia, 1946, p. 29.
59 *Ibid.*, p. 33.
60 Jensen, A. R., *Hainuwele,* Frankfurt am Main, 1933, pp. 54–56.

flow attracted the snake while that of the younger sister stopped it. Finally the python pushed her head in through the door and swallowed the two sisters and the child. The python returned to the well and standing upright talked to the other pythons. Then the country was flooded.[61]

In the Murngin version of this myth Yurlunggur is a male, the Big Father. When the menstrual blood dropped into the pool Yurlunggur smelled the odor of the blood. He raised his head and smelled again and again. He advanced slowly in snake form and as the snake advanced so also the flood. The sisters sang to prevent the flood (snake) from swallowing them. *But he crawled into the camp and they fell into a deep sleep from his magic.* He then swallowed them and finally he regurgitated them.[62]

If we take these two myths together we must come to the conclusion that they are really based on two different dreams, one male, one female. The male dream must be that the dreamer—the snake—has intercourse with the woman, goes into her (i.e., is asleep) and his semen is the flood. In the female version the woman is excited when her blood flows, i.e., she is in her own vagina and in her mother's uterus in her dream. The flood is here the menstrual blood.[63]

We should also compare the Sumerian version of the flood myth.

Ea tells Enlil how he caused Utnapishtim, "the exceedingly wise one," to have a dream by which he learned the plan of the gods to send a flood.[64]

Fire and water and the sun and the culture hero all merge into each other in these myths. In order to make this clearer we shall now analyze once more the myth of Maui.

Maui is the youngest of many brothers. He does not know where his father and mother live because mother only comes to him to sleep, and at dawn she leaves. Maui, the youngest, was really an afterbirth thrown away by his mother but kept alive by the foam of the sea. He recounts how his ancestor Great Father Sky had rescued him and stripped off the encircling jelly fish. But he said to his mother, "From the time I was in your womb I had heard the names of your first-born children," and then he enumerated them and added, "and I am Maui, the baby." He now slept next to his mother, but he was always very curious. Where did she go when she left him at daylight?

"As soon as his mother got outside the house he jumped up and

61 Elkin, A. P. and Berndt, C. and R., *Art in Arnhem Land,* Chicago, 1939, p. 32.
62 Warner, W. Lloyd, *A Black Civilization,* New York, 1937, pp. 250-257.
63 The proofs for this interpretation are derived from an unpublished manuscript of R. and C. Berndt.
64 Langdon, S. H., *The Mythology of All Races, Semitic,* V, Boston, 1931, p. 222.

peeped after her through the doorway of bright light. Whilst he was *watching her the old woman* reached down to a tuft of rushes and snatching it from the ground *dropped into a hole underneath it* and clapping the rushes on the hole again, disappeared." *Maui followed her and discovered a beautiful open cave running quite deep into the earth. He wakes his brothers and tells them they have slept enough.* He decides that he will go and find their parents. He transforms himself into the shape of a beautiful pigeon.

"What made him now look so well in this shape was the belt of his mother and her apron which he stole while *she was sleeping*," the white mark on the breast of the pigeon is the belt of Maui's mother.

He flew to the cave which his mother had run down into but it was very narrow. He had to dip his wings twice but as he flew the cave widened and he dashed straight on.[65] In the Mangaia version mother and following her the son descend to the netherworld, i.e., open a rock by means of an incantation.

> Buataranga[66] descend thou bodily through the chasm
> The rainbow like must be obeyed
> As two dark clouds parting at dawn
> Open, open up my road to the netherworld ye fierce ones.

Maui passes through in the form of a red pigeon minus his tail which is grabbed by the two fierce guardians of the netherworld. When he obtains the fire he extinguishes it in water several times. Finally, however, he started such a conflagration that all the netherworld was in flames, the rocks cracked and split with the heat. He re-enters the red pigeon, the rock opens once more and he flies back to the upper world. The flames follow him or precede him and threaten to consume the land of Rangi and Mokoiro. Somehow they quench the flames, how is not said in the story.[67] Maui keeps thrusting the fire-brands into the pool. Maui takes the fire-brand into his hands, it burns him and he jumps into the sea. "When he sank in the waters, the sun for the first time set, and darkness covered the earth. When he found that all was night, he immediately pursued the sun and brought him back in the morning."[68]

In this solar periodicity of Maui we see the projection of sleep and awakening to a cosmic plane. The water-fire symbolism at the end of the myth is the vesical awakening dream. Nor can there be any doubt about the pigeon and the portals of the netherworld.

In Tuamotu we get the following genealogy of Maui.

65 Grey, G., *Polynesian Mythology*, London, 1855, pp. 16–24.
66 Maui's mother.
67 Gill, W. W., *Myths and Songs from the South Pacific*, London, 1876, pp. 51–57.
68 White, I., *Ancient History of the Maori*, Wellington, 1887–1888, II, pp. 76, 115.

His grandfather is *Tane te vai ora* (Male principle of the water of life), his grandmother Sacred entrance, their children are "Smeared with filth." "Offspring of the mons veneris." "Sexual organs" and then the third generation.

Wonder worker[69] the first, Maui, wonder worker the between, Maui wonder worker the later, and the hero of our myths Maui tiki tiki ataraga (Maui the *tumid* begat of Ataraga).[70]

In the Tuamotu version of the story Ataraga is the father of Maui. "Then Hua-hega turned towards Ataraga and she saw his manly staff rampant with desire."[71]

The dream origin of this myth gains added probability from the etymology of this name Ataraga = Shadow ascending or "cloud, reflection, semblance."[72] "Ataraga, however, would not give his consent[73] so they all slept and when night was far advanced Maui sat up and took the girdle of Ataraga and wrapped it about himself and then went to sleep again." (But Ataraga awakes and takes the girdle back again.)

"Maui went to the place where they had vanished (his parents) and stamped upon it."

"Open the gate," he shouted. Mue o is the guardian of the gate. Mu means silence, o signifies "to penetrate, intrude into; to be swallowed up, engulfed in."[74]

Thus Maui, the tumid phallic hero, penetrates into the gate of silence or sleep. The song of the begetting of Maui, Passion song of the Maidens, makes the meaning of the gate quite clear.

First voice:

Te kiri vi te kiri vi (The difficult entrance, the veiled gateway).
Kiri vi is tightly stretched skin, *the reference is to the hymen.*
Now it is stormed is carried by assault

Chorus:

The intruder thrusts against the nub of desire
Here is a maid; there below is the cleft portal, etc.[75]

We recognize the basic dream with the hero flying into the "vagina

---

[69] Maui = wonder worker.
[70] Stimson, I. F., *The Legends of Maui and Tahaki*, Honolulu, 1934, p. 91.
[71] *Ibid.*, p. 8.
[72] *Ibid.*, p. 91.
[73] To Maui going to the netherworld.
[74] *Ibid.*, p. 94.
[75] *Ibid.*, pp. 5 and 92; cf. also Róheim, "The Garden of Eden," *Psychoanalytic Review*, XXVII, p. 184; idem, "Fire in the Dragon," *Imago*, VII, No. 2; Westervelt, W. D., *Legends of Maui*, Honolulu, 1910; Luomala, K., "Maui of a Thousand Tricks," *Bernice P. Bishop Museum Bulletin*, Honolulu, 1949, p. 198.

of sleep." The awakening is indicated by allusions to the sun, the vesical stimulus by water and fire. I have discussed an Eastern European folk tale called *Serpent and Daughters* by Panzer, and *Dragon Family* by Solymossy.[76]

Once upon a time there was a country in which there was no sun, no moon, no stars. The king said that anyone who brought back the sun, moon and stars could have whatever he asked for. A widow had three sons and the youngest was called Beautiful Wing Meadow.[77] He asks for a carriage and a ton of gold. He takes the gold to Smith of the Land, an elderly but powerful man. By the order of the king, boil it till I return—he says. The hero rode with his brothers.

They came to a bridge; there they hit a fire and *went to sleep*. After midnight the hero was awake. On the bridge he wrestled with the seven-headed dragon. The dragon's horse shone like the stars and when Szép-mezöszárnya killed him the stars were back on the sky. The same happens with the nine-headed dragon and the moon. With the twelve-headed dragon things are more difficult. They are equal in wrestling. Then the hero becomes a wooden wheel, the dragon an iron wheel. Again there is no decision. Now the hero is a white flame. The decision is made by a crow who flies to his two sleeping brothers. The brothers awake and pour water on the blue flame. The flame "went to sleep" (*elaludt* = Hungarian for extinguished) and Wing of the Beautiful Meadow burned his adversary to death. The dragon died and the sun was shining once more. Thus far the first half of the story. They go on wandering and they arrive at a stone castle. The hero turns a somersault and becomes a wasp. He flies in through the keyhole and there he sees the wives and the mother-in-law (usually mother of the dragons). *The dragon wives wake their mother.* She asks for water to *wash in.* They vow revenge for the death of their husbands. The oldest daughter is going to be a pear tree. There will be a famine, people will want to eat the pears. But he who eats the fruit must die. The next will be a spring; anyone who drinks this water will die. The third a bridge—anyone who crosses it must be burned to death by fire.

The hero turns another somersault, becomes human once more and the three brothers continue their wandering. They see the pear tree, he plunges his sword into it. The tree becomes one mass of blood and col-

---

[76] Panzer, F., "Beowulf," *Studien zur germanischen Sagengeschichte,* I, München, 1910, p. 101; Solymossy, S., "A sárkánycsalád" (The Dragon Family), *Ethnographia,* 1928.

[77] Horger, A., *Hétfalusi csángó mesék* (Csángó Folktales of Hetfalu), *Magyar Nép-költési Gyütemény* (Hungarian Folklore Publications), X, 1908, pp. 407–416. The Rumanian versions have similar names for the hero; Sainenu, L., *Basmele Romane* (Rumanian Folk Tales), Bucharest, 1895, pp. 540–556.

lapses. The same thing happens with the spring and the fire—the hero takes care of them all with his sword.

Now the old she-dragon spouting fire sets out to pursue them. The magic flight follows.[78]

They arrive at the castle of Smith of the Country with the she-dragon still after them.

Open the gate, Smith of the Land, he shouts. When the she-dragon arrives she digs a hole under the gate and sticks her head in. They pour the burning gold on her head, she dies. Marriage and happy end.[79]

The Hungarian and Rumanian versions all contain the episode of the missing sun, moon and stars, the Rumanians add Eléna Cosin-zéna, the fairy queen abducted by the dragons and recaptured by the hero.[80] In one of the Rumanian versions we find a Field of sleep and a Field of flowers.[81] In a Russian story the three heroes are Ivan, son of the Tsar, Ivan, son of the Maid and Ivan, Son of a Cow. They enter the revolving hut and then they have to stay awake on a bridge. The two elder brothers fall asleep and Ivan, the Son of the Cow, deals with the first danger, a jug of water that dances on the bridge. The hero cuts the jug to pieces and the dragon appears. When the final battle is fought the hero needs his brothers' help. They are asleep in a hut. He throws his boots at the hut, the hut collapses but they go on sleeping. Then he throws a piece broken off his mace at the stables, and the three horses run out and help him to kill the dragon.

Next morning the brothers awoke and lo and behold! the hut is in pieces, the plates are full of blood.

The hero also awakes under the bridge and reproaches them for their long sleep. The hut is again as it was before and there is food on the plates.[82]

The old dragon mother is the famous Baba Yaga. The three dragon wives metamorphose themselves into a well, a bed, a beautiful garden and a hut in which they would sleep. Baba Yaga herself is a sow who will eat them. She swallows the two brothers. The sow sticks her tongue in through the gate and is at the mercy of the twelve smiths. Finally the hero compels her to vomit the brothers and their horses and kills her. In a Slowak story the land is plunged into darkness because the sun-horse is missing. This is the ending: "When they crossed the frontier

[78] Cf. "The Way Back."

[79] Cf. a previous analysis of this folk tale, Róheim, "The Story of the Light That Disappeared," *Samiksa,* I, No. 1.

[80] Sainenu, *op. cit.,* p. 550.

[81] *Ibid.,* p. 555.

[82] Afanassjev, M., *Russische Volksmärchen,* Wien, 1906, pp. 137–155.

of the dark realm, flashes flew in all directions from the horse's forehead and everything came to life again, beautiful regions rejoiced and blossomed with the flowers of spring."[83]

It is clear enough that we have to do with a story based on a dream. The brothers are aspects of the same person. When the story says that two are asleep and one is awake, that is the same as saying while a person is asleep his soul experiences various things, i.e., he is dreaming. The sun disappears, this is sleep, the sun reappears, this is awakening.

Some aspects of the dream have been emphasized in my paper on "The Story of the Light That Disappeared." Notably it is clear that in the person of the Smith we have the "good" paternal imago. In that of the mother of the dragons, or, in Russian, frequently the Baba Yaga, we have the bad or phallic mother. But this negative oedipal configuration only serves to obliterate the positive oedipal aspect, the dragon as enemy, the fairy queen or the king's daughter as bride. The struggle takes place on a *bridge* and frequently hero and dragon are represented as wrestling, pushing each other into the soil. The phallic nature of the bridge indicates that the dream is also a masturbation dream. In some versions the hero or rather his brothers are swallowed by the mother image and regurgitated. The hut in which they sleep, the smith's house in which they find refuge are all various symbolizations of intrauterine sleep. The moment of falling asleep is symbolized by the revolving hut (castle) and by the hero and dragon as wheels. What awakens the dreamer? Since he and the dragon become flames, since a raven brings water to extinguish the flame, since where there is a bridge there must be water, since the mother of the dragons ends by having burning gold poured on her tongue or in her mouth we recognize that this is another story based on a vesical dream.

The symbolism of the vesical dream is so typical that there is little chance of being mistaken in the interpretation. The increasing volume of water (or the growing fish), the running or escaping of the hero (heroine) or dreamer, the womb symbolism, phallic traits, moreover a combination of fire and water are the characteristics of the vesical dream. The fact that our stories frequently mention one or more of the *dramatis personae* as sleeping, or relate the whole thing as a dream, makes it quite clear that what we have here is not a parallelism of unconscious symbolism in dreaming and in inventing a story, but a type of narrative or several types of narratives that were actually retellings of vesical awakening dreams.

[83] Wratislaw, A. H., *Sixty Folk Tales from Exclusively Slavonic Sources,* 1889, London, p. 82; Wenzig, I., *Westslawischer Märchenschatz,* Leipzig, 1857, p. 182.

IV. The Water Carriers in the Moon

A simple narrative of the etiological type explains the spots on the surface of the moon. Variations of the theme of the water carriers in the moon occur from Ireland to New Zealand.

(1) *Ireland.* According to the Irish two boys are visible in the moon carrying a bucket of water.[1]

(2) *Westfalia.* A boy with a bucket is visible in the moon.[2]

(3) *Mecklenburg.* A girl was playing around with a lad. Once they went on the roof wishing to dash a bucket of water at the moon. While they were trying to do this, the moon fell down on the girl and the boy, and they were both burned.[3]

(4) *German* (Locality not given). A thief stole two buckets. On his way home a man followed the thief, who ran and the man ran after him. Turning round he saw that it was only his own shadow. He cursed the moon and splashed the water from his bucket up toward the moon—but in the same moment he flew up to the moon with both buckets. You can still see him there.[4]

(5) *Rantum.* The Man in the Moon is a giant. When the tide is in he is bent over because he is scooping the water up and pouring it down again. At ebb tide he stands straight and rests—that is how the water can flow back.[5]

(6) Edda Mani rules the moon at full moon and new moon. He took two children from the earth, Bil and Hiuki, because they came from the well Byrgir and carried the bucket on their shoulders. These children follow the moon. You can see this from the earth.[6]

(7) *Jämteland, Sweden.* We see two very old men in the moon. They wanted to extinguish the moonlight with a bucket of water. Therefore they stuck to the moon and must now be visible there and ashamed forever.[7]

(8) *Södraswerge, Sweden.* People see two men carrying a bucket on a yoke.[8]

---

[1] Theen, H., *Am Urquell*, Wien, 1892, p. 9.

[2] Bartels, M., *Zeitschrift des Vereins für Volkskunde*, VII, 1897, p. 110.

[3] Wossidlo, R., "Das Naturleben im Munde des Mecklenburger Volkes," *Zeitschrift des Vereins für Volkskunde*, V, 1895, p. 429.

[4] Wagner, W., *Unsere Vorzeit, Germanische Göttersagen*, Leipzig, 1907, pp. 392, 393.

[5] Theen, *op. cit.*, p. 290, quoting Müllenhoff, K., *Sagen, Märchen und Lieder der Herzogtümer Schleswig-Holstein und Lauenburg*, 1845, p. 360.

[6] Simrock, K., *Die Edda*, Stuttgart, 1896, p. 255.

[7] Theen, *op. cit.*, p. 35. (*Cavallius Wärend och Wirdarne.*)

[8] Grimm, *Deutsche Mythologie*, II, Berlin, 1877, p. 598; Hassencamp, R., "Die Mondflecken in Sage und Mythologie," *Globus*, XXIII, 1873, p. 108.

(9) *Gestriktland, Sweden.* Two old people with a can of soot, they wanted to cover the moon with soot, then it could not give them away when they stole something at night. They stuck fast and stayed there till doomsday.[9]

(10) *Lapp* (Rite Lapmark Arjeploug). A man and a woman wanted to steal at night but the moon was too bright. They wanted to cover the moon with soot, which angered the moon so that he pulled them up.[10]

(11) *Estonian.* A maid had to work very hard. Even on the eve of Sunday, she had to heat the bathroom and to carry the water from the well. She sighed:

> Dear Moon, marry me
> Sun, save me.

She is visible in the moon today with the bucket of water and the branches used for the bath (Turkish bath).

(12) *Estonian.* A girl who went to get water from the well saw the moon reflected in the water, she said her buttocks were prettier than the moon. To punish her she stays in the moon forever.[11]

(13) *Estonian* (Oesel). The moon shone too brightly for the thieves, they wanted to cover it with soot. God punished them by putting them into the moon. They are there forever with the bucket of soot. This explains the black spots.[12]

(14) *Estonian.* One Saturday evening a woman went very late to the river to fetch water. The moon shone brightly in the sky and she said, "Why do you stand gaping up there? You'd better come and help me carry water. I must work here and you dawdle about above."

Suddenly the moon came down from above. He seized the woman and took her with him into the sky. There she still stands with her two pails as a warning to everybody not to work too late in the evening on holidays.[13]

(15) *Estonian.* A peasant went with his wife on Saturday evening to steal something. They intended to go into a barn. But he said, "The moon is too bright! Let us climb this haystack and then we can put some pitch on

9 Theen, *op. cit.,* p. 35.

10 Halász, I., *Sved Lapp Nyelv, Nepköltési Gyüjtemény* (Language of Lapps in Sweden, Folklore). Budapest, 1893, V, p. 3.

11 Hurt, J., *Ueber estnische Himmelskunde,* Tartu 1900, p. 13 quoted by Loorits, O., *Grundzüge des estnischen Volksglaubens,* Skrifter Utgivna av Kungl, Gustav Adolfs Akademien, 18:1, Lund, 1949, p. 427.

12 Holzmayer, A. B., "Osiliana," *Verhandlungen der gelehrten Estnischen Gesellschaft zu Dorpat,* 1873, VII, p. 46; Wiedmann, F. J., *Aus dem inneren und äusseren Leben der Esten,* 1876, p. 488.

13 Jannsen, H., *Märchen und Sagen des Estnischen Volkes,* p. 175; Kirby, A., *The Hero of Esthonia,* London, 1895, II, p. 37.

the moon before it climbs higher." But they could not do it and are still visible in the moon with the yoke and the bucket of pitch.[14]

(16) *Estonian.* A young married couple could not sleep because of the moon. They decided to climb up and cover the moon with soot. But they stuck to the moon and are still to be seen there. In old times the moon was not as far away as now—it could be reached by a ladder.[15]

(17) *Estonian.* A pure maiden was rewarded for her purity by being lifted into the moon.[16]

(18) *Estonian.* The following story, although it is not told about the moon, nevertheless belongs to the group of stories we are discussing. Seven stars in the sky (probably the Dipper) are called "poles" because they carry water. The king of the northland had an only daughter. She was always carrying water from the ocean in a golden bucket. Being a very good girl she was raised into the sky. Both the king and the queen dreamed that they would see her in the sky and that is what happened.[17]

(19) *Livland.* A girl is raised to the moon either for pointing at the moon or for showing her buttocks to the moon or for comparing the moon to her buttocks.[18]

(20) *Votyak.* An evil stepmother sent her daughter to fetch water. It was in the period between Christmas and Epiphany. She cried and wanted to commit suicide. She jumped on the frozen lake but she did not sink in the water. In her despair she prayed to the moon to help her and there she is still with the bucket of water.[19]

(21) *Votyak.* An orphan lives with her brothers and sisters-in-law. She was carrying two buckets on her back held together by a yoke. She had to go to a creek to fetch water and while doing so she cried and prayed to god to take her up into heaven and save her from her oppressors. She is now visible with the yoke and the buckets in the moon.

(22) *Tshuvash.* A stepmother was always scolding her stepdaughter. God pitied her and put her into the moon. There she is even now with a bucket of water.[20]

(23) *Tartars of Kasan.* Three times a year the gates of heaven are open for a second, and in this second Allah grants all wishes. A girl was carrying water in a bucket. She looked up at the moon and wished she were there. Allah granted her wish, and there she is with her bucket.[21]

[14] Loorits, *op. cit.*, p. 428.   [15] *Ibid.*, p. 429.

[16] Kirby, *op. cit.*, II, pp. 34, 35; Loorits, *op. cit.*, p. 427.

[17] Loorits, *op. cit.*, pp. 534, 535.   [18] *Ibid.*, p. 427.

[19] Munkacsi, B., *Votják népköltészeti hagyományok* (Votják Traditions), Budapest, 1887, p. 37.

[20] Meszaros, G., *A Csuvas Ósvallás Emlékei* (Tshuvash Heathenism), Budapest, 1909, p. 82.

[21] *Ibid.*, p. 83.

(24) *Yakut*. A chief adopted an orphan but his wife kept torturing her. She went to get water but her feet got entangled into a willow; she fell and the water poured out of the bucket. The lake was frozen now and she dared not go home without water. She prayed to the moon to rescue her, and both sun and moon came from the sky to woo her. They fought and the sun was victorious. But the moon argued that the girl was his because he ruled over the night. The sun ceded the point. There she is now in the moon with the willow tree she held on to in her anxiety and the bucket of water.[22]

(25) *Yakut*. Like (24); the only difference is that the girl is supposed to die from time to time with the moon.[23]

(26) *Yakut*. The moon pitied the orphan girl, and there she is with her willow bush, yoke, and bucket. She was carrying water under a willow.[24]

(27) *Yakut*. A brother and sister are sent to fetch water. They gazed at the moon till he became angry and snatched them to him. The Yakuts never allow their children to watch the full moon.[25]

(28) *Yakut*. The moon took a young orphan girl who was mistreated by her mother-in-law. It was a very cold night and the mother-in-law made her fetch water and made her do it barefoot. The moon carried her up with a bucket while she was going to get water with the pails in her hand. When the orphan girl grows the moon grows also. When the moon is waning, it has gone into a house where it lives with the girl. At full moon the moon and the girl go to get water.[26]

(29) *Buryat*. Same as (24) of the Yakut.[27]

(30) *Altai Tartar*. An old man who used to be a great cannibal lives in the moon. To free the earth from such a danger the moon descended, and he found the cannibal picking berries from a hawthorn. The man-eater and the hawthorn can still be seen in the moon.[28]

(31) *Yogul*. In old times the moon ate little children. That is why they are visible in the moon now.[29]

(32) *Buryat*. The girl who is taken to the moon here becomes the

[22] Winter, A. C., "Die Mondmythe der Jakuten," *Globus*, LXXXIV, 1903, p. 383; Owtskinikov, W., in *Etnograficeskoje Obozrjenie*, III, 1897.

[23] Winter, *loc. cit.*

[24] Petri, E., "Neueres über die Jakuten," *Petermann's Mitteilungen*, XXXIII, 1887, p. 102, quoting Pripusow.

[25] Holmberg, U., *Finno Ugric, Siberian Mythology of All Races*, IV, Boston, 1927, p. 423, quoting Russian sources.

[26] Sieroszewski, W., "Du Chamanisme d'apres les croyances des Yakoutes," *Revue de l'Histoire des Religions*, XLVI, 1902, p. 216.

[27] Holmberg, *op. cit.*, p. 423.

[28] *Ibid.*, pp. 423, 424.

[29] Munkácsi, *Vogul Népköltési Gyüjtemény*, IV, Budapest, 1896, p. 414.

eskin (owner) of both sun and moon. Stepmother curses her two daughters. "I wish the sun or moon would take you." The girl held on to the bush, but when the sun grabbed her a part of the bush came off. The girl with the bush is in the moon, and she is the *eskin* of the moon. They draw her image on the boxes of their shamans.[30]

(33) *Buryat*. Same as (32). Both the bush and the bucket of water are there with the girl.[31]

(34) *Tungus*. The girl complains about hard work, and the moon raises her up with the bucket of water.

(35) *Gold*. A severe mother curses her daughter who is slow in coming home and says, "I hope the moon takes you."

(36) *Gilyaks*. A girl is in the moon with two buckets of water on her shoulders.[32]

(37) *Ainu*. A lazy boy refuses to obey his parents. The gods become angry and put him into the moon as a warning. They tell him to fetch water. He says to the doorpost, "You are lucky, you don't have to fetch water." He says the same to a small fish. But when he said the same to the salmon, he was grabbed and taken to the moon.[33]

(38) *Ainu*. Elder sister fetches water every night, and it is she who brings up her brother. One night she does not return. He questions the willowbush thicket who says, "Thy sister went up to the moon and got married to the man in the moon." He ascends to the moon on an arrow chain, and there he finds his sister who is now very beautiful and has a little daughter.

The Moon said, "I am a god, and I wanted to have thy sister. Therefore I took her who was handling the pails and the scoop to my house. There I married her, and we are living very happily. Take my child now and marry her, though she be miserable; then wilt thou at least have somebody to fetch thy water."[34]

(39) *British Columbia* (tribe not mentioned). One night a child of the chief class awoke and cried for water. "Mother, give me a drink," but the mother heeded not. The moon came down and gave the child a drink. Then they took an underground passage and went up to the sky. The

---

[30] *Globus,* LII, 1887, p. 252.

[31] Bastian, A., "Ein Besuch bei burjätischen Schamanen," *Geographische und ethnographische Bilder,* Berlin, 1873, p. 316; Peschel, O., "Über dem Mann im Monde," *Abhandlungen zur Erd- und Völkerkunde,* II, 1878, Leipzig, p. 329.

[32] Harva, Uno, "Die religiösen Vorstellungen der Altaischen Völker," *F. F. Communications,* 125, Helsinki, 1938, p. 185, quoting Russian sources.

[33] Batchelor, I., *The Ainu and Their Folklore,* London, 1901, pp. 67, 68.

[34] Pilsudski, B., "Ainu Folk Lore," *Journal of American Folk-Lore,* XXV, 1912, pp. 73, 74.

child is visible in the moon. In its hand it holds a round basket which it held when it went to sleep.[35]

(40) *Tlingit*. Two girls went to fetch water. One of them said, "The moon looks like my grandmother's labret." The one who said this was immediately cut to pieces. The other one is visible in the moon with a bucket of water.[36]

(41) *Tlingit*. The moon spots are two children who made fun of the moon when they went to fetch water. The moon grabbed them and there they are today.[37]

(42) *Kwakiutl*. A woman lived with her daughter in Tlamnos. The daughter was beautiful and the moon man decided to take her. He descended from the sky and asked the mother for water. She sent her daughter to the well but as soon as she stepped out of the house the moon eloped with her. The mother was sad and went to Nanete. The same thing happened with her second daughter.[38]

(43) *Awikyenoq*. A young girl was taking care of her brother while her mother had left to fish for *olachen*. The little boy kept screaming, so she covered him with her cloak and gave him a little bucket to play with. She told him, "The moon will get you if you don't behave." This is just what happened. The boy is still there in the moon with a bucket of water.[39]

(44) *Shuswap*. The moon was a handsome man; his wife's name was Wala and they had many children (the stars). They wandered and Wala followed her husband. She had a huge birchbark bucket on her back and a snow shovel in her hand. She used her shovel for filling her bucket with snow to melt it for water. This was the only kind of water they could get in wintertime. One night she pestered her husband, "Where are we going to camp tomorrow?" She repeated this question so often that the moon got angry and said, "On my face!" So that is where she is—on the moon's face with a birchbark bucket and a snow shovel.[40]

(45) *Thompson River*. The moon was formerly a handsome white-faced Indian. The stars were his friends. The Hare was his younger sister (according to others, the Frog). Once upon a time he called the Pleiades

[35] Harley, T., *Moon Lore*, London, 1885, p. 36, from *The Church Missionary Intelligencer*, 1865, p. 116.

[36] Swanton, I. R., "Social Condition, Beliefs and Linguistic Relationship of the Tlingit Indians," XXVI, Report, *Bureau of American Ethnology*, 1904/1905, p. 453.

[37] Krause, A., *Die Thlinkit Indianer*, Jena, 1885, pp. 270, 271.

[38] Boas, F., *Indianische Sagen von der Nordpazifischen Küste Amerikas*, Berlin, 1895, p. 191. (Also *Globus*, LIV, 1888, p. 14.)

[39] *Ibid.*, p. 217.

[40] Teit, T., "The Shuswap" (Jesup North Pacific Expedition, II, Part VII), *Mem. Amer. Mus. Nat. Hist.*, IV, 1909, p. 653.

and all the other stars to his house but only the star sister came. After the guests had arrived the moon sent his younger sister to fetch water. She took the water buckets and left. Soon she returned carrying a bucket in each hand. When she had entered she said to her brother, "There is no place for me to sit." Her elder brother replied, "Sit here on my face for there is no room elsewhere." His sister jumped on to his face. If the moon had not joked in this manner, he would now be much brighter for his sister is darkening his brightness. The woman may still be seen sitting on the moon's face holding her water buckets, and because the Pleiades gathered in his house they form a cluster up to this day and travel the way they are now. They are the moon's closest friends.[41]

(46) *Lillooet*. Three Frog sisters lived in a swamp. Snake and Beaver wished to marry one of the Frog girls. While she was *asleep* they crawled on her. She awoke and called them bad names. Beaver cried, but although his father asked him to stop crying because it would rain too much, he insisted. The swamp was flooded and the Frogs got cold. The water now ran in a regular stream. The Frogs swam downstream until they *reached a whirlpool which sucked them in and they descended to the house of the Moon*. The Moon invited them to sit by the fire. They refused. "We wish to sit there," pointing at him. They jumped on his face and the Frog's sisters are still there seated on his face.[42]

(47) *Shuswap*. The Moon had two wives, Wala and Tsitalka. The second wife had no children and she was the favorite. Wala said, "Where shall I go with my children?" The Moon got angry and said, "Sit on my eyes." She did and that is where she is now in the Moon. You can also see the man—his legs and the pack he is carrying on his back.[43]

(48) *Bilqula*. A husband sent his wife into the forest to gather berries. One day she met the Man in the Moon. She had intercourse with him and brought no berries home. When this happened several times her husband got suspicious. He went after her and saw what she was doing. He put his wife's dress on and went to meet the Moon Man. He cut his head off and then called all the people, but nobody recognized it. The Moon Man's father was the Sun. He came down in search of his son. He was terribly angry and made a conflagration. All human beings perished; the rivers were dry. Only the mistress of the Moon Man survived. She took a bucket and dipped it into the water. When the fire had dried up all the other

[41] Teit, T., "Traditions of the Thompson River Indians of British Columbia," *Mem. Am. F. L. S.*, VI, 1898, pp. 91, 92.

[42] Teit, T., "Traditions of the Lillooet Indians of British Columbia," *Journal of American Folk-Lore*, XXV, 1912, pp. 298, 299.

[43] Boas, F., *Indianische Sagen*, p. 15. This latter trait is like the Man in the Moon in Europe with faggots on his back. Dähnhardt, O., *Natursagen*, 1907; Roscher, *Selene und Verwandtes*, Leipzig, 1890, p. 183.

waters she poured it out and there were many little fish in it which grew and multiplied quickly.[44]

(49) *Haida.* A man called Eethlinga is visible in the Moon with his bucket of water and the salal-bush he was hanging onto when he got pulled up by the Moon. In clear weather you can see him in the full. Rain comes when he pours the water from his bucket.[45]

(50) *Haida.* A woman used to point her fingers at a certain star as a sign of contempt for which she was taken up to a house in the sky and hung in the smoke hole. Her brothers made an image of her, hung it in her place and thus got her back. But then she pointed at the Moon and was carried up there with the bucket of water she was carrying and she held on to the salal bushes in order to stop herself.[46]

(51) *Ceram.* There was a girl called Dabike. At her first menstruation she went into the menstrual hut. Three days later she came out and went to a well to wash her sarong. In the water she saw a ray of the Sun. She got frightened and called the people, "I see something, maybe it is the Sun." But they saw nothing. This was repeated three times.

The fourth time the Sun came he got hold of Dabike. He pulled her legs and dragged her down into the earth. She disappeared altogether. A voice was heard, "I am the Sun and my name is Tuale. In three days you shall see your child in the sky."

Three days later they saw Dabike, the Moon.[47]

(52) *Vaitupu, Polynesia.* There is a little boy called Terete in the Moon. His parents took him in a fit of crying to look at the rising moon. He was quiet directly. They concluded that he wished to go there and so his father went off one morning in a canoe and handed him in as the moon was rising (boat instead of bucket of water).[48]

(53) *Nanumea, Polynesia.* A little boy called Tapirinoko cried to go to the Sun. His father took him in a canoe to the Sun as it was rising, but the boy shrank back—it was too hot. Then he cried to be taken to the Moon and there it was too cold. But the Moon persuaded him to stay, so there he is.[49]

(54) *Pelau.* A man left home to fish (usually "carrying water"). His wife was angry and, raising her arms toward the moon, she said, "Moon, take your child." But when the Moon really descended and demanded the

[44] Boas, F., *Indianische Sagen,* p. 247.

[45] Niblack, A. P., *The Coast Indians of Southern Alaska and Northern British Columbia,* 1890, p. 323.

[46] Swanton, F., "Contributions to the Ethnology of the Haida," *Jesup North Pacific Expedition,* V, 1905, pp. 217, 218; Boas, F., *Tsimshian Texts,* p. 86.

[47] Jensen, A. E., *Hainuwele,* Frankfurt am Main, 1939, p. 53.

[48] Turner, G., *Samoa a Hundred Years Ago,* London, 1884, p. 284.

[49] *Ibid.,* p. 292.

child, she was frightened and asked him to wait till her husband was back. All three are visible in the moon.[50]

(55) *Maori*. Rona fell into a well. In falling he tried to hold on to a tree. This is how we see him in the moon.[51]

(56) The *Maori* say, "Remember what happened to Rona because she cursed the Moon." Rona went for water on a moonlit night. But just as she was about to bend down, the moon disappeared behind a cloud and she stumbled and fell. "Damned Moon," she said, "can't you give light?" The Moon got angry, came down from the sky, and chased her. She climbed up a tree that grew near the river, but the Moon dug up the tree by its roots and took woman and tree up to the Moon.[52]

(57) *Maori*. In ancient times, before the Moon lit the sky, Rona went to get water from a lake. He stumbled and fell in the dark and he was lame so that he could not walk home. While he was in this situation, he felt that the Moon was attacking him. He tried to escape by climbing up a tree, but this was in vain because the Moon dug the tree out, and there he is today hanging on to the tree in the Moon.[53]

(58) *Maori*. Rona went with several buckets to get water and cursed the Moon for not giving light (this was the first curse). She was punished by being raised into the Moon. There she is with several buckets of water. They also say that Rona and her sister Tangarou-a-roto are the wives of the Moon.[54]

(59) *Maori, Rarawa tribe*. Rona is a woman. She wants water for the oven where she is cooking for the family. Her name means tied or strangled. She stumbled in the dark and cursed the Moon. The calabash and a ngaio tree (*Myoporum laetum*) which she held for protection and the rocks near to which the tree was growing are all visible at full moon.[55]

(60) *Maori Nga-ti hau*. An ancestor called Rona was very thirsty. All the little brooks near his home were dry so he had to go further to get water. It was dark so he wanted to wait till the Moon rose. "When will the cooked-headed Moon shine?" [Cooked head is a terrible insult] he said.

50 Bastian, A., "Die Religion der Pelauer," *Allerlei aus Volks- und Menschenkunde,* Berlin, 1888, p. 58.

51 de Rienzi, D., *Ozeanien.*

52 Waitz, G., *Anthropologie der Naturvölker,* VI, Leipzig, 1872, pp. 89, 90; Grey, G., *Proverbial and Popular Sayings of the Ancestors of the New Zealand Race,* Capetown, 1857, p. 50; Davis, C. O., *Maori Mementos,* Auckland, 1855, p. 165.

53 Taylor, R., *Te ika a Maui, or New Zealand and Its Inhabitants,* London, 1855, p. 95; cf. Polack, I. S., *Manners and Customs of the New Zealanders,* London, 1840, pp. 244, 245.

54 Best, E., "Notes on Maori Mythology," *Journal of the Polynesian Society,* VIII, pp. 100, 101.

55 White, J., *The Ancient History of the Maori, His Mythology and Traditions,* Wellington, 1887, II, p. 20.

The Moon drew him up with his calabashes and a ngaio tree he had taken hold of.[56]

(61) *Nga-i-tahu Maori*. Rona is the ruler of Sun and Moon. Rona eats the Moon, and the Moon eats Rona. When both are exhausted, they bathe in the "Waiora Tane" (living water of Tane) and are rejuvenated. Rona and Tu-raki (Garb of Heaven) are both rulers of the Moon.[57]

(62) *Maori*. Rona was a lazy man. He quarreled with his wife Hine horo-matai (the daughter who swallows all she obtains without asking). A god called Hoka (Screen) descended from the sky to smash her house to bits. One day when she was in her boat with her children, Rona called her because he wanted to beat her. Hoka beat Rona. The children got very thirsty. Hine horo-matai went with her two calabashes to get water for them, but as she advanced the water dried up. Finally when she was close to the moon, she threw one of her calabashes at it (visible in the moon). Her husband chased her; she escaped into the Sun and then to the Moon and then back home. There she set fire to her house and died in the fire with her children. Rona is in the Moon looking in vain for wife and children.

(63) *Nga i tahu Maori*. Rona is in a boat on the sea. His wife has an affair with a god called Hoka. He catches them and cuts a piece of Hoka's flesh off and makes her eat it. He sends her to get water, but as she advances with her children the water recedes. She throws the two children into the water. Rona rescues them in his boat. Finally they all perish in the fire, as above, excepting Rona. He is determined to go to the Sun, but not being able to get near it he joined himself to the Moon and began at once to eat the Moon and this he continued until the Moon was all consumed.[58]

(64) *Nga-puhi Maori*. Rona is a woman. The name means "To confine with cords." The Moon is shining. She goes to get food for her children. Stumbling, curse ("Cooked-headed Moon"). Visible in the Moon "with ngaio tree and gourd."[59]

Diffusion or Independent Origin

If we look at these stories in an attempt to find out something about their history, we first distinguish a group of narratives to be called henceforth "the Edda stories."

In most of these stories we find two people in the Moon with a bucket of water (1, 4, 6, 7, 8). In (2) it is only a baby and in (3) a girl and a boy, in (4) a man and his shadow, in (9) pitch (pitch is substituted for

---

[56] *Ibid.*, II, p. 21.
[58] White, *op. cit.*, II, pp. 23–26.
[57] *Loc. cit.*
[59] *Ibid.*, II, p. 26.

water) the aim being to extinguish the light, the purpose stealing. This we find also in (10) and (13, 15, 16). Some of these "pitch" variants are on the fringe of Ural-Altaian people, and as they agree so well with the general "Man in the Moon" type of European folklore,[60] we may well assume that they are of Germanic origin. Ural-Altaian people have a recognizable "water-carrier" story of their own. In these stories we find a girl as the heroine and three elements that are absent in the Germanic version: (a) the erotic moon as wooer (11, 17, 18, 24, 25, 28), (b) the evil stepmother or hard work (20, 21, 22, 24, 25, 26, 28, 32), (c) the tree or bush that she held on to (11, 24, 25, 26, 32, 33, 38, 49, 50).

Two stories should be mentioned here from Estonia (12) and Livland (19). In these the girl either derisively shows her buttocks to the Moon or vaunts the beauty of her buttocks as compared to the Moon. Freud interpreted a dream of his patient who sees the Moon reflected in water in this sense, "la lune" being a French colloquialism for the buttocks.[61]

One story (18) certainly shows traces of literary adaptation and instead of the Moon we have the Pleiades. It is significant, however, that the sky ascent has been dreamed by the king and queen.

(37) and (38)—The Ainu versions are peculiar. They contain the conflict with the parents, but it is the children who are to blame, not the parents. The erotic motive reappears with the peculiar ending of a double marriage with the Moon. The story is probably derived from Asia.

The American versions are all in the Northwest. They might be of independent origin, or they might be imported from Asia. The marriage motive reappears in (42, 44, 45, 47), but the stepmother motive is absent. The motive of sacrilege, i.e., offending the Moon by staring, saying something or a defiant gesture (12, 14, 19, 27) recurs here (40, 50). The derisive exclamation attributed to the Moon (44, 46, 47) may be a derivative of this motive. Hanging on to a bush reappears as a trait added to the bucket of water (49, 50). This would tip the scales in favor of an American origin. It is noteworthy that in (39) the story starts with a thirsty child and a child that is going to sleep. The underground passage (39) and the descent to the Moon in a whirlpool (46) probably mean the same thing.

Finally we have the New Zealand version. Rona, the hero or heroine is sometimes male, sometimes female. We find the tree or bush added to the bucket of water—a prominent trait of the Asiatic versions in (56, 57, 58, 61, 64). Sacrilege occurs in (57, 59, 61, 64). On the whole I would be disposed to assume diffusion from somewhere in Asia although it is a far

[60] Dähnhardt, *Natursagen*, 1907, I, pp. 254–256; Harley, *op. cit.*, pp. 5–53.
[61] Freud, S., *Gesammelte Schriften*, III, p. 120.

cry from New Zealand to the Ural-Altaic versions. New traits of interest are: the water is needed for quenching thirst (59, 62), the rival god (62, 63), being in a boat (62, 63), the fire (62, 63). The cannibal motive (62, 63)[62] recalls Ural-Altaic versions (30, 31). Falling into a well (55) is like the descent into a whirlpool (46). The child offered to the Moon (52, 53, 54) is new and significant.

There are other reasons that favor the assumption of diffusion from Asia to New Zealand. Anderson has shown a similar case of a related story connecting Mongols, Tartars, Buryats with Palau. God wishes to make human beings immortal and dispatches a bird to bring them the water of life, but through the intervention of another bird the water gets spilt on a tree, and the tree gets the benefit of it instead of mankind.[63] In Tahiti the Moon was regarded as the wife of the Sun or a beautiful land in which the Aoatree grows.[64] By bathing in the life-giving water of Tane the Moon achieves immortality in Hawaii.[65] In India the Soma is closely connected with the Moon. The Soma is the creeper called *Asclepias acida* or *Barcostemma viminalis*. According to other authorities it is *Sarcostemma intermedium*. It has a milky juice. Moreover, when they drink it, they mix it with grain and milk.[66] In Vedic times the Moon was regarded as a receptacle filled with Soma, the mythical draught of immortality.[67] The Moon grows to give sustenance to the gods, it is a drop, a well, an ocean full of food for the gods.[68] For half a month the moon is the food of the gods, in the other half it feeds the ancestors.[69] In Polynesia the stars are the ancestors and their food is the moon. The moon is the abode of the souls of dead chiefs.[70] Moreover, Tahu, the demon, who swallows the Moon when there is an eclipse and who owes his immortality to the Amrita contained in the moon, is the patron god of the fire walkers.[71] In Tonga it is the Moon goddess Hina.[72] The Ava tree and the water of life (above) correspond to the Soma in the moon. In Mina-

---

[62] Omnivorous woman in (61).

[63] Anderson, W., "Ein sonderbarer Fall von Sagenverwandtschaft," *Mitra*, 1914, pp. 37–40; *idem*, "Der auf Bäume verschüttete Unsterblichkeitstrank," *Zeitschrift für Ethnologie*, LII/LIII, 1921, pp. 430–433.

[64] Ellis, W., *Polynesian Researches*, II, 1830, p. 415.

[65] Westervelt, W. D., *Legends of Maui*, Honolulu, 1910, p. 134.

[66] Hillebrandt, A., *Vedische Mythologie*, Breslau, 1891, I, pp. 4–14.

[67] *Ibid.*, I, pp. 300–319.

[68] *Ibid.*, I, p. 275.

[69] *Ibid.*, I, p. 292.

[70] Waitz, T., *Anthropologie der Naturvölker*, 1870, V, Part 2, p. 197; Turner, G., *Nineteen Years in Polynesia*, 1861, pp. 529–531.

[71] Crooke, W., *The Popular Religion and Folklore of Northern India*, 1896, I, p. 19.

[72] Westervelt, W. D., *Legends of Maui*, Honolulu, 1910, p. 169.

hasa the Waringin tree is sacred (*Ficus benjamina*).[73] In the moon smoke is visible that looks like this tree or the tree itself is supposed to grow in the moon. In Timor, a man sits under a tree in the moon. He is spinning a yarn that keeps the world in its place.[74] The Mantra in Malacca say that the dark spots in the moon are a tree beneath which sits the Moon man who is the enemy of mankind and who is continually knotting strings together to make nooses wherewith to catch them, but some mice bite through the strings and that is why he does not succeed.[75] In Mentawei the Moon man wants to come down to earth on a rope, the mice prevent him by gnawing the rope off.[76] In another version the old man becomes the protector of mankind. He keeps chopping off the plants which would grow up to the sky and thereby prevents a catastrophy, namely, the closing up of earth and sky. He not only cuts the shoots but also eats them. The sky is a great pot suspended by a string. Should the string break everything would be crushed.[77] The Besisi see fruit trees in the moon, the nourishment of the deceased. They are protected against the attacks of a tiger by the moon ancestor Gaffer Enkok.[78] In Palau the people in the moon eat the oranges that grow on a tree.[79] In Naaru a girl climbs into the moon on a tree.[80] In Nuguria and other small islands on the fringe of Melanesia Mataga, the spirit of the moon is seated there making a cord out of the bark of the coco palm.[81] In Timor an old woman is making clothes in the moon.[82] In Samoa the moon was inhabited by Sina and her child. She was busy one evening with mallet in hand beating out on a board of the paper mulberry with which to make native cloth. It was during a *time of famine*. The moon was just rising and reminded her of a great breadfruit, looking up to it she said, "Why cannot you come down and let my child have a bit of you?" The moon was indignant at the thought of being eaten,[83] came down and took up her child, board, mallet and all. They are all visible in the full moon.[84]

73 Bastian, A., *Indonesien, Molukken,* I, p. 102; Sumatra, III. Cf. also Bastian, *Reisen im indischen Archipel,* Leipzig, 1866–1871, p. 479.

74 Wilken, *Verspreide Geschriften,* 1912, III, p. 165, IV, p. 406.

75 Skeat, W. W. and Blagden, Ch. O., *Pagan Races of the Malay Peninsula,* 1906, II, p. 319.

76 Maass, A., *Bei liebenswürdigen Wilden,* Berlin, 1902, p. 93.

77 Skeat and Blagden, *op. cit.,* II, p. 320.

78 *Idem,* II, pp. 298–300.

79 Bastian, *Indonesien: Die Molukken,* I, p. 47, quoting Kubary.

80 Hambruch, P., *Nauru,* 1914, I, p. 435.

81 Parkinson, R., *Dreissing Jahre in der Südsee,* Stuttgart, 1907, p. 525; *idem,* "Nachträge zur Ethnographie der Ontong-Java-Inseln," *Internationales Archiv für Ethnographie,* XI, 1898, p. 196.

82 Bastian, *Inselgruppen in Ozeanien,* Berlin, 1883, p. 38.

83 Cf. above "cooked-headed moon."

84 Turner, *Samoa, A Hundred Years Ago,* London, 1884, p. 203.

The details are important. The moon looks like a breadfruit in Tahiti. Hina, the moon conceives the breadfruit trees of Tangaroa and Uro is born. In Mangaia Ina is in the moon, in a clear night you can see her there with her *never-failing oven of food,* her tongs of a split cocoanut branch to enable her to adjust the live coals without burning her fingers.

Ina makes resplendent cloth, i.e., the clouds the great stones needed for the tapa are also visible. As soon as her tapa is well beaten she stretches it out to dry the upper part of the blue sky.[85] According to another Samoan story two young men are in the moon, one climbed up on a tree, the other on smoke.[86] We saw above that in the Moluccas the smoke in the moon is shaped like a tree. The tapa is paralleled in Upper India where the dark spots of the moon represent an old woman working on her spinning wheel.[87]

By saying that there is a remarkable degree of uniformity in some of these etiological myths and that this uniformity is probably due to common origin we have not solved the problem of what that common origin might be. The school which interprets these images as derived from nature[88] reminds one forcibly of the dialogue between Hamlet and Polonius.

> Hamlet: "Do you see yonder cloud that's almost in shape of a camel?
> Polonius: By the mass it's like a camel indeed.
> Hamlet: Me thinks it is like a weasel.
> Polonius: Very like a weasel.
> Hamlet: Or like a whale?
> Polonius: Very like a whale."
>
> (*Hamlet* III, Scene 2.)

In other words the spots can be man or woman or child or bucket or frog or anything and it is the story that determines what we see in it and not the spots themselves. In (34) a child awakes and cries for water. Mother refuses to give the child a drink—the child falls asleep again and dreams (this we insert by way of interpretation) that it goes up to the moon through an underground passage (basic dream). It is still holding the basket it held when it went to sleep. In (16) we are told that a couple cannot sleep because of the moon and therefore goes toward the moon, in (18) it is represented as a dream, in (26) we find mortals gazing at the moon. We conjecture that this nocturnal event is again based on a

85 Gill, W. W., *Myths and Songs of the South Pacific,* London, 1876, pp. 45, 46.
86 Turner, *op. cit.,* p. 205.
87 Crooke, W., *The Popular Religion and Folk-Lore of Northern India,* 1896, I, p. 14.
88 Cf. Ehrenreich, P., *Die Mythen und Legenden der südamerikanischen Urvölker,* 1905, p. 69; Kunike, H., "Amerikanische und Asiatische Mondbilder," *Mythologische Bibliothek,* VIII, 4, p. 30.

dream experience or on dreaming and sleepwalking called *Mondsucht* in German. Sadger has shown that these sleepwalkers, in the two cases analyzed, were really walking in their sleep looking for the toilet because they had to urinate. Sleepwalking is therefore very similar to the urethral awakening dream. A hysterical patient relates how in her childhood she would get out of bed and look for the nightchamber, but being unable to find it in her sleep she would urinate on the floor.[89] She would also open the window or door and gaze at the moon.[90] At the age of four or five she had fantasies of going up to the moon. Later she imagined that the moon was paradise where boys and girls could go naked and indulged in free love.[91]

A male patient also reports about getting up in moonlit nights and urinating in a box or in the shoes of a friend.[92]

According to Ellis, "The actions carried out in the somnambulistic condition are not usually co-ordinated with the action of higher emotions: thus a young woman was impelled by a distended bladder while still asleep to get out of bed and proceeded to carry out the suggested action, but without further precaution on to the floor."[93] It is safe to assume that the flood that arises from crying in (41) is really a urethral flood and that our stories are intrinsically related to flood myths. The receding water (56) would be a "representation by the opposite" of the increasing volume of water in the flood myths. This type of story is also suggested by the versions in which we find the moon hero or heroine in a boat with children.

In a Tshimshian story a man called "the only seeing fire" wants to go up to the moon in order to be made beautiful and healthy. He accomplishes this by shooting one arrow after the other up into the sky. Each arrow fits into the other (Arrow chain). The moon gives him the following message: "If human beings continue to do evil things I shall kill them. They should not gaze at the moon when they urinate into the river."[94]

According to a myth of the Gogia Pardhan Bhagavan (Creator) wanted to urinate. There was nowhere for him to do it for he would drown the whole earth. But as he could wait no longer he got a great bamboo, cut the top and bottom and urinated into it. In the Underworld there was a lake called Kulitpar. Bhagavan closed the bamboo and put it there.

[89] Sadger, I., "Nachtwandeln und Mondsucht," *Schriften zur angewandten Seelenkunde,* XVI, 1914, p. 8.

[90] *Ibid.,* p. 20.   [91] *Ibid.,* p. 27.

[92] *Ibid.,* p. 37.

[93] Ellis, H., *The World of Dreams,* London, 1911, p. 96.

[94] Boas, *Indianische Sagen,* p. 279.

In that place where the bamboo full of Bhagavan's urine was put Rawan, Maharawan and Madodro were born. The spangle from Bhagavan's forehead fell into the urine and turned into the Sun and Moon.[95]

That dreams and the moon should have something to do with each other is *a priori* probable. Endymion, beloved by the moon goddess Selene, receives two gifts from Zeus, eternal youth and eternal sleep. While asleep he has intercourse with Selene.[96]

The dream character of this myth is quite obvious. The Greeks, who identified Pan with Ephialtes, the demon of the nightmare,[97] also told the story about Pan seducing Selene, or eloping with Selene.[98] In Aztec mythology the women who die in childbed, carry the crescent in their nose and cause nightmares.[99] In Japan the moon god is Tonki Yomi and Yume or Yome is the word for dream.[100]

We assume that our tales are (a) based on dreams, and (b) that the type of dream that evolves into this story is the vesical awakening dream.

Coitus and birth, as Rank has shown, are the contributions of the unconscious to the vesical dream. The amorous disposition of the moon is evident in several stories, in some we find dream elements that look like intrauterine regression or the basic dream. Thus we find the underground passage in (39) and the whirlpool that takes the frog down into the moon house in (46). There is reason to assume that the bucket containing the water is originally not carried by the children but that the children are in the vessel, i.e., in the womb. The frog in the moon or the moon as a frog is a parallel story to our water carriers in the moon. The Arapaho also tell the story of the frog in or on the moon. It represents the menstrual flow of the woman. "The frog is like a pregnant woman," and it symbolizes the growth of mankind. What is visible in the moon are the traces of the first menstruation."[101] According to the Ute there is a frog in the moon, or the moon was originally a frog.[102] In Mexican hieroglyphics the moon is represented by a snail because human beings come out of their mother the way a snail comes out of its shell. In Mayan inscriptions the moon god is represented by an old, bald-headed god in a

95 Elwin, V., *Myths of Middle India*. London, 1949, p. 60.

96 *Roscher's Lexikon,* "Endymion."

97 Roscher, W. H., *Ephialtes,* XX, Abh. d. phil-hist. Classe der Königl. Sächs. Ak. d. Wiss., Leipzig, 1900, No. II, p. 67.

98 *Idem, Selene und Verwandtes,* Leipzig, 1890, pp. 4, 148.

99 Kunike, H., "Sonne, Mond und Sterne im alten Mexiko," *Zeitschrift für Ethnologie,* 1911, p. 928.

100 Florenz, K., *Japanische Mythologie,* 1901, p. 27.

101 Dorsey, G. A., *The Arapaho Sun Dance,* 1903, pp. 175, 212.

102 Powell, I. W., "Sketch of the Mythology of the North Indians," *Bureau of Am. Ethn. Report,* I, Washington, D.C., 1881, p. 467.

tortoise shell.[103] The tortoise man seen by the Teton in the moon[104] may be connected with all this. Among some tribes the frog is the animal that devours the moon at the eclipse. In a Luiseno myth the moon is killed by the magic of Wahawut, the frog who is described either as an ugly or as a beautiful woman.[105] According to the Takelma frogs and lizards devour the moon when she is waning but she rises again as the new moon.[106]

According to the Ipurina in Brazil the spots on the moon are a toad[107] and the Karaja have the same explanation.[108]

The Yuchi say in an eclipse the toad starts to eat the moon. He gets big and the moon diminishes. They frighten the toad away with noise and then the moon gets big again.[109] A Maidu myth is of interest although the Frog is opposed by the Sun instead of the Moon. Sun kills Frog's children and Frog sets out in pursuit. Sun made a patch of willow grow up behind her so that anyone who followed would stop to pick some. The old woman forgot what she had come for and picked willows. Then she remembers and starts out in pursuit once more. Frog swallows Sun. But Sun grows larger and bursts Frog in two.[110] The toad swallows both Sun and Moon, that is an eclipse according to the Maidu and Cherokee.[111]

Frog or toad occur in connection with the moon in other areas. In Buin we are told how two big chiefs arranged a feast in the hills of the ghosts. When the toad arrived and saw how the others were all decorated and looked fine, she died of envy and this is how death first came into the world. *The toad came from the moon, from the sleeping place in the moon.* The chief called Kogituku (i.e., he who drives away) who is the son of the toad and lives in the halls of the moon. When the toad appears as morning-star, they burn the dead.[112]

In China we find the toad again in the moon. The beautiful fairy

103 Loewenthal, I., "Zur Mythologie des jungen Helden und des Feuerbringers," *Zeitschrift für Ethnologie*, L, 1918, p. 48; Seler, B., "Die Tierbilder der mexikanischen und der Maya Handschriften," *Zeitschrift für Ethnologie*, XLII, 1910, pp. 50, 284.

104 Dorsey, J. O., "A Study of Siouan Cults," *Bureau of Am. Eth. Annual Report,* XI, p. 467.

105 Du Bois, "The Religion of the Luiseno Indians of Southern California," *Univ. Cal. Publ. in Am. Arch. and Ethn.,* VIII, 1908, p. 132.

106 Sapir, E., "Takelma Texts," *Univ. Penna. Anthr. Publ.,* II, No. 1, Philadelphia, 1909, p. 197.

107 Ehrenreich, P., "Beiträge zur Völkerkunde Brasiliens," *Mitteilungen für Völkerkunde,* Berlin, 1891, p. 45.

108 Krause, F., *In den Wildnissen Brasiliens,* Leipzig, 1911, p. 339.

109 Speck, Frank G., "Ethnology of the Yuchi Indians," *Univ. Penns. Publ.,* Vol. I, No. 1, 1909, p. 110.

110 Dixon, R. B., "Maidu Myths," *Bull. Am. Mus. Nat. Hist.,* XVII, 1902, pp. 77, 78.

111 *Ibid.,* XVI, 1901, p. 2; Mooney, J., "Myths of the Cherokee," *Ann. Rep. Bureau Am. Ethn.,* XIX, 1900, p. 257.

112 Thurnwald, R., *Forschungen auf den Salomo Inseln und dem Bismarck Archipel,* I, Berlin, 1912, p. 315.

of the moon sometimes appears in the form of a toad.[113] Mongols and Kalmuks see fish and frogs in the moon.[114] The Chinese toad in the moon may be used to explain the spots or the eclipse.[115]

The spots are also explained as representing menstruation. The Arapaho see in the moon either the toad as a pregnant woman or the marks of the first menstruation. "The first menstruation happened with the woman who eloped with the moon by their connection. The flow or menstruation means the child. The sweat water is the blood shed by the woman."[116] In the New Hebrides according to Seniang tradition the moon is closely associated with childbirth. The marks on its surface are the afterbirth and at the first full moon after delivery people will point at it and say, "Look, there is the placenta."[117]

I obtained the following story in the village of Sipupu on Normanby Island: There was an old witch who lived with her granddaughter. They went to the garden to drive the birds away. She took her vulva and put it on the top of her head so that it gave light. All the others were astonished. They went to sleep (the witch and her granddaughter) and then they came again before daybreak with their light. The other people took the light away. She was delivered of a child and they performed the smoking ritual for her. As soon as her son was born he had intercourse with his mother while her blood was still flowing. The child went up and became the moon. When women are menstruating they are having intercourse with the moon and men stay away from them. The moon is also regarded as the light itself, as the *kaya* kept by witches in their vulva.[118]

The Kiwai have a similar myth: Ganumi was an infant when his mother became pregnant again. This turned her milk so he did not like it. She gave Ganumi the blood that had been stained by her second delivery to lie upon. The blood changed him into a red parrot.

The red parrot flew away and landed on a sago tree over a water-hole where it saw its reflection in the water.

Girls came to draw water and one of them called Gebae saw the reflection of the parrot. She dove, but she caught nothing. Then they saw the real bird, caught it and put it in a basket. At night he became a man,

---

[113] Wilhelm, R., *Chinesische Volksmärchen*, Jena, 1913, p. 390.

[114] Bergmann, B., *Nomadische Streifereien unter den Kalmücken*, Riga, 1804, III, p. 204.

[115] de Groot, J. J. M., "Les Fêtes anuellement célébrées à Emoui," *Annales du Musée Guimet*, XXII, Paris, 1886, p. 493.

[116] Dorsey, *The Arapaho Sun Dance*, 1903, p. 173.

[117] Deacon, A. B., *Malekula: A Vanishing People in the New Hebrides*, London, 1934, p. 235.

[118] Cf. Róheim, "Witches of Normanby Island," *Oceania*, XVIII, 1948, p. 280.

had connection with Gebae and in the morning he became a bird again. Gebae became pregnant and the parrot (Ganumi) flew away.

The girl's parents and other people wanted to kill him. He called for his mother and she tried to get hold of him in order to hide him in her basket. She unfastened the string with which her grass petticoat was tied on and threw one end up to Ganumi but it was too short. Then she did the same thing with the navel cord which she had preserved since his birth. Genumi now told his mother that he was the moon. Then he said, "You throw that to me." She flung one end of the navel cord up to him, holding the other tightly in her hand. She meant to draw him down from the tree and to put him in her basket. But he gave a pull to the cord, the tree bent toward his mother and the next moment he hurled his mother up to the sky and hoisted himself up after her. She caught hold of him and put him in her basket and there she is still carrying him in the sky.

"When Ganumi's face peeps out a little from his mother's basket he appears as the new moon and gradually more and more of his face will appear. Sometimes the mother hides the basket behind her and then the moon cannot be seen at all. The mother herself is invisible except her fingers which are sometimes outlined against Ganumi's face and they are the spots in the moon. *Ganumi married his own mother.*"

The tale is generally known and the conversation held between the bird and the girl is often quoted between lovers.[119]

In this myth we have women who go to draw water as in the story of the water carriers in the moon. The moon is first identified with a frustrated infant, then at the end with an infant in *utero* for the basket of his mother, especially since it is combined with the navel cord, can mean nothing else. The moon or the man in the moon is clearly in the intrauterine situation. Considering what we have found about dream symbolism it is doubly significant to observe that in the intrauterine situation he can also be having intercourse with his mother.

Other myths of the Kiwai identify the moon man with heroes of the Moses, Oedipus, Romulus type, i.e., the child floating on the water.

An old married couple have a child and people make them ashamed. The child Ganumi was put in a bowl and the bowl floated on the water. A girl named Gebae had born a child with bad sores. When the basin came floating in she picked Ganumi up and let her own child drown.

"Once after seeing two girls with their petticoats in disorder, Ganumi, who was still a little boy, cried, 'Mother, I want that red thing.'"

119 Landtman, G., "The Folk-Tales of the Kiwai Papuans," *Acta Societatis Scientiarum Fennicae Tomus*, XLVII, Helsingfors, 1917, pp. 484–486.

Red Flowers, fruit, etc., he rejects. Finally he was put to sleep between the two girls but he was too small for intercourse. Therefore they were dissatisfied with him and put him on top of a sago palm. A red-feathered bird named *wiowio* (cf. his mother's name in another version) alighted above him and her droppings made him grow feathers so that he became a wiowio bird.

Now all the girls wanted him but he only yielded to Gebae, his foster mother. Then because he was ashamed at the idea of having slept with his mother he jumped into the water and hid for a month among the water spirits. When he came home all the women rejected him, they all told him to go to his mother. One night he and his mother ran away into the bush and then climbed up into the sky by means of Ganumi's navel cord (the foster mother idea is here forgotten).[120]

There are several other versions. In one of these the first coitus happens when he goes with his mother to fetch water and his mother catches sight of his penis. *Finally he went and caught a large shark and taking out the intestines turned the fish into a canoe.* He cut off the tail and turned it into a paddle. He wanted to get up to heaven and for this purpose he was trying to find the place where *sky and earth meet.* Then he used a porpoise as his canoe. Finally he stood up on the porpoise and with the help of the elastic dorsal fin jumped up into heaven. In another story he travels *in a fish* called *kasi* and the fish finally throws him up on the shore. He goes up to the sky with his mother by means of his navel cord.

In another story the moon wants only girls with fine round breasts.[121]

A brief version of this myth is given by Beaver. According to the Wadaba, Sagome is the Man in the Moon. When he grew up he fell in love with his mother but she refused. Sagome became annoyed and climbed up a sago palm to the moon. As he climbed the tree became longer and longer till it reached the moon.[122]

The Mono Alu have a somewhat confused version because it does not, at least ostensibly, explain the origin of the Man in the Moon.

The children went to wash in the river and they saw the reflection of a karakai fruit. They could not get it by diving for it, till finally they looked up and saw an old woman who was eating the fruit. They picked a lot of fruit for her but she kept eating, finally her belly swelled and she died. They cut out her cunnus and took it away to an old man. "O grandfather! Cook our food," they said. But he ate it himself although she was *loa* (taboo) to him. When the children reproach him for this, he wants

120 *Ibid.*, p. 487.
121 *Ibid.*, pp. 488, 489.
122 Beaver, W. N., *Unexplored New Guinea,* London, 1920, pp. 150, 151.

to kill them. They climb up various trees, he fells the trees with his axe. Murila, the Man in the Moon, lets his rope down and they climb up to him on the rope. But a bird brings the children back and the old man eats them.[123]

I think we are justified in assuming that the buckets or other receptacles in the moon symbolize the uterus. The children who carry the vessels were originally carried by or in the vessels.

In Mexican hieroglyphics the moon appears as a vessel made of bones filled with water.[124] The Arapaho who also see the symbols of the toad and of pregnancy in the moon also talk of a kettle in the moon.[125] According to the Cegiha the moon is a woman with a kettle on her arm.[126]

The first thing these stories teach us is that the light on the firmament, i.e., the moon is the vulva. The basket or any other receptacle is the same because the moon man is in it and because it is tied to his mother by the navel cord. The journey of the hero in the shark (Sun God in the Fish as Frobenius[127] called it) is again the intrauterine situation. The moon as the child in the floating bowl again links moon myths and flood myths. Fetching water occurs in these myths as in the stories about the water carriers in the moon. The bird transformation suggests the flying or basic dream.

We assume that the nucleus of the myth was a waking dream. The somatic stimulus in this dream was thirst and vesical pressure. But there is always a conflict between falling asleep and awakening. The tendency to go on sleeping would be represented by uterine regression, symbolized in this case by the moon.

And the bush? The hanging on to the bush is what we have seen in our patients, anxiety, holding on to the state of being awake, resistance to falling asleep.

A child is thirsty and wants to urinate. It dreams that it goes to get water in a basket, that it wades in water, or pours it or is in a boat and then it is in the moon (i.e., in mother).

In Hungarian folk belief a bird called Markaláb eats the moon (Szeged). The bird is supposed to be like a parrot. "When it has digested

[123] Wheeler, G. C., *Mono Alu Folklore,* London, 1926, pp. 175–178.
[124] Seler, E., *Gesammelte Abhandlungen,* I, p. 436, III, pp. 249, 315, 318, 337, 489, 490.
[125] Mooney, J., "The Ghost Dance Religion," *Bureau Am. Ethn.,* XIII, Report 1896, p. 1006.
[126] Dorsey, "The Cegiha Language," *Contributions to North American Ethnology,* VI, 1890, p. 328.
[127] Frobenius L., *Zeitalter des Sonnengottes,* Berlin, 1904.

the light, it regurgitates it like a dove feeding its young from its own mouth."[128] According to another version the animal that is eating the moon is a poodle or lion. This is what the people of Göcsej believe.[129] If these monsters could finish up the moon that would be the end of the world. If you pour water into a white plate you can see wolves in it, they are biting the moon.[130]

Philology soon solves the riddle regarding the meaning of the word Markoláb. At Kassa a person who is of evil disposition and can turn into a wolf is called a "varkolács."[131] At Gernyeszeg they hurry to baptize the children because if they die without baptism they will eat the moon.[132] A dragon eats the sun at Kalotaszeg, but at Aranyosszék and Kalotaszeg both sun and moon are also eaten by the spirits of unbaptized children.[133] The Croats believe that the werewolf is the ghost of an unbaptized child.[134] The Palóc in Northern Hungary call a child that is unbaptized "wolf," after baptism "lamb." The Russians (Huzuls) in Máramaros say that the moon is inhabited by wolves who keep eating it till nothing is left. Then the moon somehow revives and then they eat it again.[135] The Rumanians say that the *vercolaci* are wolves in the moon who eat the moon in the eclipse.[136] However, besides being wolves in the moon they are also ghosts of children who died without baptism.[137] According to Serbians the *vukodlak* is a kind of vampire. It goes to the living to suck their blood and it leaves its grave at *full moon*.[138] Russian incantations

---

128 Kálmány, L., *A hold nyelvhagyomanyainkban* (Moon Lore), Phil. Dept. of the Hungarian Academy of Sciences, XIV, 1887, p. 14.

129 Gönczi, F., *Göcsej*, Budapest, 1914, p. 186.

130 Janko, J., *A Balaton mellékének neprajza* (Ethnography of the Balaton), Budapest, 1902, p. 406.

131 *Magyarorszag Vármegyéi es Városai* (Counties and Cities of Hungary). County Abanj, 1896, p. 207.

132 Elekes, S. "Gernyeszegi babonák és népszokások" ("Superstitions and Popular Customs in Gernyeszeg"), *Ethnographia*, VI, 1896, p. 19.

133 Istvánffy, G., "A borsodmegyei palócok" ("The Palóc people of Borsod"), *Ethnographia*, XXII, 1911, p. 277.

134 Margalits, E., "Horvat népszohasok és babonák Belovár Körös megyeben" ("Croatian Customs and Superstitions in Belovár Körös"), *Ethnographia*, X, 1899, p. 124; Jankó, J., *Torda Aranyosszék magyar népe* (The Hungarians of Torda Aranyosszék), Budapest, 1901, p. 232; Lázár, J., *Alsófehér Vármegye magyar népe* (The Hungarians of Alsófehér), Budapest, 1896, p. 101.

135 Kaindl, R. F., *Die Huzulen*, Wien, 1894, p. 97.

136 Moldovan, G., "A románok" (The Rumanians), *Az Osztrák Magyar Monarchia* (The Austro-Hungarian Monarchy): *Magyarorszag* (Hungary), VII, p. 424.

137 Wlislocki, H. von, "Quälgeister im Volksglauben der Rumänen," *Am Urquell*, 1895, p. 90; Pávay, V. F., "Oláhlapádi babonák és népies gyógy módok" (Superstition and Popular Cures of Oláhlapád), *Ethnographia*, XVIII, 1907, pp. 218, 219.

138 Hadzsics, I., "Délmagyarországi szerbek" (Serbs in Southern Hungary), *The Austro-Hungarian Monarchy, Hungary*, VI, p. 639.

refer to the moon as the patron of the *virkolak*.[139] In 1262 the Southern Slavs believed that the *vlkodlak*—that is, human beings who had changed into wolves—were eating the moon.[140]

In the moon lore of other people we frequently find ogres, dragons and witches eating the moon and causing the eclipse.

Hungarians at Besenyötelke believe that the witch takes the sun off the sky, that is an eclipse.[141] A stone put in the mouth of the buried shaman (*táltos*) is supposed to prevent him from eating the moon.[142] This is important because a *táltos* is a boy born with a tooth and nursed by his mother for seven years.[143] The Tshuvash say that a *vuber* eats the moon in an eclipse. The *vuber* is the cause of nightmares by pressing on the sleeper. Calves can get the *vuber* too, it prevents them from taking the udder.[144] In Turkish folklore the moon is taken off the sky by the witch.[145] According to Radloff the Lebed Tartars believe that the "seven-headed Yälbägän eats the moon. This is also the ogre of their folk tales who eats children.[146] The usual belief is that mythical beings, dragons or wolves eat the moon.[147] At Halmahera, however, the souls of dead children play with the moon and an eclipse happens when the dragon eats these souls.[148]

The sum total of all this is that these mythical monsters are projected images of infantile aggression or sucking and the moon a symbol of the breast.

According to the Rumanians the souls of unbaptized children, the *moroiu* (the equivalent of the *varcolaci*) comes out of the grave to suck their mothers' breasts. Should it meet a human being or animal it will jump on it and tear it to pieces.[149] At Vörösvár: look into a vessel filled

[139] Russwurm, C., "Aberglaube aus Russland," *Zeitschrift für deutsche Mythologie und Sittenkunde*, IV, 1859, p. 156.

[140] Mansikka, V. Z., "Die Religion der Ostslaven," *F. F. Communications*, 1922, p. 95.

[141] Berze-Nagy, I., "Babonák, babonás alakok és szokásak Besenyötelkén" (Superstitions and Customs in Besenyötelke), *Ethnographia*, XXI, 1910, p. 28.

[142] Ipolyi, A., *Magyar Mythologia* (Hungarian Mythology), Budapest, 1854, p. 449.

[143] Róheim, "Hungarian Shamanism," *Psychoanalysis and the Social Sciences*, III, 1951, p. 143.

[144] Mészáros, G., *A csuvas öscallás emlékei* (Survivals of Tshuvash Heathenism), Budapest, 1909, pp. 82, 285, 286.

[145] *Idem*, "As oszmán tötök népbabo-nái" (Superstitions of the Turks), *Ethnographia*, XVIII, 1906, p. 29.

[146] Radloff, W., *Aus Sibirien*, Leipzig, 1893, I, pp. 372, 373.

[147] Lasch, R., "Die Finsternisse in der Mythologie und im religiösen Brauch der Völker," *Archiv für Religionswissenschaft*, III, 1900, pp. 97–152.

[148] Campen, *Tijdschrift v. Ind. Taal Land en Volkenk.*, XXVII, p. 439, XXVIII, p. 397 quoted by Lasch, *op. cit.*, p. 132.

[149] Herrmann, A., *A hegyek kultusza Erdély népeinél* (The Cult of Mountains among the People of Erdély), Budapest, 1891, pp. 49, 50.

with water when there is an eclipse and you shall see a child eating the moon.[150]

The child who "eats" the mother may appear in inverted form as the cannibal moon. The Mantra say that the stars are the children of the moon and formerly the sun had as many. But since they feared that mankind could not support so much brightness and heat they agreed to devour their children. The moon, however, hid hers (the stars) and made the sun eat up her own.[151]

After this *detour* we can go back again to the text of our stories.

In (1) we have two boys, in (4) two buckets, in (6) two children, in (7) two old men, in (8) two men, in (10) a man and a woman, in (15) man and wife, in (16) the same, in (27) brother and sister, in (40) two girls, in (41) two children.

Perhaps the prevalence of the number two means the two breasts. This conjecture might explain why in most of the stories the mortals visible in the moon are not really in but *on* the moon like an infant on its mother's breast. The buttocks occurring in (12) and (19) might very well be the breasts displaced to the opposite pole of the body. Thirst is mentioned in (39, 42, 60, 62), cooking food for the children in (59, 64). The name of one of the heroines is "daughter who swallows all" (62), and cannibalism occurs in (30, 31).

We may assume two fundamental dream *nuclei* to the whole story. One, which we have discussed above, is simply the imagery of uterine regression, of falling asleep with some genital overtones. The other represents suckling, or being on the breast,[152] waking in sleeping, hanging on to the object world. In this sense the simple wish fulfillment dreams of children about eating[153] are also not so simple; their defense function consists in warding off uterine regression. It is possible that at a very early stage these dreams have the same function that genital dreams have at a later, but still fairly early stage. In genitality itself, as Ferenczi has shown,[154] we find a fusion of the regressive and oral object directed trends.

As far as our stories are concerned the genital content frequently covers the regressive. We have already mentioned the stories in which we have a girl in the moon as wife of the Moon Man. In (62) and (63) Rona has a rival Hoka. This god breaks his house down. In Mangaia a compliment paid by the husband to the wife is to call her a "well-thatched

150 Róheim, *Magyar Néphit és Népszokások,* Budapest, 1925, 1, p. 33. (Unpublished M.S. of the Hungarian F.F.)

151 Skeat, W. W., and Blagden, C. O., *Pagan Races of the Malay Peninsula,* London, 1906, II, p. 320.

152 Lewin, B., *The Psychoanalysis of Elation,* New York, 1950.

153 Freud, *Gesammelte Schriften,* III, p. 203.

154 Ferenczi, *Versuch einer Genitaltheorie,* Vienna, 1924.

house,"[155] and in Tami to go under the roof of other people's houses means to seduce the wives of your friends.[156] When he cuts off a part of the god's flesh (63) we can guess that by this they mean a symbolic castration. In another story belonging to this cycle the state of being castrated appears once more but this time it is the woman. Hina wanted to be rid of her husband and children and started climbing up to the moon. Higher and higher she climbed. Her husband leaped after her and the lower part of her leg remained in his hands. Hina with her calabash limped into the moon. From the loss of a part of her leg she is called "Lono-moku, the crippled Lono."[157] It is possible that the torn bush or the bush dug out by its roots and held by the man or woman in the moon, may signify also a phallos, i.e., castration anxiety. To tear one's self off (*sich eins abreissen*) is the German equivalent of the American "jerking off."[158] We find the bush or tree in (24, 25, 26, 32, 55, 56, 57, 59, 60, 64). With the exception of (57) and (60) the person who is holding on to the tree or bush is always a woman. Since there is so much indecision about the sex of Rona (57) and (60) the two stories can be discounted. The woman having the bush in her hand or having torn it off would then mean castration anxiety in connection with the moon mother. Certain obscure passages of Polynesian cosmology might be interpreted as meaning masturbation and masturbation anxiety.

In Hawaii: "He strewed the seeds, finest seeds of stars in the heavens / Strewed fine seeds of gods, the sun became a god / Strewed the seeds from Hina, Lono-muku was formed like a jelly."[159] He throws the seed Makalii, the god throws the seed, the Moon (Hina) throws the seed, misled by Lono-muku.[160]

This is the story of Hänsel and Gretel. Once upon a time when food was very scarce a poor man and his wife decided to get rid of their children. The stepmother wants to do it, the father is reluctant.

The children had gone to bed hungry and could not fall asleep. They heard what the grownups said about them.

Hänsel gathers some pebbles in the morning saying that this will help them. The parents *take them deep into the forest* and give each child a small loaf. The children fall asleep. But then they awake and

155 Gill, W. W., *Myths and Songs from the South Pacific*, 1876, p. 63.

156 Bamler, G., "Tami," in Neuhass, R., *Deutsch Neu Guinea*, Berlin, 1911, III, p. 504.

157 Westervelt, W. D., *Legends of Maui*, Honolulu, 1910, pp. 168, 169; Bastian, A., *Inselgruppen in Ozeanien*, 1883, p. 231.

158 Cf. Stekel, *Die Sprache des Traumes,* 1911, p. 202; Jung, C. G., *Wandlungen und Symbole der Libido*, 1912, p. 164.

159 Tregear, E.: "The Creation Song of Hawaii," *Journal of the Polynesian Society*, IX, p. 45.

160 Bastian, A., *Heilige Sage der Polynesier*, Leipzig, 1881, p. 275.

when the moon has risen they find their way back home with the aid of the pebbles. This is repeated several times and each time the parents take them deeper and deeper into the woods. A beautiful snow-white bird leads them to a house of bread and sugar. While they start eating it they hear a voice from the inside, "Who is eating my house?" They reply, "Der Wind, der Wind, Das himmlische Kind." (It is the wind, the child of heaven.)

The door opens and an aged woman appears leaning on her crutch. She is very friendly and inside they find all sorts of good things to eat and nice beds to sleep in. She locks Hänsel in a cage and starts fattening him up. Hänsel gets all the good food and his sister only what is peeled off. The boy had to stick his finger out through the bars all the time so as to show how fat he was. But he kept sticking a little piece of bone out just so as to delude the old witch. Finally she decides to eat them both. Gretel is to be pushed into the oven. Pleading ignorance of how to sit on the shovel, she pushes the old witch head first into the oven. Hänsel jumps out of his cage like a bird. They escape and arrive at a big lake. A white duck carries them across, and they arrive in their father's house with all the jewels they have brought from the witch's house. The stepmother is dead and they live happily ever afterwards (Grimm, 15).

We can assume two fundamental dreams dreamed maybe at the same time as basic elements of this story.

(a) The child is hungry, it dreams of food;

(b) The child represents sleep in the dream imagery, it dreams of uterine regression. This is represented by the oven. In Silesia, when they expect a delivery they say, "Der Backofen wird bald einfallen" (the oven will collapse). If they wish a person to be different they say he has to be baked again.[161]

The first dream contains oral aggression and talio anxiety, hence the children as monsters eating the moon, and in talio form the cannibal witch. The vesical awakening dream is at the same time a rescue from anxiety and the frontier of fairyland and reality, or the land of mortals is the moment of awakening. The moon is part of the waking stimulus for those who sleep in the open, but on account of its association with the vulva (menstruation) it also represents sleep and regression. But why is the pursuing mother imago so often detained by food? Because eating in a dream is a partial awakening (object-directed trend), at the same time, however, a guardian of sleep through hallucinatory wish fulfillment (obstacle flight).[162]

[161] Drechsler, P., *Sitte, Brauch und Volksglaube in Schlesien*, Leipzig, 1903, I, p. 181.

[162] Cf. chapter "The Way Back."

The following Russian folk tale from the Voronej Government illustrates these points.

There once lived an old couple, and they had a little boy called Ivashko. He wants to catch some fish, and they put him in a boat. Out in the boat he says:

> Canoe, canoe, float a little farther,
> Canoe, canoe, float a little farther,

and the canoe floated always farther and farther. (Flood myth, water carriers, end of obstacle flight in water.)

A witch learned to imitate his mother's voice and she catches him intending to eat him. He pitches Alentio, the witch's daughter, into the oven. She eats her own daughter. Then she sees Ivashko seated on an oak tree. She gnawed the oak, and just when she was about to gnaw it through Ivashko jumped on another tree. (Repeated.) He sees swans and geese flying past and sings:

> O my swans and geese,
> Take me on your pinions,
> Bear me to my father and mother.
> There to eat and drink and live in comfort.
> The father said at home to the mother,

"I dreamed that swans and geese had brought our Ivashko home on their wings."[163]

In a somewhat parallel story Ivan is escaping from his cannibal sister. A brush is transformed into mountains, a comb into trees, and apples rejuvenate old women. He waves his handkerchief, and there is a deep lake. In the last moment he escapes; the Sun's sister opens her house and here the witch cannot get him. In another story death is in search of a man who escapes into the land where there is no death, i.e., the Moon.[164]

We have seen above that the objects thrown back in the obstacle flight are urine, excrements, and the genitalia. The internal pressure in the first two cases is dealt with by representing it as being outside, while the third shows, like the flight of the birds, the genitalization of anxiety.

[163] Ralston, W. R. S., *Russian Folk Tales,* London, 1873, pp. 163–167.
[164] *Ibid.,* pp. 170–176.

IX

THE DANAIDS, WORK AND PUNISHMENT

After coitus with her husband a young woman dreams: "I am touching or counting buttons, innumerable buttons." She had not achieved orgasm and was masturbating in her dream. The button is her clitoris. The Danaids are the fifty daughters of Danaos. Acting upon their father's orders, they killed their husbands in the bridal night. Their punishment is that in Hades they have to carry water forever in a barrel that has a hole in it.[1] According to Waser the punishment fits the crime. Virgins are condemned to carry water forever because the λοντροφερειν (carrying water for the bath of the bride) is part of the marriage ceremony.[2] But we have to go further than this. What they have missed is not the marriage ceremony but marriage itself, and the vessel for water with a hole in it symbolizes the vulva which ought to have had a hole in it.

The Tim tell a story of a woman, who, because there is no vessel in the house, has to carry water for the spider in her own vulva.[3]

In a Tamul story about the goddess smallpox, Man, we are told that she was so holy that sand automatically formed itself in the form of an earthen vessel. However, one day she saw the reflection of a Gandharva in the water and she thought: "How beautiful." She had sinned and she could not form a vessel any more.[4]

This carrying of water as an endless task is the punishment of dead virgins in the other world. In Patschkau they believe the spinsters after their death must scrub the steeple of the church at Patschkau, and men who die unmarried (without sex) must carry the water in sieves. Spinsters must also scrub the *Magdalenbrücke* because during their lifetime they refused to scrub and do housework (the real meaning is the opposite; they did too much "scrubbing"[5]). At midnight they haunt the bridge.[6]

[1] *Roscher's Lexikon*, "Danaiden."

[2] Waser, O., "Über die äusseren Erscheinungsformen der Seele," *Archiv für Religionswissenschaft*, XVI, 1913, p. 353; idem, *Schweizeriches Archiv für Volkskunde*, II, 1898, pp. 55 *et. seq.*

[3] Frobenius, L., *Der Schwarze Dekameron*, quoted by Schultz, W., *Einleitung des Popul Wuh*, Berlin, 1913, Mythologische Bibliothek, VI, 2, p. 79.

[4] Fröhlich, R., *Tamulische Volksreligion*, Berlin, n.d., p. 22.

[5] I.e., masturbation.

[6] Drechsler, P., *Sitte, Brauch und Volksglaube in Schlesien*, Breslau, 1903, I, p. 282; Kühnau, *Schlesische Sagen*, Breslau, 1913, III, pp. 46–47.

Men who die unmarried are busy piling up the fog on a certain hill in Tyrol; they stack it up as if it were hay. When everything looks as if the work were finished, the Sun comes and dispels the fog and they have to start again. Other jobs given to them are salting rocks, pulling a wire through the snouts of the smallest ants and chewing the feces of geese till they turn from black to white. Spinsters are measuring the length and breadth of the swamp with their fingers.[7]

The work is endless and its duration is the punishment. The meaning of drawing a wire through a tiny hole is evident. The sexual symbolism of salt is well known;[8] to "salt" a rock is a punishment for not having "salted" a woman. Geese probably symbolize the female, and the passage about goose excreta is an anal version of the impossible task. The activity of the spinsters is obvious if we substitute their own genitalia for the swamp; they are continuously "measuring" it with their fingers. These tasks set in the other world are very similar to certain dreams called, *Beschäftigungstraum* (dream of work—really endless work) in psychoanalytic literature.

A patient of Tausk's, analyzed because of impotency, reported the following dream: It is early morning. He feels he must help his mother who has to do some household work. He decides that from now on he "will be good." He doubts whether he is grown up or still a child. He is turning over the pages of a big book; at the same time he wonders how he got out of bed. The task is somehow connected with another task. The faucet in the kitchen should be scrubbed till it is quite clean (*der Wasserleitungshahn in der Küche blank geputzt werden soll*). He turns the pages in haste, his speed keeps increasing, but they are glued to each other and it is always more and more difficult to turn them. The number of pages keeps increasing. He carries dust rags into the kitchen and this seems to be the same thing as the other tasks. The faucet is still not clean. The big book—he now recognizes—contains the assets and liabilities of last week. For a moment this reduces his anxiety. Then he notices he must still clean the faucet. Somehow making up the accounts is connected with the cleaning and he must start all over. Then the task is again to learn French and everything goes well and quietly. His tongue gets twisted and he is again anxious. Awakening.[9]

Tausk explains that this patient grew up in a family where the

7 Alpenburg, V., *Mythen und Sagen Tirols,* Wien, 1857, pp. 350–351.

8 Jones, E., "Das Salz in Glaube und Brauch der Völker," *Imago* I, p. 361; Eitrem, *Opferritus und Voropfer der Griechen und Römer* (1915), Videnskapsselkapets Skrifter II, Hist. Filos. Klasse, 1914, No. 1, p. 329; Storfer, A. J., *Marias Jungfräuliche Mutterschaft,* Wien, 1914, pp. 97–98.

9 Tausk, V., "Zur Psychologie des Alkoholischen Beschäftigungsdelirs," *Internationale Zeitschrift für ärztliche Psychoanalyse,* III, 1915, pp. 207–208.

mother often cried because of the way the father treated her. She never confessed the real cause; she said her children made her cry, but he really knew quite well what was going on, although he pretended not to know. To mask his love for his mother he became obstinate and disagreeable, and she complained to father, who would then punish him.

He remembers the following dream at an early age: Mother complained about too much housework. In a half-awake state he got out of bed and went into the kitchen to clean the faucet and thereby to help mother. But his mother was still in the kitchen and she took him back to bed.

The children used to call the penis *Wasserleitungshahn* (cock where the water flows) i.e., the faucet. Moreover, *putzen, scheuern* (to scrub), are slang words for masturbation. This is sufficient to explain the task of cleaning or scrubbing the faucet. The book reminds him of a big book he used to read at home while his mother sat close by, and also of the saying, "to turn the pages of a book with two pages," i.e., coitus. The problem therefore consists in co-ordinating the cock and the book, the penis and the vagina. "To be good," a decision frequently made in childhood, always meant to stop masturbating. To do accounts or to learn a foreign language are introduced as sublimation of masturbation. The anxiety that he will not get ready is the fear of impotency, or anxiety connected with masturbation and oedipal fantasies.[10]

Considering the fact that the beliefs about spinsters, bachelors, etc., are about the hereafter, they may well have originated in dreams.[11] Laistner correctly interpreted the sexual meaning of these eternal tasks. If spinsters have to patch trousers, this means that they have to make up for what they failed to do in their lifetime. Bachelors pulling wires through the nostrils of tiny ants; *"infibulare formicabile illud vulvae, i.e. cristam."*[12]

There is also direct proof in European folklore for the dream origin of the motive "endless work." The following is a story from the Pyrenees. On St. Agatha's Eve a woman stayed up late to spin. At nine o'clock someone knocked at the door. A strange woman came in. She said: "I will spin too." She was given wool and set to work. *She spun at a furious speed, four times faster than her hostess.* The hostess was frightened and ran to a neighbor for advice. The neighbor advised her to go back and cry as she entered: "The cemetery is on fire." The strange woman ran out immediately crying, "To my little home." But she came back to say

---

10 *Ibid.*, pp. 209–218.
11 Cf. above the chapters "Animism" and "Descensus Averni."
12 Laistner, L., *Nebelsagen*, Stuttgart, 1879, p. 229.

that the woman had just saved her life because what she was spinning was her shroud.[13]

A story of Barra in Scotland relates how a woman was in a hurry to have her stock of wool spun and made into cloth, and one night she secretly wished to have some women to help her. So the following morning there appeared at her house six or seven fairy women in green robes, all alike, chanting: "A wool card and a spinning wheel." And then they all set to work, and by midday the cloth was going through the process of the hand loom. But they were not satisfied with finishing the work the woman had set before them but asked for new employment. She got anxious and began to wonder how to get rid of the fairy women. An old man gave her this advice: "Go you in and tell them to spin the sand and if then they do not move, yell, 'Dun Borve is on fire.' " The fairy women disappear and she hears them wailing, "Dun Borve is on fire! Dun Borve is on fire! and what will become of our hammers and anvil for there was a smithy in the fairy dwelling."[14]

In the Ukraine, working on Friday evening is a great sin; spinning is even worse. "Angry Friday" punishes those who disregard this taboo. If a woman spins on Friday, "Friday" will appear to her and will spin with such vehemence that you can hear it everywhere. A girl was spinning on Friday. A woman appeared in the window: "You are spinning?" she asked. "Yes, I am spinning." She must fill many spindles during the night otherwise the Pjatnica (Friday) will kill her in the morning. She puts only one thread on each spindle and that is how she escapes.[15] The same author tells us that Holy Friday appears in dreams. In Russia the Synod of 1551 A.D. forbids the worship of the "Nedelja" (Sunday) or "Pjatnica" (Friday).[16]

A Rumanian story makes it quite clear that the demon woman appears while the mortal is asleep. A woman was cleaning the oven on Tuesday night. The Tuesday Woman came, and, while she was asleep, the demon woman wanted to cut off her hair. The woman awoke.[17]

Another woman felt something pressing on her while asleep (nightmare). A tall woman made her get out of the bed and climb up the wall.[18]

If a Huzul mother cannot make her child go to sleep she sings:

[13] Alford, V., "The Cat Saint," *Folk-Lore* LII, 1941, pp. 178–179, quoted by Róheim, "Saint Agatha and the Tuesday Woman," *International Journal of Psycho-Analysis*, XXVII, 1946, pp. 119–120.

[14] Wentz, W. Y., Evans, *The Fairy Faith in Celtic Countries*, London, 1911, p. 110.

[15] Vasiljev, N., "Antropomorficheskeja Predstavlenije V. Verovanijach Ukrainskavo Naroda" (Anthropomorphic Beliefs of the Ukrainian People), *Etnograficheskoje Obozrjenie*, I, 1890, p. 96.

[16] *Ibid.*, p. 96.   [17] *Ibid.*, III, 1892.

[18] Szabo, J., "As olahok kedd asszonya" (The Tuesday Woman of the Rumanians), *Ethnographia*, XXI, 1910, p. 172.

> Pjetnonjko-givjonka (Friday Little Girl)
> forgive my soul
> For I want to put my child to sleep
> Friday Little Girl forgive my soul
> Even if I have many sins
> May I sing her to sleep.[19]

This is significant because it shows that these apparitions originate in dreams, and because of the mother whose guilt prevents the child from falling asleep. The Tuesday Woman of the Rumanians punishes those who work on Tuesday eve by making their dreams full of anxiety or by making them work endlessly (i.e., in their dream), or by pulling their hair, or by flying away with them.[20]

In Masuria, spinning is forbidden from Christmas to Twelfth Night and on the eve of several other holidays. If somebody spins on Thursday eve after supper the nightmare will come and continue the spinning. If anyone spins or weaves on this evening, the devil will continue the work after the person has gone to bed.[21] Hungarians have the same taboo and belief—it is the devil who throws the empty spindles in through the window.[22] In Lithuania the same Thursday taboo is connected with the Laume. This is the Lithuanian name of the nightmare. The Laume would come and spin all night and then disappear when the cock crowed.[23]

Another taboo is spinning in the moonlight, at least in some parts of Germany. A woman spun at Gamburg. It was full moon. A small white man came into the room. He brought innumerable spindles and said that if she did not finish these within an hour he would twist her neck. She put just one thread on each spindle—thus she was saved. In a similar story with the same trick, the spindles are thrown into the room by the moon, and the moon says, "Don't do it again, for the day is yours, the night is mine."[24]

Laistner is right in emphasizing the connecting links that unite the moon and the nightmare. Sleepwalkers (in German, *mondsüchtig*) are regarded as nightmare beings, and the nightmares in the Upper Palatinate will only occur when the moon has risen.[25]

Why is spinning so frequently taboo or the taboo most emphasized? One obvious reason is that in the past all over Europe the girls would spin their flax in a room and it was in these rooms that the boys would

---

19 *Ibid.*, pp. 168–169. 20 *Ibid.*, p. 36.

21 Toeppen, M., *Aberglauben aus Masuren*, Danzig, 1867, p. 102.

22 Tpolyi, A., *Magyar Mythologia*, Budapest, 1854, p. 54; Wlislocki, H., *Volksglaube und religiöser Brauch der Magyaren*, Münster i. W., 1893, p. 166.

23 Laistner, L., *Das Räthsel der Sphinx*, 1889, II, pp. 315–316.

24 *Ibid.*, II, p. 317; Schönwerth, F., *Aus der Oberpfalz*, 1857, I, p. 418.

25 Laistner, *op. cit.*, II, p. 318.

come courting. Four or five houses in a village would be rivals as to which spinning room could attract a larger clientele of lads.[26] According to Rumanian belief, coitus was also taboo on Tuesday eve. A shepherd lad was on his way to his girl friend on Tuesday eve. He had lustful thoughts. The "Tuesday Evening" (Tuesday Woman) got hold of him and nearly killed him with protracted coitus. He was rescued by a mass.[27]

The eternal work might, therefore, very well be a wish for eternal lust, be it in the form of coitus or masturbation. Spinning is, of course, pre-eminently woman's work, but it is also something done with their hands. In many cases these taboos, and especially that of spinning, are connected with a mother imago, such as Frau Holle or the Virgin Mary.

In the Hungarian county of Baranya any woman who combs her hair on Good Thursday is pulling the heart of the Virgin Mary.[28] The Hungarian Tuesday Woman is really the Virgin Mary in Csallóköz and Saint Anne in Szeged.[29] The Russians frequently identify these personified taboos with the Virgin Mary. Friday eve and Sunday eve are both under the protection of the Negilja (Sunday). Sunday is a thin, black-haired woman—with the usual spindle motive. The Virgin Mary was tired and desired to rest; Monday and all the days of the week rejected her. Finally she was accepted by Sunday. Since that time Sunday is under the protection of the Virgin Mary.[30] The Bosniaks say that "Holy Sunday" is full of wounds, stabbed by people who work on Sunday or Friday. Rumanian women do not sew because they might wound Holy Friday with their needles.[31] The Serbs say that each movement with the scythe is a cut on the body of Sunday.[32]

Beside the spinning we have with about equal frequency the taboo on washing. A Rumanian woman was spinning on Tuesday eve. A tall woman came in to help. Then she said she would also help with the washing. The hostess went to a neighbor to get a big kettle. The other woman said: "Take care, that is the Tuesday Evening. She will kill you. Run home and shout: 'The hills and forests are on fire,' and then when the demon woman rushes out, turn every pot so that their open-

---

26 Róheim, *Psychoanalysis and Anthropology*, pp. 376–377.

27 Szabó, *op. cit.*, XXI, 1910, p. 234.

28 Róheim, *Adalékok magyar néphithez* (Contributions to Hungarian Folk Belief), Budapest, 1913, p. 39.

29 Berze Nagy, J., *Baranyai magyar néphagyományok* (Hungarian Folk Traditions of Baranya), Pecs, 1940, III, p. 281.

30 Oniscuk, A., "Narodnij kalendar u Zelenici, Materiali do Ukrainskoj," *Etnologii*, XXV, 1912, p. 718; Zovko, J., "Ursprungsgeschichten und andere Volksmeinungen," *Mitteilungen aus Bosnien und der Herzegovina*, I, 1893, p. 442.

31 Oniscuk, *op. cit.*, XV, 1892, pp. 7–8.

32 Tuga, V., *A magyar szent korona országaiban élö szerbek* (Serbs in Hungary), Budapest, 1913, p. 73.

ing should be on the ground."[33] A woman washed on Tuesday Eve. She also drank some water. The Tuesday evening twisted her mouth. It stayed crooked.[34]

Another woman was washing a shirt on Tuesday evening. The Tuesday Evening appeared in the shape of a grey dog. It urinated and defecated in the room and disappeared. Another woman was also washing a shirt. The Tuesday Evening appeared and offered to help but she shoved the hostess' head into the kettle; in one version the hostess is burned to death, in another she is drowned. In a third story the trough is put on her head and the Tuesday Evening shakes her.[35]

Fire and water are often combined in these stories. The Tuesday Evening sets the tow on fire, makes the woman drowsy, and pours the water out of the bucket. Then she puts the bucket on the head of the hostess.[36] In another story Tuesday Evening said: "Do you see this kettle full of hot water? I shall pour it all over you because you work on the eve of Tuesday." Her husband came to the rescue with his axe. Tuesday Evening ran away.[37]

The work is washing, the apparition is a supernatural woman and the story ends when fire is mentioned.

In another Rumanian story a woman was washing on Tuesday evening. A tall woman opened the door. "I have come to help you," she said. But the help was peculiar, to say the least. For the strange woman returned with a board torn out of a fence, and the board was on fire. The frightened housewife ran to her neighbor, *a midwife*, for advice. The advice she got was to run back and shout: "The hills of Galarea are burning." The strange woman rushed out screaming: "My children will perish in the flames!"

The midwife then told her to turn every pot upside down except one. The Tuesday Witch came back; she wanted to come in. She called on the pots to help her, but they did not open the door. The one pot that had not been turned upside down tried to help her but it broke its leg in the attempt.[38] In the Ukraine the woman is getting ready to soak her lye on a Wednesday. She told the woman that this was forbidden on Wednesday. "Take care of the hot water," she said, "and put your children into the pot." The human woman pretended to go for firewood. But she came back and said: "Listen, hag, the hills and valleys are on fire and the children are in the midst of it."[39]

[33] Szabo, *op. cit.*, 1906, XVII, p. 54.   [34] *Ibid.*, p. 170.
[35] *Ibid.*, p. 171.   [36] *Ibid.*, p. 167.
[37] *Ibid.*, p. 168.
[38] Roska, M., "Keddi boszorkany" (Tuesday Witch), *Ethnographia*, XXIII, 1912, pp. 98–99. Nearly the same told in Szabo, *op. cit.*, XXI, 1910, p. 234.
[39] Oniscuk, *op. cit.*, pp. 11–12.

The story ends in fire and has something to do with the children. One thing is evident: the woman who goes to a midwife for advice, or wants to put her children in the cauldron is the one who dreams the apparition, the dream ends with fire and children.

In Macedonia clothes are not washed on Wednesday and Friday, and especially are the people warned not to indulge in ablutions on Friday.[40] Spinning and washing may be combined.

In Brahlsdorf in Mecklenburg, a peasant woman complains that she cannot finish her spinning. *To her great amazement more and more spinning women come to help her.* The spinning is soon finished. Now they want a big cauldron to boil and wash the tow. Her neighbor tells her that "those who come from under the earth (*die Unterirdischen*)" really want to boil her in the cauldron. She must shout through the door: "The Butterhill is burning, the Butterhill is burning." They all run because that is their *exit* from the nether world to this world.[41]

In one of the stories from the Pyrenees, a woman announced that she was going to do her washing. Her neighbor warned her that this was Saint Agatha's day and that washing was forbidden. She replied impatiently, *"Santo Gato gatara e la ruscado se fara."* (Saint Cat shall kitten and I shall have my wash.) Immediately a cat[42] appeared in the chimney corner. There were many cauldrons and the cat kept crying, "Empty it, empty it." The terrified woman ran to a neighbor. She was told to go to the *window* and before she empties the last cauldron to shout, "The cemetery is on fire." The cat howled, "To my little home," and fled.

The Russians tell the story about Wednesday. A young housewife was spinning. It was the night between Tuesday and Wednesday. After midnight when the first cock crew, she was *sleepy*. She laid down her satchel—but without crossing herself, and said, "Mother Wednesday lend me thy aid that I may get up early in the morning and finish my spinning." And she went to sleep. Long before it was light she heard something moving in the room. The room was lighted up. A splint of fir was burning in the cresset, and the fire was lighted in the stove. A woman wearing a white towel and headdress was moving up and down getting things ready. Presently she came to the young woman and roused her. "Get up," she said. "I have spun the linen and woven thy web. Now let us bleach it and set it in the oven. The oven is heated. Go to the brook and draw water." The woman went with a couple of pails for water. Everybody was still asleep in the village. She was afraid and went to an

---

[40] Abbott, G. F., *Macedonian Folklore*, Cambridge, 1903, p. 190.

[41] Bartsch, K., *Sagen, Märchen und Gebräuche aus Mecklenburg*, Wien, 1879, I, pp. 48, 49.

[42] Saint Agatha and Gato: cat is a pun.

old woman for advice. The old woman tells her, "Go and beat thy pails together in the front of the house and cry, 'Wednesday's children have been burned at sea.'" (Cf. water and fire combined.) This is what happened, and Wednesday rushed out. But she came running back crying, "Let me in! I have spun thy linen, now I will black it!" But the woman did not let her in. When the cock crew she uttered a shrill cry and disappeared.[43]

The exit from the nether world, the cat having kittens, the window or door or pot are all the same thing.

The dream usually ends with fire and the danger to the child. Fire in dreams, as we have seen frequently, symbolizes urine—the Tuesday Evening in the form of a dog urinates into the room; the Murawa of the Vends urinates on those women who have not finished their spinning by Christmas Eve.[44] Moreover, fire in these myths is frequently combined with water which makes the interpretation even more probable. We have here again an awakening dream of the vesical type, the image of endless work being the delaying action, the symbolization of the process of urinating.

The Kaukas of the Lithuanians are a kind of nightmare demon. The sleeper can get rid of them by telling them to carry water in a sieve.[45]

In European folklore we find parallels to the Danaids. In the Harz mountains, Frau Holle carries water in two buckets from the brook to the hill. On the hill there is a bottomless barrel. She will rest only when the barrel is filled.[46] In a story of the Italian Tyrol, twelve women were spinning. They did not stop at midnight. Frau Berta, with the long nose, came in and then another, and another; twelve in all. They sat down on the chair, the women trembling with fear rose from their seats. "Now we shall wash the first," Frau Berta said. "Bring us pails!" But the women knew that the Bertas intended to boil them in those pails. Instead of pails, they gave them two baskets—in which they, of course, could not carry the water.[47]

In Silesia we have the ghost of the Fiebigtal. She will only be at rest when she manages to scoop all the water out of the lake with a bottomless pail. She meets wanderers at dawn and her head starts swelling

[43] Ralston, W. R. S., *Russian Folktales,* London, 1873, pp. 201–203.
[44] Schulenburg, W. von, *Wendische Volkssagen und Gebräuche,* Berlin, 1880, p. 250.
[45] Laistner, *op. cit.,* I, p. 288.
[46] Pröhle, H., *Harzsagen,* Leipzig, 1856, I, p. 156.
[47] Schneller, *Märchen und Sagen aus Walschtirol,* pp. 200–201, quoted by Laistner, *op. cit.,* I, p. 323.

till it becomes a pail.[48] The task of another ghost is to gather all the needles in a forest of pine trees in a basket that has no bottom.[49] Counting, as we have seen in the dream quoted above, is another form of the same thing. A perjurer in Oldenburg is condemned to scoop out a well with a bottomless pail or to count all the grain stalks in the valley.[50] This type of carrying water is frequently connected with Holda and similar beings.[51] Counting, which was originally part of the awakening dream, then becomes an incantation to ban evil spirits—spirits who originate in the same kind of dream work. The spirit must count all the bushes, all the twigs, all the leaves, and all the stars in heaven—but it makes a curious condition before it agrees to this pact. After each counting it will come nearer by one *cock's-step*.[52] Obviously this is derived from the crowing cock that ends the rule of these beings of the dream.

The spirit frequently has to collect small seeds, thus projecting the masturbation from the dreamer to the supernatural being. A Rumanian strew poppy seeds on St. George's Eve on the ground, at the entrance of the stables; the witches will have to pick them all up before they can come in and bewitch the cows.[53] At Nagytárkány, Hungarians use millet for the same purpose. At Eger it is the ghosts who have to pick it up. At Hegyalja it is again the witches; by the time she finishes her task, her time is up. At Retközberencs the cock will crow before they can finish.[54] In Styria the Schratt (nightmare demon) must count the grains of millet before it can harm the horses.[55] In Corsica they get rid of the lutin by mixing wheat with other grains; it has to put each into a separate bag.[56] The sexual significance of these seeds and grains becomes obvious if we quote cases in which they are used for love or fertility magic.

In Felménet a young girl who goes to Midnight Mass at Christmas Eve strews poppy seeds from her house to church. On her way back, her true love will greet her.[57] At Privigye peas are strewn on the floor.

48 Kühnau, R., *Schlesische Sagen,* Breslau, 1910, I, p. 445.

49 *Ibid.,* p. 446.

50 Strackerjan, L., *Aberglaube und Sagen aus dem Herzogtum Oldenburg,* 1909, I, pp. 257–258, 260.

51 Waschnitius, V., *Perht, Holda und vervandta Gestalten,* Sitzungsberichte der Kais. Akd. Wiss., Vol. 174, No. 2, 1913, p. 113.

52 Strackerjan, *loc. cit.*

53 Moldovan, G., *A magyarországi románok* (Rumanians in Hungary), Budapest, 1913, p. 283.

54 Róheim, *Adalekok a magyar nephithez* (Manuscripts collected by the Hungarian section of the Folklore Fellows), p. 246.

55 Schlossar, A., "Sagen vom Schratel aus Steiermark," *Zeitschrift für Volkskunde,* II, 1930, p. 377.

56 Sebillot, P., *Le Folklore de France,* III, 1904, p. 486. For further data, cf. my book quoted above.

57 Róheim, *Adalekok,* p. 245.

Each hen will lay as many eggs as it has eaten peas.[58] In Auvergne seeds ward off the evil eye because the sorcerer cannot distinguish male and female seeds. In Gironde seeds of millet worn in one's shoes ward off magic that might make the wearer impotent. In Perigord all will be well in the bridal night if you put millet into your wife's pocket.[59] Endless work or counting may mean the prolongation of sleep as against the vesical pressure or masturbation in the dream which delays or never achieves orgasm. In many European legends we find a being who is condemned to do something forever in the moon. These men or women are always guilty of having worked on the Sabbath. In Dithmarschen a woman spun on Sunday. God said, "Don't you know this is Sunday? From now on you shall sit in the moon."[60] The Southern Slavs tell the story of a girl who spun late Sunday evening in the moonshine. She will always be spinning in the moon.[61] But sometimes it is a girl who refuses to spin and wants to dance all the time. Her mother curses her and she is dancing in the moon.[62]

In the Ardennes (Belgium) a young girl danced on a holiday and broke her promise to return in time to her mother. She danced in the churchyard at full moon. She is there in the moon spinning the web of the Virgin forever.[63]

In Hungary, Cziczelle and David were sent by their mother to church. Instead they went to an inn to dance. Now they are dancing in the moon forever.[64]

We have seen some instances above in which the Penelope or Danaid motive is projected to the moon. The Mentawei say that a man called Sikobut spins a rope in the moon. The rope reaches down to the earth. But a mouse bites it off every night and that is why the man in the moon cannot come down to the earth.[65]

I assume that the eternal work in the moon is not derived from a direct observation of nature but from dream elements; it may be the awaking dream or obstacle dreams that are refound in natural phenom-

---

58 Sztancsek, L., "Privigye vidékén gyüjtott babonák" (Superstitions of Privigye), *Ethnographia*, 1909, p. 300.

59 Sebillot, *op. cit.*, III, pp. 486–487.

60 "Am Urquell," 1893, p. 54.

61 Krauss, F. S., *Volksglaube und religiöser Brauch der Südslaven*, Münster i. W., 1890, p. 13. Krauss remarks that maybe this is identical with the woman who spun on Wednesday eve and now haunts everywhere as the Wednesday Woman.

62 Schonwerth, Fr., *Aus der Oberpfalz*, II, 1859, p. 69. Cf. *supra* "The Water Carriers in the Moon."

63 Sebillot, *op. cit.*, I, pp. 17–18.

64 Kálmánz, L., *A hold nyelvha gyoman ainkbay* (The Moon in Our Traditions). Budapest, 1887, p. 17.

65 Maass, A., *Bei liebenswürdigen Wilden* (Mentawei), 1902, p. 93.

ena. However, we have so far touched only the surface of our dreams. We see that they are vesical dreams[66]—and that the fire as ending has something to do with the children. Since vesical dreams are regularly birth dreams or dreams of delivery, one would assume that the children are about to be born—but the opposite is the case—they are in danger. This takes us to another aspect of our dreams, viz., just the fact that they are punishment dreams. We know from Freud and then from Jekels and Bergler that the dream is a reaction to the unfinished task, i.e., to the superego reproach of the previous day.[67] The unfinished task is work that is not done and here it seems to be overzeal in working—rationalized as working on a holiday—that causes the punishment. But if we look a little closer, we come to the conclusion that the part of the narrative in which the woman is working must also have been part of the original dream. In other words, a girl is worried, feels guilty because she has not finished her work—in her dream she continues to work. German folklore has a technical term for this kind of work: *es arbeitet nach* (it works after). If human work is not finished "in God's name" then this "after work" sets in. It is an uncanny business, the work of the devil. Carts roll on the streets, flails make a noise in barns, wood is being chopped, the spinning goes on, the hammer sounds in the smithy. You can see the devil somewhere; he is mending his trousers. *Nacharbeiten* takes place where people have been cursing too much or where they did not stop when the bells tolled for prayer.[68]

But there is another form of this nightwork. Once upon a time there was a miller in Tyrol in the village of Hurlach. He went to bed early, but by the time he got up, all the work was done in the mill. A dwarf (Nörglein) did it. But when the miller's wife gave him new clothes for his reward, he disappeared forever. When the Nörglein in these stories gets clothes, he starts to cry and is gone.[69] Another dwarf was also in a mill; the mill was grinding corn, day and night.[70] At night the mill went on grinding—this was the dwarf at work.[71]

On the Isle of Man, the *fenodyree* corresponds to the Norg. He is a hairy, clumsy fellow, but he works for people and he will thresh a whole barnful of corn in a single night. Just like his German cousins, he leaves when he receives his reward.[72]

[66] On the anal elements in these dreams, cf. Róheim, *Mondmythologie und Mondreligion*, Wien, 1927, p. 63.

[67] Jekels, L. and Bergler, E., "Instinct Dualism in Dreams," *Psychoanalytic Quarterly*, IX, 1930.

[68] Laistner, *op. cit.*, II, p. 71.

[69] Zingerle, Ignaz V., *Sagen aus Tirol*, Innsbruck, 1891, p. 58.

[70] *Ibid.*, p. 57.   [71] *Ibid.*, p. 60.

[72] Rhys, John, *Celtic Folklore, Welsh and Manx*, Oxford, 1901, I, pp. 286-287, 324.

The grinding dwarfs look more like coitus than work. This spirit is part of a dream. Reality dispels it (the reward). If we regard the spinning of our peasant women in this light, it will be easier to understand the meaning of the supernatural interference.

The Tuesday Woman is a huge hairy woman with big breasts.[73] The martyrdom of St. Agatha is that she had her breasts torn off.[74] If "work" is masturbation or some other infantile erotic equivalent, we can see how the superego, as represented by the mother imago, intervenes once more and turns pleasure into punishment. But this supernatural being also represents the dreamer herself. The speed of the work increases and fire means that the demon rushes out. The sleeper goes to urinate and awakes. The urethral, as usual, goes with the latent content of birth, but instead of the children being born, they are in danger of dying.

At the same time we see that if the pots are upside down, the Tuesday Woman cannot enter, the sleeper cannot go into a pot, cannot continue to sleep. The story also contains elements of the simple *oral dream* —but in reverse. The dreamer is in danger of being cooked and eaten by the Tuesday Woman. The demon woman throws a horse's head in through the window and says, "Eat this if you are hungry."[75] More frequently, however, the oral is represented in reverse—the woman is going to be boiled and eaten by the Tuesday Woman.

In the fifth century B.C., Polygnot painted certain murals for Delphi. Pausanias describes them. We see Tityos, Tantalos, Sisyphus and Oknos.[76]

Tityos is the symbol of genital libido unchecked. The son of Zeus by Gaia, he was hidden in the earth (i.e., in his mother) by Zeus because of the jealousy of Hera. He rapes Leto, another wife of Zeus, and another earth goddess, and his punishment was that he was stretched out on the ground covering nine acres (the earth again)[77] with two vultures on each side devouring his liver. The liver was the seat of the libido and would grow again when the vultures devoured it. Ti-tu-os, whose name means "the swollen," is a second Oedipus, but with castration anxiety, as personified by the vultures. The crime—the growing penis—and the punishment—bitten off lust forever.

Oknos is a man weaving a rope, but what he weaves is eaten up by a she ass behind him. In real life Oknos was a man who worked a lot

73 Roska, M., "Keddi boszorkány" (Tuesday Witch), *Ethnographia*, 1906, p. 19.
74 Alford, V., "The Cat Saint," *Folklore*, LII, 1941, p. 161.
75 Oniscuk, *op. cit.*, XV, 1912, pp. 11–12.
76 Rohde, E., *Psyche*, Tübingen, 1907, I, p. 318.
77 *Roscher's Lexikon*, "Tityos," p. 1054.

but his wife was a spendthrift and squandered all he made. The same pictures show also women carrying water—the Danaids, or something equivalent to them—in fact we see that the women are in close contact with the animal.[78] It is clear that Oknos is but a less heroic version of Tityos; he has to use his hand to twist the rope (masturbation). But do what he may, the she ass, or the women, frustrate his efforts. Among the many things that Bachofen says about Oknos, some are worth quoting. He reminds us of the tendency to confuse *onos* (ass) and Oknos, and of the duality in the nature of Oknos who usually symbolizes incessant work, but sometimes laziness and always indecision.[79] Oknos is represented in a swamp and a heron is also called Oknos. The heron is one of the birds that live in swamps or among the reeds, like the stork. Bachofen regards the bird Oknos as phallic.[80] There can certainly be no doubt about the sexual significance of the ass in Greek mythology, and the she ass that chews the rope would be the female complement to the phallic Oknos-Onos.[81] Since twisting the rope is masturbation, both the ass and the ass-driver (Oknos) are lame, i.e., castrated.[82]

The parallel with the washing, water carrying and spinning both in the stories revolving around tabooed days and the moon stories, and the spinning or rope making in the same is obvious. Some of our narratives go back to oral dreams or are motivated by thirst and waking dreams, and here we have the myth of Tantalos.

Tantalos stole nectar and ambrosia; his punishment is eternal hunger. The fruit he is about to eat disappears when he touches it. According to other versions he is punished because he slew his son Pelops and dared to offer him to the gods.[83] But the myth of Tantalos is more complicated because the other punishment that threatens him is a rock that might fall and crush him at any moment. This becomes understandable only if we know that Tantalos or Taltalos is really Atlas and Atlas is really identical with Kronos who separates his parents Heaven and Earth.[84] The rock that might crush him would therefore be Heaven itself.

Another member of this group is Ixion. This hero was the first to kill

---

[78] *Roscher's Lexikon*, "Oknos," p. 821. On the Danaids and the fate of spinsters in European folklore, cf. the remark of Harrison that carrying water in a sieve was an ancient test of virginity. Harrison, J. E., *Prologemena to the Study of Greek Religion*, Cambridge, 1908, p. 621.

[79] Bachofen, J. J., *Versuch über die Gräbersymbolik der Alten*, Basel, 1925, pp. 301–306.

[80] *Ibid.*, p. 355.

[81] *Ibid.*, pp. 374–375.

[82] Harrison, *op. cit.*, p. 618.

[83] Gruppe, O., *Griechische Mythologie und Religionsgeschichte*, Berlin, 1906, I, p. 656; *Roscher's Lexikon*.

[84] Marót, K., "Ατλασόλοοφρων," *Philologische Wochenschrift*, 1926, p. 588.

a relative, the father of his bride Dia. Zeus, however, gives him immortality and a seat at his table. He falls in love with Hera. Zeus, in order to test him, forms a cloud in the shape of the goddess. He has intercourse with this image and procreates Kentauros.

He is tied to a winged fiery wheel made fast by serpents and perpetually revolving in mid-air. Moreover, he is being scourged and a voice says, "One should respect benefactors."[85]

Laistner brings convincing evidence to show that we have to do with a trait that originally belongs to the nightmare.

In Lauenburg in Pomerania, people see a fiery wheel of a plough which looks as if it were headed straight toward them. The Kashobs say that the "Mahot" (Nightmare) rolls in the air in the shape of a fiery wheel, crying, "Dselut, dselut," or whistling or cracking.[86] The ghostly wheel in Saterland is called a screaming thing. The noise it makes is too terrible. Everybody trembles who hears it. It can be gigantic or small, and it breaks everything to pieces if it falls to the ground. There again it has something to do with murder.[87] In Silesia a ghost is represented by a wheel rolling in the air.[88] In Mecklenburg, a coachman kills a serpent, the old serpent turns itself into a kind of wheel in pursuit of the man.[89]

Many etymologies have been given by Laistner and others for Ixion. Roscher suggests a derivation from $ἱποῦσδαι$ "to hurt, to press" meaning the nightmare who presses, but also connected with the word $ἰσχύς$ or $ἰξύς$ equals strength, virility.[90] Benseler suggests $ἰξύς$ = Libidinous. The only thing we have to add to this is that the rotating movement (the solar wheel)[91] clearly symbolizes coitus. "The punishment fits the crime." The raper of Hera is condemned to eternal coitus. My patients have frequently described the process of falling asleep as a kind of rotating, and also identified it with falling back into the womb, orgasm, dying.

The Iroquois say that the woman in the moon was unhappy because she did not know when the end of the world would come. For this she was transported into the moon where to this day she is to be seen, weaving a forehead strap. Once a month she stirs the boiling kettle of hominy during which occupation the cat, over by her side, unravels her net, so that she must continue her work until the end of time.[92]

The dream image is masturbation or delayed urinating. Anxiety is

---

85 *Roscher's Lexikon*, "Ixion."

86 Laistner, *op. cit.*, I, p. 299.

87 Strackerjan, *op. cit.*, I, pp. 294–295.

88 Kühnau, *op. cit.*, I, p. 49.

89 Bartsch, *op. cit.*

90 *Roscher's Lexikon*, "Ixion," p. 771.

91 Cf. Cook, A. B., *Zeus*, on "Ixion."

92 Smith, E. A., *Myths of the Iroquois*, Bureau of American Ethnology, II, 1880–1881, p. 87.

connected with the orgasm or urination—the end of the world originally, awakening. But the guilt feeling connected with enuresis or masturbation, regressing even to the simple eating dream, transforms what was meant to be prolonged pleasure (a few more seconds of sleep) into eternal punishment.

X

GHOSTS AT MIDNIGHT

I. Feralis exercitus

Tacitus describes the military tricks used by one of the Germanic tribes, the Harii.

"Ceterum Harii, super vires quibus enumeratos paulo ante populos antecedunt, truces, insitae feritati ante ac tempore lenocinantur, nigra scuta: tincta corpora; atras ad proelia noctes legunt ipsaque formidine atque umbra *feralis exercitus* terrorem inferant nullo hostium sustinente novum ut velut infernum aspectum."[1]

The night belongs to the hosts of the nether world.

In 1248, the French people believed in the army of the Hellequin. The Spanish people called the same phenomenon *exercitus antiquus.* Peasants at the crossway would see an army of innumerable warriors. But if they stepped off the crossway into the field, the army just rushed past them and nothing happened.

The Letts see the souls of dead warriors continuing their battles in the Aurora Borealis. In Thüringia they say that the Croats and the Swedes fought a battle there and every year at the anniversary of the battle the dead soldiers awake and start it all over again.[2]

According to Norwegian beliefs, souls that are not good enough for heaven and not bad enough for hell must keep riding till doomsday. They are led by a woman called Guroryme or Reisarowa. Their front side looks normal but behind there is nothing but a long tail. The horses are black with fiery eyes and their riders whip them with rods of fire.[3]

Grimm quotes a story of this type from Elenburg. A peasant walking home drunk hears the words "middle of the road" but he pays no attention. Suddenly a tall man on a white horse is standing in his way. "Are you strong?" the apparition asks. "Then let us pull." The peasant starts a tug of war with Wod, holding one end of an iron chain with Wod at the other end. Wod swings the mortal skyward, but he manages to tie the chain to an oak. Pull as he might, the demon could not pull the oak

[1] Tacitus, *Germania,* 43. L. Weniger, *"Feralis Exercitus," Archiv für Religionswissenschaft,* IX, p. 202.

[2] Grimm, *Deutsche Mythologie,* II, p. 785.

[3] *Ibid.,* p. 775.

out by the roots. His dogs kept barking, his horses neighed, but he could do nothing. A stag falls from the air and as a reward for his strength the peasant gets the hindpart. He has to take one boot off to carry it home. As he went homeward, the meat kept increasing in weight. With bent back and covered with perspiration he finally arrived at home.[4]

The typical nightmare frequently contains this feeling of oppressive weight.

The Wends tell the following story about the "night huntsman." A man was going from Sydow to Ströblitz. He saw a man on horseback galloping past him. The horse was black as night, the nostrils and hoofs were emitting fire. He was so afraid that he hardly dared to breathe. The rider galloped into the forest above the tree tops. The trees bent down to give way to him. When he had passed they stood erect once more. When the apparition had disappeared the man tried to get into the forest, but it was too dense; he could make no headway. He struggled on until dawn, but in the morning he found he was still in the same place.[5]

Here we clearly have a dream narrative. The galloping horseman, the anxiety and the inability to move (*Hemmungstraum*). In the morning he is of course still at the same place where the dream started.

Another man told the following story. He was very tired and went *to sleep* in his buggy on the fields. But he awoke on hearing a terrific noise as if cannons were being fired and a whole pack of dogs barking. That was the *black hunt,* and they kept chasing round his buggy until dawn.[6]

This is quite a clear rendering of a dream. The man is asleep and the apparition ends at dawn. A young cowboy goes to sleep and loses his herd. He sees the carriage of the *Nachtjäger* in the air above the trees. It was the previous inspector who had committed suicide with his head hanging out of the carriage.[7]

The following is a similar story from Karinthia. A young lad refused to believe in the wild hunt. He went to sleep in the barn thinking that he would see what was going on through a chink in the wall. But *he fell asleep* and *then* he heard the galloping horses and many voices. He shouted, "Give me a bit too." They threw him a horse's leg and he was frightened. The priest told him to bury it in the dungheap, and if he had not done that the wild hunt would have returned and torn him to pieces.[8]

In Saxony, we have the following belief. The night-raven is a big

4 *Ibid.,* p. 771.
5 Veckenstedt, E., *Wendische Sagen, Märchen und abergläubische Gebräuche,* Graz, 1880, pp. 35, 36.
6 *Ibid.,* p. 36.   7 *Ibid.,* p. 40.
8 Graber, G., *Sagen aus Kärnten,* Leipzig, 1914, pp. 82, 83.

strong bird. It flies only at night. Maybe it is a bird of iron; at any rate, it has iron or metal wings with which it beats those to death who imitate it. A shepherd slept outside with his herd and imitated the sound made by the raven, and the raven would have killed him if he had not hidden behind nine windbreaks.[9]

The setting guarantees the dream as a basic element of the myth. The raven is the father imago whom the dreamer is not supposed to imitate (i.e., rival), and the *nine* windbreaks that save him probably refer to the intrauterine situation.

These ghosts, dogs, ravens, horses are always flying or galloping in the air. Frequently one person (male) is chasing, hunting the other (some animal or a woman). In other cases a female being is seen flying, but the latent meaning is still the same. Werre (another word for Holle) flies in the Whirlwind. She offers to take a certain sorcerer to Dresden in one night, but he declines because he would have had to travel in her anus.[10]

Flying in a dream or what amounts to the same thing, seeing people who fly, is invariably a genital sensation.

In 1555, we find the following version of the aerial chase. "Dixerunt maiores nostri, . . . , concubinas sacerdotum in aere a daemonibus non aliter quam feras silvestres a canibus venaticis agitari atque tandem discerptas inveniri, quodsi hominem quispiam haec audiens venationem suo clamore adjuverit illi partem vel membrum concubinae dissectum ad januam domus mane a daemonibus suspensum."[11]

In my paper, "Die Wilde Jagd,"[12] I interpreted the myth of the Wild Huntsman as the primal scene. What I am now suggesting is that the myth is evolved from *dreams about the primal scene.*

The wild huntsman appears at night and the stories frequently mention the sleeping observer who imagines himself carried away by the aerial flight, presumably out of his bed. The call of the wild huntsman is his own anxiety, his attempt to scream and thereby to arouse himself from the anxiety dream. To repeat this call is dangerous and that would correspond to the hidden pleasure content of the nightmare, and could be interpreted as an attempt to prolong sleeping and dreaming. It seems easy to guess the infantile content of the anxiety dream. Mortals hear and see what supernaturals are doing; the child witnesses a "bloody" chase. Father Odin and the Mother of the Woods.

In Wermland, a tailor was out to shoot something from ambush.

9 Schambach, G., and Müller, W., *Niedersächsische Sagen und Märchen*, Göttingen, 1855, pp. 68, 69.

10 Waschnitius, V., *Perht, Holda und Verwandte Gestalten*, Sitzungsberichte der kaiserlichen Akademie der Wissenschaften in Wien, Vol. 174, 1903, p. 103; cf. the word *Sauarsch* applied to the whirlwind, Grimm, *op. cit.*, III, p. 91.

11 Grimm, *op. cit.*, II, p. 773.   12 In *Imago*, XII, 1926, p. 465.

The Skogsra flew past him. She had two pendant breasts which she threw behind her shoulder. She was followed by a huntsman with a couple of coalblack dogs. The huntsman returned with the Skogsra he had shot. Her legs were on his shoulder, blood was flowing from her long breasts and the dogs were licking her blood. The male has his "head" between the legs of the female and she is bleeding.[13] "At Mirow they say the black huntsman is chasing a woman. The night huntsman is after the woman of the forest. At Leitzkow in Westphalia and in Pomerania it is Woden himself who is chasing the whores. In Lower Austria, the wild huntsman chases the witches because they are the devil's concubines."

"Who is the forest woman? She can be recognized by her big breasts. The Finns call her Metsän emánta, the woman or mother of the forest. The Roumanians say Mama padurei—the mother of the forest."[14] We have a clear picture of the origin of the myth. It is a dream about the primal scene. There is another version of this anxiety dream where there is no threatening father but the dreamer as a *voyeur* flying with his witch mother.

A hired lad in Oldenburg *fell asleep*. He awoke to see his mistress and her friends, all women, in the kitchen. They rubbed their armpits with some kind of grease and said,

> "Upp and darvan
> Un nargends gägen an."

(Up and going, and nowhere knocking / ourselves /).

He wanted to follow them, but he got the incantation wrong and said, "Knock against everything." He flew out of the chimney, but knocked against everything. He was so full of wounds that he died in a few days.[15]

In the Hungarian witch trials of 1728, it was reported that a witch smeared her armpit and that of her son and then they flew out of the window. But the son shouted, "Jesus," and that is why he fell down.[16]

A Wend peasant was in love with a girl. People accused her of being a witch, so he went to see for himself. It was the night of Walpurgis, and he *pretended to have fallen asleep near the oven*. He flew out after the witches. Flying, he met *his girl friend and her mother,* and they told him

13 *Ibid.,* pp. 469, 470.   14 *Ibid.,* p. 467.

15 Strackerjan, L., *Aberglaube und Sagen aus dem Herzogtum Oldenburg,* Oldenburg, 1909, I, pp. 390, 391.

16 Komaromy, A., *Magyarországi boszorkányperek oklevéltára,* (Acts of the Hungarian Witches' Trials), Budapest, 1910, p. 416.

to go back but warned him against uttering a word while he was flying. He disobeyed them and crashed down to earth.[17]

The meeting with his girl and her mother is especially revealing. When a word is spoken the dream and the flight are ended. The relationship of the witch to the mortal who imitates her is always that of mistress to servant or hired lad.[18]

The "flying woman" type of these myths or beliefs goes back to antiquity. Hekate was the leader of the swarm of ghosts and witches. A fragment from an unidentified poet of the fourth or fifth century reads, "If you are afraid of dreams and hast conjured the chtonian Hekate."[19] Hekate's following are the souls who died before their proper time and the apparition causes anxiety at night. Hekate herself, as Rohde says, is not very different from Gorgo, Mormo, Empusa, and even conjectures the Hekate might have been regarded as the mother of Hades.[20] Moreover, Hekate appears as the gatekeeper of Hades and the mistress of Kerberos. In the *Aeneid* (VI, 255), she opens the gates of the nether world. Her appearance is accompanied by thunder and barking dogs.[21]

Farnell tells us that "Euripides who spoke of her as the daughter of Leto and called her also the queen of the phantom world; and on the black-figured vases she appears in company with Persephone, Demeter and Hermes."[22] Dogs were prominent in her ritual. They were sacrificed to her, and in one story she takes the shape of a dog.[23] This is interesting both because of our previous discussion of flying dogs in Central Australia and because a dog always follows the Wild Huntsman or his female counterparts.

The dog with the usual inversions of motives may also be a protector. A young man met Perchta on a bridge (Karinthia). She would have torn him into pieces if he had not a "four-eyed" dog (a dog with a white spot above each eye) to accompany him. She herself appears as a cow with long teeth which she keeps grinding.[24]

The Wend Dziewica hunts with her hounds, but she is also a *daemon meridianus* like the Prespolnica and other Sphinx-like beings of Vend folklore.[25]

17 Veckenstedt, *op. cit.*, p. 290.

18 Kühnau, R., *Schlesische Sagen*, Leipzig, 1911, VII, p. 89. For other parallels, cf. Róheim, *Adalékok a magyar néphithez*, Budapest, 1920, p. 50.

19 Nauck, Ed., *Tragicorum Graecorum Fragmenta*, Leipzig, 1889, p. 910, quoted in Liungman, W., "Traditionswanderungen Euphrat-Rhein," *F.F. Communications*, 119, 1938, p. 578.

20 Rohde, E., *Psyche* (4th ed.), Tübingen, 1907, II, pp. 408–411.

21 *Roscher's Lexikon*, "Hekate," p. 1895.

22 Farnell, L. R., *The Cults of the Greek States*, Oxford, 1896, II, p. 512.

23 *Ibid.*, pp. 506, 509, 510.   24 Graber, G., *op. cit.*, pp. 91, 95.

25 Veckenstedt, *op. cit.*, p. 108.

In Silesia the Wild Huntsman has a historical name. He is Dietrich von Bern or, as they say, Bern Dietrich. Dogs bark, horses neigh, trees crack when he arrives. He is the *Nachtjäger mit dem wütenden Heer*. Headless men riding on horses with stag heads, gruesome dogs, wild boars follow him.[26] The wild hunt appears as the barking of innumerable black dogs led by a headless black man.[27] The dog is not there just because it follows logically from the idea of the chase. In one of the stories of the Wild Huntsman the dogs urinate on the hidden onlooker. A mortal shouts derisively, "Hosenflecker!" (patcher of trousers) and the furious huntsman throws down a barrelful of *fiery fluid*. Water or salt water is also associated in other cases with these beings.[28]

The primal scene dream is also an urethral dream, or rather it is the other way round: the urethral pressure is transformed by the dream into a libidinal sensation and the imagery of the primal scene is evoked. In this sense, the urinating dogs or the dog have a phallic significance. In Touraine the aerial chase consists of flying dogs who chase belated peasants.[29]

A story of Silesia contains both the typical nightmare sensation (anxiety dream of choking or weight pressing on the dreamer) and the primal scene.

"Once when I was lying in bed," the informant says, "two small dogs came and a big black one. They jumped over each other. Suddenly the black one jumped into the bed and weighed down on my throat till it nearly choked me."

A female informant reports that two black dogs were lying on her at night.[30]

In Brittany, a woman saw the following apparition at night. A woman with dishevelled hair was running and crying pitifully. Her tears were blood and her feet barely touched the soil. Two dogs were chasing her, one white and one black. Each of the dogs wanted to devour her.[31]

On the other hand, the dog with its wide open devouring jaws also represents the castrating female organ.

Wales is full of "spirit hounds." "Near Wilton Crossways in the Vale of Glamorgan, one of these spirit hounds is described as having the upper part of the body in semihuman form. The other part and the lower limbs

---

[26] Kühnau, *op. cit.*, II, p. 446.
[27] *Ibid.*, II, p. 485.
[28] Laistner, L., *Das Räthsel der Sphinx*, II, p. 232.
[29] P. Sebillot, *Le Folklore de France*, Paris, 1904, I, p. 171.
[30] Kühnau, R., *Schlesische Sagen*, III, p. 114.
[31] Braz, A., *La Légende de la Mort chez les Bretons Armoricains*, Paris, 1902, I, pp. 90–92.

were those of a 'light spotted dog.' The eyes were large 'like moons' and smoke came out of its mouth."[32]

This dog is evidently not unrelated to the Sphinx and the Kerberos. In Silesia, the dog of a freemason (i.e., sorcerer) has a wide open jaw that emits fire.[33] The fiery or round eyes of these apparitions deserve special notice. Two girls walking on a bridge are frightened by a dog with fiery eyes.[34] The horses in these processions had also fiery eyes that glowed like furnaces.[35] The dreamer is *seeing* something forbidden, but he projects the fiery eye to the apparition.

Why are these "primal scenes" always connected with the wind? The mortal gets a gold coin as a reward in Hess.[36] A hand emerges from the whirlwind (*Windsbraut*) and then one should say, "Saudreck, thu'd Hand weg." ("Pig's excrement, away with your hand.")[37] The reward is usually the hind part of a horse and it is usually put on the dungheap. In some cases, the reward is mud that turns into gold.[38] The obvious conclusion is that the almost permanent association of these aerial phenomena with wind is also due to internal pressures, to the flatus.

"People say he reacts to calls by throwing corpses down, or parts of corpses. Wind and weather also have another meaning connected both with vehement breathing and with food. Swedish trolls are chased in the whirlwind by the thunder, but there is also a saying 'to compare a fart to thunder.' Naturally, the child identifies the activity of the father in the primal scene with his anal and urethral functions."[39]

The Indian parallel to the "wild huntsman" is *Rudra*, the red one, the demon of death. Oldenberg writes: "The master of the bow and arrow, Rudra, the wild huntsman, dwells in mountains and forests."[40] Rudra's sons fly through the forest "like two wolves."[41] M. Müller and others interpret the name as meaning "the roarer" or thunder.[42] Rudra is also the Lingam, the phallos.[43]

If Rudra is really the "wild huntsman" of Vedic times it would ex-

---

[32] Trevelyan, M., *Folk Lore and Folk Stories of Wales,* London, 1909, p. 52.

[33] Kühnau, R., *op. cit.,* III, p. 253.

[34] *Ibid.,* p. 326.

[35] Trevelyan, *op. cit.,* p. 49.

[36] Bindewald, T., *Oberhessisches Sagenbuch,* 1873, p. 38.

[37] Kühnau, *Schlesische Sagen,* II, p. 120.

[38] Rochholz, E. L., *Schweizersagen aus dem Aargau,* Bern, 1856, III, pp. 185, 187.

[39] Róheim, "Die Wilde Jagd," p. 471. Sources quoted there.

[40] Oldenberg, H., *Die Religion des Veda,* Berlin, 1894, p. 216.

[41] *Ibid.,* p. 219.

[42] Siecke, E., "Der Gott Rudra im Rig-Veda," *Archiv für Religionswissenschaft,* I, 1898, pp. 115, 116.

[43] Meyer, E. H., *Indogermanische Mythen,* Berlin, 1883, I, p. 224. Kama, the Tamul god of love, also shoots with bow and arrow, Fröhlich, R., *Tamulische Volksreligion,* n.d., p. 55.

plain why we find the wild huntsman again in Indonesia. Skeat writes, "The *baberek* or *birik-birik,* another nocturnal bird, is a harbinger of misfortune. This bird is said to fly in flocks at night; it has a peculiar note, and a passing flock makes a good deal of noise. If these birds are heard passing, the Perak peasant brings out a wooden platter and beats it with a knife, calling out as he does so, 'Great-grandfather, bring us their hearts.' This is an allusion to the belief that the bird *baberek* flies in the train of the Spectre Huntsman (*hautu pemburu*) who roams the forests with several ghostly dogs, and whose appearance is a forerunner of disease or death. 'Bring us their hearts' is a mode of asking for some of his game, and it is hoped that the request will delude the *hautu pemburu* into the belief that the applicants are his followers and that he will there-fore spare the household."

The baberek in this wild hunt, as Skeat says, is very similar to the white owl in the stories of the Wild Huntsman of the Harz.[44]

The Perak Malays relate the origin of the Wild Huntsman. "In former days, at Katapang, in Sumatra, there lived a man whose wife during her pregnancy was seized with a violent longing for the meat of the mouse-deer. But it was no ordinary "pelandok" that she wanted. She insisted that it should be a doe, big with male offspring and she bade her husband go and seek in the jungle for what she wanted. The man took his weapons and dogs and started, but his quest was fruitless for he had misunderstood his wife's injunctions and what he sought for was a *buck* mouse deer big with male offspring."[45] Obviously, he could not find it, but he had sworn an oath that he would not return home unsuccessful and therefore he went on killing animals and drinking their blood. Finally, since he could not find what he was looking for on the whole earth, he extended his search to the firmament. His dogs were now on the sky and he was constantly looking up at them from the earth. From this constant looking upwards his head became fixed in that position and he could no longer look down on the earth. With his head turned up-ward he still hunts the Malay forest.[46]

According to one version of the myth, his wife has joined him and they roam the forest together. Their children are born in the woods.[47] Children who meet the dogs of the Wild Huntsman get a stiff neck, can't move and keep staring upward.[48]

According to the Malays of Selangor, the Demon Huntsman is ten feet high and his face is very hairy. From nightfall, at the full moon he

44 Skeat, W. W., *Malay Magic,* London, 1900, pp. 111, 112.
45 *Ibid.,* p. 113.   46 *Ibid.,* pp. 113, 114.
47 *Ibid.,* p. 116.
48 Moszkowski, M., *Auf neuen Wegen durch Sumatra,* Berlin, 1909, p. 123.

goes hunting deer and pig. He has two dogs and he carries a spear with which he stabs people. If anyone wants to meet him, they restore half-bent trees into an erect position. At this he appears and asks, "What do you want?" and they reply, "I want my father." To this he answers, "I will be a father to you. If you are sick, send for me and I will come to you." This promise he keeps, and when they are sick he comes and cures them.[49]

This Malay Wild Huntsman has a surprising number of traits in common with his European cousin. Two traits interest us especially. One is that during his chase he is still supposed to be having intercourse with his wife. The other is that the chase after a female is the chase for a pregnant male. The inversion of "a woman with a penis" and its eternity is based on the fact that what it tries to achieve is impossible. The paternal role of the Spectral Huntsman is significant. However, whether the Indonesian Spectral Huntsman can be connected historically with his European counterpart remains doubtful.

Eating repulsive food is part of the whole Wild Huntsman complex. In a story from Tyrol, the cry of the Wild Huntsman, "Shachi, schachi" is heard at night. Everybody was paralyzed with anxiety who heard it. But one young and bold lad shouted loudly, "Schachi, schachi, give me my share (i.e., of the game you are hunting)." *Next morning,* he found one half of a corpse nailed to his door. But this lad was not frightened and in the evening he shouted, "Schachi, schachi, take it back again," and the corpse disappeared. A peasant woman also asked for her share and found a piece of a corpse at her door.[50]

People on the field hear someone screaming. They see up in the air one of the "wilde Männer" tearing a wild girl into pieces. This screaming went on all night, and next morning a piece of the wild girl was nailed to his door.[51]

If we interpret this as a nightmare or an anxiety dream, everything becomes clear. The screaming has a double meaning. We have the anxiety of the dreamer who wants to scream and the noise made in the primal scene situation. And we have also the well-known oral-sadistic interpretation of the primal scene. Father is tearing mother to pieces or eating her. The mortal, i.e., the child, who dares to say "me too" is usually punished for this oedipal audacity. The "eating" is coitus displaced upwards. In Voigtland, a woman did not know what to do with the meat, so she ate it. This made her the wife of the Wild Huntsman.[52] The inhibition

---

[49] Skeat, W. W., and Blagden, C. O., *Pagan Races of the Malay Peninsula,* London, 1906, II, p. 303.

[50] Zingerle, *Sagen aus Tirol,* Innsbruck, 1891, p. 101.

[51] *Ibid.,* pp. 109, 110.　　　　[52] Laistner, L., *op. cit.,* II, p. 239.

dream (*Hemmungstraum*) and the typical nightmare experience of having to carry something very heavy enter into this complex of narratives. The spirit immobilizes anyone who interferes with his activity and for a whole night he cannot move.

A coachman said, "Shall I come and help you to shout?" The result was that his carriage could not be moved. Another shouted, "You hunt the whole night and you don't catch a thing!" Immediately, he felt weighed down so that he could not make a move.[53] In Austria, the devil's carriage appears just when all living beings are in a deep sleep. It makes such a noise that the sleeper is *half awake* and listens wondering what it could be.[54]

This story clearly describes the relationship of the mortal and the supernatural being. He is asleep, then half awake—in other words, he is dreaming.

From Mecklenburg, we get the following story. Two lads were camping near a lake while their horses were grazing. It was nighttime and T. fell asleep but M. lit his pipe and kept watching the horses. T. had just fallen asleep when M. heard hoofs clattering and a terrible noise indicating that the Wild Huntsman was on his way. He just had time to hide behind a bush when the Wild Huntsman arrived with his dogs. The spirit went straight to the sleeper and trumpeted right into his ear. Then he galloped away.[55]

The distribution of roles between M. and T. corresponds exactly to the technique of the dream. Things actually happen to the one who is asleep, yet part of the events are described as being witnessed by the one who is awake—which makes it a myth, something that is believed in and not a dream.

In Gascony, King Arthur left the Mass at Easter when he heard his hounds who were chasing a boar. But the moment he stepped out of the church, he was lifted up into the air with his hounds and horses and followers, and there he will hunt the boar till Doomsday.[56]

Arthur in the role of the Wild Huntsman is by no means a modern belief. In Mallory, we find that Arthur rode to Camelot and there met the wife of King Lot of Orkney. "For she was a passing fair lady therefore the king cast great love unto her and desired to lie by her; so they agreed and she was his sister, on his mother's side Igraine. So there she rested

---

[53] *Ibid.*, pp. 233, 234.

[54] Vernalcken, T., *Mythen und Bräuche des Volkes in Österreich*, Vienna, 1859, pp. 97, 98.

[55] Bartsch, *op. cit.*, I, p. 14. On the connection of the wild huntsman with the army that sleeps in the mound cf. Schweda, V., *Die Sagen vom wilden Jäger und vom schlafenden Heer in der Provinz Posen*, Gnesen, 1915, p. 59.

[56] Sebillot, *op. cit.*, I, p. 168.

her a month and at last departed. Then the king dreamed a marvelous
dream of which he was sore dread. But all this time King Arthur knew
not that King Lot's wife was his sister. Thus was the dream of Arthur,
"Him thought there was come into his land griffons and serpents and
him thought they burnt and slew all the people in the land and then him
thought he fought with them and they did him passing great harm but
at the end he slew them." Arthur awakes from this dream and goes hunting. "As soon as he was in the forest the king saw a great hart afore him.
This hart will I chase said King Arthur and so he spurred his horse and
rode after long . . . whereas the king had chased the hart so long, that
his horse lost his breath and fell down dead; so he set him down at a
fountain and there he fell in great thoughts. And as he sat so he thought
he heard the noise of hounds to the sum of thirty. And with that the king
saw coming towards him the strangest beast that ever he saw or heard of;
so the beast went to the well and drank and the noise was in the beast's
belly like unto the questing of *thirty couple hounds;* but all the while the
beast drank there was no noise in the beast's belly and therewith he de-
parteth with great noise whereof the king had great marvel. And so he
was in great thought and therewith *he fell asleep.* Right so there came a
knight afoot unto King Arthur and said 'Knight full of thought and
sleepy, tell me if thou sawest a strange beast pass this way.' King Pellinore,
that is the strange knight. Then follows the strange hart on Arthur's
horse.[57] Then was the high feast made ready and the king was wedded at
Camelot unto Dame Guenever. Right so as they sat there came running
in a white hart into the hall and a white brachet next him and thirty
couple of black running hounds after him with a great cry."[58]

The wild hunt is the primal scene and the mortal who sees the chase
is frequently punished by loss of eyesight. This is, of course, the appropriate punishment for the *voyeur.* Frequently, this is done by the Wild
Huntsman hammering a peg into the person's eye, thus showing the
castration content in addition to the punishment of blindness. The peg
can only be removed a year later when the Wild Huntsman passes the
place a second time.

Plischke understood this. "These beliefs go back to the dream. People dream of being blind and they can only be cured by awakening." The
time, as Plischke observes, is displaced from a night to a year.

Another motive Plischke also interprets as originating from a dream.
Somebody looks out of the window, sees the Wild Huntsman and his

---

[57] Mallory, T., *Le Morte d'Arthur* (Everyman's Library ed., 1912), Book I, Chapter
XIX, pp. 34–36.
[58] *Ibid.,* p. 75. (Book II, Chapter V.)

head swells to inordinate proportions, and sometimes he grows antlers.[59] The phallic meaning of this dream trait is unmistakable.

The mythological conjectures made by Rhys[60] may or may not be correct, but what interests us is that the hero of the wild hunt is also the Sleeping Hero in the cave.

In Carmarthenshire, there is a steep high rock and on the top is the mouth of a very long cavern. "The entrance into it is small and low, but it gradually widens out, becoming in one place lofty and roomy with several smaller branch caves." In the cave King Arthur and his warriors lie *sleeping* with their right hands clasping the hilts of their drawn swords, ready to encounter anyone who might wish to disturb their repose.[61]

These sleeping heroes or kings in caves are always supposed to awake or to return one day, usually to rescue their nation from danger. "Yet some men say in many parts of England that King Arthur is not dead . . . and men say that he shall come again and he shall win the Holy Cross . . . But many men say that it is written upon his tomb this verse 'Hic jacet Arturus Rex quondam, Rexque futurus.' "[62]

A Welsh drover was resting on London Bridge. Then he went to an eating house on the other side of the Thames. His stick aroused a stranger's curiosity, and he took the stranger to the grassy hollow where the hazel grew from which he had cut the stick. The stranger then said that *in a dream* he had seen the hollow before and directed the drover to get a spade and pick and to dig down. They found a broad and flat stone and underneath it a flight of stairs where *they descended* and soon reached a long corridor from the roof of which a huge bell was suspended. The stranger warned the drover never to touch the bell for the consequences would be dreadful. Then they went on until a vast cavern was reached. It was filled with warriors in shining armor with shields beside them and swords unsheathed. In the midst of these warriors a circle of twelve knights surrounded a king and *all the men were asleep*. The stranger said that they were King Arthur and his knights. They were waiting there until the Black Eagle and the Golden Eagle would go to war. The clamor of the eagle warfare would make the earth tremble and cause the bell to ring so loudly that the warriors would awaken and go forth with King Arthur to destroy all the enemies of the Cymry.[63]

In Germany we have the same parallelism of galloping horses and

[59] Plischke, H., *Die Sage vom wilden Heer im deutschen Volke*, Leipzig, 1914, pp. 70, 71.

[60] Rhys, John, *Studies in the Arthurian Legend*, Oxford, 1891, pp. 154, 155.

[61] *Idem*, Celtic Folklore, *Welsh and Manx*, Oxford, 1901, II, p. 468.

[62] Mallory, *op. cit.*, p. 391. (Book XXI, chapter VII.)

[63] Trevelyan, M., *Folk Lore and Folk Stories of Wales*, London, 1909, p. 136.

complete immobility. At Klingenstein, they hear gruesome noises made by the wild army. Its men gallop around and joust with each other. Pebbles fly in the air, wells overflow with water. But after midnight they all retire. The gates of the castle are closed. In the Oldenwald, they show a castle. Whenever there is danger of war coming the last owner of the castle emerges with his army at night, making a terrible noise. The Emperor Karl is waiting in the Donnerberg with his whole army. An old man went to the hill and *fell asleep*. Then someone took him right into the hill, but he saw no soldiers there, only a church. He concluded that they must have come out of the hill. In another story King Charles retreats into the Oldenberg with his host of warriors, but from time to time they come out with a terrific clatter of arms and neighing horses. In the Wolsberg, there is a gigantic cave and in it a great king and his warriors are asleep. Once upon a time a huntsman happened to wander into the cave. The king asked him, *half dreaming,* whether the crows were still flying. He answered, "Yes, they are," whereupon the king fell asleep again. When the crow flies no more, the king and his army will come out of the mountain.[64]

We remind the reader of the dream analyzed by Freud about the wolves on the Christmas tree.[65] Wolves are seated on the tree; their immobility is the remarkable thing about them. The sleeping hero or king in the cave is also the leader of the wild hunt of the furious army—naturally, since the sleeping hero is the sleeping person in the "cave" and the galloping horseman chasing a woman is his dream.

II. The Haunted Mill

Castles haunted by virgins and other terrors of the night are familiar to everybody and it will hardly be a surprising move to interpret them as anxiety dreams or nightmares.

Schellenburg is a castle in Silesia with one of these virgins who are waiting to be rescued from damnation. The man who rescues her gets the buried treasure. Three nights he has to spend in the haunted castle and must not let himself be frightened by whatever he may see. He sees dragons, serpents and things that look like monkeys, but they all disappear with the *first rays of sunshine*. But the apparitions of the third night are so awful that he cannot stand them and he bolts before sunrise.[1]

A beautiful lady appears to a man who is chopping wood in the

64 Ranke, F., *Die deutschen Volkssagen,* Münich, 1910, IV, pp. 96–100.
65 Freud, *Gesammelte Schriften,* VIII, 1924, p. 439.
_____
1 Kühnau, R., *Schlesische Sagen,* Leipzig, 1910, I, pp. 270, 271.

hills. "Tomorrow night," she says, "you shall see me again, but I shall be a serpent. Do not get frightened. Just kill me with your axe. Then take a key from out of my mouth and open with it the gate that leads to the treasure." But when he hears the snake's terrible hissing, sees its eyes like balls of fire and the lightning coming from its mouth, he forgets what he has promised and runs as fast as he can. The serpent comes after him. He collapses, but when the hissing serpent nearly reaches him the hissing becomes a mournful song and the sound seems to vanish toward the sky.[2]

This is an oedipus who failed. If he had used his axe as Thor his hammer the beautiful lady could not have been (or could not have remained) a terrifying serpent.

In Karinthia it is a young shepherd who sees the woman with a key in her mouth. She tells him to lean on his shepherd's staff, to hold his hands so that they form a cross, and when she winds herself on his staff in the form of a serpent she will put the key in his mouth. When the decisive moment comes, he gets frightened, pushes the snake back and she disappears.[3]

The white lady, i.e., the ghost of the princess, can only be saved if somebody kisses her on the mouth when she is in the shape of a toad. Again the shepherd fails at the last moment.[4] In another case, he is supposed to hold her in his embrace for an hour, but when she changes into a huge serpent he cannot endure it.[5]

The sexual significance of these narratives is perfectly obvious. It is the phallic woman or the *mother's fantasied penis* that frightens the man. But its relation to sleep or dreams is merely a possibility. It is interesting, however, that in some of the stories that are openly based on nightmare beliefs the victory over the nightmare is achieved when her finger is firmly nailed into the wall.[6]

The next story of the serpent girl is a narrative with a happy ending. A snake gets into a peasant's waistcoat while he is in the fields and refuses to leave him unless he promises to marry her. He asks the priest for advice and is told to wait. The snake will visit him every night, but when the bells ring twelve he should raise her and keep his arm raised and stay in that position whatever may happen. He does this, and then other snakes get into the room, curl around him and hiss at him. He keeps his

2 *Ibid.*, I, pp. 255, 256.
3 Graber, G., *Sagen aus Kärnten*, 1914, p. 147.
4 Bartsch, K., *Sagen, Märchen und Gebräuche aus Mecklenburg*, Vienna, 1879, I, p. 271.
5 *Ibid.*, I, p. 272.
6 Laistner, *Das Rätsel der Sphinx*, I, p. 52. In general, beliefs in nightmares and the narratives about them do not come within the scope of this book.

arm raised and at one o'clock they all disappear. This happens again the next night. On the third night he does the same thing and the snake is transformed into a beautiful princess. He rubs his eyes, thinks it is a dream. The princess marries the peasant.[7]

The lad who maintains his erection dispels the anxiety dream in which phallic women or men disguised as women attack him—and finally, the serpent becomes the princess.

In a Basque story the Lamina (fairy) compels the peasant woman to bake her a cake every day. The peasant says that he will deal with the matter. *The fairy falls asleep* and while she is asleep he pours the hot fat under her skirt.[8]

At Gundershofen there was a mill where no one could spend more than two days at a time because of the bear that came every night. A brave lad undertook to break the spell. He was halfway between *waking and sleeping when the door* opened and a huge bear came in. The bear began to paw everything in the room and came nearer and nearer to the boy. But when he was just about to touch the lad with his paw, he swung his axe and cut the paw right off.[9]

The dream character of this narrative is made clear in the introduction. He is half asleep—it is a hypnagogic fantasy or basic dream, only not in its simple form. It is not he who goes in through the gate but the *bear* (father) and the anxiety is ended by the *phallic symbol* (axe).

The threat of the phallos is met either by another bigger phallos or by its counterpart, the vagina.

A shoemaker who used to work on the eve of Sunday or on holidays saw a horrible apparition, a big nose stuck in through the window. "Do you see this big nose?" the voice asked. The shoemaker replied, showing his last, "And have you ever seen such a big stick?"[10]

But in most of the legends (*Sagen*) and even folk tales concerned, the countermagic used against the threatening penis is the vagina.

The following is from Grimm's collection, one of the many "valiant tailor" type.

Once upon a time there was a proud princess. She refused all suitors who did not know the answer to her riddle (Sphinx or Turandot motive). The youngest tailor makes the right guess: her hair is gold and silver. But before she will accept him as her husband he has to overcome an-

---

[7] *Ibid.*, I, pp. 98–101.

[8] Hackman, O., *Die Polyphemsage in der Volksüberlieferung*, Helsingfors, 1904, p. 126.

[9] Stöber, A., *Die Sagen des Elsasses*, Strasburg, 1896, p. 334.

[10] Waschnitius, V., *Perht, Holden und verwandte Gestalten*, Vienna, 1913, p. 151; cf. also pp. 19, 30, 35, 40, 41, 45, 56, 104, 150.

other test. He must spend a night in the mill with a bear. The tailor is willing. When the bear attacks him, *he starts playing the violin*. (Some motives that belong to the tailor or gypsy and supernatural being cycle are omitted.) The bear who would like to learn how to play the fiddle is told that his claws have to be trimmed first by putting them in a vise. The bear thinks this is not too heavy a price to pay for so great an art and agrees to this condition. But of course the tailor screws the vise firmly and leaves it at that. After this victory, the princess has to agree to the marriage. However, the tailor's enemies unscrewed the vise, and while he and the princess were in the coach driving to the church the bear came after them. But the tailor knew what to do. He stood on his head, stuck his two legs out of the window and said, "Do you see this vise?" When the bear saw this, he ran for all he was worth.[11]

How did the tailor know the color of the princess' hair, if the others did not know? A variant from Saxony explains the riddle. She sees how three little pigs dance when he plays the flute, and in exchange for the pigs she sleeps with him. The three little pigs are the testicles and penis. He knows the riddle now, of course, and also the color of her hair—meaning her pubic hair.

But who is the bear? Since he has to spend a night with the animal one might assume that it is the princess herself as a nightmare. But this would be wrong. These stories and folk tales can only be understood if we assume that the bear is the father imago. Then the castration anxiety connected with masturbation (playing the violin or flute) is displaced from the dreamer to the father imago; it is he who teaches his father how to masturbate and it is his father, not he who fears the vagina. For the meaning of the vise is made quite clear by the following version.

In the upper Palatinate, at Ebnat, there was a haunted mill. If any one of the miller's lads tried to grind there he was chased by the green huntsman or water spirit. The miller hired a strong lad who had a violin. The huntsman came, the lad started to play and the huntsman wanted to learn. He put his fingers in the screw and the water spirit screamed with pain. The lad let the spirit go on one condition: that he would not haunt the mill any more. The young man married happily, and when he and his wife were in a boat on the lake they noticed the water spirit coming after them. The lad got hold of his wife and told her to stand on her head. Then he shouted to the breakers, "Here is the screw vise." The waters calmed down instantly.[12]

In Oldenburg, the mill is haunted by cats. The lad has a machine

11 Grimm, *Kinder und Hausmärchen* No. 14 Cf. also Róheim, "The Bear in the Haunted Mill," *American Imago,* V, 1948, pp. 70–82.
12 Schönwerth, F., *Aus der Oberpfalz,* Augsburg, 1869, III, p. 83.

for trimming cats' nails. He lets the cat he catches go only if it promises to avoid the mill. But the cat claims their first child as his (father imago). When the lad's wife lifts her skirts, the demon flees in complete panic.[13]

The mechanism of the dream is that of fission or displacement. A farmer meets Rübezahl in the mountains. Rübezahl, the mountain demon, demands that he receive "whatever is just happening in the house." When the farmer returns, he finds that his wife has just been delivered of a son. When Rübezahl comes to fetch the child he happens to put his hand into a vise which the farmer then screws firmly. He lets Rübezahl go on the condition that he forego his claim. But Rübezahl comes back. This time, the farmer says to his wife, "Stand on your head," and says to Rübezahl, "Do you see the vise?"[14]

The demon's name confirms our interpretation. "Zahl" is an old German word for penis; thus Rübezahl means "carrot penis." If anyone mentions his name, he is terribly offended.[15]

In a French folk tale from Lorraine a soldier who has been discharged from the army plays a game of cards in a castle with a lion. The soldier wins all the time and the lion gets furious. The lion is about to pounce on him when the soldier suggests a game of see-saw. The lion becomes interested and allows the soldier to tie him to the see-saw by his paws. The soldier swings him up to the ceiling and leaves him there. Then he persuades a wolf to stick his paw into a wedge and a fox to have a stick shoved into him, and leaves them all like that. Subsequently, he meets a girl and then sees that all three animals are coming after them. He tells her, "Let us make a see-saw." She agrees, and while they play the game the lion approaches and says, "What! the same game again? Let us run!" The wolf shouts, "Same thing again!" and he runs with the fox. The soldier of course after they have played see-saw together marries the girl.[16]

The mechanism of these stories is that the castration anxiety is displaced from the dreamer to the bear or spirit (father imago). A Hungarian story that occurs in a quite different context makes this quite clear.

Once upon a time, there was a poor farmer. He had a couple of oxen and a small farm. A bear came and gazed at him while he was ploughing. The bear said, "Don't be afraid! Tell me, why are these oxen so fat?" "That is because they are castrated," the farmer said. "All right," said the bear, "you castrate me today and I shall castrate you tomorrow." So the

13 Strackerjan, L., *Aberglaube und Sagen aus dem Herzogtum Oldenburg,* 1909, I, pp. 349, 350.

14 Loewe, R., "Weiteres über Rübezahl im heutigen Volksglauben," *Zeitschrift des Vereins für Volkskunde,* XXI, 1911, p. 150.

15 *Ibid.,* pp. 38, 39.

16 Cosquin, F., *Contes Populaires de Lorraine,* Paris, 1886, I, pp. 28–31.

farmer castrated the bear and went home. But he was very sad and refused to plough his field any more. He told his wife what had happened, and she said that she would take care of the situation. So she dressed in his clothes and went out to plough. When the bear saw the woman he got frightened at the effects of the castration and ran to get some herbs to heal the wound. He told the fox, "Go and fan the poor man with your bushy tail until I find the herbs." The fox started to fan the woman's vagina, but she got irritated and let a flatus go. The fox ran and told the bear, "I have been shot at with a gun." Then they both ran.[17]

A Russian story from Kiev is the closest parallel to this Hungarian story. The devil asks the peasant who calls himself Myself (cf. Polyphemos) how it happens that he is better at ploughing than the devil. The peasant says: "Because I am castrated." After he has performed this operation, the devil howls in vain because he says he has done it himself. In another Russian version, the devil wants to play the violin. He cannot get his little finger out of the wedge till finally the wedge tears his little finger off.[18]

But what of the mill? Why does the first dangerous and then terror-stricken ghost do its haunting just in a mill?

Near the village of Klausen (Lower Austria) there was a solitary mill. It was called "Mill of Skulls." The young miller was constantly quarreling with his wife and once asked the devil to help him to get rid of her. The devil agreed on the condition that he would have the right to use the mill every night.

Every midnight a carriage appeared drawn by six horses and driven by a man who had only one eye and was lame. They brought sacks with human skulls and started grinding them. The miller was eavesdropping and heard everything. He also heard that his own skull was to be ground next.[19] (The rest of the story does not concern us here.)

Getting rid of his wife and his skull being ground to ashes in the mill both mean the same thing: castration anxiety. The sexual symbolism of the mill where they grind corn makes all this quite clear. In a Szekely (Hungarians in Transylvania) song this is quite outspoken.

> A mill on the Kuekuelloe
> Makes a big clatter
> It makes a big clatter
> because the miller is a rogue

[17] Nagy, I. Berze, *Baranyai Magyar Néphagyományok* (Hungarian Folklore from Baranya), Pécs, 1940, II, p. 49.

[18] Hackman, O., *Die Polyphemsage in der Volksüberlieferung*, Helsingfors, 1904, pp. 124, 125.

[19] Vernaleken, T., *Mythen und Bräuche der Volkes in Österreich*, Wien, 1859, pp. 83, 84.

The Kuekuelloe is all frozen
The miller crossed on the ice
Come back, come back, my love
Because the mill grinds love.[20]

In a ballad of the same area the lovesick young man lies down to die. "I am dying for Ilona Görög," he says. His mother promises to get him a magic mill. It will grind pearls, silk and coins, and all the virgins shall come to see it. Ilona Görög will come too. The chorus says, "Don't go, Ilona. The net is spread, the fish will be caught." Then his mother promises him a miraculous steeple. It will reach as far as the Danube, and the girls shall come to see it. Finally, when the girl is told that her lover is dead, she comes herself and up he jumps and they are united in love.[21]

It is clear now why mills are frequently haunted. The revolving motion of the mill is coitus, the mill itself is the vagina. The Hungarian story of the young miller's lad near Keszthely who was in league with the devil and could make all women dance whether they wanted to or not,[22] and the German stories, evidently nightmares about the miller's wife who chokes the lads who attempt to spend a night in the mill until one of them cuts her arm off,[23] are the two sides of the picture.

The following versions show the typically dream-derived mechanism of duplicate formation.

In Schleswig, the miller's lad is awake at night in the mill. He wants something to eat and he is cooking porridge in a big kettle. His sabre is at hand. A whole swarm of cats come pouring in and they come nearer and nearer. One beautiful white cat tries to sit beside him. He dips the spoon into the porridge and throws the hot porridge in the cat's face. Then he draws his sabre and cuts her paw off. But it is not a paw, it is a woman's hand—the hand of the miller's wife[24] (i.e., mother imago).

The cat is significant because it is the typical form the witch takes in nightmare beliefs. The difference between the nightmare as belief and the dream is that it is not recognized as a dream, it is something the person who appears in the dream really does at night.

A girl in East Prussia became a cat every night without knowing it. In the morning she awoke fatigued, as if she had had a bad dream. But in her cat shape she went to the young man to whom she was engaged to

20 Kriza, John, "Vadrózsák" (Wild Roses), *Népköltési Gyüjtemény* (Collection of Hungarian Folklore), XI, Budapest, 1911, pp. 95, 96.

21 *Idem*, "Orbán et alii Székely földi gyüjtés" (Székely Folklore), *Magyar Népköltési Gyüjtemény*, III, 1882, pp. 63–67.

22 Vajkai, A., "Az ördöngös molnár legény" (The Devilish Miller Lad), *Ethnographia*, LVIII, 1947, pp. 55–69.

23 Hertz, W., *Der Werwolf*, Stuttgart, 1862, p. 71, fn. 4.

24 Laistner, *op. cit.*, II, pp. 36, 37, quoting Müllenhoff.

scratch and torture him. He bound the cat in a sack and the next morning he found his naked bride there.[25]

The night spent in the haunted mill or castle and the haunting spirit evidently have two meanings. The haunting image may also represent the mother imago in its castrating aspect.

There was a man who had a windmill, but every lad who spent a night in his mill was dead the next morning. A good-looking lad decided that he could take the job and do away with the spirits. At midnight, the cats came and started to surround him. He grabbed one of them and cut her paw off. It was the miller's wife.[26]

A further offshoot of this myth based on a dream is when instead of one we have two haunting beings. These are the stories discussed by Laistner on the basis of his nightmare theory.

There was a village in Vetschau and every night the water spirit came into the mill. The water spirit cooked and ate its fishes there. A man came who went around from one village to another exhibiting his bear. They thought that the bear might do the trick so they tied him up in the mill. At night the water spirit came again to cook its fish. The bear put its paw in the plate; the spirit rapped its paw with a spoon, whereupon the bear got hold of the water spirit and mauled it thoroughly. The spirit came back later and asked, "Have you still got the big cat?" "Yes, and she has nine young ones." "Then I am certainly not coming any more," the spirit said and jumped back into the water.[27]

This answer assigns definite roles to bear and spirit. The bear is the mother, the water man the father. The dish over which they quarrel is the vagina and the whole is a somewhat ambiguous representation of the primal scene. Both put their paw or spoon into the plate, and it is the father imago who appears to have been defeated.

In another version, the ending of the story is: "Miller, have you still got your big cat?" "Yes, she is cuddled up behind the oven and has ninety-nine young ones."[28]

The male character of the water spirit is quite clear in the following story. The water spirit is a tom cat, and his paw is chopped off by the wandering lad.[29]

The story could be summarized as follows: A lad dreams that he is visited by the father (bear) who threatens to castrate him as a punishment for masturbation. The dream solves the situation by turning tables: it is the father imago who masturbated and therefore has to be castrated.

[25] Hertz, *op. cit.*, pp. 73, 74.
[26] Veckenstedt, *op. cit.*, pp. 279, 280.
[27] *Ibid.*, p. 195; Laistner, *op. cit.*, II, pp. 15, 16.
[28] Kühnau, *op. cit.*, II, p. 223.   [29] *Ibid.*, II, pp. 221, 222.

XI

OEDIPUS REX

Laistner regards the Sphinx as a nightmare demon, i.e., as a being whose existence is based on an anxiety dream. The word seems to be a variant of πνίξ, the Greek word for nightmare. Suidas calls lascivious women sphinxes of Megara. According to Laistner, the Sphinx is a close relative of the empusa.[1]

Of Empusa we are told that she eats human flesh and at the same time appears in the shape of a beautiful woman to attract her victims. She is one of the group that go with Hekate like the Lamia, Mormo, Sphinx, etc. One leg is made of brass, one of asses' dung. According to one of the etymologies given in Roscher, the name means "the one-footed one." According to another, "the bloodsucker." Aristophanes represents her as being in a blood-inflated bladder.[2]

The sphinx of Greek tradition belongs to the same group of demons; they are all associated with death and are all female.[3] The etymology of the name is "she who chokes" and is not far removed from Strinx, a ghost-like bird of the night; Strinx again is like one of the Keres who have to be expelled at the Anthestheria. Orthos who, as we have seen above, is another Kerberos appears as her father; the Nemean lion is her brother or she is the offspring of the incestuous union of Echidna with her own son.[4] This brings her close to Jokaste herself.

In a modern Greek folk tale, a queen is sitting on a rock at Thebes. She propounds three riddles to all passers-by. If they do not know the answer she devours them, but if they can solve all three riddles she lets them pass or marries them. The prince decides that he knows all the answers. The first riddle is this: What is it that devours its own children? Answer: The ocean, because the rivers come from the ocean and flow back into it. The second riddle: It is white and black and never ages. Answer: Time consists of day and night and is always there. And the third riddle is the one solved by Oedipus.[5]

[1] Laistner, L., *Das Rätsel der Sphinx,* Berlin, 1889, I, pp. 60–65.
[2] *Roscher's Lexikon,* "Empusa."
[3] Rohde, E., *Psyche,* Tübingen, 1907, I, p. 318.
[4] *Roscher's Lexikon,* "Sphinx."
[5] Schmidt, B., *Griechische Märchen, Sagen und Volkslieder,* Leipzig, 1877, pp. 143, 144.

The answers to the first two riddles cannot be independent of the answer to the last one. Indeed, the Sphinx or Jokaste herself is the mother who devours her own son. This applies also to the second answer; the attitude toward the mother is *ambivalent* and in the unconscious it does not age. In another version of the classical myth, she is a daughter of Laios. The fact that she is sent by Hera makes her a "doublette" of the great goddess. A vase shows the image of Hermes with his staff passing between two representations of the Sphinx; they are facing each other.[6]

Wherever Hermes goes we should expect a dream or death, and the two sphinxes facing each other remind one forcibly of the Gates of the Sun in the Gilgamesh epic and of the two scorpion men who form these gates.

In a Scholion to Euripides *Phoen,* we are told that the answer to the riddle is revealed to Oedipus in a dream.[7] This justifies us in following Laistner and regarding the *meeting with the Sphinx as an anxiety dream.*

What was the latent content of this dream? I have assumed that the being who asks the riddle and the riddle itself are identical. There are many variants of the "legs" riddle. Aarne has shown that the being who had a different number of legs at various periods of its life was really two beings combined. For example:

> Two legs sat on three legs and ate one leg
> Then came four legs and took one leg from two legs
> The two legs hit four legs with three legs
> So that four legs dropped one leg.

A man sits on a three-legged stool eating a ham. A dog steals the ham, but the man hits him with the stool so that he drops it. Many variants are concerned with a pregnant cow or mare, and others with a horse and a man on its back. In this last form, the one leg is the rider's penis. The folklorist modestly observes that the riddle is obscene. In one version, however, the right answer is given. It is two people lying in one bed.[8]

The Sphinx is a female being who flies down on those it wishes to devour. It catches them with its claws, flies away with them and eats them.[9] Therefore she is the answer to the first riddle, the mother who devours her children. And if we assume that the time concept is derived from the oral frustration of the infant then time is again the Sphinx mother in person.[10]

---

[6] *Roscher's Lexikon,* "Sphinx," p. 1378.   [7] *Ibid.,* "Oedipus," p. 718.

[8] Aarne, A., *Vergleichende Rätselforschungen,* F. F. Communications, Helsinki, 1909, pp. 25, 66, 173, 179, 212.

[9] *Roscher's Lexikon,* "Sphinx," p. 1366. Cf. also on the Sphinx, Robert, C., *Oedipus,* Weidmannsche Buchhandlung, 1915, I, pp. 48–58; II, p. 17.

[10] Bergler, E. and Róheim, "The Psychology of Time Perception," *Psychoanalytic Quarterly,* XV, 1946, pp. 119–126.

Who then is Oedipus, the undaunted, who can solve the riddle and kill the nightmare? Kretschmer has the correct etymology of Oedipus, which is also in accordance with the myth. It means "swollen foot." Maybe there is some kinship between the "Swollen foot" and the seer Melampus or "Black foot." The latter appears in connection with snakes[11] which is not valid for Oedipus but is significant in the myth of Teiresias. I have shown that Teiresias and Oedipus are in a sense the same person. Teiresias is called in to see what Oedipus must unconsciously know.[12]

Bethe assumes that it is Teiresias who sends Laios to sacrifice on Mount Kithairon to Hera and that is where he is killed by Oedipus. He is thus really the cause of Laios' death. In the tragedy, Oedipus actually says this.

Oedipus
Yes, I will not refrain so fierce is my wrath
From speaking all my thought. I think that thou
Didst plot the deed and do it through the blow
Thy hand it may be dealt not. Hadst thou seen
I would have said it was thy deed alone.

But Teiresias has seen something and that is why he is blind. Teiresias has seen two snakes copulating at the crossroad and after having killed one of them he becomes transformed into a woman. This happens after he has killed the female snake. After a time he again sees the snakes copulating, but now he kills the male snake and becomes a man once more.[13]

Zeus and Hera are quarreling as usual, and this time the question is: Who obtains more pleasure from the sexual act, the male or the female? Teiresias is the only person who has actually experienced coitus in both roles, he is to be their umpire. Teiresias says the female, and Hera in her indignation punishes him by depriving him of his eyesight. Zeus to make up for this makes him a seer.[14]

The punishment and the reward are not for the decision; they are simply punishment for having witnessed the primal scene, and the reward in "seeing" is the sublimation of the primal scene.

There are other versions of the myth. Teiresias sees Athena in her bath, the goddess touches his eyes with her finger and he is blind. Charicleia, his mother, is evidently another form of Athena. We see, therefore, what we suspected anyway, that it is the voyeur who loses his eyesight.

11 *Roscher's Lexikon,* "Melampus."
12 Róheim, "Teiresias and Other Seers," *Psychoanalytic Review*, XXXIII, 1946, p. 314.
13 *Roscher's Lexikon,* "Teiresias."
14 Róheim, "Teiresias and Other Seers," p. 316.

It is also obvious that the copulating serpents are Father and Mother or Zeus and Hera. Curiously enough, it is just at Thebes that we find what we are looking for. At Thespiae in Boeotia, a figure was found with the inscription Zeus Ktesios, Zeus of the Household Property, i.e., fertility increase.[15] Hera does not appear as a snake goddess, but she is successor to a snake goddess. Her Cretan prototype has a serpent in her hand, and snakes are entwined around her headdress. Twisting around her body and arms, they serve as a girdle only to reappear in the cult of her Greek successor.[16] The parallel to the copulating snakes of Teiresias would be the primal scene dream of Oedipus, i.e., his meeting with the Sphinx. In emphasizing the connection between Oedipus and Zeus, we are thinking of the essentially oedipal content of Greek mythology.

Oedipus is buried in the sanctuary of Demeter at Eteonos. According to Kretschmer, the name Oedipus, i.e., "Swell-foot," actually means a snake.[17] It is probable that the buried hero is responsible for the growth of all living things. On a red-figured amphora from Basilicata, now in the Naples collection (Fig. 968), there is an inscription in which the grape of Oedipus apparently announces:

> Mallows and rooty asphodel upon my back I bare
> And in my bosom Oidipodas, Laios' son and heir.

Mallows and asphodel were the common vegetable food of the Boiotian peasant.[18]

The snake Oedipus is important because in medieval and modern Greek and other European folklore, the young adder is believed to kill its father.[19] By the time these beliefs arrive in America, "representation by the opposite" is functioning; snakes are believed to swallow their young in times of danger to protect them.[20]

Teiresias is blind because he has seen the primal scene and in the end Oedipus too becomes blind—he has also seen the primal scene represented by the Sphinx. The third seer is Melampus (Black Foot). Young snakes gave him the supernatural ability to see by cleaning his ears with their tongues. This they did out of gratitude because he had buried their mother. Since that time he understood the language of the birds and of

---

15 Harrison, J. E., *Themis*, Cambridge, 1927, pp. 297, 298.

16 Róheim, "Teiresias and Other Seers," p. 316.

17 Höfer in article "Oedipus" in *Roscher's Lexikon*.

18 Cook, A. B., *Zeus, A Study in Ancient Religion*, Vol. II, Part II, Cambridge, 1925, p. 1154.

19 Cf. Heller, B., "Népies es folklorsztikus elemek Zrinyi müveiben (Folklore in the Poems of Zrinyi), *Ethnographia*, XXX, 1919, p. 38; Legrand, E., *Collection des monuments pour servir a l'étude de la langue néohellenique*, Paris, 1873, pp. 10, 66.

20 Lys, Claudia de, *A Treasury of American Superstitions*, New York, 1948, p. 79.

all animals. He restored the potency of Iphiklos who had become impotent because his father who was gelding young goats threatened him with the knife. In one version, he, like Oedipus, is exposed by his mother. In another, he is nourished by serpents.[21] On a jug from Southern Italy we find Oedipus with a goatlike mask and with a big phallos, opposing the naked Sphinx, a woman with the face of a bird.[22] Now we know why "Swollen Foot" is the man who can overcome the monstrous woman who eats children or castration anxiety called forth by the primal scene. The situation is the same as in the myth of Orestes pursued by the Eumenides and rescued by the menacing bow and arrow of the Far-Shooting Phoibos Apollo.[23] In various versions of the myth, Oedipus, instead of solving the riddle or after he has solved it, stabs the Sphinx with his spear or sword. A dream with incestuous content, an erection, anxiety, transforms Jokaste into the man-eating Sphinx, but coitus still takes place in the veiled form of stabbing with a sword. The phallic hero overcomes the anxiety of the oral stage—we do grow up.

The scene of the victory of Oedipus is paralleled in *Faust*. The witch from her cauldron scatters flames toward Faust and Mephistopheles.

> *Mephistopheles*
> (reversing the brush which he has been holding and striking among the jars and glasses)
>
>> In two! in two![24]
>> There lies the brew
>> There lies the glass
>> The joke will pass
>> As time, foul ass
>> To the singing of they crew
>
> As the witch recoils he continues
>
>> Hast for the scarlet cloak no reverence
>> Dost recognize no more the tall cock's feather
>> Have I concealed this countenance?
>
> And later,
>
>> A cavalier am I, like others in my bearing
>> Thou hast no doubts about my noble blood
>> See, here's the coat of arms that I am wearing
>> (He makes an indecent gesture.)[25]

21 *Roscher's Lexikon,* "Melampus."

22 *Ibid.,* "Oedipus," p. 738.

23 Cf. Róheim, "The Panic of the Gods," *Psychoanalytic Quarterly,* XXI, 1952, pp. 92–100.

24 "Break!"—The text above is a too literal translation of *entzwei.*

25 Goethe, J. W. von, *Faust* (Modern Library Edition), New York, 1912, pp. 91, 92. (Scene VI.)

This fits in very well with another aspect of the Sphinx. She asks questions like other demons of the nightmare category and it is the mortal (i.e., the dreamer) who has to answer. From the dreams of our patients we know very well that examination dreams always reflect anxiety in connection with a sexual situation. For the men it is mostly the problem of potency; for women it may be their primal sexual anxiety, a foreign body penetrating into their own.

Laistner has connected the Sphinx with the female demons of midday as they appear in Slavic folklore. The Vends say that if somebody does not stop working in the fields at midday the Pripolnica appears to them and asks them questions about what happens to the flax from the moment it is sown in the field to the time when it is ready for reaping. If they can keep talking for an hour and answer all her questions they are safe, but if they fail to do this she cuts off their heads with a sickle or she chokes them.[26]

The Prepolnica (Midday Woman) is covered with hair, has feet like a horse but a face like a woman. If somebody cannot talk to her for an hour about flax or millet she cuts that person's head off with a sickle.[27] The Serpolnica is a wild woman; she has *unkempt long hair* and lives in a *cave* in the forest. She haunts the fields at midday from twelve to one. She is especially after young men and she asks them questions with a double meaning. If they fail to answer these questions she makes love to them and sticks her long hairy tongue into their mouths.[28]

The anonymous young men would correspond to Oedipus. Psychoanalysts have also raised the question that since the Oedipus myth contains such an uncensored version of the Oedipus complex it is probably hiding something else.

In this narrative of the Vends, the main thing is that the demon is the woman with the penis or the castrating woman. One version of the myth tells us that Laios must die because of his homosexuality. He raped Chrysippos and, according to Schol. Eur. Phoen. 60, he did the same to his son.[29] We have said above that the Sphinx is the representation of the primal scene. It follows that she is also the castrating woman with a penis.

The Serpysyja is a big woman. She walks on the fields with no head and a sickle under her arm, or a sickle is attached to her head.[30] The

---

26 Laistner, *op. cit.*, I, p. 106.
27 Veckenstedt, E., *Wendische Sagen, Märchen und abergläubische Gebräuche,* Godz, 1880, p. 106.
28 *Ibid.*, pp. 109, 110.
29 *Roscher's Lexikon*, "Oedipus," p. 711.
30 Veckenstedt, *op. cit.*, p. 106.

Dziewica, a kind of parallel to the Serpolnica, wanders in the woods followed by beautiful hounds.[31] Therefore, she must be related to the myth of the Wild Huntsman. There are also transitions from the "phallic woman" to completely male forms of the *daemon meridianus,* "the man with the sickle" (Sickle Man). He is a gruesome-looking person with fiery eyes, with one leg like a horse and one like a cow (the bisexuality!), and with long claws. He haunts the fields at noon and whosoever fails to give him the right answers to his questions will get his head cut off. He will chop anybody's head off with the sickle if that person feels guilty. A trespassing child is thrown into the river, but a grown-up person's head is cut off[32] (uterine regression vs. castration). If a person feels guilty he will be led astray by the serp, but if he does not, the serp will show him the right way. If children *go to sleep* in the evening under an oak, the serp descends from the oak and cuts their throats. If the children have *dirty feet,*[33] the serp comes and asks them all sorts of questions. The only correct answer is "Water was too expensive." If the child says anything else by mistake, the serp cuts their feet off.[34]

In the allusion to water I would assume a urethral dream. "Water was expensive" means I did not wet the bed. The punishment is castration.

At noon, the Serpel visits women who are working on the fields. If a woman fails to give the right answer she must go stark naked.[35] At Guckrow, the Perpolnica visited a *mason* and asked the usual questions. However, he refused to answer and kept boring a hole in a wooden wall. When he had finished this, he said to the demon, "You put your hands in there, it is still quite hot." He took a nail and hammered it into the demon's finger so that she could not withdraw it from the hole.[36]

Boring a hole is the latent dream thought of the male accompanied by castration anxiety; the veiling technique of the dream displaces the whole thing to the female.

In another story, when the peasant falls asleep the demon woman starts eating his horse's head. He awakes and there is a headless horse.[37]

We have mentioned above that it is through a dream that Oedipus knows the answer to the riddle. Since Jokasta is really the human aspect of the Sphinx, I think the following quotation from Sophocles should be taken quite seriously.

[31] *Ibid.,* p. 108.   [32] *Ibid.,* p. 50.
[33] *Oedipus, Melampus* (Swollen Foot, Black Foot). On Melampus, cf. also Schultz-Engle, Bernice, "Melampus and Freud," *Psychoanalytic Quarterly,* XI, 1942, pp. 83–86.
[34] Veckenstedt, *op. cit.,* p. 54. The Serp is the same kind of being as the Sphinx.
[35] *Ibid.,* p. 55.
[36] *Ibid.,* pp. 109, 110.
[37] von Schulenburg, W., *Wendisches Volksthum,* Berlin, 1882, p. 46.

Jocasta

'Tis best to live at random as one may. But
fear not thou touching wedlock with thy mother.
Many men ere now have so fared in dreams but he
to whom these things are as naught bears his life
most easily.[38]

This passage suggests an unconscious knowledge of Sophocles; he
feels his theme is related to the dream world. The part that I would
directly connect with a dream is the meeting of an unnamed hero with a
demon (the Sphinx) and his victory over the demon. This narrative was
based on a dream in which the anxiety-distorted image of the mother
and of the primal scene is the Sphinx. The hero stabs the devouring
mother with his spear or sword. The penis is the weapon of victory.

There are also traces of what I have called the *basic dream* in our
myth. Her riddle is answered; she *jumps from her rock*. This is the
moment of falling asleep which the dreamer often represents as happening to another person. Torn from its original dream context we find the
uterine regression of the hero at the end of his life. Kanzer's interpretation of the ending of Oedipus is correct. He disappears into the womb[39]
—be it the Grove of the Semnai or the temple of the mother goddess
Demeter. Why Theseus should be the only witness of his disappearance
is clear enough—Theseus is another, more sublimated Oedipus. In the
drama of the aging Oedipus, he says: "Son of Aegeus, I will unfold that
which shall be a treasure for this city, such as age can never mar. Anon,
unaided and with no hand to guide me, I will show the way to the place
where I must die. But that place reveal never unto mortal man, tell not
where it is hidden nor in what region it lies; so that it may ever make for
thee a defence better than the succouring spear of neighbours.[40] By what
doom Oedipus hath perished no man can tell save Theseus alone."[41]

Theseus is the Athenian hero and the kings of Athens, Cecrops and
Erichtonios are snake kings. The sisters of dew Aglauros, Herse and
Pandrosos are the guardians of the chest in which they keep the infant
king. The snake or child in the chest, as Jane Ellen Harrison shows at
this point, is the penis in the vagina or womb.[42]

[38] Mullahy, P., *Oedipus, Myth and Complex*, New York, 1948, p. 376.

[39] Kanzer, M., "The Passing of the Oedipus Complex in Greek Drama," *International Journal of Psycho-Analysis*, XXIX, 1948, p. 133.

The name of the sphinx is connected with the mountain Phikion and also with
Kithairon where Laios is offering a sacrifice to Hera. *Roscher's Lexikon,* "Oedipus,"
p. 716.

[40] Mullahy, *op. cit.*, p. 453.

[41] *Ibid.*, p. 456.

[42] Harrison, Jane Ellen, *Themis*, Cambridge, 1927, pp. 265–268.

Over and above the whole tragedy of Oedipus presides the god of prophecy and lustration, Phoibos Apollo. As I have shown before, Apollo himself is an Oedipus—Apollo who kills Tityos for attempting to rape his mother. Closely associated with Thebes we find Cadmos who built the Cadmea. Aided by the Sparti, he slays the dragon who is another form of Ares, i.e., the father of his bride Harmonia.[43]

Among the Baja the king is killed by his son and successor. They have sacred snakes to whom they pray for rain, and when the snake dies the king is poisoned by his son.[44] Frazer has collected further data on the subject. In Raratonga as soon as a son reached manhood, he would fight and wrestle with his father for the mastery, and if victorious he would *drive his parent in destitution from home.*[45] Among the Corannas a young man who had attained manhood would fight with his father and if he knocked him down he would become chief of the kraal.[46]

Frazer actually explains both the myth of Zeus and Kronos and that of Oedipus as based on these customs.[47]

Marriage with the king's widow is equally part of divine kingship. Canute the Dane marries Emma the widow of his predecessor Ethelred whose throne he had overturned and whose children he had driven into exile. Among the Saxons and the Varini it appears to have been a regular custom for the new king to marry his stepmother.[48]

Among the Banyoro princes might cohabit with princesses and have children by them though this was against the rule of totemic exogamy. The king might marry his sister and have children by her.[49] The King of Uganda married his half-sister. There was also a peculiar relationship between the king and his mother which looked very much like a veiled or repressed incest. The queen mother was treated in the same fashion as the king's chief wife. A stream of running water separated the court of the queen mother from the court of the king. Like the queen, the king's mother was carried on men's shoulders when traveling. She was not permitted to marry again though she might have lovers. If she had children these would be killed immediately.[50]

---

[43] Róheim, *Animism, Magic and the Divine King,* London, 1930, p. 301.

[44] Frobenius, L., *Und Afrika sprach,* Berlin, 1913, III, p. 181.

[45] Frazer, J., *The Dying God,* London, 1911, I, p. 191. Williams, J., *Narratives of Missionary Enterprises in the South Sea Islands,* London, 1836, p. 117.

[46] Campbell, J., *Travels in South Africa,* London, 1822, II, p. 276.

[47] Frazer, *op. cit.,* p. 193.

[48] Frazer, *The Magic Art,* London, 1911, II, p. 283.

[49] Frazer, *Totemism and Exogamy,* London, 1910, II, p. 523. Cf. also Hadfield, P., *Traits of Divine Kingship in Africa,* London, 1949, p. 115.

[50] Róheim, *Animism, Magic and the Divine King,* p. 239, quoting Roscoe, J., *The Baganda,* London, 1911, pp. 191, 203, 237, 347, 348.

The following ceremony performed by the rulers of Idah on ascending the throne speaks for itself. He goes to Ofokolo (birthplace) where he has intercourse with the senior wife of his predecessor.[51]

Among the Banyoro we have the following striking parallel to the Oedipus myth. The oracle said that if King Bukule's son had a daughter, the king would surely die. So he guarded his daughter in a tower, but it happened that a man from the priestly clan had intercourse with her and she had a son. The king gave the boy to the guard to be drowned, but the child's umbilical cord was tied to its wrist and when the child was cast into the river the string by which the cord was tied caught on a branch and saved the child from drowning. The boy grew up as the son of the guardsman who had attempted to kill him. Finally, a struggle ensued between the boy and the king's herdsman in which the king was killed. The regicide became king and disappeared in his old age because it was not customary for kings to die.[52]

In the kingdom of the Kerri the chief man might be killed by any son of his father's brother. Whenever his cousin wanted to do so the king had to submit and he was not allowed to resist. The cousin would strike him on the neck with a sword and the king had no say in the matter. The great men of the tribe gather round the slayer and put the king's hat on his head. Now he became the ruler. In another case reported by Evans Pritchard, the spearing was carried out by a brother. In this instance the king and his guard resisted to the uttermost. It was considered likely that the dead king's son would then slay the slayer of his father.[53]

The "Vavozve" killed the king if he showed any signs of physical decay such as loss of teeth, gray hair, failure of sight or impotency, in fact, any of the indications of advancing age. *He was waylaid on a path* (Oedipus and Laios!) and strangled with a thong of cowhide.[54]

A Shilluk king was killed when he showed signs of becoming old, notably if he failed to satisfy the demands of one of his many wives. Any royal son had the right to attempt to kill the king and if successful to reign in his stead. During the day the king was protected by his body guard and the killing could only take place at night. This was the time when he was alone with his wives. He would pass the night in constant watchfulness

[51] Seligman, C. G., *Egypt and Negro Africa,* London, 1934, p. 44.

[52] Roscoe, *The Northern Bantu,* London, 1915, p. 6.

[53] Seligman, C. G. and Brenda, *Pagan Tribes of the Nilotic Sudan,* London, 1932, pp. 426–428.

[54] Seligman, C. G., *Egypt and Negro Africa: A Study in Divine Kingship,* London, 1934, p. 31, quoting Doran, S. S., "The Killing of the Divine King in South Africa," *South African Journal of Science,* XV, 1918, p. 397.

fully armed, but it was a point of honor for him not to call for help when his rival arrived.[55]

It is quite clear now that the myth of Oedipus represents actual Theban custom. Although we may assume the same for other Greek city-kings, it seems that the custom of regicide must have survived in Thebes long after it had disappeared elsewhere. For the mysterious disappearance of Oedipus is paralleled by what happens to other divine kings. The Dakka who killed their kings buried them in great secrecy.[56] The Pharaoh did not die—a falcon flew into heaven.[57] The frequent custom of covering the king's grave with a river is an effective means of concealing his whereabouts.[58] It was evidently part of the ritual of Khazar and Hungarian royalty.[59]

Frobenius is right in calling the African king a symbol, a fantasy carried out in reality. "In direct contradiction to the customs of his subjects the king marries his own sister or daughter. The Lumba-Humbe declared that this characteristic was decisive for all genuine kings between Tanganyika and Bike. The Hausa regarded this as a matter of course but they were very much shocked by the idea of doing the same thing themselves. And everywhere where the old customs still prevail the other daughters of the king are free to fornicate in the country wherever they may. Besides the king, the "king's mother" is prominent. She may be either his real mother, aunt or elder sister, but at any rate she is regarded as the "mother of kings" and has important functions.[60]

The divine king as such everywhere represents the unconscious incestuous and narcissistic[61] desires of his subjects, and as their scapegoat suffers the punishment dictated by their own guilt feelings.[62]

One detail about the tomb of Oedipus is very much to the point. "The Aigeidai, a Theban tribe who migrated to Thera, alarmed at the abnormal rate of their infant mortality, ascribed this to the curses of Laios and Oidipous and therefore erected shrines to appease the Ἐρινύες of the murdered father and his murderous son."[63]

It is therefore justifiable to say that the immediate background of the story of Oedipus is a combination of a local dream-myth and the tradition

[55] Seligman, C. G. and Brenda, *Pagan Tribes of the Nilotic Sudan*, pp. 90, 91.

[56] Frobenius, *op. cit.*, III, p. 256.

[57] Moret, A., "La royauté dans l'Egypte primitive," *Ann. du Musée Guimet Bibl. Vulg.*, XXXVIII, 1912, p. 196.

[58] Róheim, "A kazár nagyfejedelem és a turulmonda," *Ethnographia*, XXVIII, 1917, p. 21.

[59] *Ibid.*, p. 19.

[60] Frobenius, L., *Atlas Africanus*, Berlin, n.d., II, p. 7.

[61] I am referring to his magical powers.

[62] Cf. Róheim, *Animism, Magic and the Divine King*, 1930.

[63] Farnell, L. R., *The Cults of the Greek States*, Oxford, 1909, V, p. 439.

of what once took place in the divine dynasty of Thebai. But behind this of course we have the life history of every human being. He is exposed in childhood—that is, no child regards himself as sufficiently loved by the parents. Every human being has anxiety dreams based on the primal scene. Then he grows up to adult age. He marries, that is, he "kills" his father and marries a mother substitute. But he also acquires a superego, represented in the drama by the chorus. And, finally, death ends all his troubles.

This detailed explanation of what I think must have been the antecedents of the Oedipus myth is inserted here partly because I want to show that I do not claim the dream as the only source of mythology. Myths based on actual dreams entered into combination with fantasies expressing unconscious desires or with ritual based on these fantasies.

Psychiatrists and other scholars are still fighting the Oedipus complex. James Clark Moloney declares that the Oedipus complex is Freud's fantasy, in other words, that Freud himself was the only man who ever had an Oedipus complex.

"A child abandoned when three days old would be unable to recognize his parents in later life. Ascribing intentional or even archetypical father murder and incest to the Oedipus myth expresses a projection that arose out of Freud's own bias and internal conflict."[64]

Why anyone who is so totally ignorant of mythology as the author of this remark should write about it is one of the mysteries of our age. Levin treats Oedipus as if he were Mr. Smith and not a myth.

A. L. Levin comes out with the following statement. "I infer from circumstances, and others will agree with me, that being hung in an unnatural position at the age of three days and left to perish without food or warmth which the care of a mother would bestow would leave effects on the mind of the child which would easily be mistaken by himself and everyone around him as his 'fate' or destiny."[65]

What is Levin's discovery? That "fate" means the unconscious. In other words, exactly what Freud told us. And what is Moloney saying? That Oedipus could not have recognized his parents. But Oedipus is a myth, the foster parents are duplicates of the real parents.

We may compare Fromm's view here. "If we examine the myth more closely, however, questions arise which cast some doubts on the correctness of this view [i.e., Freud's view]. The most pertinent question is: If Freud's interpretation is right we should expect the myth to tell us that Oedipus met Jocasta without knowing that she was his mother, fell in love with her, and then killed his father, again unknowingly. But there is no

64 Levin, A. I., "The Oedipus Myth in History and Psychiatry," *Psychiatry*, XI, 1948, p. 299.
65 *Ibid.*, p. 287.

indication whatsoever in the myth that Oedipus is attracted by or falls in love with Jocasta. The only reason we are given for the marriage is that she as it were goes with the throne."[66]

Lord Raglan, who also entertained rather remarkable views on this subject writes, "Let us consider the story of Oedipus. The son of a king and a queen, he is condemned to death at birth; so were Perseus and Jason. He is brought up by a king of a foreign country; so were Perseus and Theseus. He overcomes a monster and becomes king but is subsequently dethroned; the same fate befell Theseus and Bellerophon. Finally, he disappears from a hilltop; so did Theseus and Heracles," etc.[67]

It is hardly Greek mythological style to emphasize the emotions of the hero and in the case of Oedipus and Jocasta there would be sufficient reason why this should not be mentioned. We find it, however, in a veiled form since Jocasta and the Sphinx are really the same person and the desire here takes the form of a nightmare (examination dream of the Sphinx).

Lord Raglan's remark simply means that all heroic myth is oedipal; repression having been unsuccessful in the myth of Oedipus (probably on account of the divine kings of Thebes and a local dream myth of the Sphinx), the tragic conflict becomes suitable for representation in dramatic form.

Fromm's argument that the queen symbolizes the throne (and not the throne the queen) can only be accepted by those who deny the existence of infantile sexuality and the universal validity of the queen representing the mother. The real significance of all this is very clear in Celtic myth.

This is the story of Lughaid, King of Ireland. Daire, because of a prophecy that a son of his named Lughaid shall rule Ireland, names all his six sons Lughaid. He asks his Druid who shall rule Ireland, and the Druid replies: "A golden faun shall come to the assembly and whoever captures it shall rule."

When a faun appears, the six sons pursue it to Benn Edar. Lughaid, who from this is named Laighe, catches the faun (laegh). They are now lost in a magic mist and snowstorm. One of them finds a great house with a big fire, with victual and liquor in plenty, silver dishes, bedsteads of white bronze and a dreadful hag. The hag will grant food only to him who will sleep with her. He refuses. "Thou hast missed of royalty," she cries. He goes back to his brothers. One after another, the others come. She names each by nickname, but they all refuse her. At last comes Lughaid Laighe who is brave enough to enter her couch. *She forthwith becomes beautiful*

---

[66] Fromm, E., "The Oedipus Complex and the Oedipus Myth," in *The Family: Its Functions and Destiny,* edited by Ruth Nanda Anshen, New York, 1949.

[67] Lord Raglan, *Jocasta's Crime,* London, 1932, p. 193.

and says to him: "Thine is an auspicious journey for I am royalty and thou shalt have Ireland's rule."[68]

Furthermore, in the Dinshenchas of Carn Mail, we have the same myth of six or seven Lughaids and the faun they follow. "When the men were in the house . . . there entered a hag . . . she was hideous and unsightly. Taller was she than a mast upright, bigger than a sleeping hut her ear, blacker than any visage her form. . . . A change fell upon the nature of the tender youths before that obese lustful horror. Sooner than look upon her they had chosen to be buried under the earth alive." She threatens *to devour them all* if one of them does not sleep with her. Lughaid Laighe undertakes the task. As the firelight dims she changes to another wondrous shape, beyond praise. When Lughaid asks her who she is she says:

> I will tell thee, gentle youth
> With me sleep the High Kings
> I the tall slender maiden
> Am the Kingship of Alba and Erin.

To thee I have revealed myself this night but nothing more shall come of our meeting. The son thou shalt have, he it is that I shall sleep with— happier fate, I will tell thee thy son's name—lucky his lot, Lughaid shall his name be and McCon thereto."

"This is an unmistakable instance of a *fée* consorting first with a father, Lughaid Laighe and then with a son, Lughaid McCon."[69]

The Arthurian parallel to this story is the marriage of Sir Gawaine. In order to rescue King Arthur from the snares of a powerful sorcerer, he agrees to marry the sorcerer's sister who is the most hideous of women. On the marriage night, she reveals herself as beautiful as she was previously repulsive and gives her husband the choice of whether he will have her beautiful by night and hideous by day, or vice versa. Gawaine leaves the decision to the lady, whereupon she tells him that she has been laid under a spell to preserve this hideous form until she finds a knight courteous enough "to give her her will." The spell is broken and she will be beautiful both night and day.[70]

The bridal night transforms the loathesome hag into a beautiful woman. The parallel is the story of "Der Froschkönig oder der eiserne Heinrich." In this story we are told how the king's daughter in exchange for her ball of gold which has rolled into the well permits the frog to share her bed. In some versions it is not the ball of gold but clear water

[68] Brown, Arthur C. L., *The Origin of the Grail Legend*, Cambridge, Mass., 1943, p. 213.

[69] Brown, *op. cit.*, pp. 214, 215.

[70] Weston, Jessie L., *The Legend of Sir Gawain*, London, 1897, p. 48.

that the frog gives her instead of muddy water. In the English version, at midnight the frog-lover appears at the door and demands entrance:

> "Open the door, my hinny, my hart,
> Open the door, mine ain wee thing
> And mind the words that you and I spak
> Down in the meadow at the well spring."

The frog is admitted, and addresses her:

> "Take me up on your knee, my dearie
> Take me up on your knee, my dearie
> And mind the word that you and I spak
> At the cauld well sae weary."

It is genital libido that brings the disenchantment about—*si quis amat ranam, aanam putat esse Dianam*—is the mediaeval proverb also quoted by Bolte and Polivka.[71]

To say that Jocasta goes with the throne is inverting cause and effect. The throne goes with Jocasta—being a divine king symbolizes the child's idea of how an adult, i.e., somebody who actually acts out all the child's conscious or unconscious fantasies lives. A king can do anything,[72] even marry his mother. Oedipus is in a sense the same as the North American culture hero in the *vagina dentata* motive, the male who conquers anxiety (the Sphinx) and achieves genitality. For growing up inevitably means supplanting father and therefore the king is periodically killed or a scapegoat takes his place.

"Guenevere is virtually the sovereignty of Britain. She was at first the giant's wife but later, by natural development, his daughter and then daughter to the Hospitable Host (the friendly father imago). Arthur is the youthful hero who delivers her from the giant and wins with her the kingdom and a set of talismans." Brown then goes on to show that Guenevere's father is really the King of the Dead or a personification of winter and darkness.[73] The divine king as such is of course the representative of the Oedipus complex and not its origin. Mother Earth is mother, but mother is not earth.

In the appraisal of the myth we have to go back to C. Robert—with this difference: we substitute psychology for the old-style *Naturmythologie*. Robert emphasizes that Oedipus' marriage with his mother is really the core of the Greek religion.

The varying names of the mother-wife of Oedipus are just other names for the Earth-Mother Demeter.

[71] Bolte, J., and Polivka, G., *Anmerkungen zu den Kinder und Hausmärchen der Brüder Grimm*, Leipzig, 1913, p. 5.
[72] *Ibid.*, p. 7.
[73] Brown, *op. cit.*, p. 406.

"Uranos, first child of Gaia, is also her first husband. Hippias dreams that he has intercourse with his mother—and the dream is interpreted in the sense that he will be buried in his own country. Caesar in Spain dreams that same thing and the answer is: *quando mater, quam subiectam sibi vidisset non alia esset quam terra quae omnium parens haberetur,* and Elektra prays in *The Choephoroi:*

καὶ Γαῖαν αὐτήν, ἥ τὰ πάντα τίκτεται,

θρέψασά τ᾽ αὖθις τῶνδε κῦμα λαμβάνει

(and Earth herself that bringeth all things to birth and having nurtured them receiveth their increase in turn)."[74]

The Earth Goddess Demeter in whose temple the corpse of Oedipus is buried is originally his mother. His cradle was originally at Kithairon and only later was the myth displaced to Thebes.[75]

What can we add to this? It is true that uterine regression in this case is a symbolic and sublimated incest, but it is also true as Ferenczi believed that coitus in general is a partial or fantasied return to the womb.

As regards the myth of Oedipus itself, it is clearly based on two "origins." The Sphinx is a localized myth derived from an anxiety dream and the story itself a myth of the Theban divine king.

[74] Aeschylus, *Choephoroi*, translation by Herbert Weir Smyth, The Loeb Classical Library, Cambridge, 1946, Vol. II, p. 171, ll. 127, 128; Robert, C., *Oedipus*, Berlin, 1915, I, p. 45.

[75] *Ibid.*, p. 46. The Kithairon is sacred to Demeter.

XII

RETROSPECT

This book is based on what I myself experienced, on what the patients said, and on Australian mythology. "Janus" might be a fit title, for while fully admitting the Freudian construct of the dream as guardian of sleep, it emphasizes the Jekels-Bergler construct of the dream as guardian of life in sleep. My theoretical emphasis has gradually been displaced from the life-death impulse theory to another point of view, namely that going to sleep represents uterine regression and giving up the security of the object world, of the nipple, of reality. The sensations of vertigo or revolving occurring as hypnagogic phenomena might very well be explicable on this basis.[1] They also represent the undirected id, coitus, and uterine regression. The dream itself is an attempt to get out of the womb (visual) but at the same time carries with it that which it is trying to negate, like the mechanism of the return of the repressed in the function of repression. The dreamer entering a cave or room, etc., is a well-known representation of coitus, a striking confirmation of Ferenczi's theory in the *Thalassa*. The unconscious interpretation of coitus and sleep as uterine regression is due to our delayed infancy, which creates a regressive psychological superstructure of biologically conditioned phenomena. One of the differences between human beings and their animal cousins is that in mankind the biologically conditioned alternation of wakefulness and sleep, of extroversion and introversion, is complicated by memory. Thus the turning inward, the withdrawing of cathexis, becomes also a journey in time toward the past. We have a congenitally inherited type of maturation, but also a phylogenetically more recent yet also congenital resistance to maturation. When Freud says: "The vagina is valued as the abode for the penis, it is the heir to the mother's womb,"[2] this is what Ferenczi says in the *Thalassa*, this is what we mean by the regressive or human trend. But the pattern of coitus is older than our foetalization.[3] We are born with a conflict between our older and more recent heritage, and something in us

[1] Cf. Schilder, Paul, "Relations between Clinging and Equilibrium," *International Journal of Psycho-Analysis*, XX, 1939, pp. 58–63.
[2] Freud, S., "Die infantile Genitalorganisation," *Gesammelte Schriften*, V, p. 236.
[3] Cf. Huxley, J., *The Uniqueness of Man*, London, 1941, p. 13.

that is rather vaguely defined in psychoanalysis as the ego is the organic defense against this inherent conflict. This synthetic function underlies the other synthetic function of mediating between the id and the super-ego. The struggle is eternal, the result never stable.

INDEX